GENERAL MOTORS | BONNEVILLE/EIGHTY EIGHT/LE SABRE 1986-99 REPAIR MANUAL

CHILTON'S

Covers all U.S. and Canadian models of Pontiac Bonneville, Oldsmobile Delta 88, Eighty Eight, LSS and Buick LeSabre Front Wheel Drive

by Christine L. Sheeky, S.A.E.

CHILTON Automotive Books

PUBLISHED BY **HAYNES NORTH AMERICA. Inc.**

Manufactured in USA
© 1998 Haynes North America, Inc.
ISBN 0-8019-8963-9
Library of Congress Catalog Card No. 93-74835
5678901234 9876543210

Haynes Publishing Group
Sparkford Nr Yeovil
Somerset BA22 7JJ England

Haynes North America, Inc
861 Lawrence Drive
Newbury Park
California 91320 USA

ABCDE
FGHIJ
KLMN

Contents

1 GENERAL INFORMATION AND MAINTENANCE

1-2 HOW TO USE THIS BOOK
1-2 TOOLS AND EQUIPMENT
1-4 SERVICING YOUR VEHICLE SAFELY
1-5 FASTENERS, MEASUREMENTS AND CONVERSIONS
1-7 SERIAL NUMBER IDENTIFICATION
1-12 ROUTINE MAINTENANCE AND TUNE-UP
1-36 FLUIDS AND LUBRICANTS
1-47 TOWING THE VEHICLE
1-47 JUMP STARTING A DEAD BATTERY
1-48 JACKING

2 ENGINE ELECTRICAL

2-2 ELECTRONIC IGNITION SYSTEMS
2-10 FIRING ORDERS
2-10 CHARGING SYSTEM
2-14 STARTING SYSTEM
2-16 SENDING UNITS

3 ENGINE AND ENGINE OVERHAUL

3-2 ENGINE MECHANICAL
3-39 EXHAUST SYSTEM
3-41 ENGINE RECONDITIONING

4 DRIVEABILITY AND EMISSION CONTROLS

4-2 EMISSION CONTROLS
4-11 ELECTRONIC ENGINE CONTROLS
4-30 COMPONENT LOCATIONS
4-35 TROUBLE CODES
4-41 VACUUM DIAGRAMS

5 FUEL SYSTEM

5-2 BASIC FUEL SYSTEM DIAGNOSIS
5-2 FUEL LINES AND FITTINGS
5-3 GASOLINE FUEL INJECTION SYSTEM
5-13 FUEL TANK

6 CHASSIS ELECTRICAL

6-2 UNDERSTANDING AND TROUBLESHOOTING ELECTRICAL SYSTEMS
6-8 BATTERY CABLES
6-8 AIR BAG—GENERATION 1 CORPORATE SYSTEM
6-12 AIR BAG—OLDSMOBILE INFLATABLE RESTRAINT (IR) SYSTEM
6-14 HEATING AND AIR CONDITIONING
6-18 CRUISE CONTROL SYSTEMS
6-19 ENTERTAINMENT SYSTEMS
6-23 WINDSHIELD WIPERS AND WASHERS
6-28 INSTRUMENTS AND SWITCHES
6-33 LIGHTING
6-39 CIRCUIT PROTECTION
6-42 WIRING DIAGRAMS

Contents

7-2   AUTOMATIC TRANSAXLE

DRIVE TRAIN **7**

8-2   WHEELS   **8-11** REAR SUSPENSION
8-4   FRONT SUSPENSION   **8-17** STEERING

SUSPENSION AND STEERING **8**

9-2   BRAKE OPERATING SYSTEM   **9-29** TEVES MARK IV ANTI-LOCK
9-9   DISC BRAKES   BRAKE SYSTEM
9-13 DRUM BRAKES   **9-35** DELCO VI AND DELCO
9-22 PARKING BRAKE   BOSCH V ANTI-LOCK
9-23 TEVES II ANTI-LOCK BRAKE   BRAKE SYSTEMS (ABS)
          SYSTEM

BRAKES **9**

10-2 EXTERIOR   **10-8** INTERIOR

BODY AND TRIM **10**

10-23 GLOSSARY

GLOSSARY

10-27 MASTER INDEX

MASTER INDEX

SAFETY NOTICE

Proper service and repair procedures are vital to the safe, reliable operation of all motor vehicles, as well as the personal safety of those performing repairs. This manual outlines procedures for servicing and repairing vehicles using safe, effective methods. The procedures contain many NOTES, CAUTIONS and WARNINGS which should be followed, along with standard procedures to eliminate the possibility of personal injury or improper service which could damage the vehicle or compromise its safety.

It is important to note that repair procedures and techniques, tools and parts for servicing motor vehicles, as well as the skill and experience of the individual performing the work vary widely. It is not possible to anticipate all of the conceivable ways or conditions under which vehicles may be serviced, or to provide cautions as to all possible hazards that may result. Standard and accepted safety precautions and equipment should be used when handling toxic or flammable fluids, and safety goggles or other protection should be used during cutting, grinding, chiseling, prying, or any other process that can cause material removal or projectiles.

Some procedures require the use of tools specially designed for a specific purpose. Before substituting another tool or procedure, you must be completely satisfied that neither your personal safety, nor the performance of the vehicle will be endangered.

Although information in this manual is based on industry sources and is complete as possible at the time of publication, the possibility exists that some car manufacturers made later changes which could not be included here. While striving for total accuracy, the authors or publishers cannot assume responsibility for any errors, changes or omissions that may occur in the compilation of this data.

PART NUMBERS

Part numbers listed in this reference are not recommendations by Haynes North America, Inc. for any product brand name. They are references that can be used with interchange manuals and aftermarket supplier catalogs to locate each brand supplier's discrete part number.

SPECIAL TOOLS

Special tools are recommended by the vehicle manufacturer to perform their specific job. Use has been kept to a minimum, but where absolutely necessary, they are referred to in the text by the part number of the tool manufacturer. These tools can be purchased, under the appropriate part number, from your local dealer or regional distributor, or an equivalent tool can be purchased locally from a tool supplier or parts outlet. Before substituting any tool for the one recommended, read the SAFETY NOTICE at the top of this page.

ACKNOWLEDGMENTS

Portions of materials contained herein have been reprinted with the permission of General Motors Corporation, Service Technology Group.

HOW TO USE THIS BOOK 1-2
WHERE TO BEGIN 1-2
AVOIDING TROUBLE 1-2
MAINTENANCE OR REPAIR? 1-2
AVOIDING THE MOST COMMON
    MISTAKES 1-2
TOOLS AND EQUIPMENT 1-2
SPECIAL TOOLS 1-4
SERVICING YOUR VEHICLE SAFELY 1-4
DO'S 1-4
DON'TS 1-5
**FASTENERS, MEASUREMENTS AND
    CONVERSIONS 1-5**
BOLTS, NUTS AND OTHER THREADED
    RETAINERS 1-5
TORQUE 1-6
    TORQUE WRENCHES 1-6
    TORQUE ANGLE METERS 1-7
STANDARD AND METRIC
    MEASUREMENTS 1-7
SERIAL NUMBER IDENTIFICATION 1-7
VEHICLE 1-7
ENGINE 1-7
TRANSAXLE 1-11
DRIVE AXLE 1-11
**ROUTINE MAINTENANCE AND
    TUNE-UP 1-12**
AIR CLEANER (ELEMENT) 1-14
    REMOVAL & INSTALLATION 1-14
FUEL FILTER 1-14
    REMOVAL & INSTALLATION 1-14
PCV VALVE 1-14
    REMOVAL & INSTALLATION 1-14
EVAPORATIVE CANISTER 1-16
    SERVICING 1-17
BATTERY 1-17
    PRECAUTIONS 1-17
    ADJUSTMENT 1-18
    GENERAL MAINTENANCE 1-18
    BATTERY FLUID 1-18
    CABLES 1-19
    CHARGING 1-20
    REPLACEMENT 1-20
BELTS 1-20
    INSPECTION 1-20
    BELT ADJUSTMENT 1-20
    REMOVAL & INSTALLATION 1-21
HOSES 1-22
    INSPECTION 1-22
    REMOVAL & INSTALLATION 1-23
CV-BOOTS 1-24
    INSPECTION 1-24
SPARK PLUGS 1-24
    SPARK PLUG HEAT RANGE 1-25
    REMOVAL & INSTALLATION 1-25
    INSPECTION & GAPPING 1-26
SPARK PLUG WIRES 1-26
    TESTING 1-26
    REMOVAL & INSTALLATION 1-27
IGNITION TIMING 1-29
    GENERAL INFORMATION 1-29
    ADJUSTMENT 1-29
VALVE LASH 1-29
IDLE SPEED AND MIXTURE
    ADJUSTMENTS 1-29
AIR CONDITIONING SYSTEM 1-30
    SYSTEM SERVICE & REPAIR 1-30
    PREVENTIVE MAINTENANCE 1-31
    SYSTEM INSPECTION 1-31
WINDSHIELD WIPERS 1-31
    ELEMENT (REFILL) CARE &
        REPLACEMENT 1-31

TIRES AND WHEELS 1-32
    TIRE ROTATION 1-32
    TIRE DESIGN 1-32
    TIRE STORAGE 1-33
    INFLATION & INSPECTION 1-33
MAINTENANCE LIGHTS 1-34
    RESETTING 1-34
FLUIDS AND LUBRICANTS 1-36
FLUID DISPOSAL 1-36
FUEL AND ENGINE OIL
    RECOMMENDATIONS 1-36
    FUEL RECOMMENDATIONS 1-36
    OIL RECOMMENDATIONS 1-36
    OIL LEVEL CHECK 1-37
    OIL & FILTER CHANGE 1-37
AUTOMATIC TRANSAXLE 1-39
    FLUID RECOMMENDATIONS 1-39
    LEVEL CHECK 1-39
    DRAIN, FILTER SERVICE & REFILL 1-39
COOLING SYSTEM 1-41
    FLUID RECOMMENDATIONS 1-41
    LEVEL CHECK 1-42
    COOLING SYSTEM INSPECTION 1-42
    DRAIN & REFILL 1-43
    FLUSHING & CLEANING 1-44
BRAKE MASTER CYLINDER 1-44
    FLUID RECOMMENDATIONS 1-44
    LEVEL CHECK 1-44
POWER STEERING PUMP 1-45
    FLUID RECOMMENDATIONS 1-45
    LEVEL CHECK 1-45
STEERING GEAR 1-46
    FLUID RECOMMENDATIONS & LEVEL
        CHECK 1-46
SUPERCHARGER 1-46
    FLUID RECOMMENDATIONS 1-46
    LEVEL CHECK 1-46
CHASSIS GREASING 1-46
BODY LUBRICATION 1-46
    HOOD 1-46
    DOOR HINGES 1-46
    LOCK CYLINDERS 1-47
    PARKING BRAKE LINKAGE 1-47
    ACCELERATOR LINKAGE 1-47
    TRUNK LID 1-47
    BODY DRAIN HOLES 1-47
WHEEL BEARINGS 1-47
TOWING THE VEHICLE 1-47
**JUMP STARTING A DEAD
    BATTERY 1-47**
JUMP STARTING PRECAUTIONS 1-47
JUMP STARTING PROCEDURE 1-47
JACKING 1-48
JACKING PRECAUTIONS 1-48
COMPONENT LOCATIONS
    UNDERHOOD MAINTENANCE COMPONENT
        LOCATIONS—LATE MODEL 1-12
    UNDERHOOD MAINTENANCE COMPONENT
        LOCATIONS—EARLY MODEL 1-14
SPECIFICATIONS CHARTS
    VEHICLE IDIENTIFICATION CHART 1-8
    ENGINE IDENTIFICATION 1-10
    GENERAL ENGINE SPECIFICATIONS 1-11
    GENERAL ENGINE TUNE-UP
        SPECIFICATIONS 1-30
    MAINTENANCE INTERVALS 1-49
    CAPACITIES 1-50

1

GENERAL INFORMATION AND MAINTENANCE

HOW TO USE THIS BOOK 1-2
TOOLS AND EQUIPMENT 1-2
SERVICING YOUR VEHICLE SAFELY 1-4
FASTENERS, MEASUREMENTS
    AND CONVERSIONS 1-5
SERIAL NUMBER IDENTIFICATION 1-7
ROUTINE MAINTENANCE
    AND TUNE-UP 1-12
FLUIDS AND LUBRICANTS 1-36
TOWING THE VEHICLE 1-47
JUMP STARTING A DEAD BATTERY 1-47
JACKING 1-48

HOW TO USE THIS BOOK

This Chilton's Total Car Care manual for the 1986–99 Buick LeSabre, Oldsmobile Delta 88/Eighty Eight and Pontiac Bonneville is intended to help you learn more about the inner workings of your vehicle, while saving you money on its upkeep and operation.

The beginning of the book will likely be referred to the most, since that is where you will find information for maintenance and tune-up. The other sections deal with the more complex systems of your vehicle. Systems (from engine through brakes) are covered to the extent that the average do-it-yourselfer can attempt. This book will not explain such things as rebuilding a differential because the expertise required and the special tools necessary make this uneconomical. It will, however, give you detailed instructions to help you change your own brake pads and shoes, replace spark plugs, and perform many more jobs that can save you money and help avoid expensive problems.

A secondary purpose of this book is a reference for owners who want to understand their vehicle and/or their mechanics better.

Where to Begin

Before removing any bolts, read through the entire procedure. This will give you the overall view of what tools and supplies will be required. So read ahead and plan ahead. Each operation should be approached logically and all procedures thoroughly understood before attempting any work.

If repair of a component is not considered practical, we tell you how to remove the part and then how to install the new or rebuilt replacement. In this way, you at least save labor costs.

Avoiding Trouble

Many procedures in this book require you to "label and disconnect . . . " a group of lines, hoses or wires. Don't be think you can remember where everything goes—you won't. If you hook up vacuum or fuel lines incorrectly, the vehicle may run poorly, if at all. If you hook up electrical wiring incorrectly, you may instantly learn a very expensive lesson.

You don't need to know the proper name for each hose or line. A piece of masking tape on the hose and a piece on its fitting will allow you to assign your own label. As long as you remember your own code, the lines can be reconnected by matching your tags. Remember that tape will dissolve in gasoline or solvents; if a part is to be washed or cleaned, use another method of identification. A permanent felt-tipped marker or a metal scribe can be very handy for marking metal parts. Remove any tape or paper labels after assembly.

Maintenance or Repair?

Maintenance includes routine inspections, adjustments, and replacement of parts which show signs of normal wear. Maintenance compensates for wear or deterioration. Repair implies that something has broken or is not working. A need for a repair is often caused by lack of maintenance. for example: draining and refilling automatic transmission fluid is maintenance recommended at specific intervals. Failure to do this can shorten the life of the transmission/transaxle, requiring very expensive repairs. While no maintenance program can prevent items from eventually breaking or wearing out, a general rule is true: MAINTENANCE IS CHEAPER THAN REPAIR.

TOOLS AND EQUIPMENT

▶ **See Figures 1 thru 15**

Without the proper tools and equipment it is impossible to properly service your vehicle. It would be virtually impossible to catalog every tool that you would need to perform all of the operations in this book. It would be unwise for the amateur to rush out and buy an expensive set of tools on the theory that he/she may need one or more of them at some time.

The best approach is to proceed slowly, gathering a good quality set of those tools that are used most frequently. Don't be misled by the low cost of bargain tools. It is far better to spend a little more for better quality. Forged wrenches, 6 or 12-point sockets and fine tooth ratchets are by far preferable to their less expensive counterparts. As any good mechanic can tell you, there are few worse

Two basic mechanic's rules should be mentioned here. First, whenever the left side of the vehicle or engine is referred to, it means the driver's side. Conversely, the right side of the vehicle means the passenger's side. Second, screws and bolts are removed by turning counterclockwise, and tightened by turning clockwise unless specifically noted.

Safety is always the most important rule. Constantly be aware of the dangers involved in working on an automobile and take the proper precautions. Please refer to the information in this section regarding SERVICING YOUR VEHICLE SAFELY and the SAFETY NOTICE on the acknowledgment page.

Avoiding the Most Common Mistakes

Pay attention to the instructions provided. There are 3 common mistakes in mechanical work:

1. Incorrect order of assembly, disassembly or adjustment. When taking something apart or putting it together, performing steps in the wrong order usually just costs you extra time; however, it CAN break something. Read the entire procedure before beginning. Perform everything in the order in which the instructions say you should, even if you can't see a reason for it. When you're taking apart something that is very intricate, you might want to draw a picture of how it looks when assembled in order to make sure you get everything back in its proper position. When making adjustments, perform them in the proper order. One adjustment possibly will affect another.

2. Overtorquing (or undertorquing). While it is more common for overtorquing to cause damage, undertorquing may allow a fastener to vibrate loose causing serious damage. Especially when dealing with aluminum parts, pay attention to torque specifications and utilize a torque wrench in assembly. If a torque figure is not available, remember that if you are using the right tool to perform the job, you will probably not have to strain yourself to get a fastener tight enough. The pitch of most threads is so slight that the tension you put on the wrench will be multiplied many times in actual force on what you are tightening.

There are many commercial products available for ensuring that fasteners won't come loose, even if they are not torqued just right (a very common brand is Loctite®). If you're worried about getting something together tight enough to hold, but loose enough to avoid mechanical damage during assembly, one of these products might offer substantial insurance. Before choosing a threadlocking compound, read the label on the package and make sure the product is compatible with the materials, fluids, etc. involved.

3. Crossthreading. This occurs when a part such as a bolt is screwed into a nut or casting at the wrong angle and forced. Crossthreading is more likely to occur if access is difficult. It helps to clean and lubricate fasteners, then to start threading the bolt, spark plug, etc. with your fingers. If you encounter resistance, unscrew the part and start over again at a different angle until it can be inserted and turned several times without much effort. Keep in mind that many parts have tapered threads, so that gentle turning will automatically bring the part you're threading to the proper angle. Don't put a wrench on the part until it's been tightened a couple of turns by hand. If you suddenly encounter resistance, and the part has not seated fully, don't force it. Pull it back out to make sure it's clean and threading properly.

Be sure to take your time and be patient, and always plan ahead. Allow yourself ample time to perform repairs and maintenance.

experiences than trying to work on a vehicle with bad tools. Your monetary savings will be far outweighed by frustration and mangled knuckles.

Begin accumulating those tools that are used most frequently: those associated with routine maintenance and tune-up. In addition to the normal assortment of screwdrivers and pliers, you should have the following tools:

• Wrenches/sockets and combination open end/box end wrenches in sizes ⅛–¾ in. and/or 3mm–19mm ¹³⁄₁₆ in. or ⅝ in. spark plug socket (depending on plug type).

➡ **If possible, buy various length socket drive extensions. Universal-joint and wobble extensions can be extremely useful, but be careful when using them, as they can change the amount of torque applied to the socket.**

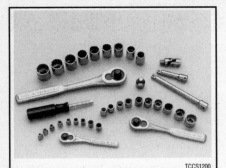

Fig. 1 All but the most basic procedures will require an assortment of ratchets and sockets

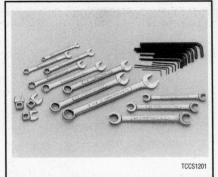

Fig. 2 In addition to ratchets, a good set of wrenches and hex keys will be necessary

Fig. 3 A hydraulic floor jack and a set of jackstands are essential for lifting and supporting the vehicle

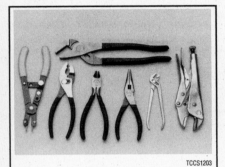

Fig. 4 An assortment of pliers, grippers and cutters will be handy for old rusted parts and stripped bolt heads

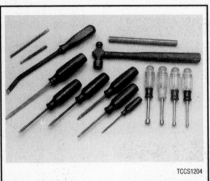

Fig. 5 Various drivers, chisels and prybars are great tools to have in your toolbox

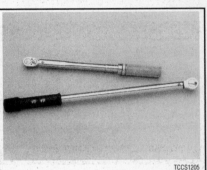

Fig. 6 Many repairs will require the use of a torque wrench to assure the components are properly fastened

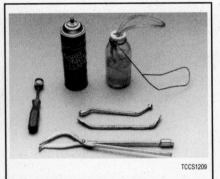

Fig. 7 Although not always necessary, using specialized brake tools will save time

Fig. 8 A few inexpensive lubrication tools will make maintenance easier

Fig. 9 Various pullers, clamps and separator tools are needed for many larger, more complicated repairs

Fig. 10 A variety of tools and gauges should be used for spark plug gapping and installation

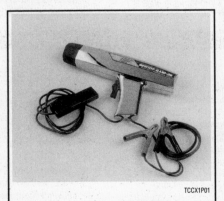

Fig. 11 Inductive type timing light

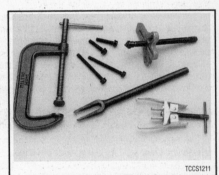

Fig. 12 A screw-in type compression gauge is recommended for compression testing

Fig. 13 A vacuum/pressure tester is necessary for many testing procedures

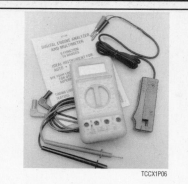

Fig. 14 Most modern automotive multimeters incorporate many helpful features

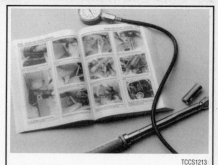

Fig. 15 Proper information is vital, so always have a Chilton Total Car Care manual handy

- Jackstands for support.
- Oil filter wrench.
- Spout or funnel for pouring fluids.
- Grease gun for chassis lubrication (unless your vehicle is not equipped with any grease fittings)
- Hydrometer for checking the battery (unless equipped with a sealed, maintenance-free battery).
- A container for draining oil and other fluids.
- Rags for wiping up the inevitable mess.

In addition to the above items there are several others that are not absolutely necessary, but handy to have around. These include an equivalent oil absorbent gravel, like cat litter, and the usual supply of lubricants, antifreeze and fluids. This is a basic list for routine maintenance, but only your personal needs and desire can accurately determine your list of tools.

After performing a few projects on the vehicle, you'll be amazed at the other tools and non-tools on your workbench. Some useful household items are: a large turkey baster or siphon, empty coffee cans and ice trays (to store parts), a ball of twine, electrical tape for wiring, small rolls of colored tape for tagging lines or hoses, markers and pens, a note pad, golf tees (for plugging vacuum lines), metal coat hangers or a roll of mechanic's wire (to hold things out of the way), dental pick or similar long, pointed probe, a strong magnet, and a small mirror (to see into recesses and under manifolds).

A more advanced set of tools, suitable for tune-up work, can be drawn up easily. While the tools are slightly more sophisticated, they need not be outrageously expensive. There are several inexpensive tach/dwell meters on the market that are every bit as good for the average mechanic as a professional model. Just be sure that it goes to a least 1200–1500 rpm on the tach scale and that it works on 4, 6 and 8-cylinder engines. The key to these purchases is to make them with an eye towards adaptability and wide range. A basic list of tune-up tools could include:

- Tach/dwell meter.
- Spark plug wrench and gapping tool.
- Feeler gauges for valve adjustment.
- Timing light.

The choice of a timing light should be made carefully. A light which works on the DC current supplied by the vehicle's battery is the best choice; it should have a xenon tube for brightness. On any vehicle with an electronic ignition system, a timing light with an inductive pickup that clamps around the No. 1 spark plug cable is preferred.

In addition to these basic tools, there are several other tools and gauges you may find useful. These include:

- Compression gauge. The screw-in type is slower to use, but eliminates the possibility of a faulty reading due to escaping pressure.
- Manifold vacuum gauge.
- 12V test light.
- A combination volt/ohmmeter
- Induction Ammeter. This is used for determining whether or not there is current in a wire. These are handy for use if a wire is broken somewhere in a wiring harness.

As a final note, you will probably find a torque wrench necessary for all but the most basic work. The beam type models are perfectly adequate, although the newer click types (breakaway) are easier to use. The click type torque wrenches tend to be more expensive. Also keep in mind that all types of torque wrenches should be periodically checked and/or recalibrated. You will have to decide for yourself which better fits your pocketbook, and purpose.

Special Tools

Normally, the use of special factory tools is avoided for repair procedures, since these are not readily available for the do-it-yourself mechanic. When it is possible to perform the job with more commonly available tools, it will be pointed out, but occasionally, a special tool was designed to perform a specific function and should be used. Before substituting another tool, you should be convinced that neither your safety nor the performance of the vehicle will be compromised.

Special tools can usually be purchased from an automotive parts store or from your dealer. In some cases special tools may be available directly from the tool manufacturer.

SERVICING YOUR VEHICLE SAFELY

▶ See Figures 16, 17 and 18

It is virtually impossible to anticipate all of the hazards involved with automotive maintenance and service, but care and common sense will prevent most accidents.

The rules of safety for mechanics range from "don't smoke around gasoline," to "use the proper tool(s) for the job." The trick to avoiding injuries is to develop safe work habits and to take every possible precaution.

Do's

- Do keep a fire extinguisher and first aid kit handy.
- Do wear safety glasses or goggles when cutting, drilling, grinding or prying, even if you have 20–20 vision. If you wear glasses for the sake of vision, wear safety goggles over your regular glasses.
- Do shield your eyes whenever you work around the battery. Batteries contain sulfuric acid. In case of contact with, flush the area with water or a mixture of water and baking soda, then seek immediate medical attention.
- Do use safety stands (jackstands) for any undervehicle service. Jacks are for raising vehicles; jackstands are for making sure the vehicle stays raised until you want it to come down.
- Do use adequate ventilation when working with any chemicals or hazardous materials. Like carbon monoxide, the asbestos dust resulting from some brake lining wear can be hazardous in sufficient quantities.
- Do disconnect the negative battery cable when working on the electrical system. The secondary ignition system contains EXTREMELY HIGH VOLTAGE. In some cases it can even exceed 50,000 volts.
- Do follow manufacturer's directions whenever working with potentially hazardous materials. Most chemicals and fluids are poisonous.
- Do properly maintain your tools. Loose hammerheads, mushroomed punches and chisels, frayed or poorly grounded electrical cords, excessively

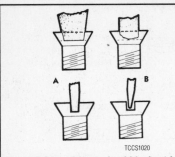

Fig. 16 Screwdrivers should be kept in good condition to prevent injury or damage which could result if the blade slips from the screw

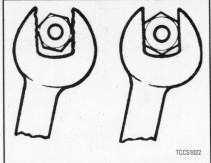

Fig. 17 Using the correct size wrench will help prevent the possibility of rounding off a nut

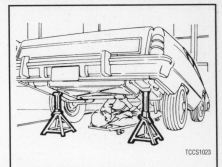

Fig. 18 NEVER work under a vehicle unless it is supported using safety stands (jackstands)

worn screwdrivers, spread wrenches (open end), cracked sockets, slipping ratchets, or faulty droplight sockets can cause accidents.

• Likewise, keep your tools clean; a greasy wrench can slip off a bolt head, ruining the bolt and often harming your knuckles in the process.

• Do use the proper size and type of tool for the job at hand. Do select a wrench or socket that fits the nut or bolt. The wrench or socket should sit straight, not cocked.

• Do, when possible, pull on a wrench handle rather than push on it, and adjust your stance to prevent a fall.

• Do be sure that adjustable wrenches are tightly closed on the nut or bolt and pulled so that the force is on the side of the fixed jaw.

• Do strike squarely with a hammer; avoid glancing blows.

• Do set the parking brake and block the drive wheels if the work requires a running engine.

Don'ts

• Don't run the engine in a garage or anywhere else without proper ventilation—EVER! Carbon monoxide is poisonous; it takes a long time to leave the human body and you can build up a deadly supply of it in your system by simply breathing in a little at a time. You may not realize you are slowly poisoning yourself. Always use power vents, windows, fans and/or open the garage door.

• Don't work around moving parts while wearing loose clothing. Short sleeves are much safer than long, loose sleeves. Hard-toed shoes with neoprene soles protect your toes and give a better grip on slippery surfaces. Watches and jewelry is not safe working around a vehicle. Long hair should be tied back under a hat or cap.

• Don't use pockets for toolboxes. A fall or bump can drive a screwdriver deep into your body. Even a rag hanging from your back pocket can wrap around a spinning shaft or fan.

• Don't smoke when working around gasoline, cleaning solvent or other flammable material.

• Don't smoke when working around the battery. When the battery is being charged, it gives off explosive hydrogen gas.

• Don't use gasoline to wash your hands; there are excellent soaps available. Gasoline contains dangerous additives which can enter the body through a cut or through your pores. Gasoline also removes all the natural oils from the skin so that bone dry hands will suck up oil and grease.

• Don't service the air conditioning system unless you are equipped with the necessary tools and training. When liquid or compressed gas refrigerant is released to atmospheric pressure it will absorb heat from whatever it contacts. This will chill or freeze anything it touches.

• Don't use screwdrivers for anything other than driving screws! A screwdriver used as an prying tool can snap when you least expect it, causing injuries. At the very least, you'll ruin a good screwdriver.

• Don't use an emergency jack (that little ratchet, scissors, or pantograph jack supplied with the vehicle) for anything other than changing a flat! These jacks are only intended for emergency use out on the road; they are NOT designed as a maintenance tool. If you are serious about maintaining your vehicle yourself, invest in a hydraulic floor jack of at least a 1½ ton capacity, and at least two sturdy jackstands.

FASTENERS, MEASUREMENTS AND CONVERSIONS

Bolts, Nuts and Other Threaded Retainers

▶ See Figures 19 and 20

Although there are a great variety of fasteners found in the modern car or truck, the most commonly used retainer is the threaded fastener (nuts, bolts, screws, studs, etc.). Most threaded retainers may be reused, provided that they are not damaged in use or during the repair. Some retainers (such as stretch bolts or torque prevailing nuts) are designed to deform when tightened or in use and should not be reinstalled.

Whenever possible, we will note any special retainers which should be replaced during a procedure. But you should always inspect the condition of a retainer when it is removed and replace any that show signs of damage. Check all threads for rust or corrosion which can increase the torque necessary to achieve the desired clamp load for which that fastener was originally selected. Additionally, be sure that the driver surface of the fastener has not been compromised by rounding or other damage. In some cases a driver surface may become only partially rounded, allowing the driver to catch in only one direction. In many of these occurrences, a fastener may be installed and tightened, but the driver would not be able to grip and loosen the fastener again.

If you must replace a fastener, whether due to design or damage, you must ALWAYS be sure to use the proper replacement. In all cases, a retainer of the same design, material and strength should be used. Markings on the heads of

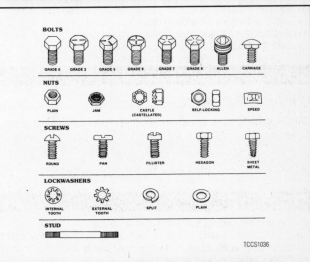

Fig. 19 There are many different types of threaded retainers found on vehicles

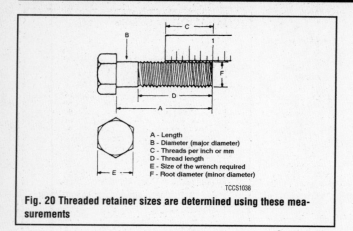

A - Length
B - Diameter (major diameter)
C - Threads per inch or mm
D - Thread length
E - Size of the wrench required
F - Root diameter (minor diameter)

TCCS1038

Fig. 20 Threaded retainer sizes are determined using these measurements

most bolts will help determine the proper strength of the fastener. The same material, thread and pitch must be selected to assure proper installation and safe operation of the vehicle afterwards.

Thread gauges are available to help measure a bolt or stud's thread. Most automotive and hardware stores keep gauges available to help you select the proper size. In a pinch, you can use another nut or bolt for a thread gauge. If the bolt you are replacing is not too badly damaged, you can select a match by finding another bolt which will thread in its place. If you find a nut which threads properly onto the damaged bolt, then use that nut to help select the replacement bolt.

✳✳ WARNING

Be aware that when you find a bolt with damaged threads, you may also find the nut or drilled hole it was threaded into has also been damaged. If this is the case, you may have to drill and tap the hole, replace the nut or otherwise repair the threads. NEVER try to force a replacement bolt to fit into the damaged threads.

Torque

Torque is defined as the measurement of resistance to turning or rotating. It tends to twist a body about an axis of rotation. A common example of this would be tightening a threaded retainer such as a nut, bolt or screw. Measuring torque is one of the most common ways to help assure that a threaded retainer has been properly fastened.

When tightening a threaded fastener, torque is applied in three distinct areas, the head, the bearing surface and the clamp load. About 50 percent of the measured torque is used in overcoming bearing friction. This is the friction between the bearing surface of the bolt head, screw head or nut face and the base material or washer (the surface on which the fastener is rotating). Approximately 40 percent of the applied torque is used in overcoming thread friction. This leaves only about 10 percent of the applied torque to develop a useful clamp load (the force which holds a joint together). This means that friction can account for as much as 90 percent of the applied torque on a fastener.

TORQUE WRENCHES

♦ See Figure 21

In most applications, a torque wrench can be used to assure proper installation of a fastener. Torque wrenches come in various designs and most automotive supply stores will carry a variety to suit your needs. A torque wrench should be used any time we supply a specific torque value for a fastener. Again, the general rule of "if you are using the right tool for the job, you should not have to strain to tighten a fastener" applies here.

Beam Type

The beam type torque wrench is one of the most popular types. It consists of a pointer attached to the head that runs the length of the flexible beam (shaft) to a scale located near the handle. As the wrench is pulled, the beam bends and the pointer indicates the torque using the scale.

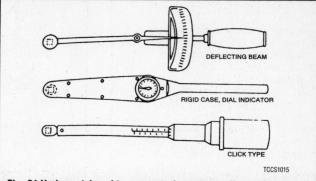

DEFLECTING BEAM

RIGID CASE, DIAL INDICATOR

CLICK TYPE

TCCS1015

Fig. 21 Various styles of torque wrenches are usually available at your local automotive supply store

Click (Breakaway) Type

Another popular design of torque wrench is the click type. To use the click type wrench you pre-adjust it to a torque setting. Once the torque is reached, the wrench has a reflex signaling feature that causes a momentary breakaway of the torque wrench body, sending an impulse to the operator's hand.

Pivot Head Type

♦ See Figure 22

Some torque wrenches (usually of the click type) may be equipped with a pivot head which can allow it to be used in areas of limited access. BUT, it must be used properly. To hold a pivot head wrench, grasp the handle lightly, and as you pull on the handle, it should be floated on the pivot point. If the handle comes in contact with the yoke extension during the process of pulling, there is a very good chance the torque readings will be inaccurate because this could alter the wrench loading point. The design of the handle is usually such as to make it inconvenient to deliberately misuse the wrench.

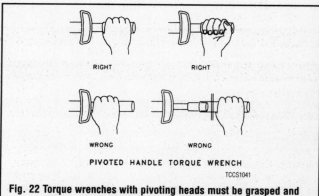

RIGHT   RIGHT

WRONG   WRONG

PIVOTED HANDLE TORQUE WRENCH

TCCS1041

Fig. 22 Torque wrenches with pivoting heads must be grasped and used properly to prevent an incorrect reading

➡**It should be mentioned that the use of any U-joint, wobble or extension will have an effect on the torque readings, no matter what type of wrench you are using. For the most accurate readings, install the socket directly on the wrench driver. If necessary, straight extensions (which hold a socket directly under the wrench driver) will have the least effect on the torque reading. Avoid any extension that alters the length of the wrench from the handle to the head/driving point (such as a crow's foot). U-joint or wobble extensions can greatly affect the readings; avoid their use at all times.**

Rigid Case (Direct Reading)

A rigid case or direct reading torque wrench is equipped with a dial indicator to show torque values. One advantage of these wrenches is that they can be held at any position on the wrench without affecting accuracy. These wrenches are often preferred because they tend to be compact, easy to read and have a great degree of accuracy.

TORQUE ANGLE METERS

Because the frictional characteristics of each fastener or threaded hole will vary, clamp loads which are based strictly on torque will vary as well. In most applications, this variance is not significant enough to cause worry. But, in certain applications, a manufacturer's engineers may determine that more precise clamp loads are necessary (such is the case with many aluminum cylinder heads). In these cases, a torque angle method of installation would be specified. When installing fasteners which are torque angle tightened, a predetermined seating torque and standard torque wrench are usually used first to remove any compliance from the joint. The fastener is then tightened the specified additional portion of a turn measured in degrees. A torque angle gauge (mechanical protractor) is used for these applications.

Standard and Metric Measurements

♦ See Figure 23

Throughout this manual, specifications are given to help you determine the condition of various components on your vehicle, or to assist you in their installation. Some of the most common measurements include length (in. or cm/mm), torque (ft. lbs., inch lbs. or Nm) and pressure (psi, in. Hg, kPa or mm Hg). In most cases, we strive to provide the proper measurement as determined by the manufacturer's engineers.

Though, in some cases, that value may not be conveniently measured with what is available in your toolbox. Luckily, many of the measuring devices which are available today will have two scales so the Standard or Metric measurements may easily be taken. If any of the various measuring tools which are available to you do not contain the same scale as listed in the specifications, use the accompanying conversion factors to determine the proper value.

The conversion factor chart is used by taking the given specification and multiplying it by the necessary conversion factor. For instance, looking at the first line, if you have a measurement in inches such as "free-play should be 2 in." but your ruler reads only in millimeters, multiply 2 in. by the conversion factor of 25.4 to get the metric equivalent of 50.8mm. Likewise, if the specification was given only in a Metric measurement, for example in Newton Meters (Nm), then look at the center column first. If the measurement is 100 Nm, multiply it by the conversion factor of 0.738 to get 73.8 ft. lbs.

CONVERSION FACTORS

LENGTH–DISTANCE

Inches (in.)	x 25.4	= Millimeters (mm)	x .0394	= Inches
Feet (ft.)	x .305	= Meters (m)	x 3.281	= Feet
Miles	x 1.609	= Kilometers (km)	x .0621	= Miles

VOLUME

Cubic Inches (in3)	x 16.387	= Cubic Centimeters	x .061	= in3
IMP Pints (IMP pt.)	x .568	= Liters (L)	x 1.76	= IMP pt.
IMP Quarts (IMP qt.)	x 1.137	= Liters (L)	x .88	= IMP qt.
IMP Gallons (IMP gal.)	x 4.546	= Liters (L)	x .22	= IMP gal.
IMP Quarts (IMP qt.)	x 1.201	= US Quarts (US qt.)	x .833	= IMP qt.
IMP Gallons (IMP gal.)	x 1.201	= US Gallons (US gal.)	x .833	= IMP gal.
Fl. Ounces	x 29.573	= Milliliters	x .034	= Ounces
US Pints (US pt.)	x .473	= Liters (L)	x 2.113	= Pints
US Quarts (US qt.)	x .946	= Liters (L)	x 1.057	= Quarts
US Gallons (US gal.)	x 3.785	= Liters (L)	x .264	= Gallons

MASS–WEIGHT

Ounces (oz.)	x 28.35	= Grams (g)	x .035	= Ounces
Pounds (lb.)	x .454	= Kilograms (kg)	x 2.205	= Pounds

PRESSURE

Pounds Per Sq. In. (psi)	x 6.895	= Kilopascals (kPa)	x .145	= psi
Inches of Mercury (Hg)	x .4912	= psi	x 2.036	= Hg
Inches of Mercury (Hg)	x 3.377	= Kilopascals (kPa)	x .2961	= Hg
Inches of Water (H$_2$O)	x .07355	= Inches of Mercury	x 13.783	= H$_2$O
Inches of Water (H$_2$O)	x .03613	= psi	x 27.684	= H$_2$O
Inches of Water (H$_2$O)	x .248	= Kilopascals (kPa)	x 4.026	= H$_2$O

TORQUE

Pounds–Force Inches (in-lb)	x .113	= Newton Meters (N·m)	x 8.85	= in-lb
Pounds–Force Feet (ft-lb)	x 1.356	= Newton Meters (N·m)	x .738	= ft-lb

VELOCITY

Miles Per Hour (MPH)	x 1.609	= Kilometers Per Hour (KPH)	x .621	= MPH

POWER

Horsepower (Hp)	x .745	= Kilowatts	x 1.34	= Horsepower

FUEL CONSUMPTION*

Miles Per Gallon IMP (MPG)	x .354	= Kilometers Per Liter (Km/L)	
Kilometers Per Liter (Km/L)	x 2.352	= IMP MPG	
Miles Per Gallon US (MPG)	x .425	= Kilometers Per Liter (Km/L)	
Kilometers Per Liter (Km/L)	x 2.352	= US MPG	

*It is common to covert from miles per gallon (mpg) to liters/100 kilometers (1/100 km), where mpg (IMP) x 1/100 km = 282 and mpg (US) x 1/100 km = 235.

TEMPERATURE

Degree Fahrenheit (°F)	= (°C x 1.8) + 32
Degree Celsius (°C)	= (°F − 32) x .56

TCCS1044

Fig. 23 Standard and metric conversion factors chart

SERIAL NUMBER IDENTIFICATION

Vehicle

♦ See Figures 24 and 25

The Vehicle Identification Number (VIN) is a seventeen-digit alpha/numeric sequence stamped on a plate which is located at the top, left-hand side of the instrument panel.

As far as the car owner is concerned, many of the digits in the VIN are of little or no value. At certain times, it may be necessary to refer to the VIN to interpret certain information, such as when ordering replacement parts or determining if your vehicle is involved in a factory service campaign (recall). In either of these instances, the following information may be helpful:

• 1st digit—indicates the place of manufacture. A **1** designates the USA; **2** designates Canada.
• 8th digit—indicates the type and the manufacturer of the original engine which was installed in the vehicle (see Engine).
• 10th digit—indicates the model year of the vehicle. **J** designates a 1988 model, **K** is for 1989, and so on.
• 11th digit—indicates the specific plant at which the vehicle was assembled.
• 12th–17th digits—this is the plant sequential number, which identifies the specific number of each vehicle within a production run. In the event of engineer-

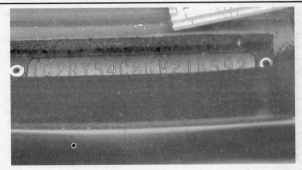

Fig. 24 The VIN is a 17-digit sequence stamped into a plate, visible through the windshield

89631P23

ing change or a recall involving only a certain quantity of vehicles within a production run, the affected vehicles can be identified.

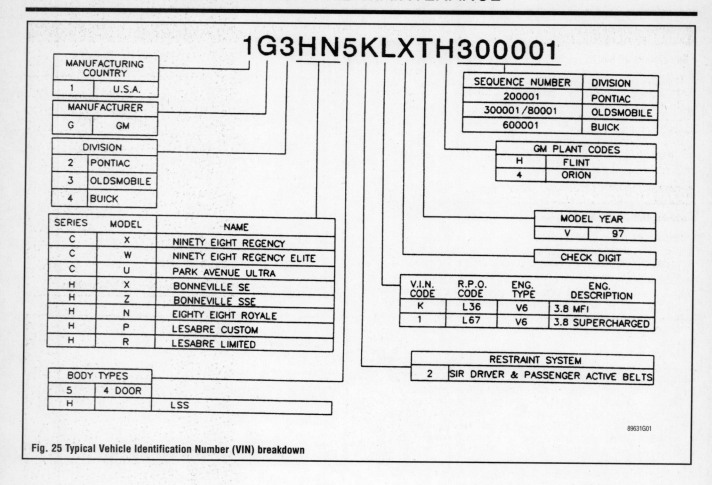

Fig. 25 Typical Vehicle Identification Number (VIN) breakdown

VEHICLE IDENTIFICATION CHART

Engine Code						Model Year	
Code	Liters	Cu. In. (cc)	Cyl.	Fuel Sys.	Eng. Mfg.	Code	Year
L	3.0	181 (2967)	6	MFI	Buick	G	1986
B	3.8	231 (3786)	6	SFI	Buick	H	1987
C	3.8	231 (3786)	6	MFI	Buick	J	1988
L	3.8	231 (3786)	6	SFI	Buick	K	1989
3	3.8	231 (3786)	6	SFI	Buick	L	1990
K	3.8	231 (3786)	6	MFI	Buick	M	1991
1	3.8	231 (3786)	6	SFI ①	Buick	N	1992
						P	1993
						R	1994
						S	1995
						T	1996
						V	1997
						W	1998
						X	1999

MFI - Multi-port electronic Fuel Injection
SFI - Sequential Fuel Injection

① Supercharged engine

89631C01

Engine

▶ See Figures 26 and 27

The engine code is represented by the eighth character in the VIN and identifies the engine type, displacement, fuel system and manufacturing division.

The engine identification code is either stamped onto the engine block or found on a label affixed to the engine. This code supplies information about the manufacturing plant location and time of manufacture.

The engine identification code will sometimes be required to order replacement engine parts. Refer to the accompanying illustrations to determine the code location for your engine.

Transaxle

▶ See Figures 28 and 29

Similar to the engine identification code, the transaxle identification code supplies information about the transaxle, such as the manufacturing plant, Julian date of manufacture, shift number and model. The location for the transaxle code is shown in the accompanying illustrations.

Drive Axle

The drive axle code is stamped onto the axle shaft near the CV-boot.

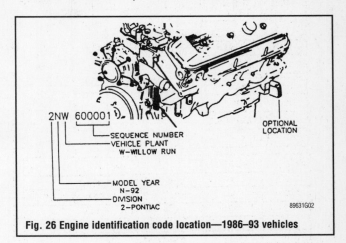

Fig. 26 Engine identification code location—1986–93 vehicles

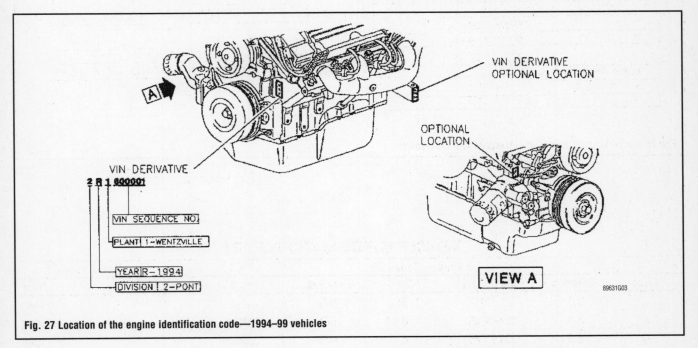

Fig. 27 Location of the engine identification code—1994–99 vehicles

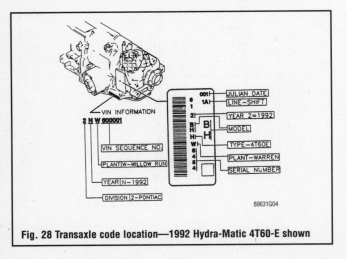

Fig. 28 Transaxle code location—1992 Hydra-Matic 4T60-E shown

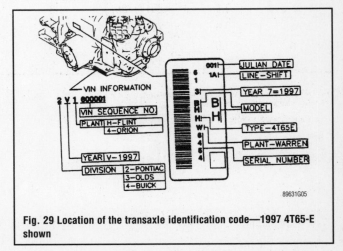

Fig. 29 Location of the transaxle identification code—1997 4T65-E shown

ENGINE IDENTIFICATION

Year	Model	Engine Displacement Liters (cc)	Engine Series (ID/VIN)	Fuel System	No. of Cylinders	Engine Type
1986	LeSabre	3.0L (2967)	L	MFI	6	OHV
	LeSabre	3.8L (3786)	B	SFI	6	OHV
	LeSabre	3.8L (3786)	3	SFI	6	OHV
	Delta 88	3.0L (2967)	L	MFI	6	OHV
	Delta 88	3.8L (3786)	B	SFI	6	OHV
	Delta 88	3.8L (3786)	3	SFI	6	OHV
1987	Bonneville	3.8L (3786)	3	SFI	6	OHV
	LeSabre	3.8L (3786)	3	SFI	6	OHV
	Delta 88	3.8L (3786)	3	SFI	6	OHV
1988	Bonneville	3.8L (3786)	C	MFI	6	OHV
	Bonneville	3.8L (3786)	3	SFI	6	OHV
	LeSabre	3.8L (3786)	C	MFI	6	OHV
	LeSabre	3.8L (3786)	3	SFI	6	OHV
	Delta 88	3.8L (3786)	C	MFI	6	OHV
	Delta 88	3.8L (3786)	3	SFI	6	OHV
1989	Bonneville	3.8L (3786)	C	MFI	6	OHV
	LeSabre	3.8L (3786)	C	MFI	6	OHV
	Eighty Eight	3.8L (3786)	C	MFI	6	OHV
1990	Bonneville	3.8L (3786)	C	MFI	6	OHV
	LeSabre	3.8L (3786)	C	MFI	6	OHV
	Eighty Eight	3.8L (3786)	C	MFI	6	OHV
1991	Bonneville	3.8L (3786)	C	MFI	6	OHV
	LeSabre	3.8L (3786)	C	MFI	6	OHV
	Eighty Eight	3.8L (3786)	C	MFI	6	OHV
1992	Bonneville	3.8L (3786)	L	SFI	6	OHV
	Bonneville	3.8L (3786)	1	SFI-S	6	OHV
	LeSabre	3.8L (3786)	L	SFI	6	OHV
	Eighty Eight	3.8L (3786)	L	SFI	6	OHV
1993	Bonneville	3.8L (3786)	L	SFI	6	OHV
	Bonneville	3.8L (3786)	1	SFI-S	6	OHV
	LeSabre	3.8L (3786)	L	SFI	6	OHV
	Eighty Eight	3.8L (3786)	L	SFI	6	OHV
1994	Bonneville	3.8L (3786)	L	SFI	6	OHV
	Bonneville	3.8L (3786)	1	SFI-S	6	OHV
	LeSabre	3.8L (3786)	L	SFI	6	OHV
	Eighty Eight	3.8L (3786)	L	SFI	6	OHV
1995	Bonneville	3.8L (3786)	K	MFI	6	OHV
	Bonneville	3.8L (3786)	1	SFI-S	6	OHV
	LeSabre	3.8L (3786)	L	SFI	6	OHV
	Eighty Eight	3.8L (3786)	K	MFI	6	OHV
	Eighty Eight	3.8L (3786)	1	SFI-S	6	OHV
1996	Bonneville	3.8L (3786)	K	MFI	6	OHV
	Bonneville	3.8L (3786)	1	SFI-S	6	OHV
	LeSabre	3.8L (3786)	K	MFI	6	OHV
	Eighty Eight	3.8L (3786)	K	MFI	6	OHV
	Eighty Eight	3.8L (3786)	1	SFI-S	6	OHV
1997	Bonneville	3.8L (3786)	K	MFI	6	OHV
	Bonneville	3.8L (3786)	1	SFI-S	6	OHV
	LeSabre	3.8L (3786)	K	MFI	6	OHV
	Eighty Eight	3.8L (3786)	K	MFI	6	OHV
	Eighty Eight	3.8L (3786)	1	SFI-S	6	OHV
1998	Bonneville	3.8L (3786)	K	MFI	6	OHV
	Bonneville	3.8L (3786)	1	SFI-S	6	OHV
	LeSabre	3.8L (3786)	K	MFI	6	OHV
	Eighty Eight	3.8L (3786)	K	MFI	6	OHV
	Eighty Eight	3.8L (3786)	1	SFI-S	6	OHV
1999	Bonneville	3.8L (3786)	K	MFI	6	OHV
	Bonneville	3.8L (3786)	1	SFI-S	6	OHV
	LeSabre	3.8L (3786)	K	MFI	6	OHV
	Eighty Eight	3.8L (3786)	K	MFI	6	OHV
	Eighty Eight	3.8L (3786)	1	SFI-S	6	OHV

MFI - Multi-port Fuel Injection
SFI - Sequential Fuel Injection
SFI-S - Sequential Fuel Injection, Supercharged engine
OHV - OverHead Valve

89631C00

GENERAL ENGINE SPECIFICATIONS

Year	Engine ID/VIN	Engine Displacement Liters (cc)	Fuel System Type	Net Horsepower @ rpm	Net Torque @ rpm (ft. lbs.)	Bore x Stroke (in.)	Compression Ratio	Oil Pressure @ rpm
1986	L	3.0L (2967)	MFI	125 @ 4900	150 @ 2400	3.800 x 2.660	9.0:1	37 @ 2400
	B	3.8L (3786)	SFI	140 @ 4400	200 @ 2000	3.800 x 3.400	8.5:1	37 @ 2000
	3	3.8L (3786)	SFI	150 @ 4400	200 @ 2000	3.800 x 3.400	8.5:1	37 @ 2000
1987	3	3.8L (3786)	SFI	165 @ 5200	210 @ 2000	3.800 x 3.400	8.5:1	37 @ 2400
1988	C	3.8L (3786)	MFI	165 @ 5200	210 @ 2000	3.800 x 3.400	8.5:1	37 @ 2400
	3	3.8L (3786)	SFI	165 @ 5200	210 @ 2100	3.800 x 3.400	8.5:1	37 @ 2400
1989	C	3.8L (3786)	MFI	165 @ 5200	210 @ 2100	3.800 x 3.400	8.5:1	37 @ 2400
1990	C	3.8L (3786)	MFI	165 @ 5200	210 @ 2000	3.800 x 3.400	8.5:1	40 @ 1850
1991	C	3.8L (3786)	MFI	165 @ 5200	210 @ 2100	3.800 x 3.400	8.5:1	60 @ 1850
1992	L	3.8L (3786)	SFI	170 @ 4800	220 @ 3200	3.800 x 3.400	8.5:1	60 @ 1850
	1	3.8L (3786)	SFI-S	205 @ 4400	260 @ 2600	3.800 x 3.400	8.5:1	60 @ 1850
1993	L	3.8L (3786)	SFI	170 @ 4800	220 @ 3200	3.800 x 3.400	8.5:1	60 @ 1850
	1	3.8L (3786)	SFI-S	205 @ 4400	260 @ 2600	3.800 x 3.400	8.5:1	60 @ 1850
1994	L	3.8L (3786)	SFI	170 @ 4800	220 @ 3200	3.800 x 3.400	8.5:1	60 @ 1850
	1	3.8L (3786)	SFI-S	205 @ 4400	260 @ 2600	3.800 x 3.400	8.5:1	60 @ 1850
1995	L	3.8 (3786)	SFI	170 @ 4800	220 @ 3200	3.800 x 3.400	8.5:1	60 @ 1850
	K	3.8 (3786)	MFI	205 @ 5200	230 @ 4000	3.800 x 3.400	9.4:1	60 @ 1850
	1	3.8L (3786)	SFI-S	240 @ 5200	280 @ 3200	3.800 x 3.400	8.5:1	60 @ 1850
1996	K	3.8L (3786)	MFI	205 @ 5200	230 @ 4000	3.800 x 3.400	9.4:1	60 @ 1850
	1	3.8L (3786)	SFI-S	240 @ 5200	280 @ 3200	3.800 x 3.400	8.5:1	60 @ 1850
1997	K	3.8L (3786)	MFI	205 @ 5200	230 @ 4000	3.800 x 3.400	9.4:1	60 @ 1850
	1	3.8L (3786)	SFI-S	240 @ 5200	280 @ 3200	3.800 x 3.400	8.5:1	60 @ 1850
1998	K	3.8L (3786)	MFI	205 @ 5200	230 @ 4000	3.800 x 3.400	9.4:1	60 @ 1850
	1	3.8L (3786)	SFI-S	240 @ 5200	280 @ 3200	3.800 x 3.400	8.5:1	60 @ 1850
1999	K	3.8L (3786)	MFI	205 @ 5200	230 @ 4000	3.800 x 3.400	9.4:1	60 @ 1850
	1	3.8L (3786)	SFI-S	240 @ 5200	280 @ 3200	3.800 x 3.400	8.5:1	60 @ 1850

89631C09

ROUTINE MAINTENANCE AND TUNE-UP

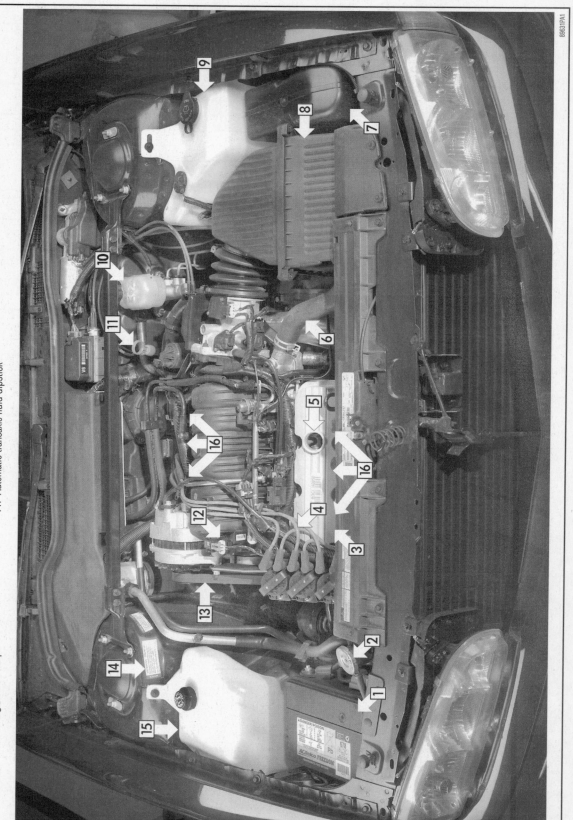

UNDERHOOD MAINTENANCE COMPONENT LOCATIONS—LATE MODEL

1. Battery
2. Radiator cap
3. Engine oil dipstick (located behind radiator shroud)
4. Spark plug wires
5. Engine oil fill cap
6. Upper radiator hose
7. Evaporative canister (located behind radiator)
8. Air cleaner assembly
9. Windshield washer fluid reservoir
10. Brake master cylinder
11. Automatic transaxle fluid dipstick
12. PCV valve (located under MAP sensor)
13. Accessory drive belt
14. Coolant specification label
15. Coolant recovery (overflow) reservoir
16. Spark plugs

UNDERHOOD MAINTENANCE COMPONENT LOCATIONS—EARLY MODEL

1. Battery
2. Radiator cap
3. Accessory belt routing
4. Spark plug wires
5. Engine oil fill cap
6. Upper radiator hose
7. Air cleaner assembly
8. Brake master cylinder
9. Automatic transaxle fluid dipstick
10. Spark plugs
11. Power steering fluid reservoir
12. Accessory drive belts
13. Coolant recovery (overflow) reservoir
14. Windshield washer fluid reservoir
15. Evaporative canister (located under air duct)

89631PA2

Proper maintenance and tune-up is the key to long and trouble-free vehicle life, and the work can yield its own rewards. Studies have shown that a properly tuned and maintained vehicle can achieve better gas mileage than an out-of-tune vehicle. As a conscientious owner and driver, set aside a Saturday morning, say once a month, to check or replace items which could cause major problems later. Keep your own personal log to jot down which services you performed, how much the parts cost you, the date, and the exact odometer reading at the time. Keep all receipts for such items as engine oil and filters, so that they may be referred to in case of related problems or to determine operating expenses. As a do-it-yourselfer, these receipts are the only proof you have that the required maintenance was performed. In the event of a warranty problem, these receipts will be invaluable.

The literature provided with your vehicle when it was originally delivered includes the factory recommended maintenance schedule. If you no longer have this literature, replacement copies are usually available from the dealer. A maintenance schedule is provided later in this section, in case you do not have the factory literature.

Air Cleaner (Element)

Regular air cleaner element replacement is a must, since a partially clogged element will cause a performance loss, decreased fuel mileage, and engine damage if enough dirt gets into the cylinders and contaminates the engine oil.

REMOVAL & INSTALLATION

▶ **See Figures 30 thru 35**

The removal of air filter assembly will vary slightly for different year and different engine. The following procedure can be altered as you see fit for your specific vehicle.

1. Disconnect the negative battery cable.
2. If necessary to remove the air cleaner assembly cover, disconnect the air duct tube clamp to the throttle body and slip the duct off.
3. Unfasten the bolts/screws, or retaining clips, then remove the air cleaner cover. The cover should be easy to remove, if not look to see if you missed a hidden clip or screw.
4. Lift the air cleaner element from the housing.
5. Clean the air cleaner housing to remove any remaining dirt. Inspect the element for dirt, dust and/or water and replace if necessary.

To install:

➡**When installing the new filter make certain not to bend or tear the paper element.**

6. Place the new element in the air cleaner housing.
7. Position the cover over the air cleaner assembly and secure with the retaining clips or screws, as applicable.
8. If removed, install the air cleaner assembly cover.
9. Connect the negative battery cable.

Fuel Filter

✳✴ CAUTION

To reduce the risk of fire and personal injury, it is necessary to relieve the fuel system pressure before servicing any fuel system component. If this procedure is not performed, fuel may be sprayed out of the connection under pressure. Cover fuel hose connections with a shop towel before disconnecting to catch any residual fuel that may still be in the line. Always keep a dry chemical (Class B) fire extinguisher near the work area.

The fuel filter is located in the fuel feed line attached to the frame rail, at the rear of the vehicle. The fuel filter may be either a quick-connect or threaded fitting type. Check your vehicle to see which type it has and proceed accordingly.

REMOVAL & INSTALLATION

▶ **See Figures 36, 37, 38 and 39**

✳✴ CAUTION

Observe all applicable safety precautions when working around fuel. Whenever servicing the fuel system, always work in a well ventilated area. Do not allow fuel spray or vapors to come in contact with a spark or open flame. Keep a dry chemical fire extinguisher near the work area. Always keep fuel in a container specifically designed for fuel storage; also, always properly seal fuel containers to avoid the possibility of fire or explosion.

1. Relieve the fuel system pressure, as outlined in Section 5 of this manual.
2. If not already done, disconnect the negative battery cable.
3. Raise and safely support the vehicle.

➡**To reduce fuel spillage, place a shop towel over the fuel lines before disconnecting.**

4. If equipped with quick-connect fuel line fittings, perform the following:
   a. Grasp the filter and 1 fuel line fitting. Twist the quick-connect fitting ¼ turn in each direction to loosen any dirt within the fitting. Repeat for the other fuel line fitting.
   b. Use compressed air, blow out dirt from the quick-connect fittings at both ends of the fuel filter.
   c. To disconnect plastic fuel line fittings, squeeze the plastic tabs of the male end of the connector and pull the connector apart. Repeat for the other fitting.
   d. To disconnect metal fuel line fittings, choose the proper size tool from a suitable quick-connect tool set, for the size of the quick-connect fitting. Insert the tool into the female connector, then push inward with the tool in order to release the locking tabs. Pull the connection apart.
5. If equipped with threaded fuel line fittings, perform the following:
   a. Use a back-up wrench to disconnect the fuel lines from the filter.
6. Loosen the filter bracket attaching screw/bolt, then slide the filter from the bracket.

To install:

7. If necessary, remove the protective caps from the new fuel filter. Position the filter in the bracket. Using new O-rings, install the fuel lines to the filter.
8. For filters with quick-connect lines, perform the following:
   a. Apply a few drops of clean engine oil to the male fuel pipe end.
   b. Push both sides of the quick-connect fitting together in order to cause the retaining tabs/fingers to snap into place.
   c. Once installed, pull on both sides of the quick-connect fitting to ensure connector is secure.
   d. If equipped, reposition the dust cover over the quick-connect fitting.
9. For filters with threaded fuel lines, use a back-up wrench to prevent the filter from turning, then tighten the fittings to 22 ft. lbs. (30 Nm).
10. Securely tighten the fuel filter bracket retaining screw/bolt.
11. Carefully lower the vehicle.
12. Connect the negative battery cable, and check for leaks as follows:

PCV Valve

REMOVAL & INSTALLATION

➡**When replacing a PCV valve, you MUST use the correct valve. Many valves look alike on the outside, but have different mechanical values. Putting an incorrect PCV valve on a vehicle can cause a great deal of driveability problems. The engine computer assumes the valve is the correct one and may overadjust ignition timing or fuel mixture.**

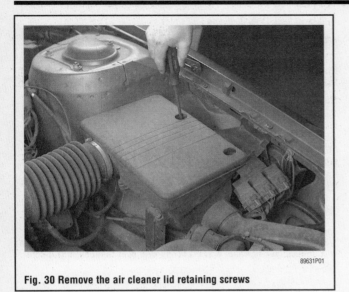

Fig. 30 Remove the air cleaner lid retaining screws

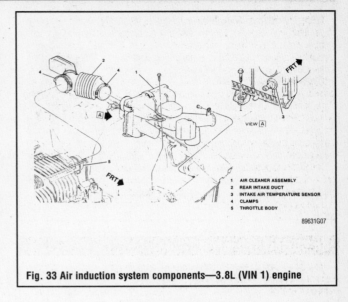

1 AIR CLEANER ASSEMBLY
2 REAR INTAKE DUCT
3 INTAKE AIR TEMPERATURE SENSOR
4 CLAMPS
5 THROTTLE BODY

Fig. 33 Air induction system components—3.8L (VIN 1) engine

Fig. 31 Lift the air cleaner cover off, then remove the element from the housing

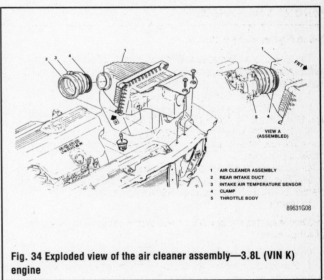

1 AIR CLEANER ASSEMBLY
2 REAR INTAKE DUCT
3 INTAKE AIR TEMPERATURE SENSOR
4 CLAMP
5 THROTTLE BODY

Fig. 34 Exploded view of the air cleaner assembly—3.8L (VIN K) engine

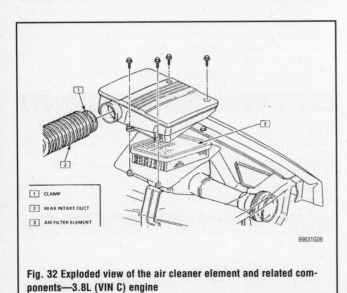

1 CLAMP
2 REAR INTAKE DUCT
3 AIR FILTER ELEMENT

Fig. 32 Exploded view of the air cleaner element and related components—3.8L (VIN C) engine

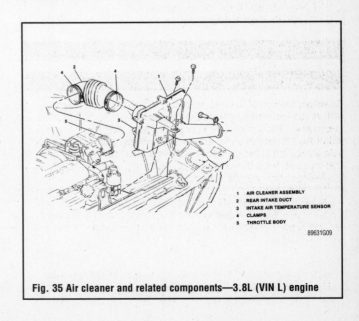

1 AIR CLEANER ASSEMBLY
2 REAR INTAKE DUCT
3 INTAKE AIR TEMPERATURE SENSOR
4 CLAMPS
5 THROTTLE BODY

Fig. 35 Air cleaner and related components—3.8L (VIN L) engine

Fig. 36 The fuel filter is mounted on the frame rail, just forward of the rear wheel

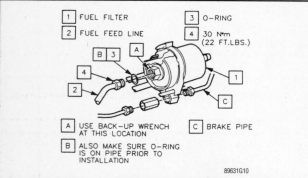

Fig. 37 Some early model vehicles have fuel filters with threaded fuel lines—1991 vehicle shown

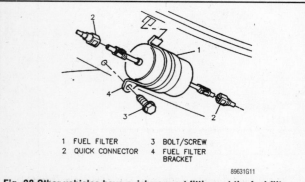

Fig. 38 Other vehicles have quick-connect fittings at the fuel filter—1995 vehicle shown

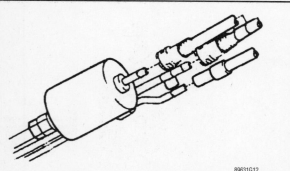

Fig. 39 Some vehicles, such as 1997–99 models, have filters with quick-connect and threaded fittings

3.0L and 3.8L (VIN 3, B and C) Engines

▶ **See Figures 40, 41 and 42**

1. Remove the PCV valve from the grommet in the valve (rocker arm) cover or intake manifold, as applicable.
2. Disconnect the PCV valve from the breather hose.
To install:
3. Connect the new PCV valve into the breather hose.
4. Install the PCV valve into the grommet in the valve (rocker arm) cover.

3.8L (VIN 1) Engine

▶ **See Figure 43**

1. Disconnect the negative battery cable.
2. If necessary, remove the cosmetic cover from the fuel rail and intake manifold.
3. While holding the access cover down with your finger to keep the spring from pushing the cover off, unfasten the cover retaining bolts.
4. Lift the cover and gasket off slowly.
5. Remove the spring and valve, with the O-ring, from the intake manifold. Inspect the O-ring and replace if damaged.
To install:
6. Install the PCV valve and O-ring, then position the spring.
7. Position a new gasket, then install the cover and secure with the retaining screws.
8. If equipped, install the cosmetic cover.
9. Connect the negative battery cable.

3.8L (VIN L) Engine

▶ **See Figure 44**

1. Disconnect the negative battery cable.
2. Remove the sight shield from the fuel rail and intake manifold.
3. Press down on the access cover and rotate it ¼ turn counterclockwise.
4. Slowly lift off the cover and O-ring.
5. Remove the spring and PCV valve with the O-ring from the intake manifold. Inspect the O-rings and replace if necessary.
To install:
6. Install the PCV valve; replace the O-ring if necessary.
7. Install the spring.
8. Install the O-ring and cover. Hold the cover in place, then rotate it ¼ turn clockwise to lock it into position.
9. Install the sight shield to the fuel rail and intake manifold.
10. Connect the negative battery cable.

3.8L (VIN K) Engine

▶ **See Figure 45**

1. Disconnect the negative battery cable.
2. Remove the sight shield from the fuel rail and intake manifold.
3. For 1996–99 vehicles, remove the MAP sensor.
4. Using a ½ in. (1995 vehicles) or 16mm (1996–99 vehicles) socket, press the access cover down and rotate ¼ turn counterclockwise.
5. Lift the cover and O-ring off slowly.
6. Remove the spring and valve with the O-ring from the intake manifold. Inspect the O-ring for damage and replace if necessary.
To install:
7. Position the PCV valve and O-ring.
8. Install the spring.
9. Fasten the cover and O-ring.
10. If necessary, install the MAP sensor.
11. Install the sight shield.
12. Connect the negative battery cable.

Evaporative Canister

This system is designed to limit gasoline vapor, which normally escapes from the fuel tank and intake manifold, from discharging into the atmosphere. Vapor absorption is accomplished through the use of the charcoal canister, which stores the vapors until they can be removed and burned in the combustion process.

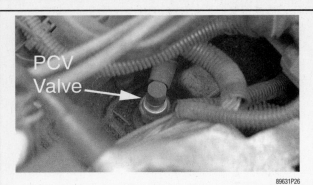

Fig. 40 The PCV valve on the 3.8L (VIN C) engine is mounted in the intake manifold

Fig. 41 Remove the PCV valve from its grommet, disconnect the vacuum hose, then remove the valve from the vehicle

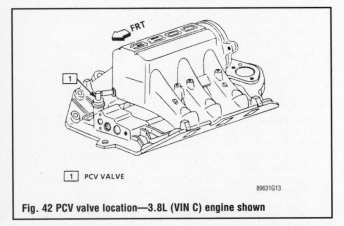

1 PCV VALVE

Fig. 42 PCV valve location—3.8L (VIN C) engine shown

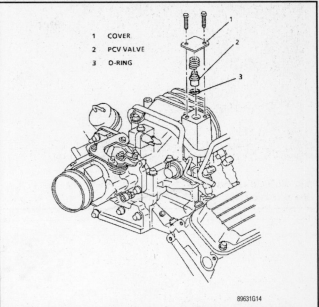

1 COVER
2 PCV VALVE
3 O-RING

Fig. 43 The PCV valve on the 3.8L (VIN 1) engine is located under a cover

1 COVER
2 COVER O-RING
3 SPRING
4 CRANKCASE VENTILATION VALVE
5 O-RING

Fig. 44 Exploded view of the PCV valve and related components—3.8L (VIN L) engine

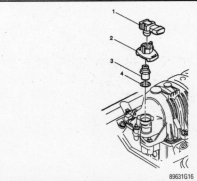

Fig. 45 For 1996–99 3.8L (VIN K) engines, you must first remove the MAP sensor (1) and cover (2), then the PCV valve (3) and O-ring (4)

SERVICING

♦ **See Figures 46 and 47**

The evaporative canister does not require periodic service. Check the hoses and canister for cracks and/or other damage. For canister removal and installation procedures, please refer to Section 4 of this manual.

Battery

PRECAUTIONS

Always use caution when working on or near the battery. Never allow a tool to bridge the gap between the negative and positive battery terminals. Also, be

Fig. 46 The EVAP canister is found at the left front corner of the engine compartment, under the air duct

89631P28

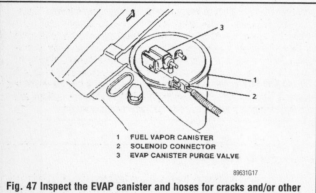

1 FUEL VAPOR CANISTER
2 SOLENOID CONNECTOR
3 EVAP CANISTER PURGE VALVE

89631G17

Fig. 47 Inspect the EVAP canister and hoses for cracks and/or other damage

careful not to allow a tool to provide a ground between the positive cable/terminal and any metal component on the vehicle. Either of these conditions will cause a short circuit, leading to sparks and possible personal injury.

ADJUSTMENT

Do not smoke, have an open flame or create sparks near a battery; the gases contained in the battery are very explosive and, if ignited, could cause severe injury or death.

All batteries, regardless of type, should be carefully secured by a battery hold-down device. If this is not done, the battery terminals or casing may crack from stress applied to the battery during vehicle
operation. A battery which is not secured may allow acid to leak out, making it discharge faster; such leaking corrosive acid can also eat away at components under the hood.

Always visually inspect the battery case for cracks, leakage and corrosion. A white corrosive substance on the battery case or on nearby components would indicate a leaking or cracked battery. If the battery is cracked, it should be replaced immediately.

GENERAL MAINTENANCE

▶ **See Figure 48**

A battery that is not sealed must be checked periodically for electrolyte level. You cannot add water to a sealed maintenance-free battery (though not all maintenance-free batteries are sealed); however, a sealed battery must also be checked for proper electrolyte level, as indicated by the color of the built-in hydrometer "eye."

Always keep the battery cables and terminals free of corrosion. Check these components about once a year. Refer to the removal, installation and cleaning procedures outlined in this section.

Keep the top of the battery clean, as a film of dirt can help completely discharge a battery that is not used for long periods. A solution of baking soda and

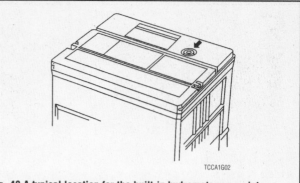

TCCA1G02

Fig. 48 A typical location for the built-in hydrometer on mainte-nance-free batteries

water may be used for cleaning, but be careful to flush this off with clear water. DO NOT let any of the solution into the filler holes. Baking soda neutralizes battery acid and will de-activate a battery cell.

Batteries in vehicles which are not operated on a regular basis can fall victim to parasitic loads (small current drains which are constantly drawing current from the battery). Normal parasitic loads may drain a battery on a vehicle that is in storage and not used for 6–8 weeks. Vehicles that have additional accessories such as a cellular phone, an alarm system or other devices that increase parasitic load may discharge a battery sooner. If the vehicle is to be stored for 6–8 weeks in a secure area and the alarm system, if present, is not necessary, the negative battery cable should be disconnected at the onset of storage to protect the battery charge.

Remember that constantly discharging and recharging will shorten battery life. Take care not to allow a battery to be needlessly discharged.

BATTERY FLUID

Check the battery electrolyte level at least once a month, or more often in hot weather or during periods of extended vehicle operation. On non-sealed batteries, the level can be checked either through the case on translucent batteries or by removing the cell caps on opaque-cased types. The electrolyte level in each cell should be kept filled to the split ring inside each cell, or the line marked on the outside of the case.

If the level is low, add only distilled water through the opening until the level is correct. Each cell is separate from the others, so each must be checked and filled individually. Distilled water should be used, because the chemicals and minerals found in most drinking water are harmful to the battery and could significantly shorten its life.

If water is added in freezing weather, the vehicle should be driven several miles to allow the water to mix with the electrolyte. Otherwise, the battery could freeze.

Although some maintenance-free batteries have removable cell caps for access to the electrolyte, the electrolyte condition and level on all sealed maintenance-free batteries must be checked using the built-in hydrometer "eye." The exact type of eye varies between battery manufacturers, but most apply a sticker to the battery itself explaining the possible readings. When in doubt, refer to the battery manufacturer's instructions to interpret battery condition using the built-in hydrometer.

➡**Although the readings from built-in hydrometers found in sealed batteries may vary, a green eye usually indicates a properly charged battery with sufficient fluid level. A dark eye is normally an indicator of a battery with sufficient fluid, but one which may be low in charge. And a light or yellow eye is usually an indication that electrolyte supply has dropped below the necessary level for battery (and hydrometer) operation. In this last case, sealed batteries with an insufficient electrolyte level must usually be discarded.**

Checking the Specific Gravity

▶ **See Figures 49, 50 and 51**

A hydrometer is required to check the specific gravity on all batteries that are not maintenance-free. On batteries that are maintenance-free, the specific gravity is checked by observing the built-in hydrometer "eye" on the top of the battery case. Check with your battery's manufacturer for proper interpretation of its built-in hydrometer readings.

Fig. 49 On non-maintenance-free batteries, the fluid level can be checked through the case on translucent models; the cell caps must be removed on other models

Fig. 50 If the fluid level is low, add only distilled water through the opening until the level is correct

Fig. 51 Check the specific gravity of the battery's electrolyte with a hydrometer

---

> ### ✳✳ CAUTION
>
> **Battery electrolyte contains sulfuric acid. If you should splash any on your skin or in your eyes, flush the affected area with plenty of clear water. If it lands in your eyes, get medical help immediately.**

The fluid (sulfuric acid solution) contained in the battery cells will tell you many things about the condition of the battery. Because the cell plates must be kept submerged below the fluid level in order to operate, maintaining the fluid level is extremely important. And, because the specific gravity of the acid is an indication of electrical charge, testing the fluid can be an aid in determining if the battery must be replaced. A battery in a vehicle with a properly operating charging system should require little maintenance, but careful, periodic inspection should reveal problems before they leave you stranded.

As stated earlier, the specific gravity of a battery's electrolyte level can be used as an indication of battery charge. At least once a year, check the specific gravity of the battery. It should be between 1.20 and 1.26 on the gravity scale. Most auto supply stores carry a variety of inexpensive battery testing hydrometers. These can be used on any non-sealed battery to test the specific gravity in each cell.

The battery testing hydrometer has a squeeze bulb at one end and a nozzle at the other. Battery electrolyte is sucked into the hydrometer until the float is lifted from its seat. The specific gravity is then read by noting the position of the float. If gravity is low in one or more cells, the battery should be slowly charged and checked again to see if the gravity has come up. Generally, if after charging, the specific gravity between any two cells varies more than 50 points (0.50), the battery should be replaced, as it can no longer produce sufficient voltage to guarantee proper operation.

CABLES

◆ See Figures 52 thru 57

Once a year (or as necessary), the battery terminals and the cable clamps should be cleaned. Loosen the clamps and remove the cables, negative cable

Fig. 52 Loosen the battery cable retaining nut . . .

Fig. 53 . . . then disconnect the cable from the battery

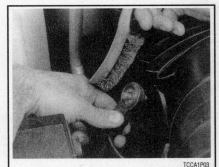

Fig. 54 A wire brush may be used to clean any corrosion or foreign material from the cable

Fig. 55 The wire brush can also be used to remove any corrosion or dirt from the battery terminal

Fig. 56 The battery terminal can also be cleaned using a solution of baking soda and water

Fig. 57 Before connecting the cables, it's a good idea to coat the terminals with a small amount of dielectric grease

first. On batteries with posts on top, the use of a puller specially made for this purpose is recommended. These are inexpensive and available in most auto parts stores. Side terminal battery cables are secured with a small bolt.

Clean the cable clamps and the battery terminal with a wire brush, until all corrosion, grease, etc., is removed and the metal is shiny. It is especially important to clean the inside of the clamp thoroughly (an old knife is useful here), since a small deposit of foreign material or oxidation there will prevent a sound electrical connection and inhibit either starting or charging. Special tools are available for cleaning these parts, one type for conventional top post batteries and another type for side terminal batteries. It is also a good idea to apply some dielectric grease to the terminal, as this will aid in the prevention of corrosion.

After the clamps and terminals are clean, reinstall the cables, negative cable last; DO NOT hammer the clamps onto battery posts. Tighten the clamps securely, but do not distort them. Give the clamps and terminals a thin external coating of grease after installation, to retard corrosion.

Check the cables at the same time that the terminals are cleaned. If the cable insulation is cracked or broken, or if the ends are frayed, the cable should be \replaced with a new cable of the same length and gauge.

CHARGING

❈❈ CAUTION

The chemical reaction which takes place in all batteries generates explosive hydrogen gas. A spark can cause the battery to explode and splash acid. To avoid serious personal injury, be sure there is proper ventilation and take appropriate fire safety precautions when connecting, disconnecting, or charging a battery and when using jumper cables.

A battery should be charged at a slow rate to keep the plates inside from getting too hot. However, if some maintenance-free batteries are allowed to dis-charge until they are almost "dead," they may have to be charged at a high rate to bring them back to "life." Always follow the charger manufacturer's instructions on charging the battery.

REPLACEMENT

When it becomes necessary to replace the battery, select one with an amperage rating equal to or greater than the battery originally installed. Deterioration and just plain aging of the battery cables, starter motor, and associated wires makes the battery's job harder in successive years. The slow increase in electrical resistance over time makes it prudent to install a new battery with a greater capacity than the old.

Belts

INSPECTION

▶ **See Figures 58, 59, 60, 61 and 62**

Inspect the belts for signs of glazing or cracking. A glazed belt will be perfectly smooth from slippage, while a good belt will have a slight texture of fabric visible. Cracks will usually start at the inner edge of the belt and run outward. All worn or damaged drive belts should be replaced immediately. It is best to replace all drive belts at one time, as a preventive maintenance measure, during this service operation.

BELT ADJUSTMENT

Belt tension is maintained by the automatic tensioner and is NOT adjustable. If the belt slips or is out of minimum tension range, you need a new belt. To inspect the belt's tension, perform the following:

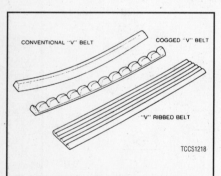

Fig. 58 There are typically 3 types of accessory drive belts found on vehicles today

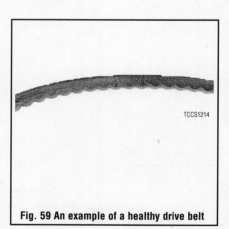

Fig. 59 An example of a healthy drive belt

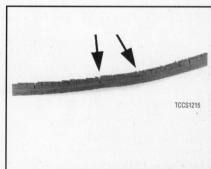

Fig. 60 Deep cracks in this belt will cause flex, building up heat that will eventually lead to belt failure

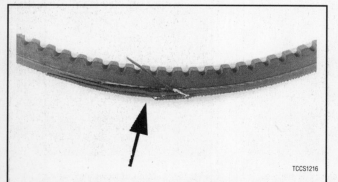

Fig. 61 The cover of this belt is worn, exposing the critical reinforcing cords to excessive wear

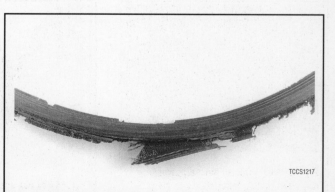

Fig. 62 Installing too wide a belt can result in serious belt wear and/or breakage

Tension Measurement

1986–92 VEHICLES

1. Inspect the tensioner markings to see if the belt is within operating lengths. Replace the belt if it is excessively worn or is outside of the tensioner's operating range.

2. Run the engine with all of the accessories off for until the engine is warmed up. Shut the engine **OFF**. Using a belt tension gauge No. J 23600-B or equivalent, placed halfway between the alternator and A/C compressor (if equipped), or between the power steering pump and the crankshaft pulley (if not equipped with A/C), measure the belt tension. Note the reading.

3. With the accessories off, start the engine and allow to stabilize for 15 seconds. Turn the engine **OFF**. Using a 18mm box end wrench, apply clockwise force to the tensioner pulley bolt. Release the force and record the tension immediately, without disturbing the belt tensioner position.

4. Using the 18mm wrench, apply counterclockwise force to the tensioner pulley bolt and fully raise the pulley to eliminate all tension. Slowly lower the pulley to the belt and take a tension reading without disturbing the belt tensioner position.

5. Average the three readings. If the average of the three readings is lower than 67 lbs. (298 N), and the belt is within the tensioner's operating range, replace the belt tensioner.

1993–99 VEHICLES

1. Run the engine, with no accessories on, until it is warmed up or for about 10 minutes.

2. Shut the engine **OFF**, then check the belt tension using J 23600-B or equivalent belt tension gauge. Place the belt tension gauge as follows:

   a. Except supercharged engines: Place the gauge halfway between the alternator and the power steering pump.

   b. Supercharged engines: Place the gauge halfway between the supercharger and the idler pulley.

3. Note the reading, then remove the gauge.

4. Start the engine, with the accessories off, and allow the system to stabilizer for 15 seconds, then shut the engine **OFF**. Using a 15mm or 18mm socket, as applicable, apply clockwise force (tighten) to the tensioner pulley bolt. Release the force, then immediately record the tension reading without disturbing the belt tensioner position.

5. Using the 15mm or 18mm socket, as applicable, apply counterclockwise force to the tensioner pulley bolt and raise the pulley to eliminate all tension. Slowly lower the pulley to the belt and take a tension reading without disturbing the belt tensioner position.

6. Average the three readings. If the average is not between 50–70 lbs. (225–315 N) and the belt is within the tensioner's operating range, replace the tensioner.

REMOVAL & INSTALLATION

▶ **See Figures 63 thru 69**

1. Disconnect the negative battery cable.
2. Remove the belt guard or coolant recovery reservoir as required.

3. For 1996–99 supercharged engines, perform the following:

   a. Raise and safely support the vehicle.

   b. Remove the right-hand splash shield.

   c. Remove the connector from the crank sensor.

4. For 1996–99 vehicles, remove the engine mounting bracket lower nut, stud and spacer. Carefully lower the vehicle.

✳✳ CAUTION

To avoid personal injury when rotating the serpentine belt tensioner, use a tight fitting wrench that is at least 24 in. (61cm) long.

5. Take note of the belt's routing. Lift or rotate the tensioner using a suitable sized breaker bar in the square opening or box end wrench on the pulley nut. Remove the belt from the pulleys.

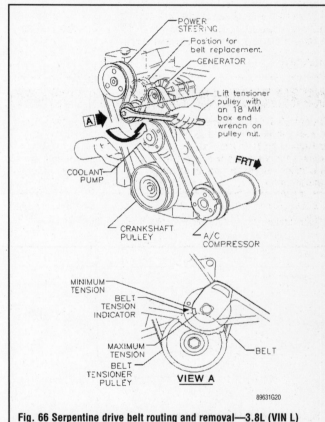

Fig. 66 Serpentine drive belt routing and removal—3.8L (VIN L) engine shown, VIN C similar

Fig. 63 Many vehicles have an accessory drive belt routing label affixed to the radiator shroud

Fig. 64 You can use a box-end wrench on the pulley nut to rotate the tensioner . . .

Fig. 65 . . . then remove the belt from the pulleys

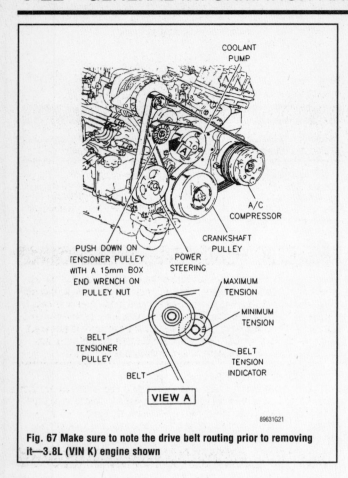

Fig. 67 Make sure to note the drive belt routing prior to removing it—3.8L (VIN K) engine shown

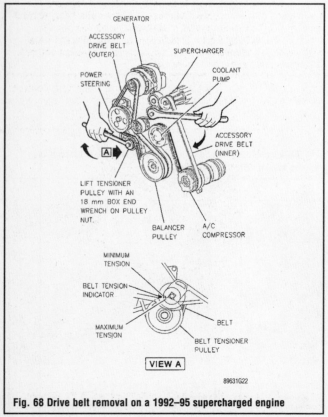

Fig. 68 Drive belt removal on a 1992–95 supercharged engine

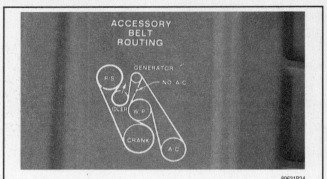

Fig. 69 Many vehicles have a label you can check to be sure the belt is installed and routed correctly

To install:

➡ Be sure the belt is aligned into the proper grooves of the accessory drive pulleys.

6. Lift the tensioner, and install the belt onto pulleys. Make sure the belt is routed properly.

7. For 1996–99 vehicles, raise and safely support the vehicle. Install the engine mounting bracket lower spacer, stud and nut.

8. For 1996–99 supercharged engines, perform the following:
   a. Attach the connector to the crank sensor.
   b. Install the right-hand splash shield, then carefully lower the vehicle.
9. Install the belt guard or reservoir.
10. Connect the negative battery cable.

Hoses

INSPECTION

▶ See Figures 70, 71, 72 and 73

Upper and lower radiator hoses along with the heater hoses should be checked for deterioration, leaks and loose hose clamps at least every 15,000 miles (24,100km). It is also wise to check the hoses periodically in early spring and at the beginning of the fall or winter when you are performing other maintenance. A quick visual inspection could discover a weakened hose which might have left you stranded if it had remained unrepaired.

Whenever you are checking the hoses, make sure the engine and cooling system are cold. Visually inspect for cracking, rotting or collapsed hoses, and replace

Fig. 70 The cracks developing along this hose are a result of age-related hardening

Fig. 71 A hose clamp that is too tight can cause older hoses to separate and tear on either side of the clamp

Fig. 72 A soft spongy hose (identifiable by the swollen section) will eventually burst and should be replaced

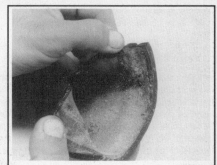

Fig. 73 Hoses are likely to deteriorate from the inside if the cooling system is not periodically flushed

as necessary. Run your hand along the length of the hose. If a weak or swollen spot is noted when squeezing the hose wall, the hose should be replaced.

REMOVAL & INSTALLATION

▶ See Figures 74 and 75

✳ CAUTION

Disconnect the negative battery cable or fan motor wiring harness connector before replacing any radiator/heater hose. The fan may come on even though the ignition has been turned off.

1. Disconnect the negative battery cable.
2. Remove the radiator pressure cap.

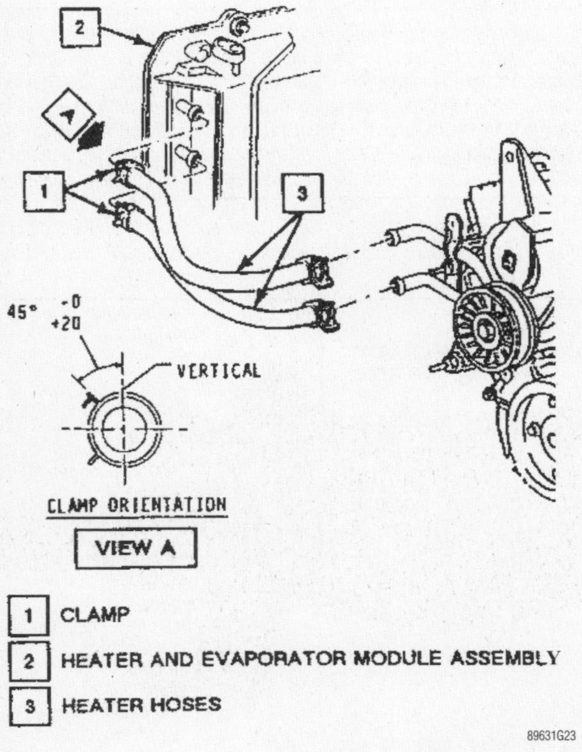

✳ CAUTION

Never remove the pressure cap while the engine is running, or personal injury from scalding hot coolant or steam may result. If possible, wait until the engine has cooled to remove the pressure cap. If this is not possible, wrap a thick cloth around the pressure cap and turn it slowly to the stop. Step back while the pressure is released from the cooling system. When you are sure all the pressure has been released, use the cloth to turn and remove the cap.

3. If necessary, remove the lower air dam.
4. Position a clean container under the radiator and/or engine draincock or plug, then open the drain and allow the cooling system to drain to an appropriate level. For some upper hoses, only a little coolant must be drained. To remove hoses positioned lower on the engine, such as a lower radiator hose, the entire cooling system must be emptied.

✳ CAUTION

When draining coolant, keep in mind that cats and dogs are attracted by ethylene glycol antifreeze, and are quite likely to drink any that is left in an uncovered container or in puddles on the ground. This will prove fatal in sufficient quantity. Always drain coolant into a sealable container. Coolant may be reused unless it is contaminated or several years old.

5. Loosen the hose clamps at each end of the hose requiring replacement. Clamps are usually either of the spring tension type (which require pliers to

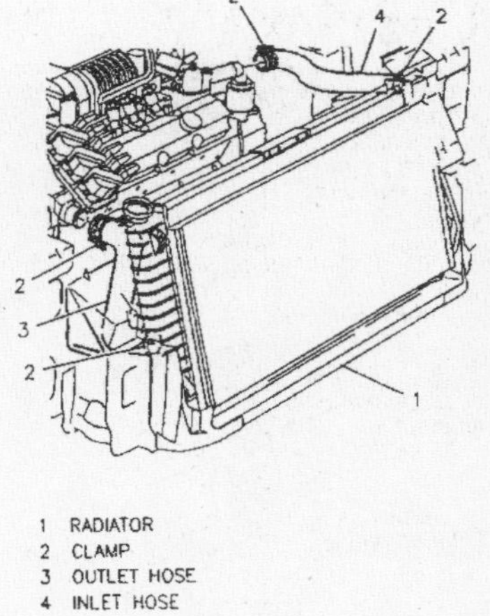

Fig. 74 Typical heater hose locations

Fig. 75 There is an inlet and outlet hose connected to the radiator

45° -0 +20
VERTICAL

CLAMP ORIENTATION

VIEW A

1 CLAMP
2 HEATER AND EVAPORATOR MODULE ASSEMBLY
3 HEATER HOSES

1 RADIATOR
2 CLAMP
3 OUTLET HOSE
4 INLET HOSE

squeeze the tabs and loosen) or of the screw tension type (which require screw or hex drivers to loosen). Pull the clamps back on the hose away from the connection.

6. Twist, pull and slide the hose off the fitting, taking care not to damage the neck of the component from which the hose is being removed.

➡If the hose is stuck at the connection, do not try to insert a screwdriver or other sharp tool under the hose end in an effort to free it, as the connection and/or hose may become damaged. Heater connections especially may be easily damaged by such a procedure. If the hose is to be replaced, use a single-edged razor blade to make a slice along the portion of the hose which is stuck on the connection, perpendicular to the end of the hose. Do not cut deep so as to prevent damaging the connection. The hose can then be peeled from the connection and discarded.

7. Clean both hose mounting connections. Inspect the condition of the hose clamps and replace them, if necessary.

To install:

8. Dip the ends of the new hose into clean engine coolant to ease installation.

9. Slide the clamps over the replacement hose, then slide the hose ends over the connections into position.

10. Position and secure the clamps at least ¼ in. (6.35mm) from the ends of the hose. Make sure they are located beyond the raised bead of the connector.

11. Close the radiator or engine drains and properly refill the cooling system with the clean drained engine coolant or a suitable mixture of ethylene glycol coolant and water.

12. If removed, install the lower air dam.

13. Connect the negative battery cable.

14. If available, install a pressure tester and check for leaks. If a pressure tester is not available, run the engine until normal operating temperature is reached (allowing the system to naturally pressurize), then check for leaks.

❋❋ CAUTION

If you are checking for leaks with the system at normal operating temperature, BE EXTREMELY CAREFUL not to touch any moving or hot engine parts. Once temperature has been reached, shut the engine OFF, and check for leaks around the hose fittings and connections which were removed earlier.

CV-Boots

INSPECTION

▶ See Figures 76 and 77

The CV (Constant Velocity) boots should be checked for damage each time the oil is changed and any other time the vehicle is raised for service. These

Fig. 76 CV-boots must be inspected periodically for damage

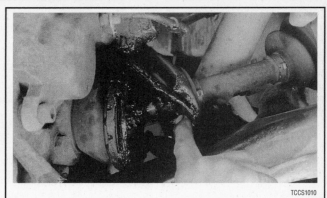

Fig. 77 A torn boot should be replaced immediately

boots keep water, grime, dirt and other damaging matter from entering the CV-joints. Any of these could cause early CV-joint failure which can be expensive to repair. Heavy grease thrown around the inside of the front wheel(s) and on the brake caliper/drum can be an indication of a torn boot. Thoroughly check the boots for missing clamps and tears. If the boot is damaged, it should be replaced immediately. Please refer to Section 7 for procedures.

Spark Plugs

▶ See Figure 78

A typical spark plug consists of a metal shell surrounding a ceramic insulator. A metal electrode extends downward through the center of the insulator and protrudes a small distance. Located at the end of the plug and attached to the side of the outer metal shell is the side electrode. The side electrode bends in at a 90° angle so that its tip is just past and parallel to the tip of the center electrode. The distance between these two electrodes (measured in thousandths of an inch or hundredths of a millimeter) is called the spark plug gap.

The spark plug does not produce a spark but instead provides a gap across which the current can arc. The coil produces anywhere from 20,000 to 50,000 volts (depending on the type and application) which travels through the wires to the spark plugs. The current passes along the center electrode and jumps the gap to the side electrode, and in doing so, ignites the air/fuel mixture in the combustion chamber.

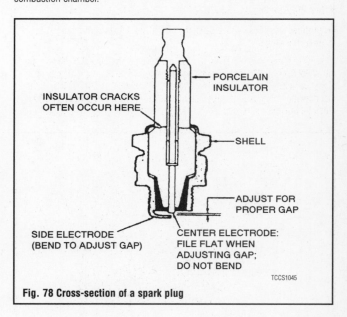

Fig. 78 Cross-section of a spark plug

SPARK PLUG HEAT RANGE

▶ **See Figure 79**

Spark plug heat range is the ability of the plug to dissipate heat. The longer the insulator (or the farther it extends into the engine), the hotter the plug will operate; the shorter the insulator (the closer the electrode is to the block's cooling passages) the cooler it will operate. A plug that absorbs little heat and remains too cool will quickly accumulate deposits of oil and carbon since it is not hot enough to burn them off. This leads to plug fouling and consequently to misfiring. A plug that absorbs too much heat will have no deposits but, due to the excessive heat, the electrodes will burn away quickly and might possibly lead to preignition or other ignition problems. Preignition takes place when plug tips get so hot that they glow sufficiently to ignite the air/fuel mixture before the actual spark occurs. This early ignition will usually cause a pinging during low speeds and heavy loads.

The general rule of thumb for choosing the correct heat range when picking a spark plug is: if most of your driving is long distance, high speed travel, use a colder plug; if most of your driving is stop and go, use a hotter plug. Original equipment plugs are generally a good compromise between the 2 styles and most people never have the need to change their plugs from the factory-recommended heat range.

```
THE SHORTER          THE LONGER
THE PATH, THE        THE PATH, THE
FASTER THE           SLOWER THE
HEAT IS DIS-         HEAT IS DIS-
SIPATED AND          SIPATED AND
THE COOLER           THE HOTTER
THE PLUG             THE PLUG

HEAVY LOADS,         SHORT TRIP
HIGH SPEEDS          STOP-AND-GO

SHORT Insulator Tip  LONG Insulator Tip
Fast Heat Transfer   Slow Heat Transfer
LOWER Heat Range     HIGHER Heat Range
COLD PLUG            HOT PLUG

                              TCCS1046
```

Fig. 79 Spark plug heat range

REMOVAL & INSTALLATION

▶ **See Figures 80, 81, 82 and 83**

➡ **On these vehicles, you probable need a ⅝ in. spark plug socket to remove the plugs.**

A set of spark plugs usually requires replacement after about 20,000–30,000 miles (32,000–48,000 km), depending on your style of driving. On some later model vehicles, the replacement interval is 100,000 miles (160,000 km). In normal operation plug gap increases about 0.001 in. (0.025mm) for every 2500 miles (4000 km). As the gap increases, the plug's voltage requirement also increases. It requires a greater voltage to jump the wider gap and about two to three times as much voltage to fire the plug at high speeds than at idle. The improved air/fuel ratio control of modern fuel injection combined with the higher voltage output of modern ignition systems will often allow an engine to run significantly longer on a set of standard spark plugs, but keep in mind that efficiency will drop as the gap widens (along with fuel economy and power).

When you're removing spark plugs, work on one at a time. Don't start by removing the plug wires all at once, because, unless you number them, they may become mixed up. Take a minute before you begin and number the wires with tape.

1. Disconnect the negative battery cable, and if the vehicle has been run recently, allow the engine to thoroughly cool.

2. If necessary, remove the retainer, then lift the engine cover off for access to the spark plugs and wires.

✳✳ CAUTION

Make sure you thoroughly wash your hands after handling coated spark plugs, especially if you are a smoker. The spark plug coating itself is a non-hazardous material and incidental contact will not have any negative effects. However, exposure to polymer vapors, which result from the contamination of tobacco products and the subsequent burning of the polymer could cause symptoms similar to the flu and should be avoided.

3. Carefully twist the spark plug wire boot ½ turn in each direction to loosen it, then pull upward and remove the boot from the plug. Be sure to pull on the boot and not on the wire, otherwise the connector located inside the boot may become separated.

4. Using compressed air, blow any water or debris from the spark plug well to assure that no harmful contaminants are allowed to enter the combustion chamber when the spark plug is removed. If compressed air is not available, use a rag or a brush to clean the area.

➡ **Remove the spark plugs when the engine is cold, if possible, to prevent damage to the threads. If removal of the plugs is difficult, apply a few drops of penetrating oil or silicone spray to the area around the base of the plug, and allow it a few minutes to work.**

5. Using a spark plug socket that is equipped with a rubber insert to properly hold the plug, turn the spark plug counterclockwise to loosen and remove the spark plug from the bore.

✳✳ WARNING

Be sure not to use a flexible extension on the socket. Use of a flexible extension may allow a shear force to be applied to the plug. A shear force could break the plug off in the cylinder head, leading to costly and frustrating repairs.

To install:

6. Inspect the spark plug boot for tears or damage. If a damaged boot is found, the spark plug wire must be replaced.

7. Using a wire feeler gauge, check and adjust the spark plug gap. When using a gauge, the proper size should pass between the electrodes with a slight drag. The next larger size should not be able to pass while the next smaller size should pass freely.

8. Carefully thread the plug into the bore by hand. If resistance is felt before the plug is almost completely threaded, back the plug out and begin threading again. In small, hard to reach areas, an old spark plug wire and boot could be used as a threading tool. The boot will hold the plug while you twist the end of the wire and the wire is supple enough to twist before it would allow the plug to crossthread.

✳✳ WARNING

Do not use the spark plug socket to thread the plugs. Always carefully thread the plug by hand or using an old plug wire to prevent the possibility of crossthreading and damaging the cylinder head bore.

9. Carefully tighten the spark plug. If the plug you are installing is equipped with a crush washer, seat the plug, then tighten about ¼ turn to crush

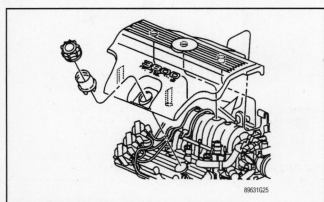

Fig. 80 Exploded view of the engine cover mounting

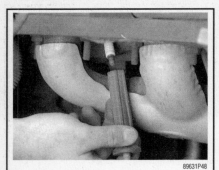

Fig. 81 Twist the spark plug boot ½ turn, then disconnect the wire from the plug by pulling on the boot

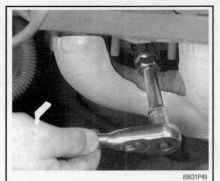

Fig. 82 Use a ratchet with a spark plug socket to loosen . . .

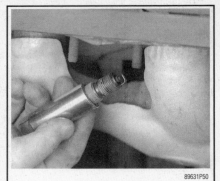

Fig. 83 . . . and remove the spark plug from the cylinder head

the washer. If you are installing a tapered seat plug, tighten the plug to specifications provided by the vehicle or plug manufacturer.

➡On these engines, aluminum heat shields are used over the spark plug boots on cylinders located near the exhaust tubing. Make sure the heat shield are fully seated during installation.

10. Apply a small amount of silicone dielectric compound to the end of the spark plug lead or inside the spark plug boot to prevent sticking, then install the boot to the spark plug and push until it clicks into place. The click may be felt or heard, then gently pull back on the boot to assure proper contact.

11. If necessary, position the engine cover, then secure it in place using the retainer.

12. Connect the negative battery cable.

INSPECTION & GAPPING

▶ See Figures 84, 85, 86 and 87

Check the plugs for deposits and wear. If they are not going to be replaced, clean the plugs thoroughly. Remember that any kind of deposit will decrease the efficiency of the plug. Plugs can be cleaned on a spark plug cleaning machine, which can sometimes be found in service stations, or you can do an acceptable job of cleaning with a stiff brush. If the plugs are cleaned, the electrodes must be filed flat. Use an ignition points file, not an emery board or the like, which will leave deposits. The electrodes must be filed perfectly flat with sharp edges; rounded edges reduce the spark plug voltage by as much as 50%.

Check spark plug gap before installation. The ground electrode (the L-shaped one connected to the body of the plug) must be parallel to the center electrode and the specified size wire gauge (please refer to the Tune-Up Specifications chart for details) must pass between the electrodes with a slight drag.

➡NEVER adjust the gap on a used platinum type spark plug.

Always check the gap on new plugs as they are not always set correctly at the factory. Do not use a flat feeler gauge when measuring the gap on a used plug, because the reading may be inaccurate. A round-wire type gapping tool is the best way to check the gap. The correct gauge should pass through the electrode gap with a slight drag. If you're in doubt, try one size smaller and one larger. The smaller gauge should go through easily, while the larger one shouldn't go through at all. Wire gapping tools usually have a bending tool attached. Use that to adjust the side electrode until the proper distance is obtained. Absolutely never attempt to bend the center electrode. Also, be careful not to bend the side electrode too far or too often as it may weaken and break off within the engine, requiring removal of the cylinder head to retrieve it.

Spark Plug Wires

TESTING

▶ See Figure 88

At every tune-up/inspection, visually check the spark plug cables for burns cuts, or breaks in the insulation. Check the boots and the nipples on the coil. Replace any damaged wiring.

Every 50,000 miles (80,000 km) or 60 months, the resistance of the wires should be checked with an ohmmeter. Wires with excessive resistance will cause misfiring, and may make the engine difficult to start in damp weather.

To check resistance, disconnect the spark plug wires from the coil and spark plug. Connect one lead of an ohmmeter to an electrode within the cap; connect the other lead to the corresponding spark plug terminal (remove it from the spark plug for this test). Replace any wire which shows a resistance over 30,000 ohms. The following chart gives resistance values as a function of length. Generally speaking, however, resistance should not be considered the outer limit of acceptability.

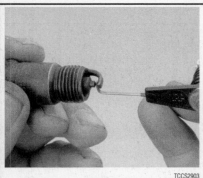

Fig. 84 Checking the spark plug gap with a feeler gauge

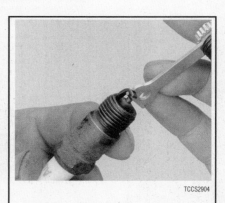

Fig. 85 Adjusting the spark plug gap

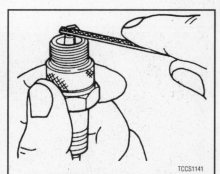

Fig. 86 If the standard plug is in good condition, the electrode may be filed flat— WARNING: do not file platinum plugs

A **normally worn** spark plug should have light tan or gray deposits on the firing tip.

A **carbon fouled** plug, identified by soft, sooty, black deposits, may indicate an improperly tuned vehicle. Check the air cleaner, ignition components and engine control system.

This spark plug has been **left in the engine too long,** as evidenced by the extreme gap. Plugs with such an extreme gap can cause misfiring and stumbling accompanied by a noticeable lack of power.

An **oil fouled** spark plug indicates an engine with worn poston rings and/or bad valve seals allowing excessive oil to enter the chamber.

A **physically damaged** spark plug may be evidence of severe detonation in that cylinder. Watch that cylinder carefully between services, as a continued detonation will not only damage the plug, but could also damage the engine.

A **bridged or almost bridged** spark plug, identified by a build up between the electrodes caused by excessive carbon or oil build-up on the plug.

TCCA1P40

Fig. 87 Inspect the spark plug to determine engine running conditions

- 0–15 in. (0–38cm): 3,000–10,000 ohms.
- 15–25 in. (38–64cm): 4,000–15,000 ohms.
- 25–35 in. (64–89cm): 6,000–20,000 ohms.
- Over 35 in. (89cm): 25,000 ohms.

It should be remembered that resistance is also a function of length; the longer the wire, the greater the resistance. Thus, if the wires on your car are longer than the factory originals, resistance will be higher, quite possibly outside these limits.

REMOVAL & INSTALLATION

♦ **See Figures 89, 90 and 91**

➡**If all of the wires must be disconnected from the spark plugs or from the ignition coil pack at the same time, be sure to tag the wires to assure proper reconnection.**

1. Disconnect the negative battery cable, and if the vehicle has been run recently, allow the engine to thoroughly cool.

TCCS1009

Fig. 88 Checking individual plug wire resistance with a digital ohmmeter

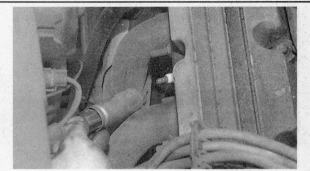

89631P47

Fig. 89 Pull the spark plug wire off the plug by the boot, NOT the wire

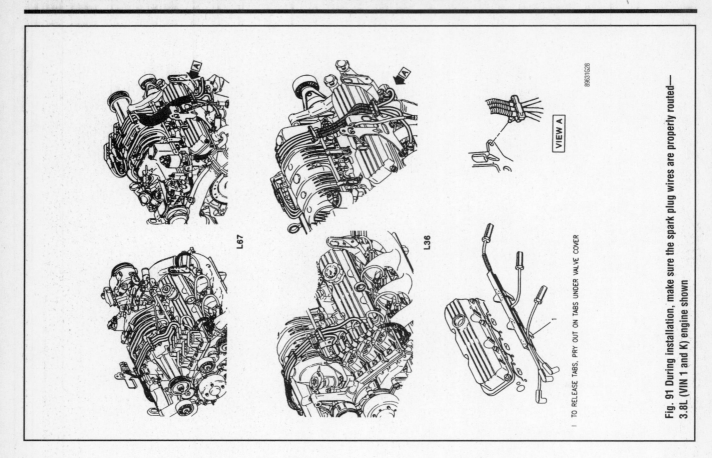

L67

L36

VIEW A

1 TO RELEASE TABS, PRY OUT ON TABS UNDER VALVE COVER

Fig. 91 During installation, make sure the spark plug wires are properly routed—3.8L (VIN 1 and K) engine shown

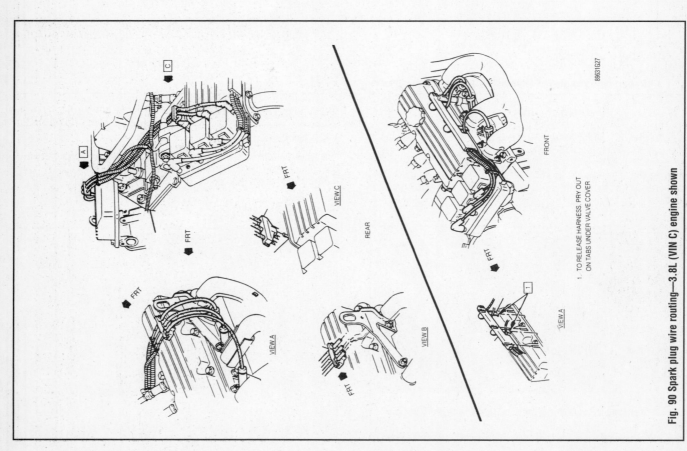

VIEW C

VIEW A

VIEW B

FRT

REAR

FRONT

1. TO RELEASE HARNESS, PRY OUT ON TABS UNDER VALVE COVER

Fig. 90 Spark plug wire routing—3.8L (VIN C) engine shown

2. If equipped, remove the retainer, then lift the engine cover off for access to the spark plug wires.

When installing a new set of spark plug cables, replace the cables one at a time so there will be no mix-up. Start by replacing the longest cable first.

3. Carefully twist the spark plug wire boot ½ turn in each direction to loosen it, then pull upward and remove the boot from the plug. Be sure to pull on the boot and not on the wire, otherwise the connector located inside the boot may become separated. Repeat the process to disconnect the wire from the ignition coil.

To install:

➡**On these engines, aluminum heat shields are used over the spark plug boots on cylinders located near the exhaust tubing. Make sure the heat shield are fully seated during installation.**

4. Install the boot firmly over the spark plug and push until it clicks into place. The click may be felt or heard, then gently pull back on the boot to assure proper contact. Route the wire exactly the same as the original, through all convolute tubing and clamped in all holders. Insert the nipple firmly onto the tower on the ignition coil. Be sure to apply silicone dielectric compound to the spark plug wire boots and tower connectors prior to installation.

5. Repeat the process for each cable, making sure ends snap into place.

6. If necessary, position the engine cover, then secure it in place using the retainer.

7. Connect the negative battery cable.

Ignition Timing

GENERAL INFORMATION

▶ **See Figure 92**

Ignition timing is the point at which each spark plug fires in relation to its respective piston, during the compression stroke of the engine.

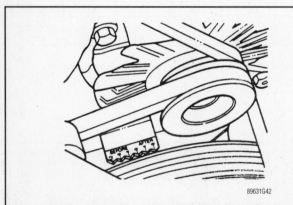

89631G42

Fig. 92 Timing mark location. Note that ignition timing is NOT adjustable

As far as ignition timing is concerned, the position of the piston can be related (in degrees) to the following reference terms: Top Dead Center (TDC), After Top Dead Center (ATDC), and Before Top Dead Center (BTDC). The movement of the piston is expressed in degrees due to the rotation of the crankshaft. Even though the crankshaft turns 720° to complete one entire 4-stroke cycle, all we're concerned about here is the compression stroke, since this is when the ignition of the air/fuel mixture takes place (or more accurately, should take place).

Because it takes a fraction of a second for the spark (at the spark plug) to ignite the air/fuel mixture and for the mixture to burn completely, the spark should ideally occur just before the piston reaches TDC. If the spark didn't occur until exactly TDC or ATDC, the piston would already be on its way down before the mixture explosion would not exert as much downward force on the piston as it would if the ignition timing was properly set. The result of this would be reduced power and fuel economy.

Should ignition of the air/fuel mixture occur too far BTDC (advanced), the mixture explosion will try to force the piston downward before it can mechanically do so. This contest between the explosion forcing the piston downward and the crankshaft forcing the piston upward will result in a pinging sound if you're lucky; severe engine damage if you're not so lucky. If you experience pinging, check with a trusted mechanic to determine if the pinging is mild or severe. Only a trained car mechanic can safely determine this.

➡**Pinging can also be caused by inferior gasoline, since lower octane gas burns at a faster, more uncontrolled rate than a higher octane fuel.**

ADJUSTMENT

All of the vehicles covered by this manual are equipped with a distributorless ignition system. The system consists of a coil pack, ignition module, crankshaft reluctor or interrupter ring(s), magnetic sensor and a computer control module (ECM or PCM, depending upon year of vehicle). Timing advance and retard are accomplished through the ECM with the Electronic Spark Timing (EST) and Electronic Spark Control (ESC) circuitry. No ignition timing adjustment is necessary or possible.

Valve Lash

All models utilize an hydraulic valve lifter system to obtain zero lash. No adjustment is necessary. An initial adjustment is required anytime that the lifters are removed or the valve train is disturbed, this procedure is covered in Section 3.

Idle Speed and Mixture Adjustments

All engines' idle speed and mixture is electronically controlled by the computerized fuel injection system. Adjustment are neither necessary nor possible. All threaded throttle stop adjusters are factory set and capped to discourage any tampering; in some areas, tampering is illegal. In most cases, proper diagnosis and parts replacement will straighten out any problems concerning this subject.

GASOLINE ENGINE TUNE-UP SPECIFICATIONS

Year	Engine ID/VIN	Engine Displacement Liters (cc)	Spark Plugs Gap (in.)	Ignition Timing (deg.)		Fuel Pump (psi)	Idle Speed (rpm)		Valve Clearance	
				MT	AT		MT	AT	In.	Ex.
1986	L	3.0 (2967)	0.045	—	①	34-44	—	②	HYD	HYD
	B	3.8L (3786)	0.045	—	①	25-35	—	②	HYD	HYD
	3	3.8L (3786)	0.045	—	①	25-35	—	②	HYD	HYD
1987	3	3.8L (3786)	0.045	—	①	25-35	—	②	HYD	HYD
1988	C	3.8L (3786)	0.060	—	①	31-42	—	②	HYD	HYD
	3	3.8L (3786)	0.045	—	①	25-35	—	②	HYD	HYD
1989	C	3.8L (3786)	0.060	—	①	41-47	—	②	HYD	HYD
1990	C	3.8L (3786)	0.060	—	①	41-47	—	②	HYD	HYD
1991	C	3.8L (3786)	0.060	—	①	41-47	—	②	HYD	HYD
1992	L	3.8L (3786)	0.060	—	①	41-47	—	②	HYD	HYD
	1	3.8L (3786)	0.060	—	①	41-47	—	②	HYD	HYD
1993	L	3.8L (3786)	0.060	—	①	41-47	—	②	HYD	HYD
	1	3.8L (3786)	0.060	—	①	41-47	—	②	HYD	HYD
1994	L	3.8L (3786)	0.060	—	①	41-47	—	②	HYD	HYD
	1	3.8L (3786)	0.060	—	①	41-47	—	②	HYD	HYD
1995	L	3.8 (3786)	0.060	—	①	41-47	—	②	HYD	HYD
	K	3.8 (3786)	0.060	—	①	41-47	—	②	HYD	HYD
	1	3.8L (3786)	0.060	—	①	41-47	—	②	HYD	HYD
1996	K	3.8L (3786)	0.060	—	①	41-47	—	②	HYD	HYD
	1	3.8L (3786)	0.060	—	①	41-47	—	②	HYD	HYD
1997	K	3.8L (3786)	0.060	—	①	41-47	—	②	HYD	HYD
	1	3.8L (3786)	0.060	—	①	41-47	—	②	HYD	HYD
1998	K	3.8L (3786)	0.060	—	①	41-47	—	②	HYD	HYD
	1	3.8L (3786)	0.060	—	①	41-47	—	②	HYD	HYD
1999	K	3.8L (3786)	0.060	—	①	41-47	—	②	HYD	HYD
	1	3.8L (3786)	0.060	—	①	41-47	—	②	HYD	HYD

NOTE: The Vehicle Emission Control Information Label often reflects specification changes made during production. The label figures must be used if they differ from those in this chart.

HYD - Hydraulic

① The ignition timing is controlled by the PCM and is not adjustable.

② Idle speed is controlled by the PCM; adjustments are neither necessary nor possible.

89631C04

Air Conditioning System

SYSTEM SERVICE & REPAIR

♦ See Figure 93

➡ It is recommended that the A/C system be serviced by an EPA Section 609 certified automotive technician utilizing a refrigerant recovery/recycling machine.

The do-it-yourselfer should not service his/her own vehicle's A/C system for many reasons, including legal concerns, personal injury, environmental damage and cost.

According to the U.S. Clean Air Act, it is a federal crime to service or repair (involving the refrigerant) a Motor Vehicle Air Conditioning (MVAC) system for money without being EPA certified. It is also illegal to vent R-134a refrigerant into the atmosphere. State and/or local laws may be more strict than the federal regulations, so be sure to check with your state and/or local authorities for further information.

➡ Federal law dictates that a fine of up to $25,000 may be levied on people convicted of venting refrigerant into the atmosphere.

When servicing an A/C system you run the risk of handling or coming in contact with refrigerant, which may result in skin or eye irritation or frostbite.

Fig. 93 There are probably some A/C warning labels in your engine compartment

Although low in toxicity (due to chemical stability), inhalation of concentrated refrigerant fumes is dangerous and can result in death; cases of fatal cardiac arrhythmia have been reported in people accidentally subjected to high levels of refrigerant. Some early symptoms include loss of concentration and drowsiness.

Also, some refrigerants can decompose at high temperatures (near gas heaters or open flame), which may result in hydrofluoric acid, hydrochloric acid and phosgene (a fatal nerve gas).

It is usually more economically feasible to have a certified MVAC automotive technician perform A/C system service on your vehicle.

PREVENTIVE MAINTENANCE

Although the A/C system should not be serviced by the do-it-yourselfer, preventive maintenance should be practiced to help maintain the efficiency of the vehicle's A/C system. Be sure to perform the following:
• The easiest and most important preventive maintenance for your A/C system is to be sure that it is used on a regular basis. Running the system for five minutes each month (no matter what the season) will help ensure that the seals and all internal components remain lubricated.

➡**Some vehicles automatically operate the A/C system compressor whenever the windshield defroster is activated. Therefore, the A/C system would not need to be operated each month if the defroster was used.**

• In order to prevent heater core freeze-up during A/C operation, it is necessary to maintain proper antifreeze protection. Be sure to properly maintain the engine cooling system.
• Any obstruction of or damage to the condenser configuration will restrict air flow which is essential to its efficient operation. Keep this unit clean and in proper physical shape.

➡**Bug screens which are mounted in front of the condenser (unless they are original equipment) are regarded as obstructions.**

• The condensation drain tube expels any water which accumulates on the bottom of the evaporator housing into the engine compartment. If this tube is obstructed, the air conditioning performance can be restricted and condensation buildup can spill over onto the vehicle's floor.

SYSTEM INSPECTION

Although the A/C system should not be serviced by the do-it-yourselfer, system inspections should be performed to help maintain the efficiency of the vehicle's A/C system. Be sure to perform the following:

The easiest and often most important check for the air conditioning system consists of a visual inspection of the system components. Visually inspect the system for refrigerant leaks, damaged compressor clutch, abnormal compressor drive belt tension and/or condition, plugged evaporator drain tube, blocked condenser fins, disconnected or broken wires, blown fuses, corroded connections and poor insulation.

A refrigerant leak will usually appear as an oily residue at the leakage point in the system. The oily residue soon picks up dust or dirt particles from the surrounding air and appears greasy. Through time, this will build up and appear to be a heavy dirt impregnated grease.

For a thorough visual and operational inspection, check the following:
• Check the surface of the radiator and condenser for dirt, leaves or other material which might block air flow.
• Check for kinks in hoses and lines. Check the system for leaks.
• Make sure the drive belt is properly tensioned. During operation, make sure the belt is free of noise or slippage.
• Make sure the blower motor operates at all appropriate positions, then check for distribution of the air from all outlets.

➡**Remember that in high humidity, air discharged from the vents may not feel as cold as expected, even if the system is working properly. This is because moisture in humid air retains heat more effectively than dry air, thereby making humid air more difficult to cool.**

Windshield Wipers

ELEMENT (REFILL) CARE & REPLACEMENT

▶ **See Figures 94, 95 and 96**

For maximum effectiveness and longest element life, the windshield and wiper blades should be kept clean. Dirt, tree sap, road tar and so on will cause streaking, smearing and blade deterioration if left on the glass. It is advisable to wash the windshield carefully with a commercial glass cleaner at least once a month. Wipe off the rubber blades with the wet rag afterwards. Do not attempt to move wipers across the windshield by hand; damage to the motor and drive mechanism will result.

To inspect and/or replace the wiper blade elements, place the wiper switch in the **LOW** speed position and the ignition switch in the **ACC** position. When the wiper blades are approximately vertical on the windshield, turn the ignition switch to **OFF**.

Examine the wiper blade elements. If they are found to be cracked, broken or torn, they should be replaced immediately. Replacement intervals will vary with usage, although ozone deterioration usually limits element life to about one year. If the wiper pattern is smeared or streaked, or if the blade chatters across the glass, the elements should be replaced. It is easiest and most sensible to replace the elements in pairs.

If your vehicle is equipped with aftermarket blades, there are several different types of refills and your vehicle might have any kind. Aftermarket blades and arms rarely use the exact same type blade or refill as the original equipment. Regardless of the type of refill used, be sure to follow the part manufacturer's

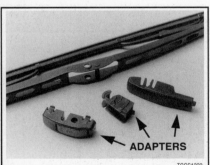

TCCS1223

Fig. 94 Most aftermarket blades are available with multiple adapters to fit different vehicles

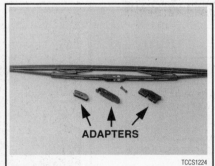

TCCS1224

Fig. 95 Choose a blade which will fit your vehicle, and that will be readily available next time you need blades

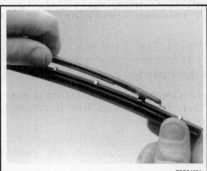

TCCS1231

Fig. 96 When installed, be certain the blade is fully inserted into the backing

instructions closely. Make sure that all of the frame jaws are engaged as the refill is pushed into place and locked. If the metal blade holder and frame are allowed to touch the glass during wiper operation, the glass will be scratched.

Tires and Wheels

Common sense and good driving habits will afford maximum tire life. Make sure that you don't overload the vehicle or run with incorrect pressure in the tires. Either of these will increase tread wear. Fast starts, sudden stops and sharp cornering are hard on tires and will shorten their useful life span.

➡**For optimum tire life, keep the tires properly inflated, rotate them often and have the wheel alignment checked periodically.**

Inspect your tires frequently. Be especially careful to watch for bubbles in the tread or sidewall, deep cuts or underinflation. Replace any tires with bubbles in the sidewall. If cuts are so deep that they penetrate to the cords, discard the tire. Any cut in the sidewall of a radial tire renders it unsafe. Also look for uneven tread wear patterns that may indicate the front end is out of alignment or that the tires are out of balance.

TIRE ROTATION

▶ **See Figure 97**

Tires must be rotated periodically to equalize wear patterns that vary with a tire's position on the vehicle. Tires will also wear in an uneven way as the front steering/suspension system wears to the point where the alignment should be reset.

Rotating the tires will ensure maximum life for the tires as a set, so you will not have to discard a tire early due to wear on only part of the tread. Regular rotation is required to equalize wear.

When rotating "unidirectional tires," make sure that they always roll in the same direction. This means that a tire used on the left side of the vehicle must not be switched to the right side and vice-versa. Such tires should only be rotated front-to-rear or rear-to-front, while always remaining on the same side of the vehicle. These tires are marked on the sidewall as to the direction of rotation; observe the marks when reinstalling the tire(s).

Some styled or "mag" wheels may have different offsets front to rear. In these cases, the rear wheels must not be used up front and vice-versa. Furthermore, if these wheels are equipped with unidirectional tires, they cannot be rotated unless the tire is remounted for the proper direction of rotation.

➡**The compact or space-saver spare is strictly for emergency use. It must never be included in the tire rotation or placed on the vehicle for everyday use.**

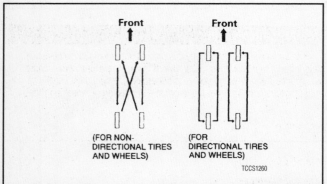

Fig. 97 Compact spare tires must NEVER be used in the rotation pattern

TIRE DESIGN

▶ **See Figure 98**

For maximum satisfaction, tires should be used in sets of four. Mixing of different brands or types (radial, bias-belted, fiberglass belted) should be avoided.

In most cases, the vehicle manufacturer has designated a type of tire on which the vehicle will perform best. Your first choice when replacing tires should be to use the same type of tire that the manufacturer recommends.

When radial tires are used, tire sizes and wheel diameters should be selected to maintain ground clearance and tire load capacity equivalent to the original specified tire. Radial tires should always be used in sets of four.

✱✱ CAUTION

Radial tires should never be used on only the front axle.

When selecting tires, pay attention to the original size as marked on the tire. Most tires are described using an industry size code sometimes referred to as P-Metric. This allows the exact identification of the tire specifications, regardless of the manufacturer. If selecting a different tire size or brand, remember to check the installed tire for any sign of interference with the body or suspension while the vehicle is stopping, turning sharply or heavily loaded.

Snow Tires

Good radial tires can produce a big advantage in slippery weather, but in snow, a street radial tire does not have sufficient tread to provide traction and control. The small grooves of a street tire quickly pack with snow and the tire behaves like a billiard ball on a marble floor. The more open, chunky tread of a snow tire will self-clean as the tire turns, providing much better grip on snowy surfaces.

To satisfy municipalities requiring snow tires during weather emergencies, most snow tires carry either an M + S designation after the tire size stamped on the sidewall, or the designation "all-season." In general, no change in tire size is necessary when buying snow tires.

Most manufacturers strongly recommend the use of 4 snow tires on their vehicles for reasons of stability. If snow tires are fitted only to the drive wheels, the opposite end of the vehicle may become very unstable when braking or turning on slippery surfaces. This instability can lead to unpleasant endings if the driver can't counteract the slide in time.

Note that snow tires, whether 2 or 4, will affect vehicle handling in all non-snow situations. The stiffer, heavier snow tires will noticeably change the turning and braking characteristics of the vehicle. Once the snow tires are installed, you must re-learn the behavior of the vehicle and drive accordingly.

➡**Consider buying extra wheels on which to mount the snow tires. Once done, the "snow wheels" can be installed and removed as needed. This eliminates the potential damage to tires or wheels from seasonal removal and installation. Even if your vehicle has styled wheels, see if inexpensive steel wheels are available. Although the look of the vehicle will change, the expensive wheels will be protected from salt, curb hits and pothole damage.**

TIRE STORAGE

If they are mounted on wheels, store the tires at proper inflation pressure. All tires should be kept in a cool, dry place. If they are stored in the garage or basement, do not let them stand on a concrete floor; set them on strips of wood, a mat or a large stack of newspaper. Keeping them away from direct moisture is of paramount importance. Tires should not be stored upright, but in a flat position.

INFLATION & INSPECTION

▶ **See Figures 99 thru 104**

The importance of proper tire inflation cannot be overemphasized. A tire employs air as part of its structure. It is designed around the supporting strength of the air at a specified pressure. For this reason, improper inflation drastically reduces the tire's ability to perform as intended. A tire will lose some air in day-to-day use; having to add a few pounds of air periodically is not necessarily a sign of a leaking tire.

Two items should be a permanent fixture in every glove compartment: an accurate tire pressure gauge and a tread depth gauge. Check the tire pressure (including the spare) regularly with a pocket type gauge. Too often, the gauge on the end of the air hose at your corner garage is not accurate because it suffers too much abuse. Always check tire pressure when the tires are cold, as pressure increases with temperature. If you must move the vehicle to check the

Fig. 98 P-Metric tire coding

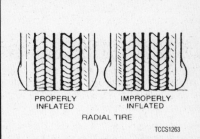

Fig. 99 Tires with deep cuts, or cuts which bulge, should be replaced immediately

PROPERLY INFLATED   IMPROPERLY INFLATED

RADIAL TIRE

TCCS1263

Fig. 100 Radial tires have a characteristic sidewall bulge; don't try to measure pressure by looking at the tire. Use a quality air pressure gauge

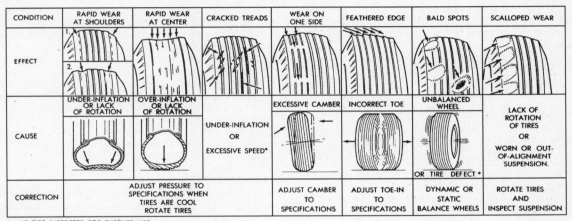

Fig. 101 Common tire wear patterns and causes

tire inflation, do not drive more than a mile before checking. A cold tire is generally one that has not been driven for more than three hours.

A plate or sticker is normally provided somewhere in the vehicle (door post, hood, tailgate or trunk lid) which shows the proper pressure for the tires. Never counteract excessive pressure build-up by bleeding off air pressure (letting some air out). This will cause the tire to run hotter and wear quicker.

✳ CAUTION

Never exceed the maximum tire pressure embossed on the tire! This is the pressure to be used when the tire is at maximum loading, but it is rarely the correct pressure for everyday driving. Consult the owner's manual or the tire pressure sticker for the correct tire pressure.

Once you've maintained the correct tire pressures for several weeks, you'll be familiar with the vehicle's braking and handling personality. Slight adjustments in tire pressures can fine-tune these characteristics, but never change the cold pressure specification by more than 2 psi. A slightly softer tire pressure will give a softer ride but also yield lower fuel mileage. A slightly harder tire will give crisper dry road handling but can cause skidding on wet surfaces. Unless you're fully attuned to the vehicle, stick to the recommended inflation pressures.

All automotive tires have built-in tread wear indicator bars that show up as ½ in. (13mm) wide smooth bands across the tire when 1⁄16 in. (1.5mm) of tread remains. The appearance of tread wear indicators means that the tires should be replaced. In fact, many states have laws prohibiting the use of tires with less than this amount of tread.

You can check your own tread depth with an inexpensive gauge or by using a Lincoln head penny. Slip the Lincoln penny (with Lincoln's head upside-down)

into several tread grooves. If you can see the top of Lincoln's head in 2 adjacent grooves, the tire has less than 1⁄16 in. (1.5mm) tread left and should be replaced. You can measure snow tires in the same manner by using the "tails" side of the Lincoln penny. If you can see the top of the Lincoln memorial, it's time to replace the snow tire(s).

Maintenance Lights

Some of the vehicles covered by this manual utilize various maintenance lights in order to let the driver know when it is time to perform certain basic maintenance items. After the service is performed, the light must usually be reset. Please refer to the following information for the proper resetting procedures.

RESETTING

Pontiac Bonneville

1989–90 VEHICLES

The **SERVICE REMINDER** portion of the Driver Information Center (DIC) display shows how many miles remain until service is needed. When the **RESET** button is pressed twice, the type of service and the number of miles remaining until that service is needed, will be displayed. Each time the **RESET** is pressed, another type of service and the miles remaining for it will be displayed.

With the ignition switch in the **RUN**, **BULB TEST**, or **START** positions, voltage is applied from the ECM fuse through the pink/black wire to the Electronic Control Module (ECM). As the vehicle is driven, the speed sensor sends

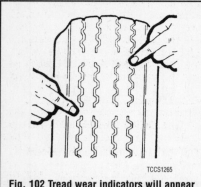

Fig. 102 Tread wear indicators will appear when the tire is worn

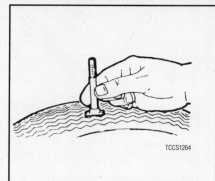

Fig. 103 Accurate tread depth indicators are inexpensive and handy

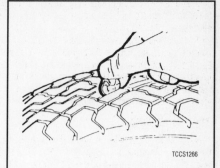

Fig. 104 A penny works well for a quick check of tread depth

electrical pulses to the ECM. The ECM sends a signal to the speed signal input of the DIC module. The DIC module converters the pulses into miles. The module subtracts the miles traveled from the distance remaining for each item of the service reminder.

When the miles remaining for a service approaches zero, that service will be displayed on the DIC display. All 4 types of services can be shown at the same time.

To reset the service light, it will be necessary to subtract the mileage from the service interval light that is illuminated. The miles remaining for a certain type of service can be decreased by holding the **RESET** button, the miles will be decreased in steps of 500 miles, every 5 seconds. In the first step, the miles will decrease to a multiple of 500. For example, 2,880 miles will decrease to 2,500 miles. If the **RESET** button is held in and the miles remaining reach zero, the DIC display will shown the service interval for the service selected. The service intervals are as follows:

1. Change Oil—7,500 miles
2. Oil Filter Change—7,500 miles
3. Next Filter Change—15,000 miles
4. Rotate Tires—7,500 miles
5. Next Tire Rotation—15,000 miles
6. Tune Up—30,000 miles

If the **RESET** button is still held down, the miles will decrease in steps of 500 miles from the service interval. When the **RESET** button is released, the mile display shown will be the new distance until the service should be performed.

When a service distance reaches zero, the service reminder item will be displayed. If the service interval is reset within 10 miles, the display will go out immediately. If more than 10 miles passes before the service interval is reset, the item will remain displayed for another 10 miles after being reset before going out.

➡On some models, it may be necessary to depress the SYSTEM RECALL button in order to display the service interval light on the driver information center, in order to be able to decrease the mileage from it to reset the interval light.

1991–93 VEHICLES

▶ See Figure 105

The Driver Information Center (DIC) lights up for a few seconds when the ignition is turned **ON**. To see the entire DIC, press and release the DIC button to the right of the display. The system is divided into 4 main systems: Function Monitor, Lamp Check, Security and Service Reminder. These systems monitor the following:

1. FUNCTION MONITOR:
    a. Checks windshield washer fluid. Message comes ON when fluid is less than 40 percent full.

b. Checks the engine coolant level. Message comes ON when coolant level has fallen to about half full.

c. Checks the fuel level. Message comes ON when approximately 2½ gallons of fuel remain.

2. LAMP CHECK:
    a. Checks headlights, turn signal, brake lights and tail lights.

b. Message comes ON if a problem exists at 1 of the lights. The problem area is indicate on the vehicle outline shown on the DIC. Note that if a burned out bulb is replaced, then warning light will stay on until the bulb is energized or turned on.

3. SECURITY:
    a. Checks if the doors are fully closed. The problem area is indicated on the vehicle outline shown on the DIC.

b. Checks if hood or trunk isn't fully closed.

4. SERVICE REMINDER:
    a. Lets vehicle operator know when to have the following service work done: Change engine oil, change oil filter, rotate tire and have engine tune-up.

b. The figures at the bottom of the DIC show the number of miles remaining before the work should be done.

To use the service reminder, you must first decide which service items to check. For example, if you want to knock when to next rotate the tires, push and hold the DIC button until the **SERVICE REMINDER** light comes ON. Then,

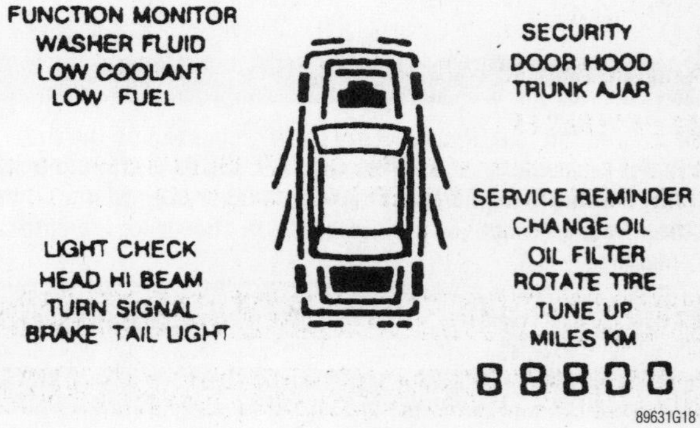

FUNCTION MONITOR
WASHER FLUID
LOW COOLANT
LOW FUEL

SECURITY
DOOR HOOD
TRUNK AJAR

LIGHT CHECK
HEAD HI BEAM
TURN SIGNAL
BRAKE TAIL LIGHT

SERVICE REMINDER
CHANGE OIL
OIL FILTER
ROTATE TIRE
TUNE UP
MILES KM

Fig. 105 Typical Driver Information Center (DIC) display

push and release the DIC button until **ROTATE TIRES** appears. The number at the bottom then shows how many miles there are to go before the tires should be rotates.

To reset the service reminder, push the DIC until the service item desired appears and do not release the button. In 5–10 seconds the display will start to count down, 500 miles at a time. When the display reads the distance you wish to set, release the button. Note that sometimes a service reminder display will stay ON even though it has been reset, but the reminder should go OFF after the vehicle has been driven about 10 miles.

1994–99 VEHICLES

Vehicles equipped with an **ENGINE OIL LIFE INDEX**, the display located on the Driver Information Center (DIC). The PCM determines approximately when the engine oil should be changed by calculating information based on vehicle speed, coolant temperature and engine RPM. Once the PCM determines it is time to change the engine oil, it will illuminate the **CHANGE OIL SOON** light on the DIC. This indicates the remaining oil life is below 10% (not to be confused with oil level). On a new vehicle or one that has been reset, the oil life is 100%. This percentage will slowly decrease based on the inputs the PCM receives. When oil life reaches the 0% mark, the PCM will illuminate the **CHANGE OIL NOW** light on the DIC. At this time, both messages will be displayed accompanied by a slow 5 second audible chime. The reset button must be pressed to acknowledge each of these messages. If a steady **CHANGE OIL SOON** light persists, this indicates a diagnostic trouble code has been set, specifying a possible shorted switch.

Remaining oil life percentage can be displayed by pressing the OIL button on the DIC and advancing through the messages until the oil life index is displayed. The oil life index will not detect abnormal conditions such as excessively dust or engine malfunctions that could otherwise affect the engine oil life.

After the engine oil has been changed, display the oil life index on the DIC, then hold the **RESET** button for at least 5 seconds. When a DIC message of **RESET** is displayed and the oil life index equals 100%, the reset is complete.

Buick LeSabre

1994 VEHICLES

After the engine oil has been changed, the Engine Oil Monitor must be reset. The reset button is located in the glove compartment. Reset as follows:

1. With the ignition key in the **RUN** position, push the reset button, hold it in for at least 5 seconds but not more than 60 seconds.

2. The CHANGE OIL SOON light will flash 4 times and then go off. This indicates that the Oil Life Monitor System has been reset.

1995–99 VEHICLES

For information on these vehicles, please refer to the procedure for 1994–99 Pontiac Bonnevilles.

Oldsmobile Delta 88

1989–93 VEHICLES

Vehicles equipped with an **ENGINE OIL LIFE INDEX** display as part of the **DRIVER INFORMATION SYSTEM (DIS)**, have a display that will show when to change the engine oil.

The oil change interval is determines by the DIS and will usually fall at or between the 2 recommended intervals of 3,000 and 7,500 miles, but it could be shorter than 3,000 miles under some severe driving conditions. The DIS will also signal the need for an oil change at 7,500 miles or 1 year passed since the last oil change. If the DIS does not indicate the need for an oil change after 7,500 miles or one year or if the **ENGINE OIL LIFE INDEX** display fails to appear, the oil should be changed and the driver information system serviced.

When the **ENGINE OIL LIFE INDEX** reaches 10 percent or less, the **CHANGE OIL** light display will function as a reserve trip odometer (indicating the distance to an oil change). Until the **ENGINE OIL LIFE INDEX** reset is performed, the driver information system will display the distance to the oil change and sound a beep when the ignition switch is turned to the **ACCESSORY** or **RUN** position the first time each day.

When the distance to the next oil change reaches zero, the driver information system will display the **CHANGE OIL NOW** light. Until an **ENGINE OIL LIFE INDEX** reset is performed, the driver information system will display the **CHANGE OIL NOW** light and sound a beep when the ignition switch is turned to the **ACCESSORY** or **RUN** position at the beginning of each day.

The driver information system will not detect dusty conditions or engine malfunctions which may affect the engine oil. If driving in severe conditions exist, be sure to change the engine oil every 3,000 miles or 3 months, whichever comes first, unless instructed otherwise by the driver information system. The driver information center does not measure the engine oil level. It still remains your responsibility to check the engine oil level. After the oil has been changed, the **ENGINE OIL LIFE INDEX** light must be reset. Resetting is performed as follows:

1. The **ENGINE OIL LIFE INDEX** can be reset by pressing the **RESET** and **OIL** buttons simultaneously for at least 5 seconds on the **ENGINE OIL LIFE INDEX** display. The driver information system will reset the **ENGINE OIL LIFE INDEX** to 100 percent and display an index of 100 percent.

1994–99 VEHICLES

Vehicles which are equipped with a Drivers Information Center (DIC) and have an Oil Life Index, will require the Oil Life Indicator to be reset after each oil change.

Press the **SEL** to select **OIL**. Press SEL if necessary to display the oil life. The display will show a reading of the estimated oil life left. Example: OIL LIFE 85%. When the remaining oil life is 9% or less, the display will show **CHANGE OIL SOON**. Then, a tone will sound and the **CHANGE OIL SOON** message will display each time the vehicle is started.

When the oil life is zero, a tone will sound and the display will show, **CHANGE OIL NOW**. Then, when the vehicle is started a tone will sound and the **CHANGE OIL NOW** message will display each time the vehicle is started. Reset the Oil Life Display as follows:

a. Acknowledge all diagnostic messages in the Drivers Information Center (DIC) by pressing **RESET**.

b. Press the **SEL** button on the left to select **OIL**. Press the **SEL** button on the right if necessary to display oil life.

c. Press and hold the **RESET** button for about 5 seconds. Once the oil life index has been reset, a **RESET** message will be displayed and then oil life will change to 100%.

Be careful not to reset the oil life accidentally at any time other than when the oil has just been changed. It cannot be reset accurately until the next oil change.

FLUIDS AND LUBRICANTS

Fluid Disposal

Used fluids such as engine oil, transmission fluid, antifreeze and brake fluid are hazardous wastes and must be disposed of properly. Before draining any fluids, consult with your local authorities; in many areas, waste oil, antifreeze, etc. is being accepted as a part of recycling programs. A number of service stations and auto parts stores are also accepting waste fluids for recycling.

Be sure of the recycling center's policies before draining any fluids, as many will not accept different fluids that have been mixed together.

Fuel and Engine Oil Recommendations

FUEL RECOMMENDATIONS

➡**Some fuel additives contain chemicals that can damage the catalytic converter and/or oxygen sensor. Read all of the labels carefully before using any additive in the engine or fuel system.**

All of the vehicles covered by this manual are designed to run on unleaded fuel. The use of a leaded fuel in a car requiring unleaded fuel will plug the catalytic converter and render it inoperative. It will also increase exhaust backpressure to the point where engine output will be severely reduced. The minimum octane rating of the unleaded fuel being used must be at least 87, which usually means regular unleaded, but some high performance engines may require higher ratings. Fuel should be selected for the brand and octane which performs best with your engine. Judge a gasoline by its ability to prevent pinging, its engine starting capabilities (cold and hot) and general all weather performance.

As far as the octane rating is concerned, refer to the general engine specifications chart in Section 3 of this manual to find your engine and its compression ratio. If the compression ratio is 9.0:1 or lower, in most cases a regular unleaded grade of gasoline can be used. If the compression ratio is higher than 9.0:1 use a premium grade of unleaded fuel.

➡**All of the engines covered by this manual required a fuel with an octane rating of 87 or higher, except for the supercharged engine. The supercharged engine requires premium fuel with an octane rating of 92 or higher.**

The use of a fuel too low in octane (a measure of anti-knock quality) will result in spark knock. Since many factors such as altitude, terrain, air temperature and humidity affect operating efficiency, knocking may result even though the recommended fuel is being used. If persistent knocking occurs, it may be necessary to switch to a higher grade of fuel. Continuous or heavy knocking may result in engine damage.

➡**Your engine's fuel requirement can change with time, mainly due to carbon build-up, which will in turn change the compression ratio. If you engine pings, knocks or diesels (runs with the ignition OFF) switch to a higher grade of fuel. Sometimes, just changing brands will cure the problem. If it becomes necessary to retard the timing from the specifications, don't change it more than a few degrees. Retarded timing will reduce power output and fuel mileage, in addition to making the engine run hotter.**

OIL RECOMMENDATIONS

▶ **See Figures 106 and 107**

The Society Of Automotive Engineer (SAE) grade number indicates the viscosity of the engine oil and thus its ability to lubricate at a given temperature. The lower the SAE grade number, the lighter the oil; the lower the viscosity, the easier it is to crank the engine in cold weather. Oil viscosities should be chosen from those oils recommended for the lowest anticipated temperatures during the oil change interval. With the proper viscosity, you will be assured of easy cold starting and sufficient engine protection.

Multi-viscosity oils (5W-30, 10W-30 etc.) offer the important advantage of being adaptable to temperature extremes. They allow easy starting at low temperatures, yet they give good protection at high speeds and engine temperatures. This is a decided advantage in changeable climates or in long distance driving.

The American Petroleum Institute (API) designation indicates the classification of engine oil used under certain given operating conditions. Only oil designated for Service SJ, or latest superseding oil grade, should be used. Oils of the SJ type perform a variety of functions inside the engine in addition to their basic function as a lubricant. Through a balanced system of metallic detergents and polymeric dispersants, the oil prevents the formation of high and low temperature deposits and also keeps sludge and particles of dirt in suspension. Acids, particularly sulfuric acid, as well as other byproducts of combustion, are neutralized. Both the SAE grade number and the API designation can be found on the side of the oil bottle.

Synthetic Oils

There are excellent synthetic and fuel-efficient oils available that, under the right circumstances, can help provide better fuel mileage and better engine protection. However, these advantages come at a price, which can be significantly more than the price per quart of conventional motor oils.

Before pouring any synthetic oils into your car's engine, you should consider the condition of the engine and the type of driving you do. It is also wise to check the vehicle manufacturer's position on synthetic oils.

Generally, it is best to avoid the use of synthetic oil in both brand new and older, high mileage engines. New engines require a proper break-in, and the synthetics are so slippery that they can impede this; most manufacturers recommend that you wait at least 5,000 miles (8,000 km) before switching to a syn-

Fig. 106 Look for the API oil identification label when choosing your engine oil

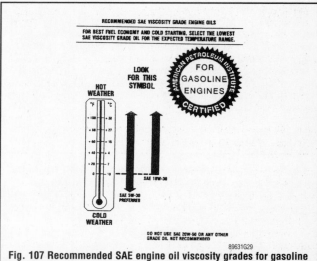

Fig. 107 Recommended SAE engine oil viscosity grades for gasoline engines

thetic oil. Conversely, older engines are looser and tend to lose more oil; synthetics will slip past worn parts more readily than regular oil. If your car already leaks oil, (due to worn parts or bad seals/gaskets), it may leak more with a synthetic inside.

Consider your type of driving. If most of your accumulated mileage is on the highway at higher, steadier speed, a synthetic oil will reduce friction and probably help deliver better fuel mileage. Under such ideal highway conditions, the oil change interval can be extended, as long as the oil filter can operated effectively for the extended life of the oil. If the filter can't do its job for this extended period, dirt and sludge will build up in your engine's crankcase, sump, oil pump and lines, no matter what type of oil is used. If using synthetic oil in this manner, your should continue to change the oil filter at the recommended intervals.

Cars used under harder, stop-and-go, short hop circumstances should always be serviced more frequently, and for these cars synthetic oil may not be a wise investment. Because of the necessary shorter change interval needed for this type of driving, you cannot take advantage of the long recommended change interval of most synthetic oils.

OIL LEVEL CHECK

▶ **See Figures 108 and 109**

Every time you stop for fuel, check the engine oil making sure the engine has fully warmed and the vehicle is parked on a level surface. Because it takes some

Fig. 108 Locate the engine oil dipstick, which should be found at the front of the engine, and pull it out of the tube

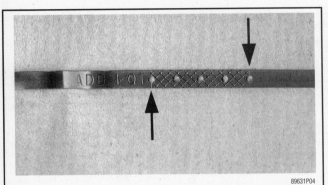

Fig. 109 The oil level should be within the crosshatched area on the dipstick (between the photo's arrows)

time for the oil to drain back to the oil pan, you should wait a few minutes before checking your oil. If you are doing this at a fuel stop, first fill the fuel tank, then open the hood and check the oil, but don't get so carried away as to forget to pay for the fuel. Most station attendants won't believe that you forgot.

1. Make sure the car is parked on level ground.
2. When checking the oil level, it is best for the engine to be at normal operating temperature, although checking the oil immediately after stopping will lead to a false reading. Wait a few minutes after turning off the engine to allow the oil to drain back into the crankcase.
3. Open the hood and locate the dipstick which will be in a guide tube mounted in the upper engine block. Pull the dipstick from its tube, wipe it clean (using a clean, lint free rag) and then reinsert it, making sure that you push it back in completely.
4. Pull the dipstick back out, hold it horizontally, and check the level at the end of the dipstick. Some dipsticks are marked with **ADD** and **FULL** lines, others with **ADD 1 QT** and **OPERATING RANGE**, or crosshatched area. In either case, the level must be above the **ADD** line. Reinsert the dipstick completely.
5. If oil must be added, it can be poured in through the rocker (valve) cover after removing the filler cap on the cover. See the oil and fuel recommendations listed earlier in this section for the proper viscosity and rating of oil to use.
6. Insert the dipstick and check the oil level again after adding any oil. Approximately one quart of oil will raise the level from the ADD mark to the FULL mark. Be sure not to overfill the crankcase and waste the oil. Excess oil will generally be consumed at an accelerated rate.

✲✲ WARNING

DO NOT overfill the crankcase. It may result in oil-fouled spark plugs, oil leaks cause by oil seal failure or engine damage due to oil foaming.

7. Be sure that the dipstick and oil filler cap are installed before closing the hood.

OIL & FILTER CHANGE

▶ **See Figures 110 thru 119**

➡**On these vehicles, you need a 14mm wrench or socket to loosen the oil pan drain plug.**

The manufacturer's recommended oil change interval is 7500 miles (12,000 km) under normal operating conditions. We recommend an oil change interval of 3000–3500 miles (4800–5600 km) under normal conditions; more frequently under severe conditions such as when the average trip is less than 4 miles (6 km), the engine is operated for extended periods at idle or low-speed, when towing a trailer or operating in dusty areas.

Always replace the oil filter every time you change the oil. For the small price of an oil filter, it's cheap insurance to replace the filter at every oil change. One of the larger filter manufacturers points out in its advertisements that not changing the filter leaves one quart of dirty oil in the engine. This claim is true and should be kept in mind when changing your oil.

1. Drive the car until the engine is at normal operating temperature. A run to the parts store for oil and a filter should accomplish this. If the engine is not hot when the oil is changed, most of the acids and contaminants will remain inside the engine.

➡**Please be considerate of the environment. Dispose of waste oil properly by taking it to a service station, municipal facility or recycling center.**

2. Run the engine until it reaches normal operating temperature. The turn the engine **OFF**.
3. Raise and safely support the front of the vehicle using jackstands.
4. Slide a pan of at least six quarts capacity under the oil pan. Wipe the drain plug and surrounding area clean using an old rag.
5. Loosen the drain plug using a ratchet, short extension and socket, or a box-wrench. The drain plug is the bolt inserted at an angle into the lowest point of the oil pan. Turn the plug out by hand, using a rag to shield your fingers from the hot oil. By keeping an inward pressure on the plug as you unscrew it, oil won't escape past the threads and you can remove it without being burned by hot oil.
6. Quickly withdraw the plug and move your hands out of the way, but be careful not to drop the plug into the drain pan, as fishing it out can be an unpleasant mess. Allow the oil to drain completely, then reinstall the drain plug. Do not overtighten the plug.
7. Wipe off the drain plug, removing any traces of metal particles. Check the condition of the plastic drain plug gasket. If it is cracked or distorted in any way, replace it. Reinstall the drain plug and gasket. Tighten the drain plug snugly.

➡**The oil filter is just about impossible to reach from above, and almost as inaccessible from below. It may be easiest to remove the front wheel to allow more room to work on some models.**

8. Place the drain pan on the ground, under the filter. Use a strap or cap type wrench to loosen the oil filter; these are available at auto parts stores. Unscrew and discard the old filter. It will be VERY HOT, so be careful.

➡**Regardless of which type wrench you decide to use, be sure to obtain the correct size; filter wrenches come in different sizes (as do oil filters), and one size does not fit all.**

9. If the oil filter is on so tightly that it collapses under pressure from the wrench, move the wrench as close to the engine as possible. If the filter hasn't torn, but can't turn, it may be to your advantage to take it to a shop before a leak develops. It is next to impossible to cut these filters off without special tools. Make sure you are turning it counterclockwise.
10. Clean off the oil filter mounting surface with a rag. Apply a thin film of clean engine oil to the filter gasket.
11. Screw the filter on by hand until the gasket makes contact. Then tighten it by hand an additional ½ to ¾ of a turn. Do not overtighten.
12. If raised, carefully lower the vehicle.
13. Refill the crankcase with the correct amount of fresh engine oil. Please refer to the Capacities chart in this section.
14. Check the oil level on the dipstick. It is normal or the level to be a bit above the full mark until the engine is run and the new filter is filled with oil. Start the engine and allow it to idle for a few minutes.

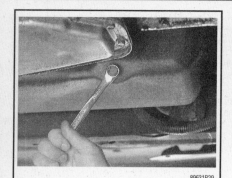

Fig. 110 Use a box end wrench to break the oil pan drain plug loose

Fig. 111 Keeping inward pressure when unthreading the drain plug helps avoid spilling hot oil all over your hand

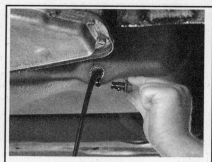

Fig. 112 Quickly withdraw the plug from the oil pan, and allow the oil to drain completely

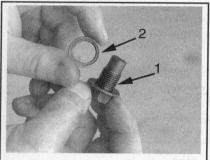

Fig. 113 Clean off and inspect the oil pan drain plug (1) and washer (2), and replace if necessary

Fig. 114 Use an oil filter wrench or adapter with a ratchet (shown) to loosen the oil filter

Fig. 115 Remember, the oil filter holds about a quart of dirty oil that will probably drip out as the filter is loosened . . .

Fig. 116 . . . so you may want to wear protective gloves when removing the filter

Fig. 117 Clean the oil filter mounting boss with a clean, lint-free rag before installing a new filter

Fig. 118 Before installing a new oil filter, lightly coat the rubber gasket with clean oil

❊❊ CAUTION

Do not run the engine above idle speed until it has built up oil pressure, as indicated when the oil light goes out.

15. Shut off the engine and allow the oil to flow back to the crankcase for a minute, then recheck the oil level. Check around the filter and drain plug for any leaks, and correct as necessary.

When you have finished this job, you will notice that you now possess four or five quarts of dirty oil. The best thing to do is to pour it into plastic jugs, such as milk or old antifreeze containers. Then, locate a service station or automotive parts store where you can pour it into their used oil tank for recycling.

➡Improperly disposing of used motor oil not only pollutes the environment, it violates Federal law. Dispose of waste oil properly.

Automatic Transaxle

FLUID RECOMMENDATIONS

When adding fluid or refilling the transaxle, use Dexron®IIE or Dexron® III automatic transmission fluid. Use of other fluids could cause erratic shifting and transmission damage.

Fig. 119 Using a funnel when adding engine oil to the crankcase will prevent making a mess

LEVEL CHECK

▶ **See Figures 120, 121 and 122**

1. Start the engine and drive the vehicle for a minimum of 15 miles (24 km).

➡**The automatic transaxle fluid level must be checked with the vehicle at normal operating temperature; 180–200°F (82–93°C). Temperature will greatly affect transaxle fluid level.**

2. Park the vehicle on a level surface.
3. Place the transaxle gear selector in **P**.
4. Apply the parking brake and block the drive wheels.
5. With the brakes applied, move the shift lever through all the gear ranges, ending in **P**.

➡**The fluid level must be checked with the engine running at slow idle, with the car level, and the fluid at least at room temperature. The correct fluid level cannot be read if you have just driven the car for a long time at high speed, city traffic in hot weather or if the car has been pulling a trailer. In these cases, wait at least 30 minutes for the fluid to cool down.**

6. Pull the dipstick, located at the rear end of the engine, out and wipe with a clean, lint-free rag.
7. Push the dipstick completely into the filler tube, then wait 3 seconds and pull the dipstick out again.
8. Check both sides of the dipstick and read the lower level. The fluid level should be in the crosshatch area.

➡**The fluid level is acceptable if it is anywhere within the crosshatch area. The fluid level does not have to be at the top of the crosshatch area. DO NOT add fluid unless the level is below the crosshatch area.**

9. Inaccurate fluid level readings may result if the fluid is checked immediately after the vehicle has been operated under any or all of the following conditions:

a. In high ambient temperatures above 90°F (32°C).
b. At sustained high speeds.
c. In heavy city traffic during hot weather.
d. As a towing vehicle.
e. In commercial service (taxi or police use).

10. If the vehicle has been operated under these conditions, shut the engine **OFF** and allow the vehicle to cool for 30 minutes. After the cool-down period, restart the vehicle and continue from Step 2.

11. If it is determined that the fluid level is low, add only enough fluid to bring the level into the crosshatch area. It generally takes less than a pint. DO NOT overfill the transaxle! If the fluid level is within specifications, simply push the dipstick back into the filler tube completely.

12. After adding fluid, if necessary, recheck the level, making sure it is within the crosshatch area. Turn the engine **OFF**, then unblock the drive wheels.

DRAIN, FILTER SERVICE & REFILL

▶ **See Figures 123 thru 133**

➡**On these vehicles, a 10mm socket is needed to loosen and remove the automatic transaxle retaining bolts.**

The car should be driven approximately 15 miles (24 km) to warm the transaxle fluid before the pan is removed.

➡**The fluid should be drained while the transaxle is warm.**

✳✳ WARNING

Use only fluid labeled Dexron®III or IIE. Use of other fluids could cause erratic shifting and transaxle damage.

1. Raise and safely support the vehicle with jackstands.
2. Place a suitable drain pan under the transaxle fluid pan.
3. Remove the fluid pan bolts/screws from the front and sides of the pan.
4. Loosen the rear bolts/screws about four turns.

✳✳ WARNING

Be careful not to damage the mating surfaces of the oil pan and case. Any damage could result in fluid leaks.

5. Lightly tap the pan with a rubber mallet or carefully pry the fluid pan loose and allow the fluid to drain.

➡**If the transaxle fluid is dark or has a burnt smell, transaxle damage is indicated. Have the transaxle checked professionally.**

6. Remove the remaining bolts, the pan, and the gasket or RTV sealant. Discard the old gasket. Use a suitable gasket scraper to clean the gasket mating surfaces.

7. For 1986–90 vehicles, inspect the fluid pan bolts, as shown in the accompanying figure, to see if they are in reusable condition.

8. Remove the filter. It may be necessary to use a long flat-bladed tool to

Fig. 120 After wiping the automatic transaxle dipstick clean, reinsert it fully into the tube

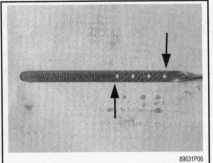

Fig. 121 Do NOT add fluid if the level is anywhere within the crosshatched area on the dipstick

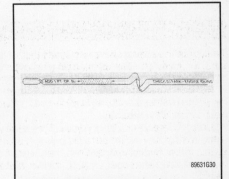

Fig. 122 If the fluid level is low, add only enough to reach the cross-hatched area.

Fig. 123 View of the automatic transaxle pan and retaining bolts—1989 Bonneville shown

Fig. 124 After removing the necessary bolts, partially loosen the 2 side bolts (see arrows)

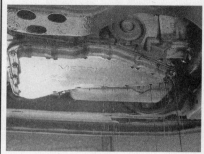

Fig. 125 Tap or pry the pan loose, then allow the fluid to drain completely

Fig. 126 After all of the fluid has drained, unfasten the remaining bolts and remove the fluid pan

Fig. 127 Remove the pan magnet and inspect it for metal shavings or chips, which may indicate excessive wear

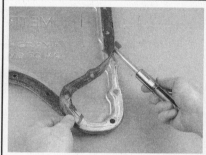

Fig. 128 Carefully remove the gasket, then install a new one prior to installation

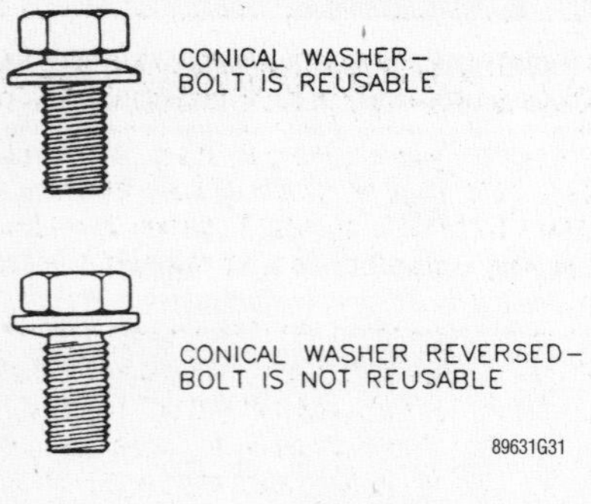

CONICAL WASHER—
BOLT IS REUSABLE

CONICAL WASHER REVERSED—
BOLT IS NOT REUSABLE

Fig. 129 On 1986–90 vehicles, you must inspect the bolts and determine if they are reusable or not

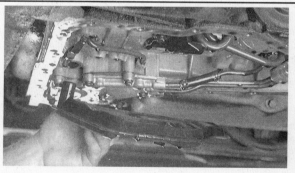

Fig. 130 Removing the filter from the transaxle

pry the filter neck out of the seal. Inspect the oil filter seal for damage or wear and replace if necessary. You may need to use special tools J 6215-B and J 23129 or equivalent to remove the seal.

9. Clean the transaxle case and oil pan gasket surfaces with solvent and dry it thoroughly. Make sure all of the old gasket material is removed.

To install:

10. Coat a new oil filter seal with a small amount of Transjel® or petroleum jelly, then install the new seal onto the filter.

11. Install the new transaxle filter and O-ring seal, locating the filter against the dipstick stop. Always replace the filter with a new one. Do not attempt to clean the old one!

12. Place a new transaxle fluid pan gasket in position in the pan.

13. Thoroughly clean and dry all bolts and bolt holes. Install the pan and tighten the bolts in a crisscross manner, starting from the middle and working outward. Tighten the bolts/screws to the following specifications:

a. 1986–90 vehicles: 15 ft. lbs. (20 Nm).

b. 1991–99 vehicles: 12–13 ft. lbs. (16–17 Nm)

14. Carefully lower the vehicle, then add the correct amount of Dexron®III, IIE, or equivalent, transmission fluid. Refer to the Capacities chart for fluid specifications.

15. Follow the fluid check procedure earlier in this section.

16. Check the pan for leaks.

Cooling System

♦ See Figure 134

✱✱ CAUTION

Never remove the radiator cap under any conditions while the engine is hot! Failure to follow these instructions could result in damage to the cooling system, engine and/or personal injury. To avoid having scalding hot coolant or steam blow out of the radia-

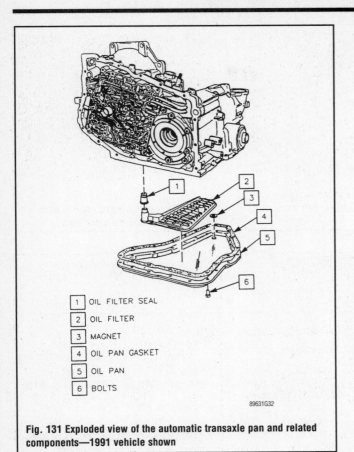

1	OIL FILTER SEAL
2	OIL FILTER
3	MAGNET
4	OIL PAN GASKET
5	OIL PAN
6	BOLTS

89631G32

Fig. 131 Exploded view of the automatic transaxle pan and related components—1991 vehicle shown

89631P22

Fig. 133 Use a long-necked funnel to add fluid through the automatic transaxle dipstick tube

tor, use extreme care whenever you are removing the radiator cap. Wait until the engine has cooled, then wrap a thick cloth around radiator cap and turn it slowly to the first stop. Step back while the pressure is released from the cooling system. When you are sure the pressure has been released, press down on the radiator cap (still have the cloth in position), turn and remove the cap.

The engine is kept cool by a liquid circulating through the engine to a radiator. In the radiator, the liquid is cooled by air passing through the radiator tubes. The coolant is circulated by a rotating water pump driven by the engine crankshaft. The complete engine cooling system consists of a radiator, recovery system, cooling fan, thermostat, water pump and serpentine belt.

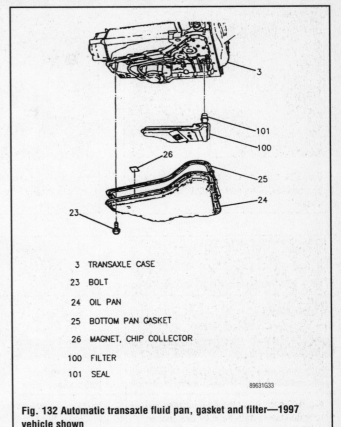

3	TRANSAXLE CASE
23	BOLT
24	OIL PAN
25	BOTTOM PAN GASKET
26	MAGNET, CHIP COLLECTOR
100	FILTER
101	SEAL

89631G33

Fig. 132 Automatic transaxle fluid pan, gasket and filter—1997 vehicle shown

FLUID RECOMMENDATIONS

✳✳ WARNING

For 1996–99 vehicles, when adding coolant, it is important that you use DEX-COOL®, an orange colored, silicate-free coolant meeting GM specifications 6277M. If silicated coolant is added to the system, premature engine, heater core or radiator corrosion may result.

The cooling system should be inspected, flushed and refilled with fresh coolant at least every 30,000 miles (48,000 km) or 24 months. If the coolant is left in the system too long, it loses its ability to prevent rust and corrosion.

When the coolant is being replaced, use a good quality antifreeze that is safe to be used with aluminum cooling system components. The ratio of antifreeze to water should always be a 50/50 mixture. This ratio will ensure the proper balance of cooling ability, corrosion protection and antifreeze protection. At this ratio, the antifreeze protection should be good to -34°F (-37°C). If greater antifreeze protection is needed, the ratio should not exceed 70% antifreeze to 30% water.

LEVEL CHECK

▶ **See Figures 135 and 136**

➡**When checking the coolant level, the radiator cap need not be removed. Simply check the coolant level in the recovery bottle or surge tank.**

Check the coolant level in the recovery bottle or surge tank, usually mounted on the inner fender. With the engine cold, the coolant level should be at the FULL COLD or between the FULL HOT and ADD level. With the engine at normal operating temperature, the coolant level should be at the FULL HOT or HOT

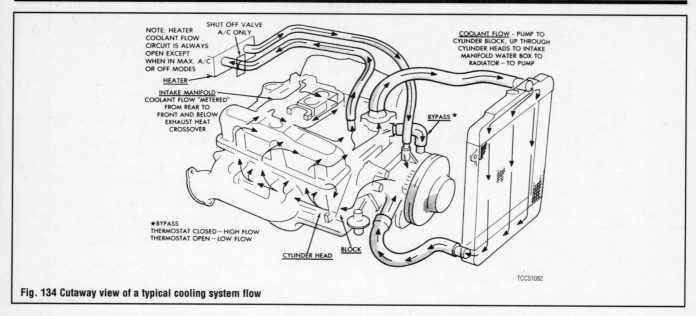

Fig. 134 Cutaway view of a typical cooling system flow

mark. Only add coolant to the recovery bottle or surge tank as necessary to bring the system up to a proper level.

> ⁕ **CAUTION**
>
> **Should it be necessary to remove the radiator cap, make sure the system has had time to cool, thereby reducing the internal pressure.**

On any vehicle that is not equipped with a coolant recovery bottle or surge tank, the level must be checked by removing the radiator cap. This should only be done when the cooling system has had time to sufficiently cool after the engine has been run. The coolant level should be within 2 in. (51mm) of the base of the radiator filler neck. If necessary, coolant can then be added directly to the radiator.

COOLING SYSTEM INSPECTION

Checking the Radiator Cap Seal

▶ **See Figure 137**

While you are checking the coolant level, check the radiator cap for a worn or cracked gasket. If the cap doesn't seal properly, fluid will be lost and the engine will overheat.

Worn caps should be replaced with a new one.

Checking the Radiator For Debris

▶ **See Figure 138**

Periodically clean any debris; leaves, paper, insects, etc. from the radiator fins. Pick the large pieces off by hand. The smaller pieces can be washed away with water pressure from a hose.

Carefully straighten any bent radiator fins with a pair of needle nose pliers. Be careful, the fins are very soft. Don't wiggle the fins back and forth too much. Straighten them once and try not move them again.

DRAIN & REFILL

▶ **See Figures 139, 140, 141, 142 and 143**

> ⁕ **CAUTION**
>
> **When draining the coolant, keep in mind that cats and dogs are attracted by ethylene glycol antifreeze and are quite likely to drink any that is left in an uncovered container or in puddles on the ground. This will prove fatal in sufficient quantity. Always drain the coolant into a sealable container. Coolant should be reused until it is contaminated or several years old. To avoid injuries from scalding fluid and steam, DO NOT remove the radiator cap while the engine and radiator are still hot.**

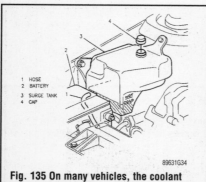

Fig. 135 On many vehicles, the coolant recovery reservoir is mounted on the fenderwell, near the battery

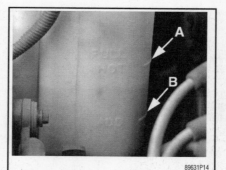

Fig. 136 Coolant level should be between the FULL HOT (A) and ADD (B) marks, depending upon the temperature

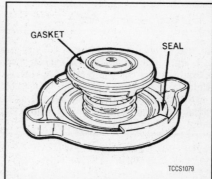

Fig. 137 Be sure the rubber gasket on the radiator cap has a tight seal

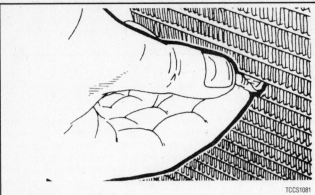

Fig. 138 Periodically removal all debris from the radiator fins

1. Make sure the engine is cool and the vehicle is parked on a level surface, remove the radiator cap by performing the following:
   a. Slowly rotate the cap counterclockwise to the detent.
   b. If any residual pressure is present, WAIT until the hissing stops.
   c. After the hissing noise has ceased, press down on the cap and continue rotating it counterclockwise to remove it.
2. Remove the recovery bottle or surge tank cap.

➡**You may want to attach a short piece of hose or tubing to the radiator drain tube to prevent the coolant from running everywhere during draining.**

3. Place a fluid catch pan under the radiator. Open the radiator drain valve, which is located at the bottom of the radiator tank, by turning it counterclock-wise. It may be wise to coat the fitting with penetrating lubricant before you attempt to turn it. Also, it's a good idea to attach a hose to the drain tube to prevent a mess. Allow the coolant to completely drain from the radiator.

4. Remove the thermostat housing cap and thermostat, or open the air bleed vent(s), if applicable.
5. Remove the drain plug(s) from the engine block (located on the engine block, above the engine oil pan) and allow the coolant to drain.
6. Allow the coolant to drain completely from the vehicle.
7. Close the radiator drain valve, then reinstall any block drains which were removed.
8. Using a 50/50 mixture of antifreeze and clean water, fill the radiator to the bottom of the filler neck and the coolant tank to the FULL mark.
9. Install the radiator cap, making sure the arrows line up over the overflow tube leading the reservoir or surge tank. Place the cap back on the recovery bottle or surge tank.
10. Start the engine. Select HEAT on the climate control panel and turn the temperature valve to full WARM. Run the engine until it reaches normal operating temperature. Check to make sure there is hot air flowing from the floor ducts.
11. Check the fluid level in the reservoir or surge tank and add as necessary.
12. If necessary, you can pressure check the cooling system for leaks.

FLUSHING & CLEANING

Several aftermarket radiator flushing and cleaning kits can be purchased at your local auto parts store. It is recommended that the radiator be cleaned and flushed of sludge and any rust build-up once a year. Manufacturer's directions for proper use, and safety precautions, come in each kit.

1. Refer to the drain and refill procedure in this section, then drain the cooling system.
2. Close the drain valve.

Fig. 139 Location of the drain valve (1) and drain hole (2)

Fig. 140 If a complete draining is required, you can remove the engine block's drain plug(s) (see arrow)

Fig. 141 Fill the radiator to the bottom of the filler neck with a 50/50 antifreeze and water mixture

Fig. 142 Also, make sure to fill the coolant recovery reservoir

Fig. 143 Cooling systems should be pressure tested for leaks periodically

➡A flushing solution may be used. Ensure it is safe for use with aluminum cooling system components. Follow the directions on the container.

3. If using a flushing solution, remove the thermostat. Reinstall the thermostat housing.

4. Add sufficient water to fill the system.

5. Start the engine and run for a few minutes. Drain the system.

6. If using a flushing solution, disconnect the heater hose that connects the cylinder head to the heater core (that end of the hose will clamp to a fitting on the firewall. Connect a water hose to the end of the heater hose that runs to the cylinder head and run water into the system until it begins to flow out of the top of the radiator.

7. Allow the water to flow out of the radiator until it is clear.

8. Reconnect the heater hose.

9. Drain the cooling system.

10. Reinstall the thermostat.

11. Empty the coolant reservoir or surge tank and flush it.

12. Fill the cooling system, using the correct ratio of antifreeze and water, to the bottom of the filler neck. Fill the reservoir or surge tank to the FULL mark.

13. Install the radiator cap, making sure that the arrows align with the overflow tube.

Brake Master Cylinder

FLUID RECOMMENDATIONS

Use only heavy duty brake fluid meeting DOT 3 specifications from a clean, sealed container. Using any other type of fluid may result in severe brake system damage.

✳✳ WARNING

Brake fluid damages paint. It also absorbs moisture from the air; never leave a container or the master cylinder uncovered longer than necessary. All parts in contact with the brake fluid (master cylinder, hoses, plunger assemblies and etc.) must be kept clean, since any contamination of the brake fluid will adversely affect braking performance.

LEVEL CHECK

◗ See Figures 144 thru 150

It should be obvious how important the brake system is to safe operation of your vehicle. The brake fluid is key to the proper operation of your vehicle. Low levels of fluid indicate a need for service (there may be a leak in the system or the brake pads may just be worn and in need of replacement). In any case, the brake fluid level should be inspected at least during every oil change, but more often is desirable. Every time you open the hood is a good time to glance at the master cylinder reservoir.

1. Make sure the vehicle is parked on a level surface, then raise the hood.

2. Wipe off the master cylinder cover before you remove it, to prevent contaminating the fluid with dirt.

➡On some models, a see-through reservoir is used, eliminating the need of removing the cylinder cover.

3. On early model vehicles, the cover is snapped into place on the master cylinder. To remove the cover, just press up on the two tabs on the side of the cover, tilt it, then remove it. Be careful not to damage the rubber seal under the cover.

4. On later model vehicles, the master cylinder cap is a screw-on type. Simply unscrew the cap (and diaphragm, if equipped), and remove it from the reservoir.

✳✳ WARNING

Clean, high quality brake fluid is essential to the safe and proper operation of the brake system. You should always buy the highest quality brake fluid that is available. If the brake fluid becomes contaminated, drain and flush the system, then refill the master cylin-

Fig. 144 Some vehicles may have a warning label on the master cylinder reservoir

Fig. 145 Use a paper towel to wipe all of the dirt from around the master cylinder cap

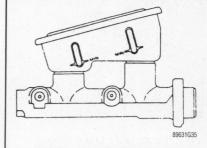

Fig. 146 On early model vehicles, the master cylinder lid is a snap-on type, and the fluid level markings are on the side of the reservoir

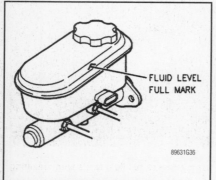

Fig. 147 On newer vehicles, the master cylinder cap screws onto the reservoir

Fig. 148 After cleaning the area, unscrew the master cylinder reservoir cap

Fig. 149 Add just enough brake fluid to bring the level up to the mark on the reservoir

Fig. 150 When adding brake fluid, only use fluid from a fresh sealed container

der with new fluid. **Never reuse any brake fluid. Any brake fluid that is removed from the system should be discarded. Also, do not allow any brake fluid to come in contact with a painted surface; it will damage the paint.**

➡**Don't leave the cover off of the master cylinder or the cap off of the brake fluid container any longer than necessary.**

5. The fluid level in each master cylinder reservoir should be ¼ in. (6mm) below the lowest edge of the filler opening or reach the marking shown in the reservoir. Use fresh brake fluid to adjust the level if necessary.

It is normal for the master cylinder fluid level to drop as the brake linings wear—⅛ in. (3mm) drop about every 10,000 miles (16,100km). If the fluid level is constantly low, the system should be checked for leaks.

6. Carefully seat the cover seal into the cover, then snap or screw the cover into place on the master cylinder. If equipped, with a snap-on lid, make sure that all four snaps latch completely.

Power Steering Pump

FLUID RECOMMENDATIONS

When adding fluid or making a complete fluid change, always use GM P/N 1050017, 1052884, power steering fluid or equivalent. DO NOT use automatic transmission fluid. Failure to use the proper fluid may cause hose and seal damage and fluid leaks.

For colder climates, another type of power steering fluid, available through GM dealerships, is available. However, the system must be flushed and bled before using the cold climate power steering fluid.

LEVEL CHECK

▶ **See Figures 151, 152, 153, 154 and 155**

The power steering fluid level should be checked at every oil change. The power steering pump and reservoir are integrated into one unit bolted to the front of the engine.

The power steering fluid reservoir is directly above the steering pump. The pump is located on top of the engine on the right (passenger's) side.

Power steering fluid level is indicated either by marks on a see through reservoir or by marks on a fluid level indicator in the reservoir cap.

If the fluid is warmed up (about 150°F/66°C), the level should be between the HOT and COLD marks or at the HOT mark.

If the fluid is cooler than 150°F (66°C), the level should be between the ADD and COLD marks.

Fig. 151 Unscrew the power steering cap/dipstick and pull it out of the reservoir to check the fluid level

Fig. 152 When the vehicle is at normal operating temperature, fluid should be added if the level is below the HOT mark

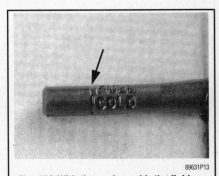

Fig. 153 With the engine cold, the fluid should reach the FULL COLD mark on the other side of the dipstick/cap

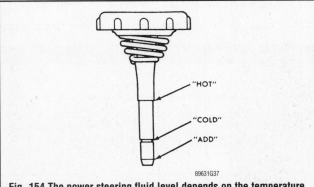

Fig. 154 The power steering fluid level depends on the temperature of the fluid

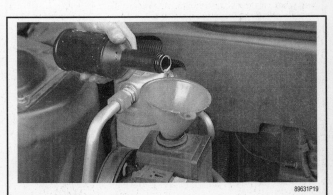

Fig. 155 If necessary, use a funnel to add fluid to the power steering fluid reservoir

Steering Gear

FLUID RECOMMENDATIONS & LEVEL CHECK

All models use integral rack and pinion power steering. The power steering pump delivers hydraulic pressure through two hoses to the steering gear itself. Refer to the preceding power steering pump fluid recommendation and level check procedures to check the steering gear fluid level.

Supercharger

FLUID RECOMMENDATIONS

When adding oil to the supercharger, use only synthetic oil, GM part no. 12345982 or equivalent.

LEVEL CHECK

▶ **See Figure 156**

✴✴ WARNING

Do NOT remove the oil plug when the engine is warm. The engine should be cool to the touch, about 2–3 hours after running. Removing the oil pump when the engine is still warm can cause hot oil to overflow. This could result in loss of oil and possible personal injury.

1. Remove the wiring harness shield or engine acoustic cover, as applicable.
2. Use a rag to clean the area around the oil fill plug before removing it.
3. Remove the oil plug. The oil level should be maintained to the bottom of the plug threads. Do not use petroleum based oil. When adding oil, use only GM part no. 12345982 synthetic oil, or equivalent. Failure to do so may cause supercharger failure.
4. After filling the supercharger to the proper level, make sure the O-ring is on the oil plug, then install the plug. Tighten the plug to 88 inch lbs. (10 Nm).
5. Install the wiring harness shield or engine acoustic cover, as applicable.

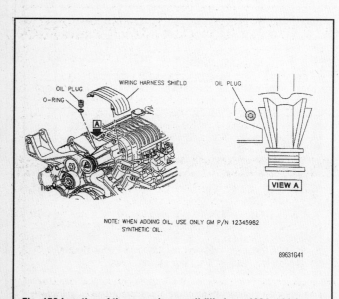

NOTE: WHEN ADDING OIL, USE ONLY GM P/N 12345982 SYNTHETIC OIL.

89631G41

Fig. 156 Location of the supercharger oil fill plug—1994 vehicle shown, other years similar

Chassis Greasing

▶ **See Figures 157 and 158**

The front suspension and steering linkage should be greased every 12 months or 7,500 miles (12,000 km) with an EP grease meeting GM specification 6031M.

If you choose to do this job yourself, you will need to purchase a hand operated grease gun, if you do not own one already, and a long flexible extension hose to reach the various grease fittings. You will also need a cartridge of the appropriate grease.

Press the fitting of the grease gun hose onto the grease fitting of the suspension or steering linkage component. Pump a few shots of grease into the fitting, until the rubber boot on the joint begins to expand, indicating that the joint is full. Remove the gun from the fitting. Be careful not to overfill the joints, which will rupture the rubber boots, allowing the entry of dirt. You can keep the grease fittings clean by covering them with a small square of tin foil.

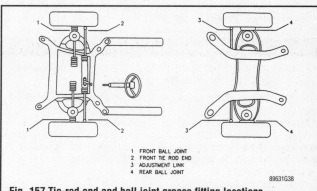

1 FRONT BALL JOINT
2 FRONT TIE ROD END
3 ADJUSTMENT LINK
4 REAR BALL JOINT

89631G38

Fig. 157 Tie-rod end and ball joint grease fitting locations— 1986–97 vehicles

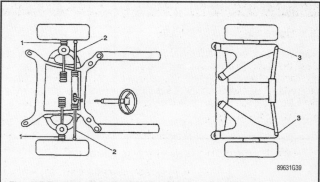

89631G39

Fig. 158 Front lower ball joint (1), front tie rod end (2) and rear tie rod end (3) grease fitting locations—1998–99 vehicles

Body Lubrication

HOOD

Clean the latch surfaces and apply clean engine oil to the latch pilot bolts and the spring anchor. Use the engine oil to lubricate the hood hinges as well. Use a chassis grease to lubricate all the pivot points in the latch release mechanism.

DOOR HINGES

The gas tank filler door, car door, and rear hatch or trunk lid hinges should be wiped clean and lubricated with clean engine oil. Silicone spray also works well on these parts, but must be applied more often. Use engine oil to lubricate the trunk or hatch lock mechanism and the lock bolt and striker. The door lock cylinders can be lubricated easily with a shot of silicone spray or one of the many dry penetrating lubricants commercially available.

LOCK CYLINDERS

Apply graphite lubricant sparingly though the key slot. Insert the key and operate the lock several times to be sure that the lubricant is worked into the lock cylinder.

PARKING BRAKE LINKAGE

Use chassis grease on the parking brake cable where is contacts the guides, links, levers, and pulleys. The grease should be a water resistant one for durability under the car.

ACCELERATOR LINKAGE

Lubricate the carburetor stud, carburetor lever, and the accelerator pedal lever at the support inside the car with clean engine oil.

TOWING THE VEHICLE

DO NOT attempt to start your car by pushing or towing as damage to the catalytic converter or other components may result. If the battery is weak, the vehicle may be jump started, using the procedure found after this section.

As long as the driveline and steering are normally operable, your car may be towed on all four wheels. If this is done, don't exceed 35 mph or travel further than 50 miles (80km). The steering wheel must be unlocked, the transaxle in Neutral, and the parking brake released. Never attach towing equipment to the bumpers or bumper brackets—the equipment must be attached to the main structural members of the car.

➡Remember that there will be no power assist for brakes and steering with the engine OFF. Also, be sure to check into state and local towing

JUMP STARTING A DEAD BATTERY

▶ See Figure 159

Whenever a vehicle is jump started, precautions must be followed in order to prevent the possibility of personal injury. Remember that batteries contain a small amount of explosive hydrogen gas which is a by-product of battery charging. Sparks should always be avoided when working around batteries, especially when attaching jumper cables. To minimize the possibility of accidental sparks, follow the procedure carefully.

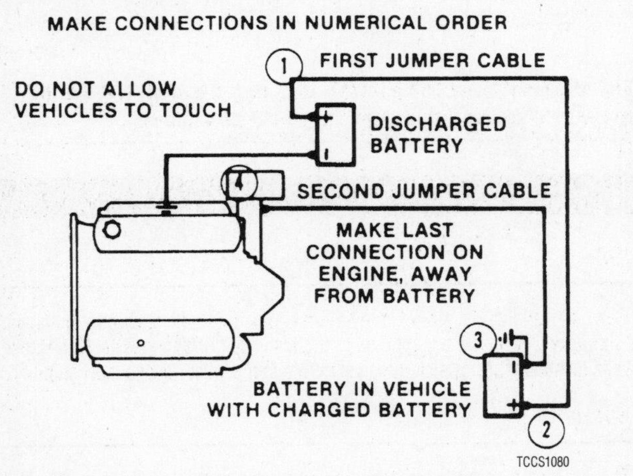

Fig. 159 Connect the jumper cables to the batteries and engine in the order shown

TRUNK LID

Spray a silicone lubricant on all of the pivot and friction surfaces to eliminate any squeaks or binds. Work the tailgate to distribute the lubricant

BODY DRAIN HOLES

Be sure that the drain holes in the doors and rocker panels are cleared of obstruction. A small screwdriver can be used to clear them of any debris.

Wheel Bearings

The H-body models are equipped with sealed hub and bearing assemblies for the front and rear wheels. The hub and bearing assemblies are non-serviceable. If the assembly is damaged, the complete unit must be replaced. Refer to Section 8 for the hub and bearing removal and installation procedure.

laws before flat-towing your vehicle.

If the car is to be towed by a wrecker, instructions supplied by the wrecker manufacturer should be followed. Because of the front wheel drive, towing on the rear wheels is preferred. If absolutely necessary, the car may be towed on the front wheels as long as the speed does not exceed 25 mph and the towing distance does not exceed 10 miles (16km).

☀☀ CAUTION

Don't exceed the speed or distance limits which are outlined here. Severe transaxle damage could result.

☀☀ CAUTION

NEVER hook the batteries up in a series circuit or the entire electrical system will go up in smoke, including the starter!

Jump Starting Precautions

• Be sure that both batteries are of the same polarity (have the same terminal, in most cases NEGATIVE grounded).
• Be sure that the vehicles are not touching or a short could occur.
• On non-sealed batteries, be sure the vent cap holes are not obstructed.
• Do not smoke or allow sparks anywhere near the batteries.
• In cold weather, make sure the battery electrolyte is not frozen. This can occur more readily in a battery that has been in a state of discharge.
• Do not allow electrolyte to contact your skin or clothing.

Jump Starting Procedure

1. Make sure that the voltages of the 2 batteries are the same. Most batteries and charging systems are of the 12 volt variety.
2. Pull the jumping vehicle (with the good battery) into a position so the jumper cables can reach the dead battery and that vehicle's engine. Make sure that the vehicles do NOT touch.
3. Place the transmissions/transaxles of both vehicles in **Neutral** (MT) or **P** (AT), as applicable, then firmly set their parking brakes.

➡**If necessary for safety reasons, the hazard lights on both vehicles may be operated throughout the entire procedure without significantly increasing the difficulty of jumping the dead battery.**

4. Turn all lights and accessories OFF on both vehicles. Make sure the ignition switches on both vehicles are turned to the **OFF** position.

5. Cover the battery cell caps with a rag, but do not cover the terminals.

6. Make sure the terminals on both batteries are clean and free of corrosion for good electrical contact.

7. Identify the positive (+) and negative (-) terminals on both batteries.

8. Connect the first jumper cable to the positive (+) terminal of the dead battery, then connect the other end of that cable to the positive (+) terminal of the booster (good) battery.

9. Connect one end of the other jumper cable to the negative (-) terminal on the booster battery and the final cable clamp to an engine bolt head, alternator bracket or other solid, metallic point on the engine with the dead battery. Try to pick a ground on the engine that is positioned away from the battery in order to minimize the possibility of the 2 clamps touching should one loosen during the procedure. DO NOT connect this clamp to the negative (-) terminal of the bad battery.

✳✳ CAUTION

Be very careful to keep the jumper cables away from moving parts (cooling fan, belts, etc.) on both engines.

10. Check to make sure that the cables are routed away from any moving parts, then start the donor vehicle's engine. Run the engine at moderate speed for several minutes to allow the dead battery a chance to receive some initial charge.

11. With the donor vehicle's engine still running slightly above idle, try to start the vehicle with the dead battery. Crank the engine for no more than 10 seconds at a time and let the starter cool for at least 20 seconds between tries. If the vehicle does not start in 3 tries, it is likely that something else is also wrong or that the battery needs additional time to charge.

12. Once the vehicle is started, allow it to run at idle for a few seconds to make sure that it is operating properly.

13. Turn ON the headlights, heater blower and, if equipped, the rear defroster of both vehicles in order to reduce the severity of voltage spikes and subsequent risk of damage to the vehicles' electrical systems when the cables are disconnected. This step is especially important to any vehicle equipped with computer control modules.

14. Carefully disconnect the cables in the reverse order of connection. Start with the negative cable that is attached to the engine ground, then the negative cable on the donor battery. Disconnect the positive cable from the donor battery and finally, disconnect the positive cable from the formerly dead battery. Be careful when disconnecting the cables from the positive terminals not to allow the alligator clips to touch any metal on either vehicle or a short and sparks will occur.

JACKING

▶ **See Figure 160**

Your vehicle was supplied with a jack for emergency road repairs. This jack is fine for changing a flat tire or other short term procedures not requiring you to go beneath the vehicle. If it is used in an emergency situation, carefully follow the instructions provided either with the jack or in your owner's manual. Do not attempt to use the jack on any portions of the vehicle other than specified by the vehicle manufacturer. Always block the diagonally opposite wheel when using a jack.

A more convenient way of jacking is the use of a garage or floor jack. You may use the floor jack to raise the front of the vehicle by placing it under the center of the front crossmember. To raise the rear of the vehicle, you can place the floor jack under the rear lower control arm (to raise one side of the vehicle), or under rear suspension support assembly (to raise the entire rear of the vehicle).

Never place the jack under the radiator, engine or transmission components. Severe and expensive damage will result when the jack is raised. Additionally, never jack under the floorpan or bodywork; the metal will deform.

Whenever you plan to work under the vehicle, you must support it on jackstands or ramps. Never use cinder blocks or stacks of wood to support the vehicle, even if you're only going to be under it for a few minutes. Never crawl under the vehicle when it is supported only by the tire-changing jack or other floor jack.

➡ **Always position a block of wood or small rubber pad on top of the jack or jackstand to protect the lifting point's finish when lifting or supporting the vehicle.**

Small hydraulic, screw, or scissors jacks are satisfactory for raising the vehicle. Drive-on trestles or ramps are also a handy and safe way to both raise and support the vehicle. Be careful though, some ramps may be too steep to drive your vehicle onto without scraping the front bottom panels. Never support the vehicle on any suspension member (unless specifically instructed to do so by a repair manual) or by an underbody panel.

Jacking Precautions

The following safety points cannot be overemphasized:
- Always block the opposite wheel or wheels to keep the vehicle from rolling off the jack.
- When raising the front of the vehicle, firmly apply the parking brake.
- When the drive wheels are to remain on the ground, leave the vehicle in gear to help prevent it from rolling.
- Always use jackstands to support the vehicle when you are working underneath. Place the stands beneath the vehicle's jacking brackets. Before climbing underneath, rock the vehicle a bit to make sure it is firmly supported.

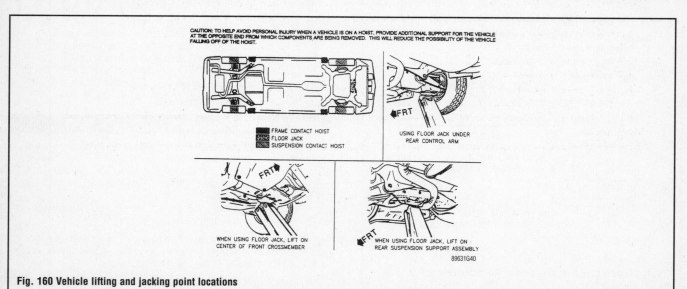

Fig. 160 Vehicle lifting and jacking point locations

NORMAL MAINTENANCE INTERVALS

TO BE SERVICED	TYPE OF SERVICE	VEHICLE MILEAGE INTERVAL (x1000)															
		7.5	15	22.5	30	37.5	45	52.5	60	67.5	75	82.5	90	97.5	105	112.5	120
Change engine oil	R	✓	✓	✓	✓	✓	✓	✓	✓	✓	✓	✓	✓	✓	✓	✓	✓
Replace engine oil filter	R	✓	✓	✓	✓	✓	✓	✓	✓	✓	✓	✓	✓	✓	✓	✓	✓
Lube the suspension grease fittings and linkages	L	✓	✓	✓	✓	✓	✓	✓	✓	✓	✓	✓	✓	✓	✓	✓	✓
Rotate and inspect the tires and wheels	S/I	✓	✓	✓	✓	✓	✓	✓	✓	✓	✓	✓	✓	✓	✓	✓	✓
Inspect the brake system components	S/I	✓	✓	✓	✓	✓	✓	✓	✓	✓	✓	✓	✓	✓	✓	✓	✓
Inspect throttle body mount torque (1987-93) vehicles	S/I	✓															
Inspect the caliper and steering knuckle	S/I		✓		✓		✓		✓		✓		✓		✓		✓
Check supercharger oil (if equipped)	S/I				✓				✓				✓				✓
Replace the air cleaner element	R				✓				✓				✓				✓
Inspect the fuel tank cap and fuel lines	S/I				✓				✓				✓				✓
Inspect the accessory drive belts	S/I								✓								✓
Inspect the PCV valve (1988-93) vehicles	S/I								✓								✓
Inspect the EGR system (1988-93) vehicles									✓								✓
Change the automatic transaxle fluid and filter	R	Every 50,000 miles, if operated in conditions listed below ①															
Inspect the spark plug wires	S/I	See note below ②															
Replace the spark plugs	R	See note below ③															
Cooling system ④	R	See note below ⑤															

R - Replace   S/I - Inspect and service, if needed   L - Lubricate   A - Adjust   C - Clean

NOTE: The services shown in this schedule up to 120,000 miles, should be performed at the same intervals after 150,000 miles.

① Change the automatic transaxle fluid and filter ONLY if the vehicle is mainly driven under on or more of the following conditions:

  a: In heavy city traffic where the outside temperatures reach 90°F (32°C) or higher.

  b: In hilly or mountainous terrain.

  c: When performing frequent trailer towing.

  d: When used as a taxi, police car or for delivery service.

② For 1986-95 vehicles, inspect the spark plug wires every 30,000 miles. For 1996-99 vehicles, inspect them every 100,000 miles

③ For 1986-95 vehicles, replace the spark plugs every 30,000 miles. For 1996-99 vehicles, replace them every 100,000 miles.

④ Drain, flush and refill the cooling system. Inspect the hoses, clean the radiator, condenser, pressure cap and neck. Pressure test the cooling system and pressure cap.

⑤ For 1986-95 vehicles, perform the cooling system service every 30,000 miles. For 1996-99 vehicles perform the service every 100,000 miles.

89631C05

SEVERE MAINTENANCE INTERVALS

TO BE SERVICED	TYPE OF SERVICE	VEHICLE MILEAGE INTERVAL (x1000)																			
		3	6	9	12	15	18	21	24	27	30	33	36	39	42	45	48	51	54	57	60
Change engine oil	R	✓	✓	✓	✓	✓	✓	✓	✓	✓	✓	✓	✓	✓	✓	✓	✓	✓	✓	✓	✓
Replace engine oil filter	R	✓	✓	✓	✓	✓	✓	✓	✓	✓	✓	✓	✓	✓	✓	✓	✓	✓	✓	✓	✓
Chassis lubrication	L		✓		✓		✓		✓		✓		✓		✓		✓		✓		✓
Rotate and inspect the tires and wheels	S/I		✓		✓		✓		✓		✓		✓		✓		✓		✓		✓
Inspect the brake system components	S/I		✓		✓		✓		✓		✓		✓		✓		✓		✓		✓
Throttle body mount bolt torque (1988-93 vehicles only)	S/I		✓																		
Inspect the caliper and steering knuckle	S/I				✓				✓				✓			✓					✓
Inspect the air cleaner element ①	S/I				✓						✓					✓					✓
Replace the air cleaner element	R										✓										✓
Check supercharger oil (if equipped)	S/I										✓										✓
Inspect the accessory drive belts	S/I																				✓
Inspect the PCV valve (1988-93 vehicles)	S/I										✓										✓
Inspect the EGR system (1988-93 vehicles)											✓										✓
Change the automatic transaxle fluid and filter	R	Every 50,000 miles, if operated in conditions listed below ②																			
Inspect the spark plug wires	S/I	See note below ③																			
Replace the spark plugs	R	See note below ④																			
Cooling system service ⑤	R	See note below ⑥																			

R - Replace   S/I - Inspect and service, if needed   L - Lubricate   A - Adjust   C - Clean

NOTE: The services shown in this schedule up to 120,000 miles, should be performed at the same intervals after 120,000 miles.

① Inspect air cleaner element if vehicle is driven under dusty conditions

② Change the automatic transaxle fluid and filter ONLY if the vehicle is mainly driven under one or more of the conditions listed under severe service.

③ For 1986-95 vehicles, inspect the spark plug wires every 30,000 miles. For 1996-99 vehicles, inspect them every 100,000 miles

④ For 1986-95 vehicles, replace the spark plugs every 30,000 miles. For 1996-99 vehicles, replace them every 100,000 miles.

⑤ Drain, flush and refill the cooling system. Inspect the hoses, clean the radiator, condenser, pressure cap and neck. Pressure test the cooling system and pressure cap.

⑥ For 1986-95 vehicles, perform the cooling system service every 30,000 miles. For 1996-98 vehicles perform the service every 100,000 miles.

FREQUENT OPERATION MAINTENANCE (SEVERE SERVICE)

If a vehicle is operated under any of the following conditions it is considered severe service:

- Towing a trailer or using a camper or car-top carrier.
- Repeated short trips of less than 5 miles in temperatures below freezing, or trips of less than 10 miles in any temperature.
- Extensive idling or low-speed driving for long distances as in heavy commercial use, such as delivery, taxi or police cars.
- Operating on rough, muddy or salt-covered roads.
- Operating on unpaved or dusty roads.
- Driving in extremely hot (over 90°) conditions.

89631C06

CAPACITIES

Year	Model	Engine ID/VIN	Engine Displacement Liters (cc)	Engine Oil with Filter	Transmission (pts.)		Drive Axle		Fuel Tank (gal.)	Cooling System (qts.)
					5-Spd	Auto.	Front (pts.)	Rear (pts.)		
1986	LeSabre	L	3.0l (2967)	4.0 ①	—	13.0	—	—	18.0	12.2
	LeSabre	B	3.8L (3786)	4.0 ①	—	13.0	—	—	18.0	12.6
	LeSabre	3	3.8L (3786)	4.0 ①	—	13.0	—	—	18.0	12.6
	Delta 88	L	3.0L (2967)	4.0 ①	—	13.0	—	—	18.0	12.2
	Delta 88	B	3.8L (3786)	4.0 ①	—	13.0	—	—	18.0	12.6
	Delta 88	3	3.8L (3786)	4.0 ①	—	13.0	—	—	18.0	12.6
1987	Bonneville	3	3.8L (3786)	4.0 ①	—	12.0 ②	—	—	18.0	13.0
	LeSabre	3	3.8L (3786)	4.0 ①	—	12.0 ②	—	—	18.0	13.0
	Delta 88	3	3.8L (3786)	4.0 ①	—	12.0 ②	—	—	18.0	13.0
1988	Bonneville	C	3.8L (3786)	4.0 ①	—	12.0 ②	—	—	18.0	13.0
	Bonneville	3	3.8L (3786)	4.0 ①	—	12.0 ②	—	—	18.0	13.0
	LeSabre	C	3.8L (3786)	4.0 ①	—	12.0 ②	—	—	18.0	13.0
	LeSabre	3	3.8L (3786)	4.0 ①	—	12.0 ②	—	—	18.0	13.0
	Delta 88	C	3.8L (3786)	4.0 ①	—	12.0 ②	—	—	18.0	13.0
	Delta 88	3	3.8L (3786)	4.0 ①	—	12.0 ②	—	—	18.0	13.0
1989	Bonneville	C	3.8L (3786)	4.0 ①	—	12.0 ②	—	—	18.0	13.0
	LeSabre	C	3.8L (3786)	4.0 ①	—	12.0 ②	—	—	18.0	13.0
	Eighty Eight	C	3.8L (3786)	4.0 ①	—	12.0 ②	—	—	18.0	13.0
1990	Bonneville	C	3.8L (3786)	4.0 ①	—	12.0 ②	—	—	18.0	13.0
	LeSabre	C	3.8L (3786)	4.0 ①	—	12.0 ②	—	—	18.0	13.0
	Eighty Eight	C	3.8L (3786)	4.0 ①	—	12.0 ②	—	—	18.0	13.0
1991	Bonneville	C	3.8L (3786)	4.0 ①	—	12.0 ②	—	—	18.0	13.0
	LeSabre	C	3.8L (3786)	4.0 ①	—	12.0 ②	—	—	18.0	13.0
	Eighty Eight	C	3.8L (3786)	5.0	—	12.0 ②	—	—	18.0	13.0
1992	Bonneville	L	3.8L (3786)	5.0	—	12.0 ②	—	—	18.0	13.0
	Bonneville	1	3.8L (3786)	5.0	—	12.0 ②	—	—	18.0	13.0
	LeSabre	L	3.8L (3786)	5.0	—	12.0 ②	—	—	18.0	13.0
	Eighty Eight	L	3.8L (3786)	5.0	—	12.0 ②	—	—	18.0	13.0
1993	Bonneville	L	3.8L (3786)	5.0	—	12.0 ②	—	—	18.0	13.0
	Bonneville	1	3.8L (3786)	5.0	—	12.0 ②	—	—	18.0	13.0
	LeSabre	L	3.8L (3786)	5.0	—	12.0 ②	—	—	18.0	13.0
	Eighty Eight	L	3.8L (3786)	5.0	—	12.0 ②	—	—	18.0	13.0
1994	Bonneville	L	3.8L (3786)	5.0	—	12.0 ②	—	—	18.0	13.0
	Bonneville	1	3.8L (3786)	5.0	—	12.0 ②	—	—	18.0	13.0
	LeSabre	L	3.8L (3786)	5.0	—	12.0 ②	—	—	18.0	13.0
	Eighty Eight	L	3.8L (3786)	5.0	—	12.0 ②	—	—	18.0	13.0
1995	Bonneville	K	3.8L (3786)	5.0	—	12.0 ②	—	—	18.0	13.0
	Bonneville	1	3.8L (3786)	5.0	—	12.0 ②	—	—	18.0	13.0
	LeSabre	L	3.8L (3786)	5.0	—	12.0 ②	—	—	18.0	13.0
	Eighty Eight	K	3.8L (3786)	5.0	—	12.0 ②	—	—	18.0	13.0
	Eighty Eight	1	3.8L (3786)	5.0	—	12.0 ②	—	—	18.0	13.0
1996	Bonneville	K	3.8L (3786)	5.0	—	12.0 ②	—	—	18.0	13.0
	Bonneville	1	3.8L (3786)	5.0	—	12.0 ②	—	—	18.0	13.0
	LeSabre	K	3.8L (3786)	5.0	—	12.0 ②	—	—	18.0	13.0
	Eighty Eight	K	3.8L (3786)	5.0	—	12.0 ②	—	—	18.0	13.0
	Eighty Eight	1	3.8L (3786)	5.0	—	12.0 ②	—	—	18.0	13.0
1997	Bonneville	K	3.8L (3786)	5.0	—	12.0 ②	—	—	18.0	13.0
	Bonneville	1	3.8L (3786)	5.0	—	12.0 ②	—	—	18.0	13.0
	LeSabre	K	3.8L (3786)	5.0	—	12.0 ②	—	—	18.0	13.0
	Eighty Eight	K	3.8L (3786)	5.0	—	12.0 ②	—	—	18.0	13.0
	Eighty Eight	1	3.8L (3786)	5.0	—	12.0 ②	—	—	18.0	13.0
1998	Bonneville	K	3.8L (3786)	4.5	—	14.8 ③	—	—	19.4	13.0
	Bonneville	1	3.8L (3786)	4.5	—	14.8 ③	—	—	19.4	13.0
	LeSabre	K	3.8L (3786)	4.5	—	14.8 ③	—	—	19.4	13.0
	Eighty Eight	K	3.8L (3786)	4.5	—	14.8 ③	—	—	19.4	13.0
	Eighty Eight	1	3.8L (3786)	4.5	—	14.8 ③	—	—	19.4	13.0
1999	Bonneville	K	3.8L (3786)	4.5	—	14.8 ③	—	—	19.4	13.0
	Bonneville	1	3.8L (3786)	4.5	—	14.8 ③	—	—	19.4	13.0
	LeSabre	K	3.8L (3786)	4.5	—	14.8 ③	—	—	19.4	13.0
	Eighty Eight	K	3.8L (3786)	4.5	—	14.8 ③	—	—	19.4	13.0
	Eighty Eight	1	3.8L (3786)	4.5	—	14.8 ③	—	—	19.4	13.0

NOTE: All capacities are approximate. Add fluid gradually and check to be sure a proper fluid level is obtained
① Additional oil may be necessary to bring the level to full. SSE models may require 1.5 additional quarts.
② Specification given is for fluid drain and refill. For transaxle overhaul, use approximately 22 pts.
③ Specification given is for fluid drain and refill. For transaxle overhaul, use approximately 20 pts.

89631C10

ENGLISH TO METRIC CONVERSION: MASS (WEIGHT)

Current **mass** measurement is expressed in pounds and ounces (lbs. & ozs.). The metric unit of mass (or weight) is the kilogram (kg). Even although this table does not show conversion of masses (weights) larger than 15 lbs, it is easy to calculate larger units by following the data immediately below.

To convert ounces (oz.) to grams (g): multiply th number of ozs. by 28
To convert grams (g) to ounces (oz.): multiply the number of grams by .035

To convert pounds (lbs.) to kilograms (kg): multiply the number of lbs. by .45
To convert kilograms (kg) to pounds (lbs.): multiply the number of kilograms by 2.2

lbs	kg	lbs	kg	oz	kg	oz	kg
0.1	0.04	0.9	0.41	0.1	0.003	0.9	0.024
0.2	0.09	1	0.4	0.2	0.005	1	0.03
0.3	0.14	2	0.9	0.3	0.008	2	0.06
0.4	0.18	3	1.4	0.4	0.011	3	0.08
0.5	0.23	4	1.8	0.5	0.014	4	0.11
0.6	0.27	5	2.3	0.6	0.017	5	0.14
0.7	0.32	10	4.5	0.7	0.020	10	0.28
0.8	0.36	15	6.8	0.8	0.023	15	0.42

ENGLISH TO METRIC CONVERSION: TEMPERATURE

To convert Fahrenheit (°F) to Celsius (°C): take number of °F and subtract 32; multiply result by 5; divide result by 9

To convert Celsius (°C) to Fahrenheit (°F): take number of °C and multiply by 9; divide result by 5; add 32 to total

Fahrenheit (F)		Celsius (C)		Fahrenheit (F)		Celsius (C)		Fahrenheit (F)		Celsius (C)	
°F	°C	°C	°F	°F	°C	°C	°F	°F	°C	°C	°F
−40	−40	−38	−36.4	80	26.7	18	64.4	215	101.7	80	176
−35	−37.2	−36	−32.8	85	29.4	20	68	220	104.4	85	185
−30	−34.4	−34	−29.2	90	32.2	22	71.6	225	107.2	90	194
−25	−31.7	−32	−25.6	95	35.0	24	75.2	230	110.0	95	202
−20	−28.9	−30	−22	100	37.8	26	78.8	235	112.8	100	212
−15	−26.1	−28	−18.4	105	40.6	28	82.4	240	115.6	105	221
−10	−23.3	−26	−14.8	110	43.3	30	86	245	118.3	110	230
−5	−20.6	−24	−11.2	115	46.1	32	89.6	250	121.1	115	239
0	−17.8	−22	−7.6	120	48.9	34	93.2	255	123.9	120	248
1	−17.2	−20	−4	125	51.7	36	96.8	260	126.6	125	257
2	−16.7	−18	−0.4	130	54.4	38	100.4	265	129.4	130	266
3	−16.1	−16	3.2	135	57.2	40	104	270	132.2	135	275
4	−15.6	−14	6.8	140	60.0	42	107.6	275	135.0	140	284
5	−15.0	−12	10.4	145	62.8	44	112.2	280	137.8	145	293
10	−12.2	−10	14	150	65.6	46	114.8	285	140.6	150	302
15	−9.4	−8	17.6	155	68.3	48	118.4	290	143.3	155	311
20	−6.7	−6	21.2	160	71.1	50	122	295	146.1	160	320
25	−3.9	−4	24.8	165	73.9	52	125.6	300	148.9	165	329
30	−1.1	−2	28.4	170	76.7	54	129.2	305	151.7	170	338
35	1.7	0	32	175	79.4	56	132.8	310	154.4	175	347
40	4.4	2	35.6	180	82.2	58	136.4	315	157.2	180	356
45	7.2	4	39.2	185	85.0	60	140	320	160.0	185	365
50	10.0	6	42.8	190	87.8	62	143.6	325	162.8	190	374
55	12.8	8	46.4	195	90.6	64	147.2	330	165.6	195	383
60	15.6	10	50	200	93.3	66	150.8	335	168.3	200	392
65	18.3	12	53.6	205	96.1	68	154.4	340	171.1	205	401
70	21.1	14	57.2	210	98.9	70	158	345	173.9	210	410
75	23.9	16	60.8	212	100.0	75	167	350	176.7	215	414

ENGLISH TO METRIC CONVERSION: LENGTH

To convert inches (ins.) to millimeters (mm): multiply number of inches by 25.4

To convert millimeters (mm) to inches (ins.): multiply number of millimeters by .04

Inches	Decimals	Milli-meters	Inches to millimeters (inches)	mm		Inches	Decimals	Milli-meters	Inches to millimeters (inches)	mm
1/64	0.051625	0.3969	0.0001	0.00254		33/64	0.515625	13.0969	0.6	15.24
1/32	0.03125	0.7937	0.0002	0.00508		17/32	0.53125	13.4937	0.7	17.78
3/64	0.046875	1.1906	0.0003	0.00762		35/64	0.546875	13.8906	0.8	20.32
1/16	0.0625	1.5875	0.0004	0.01016		9/16	0.5625	14.2875	0.9	22.86
5/64	0.078125	1.9844	0.0005	0.01270		37/64	0.578125	14.6844	1	25.4
3/32	0.09375	2.3812	0.0006	0.01524		19/32	0.59375	15.0812	2	50.8
7/64	0.109375	2.7781	0.0007	0.01778		39/64	0.609375	15.4781	3	76.2
1/8	0.125	3.1750	0.0008	0.02032		5/8	0.625	15.8750	4	101.6
9/64	0.140625	3.5719	0.0009	0.02286		41/64	0.640625	16.2719	5	127.0
5/32	0.15625	3.9687	0.001	0.0254		21/32	0.65625	16.6687	6	152.4
11/64	0.171875	4.3656	0.002	0.0508		43/64	0.671875	17.0656	7	177.8
3/16	0.1875	4.7625	0.003	0.0762		11/16	0.6875	17.4625	8	203.2
13/64	0.203125	5.1594	0.004	0.1016		45/64	0.703125	17.8594	9	228.6
7/32	0.21875	5.5562	0.005	0.1270		23/32	0.71875	18.2562	10	254.0
15/64	0.234375	5.9531	0.006	0.1524		47/64	0.734375	18.6531	11	279.4
1/4	0.25	6.3500	0.007	0.1778		3/4	0.75	19.0500	12	304.8
17/64	0.265625	6.7469	0.008	0.2032		49/64	0.765625	19.4469	13	330.2
9/32	0.28125	7.1437	0.009	0.2286		25/32	0.78125	19.8437	14	355.6
19/64	0.296875	7.5406	0.01	0.254		51/64	0.796875	20.2406	15	381.0
5/16	0.3125	7.9375	0.02	0.508		13/16	0.8125	20.6375	16	406.4
21/64	0.328125	8.3344	0.03	0.762		53/64	0.828125	21.0344	17	431.8
11/32	0.34375	8.7312	0.04	1.016		27/32	0.84375	21.4312	18	457.2
23/64	0.359375	9.1281	0.05	1.270		55/64	0.859375	21.8281	19	482.6
3/8	0.375	9.5250	0.06	1.524		7/8	0.875	22.2250	20	508.0
25/64	0.390625	9.9219	0.07	1.778		57/64	0.890625	22.6219	21	533.4
13/32	0.40625	10.3187	0.08	2.032		29/32	0.90625	23.0187	22	558.8
27/64	0.421875	10.7156	0.09	2.286		59/64	0.921875	23.4156	23	584.2
7/16	0.4375	11.1125	0.1	2.54		15/16	0.9375	23.8125	24	609.6
29/64	0.453125	11.5094	0.2	5.08		61/64	0.953125	24.2094	25	635.0
15/32	0.46875	11.9062	0.3	7.62		31/32	0.96875	24.6062	26	660.4
31/64	0.484375	12.3031	0.4	10.16		63/64	0.984375	25.0031	27	690.6
1/2	0.5	12.7000	0.5	12.70						

ENGLISH TO METRIC CONVERSION: TORQUE

To convert foot-pounds (ft. lbs.) to Newton-meters: multiply the number of ft. lbs. by 1.3

To convert inch-pounds (in. lbs.) to Newton-meters: multiply the number of in. lbs. by .11

in lbs	N-m	in lbs	N-m	in lbs	N-m	in lbs	N-m	in lbs	N-m
0.1	0.01	1	0.11	10	1.13	19	2.15	28	3.16
0.2	0.02	2	0.23	11	1.24	20	2.26	29	3.28
0.3	0.03	3	0.34	12	1.36	21	2.37	30	3.39
0.4	0.04	4	0.45	13	1.47	22	2.49	31	3.50
0.5	0.06	5	0.56	14	1.58	23	2.60	32	3.62
0.6	0.07	6	0.68	15	1.70	24	2.71	33	3.73
0.7	0.08	7	0.78	16	1.81	25	2.82	34	3.84
0.8	0.09	8	0.90	17	1.92	26	2.94	35	3.95
0.9	0.10	9	1.02	18	2.03	27	3.05	36	4.0

ENGLISH TO METRIC CONVERSION: TORQUE

Torque is now expressed as either foot-pounds (ft./lbs.) or inch-pounds (in./lbs.). The metric measurement unit for torque is the Newton-meter (Nm). This unit—the Nm—will be used for all SI metric torque references, both the present ft./lbs. and in./lbs.

ft lbs	N-m	ft lbs	N-m	ft lbs	N-m	ft lbs	N-m
0.1	0.1	33	44.7	74	100.3	115	155.9
0.2	0.3	34	46.1	75	101.7	116	157.3
0.3	0.4	35	47.4	76	103.0	117	158.6
0.4	0.5	36	48.8	77	104.4	118	160.0
0.5	0.7	37	50.7	78	105.8	119	161.3
0.6	0.8	38	51.5	79	107.1	120	162.7
0.7	1.0	39	52.9	80	108.5	121	164.0
0.8	1.1	40	54.2	81	109.8	122	165.4
0.9	1.2	41	55.6	82	111.2	123	166.8
1	1.3	42	56.9	83	112.5	124	168.1
2	2.7	43	58.3	84	113.9	125	169.5
3	4.1	44	59.7	85	115.2	126	170.8
4	5.4	45	61.0	86	116.6	127	172.2
5	6.8	46	62.4	87	118.0	128	173.5
6	8.1	47	63.7	88	119.3	129	174.9
7	9.5	48	65.1	89	120.7	130	176.2
8	10.8	49	66.4	90	122.0	131	177.6
9	12.2	50	67.8	91	123.4	132	179.0
10	13.6	51	69.2	92	124.7	133	180.3
11	14.9	52	70.5	93	126.1	134	181.7
12	16.3	53	71.9	94	127.4	135	183.0
13	17.6	54	73.2	95	128.8	136	184.4
14	18.9	55	74.6	96	130.2	137	185.7
15	20.3	56	75.9	97	131.5	138	187.1
16	21.7	57	77.3	98	132.9	139	188.5
17	23.0	58	78.6	99	134.2	140	189.8
18	24.4	59	80.0	100	135.6	141	191.2
19	25.8	60	81.4	101	136.9	142	192.5
20	27.1	61	82.7	102	138.3	143	193.9
21	28.5	62	84.1	103	139.6	144	195.2
22	29.8	63	85.4	104	141.0	145	196.6
23	31.2	64	86.8	105	142.4	146	198.0
24	32.5	65	88.1	106	143.7	147	199.3
25	33.9	66	89.5	107	145.1	148	200.7
26	35.2	67	90.8	108	146.4	149	202.0
27	36.6	68	92.2	109	147.8	150	203.4
28	38.0	69	93.6	110	149.1	151	204.7
29	39.3	70	94.9	111	150.5	152	206.1
30	40.7	71	96.3	112	151.8	153	207.4
31	42.0	72	97.6	113	153.2	154	208.8
32	43.4	73	99.0	114	154.6	155	210.2

TCCS1C03

**ELECTRONIC IGNITION
  SYSTEMS 2-2**
GENERAL INFORMATION 2-2
    SYSTEM OPERATION 2-2
    SYSTEM COMPONENTS 2-2
DIAGNOSIS AND TESTING 2-3
    SERVICE PRECAUTIONS 2-3
IGNITION COIL 2-8
    TESTING 2-8
    REMOVAL & INSTALLATION 2-8
IGNITION MODULE 2-9
    REMOVAL & INSTALLATION 2-9
CRANKSHAFT POSITION SENSOR 2-10
CAMSHAFT POSITION SENSOR 2-10
FIRING ORDERS 2-10
CHARGING SYSTEM 2-10
GENERAL INFORMATION 2-10
ALTERNATOR PRECAUTIONS 2-11
    BELT TENSION ADJUSTMENT 2-11
ALTERNATOR 2-11
    TESTING 2-11
    REMOVAL & INSTALLATION 2-12
REGULATOR 2-14
    REMOVAL & INSTALLATION 2-14
STARTING SYSTEM 2-14
GENERAL INFORMATION 2-14
STARTER 2-15
    TESTING 2-15
    REMOVAL & INSTALLATION 2-15
    SOLENOID REPLACEMENT 2-16
SENDING UNITS 2-16
COOLANT TEMPERATURE SENDER 2-16
    OPERATION 2-16
    TESTING 2-16
    REMOVAL & INSTALLATION 2-16
OIL PRESSURE SENDER 2-17
    OPERATION 2-17
    TESTING 2-17
    REMOVAL & INSTALLATION 2-17
ELECTRIC FAN SWITCH 2-17
    OPERATION 2-17
    TESTING 2-17
    REMOVAL & INSTALLATION 2-17
SPECIFICATIONS CHART
  ALTERNATOR FUNCTIONAL CHECK—
  1996–99 VEHICLES 2-12
TROUBLESHOOTING CHARTS
  STARTING SYSTEM PROBLEMS 2-18
  CHARGING SYSTEM PROBLEMS 2-18

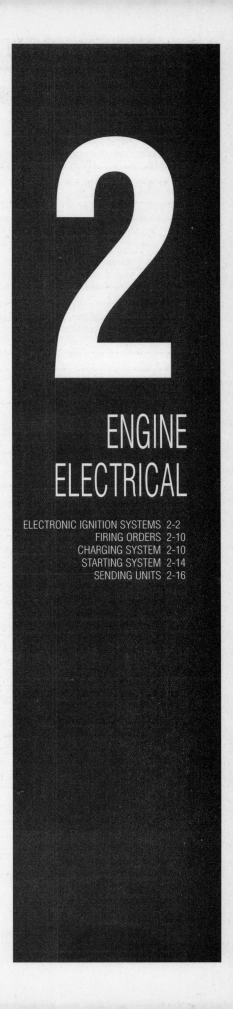

2

ENGINE
ELECTRICAL

ELECTRONIC IGNITION SYSTEMS 2-2
FIRING ORDERS 2-10
CHARGING SYSTEM 2-10
STARTING SYSTEM 2-14
SENDING UNITS 2-16

ELECTRONIC IGNITION SYSTEMS

➡️**For information on understanding electricity and troubleshooting electrical circuits, please refer to Section 6 of this manual.**

General Information

The vehicles covered by this manual are equipped with a Computer Controlled Coil (C³I) ignition system. On later models, this system may also be called the Electronic Ignition (EI) system. The C³I (or EI) system is distributorless, and consists of 3 ignition coils, an Ignition Control Module (ICM), dual crank sensor, camshaft sensor, connecting wires, and the Electronic Spark Timing (EST) portion of the Electronic Control Module (ECM).

➡️**When the term Electronic Control Module (ECM) is used in this manual, it refers to the engine control computer, regardless of whether the term Powertrain Control Module (PCM) or Electronic Control Module (ECM) is used.**

The ECM uses the EST circuit to control spark advance and ignition dwell, when the ignition system is operating in the EST mode. There are 2 modes of ignition system operation. These modes are as follows:
• Module mode—the ignition system operates independently of the ECM/PCM, with module mode spark advance always at 10 degrees BTDC. The ECM has no control of the ignition system when in this mode.
• EST mode—the ignition spark timing and ignition dwell time is fully controlled by the ECM. EST spark advance and ignition dwell is calculated by the ECM.

To control spark knock, and to use maximum spark advance to improve driveability and fuel economy, an Electronic Spark Control (ESC) system is used. This system consists of a knock sensor and the ECM. The ECM monitors the ESC signal to determine when engine detonation occurs.

SYSTEM OPERATION

The C³I ignition system uses a waste spark distribution method. Each cylinder is paired with the cylinder opposite it (1 and 4, 2 and 5, 3 and 6). The ends of each coil's secondary circuit is attached to a spark plug. These 2 plugs are on companion cylinders, cylinders that are at Top Dead Center (TDC) at the same time. The one that is on compression is said to be the "event" cylinder and the one on the exhaust stroke, the "waste" cylinder. When the coil discharges, both plugs fire at the same time to complete the series circuit.

Since the polarity of the primary and secondary windings are fixed, one plug always fires in a forward direction and the other in reverse. This is different than a conventional system firing all plugs the same direction each time. Because of the demand for additional energy; the coil design, saturation time and primary current flow are also different. This redesign of the system allows higher energy to be available from the distributorless coils, greater than 40 kilovolts at all rpm ranges.

During cranking, when the engine speed is beneath 400 rpm, the C³I module monitors the dual crank sensor sync signal. The sync signal is used to determine the correct pair of cylinders to be sparked first. Once the sync signal has been processed by the ignition module, it sends a fuel control reference pulse to the ECM.

During the cranking period, the ECM will also receive a cam pulse signal and will operate the injectors sequentially, based on true camshaft position only.

The sync signal is used only by the ignition module. It is used for spark synchronization at start-up only.

When the engine speed is below 400 rpm (during cranking), the C³I module controls spark timing. Once the engine speed exceeds 400 rpm (engine running), spark timing is controlled by the EST signal from the ECM. To control EST, the ECM uses the following inputs:
• Crankshaft position
• Engine speed (rpm)
• Coolant Temperature Sender
• Mass Air Flow
• Throttle Position Sensor
• Park/Neutral Switch
• Vehicle Speed Sensor
• ESC signal

The C³I ignition module provides proper ignition coil sequencing during both the module and the EST modes.

The ESC system is designed to retard spark timing up to 10 degrees to reduce spark knock in the engine. When the knock sensor detects spark knocking in the

engine, it sends an A/C voltage signal to the ECM, which increases with the severity of the knock. The ECM then adjusts the EST to reduce spark knock.

SYSTEM COMPONENTS

C³I Module

♦ See Figure 1

The C³I module monitors the sync-pulse and the crank signal. During cranking, the C³I module monitors the sync-pulse to begin the ignition firing sequence. During this time, each of the 3 coils are fired at a pre-determined interval based on engine speed only. Above 400 rpm, the C³I module is only use as a reference signal.

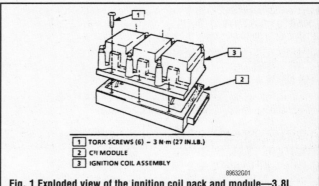

1	TORX SCREWS (6) – 3 N·m (27 IN.LB.)
2	C³I MODULE
3	IGNITION COIL ASSEMBLY

89632G01

Fig. 1 Exploded view of the ignition coil pack and module—3.8L (VIN C) engine shown

Ignition Coils

♦ See Figure 1

The ignition coil assemblies are mounted on the C³I module. Each coil distributes the spark for 2 plugs simultaneously.

Electronic Spark Control (ESC) System

The ESC system incorporates a knock sensor and the ECM. The knock sensor detects engine detonation. When engine detonation occurs, the ECM receives the ESC signal and retards EST to reduce detonation.

Electronic Spark Timing (EST) System

The EST system includes the following circuits:
• Reference circuit—provides the ECM with rpm and crankshaft position information from the C³I module. The C³I module receives this signal from the crank sensor Hall-effect switch.
• Bypass signal—above 400 rpm, the ECM applies 5 volts to this circuit to switch spark timing control from the C³I module to the ECM.
• EST signal—reference signal is sent to the ECM via the C³I module during cranking. Under 400 rpm, the C³I module controls the ignition timing. Above 400 rpm, the ECM applies 5 volts to the bypass line to switch the timing to the ECM control.

Electronic Control Module (ECM) or Powertrain Control Module (PCM)

The ECM/PCM is responsible for maintaining proper spark and fuel injection timing for all driving conditions.

Dual Crank Sensor

♦ See Figures 2 and 3

The dual crank sensor is mounted in a pedestal on the front of the engine near the harmonic balancer. The sensor consists of 2 Hall-effect switches, which

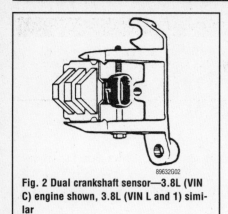

Fig. 2 Dual crankshaft sensor—3.8L (VIN C) engine shown, 3.8L (VIN L and 1) similar

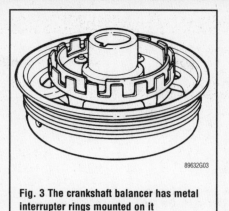

Fig. 3 The crankshaft balancer has metal interrupter rings mounted on it

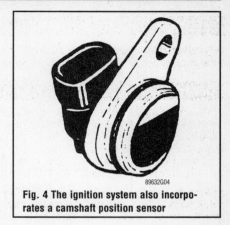

Fig. 4 The ignition system also incorporates a camshaft position sensor

depend on 2 metal interrupter rings mounted on the balancer to activate them. Windows in the interrupters activate the Hall-effect switches as they provide a path for the magnetic field between the switches' transducers and magnets.

Camshaft Sensor

▶ See Figure 4

The camshaft sensor sends signal to the ECM/PCM, which is used as a sync-pulse to trigger the injectors in the proper sequence.

Diagnosis and Testing

SERVICE PRECAUTIONS

▶ See Figures 5 thru 14

✳✳ CAUTION

The ignition coil's secondary voltage output capabilities can exceed 40,000 volts. Avoid bodily contact with the C³I high voltage secondary components when the engine is running, or personal injury may result.

➡ To avoid damage to the ECM/PCM or other ignition system components, do not use electrical test equipment such as a battery or AC-powered voltmeter, ohmmeter, etc., or any type of tester other than specified.

- Check for trouble codes, as described in Section 4. If any are found, refer to the appropriate diagnostic procedure in Section 4.
- When performing electrical tests on the system, use a high impedance multimeter or quality digital voltmeter (DVM). Use of a 12 volt test light is not recommended.
- To prevent electrostatic discharge damage when working with the ECM, do not touch the connector pins or soldered components on the circuit board.
- When handling a PROM, CAL-PAK or MEM-CAL, do not touch the component leads. Also, do not remove the integrated circuit from the carrier.
- Never pierce a high tension lead or boot for any testing purpose; otherwise, future problems are guaranteed.
- Do not allow extension cords for power tools or droplights to lie on, near or across any vehicle electrical wiring.
- Leave new components and modules in the shipping package until ready to install them.

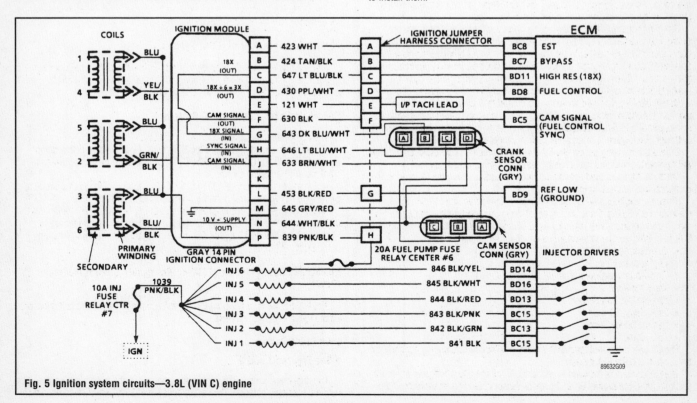

Fig. 5 Ignition system circuits—3.8L (VIN C) engine

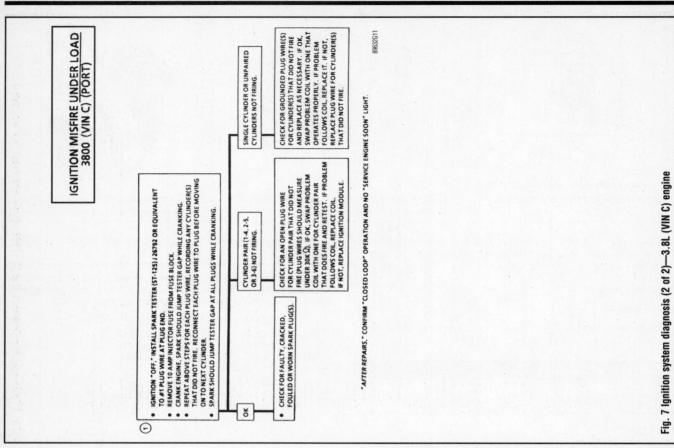

Fig. 7 Ignition system diagnosis (2 of 2)—3.8L (VIN C) engine

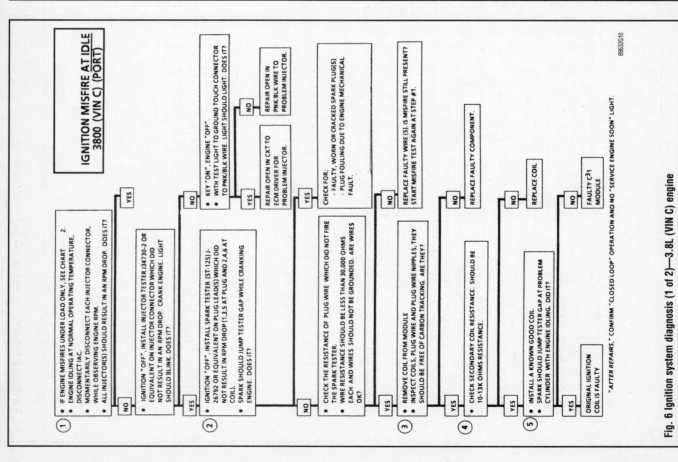

Fig. 6 Ignition system diagnosis (1 of 2)—3.8L (VIN C) engine

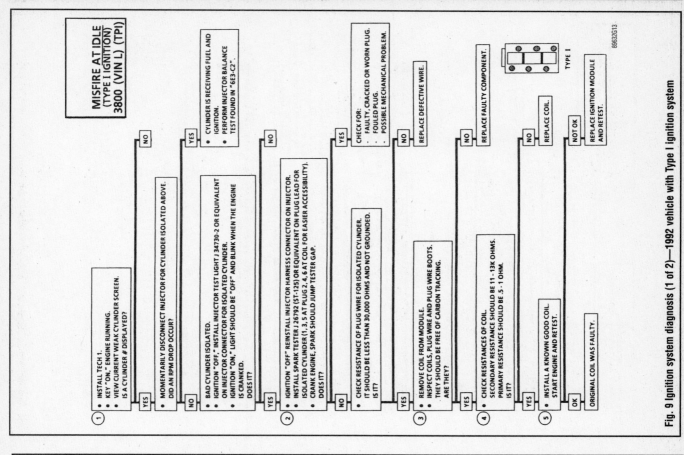

Fig. 9 Ignition system diagnosis (1 of 2)—1992 vehicle with Type I ignition system

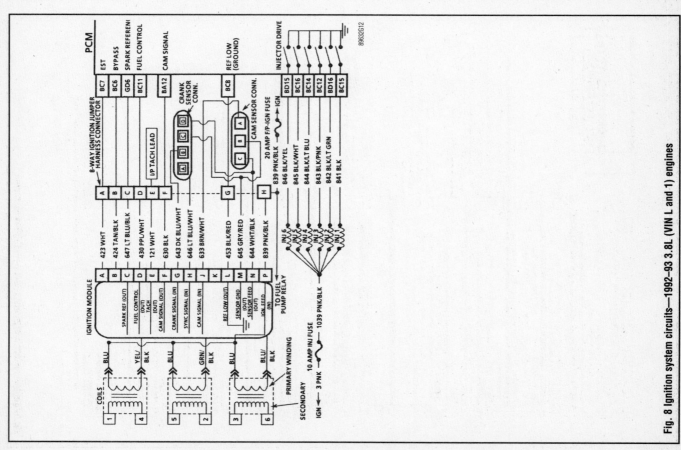

Fig. 8 Ignition system circuits—1992–93 3.8L (VIN L and 1) engines

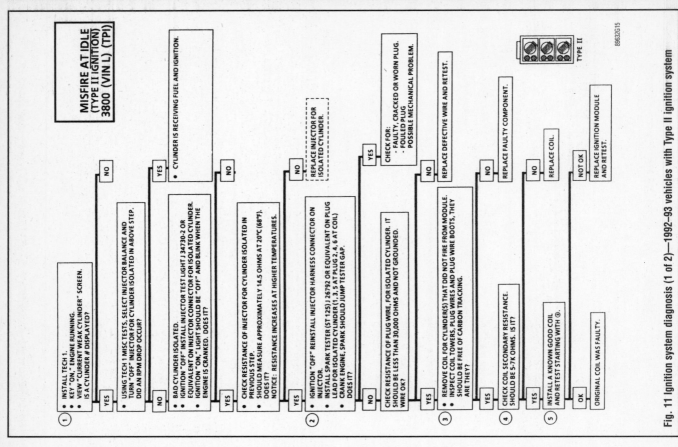

Fig. 11 Ignition system diagnosis (1 of 2)—1992–93 vehicles with Type II ignition system

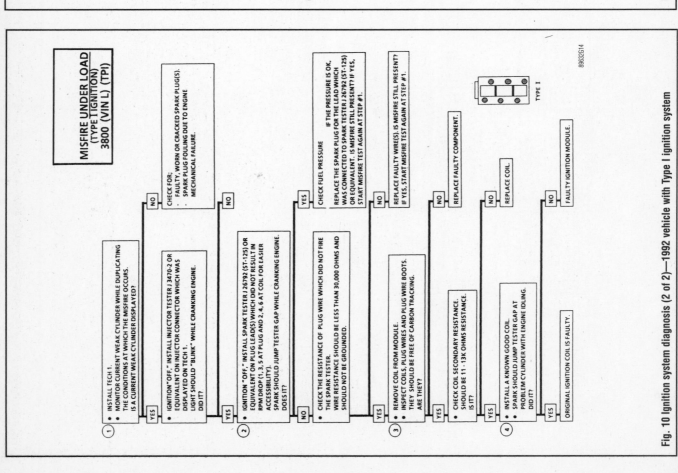

Fig. 10 Ignition system diagnosis (2 of 2)—1992 vehicle with Type I ignition system

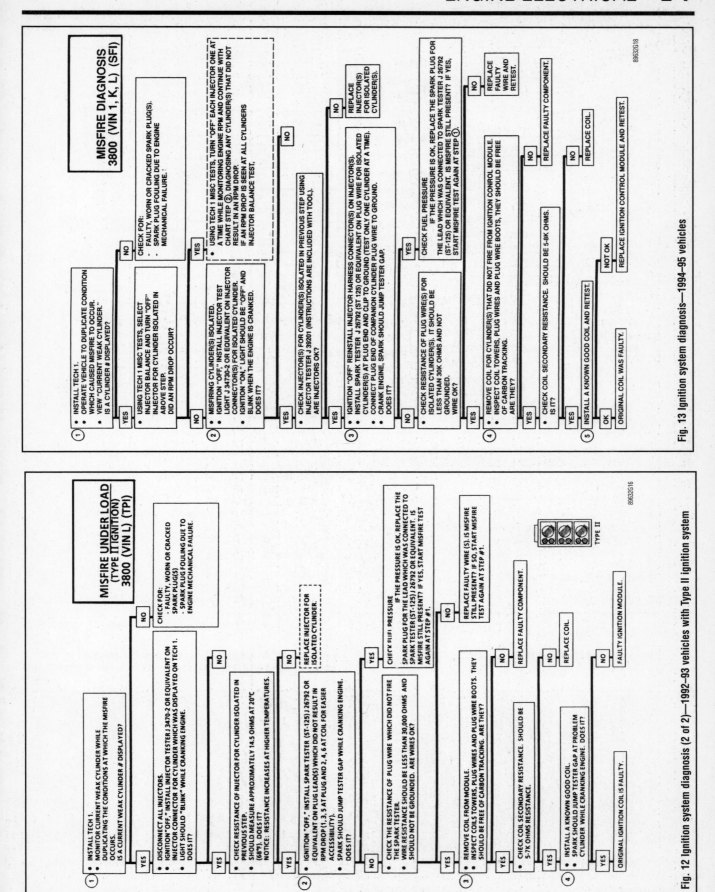

Fig. 13 Ignition system diagnosis—1994–95 vehicles

Fig. 12 Ignition system diagnosis (2 of 2)—1992–93 vehicles with Type II ignition system

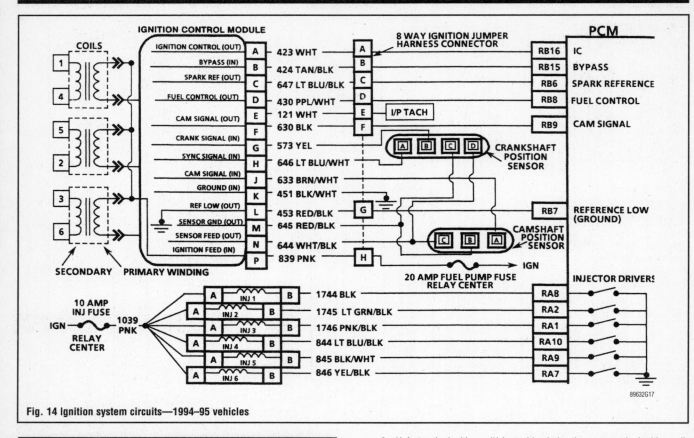

Fig. 14 Ignition system circuits—1994–95 vehicles

Ignition Coil

TESTING

1. Remove the ignition coil(s).
2. Using an ohmmeter, check the resistance between the primary terminals on the underside of the coil. The resistance should be 0.50–0.90 ohms.
3. Check the resistance between the secondary terminals. It should be 5,000–8,000 ohms.
4. If the coil failed either test, replace the coil.

REMOVAL & INSTALLATION

3.0L and 3.8L (VIN 3 and B) Engines

1. Disconnect the negative battery cable.
2. Tag and disconnect the spark plug wires.

3. Unfasten the ignition coil(s) attaching bolts, then remove the ignition coil from the module.
To install:
4. Install the coil(s) and attaching bolts.
5. Connect the spark plug wires.
6. Connect the negative battery cable.

3.8L (VIN C) Engine

♦ See Figures 15, 16, 17 and 18

1. Disconnect the negative battery cable.
2. Tag and disconnect the spark plug wires.
3. Remove the 6 retaining screws, or Torx® screws, as applicable, securing the coil to the ignition module.
4. Tilt the coil assembly back and unplug the coil-to-module connectors.
5. Remove the coil assembly.

➡Although the 3.8L engine's Type I coil pack will physically fit, the position of the number 1 coil, as noted on the coil pack, is in a different

Fig. 15 Labeling the wires before disconnecting them from the coil helps assure correct reconnection

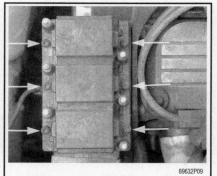

Fig. 16 After removing the wires, you can see the 6 Torx® retaining screws

Fig. 17 Unfasten the mounting screws, then lift the coil up from the ignition module and label the connectors

Fig. 18 After unplugging the connectors, you can remove the ignition coil pack from the module

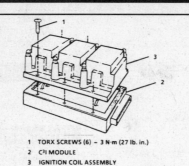

1 TORX SCREWS (6) - 3 N·m (27 lb. in.)
2 C³I MODULE
3 IGNITION COIL ASSEMBLY

Fig. 19 In 1992, there were 2 different ignition coils used: a Type I, as shown here . . .

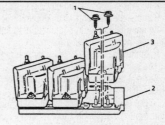

1 SCREWS (6) - 4-5 N·m (40 lb. in.)
2 IGNITION MODULE
3 IGNITION COILS (3)

Fig. 20 . . . and a Type II, shown here. Later model vehicles use the Type II

location; coil towers No. 1 and 4 on the 3800 engine are closest to the module connector.

To install:

6. Fit the coil assembly into position and attach the connectors.
7. Install the retaining screws, or Torx® screws, as applicable, and tighten to 27 inch lbs. (3 Nm).
8. Connect the spark plug wires, as tagged during removal.
9. Reconnect the negative battery cable.

3.8L (VIN L, 1 and K) Engines

♦ See Figures 19 and 20

1. Disconnect the negative battery cable.
2. Tag and disconnect the spark plug wires.
3. Remove the 2 retaining screws securing the coil to the ignition module.
4. Remove the coil assembly.

To install:

5. Fit the coil assembly to the ignition module.
6. Install the retaining screws and tighten them to 40 inch lbs. (4–5 Nm).
7. Attach the spark plug wires, as tagged during removal.
8. Reconnect the negative battery cable.

Ignition Module

REMOVAL & INSTALLATION

♦ See Figures 21 thru 26

1. Disconnect the negative battery cable.
2. Tag and disconnect the spark plug wires at the coil assembly.
3. If equipped, unfasten the connector retaining nut, then unplug the 14-way connector from the ignition module.

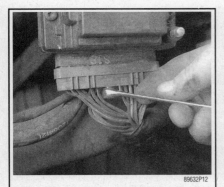

Fig. 21 If necessary, unfasten the 14-way electrical connector retaining nut . . .

Fig. 22 . . . then unplug the electrical connector from the ignition module

Fig. 23 To access the 3 retaining nuts, it may be necessary to loosen the ground straps and reposition them

Fig. 24 After unfastening the 3 nuts, remove the ignition module from the bracket

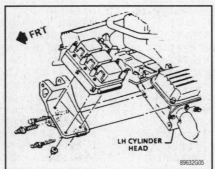

Fig. 25 Exploded view of the ignition coil and module assembly—3.8L (VIN C) engine shown

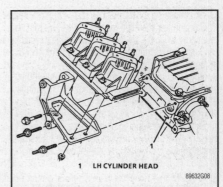

1 LH CYLINDER HEAD

Fig. 26 Ignition control module mounting—1995 3.8L (VIN 1, K and L) engines

4. If necessary, loosen and reposition the ground straps.

5. Remove the nuts and washers that retains the module to the bracket.

6. Remove the coil-to-module retaining bolts or screws. On some vehicles, the coils may be secured with Torx® screws.

7. Note the lead colors or mark for reassembly, then detach the connectors between the coil and ignition module.

8. Remove the ignition module from the vehicle.

To install:

9. Fit the coils and connectors to the ignition module and install the retaining bolts. Tighten the retainers to 27 inch lbs. (3 Nm) for 1987–91 vehicles or to 40 inch lbs. (4.5 Nm) for 1992–99 vehicles.

10. Fit the module assembly to the bracket and install the nuts and washers. Tighten to 70 inch lbs. (8 Nm).

11. Connect the spark plug wires, as tagged during removal.

12. Attach the 14-way connector to the module.

13. Connect the negative battery cable.

Crankshaft Position Sensor

For crankshaft position sensor testing and removal and installation, please refer to Section 4 of this manual.

Camshaft Position Sensor

For camshaft position sensor testing and removal and installation, please refer to Section 4 of this manual.

FIRING ORDERS

♦ **See Figures 27 and 28**

➡ **To avoid confusion, remove and tag the spark plug wires one at a time, for replacement.**

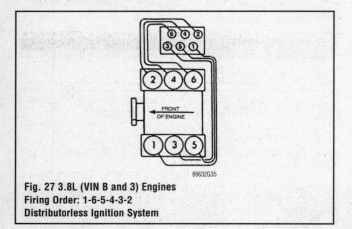

Fig. 27 3.8L (VIN B and 3) Engines
Firing Order: 1-6-5-4-3-2
Distributorless Ignition System

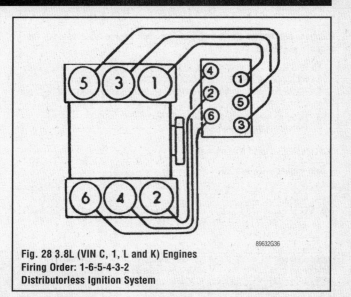

Fig. 28 3.8L (VIN C, 1, L and K) Engines
Firing Order: 1-6-5-4-3-2
Distributorless Ignition System

CHARGING SYSTEM

General Information

♦ **See Figure 29**

The automobile charging system provides electrical power for operation of the vehicle's ignition system, starting system and all electrical accessories. The battery serves as an electrical surge or storage tank, storing (in chemical form) the energy originally produced by the engine driven generator. The system also provides a means of regulating output to protect the battery from being overcharged and to avoid excessive voltage to the accessories.

The storage battery is a chemical device incorporating parallel lead plates in a tank containing a sulfuric acid/water solution. Adjacent plates are slightly dissimilar, and the chemical reaction of the two dissimilar plates produces electrical energy when the battery is connected to a load such as the starter motor. The chemical reaction is reversible, so that when the alternator is producing a voltage (electrical pressure) greater than that produced by the battery, electricity is forced into the battery, and the battery is returned to its fully charged state.

Newer automobiles use alternating current alternators, because they are more efficient, can be rotated at higher speeds, and have fewer brush problems. In an alternator, the field usually rotates while all the current produced passes only through the stator winding. The brushes bear against continuous slip rings. This causes the current produced to periodically reverse the direction of its flow. Diodes (electrical one way valves) block the flow of current from traveling in the wrong direction. A series of diodes is wired together to permit the alternating flow of the stator to be rectified back to 12 volts DC for use by the vehicle's electrical system.

The voltage regulating function is performed by a regulator. The regulator is often built in to the alternator; this system is termed an integrated or internal regulator.

An alternator differs from a DC shunt generator in that the armature is stationary, and is called the stator, while the field rotates and is called the rotor. The higher current values in the alternator's stator are conducted to the external circuit through fixed leads and connections, rather than through a rotating commutator and brushes as in a DC generator. This eliminates a major point of maintenance.

The rotor assembly is supported in the drive end frame by a ball bearing and at the other end by a roller bearing. These bearings are lubricated during assembly and require no maintenance. There are six diodes in the end frame assembly. These diodes are electrical check valves that also change the alternating current developed within the stator windings to a Direct Current (DC) at the output (BAT) terminal. Three of these diodes are negative and are mounted flush with the end frame while the other three are positive and are mounted into a strip called a heat sink. The positive diodes are easily identified as the ones within small cavities or depressions.

The alternator charging system is a negative (-) ground system which consists of an alternator, a regulator, a charge indicator, a storage battery and wiring connecting the components, and fuse link wire.

The alternator is belt-driven from the engine. Energy is supplied from the alternator/regulator system to the rotating field through two brushes to two slip-rings. The slip-rings are mounted on the rotor shaft and are connected to the field coil. This energy supplied to the rotating field from the battery is called excitation current and is used to initially energize the field to begin the generation of electricity. Once the alternator starts to generate electricity, the excitation current comes from its own output rather than the battery.

The alternator produces power in the form of alternating current. The alternating current is rectified by 6 diodes into direct current. The direct current is used to charge the battery and power the rest of the electrical system.

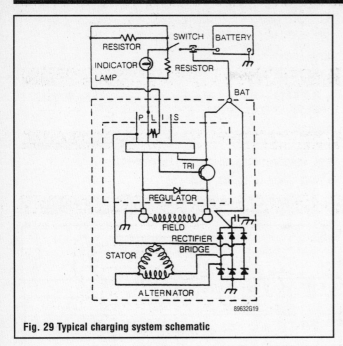

Fig. 29 Typical charging system schematic

When the ignition key is turned **ON**, current flows from the battery, through the charging system indicator light on the instrument panel, to the voltage regulator, and to the alternator. Since the alternator is not producing any current, the alternator warning light comes on. When the engine is started, the alternator begins to produce current and turns the alternator light off. As the alternator turns and produces current, the current is divided in two ways: part to the battery (to charge the battery and power the electrical components of the vehicle), and part is returned to the alternator (to enable it to increase its output). In this situation, the alternator is receiving current from the battery and from itself. A voltage regulator is wired into the current supply to the alternator to prevent it from receiving too much current which would cause it to put out too much current. Conversely, if the voltage regulator does not allow the alternator to receive enough current, the battery will not be fully charged and will eventually go dead.

The battery is connected to the alternator at all times, whether the ignition key is turned **ON** or not. If the battery were shorted to ground, the alternator would also be shorted. This would damage the alternator. To prevent this, a fuse link is installed in the wiring between the battery and the alternator. If the battery is shorted, the fuse link melts, protecting the alternator.

An alternator is better that a conventional, DC shunt generator because it is lighter and more compact, because it is designed to supply the battery and accessory circuits through a wide range of engine speeds, and because it eliminates the necessary maintenance of replacing brushes and servicing commutators.

Alternator Precautions

✳✳ CAUTION

To prevent damage to the alternator and possible to yourself, the following precautions should be taken when working with the electrical system.

1. Never reverse the battery connections.
2. Booster batteries for starting must be connected properly: positive-to-positive and negative-to-negative.
3. Disconnect the battery cables before using a fast charger; the charger has a tendency to force current through the diodes in the opposite direction for which they were designed. This burns out the diodes.
4. Never use a fast charger as a booster for starting the vehicle.
5. Never disconnect the voltage regulator while the engine is running.
6. Avoid long soldering times when replacing diodes or transistors. Prolonged heat is damaging to AC (alternating current) generators.
7. Do not use test lamps of more than 12 volts (V) for checking diode continuity.

8. Do not short across or ground any of the terminals of the AC (alternating current) generator.
9. The polarity of the battery, generator, and regulator must be matched and considered before making any electrical connections within the system.
10. Never operate the alternator on an open circuit. Make sure that all connections within the circuit are clean and tight.
11. Disconnect the battery terminals when performing any service on the electrical system. This will eliminate the possibility of accidental reversal of polarity.
12. Disconnect the battery ground cable if arc welding is to be done on any part of the car.

BELT TENSION ADJUSTMENT

All alternators used have a rated output of 100–105 amps. If the charging system is inadequate, check the serpentine belt and tensioner.

➡**The drive belt tensioner can control the belt tension over a wide range of belt lengths; however, there are limits to the tensioner's ability to compensate for various belt lengths. Installing the wrong size belt and using the tensioner outside of its operating range can result in poor tension control and damage to the tensioner, drive belt and driven components.**

Alternator

TESTING

Basic alternator testing can be done with a voltmeter. The alternator function check must be made with a known good, fully charged battery.

1986–91 Vehicles

▶ **See Figure 30**

1. Make the connections as shown in the accompanying illustration. Leave the carbon pile turned off. The ground polarity of the alternator and battery must be the same. The battery must be fully charged. If bypassing the indicator light/voltmeter circuit by leaving the 4-cavity connector detached, use a 30–500 ohm resistor between the battery and the "L" terminal.
2. Start the engine and let it idle. Turn all electrical loads OFF, then slowly increase the engine speed to 1,500 rpm. Note the voltage reading.
3. If the voltage increases above 16 volts, replace the alternator.

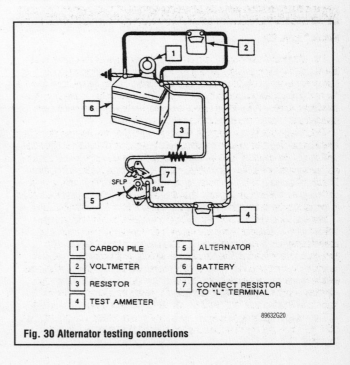

1	CARBON PILE	5	ALTERNATOR
2	VOLTMETER	6	BATTERY
3	RESISTOR	7	CONNECT RESISTOR TO "L" TERMINAL
4	TEST AMMETER		

Fig. 30 Alternator testing connections

4. If the voltage is below 16 volts, hold the engine speed at 1,500 rpm and adjust the carbon pile to obtain the maximum amperage output. Maintain the voltage above 13 volts. If the output is within 15 amperes of rated output, the alternator is good. If the output is not within 15 amperes of rated output, replace the alternator.

1992–95 Vehicles

▶ **See Figure 30**

1. Make the connections as shown in the accompanying figure. Leave the carbon pile load turned off. The alternator and battery ground polarity must be the same. Detach the alternator (4-cavity) connector, then connect a fused jumper between the positive battery terminal and the alternator terminal "I".

2. Start the engine, turn all of the electrical loads OFF, then slowly increase the engine speed to about 1,500 rpm. Note the voltage reading.

3. When the voltage is uncontrolled and increases above 16 volts, replace the alternator.

4. When the voltage is below 16 volts, hold the engine speed at 1,500 rpm. Turn on the carbon pile and adjust to obtain maximum amperage output. Maintain the voltage above 13 volts. When the output is within 15 amperes of rated

output, the alternator is good. When the output is not within 15 amperes of rated output, replace the alternator.

1996–99 Vehicles

▶ **See Figure 30**

To test the alternator on these vehicles, make the connections shown in the figure, then follow the test steps in the accompanying chart.

REMOVAL & INSTALLATION

3.0L and 3.8L (VIN 3, B, C and L) Engines

▶ **See Figures 31, 32, 33, 34 and 35**

1. Disconnect the negative battery cable.

2. Using a suitable breaker bar or ratchet, rotate the tensioner counterclockwise, then remove the serpentine drive belt. For more information regarding serpentine drive belt removal, please refer to Section 1 of this manual.

3. If necessary, remove the fuel rail cover.

Step	ALTERNATOR FUNCTIONAL CHECK - 1996-99 VEHICLES			
	Action	Value	Yes	No
1	Perform charging system message and code diagnosis. Message or code?	—		Go to Step 2.
2	Check connections at battery and alternator. Was poor connection found?	—	Repair connector as required.	Go to Step 3.
3	Is battery fully charged?	+12V	Go to Step 4.	
4	Turn all electrical loads off.	—	Go to Step 5.	—
5	Connect volt meter to alternator output.	—	Go to Step 6.	—
6	Run engine at 2500 RPM for 30 seconds.	—	Go to Step 7.	—
7	Check voltage output.	+14V*	Go to Step 8.	Replace alternator.
8	Connect inductive ammeter to the battery charging cable from the alternator at the underhood junction block.	—	Go to Step 9.	—
9	Connect carbon pile (VAT 40) across battery.	—	Go to Step 10.	—
10	Run engine at 2500 RPM.	—	Go to Step 11.	—
11	Adjust carbon pile to obtain maximum output from alternator. Note value.	Within 15 AMPS of rated output.	Alternator is good.	Replace alternator.

* Cold engine temperature voltage 14.0-16.0. Voltage should be between 13.0 and 15.0 when the engine is at operating temperature.

89632C28

Fig. 31 Remove the 2 alternator mounting bolts (see arrows)

89632P06

Fig. 32 Tilt the alternator forward to unfasten the electrical connections (see arrows) . . .

89632P07

Fig. 33 . . . then remove the alternator from the vehicle

89632P08

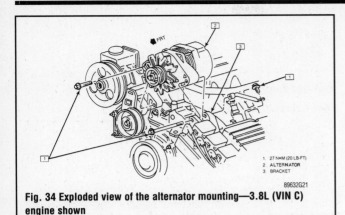

Fig. 34 Exploded view of the alternator mounting—3.8L (VIN C) engine shown

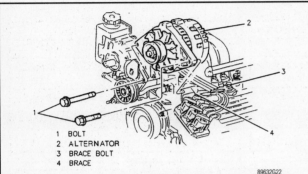

Fig. 35 Alternator-to-engine attachment—1994 3.8L (VIN L) engine shown; other years similar

4. While supporting the alternator, remove the mounting bolts.
5. Tilt the alternator forward, then label and detach the electrical connectors.
6. Remove the alternator from the vehicle.

To install:

7. Support the alternator in position, then install the alternator.
8. Install the mounting bolts and tighten to 20 ft. lbs. (27 Nm).
9. Attach the electrical connectors at the back of the alternator. Tighten the alternator output terminal nut to 93 inch lbs. (10.5 Nm) for 1987–92 vehicles, or to 66 inch lbs. (7.5 Nm) for 1993–94 vehicles.
10. If removed, install the fuel rail cover.
11. Install the serpentine drive belt and rotate the tensioner into position.
12. Connect the negative battery cable.

3.8L (VIN K) Engines

1995 VEHICLES

▶ See Figure 36

1. Disconnect the negative battery cable.
2. Use a suitable breaker bar or ratchet, rotate the tensioner, then remove the serpentine drive belt. For more information regarding drive belt removal, please refer to Section 1 of this manual.
3. Detach the alternator electrical connections.
4. Remove the two nuts and brackets from the alternator.
5. Unfasten the two bolt and one stud securing the alternator, then remove the alternator from the vehicle.

To install:

6. Position the alternator in the vehicle. Install the two bolts and one stud to secure the alternator. Tighten to 37 ft. lbs. (50 Nm).
7. Install the bracket and two nuts to the alternator. Tighten the bolts and stud to 37 ft. lbs. (50 Nm).
8. Install the electrical connections. Tighten the alternator output terminal nut to 66 inch lbs. (7.5 Nm).
9. Install the serpentine drive belt, as outlined in Section 1 of this manual.
10. Connect the negative battery cable.

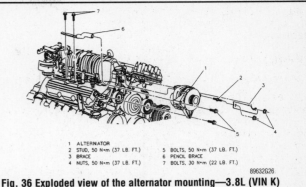

Fig. 36 Exploded view of the alternator mounting—3.8L (VIN K) engine

1996–99 VEHICLES

▶ See Figures 37 and 38

1. Disconnect the negative battery cable.
2. Remove the serpentine drive belt from the alternator.
3. Remove the engine cover.
4. Remove the front alternator support brace.
5. Remove the alternator mounting bolts.
6. Remove the rear pencil brace bolt.
7. Unfasten the output terminal nut.
8. Detach the alternator electrical connector(s).
9. Remove the alternator from the vehicle.

To install:

10. Position the alternator in the vehicle.
11. Attach the electrical connection(s) and the output terminal nut. Tighten the nut to 15 ft. lbs. (20 Nm).
12. Install the alternator mounting bolts and tighten to 37 ft. lbs. (50 Nm).
13. Install the front alternator support brace and tighten the retainers to 37 ft. lbs. (50 Nm).

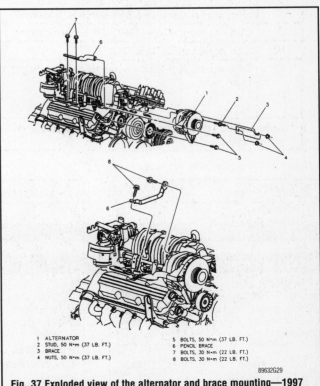

Fig. 37 Exploded view of the alternator and brace mounting—1997 3.8L (VIN K) engine shown

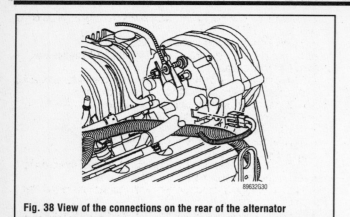

Fig. 38 View of the connections on the rear of the alternator

14. Install the rear pencil brace bolt and tighten to 22 ft. lbs. (30 Nm).
15. Install the engine cover.
16. Install the serpentine drive belt.
17. Connect the negative battery cable.

3.8L (VIN 1) Supercharged Engines

1992–95 VEHICLES

▶ See Figures 39 and 40

1. Disconnect the negative battery cable.
2. Remove the serpentine drive belt from the alternator, as outlined in Section 1 of this manual.
3. Detach the electrical connections from the alternator.
4. Unfasten the alternator mounting bolt and mounting bolt and nut.
5. Remove the alternator from the vehicle.

To install:

6. Position the alternator in the vehicle and secure with the mounting nut and bolt. Tighten to 21 ft. lbs. (29 Nm).

7. Install the remaining mounting bolt and tighten to 21 ft. lbs. (29 Nm).
8. Attach the alternator connections. Tighten the output terminal nut to 66 inch lbs. (7.5 Nm).
9. Install the serpentine drive belt.
10. Connect the negative battery cable.

1996–99 VEHICLES

▶ See Figures 38 and 41

1. Disconnect the negative battery cable.
2. Remove the serpentine drive belt from the alternator.
3. Remove the engine cover.
4. Unfasten the rear pencil brace bolts, then remove the brace.
5. Remove the alternator mounting bolts.
6. Remove the output terminal nut.
7. Detach the alternator electrical connection(s).
8. Remove the alternator from the vehicle.

To install:

9. Position the alternator in the vehicle.
10. Attach the electrical connection(s) and install the output terminal nut. Tighten the nut to 15 ft. lbs. (20 Nm).
11. Install the alternator mounting bolt and tighten to 37 ft. lbs. (50 Nm).
12. Install the rear pencil brace bolts and tighten to 22 ft. lbs. (30 Nm).
13. Install the engine cover and serpentine drive belt.
14. Connect the negative battery cable.

Regulator

REMOVAL & INSTALLATION

A solid-state regulator is mounted within the alternator. All regulator components are enclosed in a solid mold. The regulator is non-adjustable and requires no maintenance.

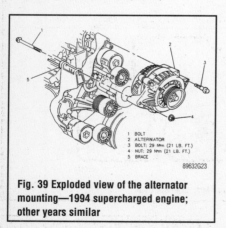

Fig. 39 Exploded view of the alternator mounting—1994 supercharged engine; other years similar

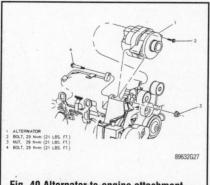

Fig. 40 Alternator-to-engine attachment—1995 3.8L (VIN 1) engine shown

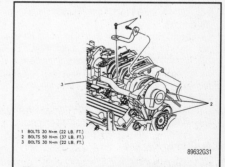

Fig. 41 Location of the alternator and brace mounting bolts—1997 supercharged engine shown

STARTING SYSTEM

General Information

The starting motor is a specially designed, direct current electric motor capable of producing a very great amount of power for its size. One thing that allows the motor to produce a great deal of power is its tremendous rotating speed. It drives the engine through a tiny pinion gear (attached to the starter's armature), which drives the very large flywheel ring gear at a greatly reduced speed. Another factor allowing it to produce so much power is that only intermittent operation is required of it. Thus, little allowance for air circulation is required, and the windings can be built into a very small space.

The starter solenoid is a magnetic device which employs the small current supplied by the starting switch circuit of the ignition switch. This magnetic action moves a plunger which mechanically engages the starter and electrically

closes the heavy switch which connects it to the battery. The starting switch circuit consists of the starting switch contained within the ignition switch, a transmission neutral safety switch or clutch pedal switch, and the wiring necessary to connect these with the starter solenoid or relay.

A pinion, which is a small gear, is mounted to a one-way drive clutch. This clutch is splined to the starter armature shaft. When the ignition switch is moved to the start position, the solenoid plunger slides the pinion toward the flywheel ring gear via a collar and spring. If the teeth on the pinion and flywheel match properly, the pinion will engage the flywheel immediately. If the gear teeth butt one another, the spring will be compressed and will force the gears to mesh as soon as the starter turns far enough to allow them to do so. As the solenoid plunger reaches the end of its travel, it closes the contacts that connect the battery and starter and then the engine is cranked.

As soon as the engine starts, the flywheel ring gear begins turning fast enough to drive the pinion at an extremely high rate of speed. At this point, the one-way clutch begins allowing the pinion to spin faster than the starter shaft so that the starter will not operate at excessive speed. When the ignition switch is released from the start position, the solenoid is de-energized, and a spring contained within the solenoid assembly pulls the gear out of mesh and interrupts the current flow to the starter.

Starter

TESTING

Basic Check

✳✳ WARNING

Never operate the starter motor than 30 seconds at a time without pausing to allow it to cool for at least two minutes. Overheating, caused by excessive cranking, will seriously damage the starter motor.

Basic starter testing can be done without tools. The problem is a bad battery and a defective starter cause the same symptoms. First test and charge the battery to confirm it is in good condition.

1. Place a voltmeter across the battery and try to start the car.
2. If starter makes no sounds and voltmeter doesn't move, check the wires from the ignition switch to the starter. Place the voltmeter on the starter wires and check for 12 volts at the little wire when the ignition is turned to **START**. The problem is most likely not the starter, but the solenoid, ignition switch, neutral safety switch or wiring to the starter.
3. If the starter clicks and the voltmeter moves very little, check the solenoid, battery cables and wire connections.
4. If the engine cranks very slow or seems to jam, the starter is the probably bad.
5. If the vehicle is hard to crank warm, but after given time to cool cranks easier, the starter is the most likely problem.
6. Before condemning the starter, always check the engine's mechanical condition. A good starter cannot crank a damaged engine, or an engine that has been extremely overheated, is low on oil, or has extremely thick and dirty oil.

No-Load Test

▶ See Figure 42

1. Make the connections as shown in the accompanying figure.
2. Close the switch and compare the RPM, current and voltage readings with the following values:
- 1987–95 vehicles with SD-250 starter: No-load test @ 10 volts—45–75 amps, RPM at drive pinion—8,600–13,000 rpm
- 1987–95 vehicles with PG-250 starter: No-load test @ 10 volts—60–90 amps, RPM at drive pinion—2,880–3,200 rpm
- 1996–99 vehicles with SD-255 starter: No-load test @ 10 volts—45–70 amps, RPM at drive pinion—8,600–13,000 rpm

Make disconnections only with the switch open. Use the test results as follows:

3. Rated current draw and no-load speed indicates normal condition of the starter motor.
4. Low free speed and high current draw indicates:
- Too much friction. Tight, dirty, or worn bushings, bent armature shaft, allowing the armature to drag.
- Shorted armature. This can be further checked on a growler after disassembly.
- Grounded armature or fields. Check further after assembly.
5. Failure to operate with high current draw indicates:
- A direct ground in the terminal or fields.
- "Frozen'|" bearings.
6. Failure to operate with low or no current draw indicates:
- Open solenoid windings.
- Open field circuit. This can be checked after disassembly by inspecting internal connections and tracing the circuit with a test lamp.
- Open armature coils. Inspect the commutator for badly burned bar after disassembly.
- Broken brush springs, worn brushes, high insulation between the commutator bars of other causes which would prevent good contact between the brushes and commutator.
7. Low no-load speed and low current draw indicates:
- High internal resistance due to poor connections, defective leads, dirty commutator and causes listed under Step 6.
8. High free speed and high current drain usually indicate shorted fields. If shorted fields are suspected, replace the field and frame assembly. Also check for shorted armature using a growler.

REMOVAL & INSTALLATION

▶ See Figures 43 thru 48

1. Disconnect the negative battery cable.
2. Raise and support the vehicle safely.
3. If necessary for access, remove the splash shield.
4. If equipped, unfasten the flywheel inspection cover bolts and remove the cover.

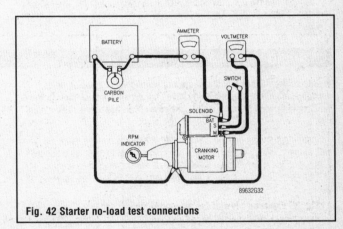

Fig. 42 Starter no-load test connections

Fig. 43 Unfasten the starter motor electrical connections. You may want to tag them first to avoid confusion

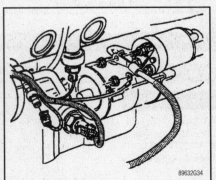

Fig. 44 Exploded view of the starter motor electrical connections

Fig. 45 The starter is attached to the engine with 2 mounting bolts (see arrows)

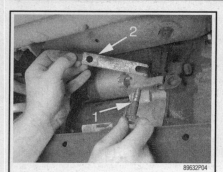

Fig. 46 Unfasten the front mounting bolt (1) and remove any necessary shims (2), noting their locations for installation

Fig. 47 Unfasten the long starter mounting bolt, then remove the starter motor from the vehicle

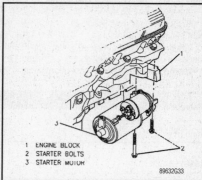

1 ENGINE BLOCK
2 STARTER BOLTS
3 STARTER MOTOR

Fig. 48 Exploded view of the starter motor mounting—1987–97 vehicles

5. Label and detach the electrical connectors from the starter.
6. It may allow more room it you remove the right side cooling fan.
7. Remove the starter-to-engine bolts, then carefully lower the starter from the vehicle.

Before installing the starter motor, make sure the electrical terminals are secure by tightening the nuts next to the cap on the solenoid battery terminal and on the "S" terminal. If these terminals are not tight in the solenoid cap, the cap may be damaged during installation of the electrical connections and cause premature starter failure.

To install:

➡Note the location of any shims so they may be replaced in the same positions upon installation.

8. Place the starter in position, then install the starter-to-engine bolts and tighten to 32 ft. lbs. (43 Nm).
9. Attach the electrical connectors to the starter, as tagged during removal. Tighten as follows:
   a. Tighten the nut on the solenoid battery terminal to 12 ft. lbs. (16 Nm).
   b. On the SD-250 and SD-255 models, tighten the nut on the "S" terminal to 22 inch lbs. (2.5 Nm).

10. If removed, install the flywheel inspection cover and secure with the retaining bolts. Tighten the flywheel cover bolts to 62 inch lbs. (7 Nm).
11. If removed, install the splash shield.
12. Carefully lower the vehicle.
13. Connect the negative battery cable.

SOLENOID REPLACEMENT

1. Remove the starter, as outlined earlier in this section.
2. Remove the screw from the field strap at the rear of the starter.
3. Remove the 2 bolts holding the solenoid to the starter.
4. Rotate the solenoid 90 degrees and remove it from the starter. Be aware that there is a large spring behind the solenoid.

To install:

5. Push solenoid and spring onto starter and rotate into position.
6. Install the mounting bolts and tighten to 60 inch. lbs. (6.5 Nm).
7. Install screw to field strap and tighten the retaining screw to 75 inch lbs. (8.5 Nm).
8. Install the starter, as outlined earlier in this section.

SENDING UNITS

➡This section describes the operating principles of sending units, warning lights and gauges. Sensors which provide information to the Electronic Control Module (ECM) are covered in Section 4 of this manual.

Instrument panels contain a number of indicating devices (gauges and warning lights). These devices are composed of two separate components. One is the sending unit, mounted on the engine or other remote part of the vehicle, and the other is the actual gauge or light in the instrument panel.

Several types of sending units exist, however most can be characterized as being either a pressure type or a resistance type. Pressure type sending units convert liquid pressure into an electrical signal which is sent to the gauge. Resistance type sending units are most often used to measure temperature and use variable resistance to control the current flow back to the indicating device. Both types of sending units are connected in series by a wire to the battery (through the ignition switch). When the ignition is turned **ON**, current flows from the battery through the indicating device and on to the sending unit.

Coolant Temperature Sender

OPERATION

The coolant temperature sender changes resistance as the coolant temperature increases and decreases.

TESTING

1. Remove the temperature sender from the engine.
2. Position the water temperature sending unit in such a way that the metal shaft (opposite end from the electrical connectors) is situated in a pot of water. Make sure that the electrical connector is not submerged and that only the tip of the sending unit's body is in the water.
3. Heat the pot of water at a medium rate. While the water is warming, continue to measure the resistance of the terminal and the metal body of the sending unit:
   a. As the water warms up, the resistance exhibited by the ohmmeter goes down in a steady manner: the sending unit is good.
   b. As the water warms up, the resistance does not change or changes in erratic jumps: the sender is bad, replace it with a new one.
4. Install the good or new sending unit into the engine, then connect the negative battery cable.

REMOVAL & INSTALLATION

1. Disconnect the negative battery cable.
2. Drain the coolant to a level below the coolant temperature sender.
3. Unplug the sender electrical connector, then unscrew the sender. The sender can usually be found mounted in the engine block or threaded into the thermostat housing/outlet or radiator.

To install:

4. Install the sender in the vehicle and tighten securely.

5. Attach the sender electrical connector.
6. Refill the cooling system to the proper level with the proper type and amount of coolant.
7. Connect the negative battery cable.

Oil Pressure Sender

OPERATION

The oil pressure sender/switch relays the engine oil pressure to the dash gauge.

TESTING

1. To test the normally closed oil pressure lamp circuit, disengage the locking connector and measure the resistance between the switch terminal (terminal for the wire to the warning lamp) and the metal housing. The ohmmeter should read 0 ohms.
2. To test the sending unit, measure the resistance between the sending unit terminal and the metal housing. The ohmmeter should read an open circuit (infinite resistance).
3. Start the engine.
4. Once again, test each terminal against the metal housing:
   a. The oil switch terminal-to-housing circuit should read an open circuit if there is oil pressure present.
   b. The sending unit-to-housing circuit should read between 15–80 ohms, depending on the engine speed, oil temperature and oil viscosity.
5. To test the oil pressure sender only, rev the engine and watch the ohms reading, which should fluctuate slightly (within the range of 15–80 ohms) as rpm increases.
6. If the above results were not obtained, replace the sending unit/switch with a new one.

REMOVAL & INSTALLATION

▶ **See Figure 49**

1. Disconnect the negative battery cable.
2. If necessary for access, raise and safely support the vehicle.

3. If necessary, drain the engine oil into a suitable container.
4. Detach the switch electrical connector.
5. Remove the switch.
To install:
6. Coat the first two or three threads with sealer. Install the switch and tighten until snug. Engage the electrical lead.
7. Carefully lower the vehicle.
8. Fill the crankcase with the proper type and amount of engine oil.
9. Connect the negative battery cable.

Electric Fan Switch

OPERATION

When the switch reaches a predetermined temperature, it closes the circuit to the relay. This energizes the relay, sending 12 volts to the fan. When the temperature decreases below the set point of the sender, the circuit opens and the voltage is no longer applied to the fan.

TESTING

1. Connect a jumper wire from the negative battery terminal to the black wire, or its terminal, on the electric fan motor.
2. Connect a jumper wire from the battery positive terminal to the remaining wire or terminal on the motor.
3. The fan should operate. If the fan does not operate, the motor may be defective and it should be replaced.

REMOVAL & INSTALLATION

▶ **See Figure 50**

1. Disconnect the negative battery cable.
2. Disconnect the switch electrical lead and remove the switch.
To install:
3. Install the switch and connect the electrical lead.
4. Connect the battery cable.

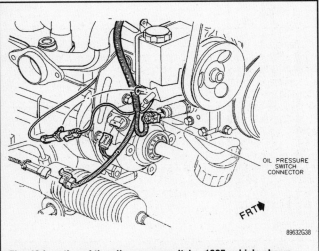

Fig. 49 Location of the oil pressure switch—1995 vehicle shown, others similar

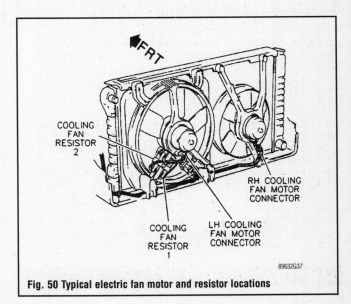

Fig. 50 Typical electric fan motor and resistor locations

Troubleshooting Basic Charging System Problems

Problem	Cause	Solution
Noisy alternator	• Loose mountings	• Tighten mounting bolts
	• Loose drive pulley	• Tighten pulley
	• Worn bearings	• Replace alternator
	• Brush noise	• Replace alternator
	• Internal circuits shorted (High pitched whine)	• Replace alternator
Squeal when starting engine or accelerating	• Glazed or loose belt	• Replace or adjust belt
Indicator light remains on or ammeter indicates discharge (engine running)	• Broken belt	• Install belt
	• Broken or disconnected wires	• Repair or connect wiring
	• Internal alternator problems	• Replace alternator
	• Defective voltage regulator	• Replace voltage regulator/alternator
Car light bulbs continually burn out—battery needs water continually	• Alternator/regulator overcharging	• Replace voltage regulator/alternator
Car lights flare on acceleration	• Battery low	• Charge or replace battery
	• Internal alternator/regulator problems	• Replace alternator/regulator
Low voltage output (alternator light flickers continually or ammeter needle wanders)	• Loose or worn belt	• Replace or adjust belt
	• Dirty or corroded connections	• Clean or replace connections
	• Internal alternator/regulator problems	• Replace alternator/regulator

TCCS2C02

Troubleshooting Basic Starting System Problems

Problem	Cause	Solution
Starter motor rotates engine slowly	• Battery charge low or battery defective	• Charge or replace battery
	• Defective circuit between battery and starter motor	• Clean and tighten, or replace cables
	• Low load current	• Bench-test starter motor. Inspect for worn brushes and weak brush springs.
	• High load current	• Bench-test starter motor. Check engine for friction, drag or coolant in cylinders. Check ring gear-to-pinion gear clearance.
Starter motor will not rotate engine	• Battery charge low or battery defective	• Charge or replace battery
	• Faulty solenoid	• Check solenoid ground. Repair or replace as necessary.
	• Damaged drive pinion gear or ring gear	• Replace damaged gear(s)
	• Starter motor engagement weak	• Bench-test starter motor
	• Starter motor rotates slowly with high load current	• Inspect drive yoke pull-down and point gap, check for worn end bushings, check ring gear clearance
	• Engine seized	• Repair engine
Starter motor drive will not engage (solenoid known to be good)	• Defective contact point assembly	• Repair or replace contact point assembly
	• Inadequate contact point assembly ground	• Repair connection at ground screw
	• Defective hold-in coil	• Replace field winding assembly
Starter motor drive will not disengage	• Starter motor loose on flywheel housing	• Tighten mounting bolts
	• Worn drive end busing	• Replace bushing
	• Damaged ring gear teeth	• Replace ring gear or driveplate
	• Drive yoke return spring broken or missing	• Replace spring
Starter motor drive disengages prematurely	• Weak drive assembly thrust spring	• Replace drive mechanism
	• Hold-in coil defective	• Replace field winding assembly
Low load current	• Worn brushes	• Replace brushes
	• Weak brush springs	• Replace springs

TCCS2C01

ENGINE MECHANICAL 3-2
ENGINE 3-5
  REMOVAL & INSTALLATION 3-5
ROCKER ARM (VALVE) COVER 3-7
  REMOVAL & INSTALLATION 3-7
ROCKER ARM/SHAFTS 3-9
  REMOVAL & INSTALLATION 3-9
THERMOSTAT 3-10
  REMOVAL & INSTALLATION 3-10
INTAKE MANIFOLD 3-11
  REMOVAL & INSTALLATION 3-11
EXHAUST MANIFOLD 3-16
  REMOVAL & INSTALLATION 3-16
SUPERCHARGER 3-19
  REMOVAL & INSTALLATION 3-19
RADIATOR 3-20
  REMOVAL & INSTALLATION 3-20
ELECTRIC COOLING FAN(S) 3-22
  TESTING 3-22
  REMOVAL & INSTALLATION 3-22
WATER PUMP 3-23
  REMOVAL & INSTALLATION 3-23
CYLINDER HEAD 3-26
  REMOVAL & INSTALLATION 3-26
OIL PAN 3-28
  REMOVAL & INSTALLATION 3-28
OIL PUMP 3-29
  REMOVAL 3-29
  INSPECTION 3-29
  INSTALLATION 3-30
CRANKSHAFT DAMPER 3-30
  REMOVAL & INSTALLATION 3-30
TIMING CHAIN COVER 3-30
  REMOVAL & INSTALLATION 3-30
FRONT COVER OIL SEAL 3-32
  REPLACEMENT 3-32
TIMING CHAIN AND SPROCKETS 3-33
  REMOVAL & INSTALLATION 3-33
CAMSHAFT, BEARINGS AND
  LIFTERS 3-35
  REMOVAL & INSTALLATION 3-35
  INSPECTION 3-35
CAMSHAFT/BALANCE SHAFT
  BEARINGS 3-35
  REMOVAL & INSTALLATION 3-35
BALANCE SHAFT 3-36
  REMOVAL & INSTALLATION 3-36
REAR MAIN OIL SEAL 3-37
  REMOVAL & INSTALLATION 3-37
FLYWHEEL AND RING GEAR 3-39
  REMOVAL & INSTALLATION 3-39
EXHAUST SYSTEM 3-39
INSPECTION 3-39
  REPLACEMENT 3-40
ENGINE RECONDITIONING 3-41
DETERMINING ENGINE CONDITION 3-41
  COMPRESSION TEST 3-41
  OIL PRESSURE TEST 3-41
BUY OR REBUILD? 3-41

ENGINE OVERHAUL TIPS 3-42
  TOOLS 3-42
  OVERHAUL TIPS 3-42
  CLEANING 3-42
  REPAIRING DAMAGED
    THREADS 3-42
ENGINE PREPARATION 3-43
CYLINDER HEAD 3-44
  DISASSEMBLY 3-44
  INSPECTION 3-45
  REFINISHING & REPAIRING 3-46
  ASSEMBLY 3-47
ENGINE BLOCK 3-47
  GENERAL INFORMATION 3-47
  DISASSEMBLY 3-48
  INSPECTION 3-48
  REFINISHING 3-50
  ASSEMBLY 3-50
ENGINE START-UP AND BREAK-IN 3-52
  STARTING THE ENGINE 3-52
  BREAKING IT IN 3-52
  KEEP IT MAINTAINED 3-52
SPECIFICATIONS CHARTS
  ENGINE SPECIFICATIONS 3-2
  TORQUE SPECIFICATIONS 3-53

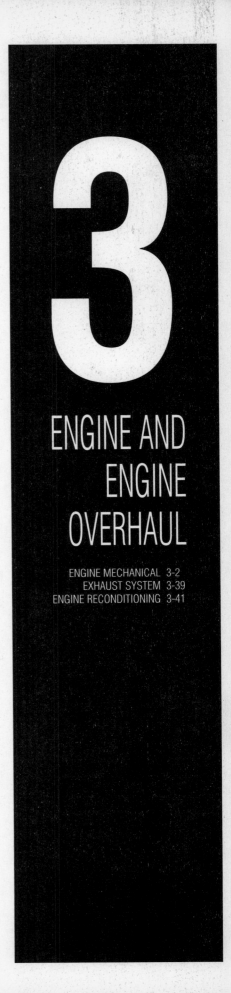

3

ENGINE AND ENGINE OVERHAUL

ENGINE MECHANICAL 3-2
EXHAUST SYSTEM 3-39
ENGINE RECONDITIONING 3-41

ENGINE MECHANICAL

1986-95 3.0L and 3.8L ENGINE SPECIFICATIONS

Description	English	Metric
General Information		
Type	90 ° V6 OverHead Valve (OHV)	
Displacement		
3.0L engines	181	3.0 (2967)
3.8L engines	231	3.8 (3786)
Number of Cylinders	6	
Bore	3.800 in.	96.52mm
Stroke		
3.0L engines	2.660 in.	67.56mm
3.8L engines	3.400 in.	86.36mm
Compression ratio		
1986-92 vehicles		
3.0L engines	9.0:1	
3.8L engines	8.5:1	
1993-95 vehicles		
VIN L & K engines	9.0:1	
VIN 1 engines	8.5:1	
Oil Pump		
Gear pocket depth	0.461-0.4625 in.	11.71-11.75mm
Gear pocket diameter	3.508-3.512 in.	89.10-89.20mm
Inner gear tip clearance	0.006 in.	0.152mm
Outer gear diameter clearance	0.008-0.015 in.	0.203-0.381mm
End clearance	0.001-0.0035 in.	0.025-0.089mm
Valve-to-bore clearance	0.0015-0.0030 in.	0.038-0.076mm
Cylinder Bore		
Diameter	3.8 in.	96.5mm
Out-of-round (max.)	0.0004 in.	0.010mm
Taper	0.0005 in.	0.013mm
Piston		
Piston clearance		
1986 vehicles	0.0008-0.0020 in.	0.020-0.051mm
1987-94 vehicles (44mm from top of piston)	0.0004-0.0022 in.	0.010-0.056mm
1995 VIN K engine (39mm from top of piston)	0.0004-0.0020 in.	0.010-0.051mm
1995 VIN 1 engine (52mm from top of piston)	0.0008-0.0024 in.	0.020-0.060mm
1995 VIN L engine (44mm from top of piston)	0.0004-0.0022 in.	0.010-0.056mm
Piston Rings		
Ring groove depth		
Top compression		
1987-94 vehicles	0.173-0.178 in.	4.389-4.519mm
1995 VIN K engine	0.158-0.163 in.	4.019-4.146mm
1995 VIN 1 engine	0.173-0.178 in.	4.392-4.522mm
1995 VIN L engine	0.169-0.174 in.	4.294-4.424mm
2nd compression		
1987-94 vehicles	0.173-0.178 in.	4.389-4.519mm
1995 VIN K engine	0.166-0.171 in.	4.214-4.341mm
1995 VIN 1 engine	0.173-0.178 in.	4.392-4.522mm
1995 VIN L engine	0.173-0.178 in.	4.389-4.519mm
Oil control		
1987-94 vehicles	0.165-0.171 in.	4.204-4.334mm
1995 VIN K engine	0.150-0.155 in.	3.814-3.941mm
1995 VIN 1 engine	0.167-0.172 in.	4.242-4.369mm
1995 VIN L engine	0.165-0.171 in.	4.204-4.334mm

89633C01

1986-95 3.0L and 3.8L ENGINE SPECIFICATIONS

Description	English	Metric
Piston Rings (cont.)		
End-gap		
Top compression		
1986 vehicles	0.010-0.020 in.	0.254-0.508mm
1987-94 vehicles	0.010-0.025 in.	0.254-0.635mm
1995 vehicles	0.012-0.022 in.	0.305-0.559mm
2nd compression		
1986 vehicles	0.010-0.020 in.	0.254-0.508mm
1987-94 vehicles	0.010-0.025 in.	0.254-0.635mm
1995 vehicles	0.030-0.040 in.	0.762-1.016mm
Oil control		
1986-94 vehicles	0.015-0.055 in.	0.381-1.397mm
1995 vehicles	0.010-0.030 in.	0.254-0.762mm
Side clearance		
Top compression		
1986 vehicles	0.0030-0.0050 in.	0.076-0.127mm
1987-94 vehicles	0.0013-0.0031 in.	0.033-0.079mm
1995 vehicles	0.0013-0.0031 in.	0.033-0.079mm
2nd compression		
1986 vehicles	0.0030-0.0050 in.	0.076-0.127mm
1987-94 vehicles	0.0013-0.0031 in.	0.033-0.079mm
1995 vehicles	0.0013-0.0031 in.	0.033-0.079mm
Oil control		
1986 vehicles	0.0035 in.	0.0889mm
1986-94 vehicles	0.011-0.0081 in.	0.028-0.206mm
1995 VIN K engine	0.0009-0.0079 in.	0.023-0.201mm
1995 VIN 1 & L engines	0.0011-0.0081 in.	0.028-0.206mm
Ring width		
Top compression		
1987-94 vehicles	0.0581-0.0589 in.	1.476-1.497mm
1995 vehicles	0.0463-0.0471 in.	1.176-1.197mm
2nd compression		
1987-94 vehicles	0.0581-0.0589 in.	1.476-1.497mm
1995 vehicles	0.0581-0.0589 in.	1.476-1.497mm
Oil control		
1987-94 vehicles	0.1122-0.1182 in.	2.850-3.002mm
1995 VIN K engine	0.073-0.079 in.	1.854-2.007mm
1995 VIN 1 & L engines	0.1122-0.1182 in.	2.850-3.002mm
Piston pin		
Diameter		
1987-94 vehicles	0.9053-0.9055 in.	22.995-23.000mm
1995 VIN K engine	0.8659-0.8661 in.	21.9950-22.0000mm
1995 VIN 1 & L engines	0.9053-0.9055 in.	22.995-23.000mm
Fit in piston		
1987-94 vehicles	0.0004-0.0008 in.	0.010-0.020mm
1995 VIN K & 1 engines	0.00008-0.0051 in.	0.0020-0.0130mm
1995 VIN L engine	0.0003-0.0006 in.	0.008-0.0155mm
Fit in rod		
1987-94 vehicles	0.007-0.0017 in.	0.018-0.043mm
1995 VIN K & 1 engines	0.0003-0.0009 in.	0.0066-0.0217mm
1995 VIN L engine	0.0007-0.0017 in.	0.0018-0.0043mm

89633C02

1986-95 3.0L and 3.8L ENGINE SPECIFICATIONS

Description	English	Metric
Crankshaft and Connecting Rods		
Crankshaft main bearings		
Journal		
Diameter (all)		
1986 vehicles		
3.0L engines	2.4995 in.	63.487mm
3.8L engines	2.4990-2.5000 in.	63.474-63.500mm
1987-95 vehicles	2.4988-2.4998 in.	63.470-63.495mm
Taper (max.)	0.0003 in.	0.008mm
run-out (max.)	0.0003 in.	0.008mm
Bearing-to-journal clearance		
1986-91 vehicles	0.0003-0.0018 in.	0.045-0.076mm
1992-94 vehicles	0.0008-0.0022 in.	0.020-0.055mm
Main bearing bore I.D.	2.687-2.688 in.	68.250-68.275mm
Crankshaft end play	0.003-0.011 in.	0.076-0.279mm
Connecting rod bearings		
Diameter	2.2487-2.2499 in.	57.117-57.147mm
Taper (max.)	0.0003 in.	0.008mm
Run-out (max.)	0.0003 in.	0.008mm
Bearing-to-journal clearance		
1986 vehicles		
3.0L engines	0.0005-0.0026 in.	0.0127-0.0660mm
3.8L engines	0.0003-0.0028 in.	0.0076-0.0711mm
1987-91 vehicles	0.0003-0.0026 in.	0.0076-0.0711mm
1992-94 vehicles	0.0008-0.0022 in.	0.020-0.055mm
Rod side clearance		
3.0L engines	0.006-0.023 in.	0.152-0.584mm
3.8L engines	0.003-0.015 in.	0.076-0.381mm
Connecting rod large end bore I.D.	2.3738-2.3745 in.	60.295-60.312mm
Camshaft		
Lobe lift		
Intake		
1986 vehicles		
VIN L and 3 engines	0.368 in.	9.34mm
VIN B engines	0.392 in.	9.96mm
1987-95 vehicles	0.250 in.	6.43mm
Exhaust	0.255 in.	6.48mm
1986 vehicles		
VIN L and 3 engines	0.384 in.	9.75mm
VIN B engines	0.392 in.	9.96mm
1987-95 vehicles	0.255 in.	6.48mm
Journal diameter		
3.0L engines	1.780-1.787 in.	45.212-45.390mm
3.8L engines	1.785-1.786 in.	45.339-45.364mm
Bearing inside diameter	1.7865-1.7885 in.	45.377-45.428mm
Bearing-to-journal clearance	0.005-0.035 in.	0.013-0.089mm

89633C03

1986-95 3.0L and 3.8L ENGINE SPECIFICATIONS

Description	English	Metric
Balance Shaft		
End play	0.0-0.008 in.	0.0-0.203mm
Radial play		
Front	0.0-0.0011 in.	0.0-0.028mm
Rear	0.0005-0.0047 in.	0.0127-0.119mm
Drive gear lash	0.002-0.005 in.	0.050-0.127mm
Bearing bore diameter		
Front	2.0462-2.0472 in.	51.973-51.999mm
Rear	1.950-1.952 in.	49.530-49.580mm
Valve System		
Lifter	Hydraulic	
Rocker arm ratio	1.6:1	
Face angle	45°	
Seat angle	45°	
Minimum margin	0.025 in.	0.635mm
Seat run-out (max.)	0.002 in.	0.050mm
Seat width		
Intake	0.060-0.080 in.	1.53-2.03mm
Exhaust	0.090-0.110 in.	2.29-2.79mm
Stem height (all)	1.935-1.975 in.	49.15-50.17mm
Stem diameter		
1986 vehicles		
Intake	0.3401-0.3412	8.64-8.67mm
Exhaust	0.3405-0.3412	8.65-8.67mm
1987-95 vehicles		
Stem clearance		
Exhaust	0.0015-0.0032 in.	0.038-0.089mm
Intake	0.0015-0.0035 in.	0.038-0.089mm
Valve spring		
Free length	1.981 in.	50.32mm
Load		
1986 vehicles		
VIN L engine	220 lbs. @ 1.34 in.	978 N @ 34.0mm
VIN B engine	90 lbs.	400 N
VIN 3 engine	105 lbs.	467 N
1987-95 vehicles		
closed	80 lbs. @ 1.75 in.	356 N @ 43.69mm
open	210 lbs. @ 1.315 in.	935 N @ 33.4mm
Installed height		
1986 vehicles	1.727 in.	43.86mm
1987-95 vehicles	1.690-1.720 in.	42.93-44.45mm
Approximate # of coils	4	
Flywheel		
Run-out (max.)	0.015 in.	0.38mm

89633C04

1996-99 3.8L ENGINE SPECIFICATIONS

Description	English	Metric
General Information		
Type	90° V-type OverHead Valve (OHV)	
Displacement	231	3.8 (3786)
Number of Cylinders	6	
Bore	3.800	96.52mm
Stroke	3.400	86.36mm
Compression ratio		
VIN K engine	9.4:1	
VIN 1 engines	8.5:1	
Oil Pump		
Gear pocket depth	0.461-0.4625 in.	11.71-11.75mm
Gear pocket diameter	3.508-3.512 in.	89.10-89.20mm
Inner gear tip clearance	0.006 in.	0.152mm
Outer gear diameter clearance	0.008-0.015 in.	0.020-0.381mm
End clearance	0.001-0.0035 in.	0.025-0.089mm
Valve-to-bore clearance	0.0015-0.0030 in.	0.038-0.076mm
Cylinder Bore		
Diameter	3.8 in.	96.5mm
Out-of-round (max.)		
1996 vehicles	0.0004 in.	0.010mm
1997-99 vehicles	0.001 in.	0.0254mm
Taper		
1996 vehicles	0.0005 in.	0.013mm
1997-99 vehicles	0.001 in.	0.0254mm
Piston		
Piston clearance (39mm from top of piston)	0.0004-0.0020 in.	0.010-0.051mm
Piston Rings		
Ring groove depth		
Top compression	0.158-0.163 in.	4.019-4.146mm
2nd compression	0.0166-0.171 in.	4.214-4.341mm
Oil control	0.150-0.155 in.	3.814-3.941mm
End gap		
Top compression	0.012-0.022 in.	0.305-0.559mm
2nd compression	0.030-0.040 in.	0.762-1.016mm
Oil control	0.010-0.030 in.	0.254-0.762mm
Side clearance		
Top compression	0.0013-0.0031 in.	0.033-0.079mm
2nd compression	0.0013-0.0031 in.	0.033-0.079mm
Oil control	0.0009-0.0079 in.	0.023-0.201mm
Ring width		
Top compression	0.0463-0.0471 in.	1.176-1.197mm
2nd compression	0.0581-0.0589 in.	1.476-1.497mm
Oil control	0.073-0.079 in.	1.854-2.007mm
Piston pin		
Diameter	0.8659-0.8661 in.	21.9950-22.0000mm
Fit in piston	0.00008-0.00051 in.	0.0020-0.0130mm
Fit in rod	0.0003-0.0009 in.	0.0066-0.0217mm
Crankshaft and Connecting Rods		
Crankshaft main bearings		
Journal		
Diameter (all)	2.4988-2.4998 in.	63.470-63.495mm
Taper (max.)	0.0003 in.	0.076mm
Runout (max.)	0.0003 in.	0.076mm

1996-99 3.8L ENGINE SPECIFICATIONS

Description	English	Metric
Crankshaft and Connecting Rods (cont.)		
Bearing-to-journal clearance		
1996-97 vehicles	0.0008-0.0022 in.	0.020-0.055mm
1998-99 vehicles		
Main bearing-to-journal clearance 1	0.0007-0.0016 in.	0.0178-0.0406mm
Main bearing-to-journal clearance 2 & 3	0.0010-0.0020 in.	0.0254-0.0508mm
Main bearing-to-journal clearance 4	0.0009-0.0018 in.	0.0229-0.0457mm
Crankshaft end play	0.003-0.011 in.	0.076-0.276mm
Connecting rod bearings		
Rod side clearance	0.003-0.015 in.	0.076-0.381mm
Rod journal diameter (all)	2.2487-2.2499 in.	57.1170-57.1475mm
Rod journal taper (max.)	0.0003 in.	0.076mm
Rod journal out-of-round (max.)	0.003 in.	0.076mm
Rod bearing clearance	0.0005-0.0026 in.	0.0127-0.0660mm
Connecting rod large end and bore I.D.	2.37378-2.3745 in.	60.295-60.312mm
Camshaft		
Lobe lift		
Intake		
1996-97 vehicles	0.250 in.	6.43mm
1998-99 vehicles	0.268 in.	6.55mm
Exhaust	0.255 in.	6.48mm
Journal diameter		
1996-97 vehicles	1.785-1.786 in.	45.339-45.364mm
1998 vehicles	1.8462-1.8448 in.	47.655-46.858mm
Bearing inside diameter		
1996-97 vehicles	1.7865-1.7885 in.	45.377-45.428mm
1998-99 vehicles		
1 & 4 inside diameter	1.8462-1.8448 in.	47.655-46.858mm
2 & 3 inside diameter	1.8481-1.8492 in.	46.977-46.942mm
Bearing-to-journal clearance		
1996-97 vehicles	0.0005-0.0035 in.	0.013-0.089mm
1998-99 vehicles	0.0016-0.0047 in.	0.041-0.119mm
Balance Shaft		
End play		
1996-97 vehicles	0.0-0.008 in.	0.0-0.203mm
1998-99 vehicles	0.0-0.0067 in.	0.0-0.171mm
Radial play		
Front		
1996-97 vehicles	0.0-0.0011 in.	0.0-0.028mm
1998-99 vehicles	0.0-0.0010 in.	0.0-0.026mm
Rear	0.0005-0.0047 in.	0.0127-0.119mm
Rear journal diameter	1.4994-1.5002 in.	38.085-38.105mm
Rear bearing-to-journal clearance	0.0005-0.0043 in.	0.0127-0.109mm
Drive gear lash		
1996-97 vehicles	0.002-0.005 in.	0.050-0.127mm
1998-99 vehicles	0.002-0.0049 in.	0.050-0.125mm
Bearing bore diameter		
Front	2.0462-2.0472 in.	51.973-51.999mm
Rear		
1996-97 vehicles	1.950-1.952 in.	49.530-49.580mm
1998-99 vehicles (in block)	1.8735-1.8745 in.	47.584-47.612mm
Bearing inside diameter (rear)	1.5007-1.5037 in.	38.118-38.194mm

1996-99 3.8L ENGINE SPECIFICATIONS

Description	English	Metric
Valve System		
Lifter	Hydraulic	
Rocker arm ratio	1.6:1	
Face angle	45°	
Seat angle	45°	
Minimum margin	0.025 in.	0.635mm
Seat runout (max.)	0.002 in.	0.050mm
Seat width		
Intake	0.060-0.080 in.	1.53-2.03mm
Exhaust	0.090-0.110 in.	2.29.2.79mm
Stem height (all)	1.935-1.975 in.	49.15-50.17mm
Stem clearance (all)	0.0015-0.0032 in.	0.038-0.089mm
Valve spring		
Free length		
1996-97 vehicles	1.981 in.	50.32mm
1998-99 vehicles	1.960 in.	49.78mm
Load - closed		
1996-97 vehicles	80 lbs. @ 1.75 in.	356 N @ 43.69mm
1998-99 vehicles	75 lbs. @ 1.72 in.	334 N @ 43.69mm
Load - open		
1996-97 vehicles	210 lbs. @ 1.315 in.	935 N @ 33.4mm
1998-99 vehicles	228 lbs. @ 1.277 in.	1014 N @ 32.4mm
Installed height	1.690-1.720 in.	42.93-44.45mm
Approximate # of coils		
1996-97 vehicles	4	
1998-99 vehicles		
Active coils	4.48	
Total coils	6.60	
Flywheel		
Runout (max.)	0.015 in.	0.38mm

89633C07

Engine

REMOVAL & INSTALLATION

In the process of removing the engine, you will come across a number of steps which call for the removal of a separate component or system, such as "disconnect the exhaust system" or "remove the radiator." In most instances, a detailed removal procedure can be found elsewhere in this manual.

It is virtually impossible to list each individual wire and hose which must be disconnected, simply because so many different model and engine combinations have been manufactured. Careful observation and common sense are the best possible approaches to any repair procedure.

Removal and installation of the engine can be made easier if you follow these basic points:

- If you have to drain any of the fluids, use a suitable container.
- Always tag any wires or hoses and, if possible, the components they came from before disconnecting them.
- Because there are so many bolts and fasteners involved, store and label the retainers from components separately in muffin pans, jars or coffee cans. This will prevent confusion during installation.
- After unbolting the transmission or transaxle, always make sure it is properly supported.
- If it is necessary to disconnect the air conditioning system, have this service performed by a qualified technician using a recovery/recycling station. If the system does not have to be disconnected, unbolt the compressor and set it aside.

- When unbolting the engine mounts, always make sure the engine is properly supported. When removing the engine, make sure that any lifting devices are properly attached to the engine. It is recommended that if your engine is supplied with lifting hooks, your lifting apparatus be attached to them.
- Lift the engine from its compartment slowly, checking that no hoses, wires or other components are still connected.
- After the engine is clear of the compartment, place it on an engine stand or workbench.
- After the engine has been removed, you can perform a partial or full teardown of the engine using the procedures outlined in this manual.

3.0L and 3.8L (VIN 3, B and C) Engines

▶ See Figures 1 thru 9

1. Properly relieve the fuel system pressure.
2. If not done already, disconnect the negative battery cable.
3. Using a scribing tool, matchmark the hood hinges and remove the hood.
4. Label and disconnect the air flow sensor wiring.
5. Remove the air intake duct. Remove the throttle cable and bracket from the throttle body. Place a clean drain pan under the radiator, open the draincock and drain the cooling system.
6. Raise and safely support the vehicle.
7. Drain the engine oil into a suitable container.
8. Remove the exhaust pipe-to-exhaust manifold bolts and separate the exhaust pipe.
9. Remove the engine mount bolts.

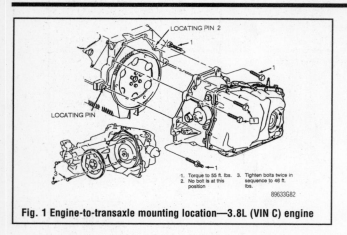

Fig. 1 Engine-to-transaxle mounting location—3.8L (VIN C) engine

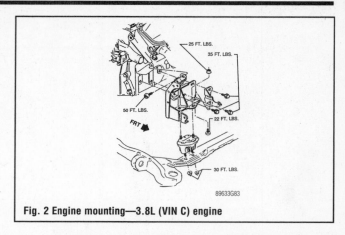

Fig. 2 Engine mounting—3.8L (VIN C) engine

Fig. 3 Once the engine is removed, it can be disassembled for rebuilding purposes

Fig. 4 Use a suitable engine hoist to slowly, and carefully, lower the engine into the engine compartment

Fig. 5 Carefully guide the engine downward into the engine compartment

Fig. 6 Make sure not to pinch any wires, or damage any components when installing the engine

Fig. 7 There are two exhaust manifold studs (one is broken on this vehicle) which must be aligned with the exhaust pipe

Fig. 8 Location of the exhaust pipe flange holes with which the studs must be aligned

10. If equipped with a driveline vibration absorber, remove the bolts and disconnect the absorber.

11. Tag and detach the electrical connectors from the starter. Remove the starter-to-engine bolts and the starter.

12. If equipped with A/C, remove the compressor mounting bolts and position aside. Do not discharge the system or disconnect the refrigerant lines.

13. Place a pan under the power steering gear. Disconnect the hydraulic lines and drain the fluid. Use a length of wire to hold the hoses aside.

14. Remove the lower transaxle-to-engine bolts.

➡**One bolt is situated between the transaxle case and the engine block. It is installed in the opposite direction to the other bolts.**

15. Remove the flywheel cover. Matchmark the flexplate-to-torque converter relationship to insure proper alignment upon installation. Remove the flexplate-to-torque converter bolts.

16. Remove the engine support bracket-to-transaxle bolts and the bracket. Lower the vehicle.

17. Attach an engine hoist to the engine lift brackets and support the engine.

18. Remove the radiator and heater hoses from the engine and position them aside.

19. Label and disconnect the hoses from the vacuum modulator and canister purge lines.

20. Tag and detach the engine electrical wiring harness(es) and position them out of way.

21. Remove the upper transaxle-to-engine bolts.

22. Carefully remove the engine from the from the vehicle with the engine hoist. Mount the engine on a suitable workstand.

To install:

23. Use the engine hoist to carefully lower the engine into the vehicle.

24. Installation of the engine is the reverse of the removal procedure. Please note the following important steps:

25. Attach all electrical connections and vacuum lines as tagged during removal, making sure the lines are routed properly.

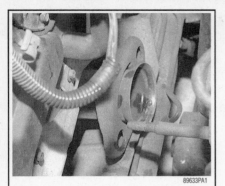

Fig. 9 You MUST align the studs with the flange holes, while lowering the engine

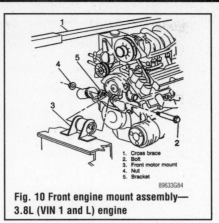

Fig. 10 Front engine mount assembly—3.8L (VIN 1 and L) engine

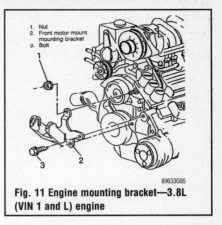

Fig. 11 Engine mounting bracket—3.8L (VIN 1 and L) engine

26. There are two studs on the exhaust manifold which must be aligned with the holes in the exhaust pipe while the engine is being lowered into the compartment. They cannot be aligned once the engine is lowered into the vehicle, as the exhaust pipe cannot be moved rearward enough to accomodate the studs.

27. Tighten the following components to specifications:
 a. Engine mount bolts: 70 ft. lbs. (95 Nm).
 b. Torque converter bolts: 46 ft. lbs. (62 Nm).
 c. Lower transaxle-to-engine bolts, tighten: 55 ft. lbs. (75 Nm).
 d. Starter mounting bolts: 35 ft. lbs. (47 Nm).

28. Install the hood assembly.

29. Connect the negative battery cable. Refill the cooling system and the crankcase.

30. Start the engine, allow it to reach normal operating temperatures and check for leaks. Check the fluid levels, and add as necessary.

3.8L (VIN L, K and 1) Engine

▶ See Figures 10 and 11

1. Properly relieve the fuel system pressure.
2. If not already done, disconnect the negative battery cable.
3. Using a marker or scribing tool, matchmark the hood hinges and remove the hood.
4. Drain the coolant and the engine oil from the vehicle into suitable containers.
5. Remove the strut tower cross brace. Disconnect the windshield washer, radiator and heater supply hoses.
6. Disconnect the wiring from the starter. Disconnect the main wiring at the harness near the relay center.
7. Remove the drive belt(s). Unbolt the power steering pump and position aside.
8. Remove the air inlet duct and the air cleaner assembly. Disconnect the throttle cable from the linkage.
9. Tag and detach the wiring harness connectors from the MAT sensor, throttle position switch, idle air control valve and oxygen sensor.
10. Disconnect the ignition coil ground strap from the fender inner panel.
11. Detach the fuel lines from the fuel rail and from the pressure regulator.
12. Disconnect the emission control hoses from the throttle body connections.
13. Tag and detach the brake booster and heater control hoses from the vacuum connections.
14. Raise and safely support the vehicle.
15. Disconnect the exhaust pipe from the right side manifold and disconnect the vacuum lines from the cruise control and servo assembly.
16. Attach a suitable engine lifting device to the engine and raise, so that it begins to support the engine.
17. If equipped with A/C, unbolt the compressor and tie it back away from the engine. If equipped with an engine oil cooler, disconnect the cooler lines.
18. Remove the front engine mount and remove the right front engine-to-transaxle bracket.
19. Use a suitable jack to support the transaxle, then remove the engine to transaxle bolts. Remove the flywheel cover.
20. Remove the torque converter-to-flywheel bolts and use a scribe to matchmark the proper flywheel-to-torque converter relationship.

21. Separate the engine from the transaxle, then remove the engine from the vehicle using a lifting device. Mount the engine on a suitable workstand.

To install:

22. Use the engine hoist to carefully lower the engine into the vehicle.
23. Installation of the engine is the reverse of the removal procedure. Please note the following important steps:
24. Attach all electrical connections and vacuum lines as tagged during removal, making sure the lines are routed properly.
25. Make sure the flywheel and converter are aligned properly before installation.
26. Fill the coolant to the proper level and refill the engine oil.
27. Connect the negative battery cable.
28. Start the engine and check for fluid or oil leakage. Check the fluid levels and add as necessary.

Rocker Arm (Valve) Cover

REMOVAL & INSTALLATION

3.0L and 3.8L (VIN 3 and B) Engines

LEFT SIDE (FRONT) COVER

1. Disconnect the negative battery cable.
2. Remove the crankcase breather tube.
3. Remove the spark plug wire harness cover, then tag and disconnect the spark plug wires from the plugs.
4. Remove the valve cover nuts, washers, seals and valve cover.
5. Using a gasket scraper or a putty knife, clean the gasket mounting surfaces.
6. To install, use a new gasket and reverse the removal procedures. Tighten the valve cover nuts to 7 ft. lbs. (10 Nm).

RIGHT SIDE (REAR) COVER

1. Disconnect the negative battery cable.
2. Remove the C$SS3I ignition coil module, the spark plug cables, the wiring connectors, the EGR solenoid wiring and vacuum hoses. Remove any fuel injection components that may interfere with the valve cover removal.
3. Remove the serpentine drive belt, as outlined in Section 1 of this manual.
4. Detach the alternator's wiring connectors, then remove the mounting bolt and swing the alternator toward the front of the vehicle.
5. Remove the power steering pump from the belt tensioner (move it aside) and the belt tensioner assembly. It is not necessary to disconnect the power steering fluid lines.
6. Remove the engine lift bracket and the rear alternator brace.
7. Drain the cooling system below the level of the heater hose, then disconnect the throttle body heater hoses.
8. Remove the valve cover nuts, the washers, the seals, the valve cover and the gasket.
9. Using a suitable gasket scraper or putty knife, clean the gasket mounting surfaces.
10. To install, use a new gasket and reverse the removal procedures. Tighten the valve cover nuts to 7 ft. lbs. (10 Nm).

3.8L (VIN 1, C and L) Engines—Except 1995–99 VIN 1 Models

LEFT SIDE (FRONT) COVER

▶ See Figures 12, 13, 14, 15 and 16

1. Disconnect the negative battery cable.
2. Remove the serpentine drive belt, as outlined in Section 1 of this manual.
3. Remove the alternator-to-brace bolt, then remove the brace.
4. Remove the spark plug wire harness and position aside.
5. Remove the valve cover retaining bolts and remove the cover. It may be necessary to tap the cover lightly with a rubber mallet in order to dislodge it. Thoroughly clean the gasket mating surfaces and clean and dry all parts.

To install:

6. Installation is the reverse of the removal procedure.
7. Place the gasket into position, apply a suitable thread-locking compound to the threads, then install the bolts and tighten them to 89 inch lbs. (10 Nm).
8. Connect the negative battery cable.
9. Run the engine and check for leaks.

RIGHT SIDE (REAR) COVER

1. Disconnect the negative battery cable.
2. Remove the accessory drive belt(s).
3. Without disconnecting the fluid lines, unbolt the power steering pump and position it aside.
4. Remove the power steering pump braces.
5. Tag and disconnect the spark plug wires.
6. For 3.8L (VIN C) engines, perform the following:
    a. Remove the EGR pipe.
    b. Remove the EGR valve and adapter from the throttle body adapter.
7. Unfasten the valve cover retaining bolts, then remove the cover. It may be necessary to tap the cover lightly with a rubber mallet in order to dislodge it. Thoroughly clean the gasket mating surfaces and clean and dry all parts.

To install:

8. Place the gasket into position, apply thread-locking compound to the threads, then install the bolts and tighten them to 89 inch lbs. (10 Nm).
9. The remainder of installation is the reverse of the removal procedure.

1995–99 3.8L (VIN K and 1) Engines

LEFT SIDE (FRONT) COVER

▶ See Figure 17

1. Disconnect the negative battery cable.
2. Remove the spark plug wire harness and position it aside.
3. Unfasten the retaining bolts, then remove the valve cover. Thoroughly clean the gasket mating surfaces and clean and dry all parts.

To install:

4. Place the gasket into position, apply threadlocking compound to the threads, then install the bolts and tighten them to 89 inch lbs. (10 Nm).
5. Move the spark plug wire into position and secure it.
6. Connect the negative battery cable.

RIGHT SIDE (REAR) COVER

1. Disconnect the negative battery cable.
2. Remove the alternator rear retaining brace.
3. Remove the spark plug wire harness and position it aside.
4. Unfasten the retaining bolts, then remove the valve cover. Thoroughly clean the gasket mating surfaces and clean and dry all parts.

To install:

5. Place the gasket into position, apply thread-locking compound to the threads, then install the bolts and tighten them to 89 inch lbs. (10 Nm).
6. Move the spark plug wire into position and secure it.
7. Remove the alternator rear retaining brace.
8. Connect the negative battery cable.

Fig. 12 Unfasten the spark plug wire harness retainer, then position the harness aside

Fig. 13 Unfasten the valve cover retainers . . .

Fig. 14 . . . then remove the valve cover from the engine (intake manifold removed, but not necessary for this procedure)

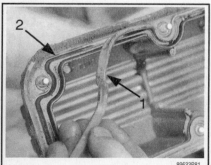

Fig. 15 Remove the gasket (1) from the groove on the underside of the valve cover (2)

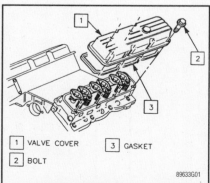

Fig. 16 Exploded view of the valve cover and gasket

1 VALVE COVER　3 GASKET
2 BOLT

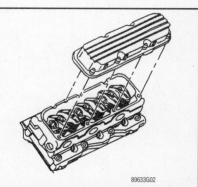

Fig. 17 Rocker arm (valve) cover mounting—1997 vehicle shown

Rocker Arm/Shafts

REMOVAL & INSTALLATION

3.0L and 3.8L (VIN 3 and B) Engines

▶ See Figure 18

1. Disconnect the negative battery cable.
2. Remove the rocker arm cover(s).
3. Remove the rocker arm shaft(s).
4. Place the shaft on a clean surface.
5. Remove the nylon rocker arm retainers. A pair of slip joint pliers is good for this.

➡ Make sure to keep all components in order for reassembly!

6. Slide the rocker arms off the shaft and inspect them for wear or damage. Keep them in order!

7. To install reverse steps 1 through 5. If new rocker arms are being installed, note that they are stamped R (right) or L (left), meaning that they be used on the right or left of each cylinder, NOT right and left cylinder banks. Each rocker arm must be centered over its oil hole. New nylon retainers must be used.

3.8L (VIN 1, C, L and K) Engines

▶ See Figures 19 thru 26

1. Disconnect the negative battery cable.
2. Remove the valve cover, as outlined earlier in this section.
3. Remove the rocker arm pedestal retaining bolts, then remove the pedestal and rocker arm assembly and place it on a clean surface.
4. If necessary, remove the pushrod guide plate, then remove the pushrods.

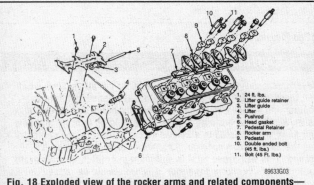

Fig. 18 Exploded view of the rocker arms and related components—3.0L and 3.8L (VIN 3 and B) engines

1. 24 ft. lbs.
2. Lifter guide retainer
3. Lifter guide
4. Lifter
5. Pushrod
6. Head gasket
7. Pedestal Retainer
8. Rocker arm
9. Pedestal
10. Double ended bolt (45 ft. lbs.)
11. Bolt (45 Ft. lbs.)

89633G03

Fig. 19 Unfasten the retainers, then remove the rocker arms

89633P72

Fig. 20 Remove the pushrod guide plate . . .

89633P73

Fig. 21 . . . then remove the pushrods

89633P74

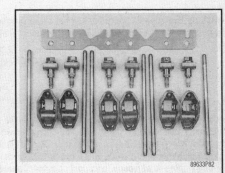

Fig. 22 Lay the valve train components out on a clean surface, in the proper orientation for installation

89633P82

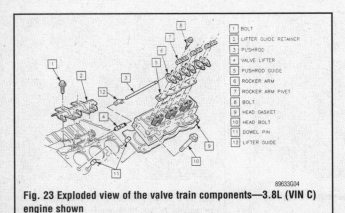

Fig. 23 Exploded view of the valve train components—3.8L (VIN C) engine shown

1. BOLT
2. LIFTER GUIDE RETAINER
3. PUSHROD
4. VALVE LIFTER
5. PUSHROD GUIDE
6. ROCKER ARM
7. ROCKER ARM PIVOT
8. BOLT
9. HEAD GASKET
10. HEAD BOLT
11. DOWEL PIN
12. LIFTER GUIDE

89633G04

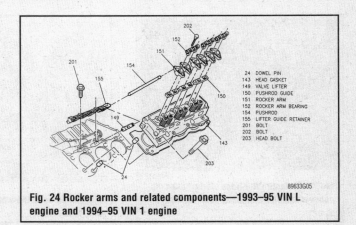

Fig. 24 Rocker arms and related components—1993–95 VIN L engine and 1994–95 VIN 1 engine

24 DOWEL PIN
143 HEAD GASKET
149 VALVE LIFTER
150 PUSHROD GUIDE
151 ROCKER ARM
152 ROCKER ARM BEARING
154 PUSHROD
155 LIFTER GUIDE RETAINER
201 BOLT
202 BOLT
203 HEAD BOLT

89633G05

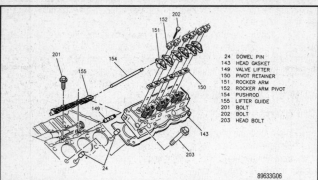

Fig. 25 Exploded view of the rocker arms and pivots—1993 supercharged engine shown

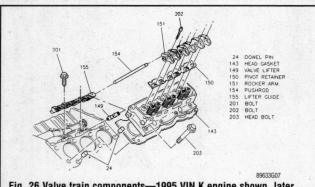

Fig. 26 Valve train components—1995 VIN K engine shown, later models similar

➡️ **Intake and exhaust pushrods are the same length. Store components in order so they can reassembled in the same location.**

5. Clean the rocker arms and pedestal bolts in a suitable solution and inspect for wear. Make sure to clean all of the thread adhesive from the rocker arm pedestal bolts.

To install:

6. If removed, install the pushrods and make sure they seat in the lifter.

➡️ **On 1996–99 vehicles, the bolts rocker arm bolts are designed to permanently stretch when tightened. The correct part number fastener must be used to replace this type of fastener. Do NOT use a bolt which is stronger in this application. If the proper bolt is not used, the parts will not be tightened correctly, and part or system damage may occur.**

7. Apply a threadlocking compound to the bolt threads before reassembly.

8. Install the pedestal and rocker arm assemblies, then tighten the retaining bolts as follows:

a. 1988–92 vehicles: 28 ft. lbs. (38 Nm).

b. 1993–94 vehicles: 19 ft. lbs. (25 Nm), plus an additional 70° with a torque angle meter.

c. 1995–99 vehicles: 11 ft. lbs. (15 Nm), plus an additional 90° with a torque angle meter.

9. Install the valve cover(s), as outlined earlier, then connect the negative battery cable.

10. Start engine and check for fluid leaks and listen for valve train noise.

Thermostat

The thermostat is used to control the flow of engine coolant. When the engine is cold, the thermostat is closed to prevent coolant from circulating through the engine. As the engine begins to warm up, the thermostat opens to allow the coolant to flow through the radiator and cool the engine to its normal operating temperature. Fuel economy and engine durability is increased when operated at normal operating temperature.

REMOVAL & INSTALLATION

▶ **See Figures 27 thru 36**

⁂ CAUTION

Never open, service or drain the radiator or cooling system when hot; the system is under pressure and will release scalding hot coolant and steam which can cause severe burns and other bodily harm. Also, when draining engine coolant, keep in mind that cats and dogs are attracted to ethylene glycol antifreeze and could drink any that is left in an uncovered container or in puddles on the ground. This will prove fatal in sufficient quantities. Always drain coolant into a sealable container. Coolant should be reused unless it is contaminated or is several years old.

1. If necessary, unfasten the retainer and remove the upper engine cover.

2. Disconnect the negative battery cable.

3. Remove the air cleaner and duct assembly.

4. Partially drain the engine cooling system, into a suitable container, to a level below the thermostat.

5. Disconnect the upper radiator hose from the water outlet.

6. If necessary, detach the electrical connections from the throttle body assembly.

7. Unfasten the water outlet attaching bolts, then remove the water outlet.

8. Remove the thermostat. Remove and discard the gasket.

9. Thoroughly clean the manifold water inlet and water outlet mating surfaces. Inspect the water outlet for corrosion or other damage, and replace if necessary.

To install:

10. Position the thermostat into the intake manifold with a new gasket.

11. Install the water outlet to the intake manifold with RTV sealer. Tighten the attaching bolts to 20 ft. lbs. (27 Nm).

12. The remainder of installation is the reverse of the removal procedure.

Fig. 27 Unfasten the hose clamp, then disconnect the radiator hose from the water outlet

Fig. 28 Remove the water outlet attaching bolt (see arrow) . . .

Fig. 29 . . . then remove the water outlet for access to the thermostat

Fig. 30 Remove the thermostat by simply lifting it out

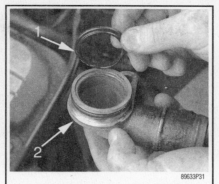

Fig. 31 Remove and inspect the top O-ring (1) from the water outlet (2) . . .

Fig. 32 . . . and do the same with the lower O-ring

Fig. 33 A water outlet that is badly corroded, such as this one, should be replaced

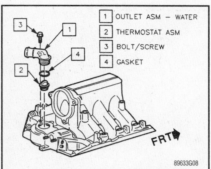

1	OUTLET ASM — WATER
2	THERMOSTAT ASM
3	BOLT/SCREW
4	GASKET

FRT

Fig. 34 Exploded view of the thermostat and housing assembly—3.8L (VIN C) engine

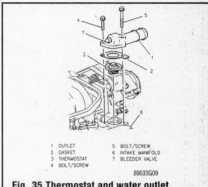

1	OUTLET	5	BOLT/SCREW
2	GASKET	6	INTAKE MANIFOLD
3	THERMOSTAT	7	BLEEDER VALVE
4	BOLT/SCREW		

Fig. 35 Thermostat and water outlet mounting—3.8L (VIN L) engine shown

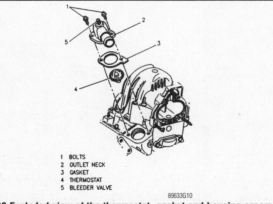

1 BOLTS
2 OUTLET NECK
3 GASKET
4 THERMOSTAT
5 BLEEDER VALVE

Fig. 36 Exploded view of the thermostat, gasket and housing assembly—1997 vehicle shown

Intake Manifold

REMOVAL & INSTALLATION

✳✳ CAUTION

When draining the coolant, keep in mind that cats and dogs are attracted by ethylene glycol antifreeze, and are quite likely to drink any that is left in an uncovered container or in puddles on the ground. This will prove fatal in sufficient quantity. Always drain the coolant into a sealable container. Coolant should be reused unless it is contaminated or several years old.

1986–90 Vehicles

3.0L AND 3.8L (VIN 3 AND B) ENGINES

◆ See Figure 37

1. Relieve the pressure in the fuel system before disconnecting any fuel line connections. Refer to the procedure in Section 5.
2. If not already done, disconnect the negative battery cable.
3. Remove the mass air flow sensor and air intake duct.
4. Remove the serpentine accessory drive belt, alternator and bracket.
5. Remove the ignition coil module, TV cable, throttle cable and cruise control cable.
6. Tag and disconnect all necessary vacuum hoses and electrical wiring.
7. Drain the cooling system into a suitable container. Disconnect the heater hoses from the throttle body and upper radiator hose.
8. Disconnect the fuel lines from the fuel rail and injectors.

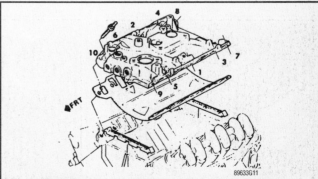

FRT

Fig. 37 You must tighten the intake manifold bolts in the proper sequence—3.0L and 3.8L (VIN 3 and B) engines

9. Unfasten the intake manifold retaining bolts and remove the intake manifold and gasket.

To install:

10. Clean the cylinder head and intake manifold surfaces from any foreign matter, nicks or heavy scratches.

11. Install the intake manifold gasket and rubber seals. Apply sealer 1050026 or equivalent, on the gasket. Apply sealer/lubricant 1052080 or equivalent, to all pipe thread fittings.

12. Carefully position the intake manifold on the cylinder block. Install the intake manifold bolts, then tighten them in sequence to 47 ft. lbs. (65 Nm).

13. The remainder of installation is the reverse of the removal procedure.

3.8L (VIN C) ENGINE

▶ See Figures 38 thru 53

1. Properly relieve the fuel system pressure, as outlined in Section 5.
2. If not already done, disconnect the negative battery cable.
3. Disconnect the fuel lines from the fuel rail.
4. Place a clean drain pan under the radiator, open the draincock and drain the cooling system.
5. Remove the serpentine drive belt, alternator and bracket.
6. Disconnect the coolant bypass hose, the heater pipe and the upper radiator hose from the intake manifold.
7. Remove the power steering pump and braces, and move them aside; do not disconnect the pressure lines.
8. Remove the vacuum hoses and tag and detach the electrical connectors from the intake manifold.
9. Remove the EGR pipe, EGR valve and adapter from the throttle body.
10. Remove the throttle body coolant pipe, the throttle body and the throttle body adapter.
11. Disconnect the rear spark plug wires. Unfasten the intake manifold-to-engine bolts and remove the manifold.
12. Remove and discard the manifold gaskets and seals, then clean the gasket mating surfaces.

Fig. 38 Unfasten the 3 mounting bolts, then remove the alternator bracket (with the ignition coil attached)

Fig. 39 Disconnect the coolant bypass hose from the intake manifold

Fig. 40 Detach the heater pipe from the intake manifold

Fig. 41 Unfasten the power steering pump brace retaining bolts

Fig. 42 Remove the power steering pump brace

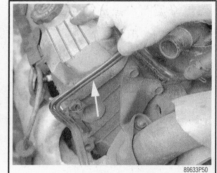
Fig. 43 The EGR pipe is located on the side of the front valve cover (see arrow)

Fig. 44 Unfasten the hose clamp, then disconnect the EGR pipe

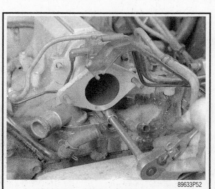
Fig. 45 Unfasten the throttle body adapter retaining bolts . . .

Fig. 46 . . . then remove the throttle body adapter

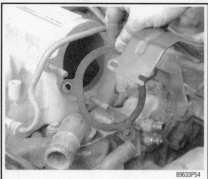

Fig. 47 Remove the throttle body adapter gasket

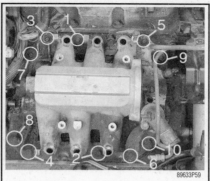

Fig. 48 Overview of the intake manifold and retaining bolt tightening sequence

Fig. 49 Remove the intake manifold retaining bolts . . .

Fig. 50 . . . then lift the manifold up and remove it from the vehicle

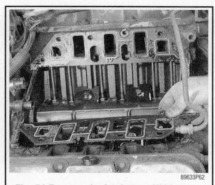

Fig. 51 Remove the intake manifold gaskets . . .

Fig. 52 . . . and the seals from each end of the manifold

Fig. 53 A piece of Scotchbrite®, or similar non-abrasive scouring pad, works well to clean the manifold gasket mating surfaces

3. Tag and disconnect the spark plug wires on the right side of the engine and set aside.

4. Remove the fuel rail from the vehicle.

5. Remove the exhaust crossover heat shield.

6. Unfasten the cable bracket-to-cylinder head mounting bolt.

7. Remove the power steering pump bracket.

8. Loosen the alternator mounting bolts, then position the alternator aside for clearance.

9. Remove the alternator bracket.

10. Disconnect the heater pipes and bypass hose.

11. Unfasten the retaining bolts, then remove the intake manifold from the vehicle. Remove and discard the gasket and thoroughly clean the gasket mating surfaces and intake manifold bolts and bolt holes.

To install:

13. Install new gaskets and the proper sealant on the ends of the manifold seals.

14. Install the intake manifold and tighten the mounting bolts, in sequence, twice to 88 inch lbs. (10 Nm).

15. Connect the rear spark plug wires.

16. Install the throttle body adapter, throttle body and throttle body coolant pipe. Tighten the bolts to 20 ft. lbs. (27 Nm).

17. The remainder of installation is the reverse of the removal procedure.

1991–97 Vehicles

EXCEPT 1995–97 VIN 1 AND K ENGINES

▶ See Figures 54 and 55

1. Remove the plastic engine cover and air intake duct.

2. Properly relieve the fuel system pressure, as outlined in Section 5 of this manual. If not already done, disconnect the negative battery cable.

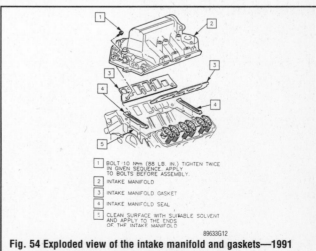

1 BOLT 10 Nm (88 LB. IN.) TIGHTEN TWICE IN GIVEN SEQUENCE. APPLY TO BOLTS BEFORE ASSEMBLY.
2 INTAKE MANIFOLD
3 INTAKE MANIFOLD GASKET
4 INTAKE MANIFOLD SEAL
5 CLEAN SURFACE WITH SUITABLE SOLVENT AND APPLY TO THE ENDS OF THE INTAKE MANIFOLD

Fig. 54 Exploded view of the intake manifold and gaskets—1991 3.8L (VIN C) engine shown, later models similar

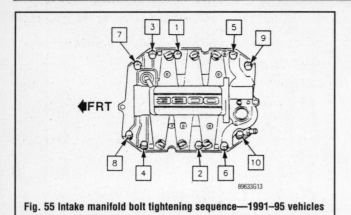

Fig. 55 Intake manifold bolt tightening sequence—1991–95 vehicles

To install:

12. Apply a suitable sealer to the ends of the manifold seals.

13. Position a new intake manifold gasket, then place the intake manifold over it. Apply a suitable threadlocking sealer to the retaining bolts, then install and tighten them twice, in the sequence shown in the accompanying figure, to 88 inch lbs. (10 Nm).

14. The remainder of installation is the reverse of the removal procedure.

1995–97 VIN K ENGINE

♦ See Figures 55, 56 and 57

➡On these engines, the upper and lower intake manifolds must be removed separately.

1. Properly relieve the fuel system pressure, as outlined in Section 5 of this manual.

2. Disconnect the negative battery cable.

3. Drain the cooling system into a suitable container.

4. Remove the fuel injector sight shield and air intake duct.

5. Tag and disconnect the spark plug wires on the right side of the engine and position aside.

6. Remove the manifold vacuum source.

7. Remove the fuel rail.

8. Remove the EGR heat shield.

9. Unfasten the cable bracket-to-cylinder head mounting bolt.

10. Disconnect the throttle cable.

11. Remove the throttle body support bracket.

12. Unfasten the upper intake manifold bolts, then remove the upper manifold.

➡This engine has two bolts which are hidden beneath the upper intake. These bolts are located in the right front and left rear corners of the lower intake manifold. This is why it is necessary to remove the upper before servicing the lower manifold.

13. Disconnect the upper radiator hose.

14. Remove the alternator, as outlined in Section 2 of this manual.

15. Remove the drive belt tensioner.

16. Remove the EGR valve outlet pipe.

17. Unfasten the intake manifold bolt, then remove the manifold from the vehicle. Remove and discard the gaskets. Thoroughly clean the gasket mating surfaces, intake manifold bolts and bolt holes.

To install:

18. Position a new gasket, then place the lower intake manifold over it. Apply a suitable threadlocking compound to the bolts, then install them. For 1995 vehicles, tighten the bolts twice, to 89 inch lbs. (10 Nm), in the sequence shown in the accompanying figure. For 1996–97 vehicles, tighten the bolts to 11 ft. lbs. (15 Nm), in the sequence shown in the accompanying figure.

19. The remainder of installation is the reverse of the removal procedure. During installation be sure to tighten the upper intake manifold-to-lower manifold retaining bolts to 89 inch lbs. (10 Nm).

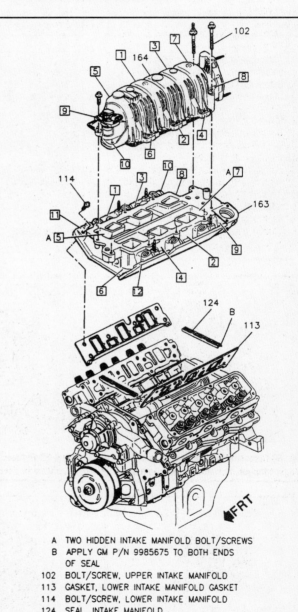

A TWO HIDDEN INTAKE MANIFOLD BOLT/SCREWS
B APPLY GM P/N 9985675 TO BOTH ENDS OF SEAL
102 BOLT/SCREW, UPPER INTAKE MANIFOLD
113 GASKET, LOWER INTAKE MANIFOLD GASKET
114 BOLT/SCREW, LOWER INTAKE MANIFOLD
124 SEAL, INTAKE MANIFOLD
163 MANIFOLD, LOWER INTAKE
164 MANIFOLD, UPPER INTAKE
☐ NUMBER IN BOX IDENTIFY TIGHTENING SEQUENCE

Fig. 57 Intake manifold bolt tightening sequence—1996–97 3.8L (VIN K) engine; VIN 1 similar

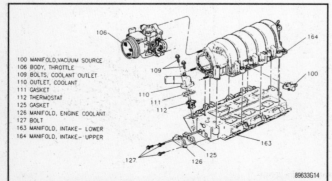

100 MANIFOLD, VACUUM SOURCE
106 BODY, THROTTLE
109 BOLTS, COOLANT OUTLET
110 OUTLET, COOLANT
111 GASKET
112 THERMOSTAT
125 GASKET
126 MANIFOLD, ENGINE COOLANT
127 BOLT
163 MANIFOLD, INTAKE – LOWER
164 MANIFOLD, INTAKE – UPPER

Fig. 56 Exploded view of the upper and lower intake manifold and gaskets—1995 3.8L (VIN K) engine

1995 VIN 1 ENGINE

▶ See Figure 55

1. Properly relieve the fuel system pressure, as outlined in Section 5 of this manual.
2. Disconnect the negative battery cable.
3. Drain the cooling system into a suitable container.
4. Remove the fuel injector sight shield and air intake duct.
5. Tag and disconnect the spark plug wires from the right side of the engine and position it aside.
6. Remove the manifold vacuum source.
7. Disconnect the fuel feed and return lines.
8. Disconnect the upper radiator hose and bypass hose.
9. Tag and detach the electrical connectors from the following components:
   a. EGR valve.
   b. Throttle Position (TP) sensor.
   c. Idle Air Control (IAC) solenoid.
   d. Fuel injectors.
   e. Manifold Air Pressure (MAP) solenoid.
10. Disconnect the EGR outlet pipe.
11. Detach the throttle and cruise cables.
12. Unbolt the throttle bracket with the power steering reservoir and position aside.
13. Remove the inner accessory drive belt.
14. Disconnect the heater hose pipe from the intake manifold.
15. Remove the tensioner bracket-to-supercharger retaining stud using the standard double nut procedure.
16. Unfasten the intake manifold bolts, then remove the intake manifold from the vehicle. If equipped, remove and discard the intake manifold gasket. Thoroughly clean the gasket mating surfaces, bolts and bolt holes.

To install:

17. Apply a suitable sealer to the ends of the manifold seals.
18. Position a new intake manifold gasket. Apply a suitable threadlocking compound to the threads of the intake manifold bolts.
19. Install the intake manifold, then secure with the mounting bolts. Tighten the bolts to 11 ft. lbs. (15 Nm).
20. The remainder of installation is the reverse of the removal procedure.

1996–97 3.8L (VIN 1) ENGINE

▶ See Figure 57

1. Disconnect the negative battery cable.
2. Raise and safely support the vehicle.
3. Remove the front splash shield.
4. Drain the engine coolant into a suitable container. Don't forget to close the radiator draincock.
5. Install the front splash shield.
6. Carefully lower the vehicle.
7. Remove the supercharger, as outlined in this section.
8. Remove the thermostat housing.
9. Disconnect the EGR tube from the intake manifold.
10. Detach the electrical connection from the temperature sensor.
11. Unfasten the retainers, then remove the intake manifold from the vehicle. If equipped, remove and discard the intake manifold gasket. Thoroughly clean the gasket mating surfaces, bolts and bolt holes.

To install:

12. Position a new gasket or seal(s), as applicable, then install the intake manifold. Install a suitable threadlocking compound to the intake manifold bolts. Install the bolts and tighten to 11 ft. lbs. (15 Nm), in the sequence shown in the accompanying figure.
13. The remainder of installation is the reverse of the removal procedure.

1998–99 Vehicles

▶ See Figures 58 thru 65

1. Properly relieve the fuel system pressure, as outlined in Section 5 of this manual.
2. If not done already, disconnect the negative battery cable.
3. Drain the engine cooling system into a suitable container.

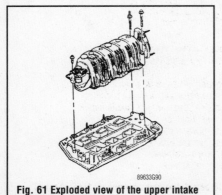

Fig. 58 Disconnect the right side spark plugs, then position the harness aside

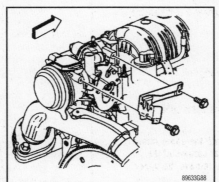

Fig. 59 Remove the bolts, then remove the accelerator control cable bracket

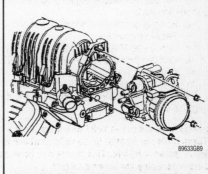

Fig. 60 Exploded view of the throttle body mounting

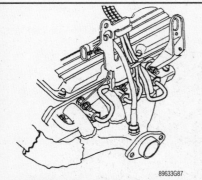

Fig. 61 Exploded view of the upper intake manifold mounting

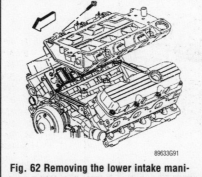

Fig. 62 Removing the lower intake manifold and gasket—VIN K engine shown, VIN 1 similar

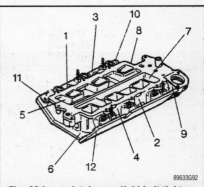

Fig. 63 Lower intake manifold bolt tightening sequence—VIN K engine

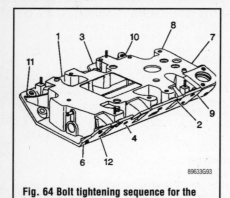

Fig. 64 Bolt tightening sequence for the lower intake manifold—VIN 1 engine

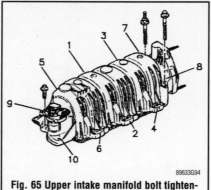

Fig. 65 Upper intake manifold bolt tightening sequence

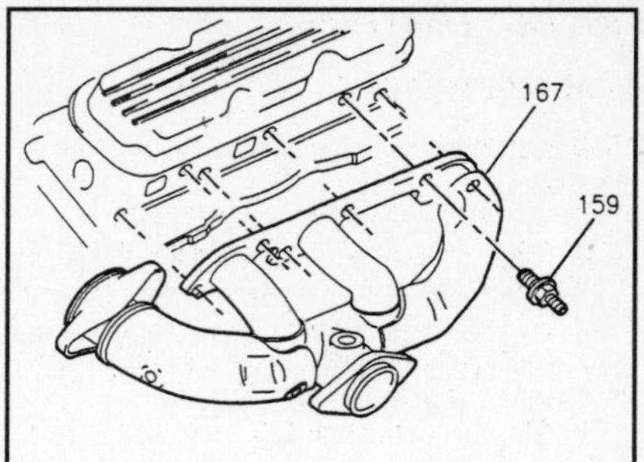

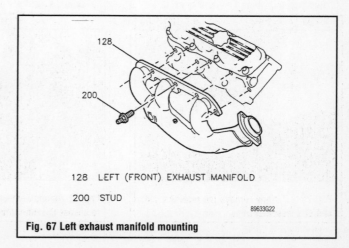

159 STUD
167 RIGHT (REAR) EXHAUST MANIFOLD

Fig. 66 Right exhaust manifold mounting

4. Tag and disconnect the right side spark plug wires, then position them aside.

5. Detach the spark plug wires from the fuel injector rail.

6. Unfasten the fuel lines from the fuel rail. Remove the mounting nuts, then remove the fuel rail from the engine.

7. Remove the accelerator control cable bracket bolts, then remove the cable bracket from the manifold.

8. Unfasten the throttle body nuts, then remove the throttle body. Remove the throttle body gasket.

➡The two bolts which hold the lower intake manifold to the cylinder head are only accessible after the upper intake manifold is removed. The bolts are found in the right front and left rear corners of the lower intake manifold. You must remove the upper intake manifold to service the lower manifold.

9. Unfasten the upper intake manifold bolts and stud, then remove the upper manifold.

10. Remove the EGR outlet pipe from the intake manifold.

11. Unfasten the lower intake manifold bolts, then remove the lower manifold and gasket.

12. Thoroughly clean the gasket mating surfaces, bolt and bolt holes.

To install:

13. Position the lower manifold gasket. Install the lower intake manifold.

14. Apply a suitable threadlocking compound to the lower manifold bolts. Install the bolts, including the 2 hidden bolts, and tighten to 11 ft. lbs. (15 Nm), in the sequence shown in the accompanying figures.

15. Install the EGR outlet pipe to the intake manifold and secure with the mounting bolt. Tighten the bolt to 21 ft. lbs. (29 Nm).

16. Position a new upper intake manifold gasket, then place the upper manifold on the gasket.

17. Install the upper intake manifold bolts, then tighten the bolts to 89 inch lbs. (10 Nm), in the sequence shown in the accompanying figure.

18. The remainder of installation is the reverse of the removal procedure. During installation, please heed the following tightening values:

• Throttle body retaining nuts—89 inch lbs. (10 Nm)
• Engine wiring harness shield bracket retaining bolt and nut—89 inch lbs. (89 Nm)
• Accelerator control cable bracket retaining bolts—12 ft. lbs. (16 Nm)
• Fuel rail nuts—89 inch lbs. (10 Nm)

Exhaust Manifold

REMOVAL & INSTALLATION

3.0L and 3.8L (VIN 3 and B) engines

▸ **See Figures 66 and 67**

1. Disconnect the negative battery cable.

➡Failure to disconnect the intermediate shaft from the rack and pinion stub shaft may result in damage to the steering gear and/or intermediate shaft.

2. Remove the pinch bolt from the intermediate shaft and separate the intermediate shaft from the stub shaft.

3. Raise and safely support the vehicle.

4. Remove the 2 bolts attaching the exhaust pipe to the manifold.

5. Carefully lower the vehicle.

6. Remove the upper engine support strut.

7. Place a jack under the front crossmember of the cradle and raise the jack until it starts to raise the vehicle.

8. Remove the 2 front body mount bolts.

9. With the cushions removed, thread the body mount bolts and retainers a minimum of 3 turns into the cage nuts.

10. Release the jack slowly.

➡To avoid damage, do not lower the cradle without it being restrained.

11. Remove the power steering pump and bracket from the cylinder head and exhaust manifold.

12. Disconnect the oxygen sensor.

13. If removing the left side exhaust manifold, remove the upper engine support strut.

14. Remove the 2 nuts retaining the crossover pipe to the exhaust manifold.

15. Remove the 6 bolts attaching the manifold to the cylinder head.

16. Remove the exhaust manifold. Carefully, clean the gasket sealing surfaces of old gasket material.

To install:

17. Install the exhaust manifold and the manifold-to-cylinder head bolts. Tighten to 37 ft. lbs. (50 Nm).

18. If the left side exhaust manifold was removed, install the crossover pipe to the manifold.

19. If the right side exhaust manifold was removed, install the upper engine support strut.

20. The remainder of installation is the reverse of the removal procedure.

21. Connect the negative battery cable. Start the engine and check for leaks.

128 LEFT (FRONT) EXHAUST MANIFOLD
200 STUD

Fig. 67 Left exhaust manifold mounting

3.8L (VIN C and L) Engine

RIGHT SIDE (REAR)

♦ See Figure 66

1. Disconnect the negative battery cable.
2. If necessary, disconnect the Mass Air Flow (MAF) sensor, air intake duct, the crankcase ventilation pipe and the IAC connector from the throttle body.
3. Label and disconnect the wires from the spark plugs. Disconnect the oxygen sensor lead.
4. For vehicles through 1992, remove the EGR pipe.
5. Unfasten the two bolts attaching the right exhaust manifold to the left exhaust manifold.
6. Remove the plastic vacuum tank mounted on the cowl.
7. Raise and safely support the vehicle.
8. Remove the catalytic converter heat shield and pipe hanger.
9. Unfasten the front exhaust pipe-to-exhaust manifold attaching nuts.
10. Separate the front exhaust pipe from the exhaust manifold.
11. Carefully lower the vehicle.
12. Remove the engine lift bracket.
13. Unfasten the exhaust manifold nuts/studs, then remove the manifold from the vehicle. If equipped, remove and discard the gasket. Thoroughly clean the gasket mating surfaces.

To install:

14. Install the exhaust manifold and secure with the nuts/studs previously removed. Tighten the exhaust manifold retainers to 38–41 ft. lbs. (51–56 Nm).
15. Install the engine lift bracket.
16. Raise and safely support the vehicle.
17. Attach the front exhaust pipe to the exhaust manifold and secure with the retaining nuts.
18. Install the catalytic converter heat shield and pipe hanger.
19. Carefully lower the vehicle.

20. The remainder of installation is the reverse of the removal procedure. During installation, please tighten the right exhaust manifold-to-left exhaust manifold bolts—15 ft. lbs. (20 Nm)
21. Connect the negative battery cable. Start the engine and check for leaks.

LEFT SIDE (FRONT)

♦ See Figures 67 thru 77

1. Disconnect the negative battery cable.
2. If necessary, remove the Mass Air Flow (MAF) sensor, air intake duct and crankcase ventilation pipe.
3. Remove any necessary brackets.
4. Remove the exhaust crossover pipe-to-exhaust manifold bolts, attaching the left and right exhaust manifolds.
5. Label and disconnect the spark plug wires.
6. Remove the exhaust manifold-to-cylinder head bolts/studs and the manifold. It may be necessary for additional clearance, to remove the oil dipstick tube, before removing the manifold..
7. Clean the gasket mounting surfaces and install a new gasket.

To install:

8. Install the exhaust manifold and tighten the manifold mounting bolts/studs to 37–41 ft. lbs. (50–56 Nm).
9. If removed, install the oil dipstick tube.
10. The remainder of installation is the reverse of the removal procedure.
11. Connect the negative battery cable. Start the engine and check for leaks.

1992 3.8L (VIN 1) Engine

RIGHT SIDE

♦ See Figure 66

1. Disconnect the negative battery cable.
2. If necessary, disconnect the Mass Air Flow (MAF) sensor, air intake duct, the crankcase ventilation pipe and the IAC connector from the throttle body.

Fig. 68 The exhaust manifold is mounted on studs and secured with retaining nuts

Fig. 69 Remove any brackets that will interfere with exhaust manifold removal

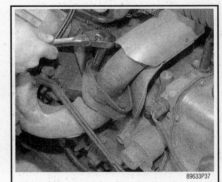

Fig. 70 Remove the exhaust crossover pipe-to-manifold retainers . . .

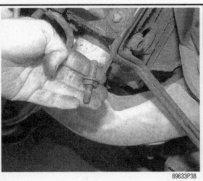

Fig. 71 . . . then remove the retaining nut and stud assemblies

Fig. 72 You may have to lift the collar up to access the other crossover pipe retainer

Fig. 73 Once the collar is moved aside, you can remove the other nut and stud retainer

Fig. 74 It may be necessary to remove the oil dipstick tube. Do so by pulling it straight out of the block

Fig. 75 After all of the retainers are removed, you can remove the exhaust manifold from the engine

Fig. 76 You can use a piece of Scotchbrite® or equivalent non-abrasive scouring pad to clean the gasket mating surfaces

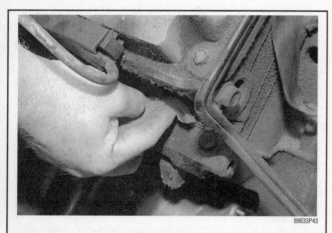

Fig. 77 Make sure to also clean the engine block mating surfaces

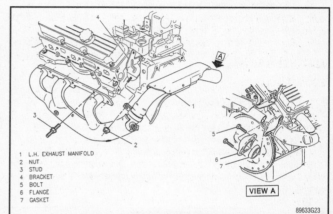

1 L.H. EXHAUST MANIFOLD
2 NUT
3 STUD
4 BRACKET
5 BOLT
6 FLANGE
7 GASKET

Fig. 78 Exploded view of the left side exhaust manifold on a 1992 supercharged engine

3. Label and disconnect the wires from the spark plugs. Disconnect the oxygen sensor lead.

4. If equipped, disconnect the heater inlet pipe from the manifold stud. If equipped, remove the transaxle oil indicator tube.

5. Remove the exhaust crossover pipe-to-exhaust manifold bolts and the pipe. Disconnect the alternator bracket, if necessary.

6. Raise and support the vehicle safely. Remove the exhaust pipe-to-manifold bolts, the exhaust manifold-to-cylinder head bolts and the manifold.

7. Remove the EGR pipe from the exhaust manifold.

8. Clean the gasket mounting surfaces.

To install:

9. Replace the EGR pipe to the exhaust manifold.

10. Install the exhaust manifold, using a new gasket. Tighten the mounting studs to 37–41 ft. lbs. (50–56 Nm).

11. The remainder of installation is the reverse of the removal procedure.

12. Connect the negative battery cable. Start the engine and check for leaks.

LEFT SIDE

▶ See Figure 78

1. Disconnect the negative battery cable.
2. Remove the 2 flange bolts and the manifold-to-bracket nut.
3. Remove the manifold to engine studs and remove the manifold.

To install:

4. Clean the gasket mounting surfaces and install a new gasket.
5. Install the exhaust manifold and tighten the manifold mounting studs to 37–41 ft. lbs. (50–56 Nm).
6. Install the manifold to bracket nut and the flange gasket. Install the flange bolts.
7. Connect the negative battery cable.
8. Start the engine and check for exhaust leaks.

1993–99 3.8L (VIN 1 and K) Engines

RIGHT SIDE (REAR)

▶ See Figures 79 and 80

1. Disconnect the negative battery cable.
2. Tag and disconnect the spark plug wires from the spark plugs.
3. If equipped with a supercharged engine, remove the throttle cable bracket. Remove the crossover pipe heat shield.
4. Remove the transaxle oil level indicator and indicator tube.
5. Detach the oxygen sensor lead.
6. Unfasten the two bolts attaching the right exhaust manifold to the crossover pipe or left exhaust manifold, as applicable.
7. Remove the vacuum reservoir, mounted on the cowl.
8. Raise and safely support the vehicle.
9. Remove the front exhaust pipe-to-exhaust manifold attaching nuts.
10. Separate the front exhaust pipe from the exhaust manifold.
11. Carefully lower the vehicle.
12. Remove the engine lift bracket.
13. Unfasten the exhaust manifold studs, then remove the manifold from the vehicle.
14. Remove and discard the gasket, then thoroughly clean the gasket mating surfaces.

To install:

15. Install a new gasket, then position the exhaust manifold. Secure with the retaining studs and tighten to 38 ft. lbs. (51 Nm) for 1993–95 vehicles or to 22 ft. lbs. (30 Nm) for 1996–99 vehicles.
16. Install the engine lift bracket.
17. Raise and safely support the vehicle.
18. Attach the front exhaust pipe to the manifold.

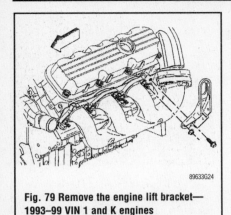

Fig. 79 Remove the engine lift bracket— 1993–99 VIN 1 and K engines

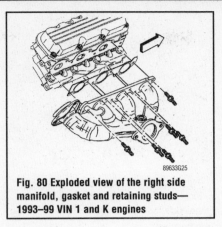

Fig. 80 Exploded view of the right side manifold, gasket and retaining studs— 1993–99 VIN 1 and K engines

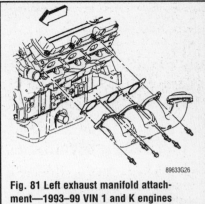

Fig. 81 Left exhaust manifold attachment—1993–99 VIN 1 and K engines

19. The remainder of installation is the reverse of the removal procedure. During installation, be sure to tighten the right exhaust manifold-to-left manifold or crossover pipe bolts to 15 ft. lbs. (20 Nm).

20. Connect the negative battery cable. Start the engine and check for leaks.

LEFT SIDE (FRONT)

▶ See Figure 81

1. Disconnect the negative battery cable.
2. Unfasten the two bolts attaching the left exhaust manifold to the crossover pipe or right exhaust manifold, as applicable.
3. Tag and disconnect the spark plug wires from the spark plugs.
4. Remove the oil level indicator and tube.
5. Remove the manifold studs and bolts, then remove the manifold from the vehicle. Remove and discard the gasket and thoroughly clean the gasket mating surfaces.

To install:

6. Install a new gasket, then position the exhaust manifold.
7. The remainder of installation is the reverse of the removal procedure. During installation, be sure to heed the following tightening specifications:

• Right exhaust manifold-to-left manifold or crossover pipe bolts—15 ft. lbs. (20 Nm)

• Manifold studs and bolts—38 ft. lbs. (51 Nm) for 1993–95 vehicles or 22 ft. lbs. (30 Nm) for 1996–99 vehicles

8. Connect the negative battery cable.

Supercharger

REMOVAL & INSTALLATION

3.8L (VIN 1) Engine

1992–95 Vehicles

▶ See Figure 82

1. Properly relieve the fuel system pressure, as outlined in Section 5 of this manual.
2. Disconnect the negative battery cable.
3. Remove the accessory drive belt from the supercharger pulley.
4. Remove the fuel injector sight shield.
5. Disconnect the fuel pipes from the fuel rail.
6. Tag and disconnect any necessary vacuum hoses.
7. Detach the electrical connectors from the fuel injectors.
8. Remove the electrical harness shield and electrical harness from the front of the supercharger.
9. Remove the fuel rail mounting bolts. Remove the fuel rail with the injectors intact.
10. Tag and detach the electrical connectors at the Idle Air Control (IAC) valve, Throttle Position (TP) sensor, Mass Air Flow (MAF) sensor, EGR, boost control solenoid and engine coolant temperature sensor. Lay the wiring harness aside.
11. Remove the air intake duct from the throttle body, and remove the EGR pipe from the supercharger.

12. Disconnect the throttle and the cruise control cables.
13. Remove the boost pressure manifold and vacuum block.
14. Remove the cable bracket.
15. Remove the tensioner bracket-to-supercharger mounting stud. The stud must be removed, or the supercharger cannot be lifted high enough to clear the supercharger from the lower intake locator pins. This could cause parts damage. To remove the stud, use a stud removal tool or jam nut procedure. The jam nut procedure consists of the following:

a. Tighten two 8mm nuts together on the stud.

b. Remove the stud by placing the wrench on the inner nut, then turn counterclockwise.

16. Remove the throttle body from the supercharger.
17. Unfasten the supercharger-to-intake manifold bolts, then remove the supercharger from the intake manifold. Remove the supercharger gasket and coolant passage O-rings. Clean the intake manifold and supercharger mating surfaces. Check that the locator pins are in the proper positions, as shown in the accompanying figure.

To install:

18. Before installing the supercharger, remove the tensioner bracket-to-supercharger stud.
19. Replace the coolant passage O-rings and the supercharger gasket. Do NOT use any sealer on the gasket!
20. Place the supercharger in position, then install the bolts finger-tight.
21. Install the tensioner bracket-to-supercharger stud. Tighten the bolts and stud as follows:

a. 1992–93 vehicles: Tighten to 19 ft. lbs. (26 Nm).

b. 1994–95 vehicles: Tighten the stud to 88 inch lbs. (10 Nm) and the bolts to 19 ft. lbs. (26 Nm).

22. If equipped, install the tensioner bracket nut and tighten to 37 ft. lbs. (50 Nm).

23. The remainder of installation is the reverse of the removal procedure. During installation, be sure to heed the following tightening specifications:

• Throttle body retainers—11 ft. lbs. (15 Nm)

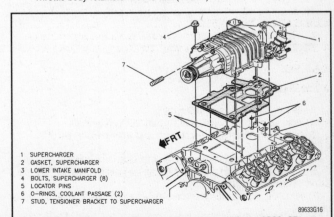

1 SUPERCHARGER
2 GASKET, SUPERCHARGER
3 LOWER INTAKE MANIFOLD
4 BOLTS, SUPERCHARGER (8)
5 LOCATOR PINS
6 O-RINGS, COOLANT PASSAGE (2)
7 STUD, TENSIONER BRACKET TO SUPERCHARGER

Fig. 82 Exploded view of the supercharger mounting—1992–95 vehicles

- Vacuum block retainers—62 inch lbs. (7 Nm)
- Fuel rail retaining bolts—15 ft. lbs. (24 Nm).

24. Connect the negative battery cable. Start the engine and check for leaks and/or noise.

1996–99 Vehicles

♦ **See Figures 83, 84, 85 and 86**

1. Properly relieve the fuel system pressure, as outlined in Section 5 of this manual.
2. If not already done, disconnect the negative battery cable.
3. Remove the engine cover.
4. Remove the air duct.
5. Remove the supercharger belt, as outlined in Section 1 of this manual.
6. Tag and disconnect the right side spark plug wires from the ignition module, then position them aside.
7. Remove the alternator brace (with the purge solenoid, if equipped).
8. For 1997–99 vehicles, disconnect the EGR wiring harness and remove the EGR wiring harness shield.
9. Detach the electrical connectors from the fuel injectors.
10. Remove the MAP sensor bracket.
11. Unfasten the fuel rail mounting bolts, then remove the fuel rail and the injectors, as an assembly.
12. Remove the boost control solenoid, as follows:
    a. Disconnect the boost source and signal hose from the solenoid.
    b. Detach the electrical connector.
    c. Unfasten the retaining nut, then remove the boost control solenoid.
13. For 1997–99 vehicles, remove the accelerator control cable bracket with the cables.
14. Unfasten the throttle body nuts and remove the throttle body.

➡ **Make sure to make note of the supercharger retainer positions for installation.**

15. Remove the supercharger retainers (bolts, studs and spacers), then remove the supercharger from the vehicle. Remove and discard the gasket, then thoroughly clean the gasket mating surfaces.

To install:

16. Install a new supercharger-to-intake gasket. Do NOT use any sealer on the gasket.
17. Position the supercharger over the gasket, then secure using the retaining bolts. Tighten the bolts to 17 ft. lbs. (23 Nm).
18. Install the MAP sensor bracket. Tighten the retaining bolts to 22 ft. lbs. (30 Nm).
19. Position the throttle body to the supercharger and install the retaining nuts. Tighten to 89 inch lbs. (10 Nm).
20. For 1997–99 vehicles, install the accelerator control cable bracket with the cables attached. Secure with the retaining bolts/screws.
21. Install the boost control solenoid, as follows:
    a. Install the boost control solenoid to the bypass actuator bracket.
    b. Install the retaining nut and tighten to 72 inch lbs. (8 Nm).
    c. Attach the electrical connector.
    d. Connect the boost vacuum source and signal hose.
22. The remainder of installation is the reverse of the removal procedure. During installation, be sure to heed the following tightening specifications:

- Fuel rail retaining nuts/bolts—89 inch lbs. (10 Nm)
- Fuel rail retaining stud—18 ft. lbs. (25 Nm)
- Alternator brace retainers—22 ft. lbs. (30 Nm)
- EGR wiring harness shield bolt/screw—89 inch lbs. (10 Nm)
- EGR wiring harness shield nut—89 inch lbs. (10 Nm)

23. Start the engine and check for leaks and proper operation.

Radiator

REMOVAL & INSTALLATION

♦ **See Figures 87 thru 98**

1. Disconnect the negative battery cable.
2. Drain the engine coolant into a suitable container.
3. If necessary for access, remove the air cleaner, mounting stud and duct.
4. Remove the upper fan mounting bolts.
5. Unfasten the retainers, then remove the upper radiator panel.

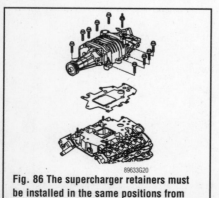

Fig. 83 Remove the boost control solenoid

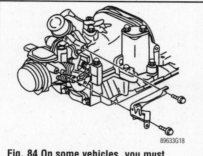

Fig. 84 On some vehicles, you must remove the accelerator control cable bracket, along with the cables

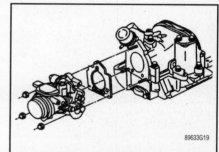

Fig. 85 Remove the throttle body-to-supercharger retainers, then remove the throttle body

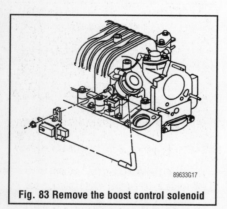

Fig. 86 The supercharger retainers must be installed in the same positions from which they were removed

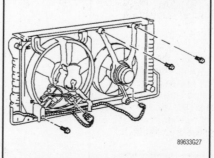

Fig. 87 On some vehicles, such as this 1998 model, remove the upper fan mounting bolts

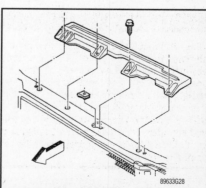

Fig. 88 Unfasten the upper radiator panel fasteners, then remove the panel

Fig. 89 Unfasten the hose clamp and disconnect the coolant reservoir hose from the radiator neck

Fig. 90 Disconnect the remaining hoses from the radiator

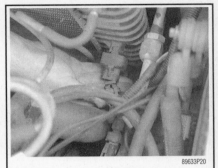

Fig. 91 On some vehicles, you must unplug the coolant sending unit electrical connector

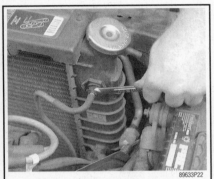

Fig. 92 Use a flare nut wrench to disconnect the upper transaxle oil cooler line

Fig. 93 Location of the lower transaxle oil cooler line fitting

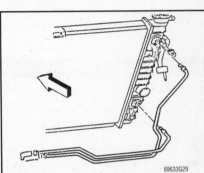

Fig. 94 If your vehicle has an automatic transaxle, disconnect the oil cooler lines from the radiator side tank

Fig. 95 Unfasten the 4 radiator upper panel retaining bolts . . .

Fig. 96 . . . then remove the upper radiator panel

Fig. 97 When removing the radiator from the vehicle, be careful not to damage the cooling fins

⁑ CAUTION

When draining the coolant, keep in mind that cats and dogs are attracted by ethylene glycol antifreeze, and are quite likely to drink any that is left in an uncovered container or in puddles on the ground. This will prove fatal in sufficient quantity. Always drain the coolant into a sealable container. Coolant should be reused unless it is contaminated or several years old. To avoid being burned, do NOT remove the thermostat housing cap while the engine is at normal operating temperature. The cooling system will release scalding fluid and steam under pressure if the cap is removed while the engine is still hot.

6. Remove the cooling fans, as outlined later in this section.
7. Disconnect the coolant reservoir hose from the radiator neck and the radiator hoses from the radiator.

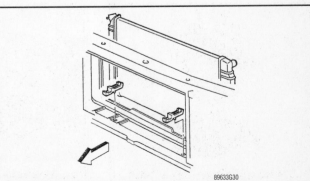

Fig. 98 Lift the radiator from the lower pads and remove it from the vehicle

8. If equipped, unplug the cooling sending unit electrical connector.

9. If equipped, disconnect the engine oil cooler lines from the radiator.

10. If equipped with an automatic transaxle, disconnect the transaxle cooler lines from the radiator side tank.

11. Unfasten the upper radiator panel retaining bolts, then remove the panel.

12. Lift the radiator up and remove from the vehicle.

To install:

13. Install the radiator in the vehicle. Make sure the bottom of the radiator is properly seated in the lower pads.

14. If equipped, install the radiator-to-radiator support attaching clamp and bolts, then tighten to 89 inch lbs. (10 Nm).

15. If equipped with an automatic transaxle, connect the transaxle cooler lines. Use a flare nut wrench to tighten the lines to 20 ft. lbs. (27 Nm).

16. Install the upper radiator panel. Tighten the retainers to 89 inch lbs. (10 Nm).

17. The remainder of installation is the reverse of the removal procedure. During installation, be sure to tighten the cooling fan attaching bolts to 89 inch lbs. (10 Nm).

18. Fill cooling system and check for leaks. Start the engine and allow to come to normal operating temperature. Recheck for leaks and refill as necessary.

Electric Cooling Fan(s)

TESTING

1. If the fan doesn't operate, disconnect the fan and apply voltage across the fan terminals. If the fan still doesn't run, it needs a new motor.

2. If the fan runs, with the jumpers but not when connected, the fan relay is the most likely problem.

3. If fan operates but a high current draw is suspected continue with the following ammeter testing.

4. Disconnect the electrical connector from the cooling fan.

5. Using an ammeter and jumper wires, connect the fan motor in series with the battery and ammeter. With the fan running, check the ammeter reading, it should be 3.4–5.0 amps; if not, replace the motor.

6. Reconnect the fan's electrical connector. Start the engine, allow it to reach temperatures above 194°F and confirm that the fan runs. If the fan doesn't run, replace the temperature switch.

REMOVAL & INSTALLATION

▶ **See Figures 99 thru 109**

1. Disconnect the negative battery cable.

❊❊ CAUTION

Always keep yours hands, clothing and tools away from the fan assembly. The electric cooling fan can start even when the engine is not running, causing personal injury.

2. Raise and safely support the vehicle.

3. Remove the retainers, then remove the splash shield.

4. Detach the fan wiring harness from the motor and fan frame.

5. Remove lower fan mounting bolts.

6. Carefully lower the vehicle.

7. If necessary, remove the fan guard and the hose support.

8. Unfasten the retaining bolts, then remove the fan assembly from the radiator support.

9. If necessary to disassemble the fan, remove the retainer(s), then separate the fan blade from the electric fan motor.

❊❊ CAUTION

In order to prevent personal injury or damage to the vehicle, you should always replace a bent, cracked or damaged fan blade or housing.

Fig. 99 Be very careful when working around the fans, as they can start running even if the engine is off!

Fig. 100 Remove the retaining bolts/screws, then remove the splash shield

Fig. 101 Remove the fan electrical connector retaining clip . . .

Fig. 102 . . . then unplug the fan electrical connector

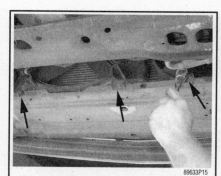

Fig. 103 Unfasten the lower fan mounting bolts. On this vehicle, there are three bolts (see arrows)

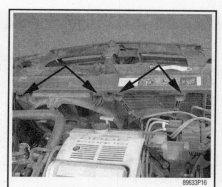

Fig. 104 Remove the 4 fan-to-radiator upper panel mounting bolts

Fig. 105 Remove the left and . . .

Fig. 106 . . . right side fan assemblies from the vehicle

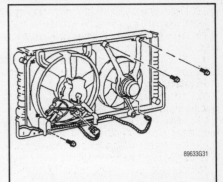

Fig. 107 Detach the fan connector and unfasten the retaining bolts

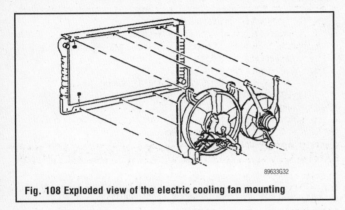

Fig. 108 Exploded view of the electric cooling fan mounting

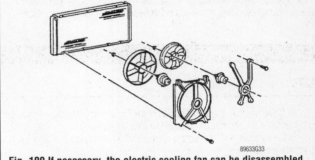

Fig. 109 If necessary, the electric cooling fan can be disassembled after removal

To install:

10. If removed, install the fan blade to the electric fan motor and secure with the retainer(s).

11. Install the fan assembly to the radiator support. Tighten the retaining bolts to 89 inch lbs. (10 Nm).

12. If removed, install the fan guard and the hose support.

13. Attach the fan wiring harness to the motor and fan frame.

14. Connect the negative battery cable.

Water Pump

REMOVAL & INSTALLATION

✷✷ CAUTION

When draining the coolant, keep in mind that cats and dogs are attracted by ethylene glycol antifreeze, and are quite likely to drink any that is left in an uncovered container or in puddles on the ground. This will prove fatal in sufficient quantity. Always drain the coolant into a sealable container. Coolant should be reused unless it is contaminated or several years old.

1986–95 Vehicles

◗ **See Figures 110 thru 123**

EXCEPT 1995 VIN 1 ENGINE

1. Disconnect the negative battery cable.
2. Drain cooling system into a suitable container.
3. Remove the serpentine drive belt, as outlined in Section 1 of this manual.

➡On some engines, removing the alternator provides better clearance for removing the water pump. For alternator removal and installation procedures, please refer to Section 2 of this manual.

4. Unfasten the water pump pulley bolts, (long bolt removed through access hole provided in the body side rail), then remove the pulley.

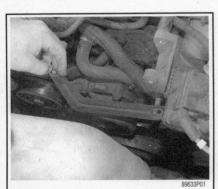

Fig. 110 After removing the alternator, remove the brace

Fig. 111 Pull the water pump pulley from the pump

Fig. 112 Use a screwdriver to loosen the hose clamp screws, then disconnect the hoses from the water pump

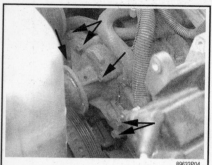

Fig. 113 Unfasten the water pump mounting bolts (see arrows for locations of top bolts) . . .

Fig. 114 . . . then remove the water pump from the engine

Fig. 115 Use a gasket scraper to carefully clean the water pump's mating surface

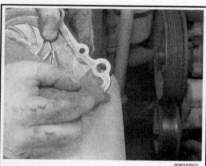

Fig. 116 You can also use Scotchbrite® or equivalent non-abrasive scouring pad to clean the water pump gasket mating surface

Fig. 117 When using a scraper to clean the gasket mating surfaces, be careful not to gouge the engine and cause leaks

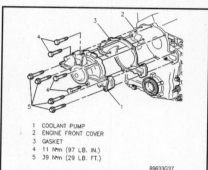

1 COOLANT PUMP
2 ENGINE FRONT COVER
3 GASKET
4 11 N•m (97 LB. IN.)
5 39 N•m (29 LB. FT.)

Fig. 118 Exploded view of the water pump mounting—1994 vehicle shown, others similar

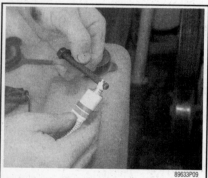

Fig. 119 Coat the bolt threads with a suitable sealing compound

Fig. 120 Place a new gasket on the water pump mounting surface

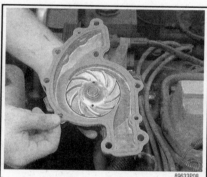

189 NUT 70 N•m (52 LB. FT.)
190 FRONT MOTOR MOUNT (TORQUE AXIS)
        MOUNTING BRACKET
191 BOLT 87 N•m (65 LB. FT.)

Fig. 121 Install the torque axis engine mount bracket and secure with the 2 bolts and nut

5. Disconnect the radiator and heater hoses from water pump.
6. For 1992–95 vehicles, remove the torque axis mount, as follows:
   a. Use a suitable engine support fixture and lifting bracket to raise the engine slightly to take the weight off of the engine mounts.
   b. Remove the through-bolt from the torque axis (front) engine mount.
   c. Lift the engine with the support fixture until the power steering reservoir touches the strut tower cross brace.
   d. Loosen the bottom two bolts on the torque axis (front) engine mount.
   e. Remove the A/C line clip and top two bolts on the torque axis engine mount, then remove the mount.
   f. Remove the 2 bolts and nut attaching the engine torque axis mount bracket assembly to the front of the engine.

➡ On some engines, when you remove the 13mm bolts, coolant will flow from the bolt holes, so make sure to position a drain pan under the pump before unfastening the bolts.

7. Remove the water pump attaching bolts, then remove the water pump from the vehicle. Remove and discard the gasket. Thoroughly clean the gasket mating surfaces.
To install:
8. Apply a suitable sealant to the bolt threads.
9. Position a new gasket, then install the water pump to the engine and tighten the retaining bolts, as follows:
   a. For 1986–94 vehicles, tighten the long bolts to 29 ft. lbs. (39 Nm) and the short bolts to 97 inch lbs. (11 Nm).
   b. For 1995 vehicles, tighten the water pump-to-block bolts to 22 ft. lbs. (30 Nm) and the water pump-to-front cover bolts to 11 ft. lbs. (15 Nm), plus an additional 80° rotation.
10. For 1992–95 vehicles, install the torque axis mount, as follows:
   a. Attach the torque axis engine mount bracket assembly to the front of the engine using the 2 bolts and nut.
   b. Replace the 2 upper bolts previously removed from the torque axis engine mount, and attach the mount and plastic clip for the A/C lines.

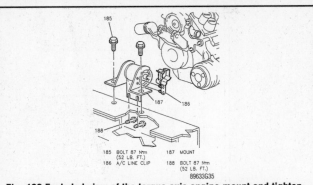

185 BOLT 87 N·m   187 MOUNT
    (52 LB. FT.)
186 A/C LINE CLIP   188 BOLT 87 N·m
                             (52 LB. FT.)

89633G35

Fig. 122 Exploded view of the torque axis engine mount and tightening specifications

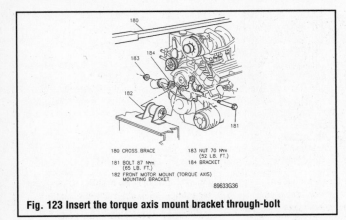

180 CROSS BRACE   183 NUT 70 N·m
                             (52 LB. FT.)
181 BOLT 87 N·m   184 BRACKET
    (65 LB. FT.)
182 FRONT MOTOR MOUNT (TORQUE AXIS)
    MOUNTING BRACKET

89633G36

Fig. 123 Insert the torque axis mount bracket through-bolt

   c. Tighten the 2 lower bolts that were previously loosened on the torque axis engine mount.

   d. Adjust the engine height to align the torque mount with the torque axis mount bracket.

   e. Insert the through-bolt, attach the retaining nut and tighten to the specifications shown in the accompanying figure. Remove the engine support and lifting fixture.

11. Install the water pump pulley and secure with the retaining bolts.

12. Connect the radiator and heater hoses to the water pump.

13. Install the serpentine drive belt.

14. Connect the negative battery cable.

15. Fill cooling system and check for leaks. Start the engine and allow to come to normal operating temperature. Check for leaks and top-off the coolant.

1995 VIN 1 ENGINE

1. Disconnect the negative battery cable.

2. Drain the cooling system into a suitable container.

3. Remove the outer and inner drive belts, as outlined in Section 1 of this manual.

4. Remove the alternator and brace.

5. Disconnect the heater hoses and pipes from the water pump.

6. Remove the pulley bracket assembly.

7. Raise and safely support the vehicle.

8. Remove the power steering pump and lines.

9. Carefully lower the vehicle.

10. Remove the torque engine mount, as follows:

   a. Remove the vacuum reservoir.

   b. Using engine support fixture J 28467-A, lifting bracket J 38854, core support wedges J 28467-350 and engine core support arm J 28467-330, raise the engine slightly to take the weight off the engine mounts.

   c. Remove the 2 bottom bolts on the torque axis engine mount.

   d. Remove the 2 through-bolts from the torque axis engine mount, then remove the mount.

   e. Raise the engine to gain clearance, then remove the engine mount bracket.

11. Unfasten the retainers and remove the water pump pulley.

12. Remove the retaining bolts, then remove the water pump from the engine.

13. Remove and discard the gasket and thoroughly clean the gasket mating surfaces.

To install:

14. Install a new gasket, then position the water pump over the gasket. Install the retaining bolts and tighten as follows:

   a. Water pump-to-block bolts: 22 ft. lbs. (30 Nm).

   b. Water pump-to-front cover bolts: 11 ft. lbs. (15 Nm), plus an additional 80° rotation.

15. Install the water pump pulley and secure with the retaining bolts.

16. Install the torque axis engine mount bracket, as follows:

   a. Install the engine mount bracket to the front of the engine.

   b. Position the torque axis engine mount to the rail.

   c. Lower the engine support fixture to align the engine mount bracket with the torque axis engine mount.

   d. Install the 2 through-bolts, attach the retaining nuts, then tighten to the specification shown in the accompanying figures. Remove the engine support fixture, lifting bracket and core support wedges and arm.

17. Raise and safely support the vehicle. The remainder of installation is the reverse of the removal procedure.

18. Bleed the power steering system. For details, please refer to Section 8 of this manual.

19. Fill cooling system and check for leaks. Start the engine and allow to come to normal operating temperature. Check for leaks and top-off the coolant.

1996–99 Vehicles

▶ See Figures 124, 125 and 126

3.8L (VIN K) ENGINE

1. Disconnect the negative battery cable.

2. Drain the cooling system into a suitable container.

3. Remove the accessory drive belt.

4. Unfasten the four 8mm water pump pulley bolts, then remove the pulley.

5. Remove the four ⅜ in. bolts and four ½ in. bolts, then remove the water pump from the engine.

6. Remove and discard the gasket and thoroughly clean the gasket mating surfaces.

To install:

7. Install a new gasket, then position the water pump over the gasket. Install the retaining bolts and tighten as follows:

   a. Tighten (1) bolts, shown in the accompanying figure, to 11 ft. lbs. (15 Nm).

   b. Tighten (2) bolts, shown in the accompanying figure, to 22 ft. lbs. (30 Nm).

8. Install the water pump pulley and secure with the four 8mm bolts.

9. Install the accessory drive belt.

10. Connect the negative battery cable.

11. Fill cooling system and check for leaks. Start the engine and allow to come to normal operating temperature. Check for leaks and top-off the coolant.

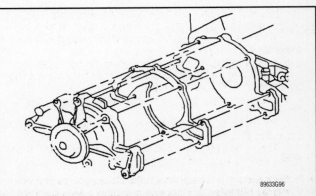

89633G96

Fig. 124 Exploded view of the water pump and gasket mounting

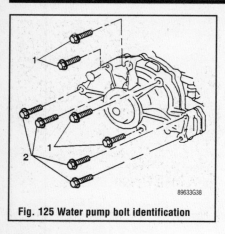

Fig. 125 Water pump bolt identification

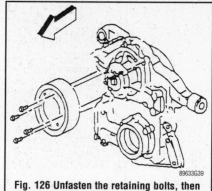
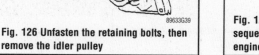

Fig. 126 Unfasten the retaining bolts, then remove the idler pulley

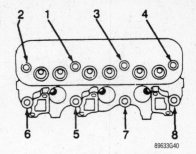

Fig. 127 Cylinder head bolt tightening sequence—3.0L and 3.8L (VIN 3 and B) engines

3.8L (VIN 1) ENGINE

1. Disconnect the negative battery cable.
2. Remove the A/C compressor splash shield. The shield is retained by six 10mm bolts and four 7mm bolts.
3. Drain the cooling system into a suitable container.
4. Remove the supercharger drive belt and the accessory drive belt.
5. Unbolt the ignition coil pack and position it out of the way.
6. Unfasten 15mm bolt, then remove the supercharger belt tensioner.
7. Install a suitable engine support fixture. Raise the engine slightly for access to the engine mount.
8. Remove the five 15mm bolts, then remove the engine mount.
9. Unfasten the two 13mm bolts, then remove the power steering pump.
10. Remove the engine mount bracket by removing the two 15mm nuts and studs, and one 19mm nut and stud.
11. Remove the idler pulley.
12. Unfasten the four 18mm bolts, then remove the water pump pulley.
13. Remove the four ⅜ in. bolts and four ½ in. bolts, then remove the water pump from the engine.
14. Remove and discard the gasket and thoroughly clean the gasket mating surfaces.

To install:

15. Install a new gasket, then position the water pump over the gasket. Install the retaining bolts and tighten to the specifications shown in the accompanying figure.
16. Install the water pump pulley and secure with the four 8mm bolts.
17. Install the idler pulley.
18. Install the engine mount bracket and secure with the two 15mm nuts and studs and one 19mm nut and stud.
19. The remainder of installation is the reverse of the removal procedure.
20. Start the engine and allow to reach normal operating temperatures. Check for leaks and top-off the coolant.

Cylinder Head

REMOVAL & INSTALLATION

3.0L and 3.8L (VIN 3 and B) engines

▶ **See Figure 127**

1. Properly relieve the fuel system pressure, as outlined in Section 5.
2. Disconnect the negative battery cable. Raise and safely support the vehicle.
3. Drain the engine coolant from the radiator and cylinder block, then carefully lower the vehicle.
4. Remove the serpentine belt, as outlined in Section 1.
5. Remove the alternator, AIR pump, oil indicator and power steering pump, as required. Position to the side.
6. Remove the throttle cable. Remove the cruise control cable, if equipped.
7. Disconnect the fuel lines and remove the fuel rail.
8. Remove the heater hoses and radiator hoses.
9. Tag and disconnect all vacuum and electrical wiring.

10. Remove the radiator and cooling fan, if necessary.
11. Remove the intake manifold and valve cover.
12. Remove the exhaust manifold(s).
13. Remove the rocker arm assembly and pushrods.
14. Unfasten the cylinder head bolts and remove the cylinder head. Remove and discard the cylinder head gasket.
15. Clean the cylinder head and block from any foreign matter, nicks or heavy scratches. Clean the cylinder head bolt threads and threads in the cylinder block. The cylinder head must be inspected before installation. Refer to the Engine Reconditioning portion of this section for details.

To install:

16. Position a new cylinder head gasket on the block.
17. Carefully guide the cylinder head into place. Coat the cylinder head bolts with a suitable sealing compound and install them.
18. Tighten the cylinder head bolts according to the following procedure:
    a. Tighten the cylinder head bolts in sequence to 25 ft. lbs. (34 Nm).
    b. Do not exceed 60 ft. lbs. (81 Nm) at any point during the next 2 steps.
    c. Using a torque angle gauge, tighten each bolt an additional 90° in sequence.
    d. Tighten each bolt an additional 90° in sequence.
19. The remainder of installation is the reverse of the removal procedure.
20. Fill cooling system and check for leaks. Start the engine and allow to come to normal operating temperature. Check for leaks and top off the coolant.

3.8L (VIN C, L, 1 and K) Engines

▶ **See Figures 128 thru 143**

1. Properly relieve the fuel system pressure, as outlined in Section 5 of this manual.
2. Remove the intake manifold, as outlined earlier in this section.
3. Remove either the right or left exhaust manifold, depending upon which cylinder head you are removing.
4. Remove the applicable valve cover for the cylinder head you are removing.
5. If you are removing the left (front) cylinder head, perform the following:
    a. Remove the ignition coil assembly.
    b. Tag and disconnect the spark plug wires.
    c. Remove the alternator and the alternator bracket.
    d. Unfasten the A/C compressor bracket bolt.
6. If removing the right (rear) cylinder head, perform the following:
    a. Unbolt the power steering pump and position aside. Do NOT disconnect the fluid lines.
    b. Remove the accessory drive belt tensioner assembly.
    c. Remove the fuel line heat shield.
7. Remove the rocker arm assemblies, guide plate and pushrods
8. If necessary, you can remove the lifter guide plate retainer, the plate, lifter guide and the lifters.
9. Unfasten the cylinder head retaining bolts, then remove the head from the engine. Remove and discard the cylinder head gasket. On 1996–99 vehicles, discard the cylinder head bolts and replace with new ones, of the same type, for installation.

➡ **The cylinder bolt hold threads can be cleaned using a ⁷⁄₁₆–4 tap.**

Fig. 128 Unfasten the retainers, then remove the rocker arms

Fig. 129 Remove the pushrod guide plate . . .

Fig. 130 . . . then remove the pushrods

Fig. 131 Unfasten the lifter guide plate retaining bolt, then remove the plate

Fig. 132 Remove the lifter guide by lifting it off . . .

Fig. 133 . . . then remove the lifter from its bore

Fig. 134 Most cylinder heads have 8 mounting bolts (see arrows)

Fig. 135 Depending upon application, remove the head bolts and inspect them for reuse, or discard them

Fig. 136 After removing the bolts, carefully lift the cylinder head from the engine block, and remove it from the vehicle

Fig. 137 If necessary, you can remove the gasket from the cylinder head after it is removed from the vehicle

Fig. 138 Use a suitable gasket scraper to remove the old gasket material from the cylinder head

Fig. 139 After shielding the cylinder bores from debris, also be sure to thoroughly clean the engine block mating surfaces

10. Clean the cylinder head and block from any foreign matter, nicks or heavy scratches. Clean the cylinder head bolt threads and threads in the cylinder block. The cylinder head must be inspected before installation. Refer to the Engine Reconditioning portion of this section for details.

To install:

✳✳ WARNING

Head gaskets are not interchangeable. Not installing the gasket with the arrow pointing to the front will cause gasket failure and, possibly, engine failure.

11. Place the cylinder head gasket on the engine block dowels with the note **THIS SIDE UP** facing the cylinder head and the arrow facing the front of the engine.

12. Place the cylinder head in position, on top of the new gasket.

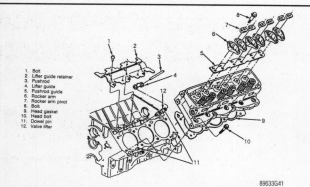

Fig. 140 Exploded view of the cylinder head and related components—3.8L (VIN L) engine shown

→On 1996–99 vehicles, the head bolts are designed to permanently stretch when tightened. the correct part number fastener MUST be used when replacing this type of bolt. Never use a bolt which is stronger in this application. If the correct bolt is not used, the parts will not be tightened correctly and component or system damage may occur.

13. Apply a suitable thread sealer to the cylinder head bolts on 1988–95 vehicles, or get new cylinder head bolts on 1996–99 vehicles, install them and tighten as follows:

a. Tighten the cylinder head bolts, in the sequence shown in the accompanying figure, to 35–37 ft. lbs. (47–50 Nm).

b. Rotate each bolt 130°, in sequence, using a torque angle meter.

c. Rotate the center 4 bolts an additional 30°, in sequence, using a torque angle meter.

14. If removed, install the lifters, guide, plate and retainer.

15. Install the pushrods, guide plate and rocker arm assemblies. Apply a suitable compound to the rocker arm pedestal bolts before assembly and tighten the bolts as follows:

a. 1988–92 vehicles: 28 ft. lbs. (38 Nm).

b. 1993–94 vehicles: 19 ft. lbs. (25 Nm), plus an additional 70° rotation.

c. 1995–96 vehicles: 11 ft. lbs. (15 Nm), plus additional 90° rotation.

16. The remainder of installation is the reverse of the removal procedure. During installation, be sure to tighten the A/C compressor bracket bolt to 52 ft. lbs. (70 Nm).

17. Fill cooling system and check for leaks. Start the engine and allow it to come to normal operating temperature. Check for leaks and top off the coolant.

Oil Pan

REMOVAL & INSTALLATION

▶ See Figures 144, 145 and 146

1. Disconnect the negative battery cable. Raise and safely support the vehicle.
2. Drain the engine oil into a suitable container.

Fig. 141 After installing a new gasket, position the cylinder head on top of the gasket

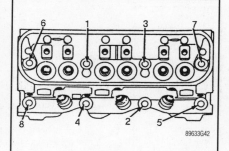

Fig. 142 Cylinder head bolts MUST be tightened in this sequence—3.8L engines, except VIN's 3 and B

Fig. 143 ALWAYS use a reliable torque wrench when tightening the cylinder head bolts!

1 CYLINDER BLOCK
2 GASKET
3 OIL PUMP PIPE AND SCREEN
4 BOLT

Fig. 144 Unfasten the retaining bolt(s), then remove the oil pump pipe and screen, if necessary

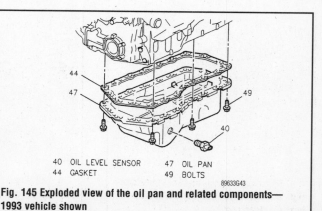

| 40 | OIL LEVEL SENSOR | 47 | OIL PAN |
| 44 | GASKET | 49 | BOLTS |

Fig. 145 Exploded view of the oil pan and related components—1993 vehicle shown

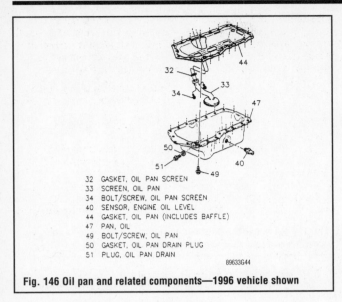

32 GASKET, OIL PAN SCREEN
33 SCREEN, OIL PAN
34 BOLT/SCREW, OIL PAN SCREEN
40 SENSOR, ENGINE OIL LEVEL
44 GASKET, OIL PAN (INCLUDES BAFFLE)
47 PAN, OIL
49 BOLT/SCREW, OIL PAN
50 GASKET, OIL PAN DRAIN PLUG
51 PLUG, OIL PAN DRAIN

89633G44

Fig. 146 Oil pan and related components—1996 vehicle shown

a. Remove the transaxle converter cover.

3. For 1986–90 vehicles, remove the starter motor from the vehicle, as outlined in Section 2.

4. Remove the oil filter.

5. If equipped, disconnect the oil level sensor.

6. For 1996–99 vehicles, remove the oil level sensor. On these vehicles, the oil level sensor must be removed prior to removing the pan. If the pan is removed first, damage to the sensor may occur.

7. Remove the oil pan-to-engine bolts and the oil pan. Remove and discard the oil pan gasket. The formed rubber oil pan gasket cannot be reused.

8. If necessary, remove the oil pump pipe and screen.

9. Thoroughly clean the gasket mounting surfaces.

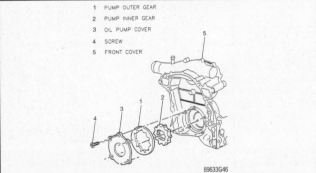

1 PUMP OUTER GEAR
2 PUMP INNER GEAR
3 OIL PUMP COVER
4 SCREW
5 FRONT COVER

89633G46

Fig. 147 The oil pump assembly is located at the front of the crankshaft

To install:

10. If removed, install the oil pump pipe and screen. Secure with the retaining bolt(s) and tighten to 89 inch lbs. (10 Nm).

11. Place a new formed rubber gasket in the oil pan flange.

12. Position the oil pan and secure with the oil pan-to-engine bolts. Tighten the bolts to 124 inch lbs. (14 Nm). Do NOT overtighten the bolts, as this will damage the oil pan, causing a leak.

13. The remainder of installation is the reverse of the removal procedure.

✳✳ WARNING

Operating the engine without the proper amount and type of engine oil will result in severe engine damage.

14. Fill the crankcase with the proper type and amount of engine oil.

15. Connect the negative battery cable, then start the engine and check for leaks. Check the oil level and add if necessary.

Oil Pump

✳✳ CAUTION

The EPA warns that prolonged contact with used engine oil may cause a number of skin disorders, including cancer! You should make every effort to minimize your exposure to used engine oil. Protective gloves should be worn when changing the oil. Wash your hands and any other exposed skin areas as soon as possible after exposure to used engine oil. Soap and water, or waterless hand cleaner should be used.

REMOVAL

▶ **See Figure 147**

1. Disconnect the negative battery cable.
2. Remove the front cover from the engine.
3. Remove the oil filter adapter, pressure regulator valve and spring.
4. Remove the oil pump cover-to-front cover screws and the cover. Remove the inner and outer pump gears.

INSPECTION

▶ **See Figures 148, 149 and 150**

1. Remove the front cover from the engine.
2. Remove the oil filter adapter, pressure regulator valve and spring.
3. Remove the oil pump cover-to-front cover screws and the cover. Remove the inner and outer pump gears.
4. Clean all parts in a suitable solvent. Remove all varnish, dirt and sludge. Thoroughly clean the gasket mating surfaces.
5. Inspect the pump cover and front cover for cracks, scoring, porous or damaged casting, damaged threads, or excessive wear. Inspect the pressure regulator for scoring, sticking in bore or burrs.

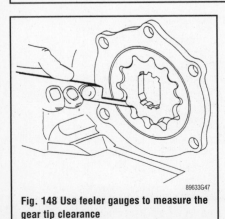

89633G47

Fig. 148 Use feeler gauges to measure the gear tip clearance

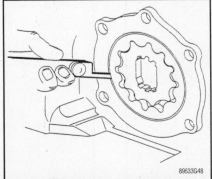

89633G48

Fig. 149 Measure the outer gear diameter clearance and compare with specifications

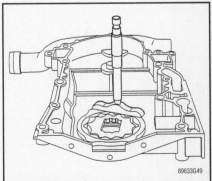

89633G49

Fig. 150 Measure the gear end clearance (gear drop-in housing)

6. Check the oil pump gears for:

   a. Inner gear tip clearance—0.006 inch (0.152mm)

   b. Outer gear diameter clearance—0.008–0.015 inch (0.203–0.381mm)

   c. Gear end clearance (gear drop in housing)—0.001–0.0035 inch (0.025–0.089mm)

   d. Pressure regulator valve-to-bore clearance—0.0015–0.003 inch (0.0015–0.003mm)

INSTALLATION

1. Using petroleum jelly, pack the pump and assemble the gears in the housing.

2. Tighten the oil pump cover-to-front cover screws to 97 inch lbs. (11 Nm).

3. Install the pressure regulator spring and valve. Install the oil filter adapter.

4. Install the front cover to the engine.

5. Connect the negative battery cable.

Crankshaft Damper

REMOVAL & INSTALLATION

▶ **See Figures 151, 152 and 153**

➡**On some vehicles, the crankshaft damper is also referred to as the crankshaft balancer or crankshaft pulley.**

1. Disconnect the negative battery cable.

2. On 1986–90 vehicles, remove the serpentine belt.

3. Raise and safely support the vehicle.

4. Right front tire and wheel assembly.

5. Remove the right front engine splash shield.

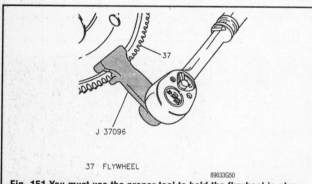

Fig. 151 You must use the proper tool to hold the flywheel in place, in order to remove the damper bolt

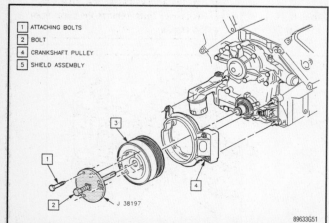

Fig. 152 Exploded view of the crankshaft pulley (damper) and related components—1991 vehicle shown

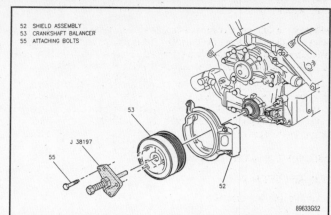

Fig. 153 The crankshaft balancer and pulley are serviced as an assembly and cannot be separated

6. Remove the flywheel or torque converter cover.

7. Use a suitable holding tool, as shown in the accompanying figure, on the flywheel to keep engine from rotating, then remove the bolt and washer from the damper.

8. For 1986–90 vehicles, remove the balancer and the key.

9. For 1991–99 vehicles, use a suitable crankshaft puller to remove the damper from the front of the engine. On 1993–99 vehicles, use ¼ inch bolts to attach the puller to the damper, then screw in ¼ in.

➡**The balancer is serviced as an assembly. The pulley cannot be removed from the balancer.**

  To install:

10. Install the key and balancer.

11. Install the bolt and washer, and while holding the flywheel stationary with the holding tool, tighten the bolt to the following specifications:

   a. For 1986–90 3.0L and 3.8L (VIN 3, B and C) engines: 220 ft. lbs. (297 Nm)

   b. For 1991 3.8L (VIN C) engines: 98–112 ft .lbs. (130–150 Nm), plus an additional 52–60° rotation.

   c. For 3.8L (VIN L, 1 and K) engines: 110 ft. lbs. (150 Nm), plus an additional 76° rotation.

12. Install the flywheel or torque converter cover.

13. Install the engine splash shield.

14. Install the tire and wheel assembly.

15. Carefully lower the vehicle.

16. If removed, install the serpentine belt.

17. Connect the negative battery cable.

Timing Chain Cover

REMOVAL & INSTALLATION

3.0L and 3.8L (VIN 3 and B) engines

1. Properly relieve the fuel system pressure.

2. If not already done, disconnect the negative battery cable.

3. Drain the cooling system into a suitable container.

4. Disconnect the lower radiator hose and the heater hose from the water pump.

5. Remove the 2 nuts from the front engine mount from the cradle, then carefully raise the engine using a suitable lifting device.

6. Remove the water pump pulley and the serpentine belt.

7. Remove the alternator and brackets.

8. Remove the balancer bolt and washer. Using a puller, remove the balancer.

9. Remove the cover-to-block bolts. Remove the 2 oil pan-to-cover bolts.

10. Remove the cover and gasket. Thoroughly clean the mating surfaces of the front cover and cylinder block.

11. After removing the timing cover, pry oil seal from front of cover. Lubricate the seal lip and install new lip seal with lip, open side of seal, facing toward the cylinder block. Carefully drive or press seal into place.

To install:

➡Remove the oil pump cover and pack the space around the oil pump gears completely with petroleum jelly. There must be no air space left inside the pump. If the pump is not packed, it may not begin to pump oil as soon as the engine is started and engine damage may result.

12. Install a new gasket to the oil pan and cylinder block. Install the front cover. Apply sealer to the threads of the cover retaining bolts and secure the cover.

13. The remainder of installation is the reverse of the removal procedure.

14. Fill cooling system and check for leaks. Start the engine and allow to come to normal operating temperature. Check for leaks and top off the coolant.

3.8L (VIN C, L, K and 1) Engines

1988–90 VEHICLES

▶ See Figures 154 thru 161

1. Disconnect the negative battery cable.
2. Drain the coolant into a clean container for reuse.
3. Remove the serpentine drive belt.
4. Disconnect the heater pipes. Disconnect the lower radiator and bypass hoses from the front cover.
5. Raise and safely support the vehicle.
6. Remove the right front tire and wheel assembly, then remove the inner splash shield.
7. Unfasten the retaining bolt, then remove the crankshaft balancer.
8. Tag and unplug the electrical connections from the camshaft sensor, crankshaft sensor and the oil pressure switch.
9. If necessary, remove the oil filter.
10. Unfasten the oil pan-to-front cover bolts.
11. Remove the front cover mounting bolts, then remove the front cover assembly. Remove and discard the gasket.
12. If necessary, you can replace the front cover oil seal at this time by carefully prying it from the cover. You can also remove the seal with the cover installed. For details, refer to the procedure located later in this section.
13. Thoroughly clean the gasket surfaces on the cover and the cylinder block.

Fig. 154 Remove the inner splash shield retaining clips, then remove the shield

Fig. 155 Unfasten the crankshaft balancer retaining bolt . . .

Fig. 156 . . . then remove the crankshaft balancer. Note the teeth on the back of the balancer

Fig. 157 Unplug the electrical connector (1) from the crankshaft position sensor (2)

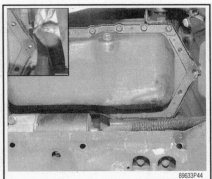
Fig. 158 Unfasten the oil pan-to-front cover retaining bolts

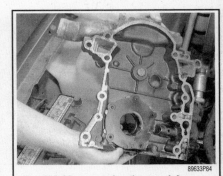
Fig. 159 After removing the remaining front cover bolts, remove the cover from the engine

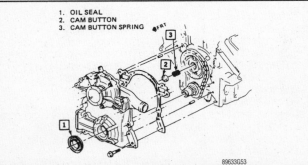
Fig. 160 Exploded view of the front cover, gasket and oil seal—1990 3.8L (VIN C) engine shown

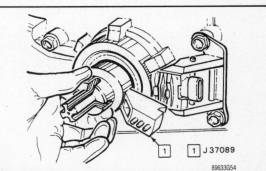
Fig. 161 There is a specific tool available for adjusting the crankshaft position sensor

To install:

14. If the front cover seal was removed, lubricate the seal lip and install new lip seal with lip, open side of seal, facing toward the cylinder block. Carefully drive or press the seal into place.

15. Position a new gasket on the cylinder block.

16. Apply a suitable sealant to the bolt threads, then install the front cover, and tighten the mounting bolts to 22 ft. lbs. (30 Nm).

17. Replace the oil pan-to-cover mounting bolts and tighten to 88 inch lbs. (10 Nm) .

18. If removed, install a new oil filter.

19. The remainder of installation is the reverse of the removal procedure. During installation, be sure to tighten the crankshaft balancer retaining bolt to 219 ft. lbs. (298 Nm).

20. Refill the cooling system and connect the negative battery cable.

21. Start the engine and check for leaks. Check the coolant level and add, if necessary.

1991–99 VEHICLES

♦ **See Figures 162, 163 and 164**

1. Disconnect the negative battery cable.

2. For 1992–99 vehicles, remove the torque axis mount, as follows:

   a. Use a suitable engine support fixture and lifting bracket to raise the engine slightly to take the weight off of the engine mounts.

   b. Remove the through-bolt from the torque axis (front) engine mount.

   c. Lift the engine with the support fixture until the power steering reservoir touches the strut tower cross brace.

   d. Loosen the bottom two bolts on the torque axis (front) engine mount.

   e. Remove the A/C line clip and top two bolts on the torque axis engine mount, then remove the mount.

   f. Remove the 2 bolts and nut attaching the engine torque axis mount bracket assembly to the front of the engine.

3. For 1996–99 vehicles, remove the torque axis mount bracket.

4. Remove the serpentine drive belt.

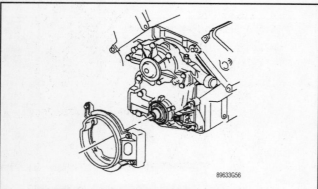

Fig. 162 Remove the crankshaft position sensor shield

5. For the 1995 VIN K engine and 1996–99 VIN 1 engines, remove the drive belt idler pulley and bracket.

6. Remove the crankshaft pulley/damper using a suitable puller, as outlined earlier in this section.

7. Remove the sensor shield, then remove the crankshaft position sensor.

8. Remove the oil pan-to-front cover bolts.

9. Remove the front cover attaching bolts, then remove the cover. Remove and discard the front cover gasket.

10. If necessary, you can replace the front cover oil seal at this time by carefully prying it from the cover. You can also remove the seal with the cover installed. For details, refer to the procedure located later in this section.

11. Thoroughly clean the gasket surfaces on the cover and the cylinder block. If the oil pan gasket is very swollen, you must remove the oil pan and replace the gasket.

12. Inspect the timing chain for overall "in and out" movement. It should not exceed 1 in. (25mm).

To install:

13. If the front cover seal was removed, lubricate the seal lip and install new lip seal with lip, open side of seal, facing toward the cylinder block. Carefully drive or press the seal into place.

14. Position a new front cover gasket on the cylinder block.

15. Apply a suitable sealant to the bolt threads, then install the front cover and the attaching bolts. Tighten the bolts to 22 ft. lbs. (30 Nm) for 1991–95 vehicles. For 1996–99 vehicles, tighten the bolts to 11 ft. lbs. (15 Nm), plus an additional 40° rotation with a torque angle meter.

16. Install the oil pan-to-front cover bolts and tighten to 124 inch lbs. (14 Nm).

17. Install the belt tensioner assembly.

18. For the 1995 VIN K and 1996–99 VIN 1 engines, install the drive belt idler pulley and bracket.

19. For 1992 vehicles, adjust the crankshaft position sensor using tool J37087 or equivalent.

20. The remainder of installation is the reverse of the removal procedure.

Front Cover Oil Seal

REPLACEMENT

♦ **See Figure 165**

➡ **This procedure covers removing the oil seal with the cover installed on the engine.**

1. Disconnect the negative battery cable.

2. Remove the drive belt.

3. Remove the crankshaft balancer-to-crankshaft bolt, then remove the crankshaft balancer/damper, as outlined earlier in this section.

4. Using a small prybar, pry the oil seal from the front cover. Be careful not to damage the sealing surfaces.

To install:

5. Clean the oil seal mounting surface. Using the proper lubricant coat the outside of the seal and the crankshaft balancer.

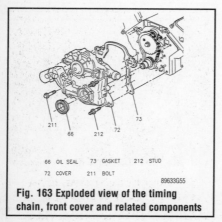

66 OIL SEAL   73 GASKET   212 STUD
72 COVER   211 BOLT

Fig. 163 Exploded view of the timing chain, front cover and related components

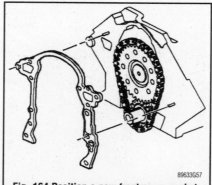

Fig. 164 Position a new front cover gasket on the cylinder block

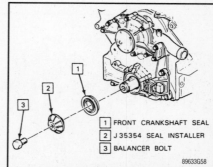

1 FRONT CRANKSHAFT SEAL
2 J35354 SEAL INSTALLER
3 BALANCER BOLT

Fig. 165 Use the crankshaft balancer bolt and a proper tool to install the front cover oil seal

6. Install the oil seal, using a suitable installation tool and the crankshaft balancer bolt. Tighten the crankshaft balancer bolt on the tool, until the seal is seated in the cover, then remove the tool.

7. Install the crankshaft balancer and secure with the mounting bolt. Tighten to the specifications given earlier in this section.

8. Install the drive belt.

9. Connect the negative battery cable.

Timing Chain and Sprockets

REMOVAL & INSTALLATION

3.0L and 3.8L (VIN 3 and B) engines

▶ See Figures 166 and 167

1. Properly relieve the fuel system pressure.
2. If not already done, disconnect the negative battery cable.
3. Remove the timing chain front cover, as outlined earlier in this section.
4. Turn the crankshaft so the timing marks are aligned.
5. Remove the crankshaft oil slinger, as required.
6. Remove the camshaft sprocket bolts.
7. Remove the camshaft sensor magnet assembly.
8. Use 2 prybars to alternately pry the camshaft and crankshaft sprocket free, along with the chain.

To install:

9. Make sure the crankshaft is positioned so the No. 1 piston is at TDC.
10. Rotate the camshaft with the sprocket temporarily installed, so the timing mark is straight down.
11. Assemble the timing chain on the sprockets with the timing marks aligned. Install the timing chain and sprocket.
12. Install the cam sensor magnet assembly.

13. Install the oil slinger with the large part of the cone toward the front of the engine, as required.
14. Install the camshaft sprocket bolt, thrust button and spring.
15. Install the timing chain damper and engine front cover.
16. Connect the negative battery cable.

3.8L (VIN 1, C, L and K) Engines

▶ See Figures 168 thru 179

1. Disconnect the negative battery cable.
2. Remove the front cover, as outlined earlier in this section.
3. On 1988–90 vehicles, remove the camshaft thrust button.
4. Align the timing marks on the sprockets, so they are as close together as possible.
5. Remove the spring/damper assembly from the center of the camshaft.
6. Remove the camshaft sprocket bolts, then remove the sprocket and timing chain as an assembly.
7. Remove the crankshaft sprocket. Clean the gasket mounting surfaces and the timing chain and sprockets.

To install:

8. If the pistons have been moved, while the timing chain was removed, perform the following:
   a. Turn the crankshaft to the No. 1 piston is at Top Dead Center (TDC).
   b. Turn the crankshaft so, with the sprocket temporarily installed, the timing mark is straight down.
9. Assemble the timing chain on the camshaft sprocket and crankshaft sprockets. Make sure to align the marks on the sprockets; they must face each other and be as close together as possible.
10. Slide the assembly onto the camshaft and crankshaft. Install the camshaft sprocket-to-camshaft bolts. Tighten the camshaft sprocket bolts to 27 ft. lbs. (37 Nm) on 1988–91 vehicles. For 1992–99 vehicles, tighten the bolts to 74 ft. lbs. (100 Nm), plus an additional 90° rotation.

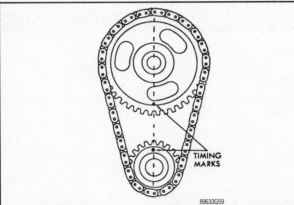

Fig. 166 The timing marks MUST be aligned before removing the timing chain

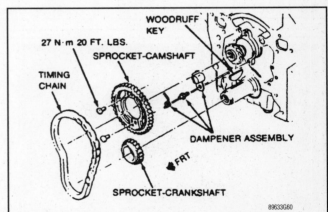

Fig. 167 Exploded view of the timing chain and related components—3.0L and 3.8L (VIN 3 and B) engines

Fig. 168 View of the timing chain after the cover is removed

Fig. 169 If equipped, remove the camshaft thrust button

Fig. 170 Align the timing marks, so they are as close together as possible, as shown by the arrows

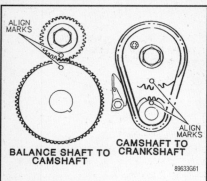

Fig. 171 The timing marks on the camshaft and crankshaft sprockets must be aligned

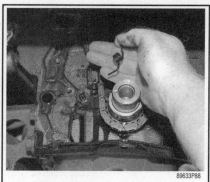

Fig. 172 Remove the spring from the center of the camshaft . . .

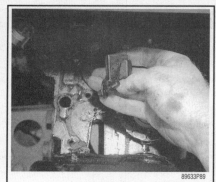

Fig. 173 . . . unfasten the retainer, then remove the damper

Fig. 174 Unfasten the 3 camshaft sprocket retaining bolts . . .

Fig. 175 . . . then remove the camshaft sprocket and timing chain as an assembly

Fig. 176 View of the camshaft gear after the camshaft sprocket and timing chain have been removed

Fig. 177 Remove the camshaft gear from the camshaft

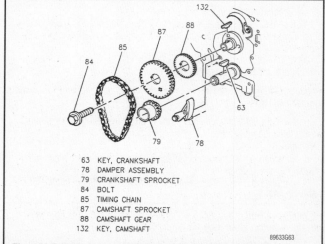

63	KEY, CRANKSHAFT
78	DAMPER ASSEMBLY
79	CRANKSHAFT SPROCKET
84	BOLT
85	TIMING CHAIN
87	CAMSHAFT SPROCKET
88	CAMSHAFT GEAR
132	KEY, CAMSHAFT

Fig. 179 Exploded view of the timing chain and related components—1993 vehicle shown, later models similar

1	37 N•M (27 LBS. FT.)
2	TIMING CHAIN
3	CAMSHAFT SPROCKET
4	CAMSHAFT GEAR
5	KEY
6	DAMPER
7	BOLT (SPECIAL) 19 N•M (14 LBS. FT.)
8	SPRING
9	CRANKSHAFT SPROCKET

Fig. 178 Exploded view of the timing chain and related components—1990 vehicle shown

➡ If equipped with 3.8L (VIN C, L or K) engines, align the camshaft sprocket mark with the balancer shaft sprocket mark.

11. Install the camshaft thrust button, if equipped, and spring/damper assembly. Tighten the bolt to 14–16 ft. lbs. (19–22 Nm).

12. Install the front cover assembly.

13. Connect the negative battery cable.

14. Refill the cooling system. Start the engine, allow it to reach normal operating temperatures and check for leaks.

Camshaft, Bearings and Lifters

REMOVAL & INSTALLATION

➡ **For the removal of the camshaft, the engine assembly will probably need to be removed from the vehicle.**

3.0L and 3.8L (VIN 3 and B) Engines

1. Properly relieve the fuel system pressure.
2. Disconnect the negative battery cable.
3. Remove the engine as outlined earlier in this section, and support it on a suitable engine stand.
4. Remove the intake manifold.
5. Remove the rocker arm covers.
6. Remove the rocker arm assemblies, pushrods and lifters, keeping the components in order for assembly.
7. Unfasten the retainers, then remove the timing chain cover.

➡ **Align the timing marks of the camshaft and crankshaft sprockets to avoid burring the camshaft journals by the crankshaft.**

8. Remove the timing chain, camshaft sensor magnet assembly and sprockets.
9. Carefully remove the camshaft from the engine.
   To install:
10. Coat the camshaft with lubricant 1052365 or equivalent, and install the camshaft.
11. Install the timing chain, camshaft sensor magnet assembly and sprockets.
12. Install the camshaft thrust button and front cover.
13. Complete installation by reversing the removal procedure.
14. Connect battery negative cable.

3.8L (Except VIN 3 and B) Engines

1988–90 VEHICLES

1. Disconnect the negative battery cable.
2. Remove the engine assembly and position in a suitable holding fixture.
3. Remove the intake manifold, the front timing cover, timing chain and sprockets.
4. Remove the valve covers, the rocker arm shaft or rocker arm assemblies, the pushrods and the hydraulic lifters.

➡ **Keep all valve components in order so they may be reinstalled in their original positions.**

5. Carefully, slide the camshaft forward, out of the bearing bores; do not damage the bearing surfaces.
   To install:
6. Clean the gasket mounting surfaces. Inspect the parts for wear and/or damage, replace if necessary.
7. Lubricate the valve lifters and camshaft with multi-lube 1052365 or equivalent, and install in the original positions.

➡ **If equipped with 3.8L (VIN C or L) engine, align the camshaft gear with the balancer shaft gear timing marks.**

8. Carefully, install the camshaft in the engine.
9. The remainder of installation is the reverse of the removal procedure.
10. Fill cooling system and check for leaks. Start the engine and allow to come to normal operating temperature. Recheck for leaks. Top-up coolant.

1991–99 VEHICLES

◆ **See Figure 180**

1. Disconnect the negative battery cable. Remove the engine assembly and position in a suitable holding fixture.

➡ **Keep all valve components in order so they may be reinstalled in their original positions.**

2. Remove the intake manifold, the valve covers, rocker arms, pushrods and valve lifters.

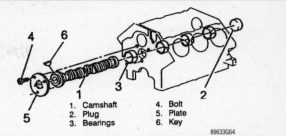

Fig. 180 Exploded view of the camshaft and related components—1991–99 vehicles

1. Camshaft
2. Plug
3. Bearings
4. Bolt
5. Plate
6. Key

89633G64

3. Remove the crankshaft pulley/balancer, crankshaft sensor cover, sensor, front timing cover, timing chain and sprockets.
4. Unfasten the camshaft thrust plate retainers, then remove the thrust plate.
5. Carefully rotate and pull the camshaft out of the camshaft bearings.
   To install:
6. Clean the gasket mounting surfaces. Inspect the parts for wear and/or damage, replace if necessary.
7. Lubricate the valve lifters and camshaft with multi-lube 1052365 or equivalent, and install in the original positions.

➡ **If equipped with 3.8L (VIN C or L) engine, align the camshaft gear with the balancer shaft gear timing marks.**

8. Carefully, install the camshaft in the engine and install the camshaft thrust plate.
9. The remainder of installation is the reverse of the removal procedure.

INSPECTION

1. Check the camshaft sprocket, keyway and threads, bearing journals and lobes for wear, galling, gouges or overheating. If any of these conditions exist, replace the camshaft.

➡ **Do NOT attempt to repair the camshaft. Always replace the camshaft and lifters as an assembly. Old valve lifters will destroy a new camshaft in less time than it took you to replace the camshaft.**

2. Camshaft Lift Measurement:
   a. Lubricate the camshaft bearings with Assembly Lube 1051396 or equivalent.
   b. Carefully install the camshaft into the block. If the cam bearings are damaged badly, set the camshaft on "V" blocks instead.
   c. Install a dial indicator J–8520 and measure the camshaft lift.
   d. Measure the bearing journals with a micrometer. Take measurements for run-out and diameter. If not within specification in the charts in the beginning of this section, replace the camshaft.

Camshaft/Balance Shaft Bearings

REMOVAL & INSTALLATION

◆ **See Figure 181**

➡ **Camshaft bearing removal should be done by a qualified machine shop because the tools needed are expensive and would not be economical to purchase for a one time usage. A machine shop can also line-bore the bearings after installation, to avoid premature camshaft and valve train wear.**

Care must be exercised during bearing removal and installation, not to damage bearings that are not being replaced.
1. Remove camshaft as outlined earlier in this section.
2. Assemble the puller screw to required length.
3. Select the proper size expanding collet and back-up nut.
4. Install the expanding collet on the expanding mandrel. Install the back-up nut.
5. Insert this assembly into the camshaft bearing to be removed. Tighten the back-up nut to expand the collet to fit the inside diameter of the bearing.

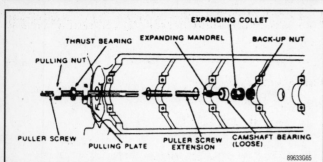

Fig. 181 Camshaft bearing replacement requires the use of several expensive tools

6. Thread the end of the puller screw assembly into the end of the expanding mandrel and collet assembly.

7. Install the pulling plate, thrust bearing, and pulling nut on the threaded end of the puller screw.

8. The bearing can then be removed by turning the pulling nut.

➡Make certain to grip the ⅝ in. hex end of the puller screw with a wrench to keep it from rotating when the pulling nut is turned. Failure to do this will result in the locking up of all threads in the pulling assembly and possible over expansion of the collet.

9. Repeat the above procedure to remove any other bearings, except the front bearing, which may be pulled from the rear of the engine.

➡When removing rear cam bearing, it is necessary to remove the plug at the back of cam bore. However, if only the front bearing is being replaced, it is not necessary to remove the plug. The front bearing can be removed by using a spacer between the pulling plate and the cylinder block.

To install:

10. Assemble the puller screw to required length.

11. Select the proper size expanding collet and back-up nut.

12. Install the expanding collet on expanding mandrel.

13. Install the back-up nut.

14. Place a new camshaft bearing on the collet and GENTLY hand tighten back-up nut to expand the collet to fit the bearing. Do not over tighten the back-up nut. A loose sliding fit between collet and bearing surface is adequate. This will provide just enough clearance to allow for the collapse which will occur when the new bearing is pulled into the engine block.

15. Slide mandrel assembly and bearing into bearing bore as far as it will go without force.

16. Thread the end of the puller screw onto the end of the mandrel. Make certain to align the oil holes in the bearing and block properly. One of the collet separation lines may be used as a reference point.

17. Install the pulling plate, thrust bearing and pulling nut on threaded end of puller screw.

18. Install bearing in the same manner as described in Steps 8 and 9 under Bearing Removal.

➡When installing rear cam bearing, install a new plug at back of cam bore. Coat the outside diameter of the plug with non-hardening sealer before installation.

Balance Shaft

REMOVAL & INSTALLATION

◆ See Figures 182 and 183

➡For the removal of the camshaft or balance shaft, the engine assembly will probably need to be removed from the vehicle.

1. Disconnect the negative battery cable. Remove the engine and secure it to a workstand.

2. Remove the flywheel-to-crankshaft bolts and remove the flywheel.

3. Remove the intake manifold.

4. Remove the lifter guide retainer.

5. Unfasten the timing chain cover-to-engine bolts, then remove the cover.

6. Remove the balancer shaft drive gear bolt.

7. Remove the camshaft sprocket and timing chain.

8. Remove the balance shaft retainer bolts, retainer and gear.

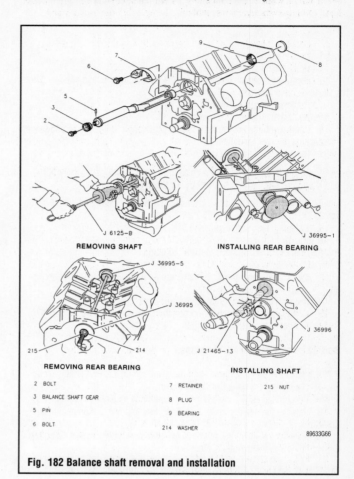

Fig. 182 Balance shaft removal and installation

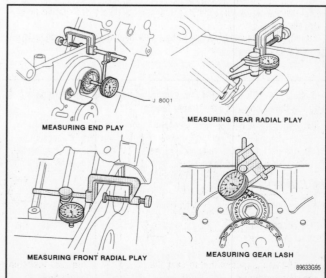

Fig. 183 You must measure the balance shaft clearances for proper specifications

9. Using a suitable slide hammer tool, pull the balance shaft from the front of the engine.

10. Remove the balance shaft rear plug by driving it from the engine.

11. Remove the balance shaft rear bearing using a suitable bearing removal and installer tool to press the rear bearing from the engine.

➡**The balance shaft and both bearings are serviced as a complete package. You must use the proper tools when replacing the bearing and shaft.**

12. Inspect the balance shaft drive gear and the camshaft drive gear for nicks and burrs.

To install:

13. Install the balance shaft gear bearing, as follows:

   a. Dip the new bearing in clean engine oil.

   b. Using the balance shaft rear bearing installer tool, press the new rear bearing into the rear of the engine.

14. Dip the front balance shaft into clean engine oil. Using the balance shaft installer tool, screw it into the balance shaft and install the shaft into the engine; remove the installer tool.

15. Temporarily install the balance shaft bearing retainer and bolts. Install the balance shaft drive gear. Apply a suitable sealer to the bolt threads, then install the bolt. Tighten the bolts to 14 ft. lbs. (20 Nm), plus an additional 35° rotation for 1986–92 vehicles. For 1993–99 vehicles, tighten the bolt to 16 ft. lbs. (22 Nm), plus an additional 70° rotation.

16. Install the rear cup plug.

17. Measure the balance shaft radial play at both the front and the rear. The end-play should be 0.00–0.008 in. (0–0.203mm).

18. Measure the balance shaft radial play at both the front and the rear and compare with the following specifications:

   a. Front: 0–0.0011 (0–0.028mm).

   b. Rear: 0.0005–0.0047 in. (0.127–0.119mm).

19. Turn the camshaft so, with the camshaft sprocket temporarily installed, the timing mark is straight down.

20. With the camshaft sprocket and the camshaft gear removed, turn the balance shaft so that the timing mark on the gear points straight down.

21. Install the camshaft gear. Align the marks on the balance shaft gear and the camshaft gear by turning the balance shaft.

22. Turn the crankshaft so that the No. 1 piston is at Top Dead Center (TDC).

23. Install the timing chain and camshaft sprocket.

24. Measure the gear lash at four places, every ¼ turn. The lash should be 0.002–0.005 in. (0.050–0.127mm).

25. Install the balance shaft front bearing retainer. Install the retainer bolts and tighten them to 22–26 ft. lbs. (30–35 Nm).

26. Install the front timing cover and the lifter guide retainer.

27. Install the intake manifold.

28. Install the flywheel assembly and tighten the bolts to the specifications given later in this section.

29. Install the engine assembly and connect the negative battery cable. Start the engine and check for leaks.

Rear Main Oil Seal

REMOVAL & INSTALLATION

1986–90 Vehicles

ROPE SEAL REPAIR

▸ **See Figures 184, 185 and 186**

1. Disconnect the negative battery cable.
2. Raise and support the vehicle safely.
3. Drain the engine oil into a suitable container.
4. Remove the oil pan, as outlined earlier in this section.
5. Remove the rear main bearing cap. Remove the oil seal from the bearing cap.

6. Insert packing tool J–21526–2 or equivalent against one end of the seal in the cylinder block. Pack the old seal in until it is tight. Pack the other end of seal in the same manner.

7. Measure the amount the seal was driven up into the block on one side and add approximately ¹⁄₁₆ inch (2mm). With a single edge razor blade, cut this amount off of the old lower seal. The bearing cap can be used as a holding fixture.

➡**A small amount of oil on the pieces of seal may be helpful when packing into the cylinder block.**

8. Install the packing guide tool J–21526–1 or equivalent, onto the cylinder block.

9. Using the packing tool, work the short pieces of the seal into the guide tool and pack into the cylinder block, until the tool hits the built-in stop. Repeat this step on the other side.

10. Remove the guide tool.

11. Install a new rope seal in the bearing cap and install the cap. Tighten the retaining bolts to 90 ft. lbs. (122 ft. lbs.)

12. Install the oil pan, then carefully lower the vehicle.

13. Fill the crankcase with the proper type and amount of engine oil.

14. Connect the negative battery cable.

ROPE HALF-SEAL REPLACEMENT

▸ **See Figures 187 and 188**

1. Remove the engine from the vehicle.
2. Remove the oil pan. Remove the rear main bearing cap-to-engine bolts and the cap.
3. Remove the old seal from the bearing cap. Clean the remains of sealer and adhesive from the upper and lower bearing groove, and clean the mating surfaces of the bearing cap.

To install:

4. Using suitable sealant, apply it to the main bearing cap seal groove and, then perform the following steps within 1 minute.

5. Using a new rope seal and a wooden dowel or hammer handle, roll the new seal into the cap so both ends project above the parting surface of the cap;

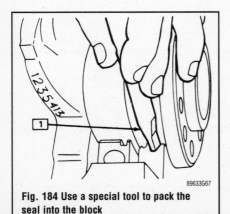

Fig. 184 Use a special tool to pack the seal into the block

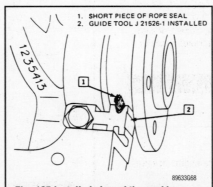

Fig. 185 Installed view of the packing guide tool

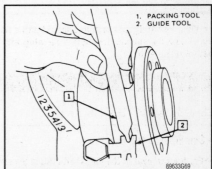

Fig. 186 Pack the short seal pieces into the block with the tool, until the tool hits the built-in stop

Fig. 187 Use a wooden dowel or equivalent tool to seat the seal in the cap

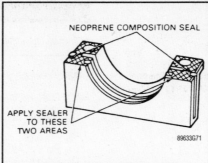

Fig. 188 Apply sealer sparingly to the areas shown, but avoid the bolt threads

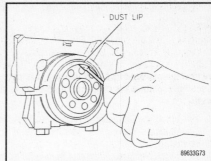

Fig. 189 Insert a small prytool through the rear main seal dust lip at the angle shown

force the seal into the groove by rubbing it down, until the seal projects above the groove not more than 1⁄16 inch.

6. Using a sharp razor blade, cut the ends off flush with the surface of the cap.
7. Using chassis grease, apply a thin coat to the seals surface.
8. To install the neoprene sealing strips (side seals), perform the following procedures:
9. Using light oil or kerosene, soak the strips for 5 minutes.

➥The neoprene composition seals will swell up once exposed to the oil and heat. It is normal for the seals to leak for a short time, until they become properly seated. The seals must not be cut to fit.

10. Place the sealing strips in the grooves on the sides of the bearing cap.
11. Apply a suitable sealer it to the main bearing cap mating surface; do not apply sealer to the bolt holes.
12. Install the main bearing cap. Torque the main bearing cap-to-engine bolts to 90 ft. lbs. (122 Nm).
13. Install the oil pan.
14. Lower the vehicle.
15. Refill the crankcase.
16. The engine must be operated at low rpm when first started, after a new seal is installed.

1991–99 3.8L (VIN C, L and 1) Engines

ONE PIECE LIP-TYPE SEAL

▶ See Figures 189, 190 and 191

1. Disconnect the negative battery cable.
2. Raise and safely support the vehicle.
3. Remove the transaxle, as outlined in Section 7 of this manual.
4. Remove the flywheel, as outlined later in this section.
5. Confirm that the rear main seal is leaking.

✶✶ WARNING

Use care when prying out the seal to avoid damage to the OD and chamfer of the crankshaft.

6. Insert a suitable prying tool through the dust lip at the angle shown in the accompanying figure. Pry the seal out by moving the handle of the tool toward the end of the crankshaft pilot. Repeat the process, as required, around the seal until it is removed.

To install:

7. Apply engine oil to the ID and OD of the new seal. Slide the new seal over the mandrel until the back of the seal bottoms squarely against the collar of the tool.
8. Align the dowel pin of the installation tool with the dowel pin in the crankshaft and attach the tool to the crankshaft by hand or by tightening the attaching screw to 60 inch lbs. (5 Nm).
9. Turn the T-handle of the tool so the collar pushes the seal into the bore. Continue turning until the collar is tight against the case. This will ensure that the seal is seated properly.
10. Loosen the T-handle of the tool until it comes to a stop. This will ensure that the collar will be in the proper position for install another new seal.
11. Remove the attaching screws.
12. Install the flywheel, as outlined later this section.
13. Install the transaxle, as outlined in Section 7.
14. Carefully lower the vehicle, then connect the negative battery cable.

1995–99 3.8L (VIN K) Engine

REAR MAIN SEAL CARRIER

▶ See Figure 192

1. Disconnect the negative battery cable.
2. Raise and safely support the vehicle. Drain the engine oil into a suitable container.
3. Remove the transaxle, as outlined in Section 7 of this manual.
4. Remove the flywheel, as outlined later in this section.
5. Remove the oil pan.
6. Unfasten the rear main seal carrier attaching bolts.
7. Remove the rear main seal carrier plate.
8. Carefully pry the rear main seal from the carrier.

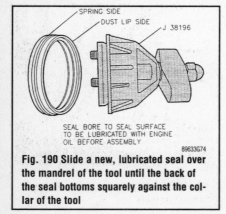

Fig. 190 Slide a new, lubricated seal over the mandrel of the tool until the back of the seal bottoms squarely against the collar of the tool

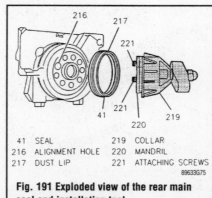

Fig. 191 Exploded view of the rear main seal and installation tool

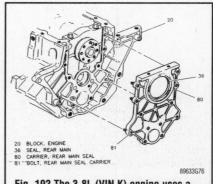

Fig. 192 The 3.8L (VIN K) engine uses a rear main seal carrier plate

To install:

➡**Proper alignment of the plate is crucial to the sealability of the rear main seal and oil pan. Take care when installing the plate to ensure the plate is properly aligned. In order to properly align the plate, use a suitable rear cover aligning tool, J 41349 or equivalent installed to the rear of the crankshaft. Check that you have equal distance between each side of the plate crank seal surface. Failure to do this may result in oil leaks.**

9. Make sure the oil seal is removed from the housing.

10. Install the housing and finger-tighten all of the bolt (loose enough to adjust the housing) to hold the housing in place.

11. Wipe a thin film of clean engine oil on both sides of the rear cover alignment tool to help in installing and removing from the crankshaft.

12. Install the rear cover alignment tool over the crankshaft; twisting or turning the tool helps in sliding it from the crankshaft.

13. Install the housing bolts and tighten to 22 ft. lbs. (30 Nm). Remove the alignment tool.

14. Place straight edge on the cylinder block oil pan flange and the housing flange. Use a feeler gauge to make sure there is no more than 0.004 in. step, high or low. If beyond specifications, repeat the preceding 4 steps and measure again. If excessive clearance is still present, replace the housing.

15. Install a new oil seal using rear main installer tool, J 38196 or equivalent.

16. Install the oil pan.

17. Install the flywheel.

18. Install the transaxle, as outlined in Section 7.

19. Carefully lower the vehicle, then connect the negative battery cable.

Flywheel and Ring Gear

REMOVAL & INSTALLATION

The ring gear is an integral part of the flywheel and is not replaceable.

1. Remove the transaxle from the vehicle, as outlined in Section 7 of this manual.

2. Mark the flywheel to the crankshaft for identification during replacement.

3. Unfasten the bolts attaching the flywheel to the crankshaft flange, then remove the flywheel.

4. Inspect the flywheel for cracks, and inspect the ring gear for burrs or worn teeth. Replace the flywheel if any damage is apparent. Remove burrs with a mill file.

To install:

5. Install the flywheel. Most flywheels will only attach to the crankshaft in one position, as the bolt holes are unevenly spaced, but use your marks as a guide.

6. Install the retaining bolts and tighten to the following specifications:

    a. 1986–91 vehicles: 61 ft. lbs. (82 Nm).

    b. 1992–94 vehicles: 11 ft. lbs. (15 Nm), plus an additional 50° rotation.

    c. 1995–99 vehicles, except 1995 3.8L (VIN K and 1) engine: 11 ft. lbs. (15 Nm), plus an additional 50° rotation.

    d. 1995 3.8L (VIN K and 1) engine: 46 ft. lbs. (62 Nm).

7. Mount a suitable dial indicator on the engine block, then check the flywheel run-out at the three attaching bosses. The crankshaft end-play must be held in one direction during this check. Run-out should not exceed 0.015 in. (0.381mm).

8. If the run-out exceeds 0.015 in. (0.381mm), try to correct by lightly tapping the high side with a rubber mallet.

9. If the condition cannot be corrected, the flywheel must be replaced.

EXHAUST SYSTEM

Inspection

▸ **See Figures 193 thru 199**

➡**Safety glasses should be worn at all times when working on or near the exhaust system. Older exhaust systems will almost always be covered with loose rust particles which will shower you when disturbed. These particles are more than a nuisance and could injure your eye.**

✳✳ CAUTION

DO NOT perform exhaust repairs or inspection with the engine or exhaust hot. Allow the system to cool completely before attempting any work. Exhaust systems are noted for sharp edges, flaking metal and rusted bolts. Gloves and eye protection are required. A healthy supply of penetrating oil and rags is highly recommended.

Your vehicle must be raised and supported safely to inspect the exhaust system properly. Placing 4 safety stands under the vehicle for support should provide enough room for you to slide under the vehicle and inspect the system completely. Start the inspection at the exhaust manifold or turbocharger pipe

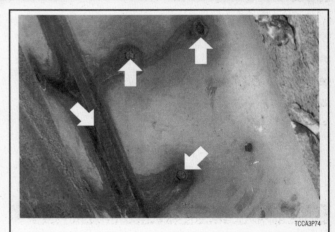

Fig. 193 Check the muffler for rotted spot welds and seams

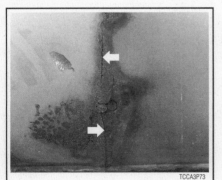

Fig. 194 Cracks in the muffler are a guaranteed leak

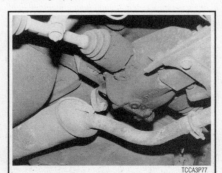

Fig. 195 Make sure the exhaust components are not contacting the body or suspension

Fig. 196 Check for overstretched or torn exhaust hangers

Fig. 197 Example of a badly deteriorated exhaust pipe

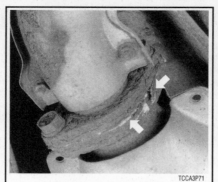

Fig. 198 Inspect flanges for gaskets that have deteriorated and need replacement

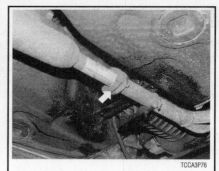

Fig. 199 Some systems, like this one, use large O-rings (donuts) in between the flanges

where the header pipe is attached and work your way to the back of the vehicle. On dual exhaust systems, remember to inspect both sides of the vehicle. Check the complete exhaust system for open seams, holes loose connections, or other deterioration which could permit exhaust fumes to seep into the passenger compartment. Inspect all mounting brackets and hangers for deterioration, some models may have rubber O-rings that can be overstretched and non-supportive. These components will need to be replaced if found. It has always been a practice to use a pointed tool to poke up into the exhaust system where the deterioration spots are to see whether or not they crumble. Some models may have heat shield covering certain parts of the exhaust system , it will be necessary to remove these shields to have the exhaust visible for inspection also.

REPLACEMENT

◆ See Figures 200, 201 and 202

There are basically two types of exhaust systems. One is the flange type where the component ends are attached with bolts and a gasket in-between. The other exhaust system is the slip joint type. These components slip into one another using clamps to retain them together.

✳✳ CAUTION

Allow the exhaust system to cool sufficiently before spraying a solvent exhaust fasteners. Some solvents are highly flammable and could ignite when sprayed on hot exhaust components.

Before removing any component of the exhaust system, ALWAYS squirt a liquid rust dissolving agent onto the fasteners for ease of removal. A lot of knuckle skin will be saved by following this rule. It may even be wise to spray the fasteners and allow them to sit overnight.

✳✳ CAUTION

Do NOT perform exhaust repairs or inspection with the engine or exhaust hot. Allow the system to cool. Exhaust systems are noted

for sharp edges, flaking metal and rusted bolts. Gloves and eye protection are required.

1. Raise and support the vehicle safely, as necessary for access. Remember that some longer exhaust pipes may be difficult to wrestle out from under the vehicle if it is not supported high enough.
2. If you haven't already, apply a generous amount of penetrating oil or solvent to any rusted fasteners.
3. On flange joints, carefully loosen and remove the retainers at the flange. If bolts or nuts are difficult to break loose, apply more penetrating liquid and give it some additional time to set. If the fasteners still will not come loose an impact driver may be necessary to jar it loose (and keep the fastener from breaking).

➡**When unbolting the headpipe from the manifold, make sure that the bolts are free before trying to remove them. If you snap a stud in the exhaust manifold, the stud will have to be removed with a bolt extractor, which often means removal of the manifold itself.**

4. On slip joint components, remove the mounting U-bolts from around the exhaust pipe you are extracting from the vehicle. Don't be surprised if the U-bolts break while removing the nuts.
5. Loosen the exhaust pipe from any mounting brackets retaining it to the floor pan and separate the components. Slight twisting and turning may be required to remove the component completely from the vehicle. You may need to tap on the component with a rubber mallet to loosen it. If all else fails, use a hacksaw to separate the parts. An oxy-acetylene cutting torch may be faster but the sparks are DANGEROUS near the fuel tank, and at the very least, accidents could happen, resulting in damage to the under-vehicle parts, not to mention yourself.
6. When installing exhaust components, you should loosely position all components before tightening any of the joints. Once you are certain that the system is run correctly, begin tightening the fasteners at the front of the vehicle and work your way back.

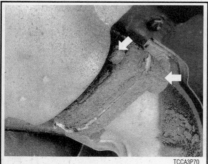

Fig. 200 Nuts and bolts will be extremely difficult to remove when deteriorated with rust

Fig. 201 Example of a flange type exhaust system joint

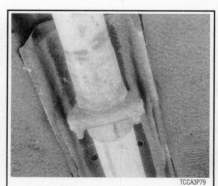

Fig. 202 Example of a common slip joint type system

ENGINE RECONDITIONING

Determining Engine Condition

Anything that generates heat and/or friction will eventually burn or wear out (for example, a light bulb generates heat, therefore its life span is limited). With this in mind, a running engine generates tremendous amounts of both; friction is encountered by the moving and rotating parts inside the engine and heat is created by friction and combustion of the fuel. However, the engine has systems designed to help reduce the effects of heat and friction and provide added longevity. The oiling system reduces the amount of friction encountered by the moving parts inside the engine, while the cooling system reduces heat created by friction and combustion. If either system is not maintained, a break-down will be inevitable. Therefore, you can see how regular maintenance can affect the service life of your vehicle. If you do not drain, flush and refill your cooling system at the proper intervals, deposits will begin to accumulate in the radiator, thereby reducing the amount of heat it can extract from the coolant. The same applies to your oil and filter; if it is not changed often enough it becomes laden with contaminates and is unable to properly lubricate the engine. This increases friction and wear.

There are a number of methods for evaluating the condition of your engine. A compression test can reveal the condition of your pistons, piston rings, cylinder bores, head gasket(s), valves and valve seats. An oil pressure test can warn you of possible engine bearing, or oil pump failures. Excessive oil consumption, evidence of oil in the engine air intake area and/or bluish smoke from the tailpipe may indicate worn piston rings, worn valve guides and/or valve seals. As a general rule, an engine that uses no more than one quart of oil every 1000 miles is in good condition. Engines that use one quart of oil or more in less than 1000 miles should first be checked for oil leaks. If any oil leaks are present, have them fixed before determining how much oil is consumed by the engine, especially if blue smoke is not visible at the tailpipe.

COMPRESSION TEST

▶ **See Figure 203**

A noticeable lack of engine power, excessive oil consumption and/or poor fuel mileage measured over an extended period are all indicators of internal engine wear. Worn piston rings, scored or worn cylinder bores, blown head gaskets, sticking or burnt valves, and worn valve seats are all possible culprits. A check of each cylinder's compression will help locate the problem.

➡**A screw-in type compression gauge is more accurate than the type you simply hold against the spark plug hole. Although it takes slightly longer to use, it's worth the effort to obtain a more accurate reading.**

1. Make sure that the proper amount and viscosity of engine oil is in the crankcase, then ensure the battery is fully charged.
2. Warm-up the engine to normal operating temperature, then shut the engine **OFF**.
3. Disable the ignition system.
4. Label and disconnect all of the spark plug wires from the plugs.
5. Thoroughly clean the cylinder head area around the spark plug ports, then remove the spark plugs.

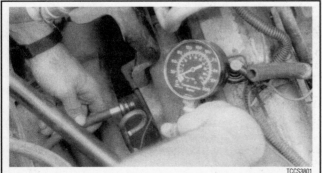

TCCS3801

Fig. 203 A screw-in type compression gauge is more accurate and easier to use without an assistant

6. Set the throttle plate to the fully open (wide-open throttle) position. You can block the accelerator linkage open for this, or you can have an assistant fully depress the accelerator pedal.
7. Install a screw-in type compression gauge into the No. 1 spark plug hole until the fitting is snug.

✳✳ WARNING

Be careful not to crossthread the spark plug hole.

8. According to the tool manufacturer's instructions, connect a remote starting switch to the starting circuit.
9. With the ignition switch in the **OFF** position, use the remote starting switch to crank the engine through at least five compression strokes (approximately 5 seconds of cranking) and record the highest reading on the gauge.
10. Repeat the test on each cylinder, cranking the engine approximately the same number of compression strokes and/or time as the first.
11. Compare the highest readings from each cylinder to that of the others. The indicated compression pressures are considered within specifications if the lowest reading cylinder is within 75 percent of the pressure recorded for the highest reading cylinder. For example, if your highest reading cylinder pressure was 150 psi (1034 kPa), then 75 percent of that would be 113 psi (779 kPa). So the lowest reading cylinder should be no less than 113 psi (779 kPa).
12. If a cylinder exhibits an unusually low compression reading, pour a tablespoon of clean engine oil into the cylinder through the spark plug hole and repeat the compression test. If the compression rises after adding oil, it means that the cylinder's piston rings and/or cylinder bore are damaged or worn. If the pressure remains low, the valves may not be seating properly (a valve job is needed), or the head gasket may be blown near that cylinder. If compression in any two adjacent cylinders is low, and if the addition of oil doesn't help raise compression, there is leakage past the head gasket. Oil and coolant in the combustion chamber, combined with blue or constant white smoke from the tailpipe, are symptoms of this problem. However, don't be alarmed by the normal white smoke emitted from the tailpipe during engine warm-up or from cold weather driving. There may be evidence of water droplets on the engine dipstick and/or oil droplets in the cooling system if a head gasket is blown.

OIL PRESSURE TEST

Check for proper oil pressure at the sending unit passage with an externally mounted mechanical oil pressure gauge (as opposed to relying on a factory installed dash-mounted gauge). A tachometer may also be needed, as some specifications may require running the engine at a specific rpm.
1. With the engine cold, locate and remove the oil pressure sending unit.
2. Following the manufacturer's instructions, connect a mechanical oil pressure gauge and, if necessary, a tachometer to the engine.
3. Start the engine and allow it to idle.
4. Check the oil pressure reading when cold and record the number. You may need to run the engine at a specified rpm, so check the specifications.
5. Run the engine until normal operating temperature is reached (upper radiator hose will feel warm).
6. Check the oil pressure reading again with the engine hot and record the number. Turn the engine **OFF**.
7. Compare your hot oil pressure reading to specification. If the reading is low, check the cold pressure reading against the chart. If the cold pressure is well above the specification, and the hot reading was lower than the specification, you may have the wrong viscosity oil in the engine. Change the oil, making sure to use the proper grade and quantity, then repeat the test.

Low oil pressure readings could be attributed to internal component wear, pump related problems, a low oil level, or oil viscosity that is too low. High oil pressure readings could be caused by an overfilled crankcase, too high of an oil viscosity or a faulty pressure relief valve.

Buy or Rebuild?

Now if you have determined that your engine is worn out, you must make some decisions. The question of whether or not an engine is worth rebuilding is largely a subjective matter and one of personal worth. Is the engine a popular one, or is it an obsolete model? Are parts available? Will it get acceptable gas mileage once it is rebuilt? Is the car it's being put into worth keeping? Would it be less expensive to buy a new engine, have your engine rebuilt by a pro, rebuild it yourself or buy a used engine from a salvage yard? Or would it be simpler and less expensive to buy another car? If you have considered all these matters, and have still decided to rebuild the engine, then it is time to decide how you will rebuild it.

➡**The editors at Chilton feel that most engine machining should be performed by a professional machine shop. Think of it as an assurance that the job has been done right the first time. There are many expensive and specialized tools required to perform such tasks as boring and honing an engine block or having a valve job done on a cylinder head. Even inspecting the parts requires expensive micrometers and gauges to properly measure wear and clearances. A machine shop can deliver to you clean, and ready to assemble parts, saving you time and aggravation. Your maximum savings will come from performing the removal, disassembly, assembly and installation of the engine and purchasing or renting only the tools required to perform these tasks.**

A complete rebuild or overhaul of an engine involves replacing all of the moving parts (pistons, rods, crankshaft, camshaft, etc.) with new ones and machining the non-moving wearing surfaces of the block and heads. Unfortunately, this may not be cost effective. For instance, your crankshaft may have been damaged or worn, but it can be machined undersize for a minimal fee.

So although you can replace everything inside the engine, it is usually wiser to replace only those parts which are really needed, and, if possible, repair the more expensive ones. Later in this section, we will break the engine down into its two main components: the cylinder head and the engine block. We will discuss each component, and the recommended parts to replace during a rebuild on each.

Engine Overhaul Tips

Most engine overhaul procedures are fairly standard. In addition to specific parts replacement procedures and specifications for your individual engine, this section is also a guide to acceptable rebuilding procedures. Examples of standard rebuilding practice are given and should be used along with specific details concerning your particular engine.

Competent and accurate machine shop services will ensure maximum performance, reliability and engine life. In most instances it is more profitable for the do-it-yourself mechanic to remove, clean and inspect the component, buy the necessary parts and deliver these to a shop for actual machine work.

Much of the assembly work (crankshaft, bearings, piston rods, and other components) is well within the scope of the do-it-yourself mechanic's tools and abilities. You will have to decide for yourself the depth of involvement you desire in an engine repair or rebuild.

TOOLS

The tools required for an engine overhaul or parts replacement will depend on the depth of your involvement. With a few exceptions, they will be the tools found in a mechanic's tool kit (see Section 1 of this manual). More in-depth work will require some or all of the following:
- A dial indicator (reading in thousandths) mounted on a universal base
- Micrometers and telescope gauges
- Jaw and screw-type pullers
- Scraper
- Valve spring compressor
- Ring groove cleaner
- Piston ring expander and compressor
- Ridge reamer
- Cylinder hone or glaze breaker
- Plastigage®
- Engine stand

The use of most of these tools is illustrated in this section. Many can be rented for a one-time use from a local parts jobber or tool supply house specializing in automotive work.

Occasionally, the use of special tools is called for. See the information on Special Tools and the Safety Notice in the front of this book before substituting another tool.

OVERHAUL TIPS

Aluminum has become extremely popular for use in engines, due to its low weight. Observe the following precautions when handling aluminum parts:
- Never hot tank aluminum parts (the caustic hot tank solution will eat the aluminum.)
- Remove all aluminum parts (identification tag, etc.) from engine parts prior to the tanking.
- Always coat threads lightly with engine oil or anti-seize compounds before installation, to prevent seizure.
- Never overtighten bolts or spark plugs especially in aluminum threads.

When assembling the engine, any parts that will be exposed to frictional contact must be prelubed to provide lubrication at initial start-up. Any product specifically formulated for this purpose can be used, but engine oil is not recommended as a prelube in most cases.

When semi-permanent (locked, but removable) installation of bolts or nuts is desired, threads should be cleaned and coated with Loctite® or another similar, commercial non-hardening sealant.

CLEANING

◆ See Figures 204, 205, 206 and 207

Before the engine and its components are inspected, they must be thoroughly cleaned. You will need to remove any engine varnish, oil sludge and/or carbon deposits from all of the components to insure an accurate inspection. A crack in the engine block or cylinder head can easily become overlooked if hidden by a layer of sludge or carbon.

Most of the cleaning process can be carried out with common hand tools and readily available solvents or solutions. Carbon deposits can be chipped away using a hammer and a hard wooden chisel. Old gasket material and varnish or sludge can usually be removed using a scraper and/or cleaning solvent. Extremely stubborn deposits may require the use of a power drill with a wire brush. If using a wire brush, use extreme care around any critical machined surfaces (such as the gasket surfaces, bearing saddles, cylinder bores, etc.). USE OF A WIRE BRUSH IS NOT RECOMMENDED ON ANY ALUMINUM COMPONENTS. Always follow any safety recommendations given by the manufacturer of the tool and/or solvent.

❋❋ CAUTION

Always wear eye protection during any cleaning process involving scraping, chipping or spraying of solvents.

An alternative to the mess and hassle of cleaning the parts yourself is to drop them off at a local garage or machine shop. They should have the necessary equipment to properly clean all of the parts for a nominal fee.

Remove any oil galley plugs, freeze plugs and/or pressed-in bearings and carefully wash and degrease all of the engine components including the fasteners and bolts. Small parts such as the valves, springs, etc., should be placed in a metal basket and allowed to soak. Use pipe cleaner type brushes, and clean all passageways in the components.

Use a ring expander and remove the rings from the pistons. Clean the piston ring grooves with a special tool or a piece of broken ring. Scrape the carbon off of the top of the piston. You should never use a wire brush on the pistons. After preparing all of the piston assemblies in this manner, wash and degrease them again.

❋❋ WARNING

Use extreme care when cleaning around the cylinder head valve seats. A mistake or slip may cost you a new seat.

When cleaning the cylinder head, remove carbon from the combustion chamber with the valves installed. This will avoid damaging the valve seats.

REPAIRING DAMAGED THREADS

◆ See Figures 208, 209, 210, 211 and 212

Several methods of repairing damaged threads are available. Heli-Coil® (shown here), Keenserts® and Microdot® are among the most widely used. All involve basically the same principle—drilling out stripped threads, tapping the

Fig. 204 Use a gasket scraper to remove the old gasket material from the mating surfaces

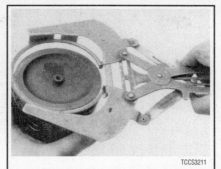

Fig. 205 Before cleaning and inspection, use a ring expander tool to remove the piston rings

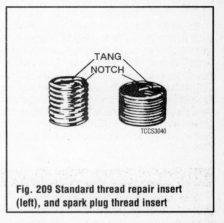

Fig. 206 Clean the piston ring grooves using a ring groove cleaner tool, or . . .

Fig. 207 . . . use a piece of an old ring to clean the grooves. Be careful, the ring can be quite sharp

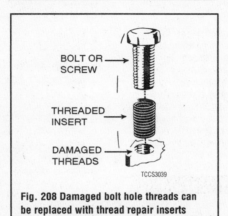

BOLT OR SCREW

THREADED INSERT

DAMAGED THREADS

Fig. 208 Damaged bolt hole threads can be replaced with thread repair inserts

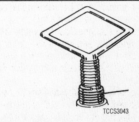

TANG

NOTCH

Fig. 209 Standard thread repair insert (left), and spark plug thread insert

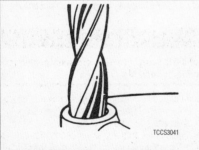

Fig. 210 Drill out the damaged threads with the specified size bit. Be sure to drill completely through the hole or to the bottom of a blind hole

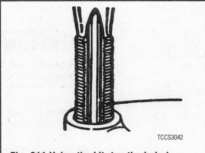

Fig. 211 Using the kit, tap the hole in order to receive the thread insert. Keep the tap well oiled and back it out frequently to avoid clogging the threads

Fig. 212 Screw the insert onto the installer tool until the tang engages the slot. Thread the insert into the hole until it is ¼–½ turn below the top surface, then remove the tool and break off the tang using a punch

hole and installing a prewound insert—making welding, plugging and oversize fasteners unnecessary.

Two types of thread repair inserts are usually supplied: a standard type for most inch coarse, inch fine, metric course and metric fine thread sizes and a spark lug type to fit most spark plug port sizes. Consult the individual tool manufacturer's catalog to determine exact applications. Typical thread repair kits will contain a selection of prewound threaded inserts, a tap (corresponding to the outside diameter threads of the insert) and an installation tool. Spark plug inserts usually differ because they require a tap equipped with pilot threads and a combined reamer/tap section. Most manufacturers also supply blister-packed thread repair inserts separately in addition to a master kit containing a variety of taps and inserts plus installation tools.

Before attempting to repair a threaded hole, remove any snapped, broken or damaged bolts or studs. Penetrating oil can be used to free frozen threads. The offending item can usually be removed with locking pliers or using a screw/stud extractor. After the hole is clear, the thread can be repaired as shown in the kit manufacturer's instructions.

Engine Preparation

To properly rebuild an engine, you must first remove it from the vehicle, then disassemble and diagnose it. Ideally you should place your engine on an engine stand. This affords you the best access to the engine components. Remove the flywheel or flexplate before installing the engine to the stand.

Now that you have the engine on a stand, and assuming that you have drained the oil and coolant from the engine, it's time to strip it of all but the necessary components. Before you start disassembling the engine, you may want to take a moment to draw some pictures, or fabricate some labels or containers to mark the locations of various components and the bolts and/or studs which fasten them. Modern day engines use a lot of little brackets and clips which hold wiring harnesses and such, and these holders are often mounted on studs and/or bolts that can be easily mixed up. The manufacturer spent a lot of time and money designing your vehicle, and they wouldn't have wasted any of it by haphazardly placing brackets, clips or fasteners on the vehicle. If it's present when you disassemble it, put it back when you assemble, you will regret not remembering that little bracket which holds a wire harness out of the path of a rotating part.

You should begin by unbolting any accessories still attached to the engine, such as the water pump, power steering pump, alternator, etc. Then, unfasten any manifolds (intake or exhaust) which were not removed during the engine removal procedure. Finally, remove any covers remaining on the engine such as the rocker arm, front or timing cover and oil pan. Some front covers may require the vibration damper and/or crank pulley to be removed beforehand. The idea is to reduce the engine to the bare necessities of cylinder head(s), valve train, engine block, crankshaft, pistons and connecting rods, plus any other `in block' components such as oil pumps, balance shafts and auxiliary shafts.

Finally, remove the cylinder head(s) from the engine block and carefully place on a bench. Disassembly instructions for each component follow later in this section.

Cylinder Head

There are two basic types of cylinder heads used on today's automobiles: the Overhead Valve (OHV) and the Overhead Camshaft (OHC). The latter can also be broken down into two subgroups: the Single Overhead Camshaft (SOHC) and the Dual Overhead Camshaft (DOHC). Generally, if there is only a single camshaft on a head, it is just referred to as an OHC head. Also, an engine with an OHV cylinder head is also known as a pushrod engine.

Most cylinder heads these days are made of an aluminum alloy due to its light weight, durability and heat transfer qualities. However, cast iron was the material of choice in the past, and is still used on many vehicles. Whether made from aluminum or iron, all cylinder heads have valves and seats. Some use two valves per cylinder, while the more hi-tech engines will utilize a multi-valve configuration using 3, 4 and even 5 valves per cylinder. When the valve contacts the seat, it does so on precision machined surfaces, which seals the combustion chamber. All cylinder heads have a valve guide for each valve. The guide centers the valve to the seat and allows it to move up and down within it. The clearance between the valve and guide can be critical. Too much clearance and the engine may consume oil, lose vacuum and/or damage the seat. Too little, and the valve can stick in the guide causing the engine to run poorly if at all,

and possibly causing severe damage. The last component all automotive cylinder heads have are valve springs. The spring holds the valve against its seat. It also returns the valve to this position when the valve has been opened by the valve train or camshaft. The spring is fastened to the valve by a retainer and valve locks (sometimes called keepers). Aluminum heads will also have a valve spring shim to keep the spring from wearing away the aluminum.

An ideal method of rebuilding the cylinder head would involve replacing all of the valves, guides, seats, springs, etc. with new ones. However, depending on how the engine was maintained, often this is not necessary. A major cause of valve, guide and seat wear is an improperly tuned engine. An engine that is running too rich, will often wash the lubricating oil out of the guide with gasoline, causing it to wear rapidly. Conversely, an engine which is running too lean will place higher combustion temperatures on the valves and seats allowing them to wear or even burn. Springs fall victim to the driving habits of the individual. A driver who often runs the engine rpm to the redline will wear out or break the springs faster then one that stays well below it. Unfortunately, mileage takes it toll on all of the parts. Generally, the valves, guides, springs and seats in a cylinder head can be machined and re-used, saving you money. However, if a valve is burnt, it may be wise to replace all of the valves, since they were all operating in the same environment. The same goes for any other component on the cylinder head. Think of it as an insurance policy against future problems related to that component.

Unfortunately, the only way to find out which components need replacing, is to disassemble and carefully check each piece. After the cylinder head(s) are disassembled, thoroughly clean all of the components.

DISASSEMBLY

▶ See Figures 213 thru 218

Before disassembling the cylinder head, you may want to fabricate some containers to hold the various parts, as some of them can be quite small (such as keepers) and easily lost. Also keeping yourself and the components organized will aid in assembly and reduce confusion. Where possible, try to maintain a components original location; this is especially important if there is not going to be any machine work performed on the components.

Fig. 213 When removing an OHV valve spring, use a compressor tool to relieve the tension from the retainer

Fig. 214 A small magnet will help in removal of the valve locks

Fig. 215 Be careful not to lose the small valve locks (keepers)

Fig. 216 Remove the valve seal from the valve stem—O-ring type seal shown

Fig. 217 Removing an umbrella/positive type seal

Fig. 218 Invert the cylinder head and withdraw the valve from the valve guide bore

1. If you haven't already removed the rocker arms and/or shafts, do so now.

2. Position the head so that the springs are easily accessed.

3. Use a valve spring compressor tool, and relieve spring tension from the retainer.

➡️**Due to engine varnish, the retainer may stick to the valve locks. A gentle tap with a hammer may help to break it loose.**

4. Remove the valve locks from the valve tip and/or retainer. A small magnet may help in removing the locks.

5. Lift the valve spring, tool and all, off of the valve stem.

6. If equipped, remove the valve seal. If the seal is difficult to remove with the valve in place, try removing the valve first, then the seal. Follow the steps below for valve removal.

7. Position the head to allow access for withdrawing the valve.

➡️**Cylinder heads that have seen a lot of miles and/or abuse may have mushroomed the valve lock grove and/or tip, causing difficulty in removal of the valve. If this has happened, use a metal file to carefully remove the high spots around the lock grooves and/or tip. Only file it enough to allow removal.**

8. Remove the valve from the cylinder head.

9. If equipped, remove the valve spring shim. A small magnetic tool or screwdriver will aid in removal.

10. Repeat Steps 3 though 9 until all of the valves have been removed.

INSPECTION

Now that all of the cylinder head components are clean, it's time to inspect them for wear and/or damage. To accurately inspect them, you will need some specialized tools:

- A 0–1 in. micrometer for the valves
- A dial indicator or inside diameter gauge for the valve guides
- A spring pressure test gauge

If you do not have access to the proper tools, you may want to bring the components to a shop that does.

Valves

▶ **See Figures 219 and 220**

The first thing to inspect are the valve heads. Look closely at the head, margin and face for any cracks, excessive wear or burning. The margin is the best place to look for burning. It should have a squared edge with an even width all around the diameter. When a valve burns, the margin will look melted and the edges rounded. Also inspect the valve head for any signs of tulipping. This will show as a lifting of the edges or dishing in the center of the head and will usually not occur to all of the valves. All of the heads should look the same, any that seem dished more than others are probably bad. Next, inspect the valve lock grooves and valve tips. Check for any burrs around the lock grooves, especially if you had to file them to remove the valve. Valve tips should appear flat, although slight rounding with high mileage engines is normal. Slightly worn valve tips will need to be machined flat. Last, measure the valve stem diameter with the micrometer. Measure the area that rides within the guide, especially towards the tip where

most of the wear occurs. Take several measurements along its length and compare them to each other. Wear should be even along the length with little to no taper. If no minimum diameter is given in the specifications, then the stem should not read more than 0.001 in. (0.025mm) below the unworn portion of the stem. Any valves that fail these inspections should be replaced.

Springs, Retainers and Valve Locks

▶ **See Figures 221 and 222**

The first thing to check is the most obvious, broken springs. Next check the free length and squareness of each spring. If applicable, insure to distinguish between intake and exhaust springs. Use a ruler and/or carpenter's square to measure the length. A carpenter's square should be used to check the springs for squareness. If a spring pressure test gauge is available, check each springs rating and compare to the specifications chart. Check the readings against the specifications given. Any springs that fail these inspections should be replaced.

The spring retainers rarely need replacing, however they should still be checked as a precaution. Inspect the spring mating surface and the valve lock retention area for any signs of excessive wear. Also check for any signs of cracking. Replace any retainers that are questionable.

Valve locks should be inspected for excessive wear on the outside contact area as well as on the inner notched surface. Any locks which appear worn or broken and its respective valve should be replaced.

Cylinder Head

There are several things to check on the cylinder head: valve guides, seats, cylinder head surface flatness, cracks and physical damage.

VALVE GUIDES

▶ **See Figure 223**

Now that you know the valves are good, you can use them to check the guides, although a new valve, if available, is preferred. Before you measure anything, look at the guides carefully and inspect them for any cracks, chips or

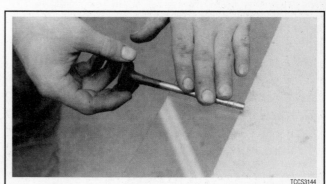
Fig. 219 Valve stems may be rolled on a flat surface to check for bends

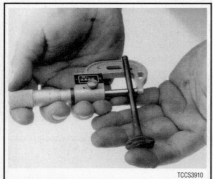
Fig. 220 Use a micrometer to check the valve stem diameter

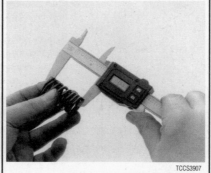
Fig. 221 Use a caliper to check the valve spring free-length

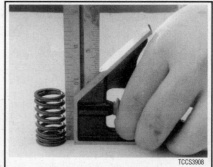
Fig. 222 Check the valve spring for squareness on a flat surface; a carpenter's square can be used

Fig. 223 A dial gauge may be used to check valve stem-to-guide clearance; read the gauge while moving the valve stem

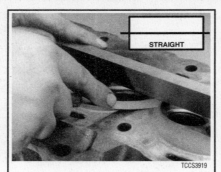

Fig. 224 Check the head for flatness across the center of the head surface using a straightedge and feeler gauge

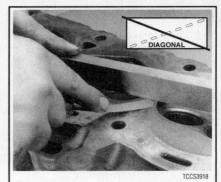

Fig. 225 Checks should also be made along both diagonals of the head surface

breakage. Also if the guide is a removable style (as in most aluminum heads), check them for any looseness or evidence of movement. All of the guides should appear to be at the same height from the spring seat. If any seem lower (or higher) from another, the guide has moved. Mount a dial indicator onto the spring side of the cylinder head. Lightly oil the valve stem and insert it into the cylinder head. Position the dial indicator against the valve stem near the tip and zero the gauge. Grasp the valve stem and wiggle towards and away from the dial indicator and observe the readings. Mount the dial indicator 90 degrees from the initial point and zero the gauge and again take a reading. Compare the two readings for an out of round condition. Check the readings against the specifications given. An Inside Diameter (I.D.) gauge designed for valve guides will give you an accurate valve guide bore measurement. If the I.D. gauge is used, compare the readings with the specifications given. Any guides that fail these inspections should be replaced or machined.

VALVE SEATS

A visual inspection of the valve seats should show a slightly worn and pitted surface where the valve face contacts the seat. Inspect the seat carefully for severe pitting or cracks. Also, a seat that is badly worn will be recessed into the cylinder head. A severely worn or recessed seat may need to be replaced. All cracked seats must be replaced. A seat concentricity gauge, if available, should be used to check the seat run-out. If run-out exceeds specifications the seat must be machined (if no specification is available given use 0.002 in. or 0.051mm).

CYLINDER HEAD SURFACE FLATNESS

▶ See Figures 224 and 225

After you have cleaned the gasket surface of the cylinder head of any old gasket material, check the head for flatness.

Place a straightedge across the gasket surface. Using feeler gauges, determine the clearance at the center of the straightedge and across the cylinder head at several points. Check along the centerline and diagonally on the head surface. If the warpage exceeds 0.003 in. (0.076mm) within a 6.0 in. (15.2cm) span, or 0.006 in. (0.152mm) over the total length of the head, the cylinder head must be resurfaced. After resurfacing the heads of a V-type engine, the intake manifold flange surface should be checked, and if necessary, milled proportionally to allow for the change in its mounting position.

CRACKS AND PHYSICAL DAMAGE

Generally, cracks are limited to the combustion chamber, however, it is not uncommon for the head to crack in a spark plug hole, port, outside of the head or in the valve spring/rocker arm area. The first area to inspect is always the hottest: the exhaust seat/port area.

A visual inspection should be performed, but just because you don't see a crack does not mean it is not there. Some more reliable methods for inspecting for cracks include Magnaflux®, a magnetic process or Zyglo®, a dye penetrant. Magnaflux® is used only on ferrous metal (cast iron) heads. Zyglo® uses a spray on fluorescent mixture along with a black light to reveal the cracks. It is strongly recommended to have your cylinder head checked professionally for cracks, especially if the engine was known to have overheated and/or leaked or consumed coolant. Contact a local shop for availability and pricing of these services.

Physical damage is usually very evident. For example, a broken mounting ear from dropping the head or a bent or broken stud and/or bolt. All of these defects should be fixed or, if unrepairable, the head should be replaced.

REFINISHING & REPAIRING

Many of the procedures given for refinishing and repairing the cylinder head components must be performed by a machine shop. Certain steps, if the inspected part is not worn, can be performed yourself inexpensively. However, you spent a lot of time and effort so far, why risk trying to save a couple bucks if you might have to do it all over again?

Valves

Any valves that were not replaced should be refaced and the tips ground flat. Unless you have access to a valve grinding machine, this should be done by a machine shop. If the valves are in extremely good condition, as well as the valve seats and guides, they may be lapped in without performing machine work.

It is a recommended practice to lap the valves even after machine work has been performed and/or new valves have been purchased. This insures a positive seal between the valve and seat.

LAPPING THE VALVES

➡Before lapping the valves to the seats, read the rest of the cylinder head section to insure that any related parts are in acceptable enough condition to continue. Also, remember that before any valve seat machining and/or lapping can be performed, the guides must be within factory recommended specifications.

1. Invert the cylinder head.
2. Lightly lubricate the valve stems and insert them into the cylinder head in their numbered order.
3. Raise the valve from the seat and apply a small amount of fine lapping compound to the seat.
4. Moisten the suction head of a hand-lapping tool and attach it to the head of the valve.
5. Rotate the tool between the palms of both hands, changing the position of the valve on the valve seat and lifting the tool often to prevent grooving.
6. Lap the valve until a smooth, polished circle is evident on the valve and seat.
7. Remove the tool and the valve. Wipe away all traces of the grinding compound and store the valve to maintain its lapped location.

✳✳ WARNING

Do not get the valves out of order after they have been lapped. They must be put back with the same valve seat with which they were lapped.

Springs, Retainers and Valve Locks

There is no repair or refinishing possible with the springs, retainers and valve locks. If they are found to be worn or defective, they must be replaced with new (or known good) parts.

Cylinder Head

Most refinishing procedures dealing with the cylinder head must be performed by a machine shop. Read the sections below and review your inspection data to determine whether or not machining is necessary.

VALVE GUIDE

➡**If any machining or replacements are made to the valve guides, the seats must be machined.**

Unless the valve guides need machining or replacing, the only service to perform is to thoroughly clean them of any dirt or oil residue.

There are only two types of valve guides used on automobile engines: the replaceable-type (all aluminum heads) and the cast-in integral-type (most cast iron heads). There are four recommended methods for repairing worn guides.

- Knurling
- Inserts
- Reaming oversize
- Replacing

Knurling is a process in which metal is displaced and raised, thereby reducing clearance, giving a true center, and providing oil control. It is the least expensive way of repairing the valve guides. However, it is not necessarily the best, and in some cases, a knurled valve guide will not stand up for more than a short time. It requires a special knurlizer and precision reaming tools to obtain proper clearances. It would not be cost effective to purchase these tools, unless you plan on rebuilding several of the same cylinder head.

Installing a guide insert involves machining the guide to accept a bronze insert. One style is the coil-type which is installed into a threaded guide. Another is the thin-walled insert where the guide is reamed oversize to accept a split-sleeve insert. After the insert is installed, a special tool is then run through the guide to expand the insert, locking it to the guide. The insert is then reamed to the standard size for proper valve clearance.

Reaming for oversize valves restores normal clearances and provides a true valve seat. Most cast-in type guides can be reamed to accept an valve with an oversize stem. The cost factor for this can become quite high as you will need to purchase the reamer and new, oversize stem valves for all guides which were reamed. Oversizes are generally 0.003–0.030 in. (0.076–0.762mm), with 0.015 in. (0.381mm) being the most common.

To replace cast-in type valve guides, they must be drilled out, then reamed to accept replacement guides. This must be done on a fixture which will allow centering and leveling off of the original valve seat or guide, otherwise a serious guide-to-seat misalignment may occur making it impossible to properly machine the seat.

Replaceable-type guides are pressed into the cylinder head. A hammer and a stepped drift or punch may be used to install and remove the guides. Before removing the guides, measure the protrusion on the spring side of the head and record it for installation. Use the stepped drift to hammer out the old guide from the combustion chamber side of the head. When installing, determine whether or not the guide also seals a water jacket in the head, and if it does, use the recommended sealing agent. If there is no water jacket, grease the valve guide and its bore. Use the stepped drift, and hammer the new guide into the cylinder head from the spring side of the cylinder head. A stack of washers the same thickness as the measured protrusion may help the installation process.

VALVE SEATS

➡**Before any valve seat machining can be performed, the guides must be within factory recommended specifications. If any machining occurred or if replacements were made to the valve guides, the seats must be machined.**

If the seats are in good condition, the valves can be lapped to the seats, and the cylinder head assembled. See the valves section for instructions on lapping.

If the valve seats are worn, cracked or damaged, they must be serviced by a machine shop. The valve seat must be perfectly centered to the valve guide, which requires very accurate machining.

CYLINDER HEAD SURFACE

If the cylinder head is warped, it must be machined flat. If the warpage is extremely severe, the head may need to be replaced. In some instances, it may be possible to straighten a warped head enough to allow machining. In either case, contact a professional machine shop for service.

CRACKS AND PHYSICAL DAMAGE

Certain cracks can be repaired in both cast iron and aluminum heads. For cast iron, a tapered threaded insert is installed along the length of the crack. Aluminum can also use the tapered inserts, however welding is the preferred method. Some physical damage can be repaired through brazing or welding. Contact a machine shop to get expert advice for your particular dilemma.

ASSEMBLY

The first step for any assembly job is to have a clean area in which to work. Next, thoroughly clean all of the parts and components that are to be assembled. Finally, place all of the components onto a suitable work space and, if necessary, arrange the parts to their respective positions.

OHV Engines

1. Lightly lubricate the valve stems and insert all of the valves into the cylinder head. If possible, maintain their original locations.
2. If equipped, install any valve spring shims which were removed.
3. If equipped, install the new valve seals, keeping the following in mind:
- If the valve seal presses over the guide, lightly lubricate the outer guide surfaces.
- If the seal is an O-ring type, it is installed just after compressing the spring but before the valve locks.
4. Place the valve spring and retainer over the stem.
5. Position the spring compressor tool and compress the spring.
6. Assemble the valve locks to the stem.
7. Relieve the spring pressure slowly and insure that neither valve lock becomes dislodged by the retainer.
8. Remove the spring compressor tool.
9. Repeat Steps 2 through 8 until all of the springs have been installed.

Engine Block

GENERAL INFORMATION

A thorough overhaul or rebuild of an engine block would include replacing the pistons, rings, bearings, timing belt/chain assembly and oil pump. For OHV engines also include a new camshaft and lifters. The block would then have the cylinders bored and honed oversize (or if using removable cylinder sleeves, new sleeves installed) and the crankshaft would be cut undersize to provide new wearing surfaces and perfect clearances. However, your particular engine may not have everything worn out. What if only the piston rings have worn out and the clearances on everything else are still within factory specifications? Well, you could just replace the rings and put it back together, but this would be a very rare example. Chances are, if one component in your engine is worn, other components are sure to follow, and soon. At the very least, you should always replace the rings, bearings and oil pump. This is what is commonly called a "freshen up".

Cylinder Ridge Removal

Because the top piston ring does not travel to the very top of the cylinder, a ridge is built up between the end of the travel and the top of the cylinder bore.

Pushing the piston and connecting rod assembly past the ridge can be difficult, and damage to the piston ring lands could occur. If the ridge is not removed before installing a new piston or not removed at all, piston ring breakage and piston damage may occur.

➡**It is always recommended that you remove any cylinder ridges before removing the piston and connecting rod assemblies. If you know that new pistons are going to be installed and the engine block will be bored oversize, you may be able to forego this step. However, some ridges may actually prevent the assemblies from being removed, necessitating its removal.**

There are several different types of ridge reamers on the market, none of which are inexpensive. Unless a great deal of engine rebuilding is anticipated, borrow or rent a reamer.

1. Turn the crankshaft until the piston is at the bottom of its travel.
2. Cover the head of the piston with a rag.

3. Follow the tool manufacturers instructions and cut away the ridge, exercising extreme care to avoid cutting too deeply.

4. Remove the ridge reamer, the rag and as many of the cuttings as possible. Continue until all of the cylinder ridges have been removed.

DISASSEMBLY

◆ **See Figures 226 and 227**

The engine disassembly instructions following assume that you have the engine mounted on an engine stand. If not, it is easiest to disassemble the engine on a bench or the floor with it resting on the bell housing or transmission mounting surface. You must be able to access the connecting rod fasteners and turn the crankshaft during disassembly. Also, all engine covers (timing, front, side, oil pan, whatever) should have already been removed. Engines which are seized or locked up may not be able to be completely disassembled, and a core (salvage yard) engine should be purchased.

If not done during the cylinder head removal, remove the pushrods and lifters, keeping them in order for assembly. Remove the timing gears and/or timing chain assembly, then remove the oil pump drive assembly and withdraw the camshaft from the engine block. Remove the oil pick-up and pump assembly. If equipped, remove any balance or auxiliary shafts. If necessary, remove the cylinder ridge from the top of the bore. See the cylinder ridge removal procedure earlier in this section.

Rotate the engine over so that the crankshaft is exposed. Use a number punch or scribe and mark each connecting rod with its respective cylinder number. The cylinder closest to the front of the engine is always number 1. However, depending on the engine placement, the front of the engine could either be the flywheel or damper/pulley end. Generally the front of the engine faces the front of the vehicle. Use a number punch or scribe and also mark the main bearing caps from front to rear with the front most cap being number 1 (if there are five caps, mark them 1 through 5, front to rear).

✳✳ WARNING

Take special care when pushing the connecting rod up from the crankshaft because the sharp threads of the rod bolts/studs will score the crankshaft journal. Insure that special plastic caps are installed over them, or cut two pieces of rubber hose to do the same.

Again, rotate the engine, this time to position the number one cylinder bore (head surface) up. Turn the crankshaft until the number one piston is at the bottom of its travel, this should allow the maximum access to its connecting rod. Remove the number one connecting rods fasteners and cap and place two lengths of rubber hose over the rod bolts/studs to protect the crankshaft from damage. Using a sturdy wooden dowel and a hammer, push the connecting rod up about 1 in. (25mm) from the crankshaft and remove the upper bearing insert. Continue pushing or tapping the connecting rod up until the piston rings are out of the cylinder bore. Remove the piston and rod by hand, put the upper half of the bearing insert back into the rod, install the cap with its bearing insert installed, and hand-tighten the cap fasteners. If the parts are kept in order in this manner, they will not get lost and you will be able to tell which bearings came form what cylinder if any problems are discovered and diagnosis is necessary.

Fig. 226 Place rubber hose over the connecting rod studs to protect the crankshaft and cylinder bores from damage

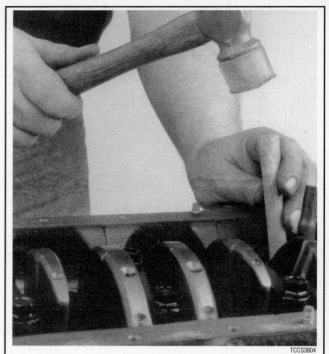

Fig. 227 Carefully tap the piston out of the bore using a wooden dowel

Remove all the other piston assemblies in the same manner. On V-style engines, remove all of the pistons from one bank, then reposition the engine with the other cylinder bank head surface up, and remove that banks piston assemblies.

The only remaining component in the engine block should now be the crankshaft. Loosen the main bearing caps evenly until the fasteners can be turned by hand, then remove them and the caps. Remove the crankshaft from the engine block. Thoroughly clean all of the components.

INSPECTION

Now that the engine block and all of its components are clean, it's time to inspect them for wear and/or damage. To accurately inspect them, you will need some specialized tools:

• Two or three separate micrometers to measure the pistons and crankshaft journals
• A dial indicator
• Telescoping gauges for the cylinder bores
• A rod alignment fixture to check for bent connecting rods

If you do not have access to the proper tools, you may want to bring the components to a shop that does.

Generally, you shouldn't expect cracks in the engine block or its components unless it was known to leak, consume or mix engine fluids, it was severely overheated, or there was evidence of bad bearings and/or crankshaft damage. A visual inspection should be performed on all of the components, but just because you don't see a crack does not mean it is not there. Some more reliable methods for inspecting for cracks include Magnaflux®, a magnetic process or Zyglo®, a dye penetrant. Magnaflux® is used only on ferrous metal (cast iron). Zyglo® uses a spray on fluorescent mixture along with a black light to reveal the cracks. It is strongly recommended to have your engine block checked professionally for cracks, especially if the engine was known to have overheated and/or leaked or consumed coolant. Contact a local shop for availability and pricing of these services.

Engine Block

ENGINE BLOCK BEARING ALIGNMENT

Remove the main bearing caps and, if still installed, the main bearing inserts. Inspect all of the main bearing saddles and caps for damage, burrs or high spots. If damage is found, and it is caused from a spun main bearing, the block will need to be align-bored or, if severe enough, replacement. Any burrs or high spots should be carefully removed with a metal file.

Place a straightedge on the bearing saddles, in the engine block, along the centerline of the crankshaft. If any clearance exists between the straightedge and the saddles, the block must be align-bored.

Align-boring consists of machining the main bearing saddles and caps by means of a flycutter that runs through the bearing saddles.

DECK FLATNESS

The top of the engine block where the cylinder head mounts is called the deck. Insure that the deck surface is clean of dirt, carbon deposits and old gasket material. Place a straightedge across the surface of the deck along its centerline and, using feeler gauges, check the clearance along several points. Repeat the checking procedure with the straightedge placed along both diagonals of the deck surface. If the reading exceeds 0.003 in. (0.076mm) within a 6.0 in. (15.2cm) span, or 0.006 in. (0.152mm) over the total length of the deck, it must be machined.

CYLINDER BORES

◊ See Figure 228

The cylinder bores house the pistons and are slightly larger than the pistons themselves. A common piston-to-bore clearance is 0.0015–0.0025 in. (0.0381mm–0.0635mm). Inspect and measure the cylinder bores. The bore should be checked for out-of-roundness, taper and size. The results of this inspection will determine whether the cylinder can be used in its existing size and condition, or a rebore to the next oversize is required (or in the case of removable sleeves, have replacements installed).

The amount of cylinder wall wear is always greater at the top of the cylinder than at the bottom. This wear is known as taper. Any cylinder that has a taper of 0.0012 in. (0.305mm) or more, must be rebored. Measurements are taken at a number of positions in each cylinder: at the top, middle and bottom and at two points at each position; that is, at a point 90 degrees from the crankshaft centerline, as well as a point parallel to the crankshaft centerline. The measurements are made with either a special dial indicator or a telescopic gauge and micrometer. If the necessary precision tools to check the bore are not available, take the block to a machine shop and have them mike it. Also if you don't have the tools to check the cylinder bores, chances are you will not have the necessary devices to check the pistons, connecting rods and crankshaft. Take these components with you and save yourself an extra trip.

For our procedures, we will use a telescopic gauge and a micrometer. You will need one of each, with a measuring range which covers your cylinder bore size.

1. Position the telescopic gauge in the cylinder bore, loosen the gauges lock and allow it to expand.

➥**Your first two readings will be at the top of the cylinder bore, then proceed to the middle and finally the bottom, making a total of six measurements.**

2. Hold the gauge square in the bore, 90 degrees from the crankshaft centerline, and gently tighten the lock. Tilt the gauge back to remove it from the bore.

3. Measure the gauge with the micrometer and record the reading.

4. Again, hold the gauge square in the bore, this time parallel to the crankshaft centerline, and gently tighten the lock. Again, you will tilt the gauge back to remove it from the bore.

5. Measure the gauge with the micrometer and record this reading. The difference between these two readings is the out-of-round measurement of the cylinder.

6. Repeat steps 1 through 5, each time going to the next lower position, until you reach the bottom of the cylinder. Then go to the next cylinder, and continue until all of the cylinders have been measured.

The difference between these measurements will tell you all about the wear in your cylinders. The measurements which were taken 90 degrees from the crankshaft centerline will always reflect the most wear. That is because at this position is where the engine power presses the piston against the cylinder bore the hardest. This is known as thrust wear. Take your top, 90 degree measurement and compare it to your bottom, 90 degree measurement. The difference between them is the taper. When you measure your pistons, you will compare these readings to your piston sizes and determine piston-to-wall clearance.

Crankshaft

Inspect the crankshaft for visible signs of wear or damage. All of the journals should be perfectly round and smooth. Slight scores are normal for a used crankshaft, but you should hardly feel them with your fingernail. When measuring the crankshaft with a micrometer, you will take readings at the front and rear of each journal, then turn the micrometer 90 degrees and take two more readings, front and rear. The difference between the front-to-rear readings is the journal taper and the first-to-90 degree reading is the out-of-round measurement. Generally, there should be no taper or out-of-roundness found, however, up to 0.0005 in. (0.0127mm) for either can be overlooked. Also, the readings should fall within the factory specifications for journal diameters.

If the crankshaft journals fall within specifications, it is recommended that it be polished before being returned to service. Polishing the crankshaft insures that any minor burrs or high spots are smoothed, thereby reducing the chance of scoring the new bearings.

Pistons and Connecting Rods

PISTONS

◊ See Figure 229

The piston should be visually inspected for any signs of cracking or burning (caused by hot spots or detonation), and scuffing or excessive wear on the skirts. The wrist pin attaches the piston to the connecting rod. The piston should move freely on the wrist pin, both sliding and pivoting. Grasp the connecting rod securely, or mount it in a vise, and try to rock the piston back and forth along the centerline of the wrist pin. There should not be any excessive play evident between the piston and the pin. If there are C-clips retaining the pin in the piston then you have wrist pin bushings in the rods. There should not be any excessive play between the wrist pin and the rod bushing. Normal clearance for the wrist pin is approx. 0.001–0.002 in. (0.025mm–0.051mm).

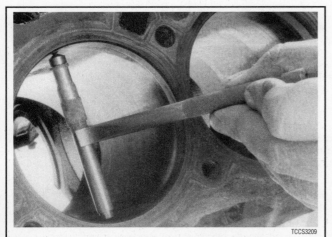

Fig. 228 Use a telescoping gauge to measure the cylinder bore diameter—take several readings within the same bore

Fig. 229 Measure the piston's outer diameter, perpendicular to the wrist pin, with a micrometer

Use a micrometer and measure the diameter of the piston, perpendicular to the wrist pin, on the skirt. Compare the reading to its original cylinder measurement obtained earlier. The difference between the two readings is the piston-to-wall clearance. If the clearance is within specifications, the piston may be used as is. If the piston is out of specification, but the bore is not, you will need a new piston. If both are out of specification, you will need the cylinder rebored and oversize pistons installed. Generally if two or more pistons/bores are out of specification, it is best to rebore the entire block and purchase a complete set of oversize pistons.

CONNECTING ROD

You should have the connecting rod checked for straightness at a machine shop. If the connecting rod is bent, it will unevenly wear the bearing and piston, as well as place greater stress on these components. Any bent or twisted connecting rods must be replaced. If the rods are straight and the wrist pin clearance is within specifications, then only the bearing end of the rod need be checked. Place the connecting rod into a vice, with the bearing inserts in place, install the cap to the rod and torque the fasteners to specifications. Use a telescoping gauge and carefully measure the inside diameter of the bearings. Compare this reading to the rods original crankshaft journal diameter measurement. The difference is the oil clearance. If the oil clearance is not within specifications, install new bearings in the rod and take another measurement. If the clearance is still out of specifications, and the crankshaft is not, the rod will need to be reconditioned by a machine shop.

➥You can also use Plastigage® to check the bearing clearances. The assembling section has complete instructions on its use.

Camshaft

Inspect the camshaft and lifters/followers as described earlier in this section.

Bearings

All of the engine bearings should be visually inspected for wear and/or damage. The bearing should look evenly worn all around with no deep scores or pits. If the bearing is severely worn, scored, pitted or heat blued, then the bearing, and the components that use it, should be brought to a machine shop for inspection. Full-circle bearings (used on most camshafts, auxiliary shafts, balance shafts, etc.) require specialized tools for removal and installation, and should be brought to a machine shop for service.

Oil Pump

➥The oil pump is responsible for providing constant lubrication to the whole engine and so it is recommended that a new oil pump be installed when rebuilding the engine.

Completely disassemble the oil pump and thoroughly clean all of the components. Inspect the oil pump gears and housing for wear and/or damage. Insure that the pressure relief valve operates properly and there is no binding or sticking due to varnish or debris. If all of the parts are in proper working condition, lubricate the gears and relief valve, and assemble the pump.

REFINISHING

▶ **See Figure 230**

Almost all engine block refinishing must be performed by a machine shop. If the cylinders are not to be rebored, then the cylinder glaze can be removed with a ball hone. When removing cylinder glaze with a ball hone, use a light or penetrating type oil to lubricate the hone. Do not allow the hone to run dry as this may cause excessive scoring of the cylinder bores and wear on the hone. If new pistons are required, they will need to be installed to the connecting rods. This should be performed by a machine shop as the pistons must be installed in the correct relationship to the rod or engine damage can occur.

Pistons and Connecting Rods

▶ **See Figure 231**

Only pistons with the wrist pin retained by C-clips are serviceable by the home-mechanic. Press fit pistons require special presses and/or heaters to remove/install the connecting rod and should only be performed by a machine shop.

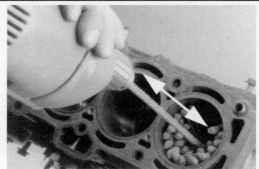

Fig. 230 Use a ball type cylinder hone to remove any glaze and provide a new surface for seating the piston rings

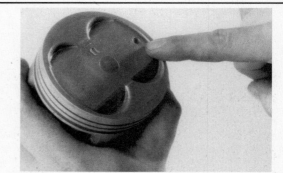

Fig. 231 Most pistons are marked to indicate positioning in the engine (usually a mark means the side facing the front)

All pistons will have a mark indicating the direction to the front of the engine and the must be installed into the engine in that manner. Usually it is a notch or arrow on the top of the piston, or it may be the letter F cast or stamped into the piston.

ASSEMBLY

Before you begin assembling the engine, first give yourself a clean, dirt free work area. Next, clean every engine component again. The key to a good assembly is cleanliness.

Mount the engine block into the engine stand and wash it one last time using water and detergent (dishwashing detergent works well). While washing it, scrub the cylinder bores with a soft bristle brush and thoroughly clean all of the oil passages. Completely dry the engine and spray the entire assembly down with an anti-rust solution such as WD-40® or similar product. Take a clean lint-free rag and wipe up any excess anti-rust solution from the bores, bearing saddles, etc. Repeat the final cleaning process on the crankshaft. Replace any freeze or oil galley plugs which were removed during disassembly.

Crankshaft

▶ **See Figures 232, 233, 234 and 235**

1. Remove the main bearing inserts from the block and bearing caps.
2. If the crankshaft main bearing journals have been refinished to a definite undersize, install the correct undersize bearing. Be sure that the bearing inserts and bearing bores are clean. Foreign material under inserts will distort bearing and cause failure.
3. Place the upper main bearing inserts in bores with tang in slot.

➥The oil holes in the bearing inserts must be aligned with the oil holes in the cylinder block.

4. Install the lower main bearing inserts in bearing caps.
5. Clean the mating surfaces of block and rear main bearing cap.
6. Carefully lower the crankshaft into place. Be careful not to damage bearing surfaces.

7. Check the clearance of each main bearing by using the following procedure:

a. Place a piece of Plastigage® or its equivalent, on bearing surface across full width of bearing cap and about ¼ in. off center.

b. Install cap and tighten bolts to specifications. Do not turn crankshaft while Plastigage® is in place.

c. Remove the cap. Using the supplied Plastigage® scale, check width of Plastigage® at widest point to get maximum clearance. Difference between readings is taper of journal.

d. If clearance exceeds specified limits, try a 0.001 in. or 0.002 in. undersize bearing in combination with the standard bearing. Bearing clearance must be within specified limits. If standard and 0.002 in. undersize bearing does not bring clearance within desired limits, refinish crankshaft journal, then install undersize bearings.

8. Install the rear main seal.

9. After the bearings have been fitted, apply a light coat of engine oil to the journals and bearings. Install the rear main bearing cap. Install all bearing caps except the thrust bearing cap. Be sure that main bearing caps are installed in original locations. Tighten the bearing cap bolts to specifications.

10. Install the thrust bearing cap with bolts finger-tight.

11. Pry the crankshaft forward against the thrust surface of upper half of bearing.

12. Hold the crankshaft forward and pry the thrust bearing cap to the rear. This aligns the thrust surfaces of both halves of the bearing.

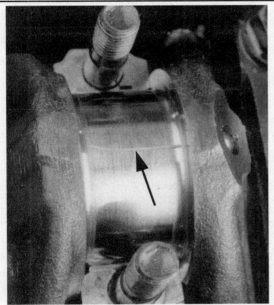

Fig. 232 Apply a strip of gauging material to the bearing journal, then install and torque the cap

13. Retain the forward pressure on the crankshaft. Tighten the cap bolts to specifications.

14. Measure the crankshaft end-play as follows:

a. Mount a dial gauge to the engine block and position the tip of the gauge to read from the crankshaft end.

b. Carefully pry the crankshaft toward the rear of the engine and hold it there while you zero the gauge.

c. Carefully pry the crankshaft toward the front of the engine and read the gauge.

d. Confirm that the reading is within specifications. If not, install a new thrust bearing and repeat the procedure. If the reading is still out of specifications with a new bearing, have a machine shop inspect the thrust surfaces of the crankshaft, and if possible, repair it.

15. Rotate the crankshaft so as to position the first rod journal to the bottom of its stroke.

Pistons and Connecting Rods

▶ See Figures 236, 237, 238 and 239

1. Before installing the piston/connecting rod assembly, oil the pistons, piston rings and the cylinder walls with light engine oil. Install connecting rod bolt protectors or rubber hose onto the connecting rod bolts/studs. Also perform the following:

a. Select the proper ring set for the size cylinder bore.

b. Position the ring in the bore in which it is going to be used.

c. Push the ring down into the bore area where normal ring wear is not encountered.

d. Use the head of the piston to position the ring in the bore so that the ring is square with the cylinder wall. Use caution to avoid damage to the ring or cylinder bore.

e. Measure the gap between the ends of the ring with a feeler gauge. Ring gap in a worn cylinder is normally greater than specification. If the ring gap is greater than the specified limits, try an oversize ring set.

f. Check the ring side clearance of the compression rings with a feeler gauge inserted between the ring and its lower land according to specification. The gauge should slide freely around the entire ring circumference without binding. Any wear that occurs will form a step at the inner portion of the lower land. If the lower lands have high steps, the piston should be replaced.

2. Unless new pistons are installed, be sure to install the pistons in the cylinders from which they were removed. The numbers on the connecting rod and bearing cap must be on the same side when installed in the cylinder bore. If a connecting rod is ever transposed from one engine or cylinder to another, new bearings should be fitted and the connecting rod should be numbered to correspond with the new cylinder number. The notch on the piston head goes toward the front of the engine.

3. Install all of the rod bearing inserts into the rods and caps.

4. Install the rings to the pistons. Install the oil control ring first, then the second compression ring and finally the top compression ring. Use a piston ring expander tool to aid in installation and to help reduce the chance of breakage.

5. Make sure the ring gaps are properly spaced around the circumference of the piston. Fit a piston ring compressor around the piston and slide the piston and connecting rod assembly down into the cylinder bore, pushing it in with the wooden hammer handle. Push the piston down until it is only slightly below

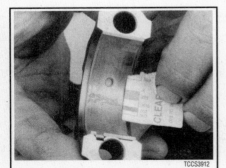

Fig. 233 After the cap is removed again, use the scale supplied with the gauging material to check the clearance

Fig. 234 A dial gauge may be used to check crankshaft end-play

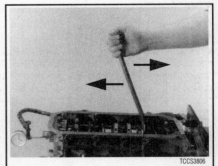

Fig. 235 Carefully pry the crankshaft back and forth while reading the dial gauge for end-play

the top of the cylinder bore. Guide the connecting rod onto the crankshaft bearing journal carefully, to avoid damaging the crankshaft.

6. Check the bearing clearance of all the rod bearings, fitting them to the crankshaft bearing journals. Follow the procedure in the crankshaft installation above.

7. After the bearings have been fitted, apply a light coating of assembly oil to the journals and bearings.

8. Turn the crankshaft until the appropriate bearing journal is at the bottom of its stroke, then push the piston assembly all the way down until the connecting rod bearing seats on the crankshaft journal. Be careful not to allow the bearing cap screws to strike the crankshaft bearing journals and damage them.

9. After the piston and connecting rod assemblies have been installed, check the connecting rod side clearance on each crankshaft journal.

10. Prime and install the oil pump and the oil pump intake tube.

11. Install the auxiliary/balance shaft(s)/assembly(ies).

Camshaft, Lifters and Timing Assembly

1. Install the camshaft.
2. Install the lifters/followers into their bores.
3. Install the timing gears/chain assembly.

Cylinder Heads

1. Install the cylinder head(s) using new gaskets.
2. Assemble the rest of the valve train (pushrods and rocker arms and/or shafts).

Fig. 236 Checking the piston ring-to-ring groove side clearance using the ring and a feeler gauge

Engine Covers and Components

Install the timing cover(s) and oil pan. Refer to your notes and drawings made prior to disassembly and install all of the components that were removed. Install the engine into the vehicle.

Engine Start-up and Break-in

STARTING THE ENGINE

Now that the engine is installed and every wire and hose is properly connected, go back and double check that all coolant and vacuum hoses are connected. Check that your oil drain plug is installed and properly tightened. If not already done, install a new oil filter onto the engine. Fill the crankcase with the proper amount and grade of engine oil. Fill the cooling system with a 50/50 mixture of coolant/water.

1. Connect the vehicle battery.
2. Start the engine. Keep your eye on your oil pressure indicator; if it does not indicate oil pressure within 10 seconds of starting, turn the vehicle **OFF**.

❋❋ WARNING

Damage to the engine can result if it is allowed to run with no oil pressure. Check the engine oil level to make sure that it is full. Check for any leaks and if found, repair the leaks before continuing. If there is still no indication of oil pressure, you may need to prime the system.

3. Confirm that there are no fluid leaks (oil or other).
4. Allow the engine to reach normal operating temperature (the upper radiator hose will be hot to the touch).
5. At this point any necessary checks or adjustments can be performed, such as ignition timing.
6. Install any remaining components or body panels which were removed.

BREAKING IT IN

Make the first miles on the new engine, easy ones. Vary the speed but do not accelerate hard. Most importantly, do not lug the engine, and avoid sustained high speeds until at least 100 miles. Check the engine oil and coolant levels frequently. Expect the engine to use a little oil until the rings seat. Change the oil and filter at 500 miles, 1500 miles, then every 3000 miles past that.

KEEP IT MAINTAINED

Now that you have just gone through all of that hard work, keep yourself from doing it all over again by thoroughly maintaining it. Not that you may not have maintained it before, heck you could have had one to two hundred thousand miles on it before doing this. However, you may have bought the vehicle used, and the previous owner did not keep up on maintenance. Which is why you just went through all of that hard work. See?

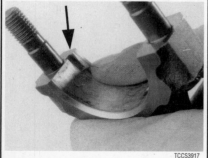
Fig. 237 The notch on the side of the bearing cap matches the tang on the bearing insert

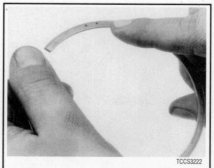
Fig. 238 Most rings are marked to show which side of the ring should face up when installed to the piston

Fig. 239 Install the piston and rod assembly into the block using a ring compressor and the handle of a hammer

TORQUE SPECIFICATIONS

Component	ft. lbs.	inch lbs.	Nm
Engine Mount Bolts			
VIN 3 and C			
Engine mount bolts	70		95
Torque converter bolts	46		62
Lower transaxle-to-engine bolts	55		75
Starter mounting bolts	35		47
Rocker Arm Cover bolts	7	89	10
Rocker Arm/Shafts			
1986-92 vehicles	28		38
1993-94 vehicles (plus an additional 70° rotation)	19		25
1995-99 vehicles (plus an additional 90° rotation)	11		15
Thermostat water outlet bolts	20		27
Intake Manifold			
1986 vehicles	32		47
1987-90 vehicles			
VIN 3 engines (in sequence)	47		65
VIN C engines			
Intake manifold bolts (tighten twice, in sequence)		88	10
Throttle body bolts	20		27
1991-99 Vehicles			
Except 1995-97 VIN 1 and K engines (tighten twice, in sequence)		89	10
1995-99 VIN K engines:			
1995 vehicles (tighten twice, in sequence)		89	10
1996-97 vehicles (in sequence)	11		15
1995-99 VIN 1 engines	11		15
Exhaust Manifold			
VIN B engines	25		34
VIN 3 and 1986 VIN L engines	37		50
VIN C and 1992-94 VIN L engines:			
exhaust manifold retainers	38-41		51-56
right-to-left exhaust manifold bolts	15		20
VIN 1 and K engines			
1992 vehicles	37-41		50-56
1993-95 vehicles	38		51
1996-99 vehicles	22		30
Supercharger			
1992-93 vehicles	19		26
1994-95 vehicles			
Studs		88	10
Bolts	19		26
Boost pressure manifold vacuum block		62	7
1996-99 vehicles			
Supercharger bolts	17		
MAP sensor bracket bolts	22		
Throttle body-to-supercharger retaining nuts		89	
Fuel rail retainers			
Nuts/bolts		89	10
Stud	18		25
Alternator brace bolts	22		30
EGR wiring harness shield bolt/screw and nut		89	10

89633C08

TORQUE SPECIFICATIONS

Component	ft. lbs.	inch lbs.	Nm
Radiator			
Radiator-to-radiator support attaching clamp and bolts		89	10
Automatic transaxle cooler line nuts	20		27
Upper radiator panel retainers		89	10
Engine fan attaching bolts		89	10
Water Pump			
1986-94 vehicles			
Long bolts	29		39
Short bolts		97	11
1995 vehicles			
Water pump-to-block bolts	22		30
Water pump-to-front cover bolts(plus an additional 80° rotation)	11		15
1996-99 vehicles			
VIN K engines			
(1) bolts, shown in figure	11		15
(2) bolts, shown in figure	22		30
VIN 1 engines	see figure in procedure		
Cylinder Head			
1986 VIN L engines			
All bolts except nos. 5, 6, 11, 12, 13, and 14	142		192
Bolt nos. 5, 6, 11, 12, 13 and 14	59		80
VIN 3 and B engines (in 4 steps)			
Step 1: Cylinder head bolts (in sequence)	25		35
Step 2: Do not exceed 60 ft. lbs. (81 Nm) at any point during the next 2 steps			
Step 3: Tighten each bolt an additional 90° in sequence		90°	
Step 4: Tighten each bolt an additional 90° in sequence.		90°	
VIN C, K, 1 and 1992-94 L engines (in 3 steps)			
Step 1: Cylinder head bolts (in sequence)	35-37		47-50
Step 2: Tighten each bolt an additional 130° in sequence		130°	
Step 3: Tighten the center 4 bolts an additional 30° in sequence		30°	
Oil Pan		124	14
Oil Pump cover-to-front cover screws		97	11
Crankshaft Damper			
1986 engines	200		271
1987-90 3.8L (VIN 3 and C) engines	220		297
1991 3.8L (VIN C) engines (plus an additional 52-60° rotation)	98-112		130-150
3.8L (VIN L, 1 and K) engines (plus an additional 76° rotation)	110		150
Timing Chain Cover			
1987-90 vehicles			
Front cover bolts	22		30
Oil pan-to-cover mounting bolts		88	10
1991-99 vehicles			
1991-95 front cover attaching bolts	22		30
1996-99 front cover attaching bolts (plus an additional 40° rotation)	11		15
Oil pan-to-front cover bolts		124	14
Timing Chain and Gears			
Camshaft sprocket bolts			
1987-91 vehicles	27		37
1992-99 vehicles (plus a 90° rotation)	74		100
Camshaft thrust button and spring/damper assembly bolt	14-16		19-22

89633C09

TORQUE SPECIFICATIONS

Component	ft. lbs.	inch lbs.	Nm
Balance Shaft			
1987-92 vehicles (plus an additional 35° rotation)	14		20
1993-98 vehicles (plus an additional 70° rotation)	16		22
Rear Main Seal			
1987-90 main bearing cap-to-engine bolts	90		122
1995-98 VIN K engine housing bolts	22		30
Flywheel			
1987-91 vehicles: 61 ft. lbs. (82 Nm).	61		82
1992-94 vehicles: 11 ft. lbs. (15 Nm), plus an additional 50<deg> rotation.	11		15
1995 VIN L engine (plus an additional 50° rotation)	11		15
1995-99 VIN K and 1 engines: 46 ft. lbs. (62 Nm).	46		62

89633C10

EMISSION CONTROLS 4-2
CRANKCASE VENTILATION SYSTEM 4-2
  OPERATION 4-2
  COMPONENT TESTING 4-2
  REMOVAL & INSTALLATION 4-3
EVAPORATIVE EMISSION
 CONTROLS 4-3
  OPERATION 4-3
  TESTING 4-4
  REMOVAL & INSTALLATION 4-4
EXHAUST GAS RECIRCULATION
 SYSTEM 4-7
  OPERATION 4-7
  TESTING 4-8
  REMOVAL & INSTALLATION 4-9
CATALYTIC CONVERTER 4-11
  OPERATION 4-11
  INSPECTION 4-11
ELECTRONIC ENGINE
CONTROLS 4-11
ELECTRONIC CONTROL MODULE
 (ECM) 4-11
  OPERATION 4-11
  REMOVAL & INSTALLATION 4-12
PROM/MEM-CAL/KS MODULE 4-13
  REMOVAL & INSTALLATION 4-13
  FUNCTIONAL CHECK 4-13
OXYGEN SENSOR 4-14
  OPERATION 4-14
  TESTING 4-14
  REMOVAL & INSTALLATION 4-15
IDLE AIR CONTROL VALVE 4-16
  OPERATION 4-16
  TESTING 4-16
  REMOVAL & INSTALLATION 4-17
COOLANT TEMPERATURE
 SENSOR 4-17
  OPERATION 4-17
  TESTING 4-17
  REMOVAL & INSTALLATION 4-18
INTAKE AIR TEMPERATURE
 SENSOR 4-19
  TESTING 4-19
  REMOVAL & INSTALLATION 4-20
MASS AIR FLOW SENSOR 4-20
  OPERATION 4-20
  TESTING 4-21
  REMOVAL & INSTALLATION 4-21
MANIFOLD ABSOLUTE PRESSURE
 SENSOR 4-22
  OPERATION 4-22
  TESTING 4-23
  REMOVAL & INSTALLATION 4-23
THROTTLE POSITION SENSOR 4-24
  OPERATION 4-24
  TESTING 4-24
  REMOVAL & INSTALLATION 4-24
  ADJUSTMENT 4-25

CAMSHAFT POSITION SENSOR 4-25
  OPERATION 4-25
  TESTING 4-25
  REMOVAL & INSTALLATION 4-25
CRANKSHAFT POSITION SENSOR 4-26
  OPERATION 4-26
  TESTING 4-26
  REMOVAL & INSTALLATION 4-26
KNOCK SENSOR 4-28
  OPERATION 4-28
  TESTING 4-28
  REMOVAL & INSTALLATION 4-28
COMPONENT LOCATIONS 4-30
TROUBLE CODES 4-35
GENERAL INFORMATION 4-35
  SCAN TOOLS 4-35
  ELECTRICAL TOOLS 4-36
DIAGNOSIS AND TESTING 4-36
  VISUAL/PHYSICAL
   INSPECTION 4-36
  INTERMITTENTS 4-36
  CIRCUIT/COMPONENT REPAIR 4-36
READING CODES 4-37
  1986-94 VEHICLES EXCEPT 1994
   MODELS WITH 16-PIN DLC 4-37
  1994 VEHICLES WITH 16-PIN DLC
   AND ALL 1995-99 MODELS 4-39
CLEARING CODES 4-39
VACUUM DIAGRAMS 4-41
COMPONENT LOCATIONS
 EMISSION CONTROL AND
  ELECTRONIC ENGINE CONTROL
  COMPONENT LOCATIONS—3.8L
  (VIN C) ENGINE 4-30
 EMISSION CONTROL AND
  ELECTRONIC ENGINE CONTROL
  COMPONENT LOCATIONS—3.8L
  (VIN K) ENGINE 4-31

4

DRIVEABILITY AND EMISSION CONTROLS

EMISSION CONTROLS 4-2
ELECTRONIC ENGINE CONTROLS 4-11
COMPONENT LOCATIONS 4-30
TROUBLE CODES 4-35
VACUUM DIAGRAMS 4-41

EMISSION CONTROLS

Crankcase Ventilation System

OPERATION

▶ **See Figures 1 and 2**

All vehicles are equipped with a Positive Crankcase Ventilation (PCV) or Crankcase Ventilation (CV) system to control crankcase blow-by vapors. The system functions as follows:

When the engine is running, a small portion of the gases which are formed in the combustion chamber leak by the piston rings and enter the crankcase. Since these gases are under pressure, they tend to escape from the crankcase and enter the atmosphere. If these gases are allowed to remain in the crankcase for any period of time, they contaminate the engine oil and cause sludge to build up in the crankcase. If the gases are allowed to escape into the atmosphere, they pollute the air with unburned hydrocarbons.

The job of the crankcase emission control equipment is to recycle these gases back into the engine combustion chamber where they are reburned.

The crankcase (blow-by) gases are recycled in the following way: as the engine is running, clean, filtered air is drawn through the air filter and into the crankcase. As the air passes through the crankcase, it picks up the combustion gases and carries them out of the crankcase, through the oil separator, through the PCV valve, and into the induction system. As they enter the intake manifold or supercharger inlet, they are drawn into the combustion chamber where they are reburned.

The most critical component in the system is the PCV valve. This valve controls the amount of gases which are recycled into the combustion chamber. At low engine speeds, the valve is partially closed, limiting the flow of gases into the intake manifold. As engine speed increases, the valve opens to admit greater quantities of gases into the intake manifold. If the valve should become blocked or plugged, the gases will be prevented from escaping from the crankcase by

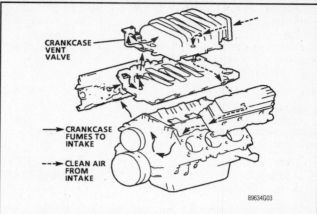

Fig. 2 Common crankcase ventilation flow—3.8L (VIN L) engine shown

the normal route. Since these gases are under pressure, they will find their own way out of the crankcase. This alternate route is usually a weak oil seal or gasket in the engine. As the gas escapes by the gasket, it also creates an oil leak. Besides causing oil leaks, a clogged PCV valve also allows these gases to remain in the crankcase for an extended period of time, promoting the formation of sludge in the engine.

A plugged PCV valve, orifice or hose may cause rough idle, stalling or slow idle speed, oil leaks, oil in the air cleaner or sludge in the engine. A leak could cause rough idle, stalling or high idle speed. The condition of the grommets in the valve cover will also affect system and engine performance.

Other than checking and replacing the PCV valve and associated hoses, there is no service required. Engine operating conditions that would direct suspicion to the PCV system are rough idle, oil present in the air cleaner, oil leaks and excessive oil sludging or dilution. If any of the above conditions exist, remove the PCV valve and shake it. A clicking sound indicates that the valve is free. If no clicking sound is heard, replace the valve. Inspect the PCV breather in the air cleaner. Replace the breather if it is so dirty that it will not allow gases to pass through. Check all the PCV hoses for condition and tight connections. Replace any hoses that have deteriorated.

COMPONENT TESTING

PCV Valve

3.0L AND 3.8L (VIN 3, B AND C) ENGINES

▶ **See Figures 3, 4 and 5**

If the engine is idling rough, check for a obstructed PCV valve or a restricted hose.

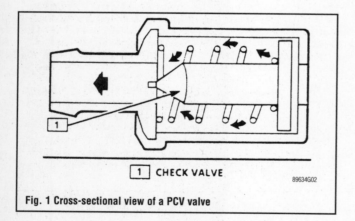

1 CHECK VALVE

89634G02

Fig. 1 Cross-sectional view of a PCV valve

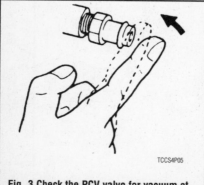

TCCS4P05

Fig. 3 Check the PCV valve for vacuum at idle

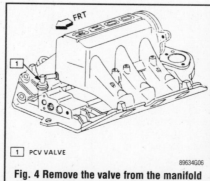

1 PCV VALVE

89634G06

Fig. 4 Remove the valve from the manifold and check for vacuum—3.8L (VIN C) engine shown

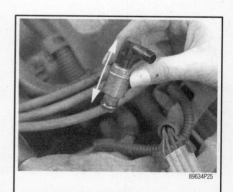

89634P25

Fig. 5 Remove and shake the PCV valve; if a rattling noise is heard, the valve is OK

1. Start the engine.
2. With the engine at normal operating temperature, run at idle.
3. Remove the PCV valve or orifice from the grommet in the valve cover or manifold and place thumb over the end to check if vacuum is present. If vacuum is not present, check for plugged hoses or manifold port. Repair or replace as necessary.
4. Stop the engine and remove the valve. Shake the valve and listen for the rattle of the check valve needle. If there is no rattle heard when the valve is shaken, replace the valve.

3.8L (VIN L, 1 AND K) ENGINES

▶ See Figure 6

➡️If the engine is idling rough, check for a plugged PCV valve, as follows:

1. Remove the PCV valve from the intake manifold.
2. Shake the valve. If you can hear rattling from the needle inside the valve, the valve is OK. If no rattle is heard, replace the PCV valve.

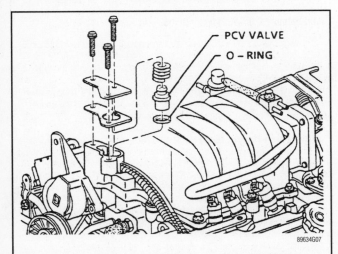

Fig. 6 Exploded view of the PCV valve mounting—1992 3.8L engine shown

PCV System

1. Check to make sure the engine has the correct PCV valve or bleed orifice.
2. Start the engine and bring to normal operating temperature.
3. Block off the PCV system fresh air intake passage.
4. Remove the engine oil dipstick and install a vacuum gauge on the dipstick tube.
5. Run the engine at 1500 rpm for 30 seconds then read the vacuum gauge with the engine at 1500 rpm.
   • If vacuum is present, the PCV system is functioning properly.
   • If there is no vacuum, the engine may not be sealed and/or is drawing in outside air. Check the grommets and valve cover or oil pan gasket for leaks.
   • If the vacuum gauge registers a pressure or the vacuum gauge is pushed out of the dipstick tube, check for the correct PCV valve or bleed orifice, a plugged hose or excessive engine blow-by.

REMOVAL & INSTALLATION

▶ See Figure 7

➡️When replacing a PCV valve you MUST use the correct valve. Many valves look alike on the outside, but have different mechanical values. Putting an incorrect PCV valve on a vehicle can cause a great deal of driveability problems. The engine computer assumes the valve is the correct one and may over adjust ignition timing or fuel mixture.

Removal and installation procedures of the PCV or CV valve is located in Section 1 of this manual.

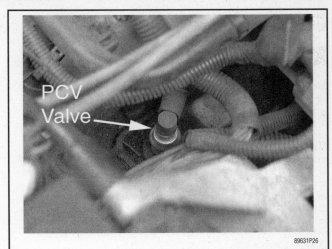

Fig. 7 On most vehicles, the PCV valve is mounted in the intake manifold

Evaporative Emission Control System

OPERATION

▶ See Figures 8, 9 and 10

The Evaporative Emission Control (EVAP) System is designed to prevent fuel tank vapors from being emitted into the atmosphere. When the engine is not running, gasoline vapors from the tank are stored in a charcoal canister, mounted under the hood. The charcoal canister absorbs the gasoline vapors and stores them until certain engine conditions are met and the vapors can be purged and burned by the engine. In some vehicles with fuel injection, any liquid fuel entering the canister goes into a reservoir in the bottom of the canister to protect the integrity of the carbon element in the canister above. Three different methods are used to control the purge cycle of the charcoal canister.

First, the charcoal canister purge cycle is controlled by throttle position without the use of a valve on the canister. A vacuum line connects the canister to a ported vacuum source on the throttle body. When the throttle is at any position above idle, fresh air is drawn into the bottom of the canister and the fuel vapors are carried into the throttle body at that port. The air/vapor flow volume is only what can be drawn through the vacuum port and is fairly constant.

Second, the flow volume is modulated with throttle position through a vacuum valve. The ported vacuum from the throttle body is used to open a diaphragm valve on top of the canister. When the valve is open, air and vapors are drawn into the intake manifold, usually through the same manifold port as

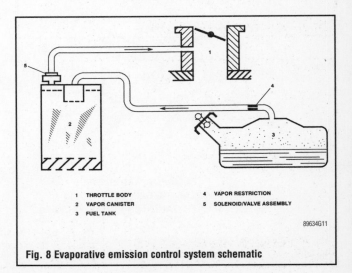

1	THROTTLE BODY	4	VAPOR RESTRICTION
2	VAPOR CANISTER	5	SOLENOID/VALVE ASSEMBLY
3	FUEL TANK		

Fig. 8 Evaporative emission control system schematic

the PCV system. With this method, the purge valve cycle is slaved to the throttle opening; more throttle opening, more purge air flow.

And third, the charcoal canister purge valve cycle is controlled by the ECM through a solenoid valve on the canister. When the solenoid is activated, full manifold vacuum is applied to the top of the purge valve diaphragm to open the valve all the way. A high volume of fresh air is drawn into the canister and the gasoline vapors are purged quickly. The ECM activates the solenoid valve when the following conditions are met:

- The engine is at normal operating temperature.
- After the engine has been running a specified period of time.
- Vehicle speed is above a predetermined speed.
- Throttle opening is above a predetermined value.

A vent pipe allows fuel vapors to flow to the charcoal canister. On some vehicles, the tank is isolated from the charcoal canister by a tank pressure control valve, located either in the tank or in the vapor line near the canister. It is a combination roll-over, integral pressure and vacuum relief valve. When the vapor pressure in the tank exceeds 0.72 psi (5 kPa), the valve opens to allow vapors

to vent to the canister. The valve also provides vacuum relief to protect against vacuum build-up in the fuel tank and roll-over spill protection.

Poor engine idle, stalling and poor driveability can be caused by an inoperative canister purge solenoid, a damaged canister or split, damaged or improperly connected hoses.

The most common symptom of problems in this system is fuel odors coming from under the hood. If there is no liquid fuel leak, check for a cracked or damaged vapor canister, inoperative or always open canister control valve, disconnected, misrouted, kinked or damaged vapor pipe or canister hoses; or a damaged air cleaner or improperly seated air cleaner gasket.

TESTING

Charcoal Canister

1. Visually check the canister for cracks or damage.
2. If fuel is leaking from the bottom of the canister, replace canister and check for proper hose routing.
3. Check the filter at the bottom of the canister. If dirty, replace the filter.

Tank Pressure Control Valve

1. Using a hand-held vacuum pump, apply a vacuum of 15 in. Hg (51 kPa) through the control vacuum signal tube to the purge valve diaphragm. If the diaphragm does not hold vacuum for at least 20 seconds, the diaphragm is leaking. Replace the control valve.
2. With the vacuum still applied to the control vacuum tube, attach a short piece of hose to the valve's tank tube side and blow into the hose. Air should pass through the valve. If it does not, replace the control valve.

Canister Purge Control Valve

1. Connect a clean length of hose to the fuel tank vapor line connection on the canister and attempt to blow through the purge control valve. It should be difficult or impossible to blow through the valve. If air passes easily, the valve is stuck open and should be replaced.
2. Connect a hand-held vacuum pump to the top vacuum line fitting of the purge control valve. Apply a vacuum of 15 in. Hg (51 kPa) to the purge valve diaphragm. If the diaphragm does not hold vacuum for at least 20 seconds the diaphragm is leaking. Replace the control valve. If it is impossible to blow through the valve, it is stuck closed and must be replaced.
3. On vehicles with a solenoid activated purge control valve, unplug the connector and use jumper wires to supply 12 volts to the solenoid connections on the valve. With the vacuum still applied to the control vacuum tube, the purge control valve should open and it should be easy to blow through. If not, replace the valve.

REMOVAL & INSTALLATION

Charcoal Canister

1986–95 VEHICLES

▶ See Figures 11 thru 16

1. Disconnect the negative battery cable.
2. For 1995 vehicles, perform the following:
   a. Remove the air cleaner box assembly.
   b. Remove the windshield washer reservoir.
   c. Remove the load level pump.
3. If equipped, detach the electrical connector.
4. Tag and disconnect the hoses from the canister.
5. Unfasten the charcoal canister retaining nut or hold-down strap.
6. Remove the canister from the vehicle.

To install:

7. Position the charcoal canister in the vehicle. Install the canister retaining nut or hold-down strap, as applicable, and tighten to 25 inch lbs. (3 Nm).
8. Connect the hoses to the canister, as tagged during removal. Refer to the Vehicle Emission Control Information label, located in the engine compartment, to make sure you have the vacuum hoses properly routed.
9. The remainder of installation is the reverse of the removal procedure.

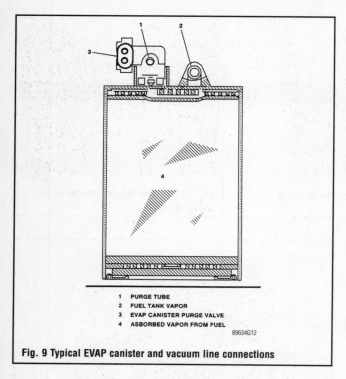

1 PURGE TUBE
2 FUEL TANK VAPOR
3 EVAP CANISTER PURGE VALVE
4 ABSORBED VAPOR FROM FUEL

89634G12

Fig. 9 Typical EVAP canister and vacuum line connections

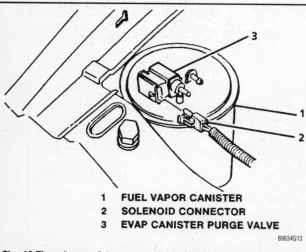

1 **FUEL VAPOR CANISTER**
2 **SOLENOID CONNECTOR**
3 **EVAP CANISTER PURGE VALVE**

89634G13

Fig. 10 There is a canister purge valve/solenoid on top of the EVAP canister

Fig. 11 EVAP canister electrical connector (1), purge solenoid (2) and vacuum hoses (3)

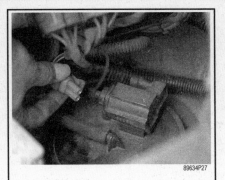

Fig. 12 Unplug the canister purge solenoid electrical connector

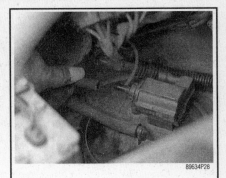

Fig. 13 Disconnect the vacuum line(s) from the purge solenoid . . .

Fig. 14 . . . and from the nipple on the canister

Fig. 15 Unfasten the canister hold-down strap retaining bolt . . .

Fig. 16 . . . then lift the canister up and out of the vehicle

1996–98 VEHICLES

1. Disconnect the negative battery cable.
2. Remove the PCM from the vehicle, as outlined later in this section.
3. For 3.8L (VIN K) engines, remove the EVAP canister vent valve/solenoid.
4. Remove the PCM bracket attaching hardware, then remove the PCM bracket.
5. Remove the EVAP canister vent valve/solenoid bracket.
6. Tag and disconnect the purge, fuel vapor, and vent lines from the EVAP canister.
7. Remove the canister from the vehicle.

To install:
8. Install the EVAP canister in the vehicle.
9. Connect the EVAP vent hose, then tighten the hose clamp securely.
10. The remainder of installation is the reverse of the removal procedure. Be certain to tighten the valve vent bracket retainers to 18 inch lbs. (2 Nm).

Canister Purge Solenoid/Valve

1986–95 VEHICLES

▶ See Figure 10

1. Disconnect the negative battery cable.

➡On some 1994–95 vehicles, it is necessary to remove the canister for access to the purge solenoid/valve.

2. If necessary, remove the EVAP canister.
3. Detach the electrical connector and hoses from the solenoid.
4. Remove the canister purge solenoid/valve from the canister.
5. Installation is the reverse of the removal procedure.

1996–98 VEHICLES

▶ See Figures 17, 18 and 19

1. Disconnect the negative battery cable.
2. Detach the electrical connector and hoses from the EVAP purge solenoid.

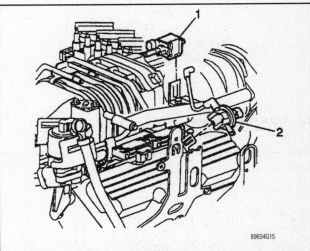

Fig. 17 Location of the EVAP purge solenoid (1) and vacuum switch (2) mounting—1996–97 vehicles

3. Bend the tab on the solenoid mounting bracket to remove the EVAP purge solenoid.
4. Installation is the reverse of the removal procedure.

Tank Pressure Control Valve

1. Disconnect the hoses from the control valve.
2. Remove the mounting hardware.
3. Remove the control valve from the vehicle.
4. Installation is the reverse of the removal procedure. Tighten the retainers to 25 inch lbs. (3 Nm).

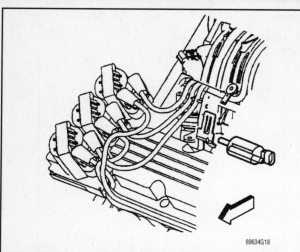

Fig. 18 After detaching the electrical connector and vacuum line, remove the purge solenoid—1998 3.8L (VIN K) engine

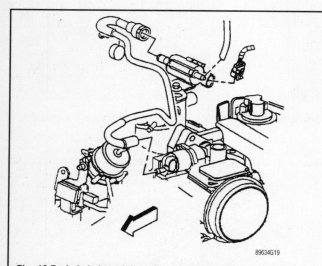

Fig. 19 Exploded view of the solenoid and related components— 1998 3.8L (VIN 1) engine

Refer to the Vehicle Emission Control Information label, located in the engine compartment, for proper routing of the vacuum hoses.

EVAP Vacuum Switch

1996–97 VEHICLES

1. Disconnect the negative battery cable.
2. Detach the electrical connector and the vacuum hoses from the EVAP vacuum switch.
3. Bend the tab on the vacuum switch mounting bracket to remove the switch.
4. Installation is the reverse of the removal procedure.

EVAP Vent Valve

♦ See Figure 20

1. Disconnect the negative battery cable.
2. Remove the PCM, as outlined later in this section.
3. Detach the EVAP canister vent valve from the vent valve bracket.
4. Unplug the canister vent valve electrical connector.
5. Loosen the vent hose clamp and remove the vent hose from the EVAP vent valve.

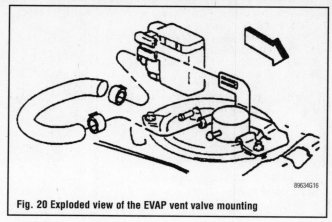

Fig. 20 Exploded view of the EVAP vent valve mounting

6. Remove the EVAP canister vent valve from the vehicle.
7. Installation is the reverse of the removal procedure.

EVAP Pipes

➡Do not try to repair the EVAP pipes or the connecting hoses. Replace any damaged hoses or pipes. If the nylon EVAP pipe becomes kinked and cannot be straightened, it must be replaced.

1996–97 VEHICLES

1. Raise and safely support the vehicle.
2. Remove the hardware retaining the EVAP pipes.
3. Inspect the location of the attaching hardware for installation.
4. Remove the EVAP pipe.
5. Inspect the pipe for bends, kinks, and cracks.
6. Installation is the reverse of the removal procedure.

➡The EVAP pipe must be properly secured in order to prevent chafing of the EVAP pipe. Always re-attach the fuel lines and fuel filter with all original type fasteners and hardware.

1998 3.8L ENGINE—ENGINE PIPES

1. Remove the fuel injector sight shield.
2. Unfasten any necessary hardware retaining the EVAP pipe.
3. Inspect the location of the attaching hardware for installation.
4. Remove the EVAP pipe/hose. Inspect the pipe/hose for bends, kinks and cracks.
5. Replace the pipes/hoses as required.
6. Installation is the reverse of the removal procedure. Make sure to properly secure the pipe in order to prevent chafing.

1998 3.8L ENGINE—CANISTER-TO-FUEL TANK PIPES

1. Properly relieve the fuel system pressure, as outlined in Section 5 of this manual.
2. If not done already, disconnect the negative battery cable.
3. Raise and safely support the vehicle.
4. Remove the fuel tank, as outlined in Section 5 of this manual.
5. Unfasten the hardware retaining the EVAP pipes, noting the location for installation.
6. Remove the in-line fuel filter.
7. Partially lower the vehicle for access to the engine compartment.
8. Remove the PCM, as outlined later in this section.
9. Remove the PCM base holder.
10. Disconnect the EVAP pipes from the canister.
11. Remove the EVAP pipes from the fuel tank.
12. Remove the EVAP pipes from the vehicle.
To install:

➡Make sure to route the replacement EVAP pipe in exactly the same orientation as the original.

13. Install the fuel tank.

➡Secure the EVAP pipe in order to prevent chafing the pipe.

14. Install the EVAP pipes to the chassis and secure with the pipe retainers. Tighten to 71 inch lbs. (8 Nm).

15. Install a new in-line fuel filter.

16. The remainder of installation is the reverse of the removal procedure.

17. Connect the negative battery cable. Turn the ignition **ON** for 2 seconds, **OFF** for 10 seconds, then **ON** again and check for fuel leaks.

Exhaust Gas Recirculation System

OPERATION

▶ **See Figure 21**

➡ **The 1992 3.8L (VIN L) engine does not use an EGR valve.**

The Exhaust Gas Recirculation (EGR) system is used to reduce oxides of nitrogen (NOx) emission levels caused by high combustion chamber temperatures. This is accomplished by the use of an EGR valve which opens, under specific engine operating conditions, to admit a small amount of exhaust gas into the intake manifold, below the throttle plate. The exhaust gas mixes with the incoming air charge and displaces a portion of the oxygen in the air/fuel mixture entering the combustion chamber. The exhaust gas does not support combustion of the air/fuel mixture but it takes up volume, the net effect of which is to lower the temperature of the combustion process. This lower temperature also helps control detonation.

The EGR valve is a mounted on the intake manifold and has an opening into the exhaust manifold. Except for the digital and linear versions, the EGR valve is opened by manifold vacuum to permit exhaust gas to flow into the intake manifold. With the digital and linear versions, the EGR valve is purely electrical and uses solenoid valves to open the flow passage. If too much exhaust gas enters, combustion will not occur. Because of this, very little exhaust gas is allowed to pass through the valve. The EGR system will be activated once the engine reaches normal operating temperature and the EGR valve will open when engine operating conditions are above idle speed and below Wide Open Throttle (WOT). On California vehicles equipped with a Vehicle Speed Sensor (VSS), the EGR valve opens when the VSS signal is greater than 2 mph (3.2 kph). The EGR system is deactivated on vehicles equipped with a Transmission Converter Clutch (TCC) when the TCC is engaged.

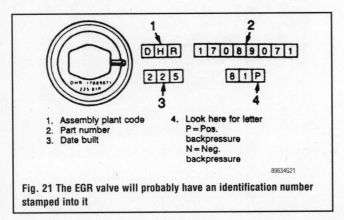

1. Assembly plant code
2. Part number
3. Date built
4. Look here for letter
   P = Pos. backpressure
   N = Neg. backpressure

89634G21

Fig. 21 The EGR valve will probably have an identification number stamped into it

Too much EGR flow at idle, cruise, or during cold operation may result in the engine stalling after cold start, the engine stalling at idle after deceleration, vehicle surge during cruise and rough idle. If the EGR valve is always open, the vehicle may not idle. Too little or no EGR flow allows combustion temperatures to get too high which could result in spark knock (detonation), engine overheating and/or emission test failure.

There are three basic types of systems as described below, differing in the way EGR flow is modulated.

Negative Backpressure EGR Valve

▶ **See Figure 22**

The negative backpressure EGR valve, used on early model vehicles, will be marked with an "N" stamped on the top side of the valve by the part number,

varies the amount of exhaust gas flow into the intake manifold depending on manifold vacuum and variations in exhaust backpressure. An air bleed valve, located inside the EGR valve assembly acts as a vacuum regulator. The bleed valve controls the amount of vacuum in the vacuum chamber by bleeding vacuum to outside air during the open phase of the cycle. The diaphragm on the valve has an internal air bleed hole which is held closed by a small spring when there is no exhaust backpressure. Engine vacuum opens the EGR valve against the pressure of a spring. When manifold vacuum combines with negative exhaust backpressure, the vacuum bleed hole opens and the EGR valve closes. This valve will open if vacuum is applied with the engine not running.

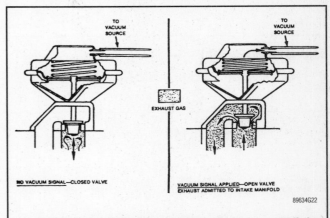

89634G22

Fig. 22 The negative backpressure EGR valve is vacuum controlled

Digital EGR Valve

▶ **See Figure 23**

The digital EGR valve, used on all 1989–93 EGR-equipped engines, is designed to control the flow of EGR independent of intake manifold vacuum. The valve controls EGR flow through 3 solenoid-opened orifices, which increase in size, to produce 7 possible combinations. When a solenoid is energized, the armature with attached shaft and swivel pintle is lifted, thereby opening the orifice.

The digital EGR valve is opened by the ECM, grounding each solenoid circuit individually. The flow of EGR is regulated by the ECM which uses information from the Engine Coolant Temperature (ECT) sensor, Throttle Position (TP) sensor and Manifold Absolute Pressure (MAP) sensor to determine the appropriate rate of flow for a particular engine operating condition.

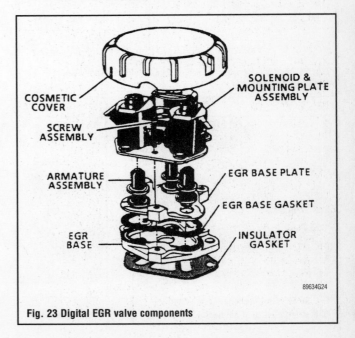

89634G24

Fig. 23 Digital EGR valve components

Linear EGR Valve

▶ See Figure 24

The linear EGR valve, used on 1994–98 engines, is designed to accurately supply EGR to an engine, independent of intake manifold vacuum. The valve controls EGR flow from the exhaust to the intake manifold through an orifice with a PCM-controlled pintle. During operation, the PCM controls pintle position by monitoring the pintle position feedback signal. The PCM uses information from the Engine Coolant Temperature (ECT) sensor, Throttle Position (TP) sensor and Mass Air Flow (MAF) sensor to determine the appropriate rate of flow for a particular engine operating condition.

TESTING

Negative Backpressure EGR Valve

1. Inspect all passages and moving parts for plugging, sticking and deposits.

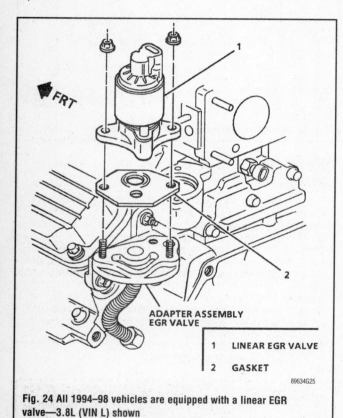

Fig. 24 All 1994–98 vehicles are equipped with a linear EGR valve—3.8L (VIN L) shown

2. Inspect the entire system (hoses, tubes, connections, etc.) for leakage. Replace any part that is leaking, hardened, cracked, or melted.
3. Run the engine to normal operating temperature, and allow the engine to idle for 2 minutes. Quickly accelerate the engine to 2,500 rpm. Visible movement of the EGR stem should occur indicating proper system function. If no movement occurs, check the vacuum source and hose.
4. To determine if gas is flowing through the system, connect a vacuum pump to the valve.
5. With the engine idling, slowly apply vacuum. Engine speed should start to decrease when applied vacuum reaches 3 in. Hg. The engine speed may drop quickly and could even stall; this indicated proper function.
6. If engine speed does not drop off, remove the EGR valve and check for plugged passages. If everything checks out, replace the valve.

Digital EGR Valve

▶ See Figures 25 thru 31

➡ **This system must be checked using a Scan tool, or similar device. Steps 4, 5 and 6 must be done very quickly, as the ECM will adjust the idle air control valve to adjust idle speed.**

1. Using a Scan tool or equivalent, check for trouble codes and solve those problems first, referring to appropriate chart elsewhere in this section.
2. Using the Scan tool, select "EGR CONTROL."
3. Run the engine to normal operating temperature, and allow the engine to idle for 2 minutes.
4. Energize EGR SOL #1; engine rpm should drop slightly.
5. Energize EGR SOL #2; the engine should have a rough idle.
6. Energize EGR SOL #3; the engine should idle rough or stall.
7. If all tests were as specified, the system is functioning properly.
8. If not, check the EGR valve, pipe, adapter, gaskets, fittings, and all passages for damage, leakage or plugging. If all is OK, replace the EGR valve assembly.
9. You can also check the resistance between the terminals using an ohmmeter, as follows:

Fig. 25 Twist the cap of the EGR valve to unlock, then lift off the cover

Fig. 26 Remove the locking clip from the EGR valve electrical connector . . .

Fig. 27 . . . then unplug the valve's electrical connector

Fig. 28 Digital EGR valve terminal identification

Fig. 29 Measure the resistance between EGR valve terminals A and D (circled in inset). In this case, the reading is 23.4 ohms

Fig. 30 Check the resistance between terminals B and D (circled in inset). In this case, the reading is 23.1 ohms

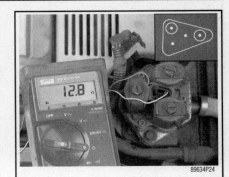

Fig. 31 Measure the resistance between terminals C and D (circled in inset). In this case, the reading is 12.8 ohms

a. Turn the EGR valve cap to unlock it, then lift it off the top of the valve.

b. Remove the EGR valve electrical connector locking clip, then detach the electrical connector.

c. Use an ohmmeter, set to the ohms scale, to measure the resistance. Compare with the following specifications:

- Terminals A and D: 20–30 ohms
- Terminals B and D: 20–30 ohms
- Terminals C and D: 10–17 ohms

Linear EGR Valve

▶ See Figure 32

To check this system, refer to the accompanying diagnostic chart for 1994–98 3.8L engines.

REMOVAL & INSTALLATION

EGR Valve

NEGATIVE BACKPRESSURE VALVE

1. Disconnect the negative battery cable.
2. Remove the air cleaner assembly.

3. Tag and disconnect the necessary hoses and wiring to gain access to the EGR valve.

4. Unfasten the EGR valve retaining bolts, then remove the EGR valve.

5. Remove and discard the gasket.

6. Carefully buff the exhaust deposits from the mounting surface and around the valve using a wire wheel.

7. Remove deposits from the valve outlet.

8. Clean the mounting surfaces of the intake manifold and valve assembly.

To install:

9. Install a new EGR gasket.

10. Position the EGR valve to the manifold, then secure with the retaining bolts. Tighten to 16 ft. lbs. (22 Nm).

11. The remainder of installation is the reverse of the removal procedure.

DIGITAL VALVE

▶ See Figures 23, 33 thru 40

1. Disconnect the negative battery cable.
2. If necessary, remove the cosmetic cover/sight shield.
3. Detach the electrical connector from the solenoid.
4. Remove the 2 base-to-flange bolts, then remove the digital EGR valve.
5. Remove and discard the EGR gasket. Thoroughly clean the gasket mating surfaces.

To install:

6. Install a new gasket, then position the EGR valve over the gasket.

7. Install the 2 base-to-flange bolts. Tighten to 17 ft. lbs. (24 Nm) for 1990–91 vehicles, or to 22 ft. lbs. (30 Nm) for 1992–93 vehicles.

8. If removed, install the cosmetic cover/sight shield.

9. Connect the negative battery cable.

Fig. 32 Linear EGR system flow check

```
① • START ENGINE.
   • SELECT MISCELLANEOUS TESTS, EGR CONTROL WITH TECH
     1 AND CYCLE THE EGR VALVE THROUGH THE 25%, 50%, 75%
     AND 100% POSITIONS.
   • RUN ENGINE ABOVE 1500 RPM; RPM SHOULD DROP AND THE
     ENGINE SHOULD RUN ROUGH AS THE EGR VALVE IS CYCLED.
     DOES IT?

   NO ──────────────────────── YES

② • KEY "ON," ENGINE "OFF."          NO TROUBLE FOUND
   • DISCONNECT EGR VALVE ELECTRICAL CONNECTOR.
   • CONNECT A TEST LIGHT BETWEEN EGR VALVE
     HARNESS CONNECTOR TERMINAL "A" AND "E".
     TEST LIGHT SHOULD BE "OFF."

   YES ──────────────────────── NO

③ • SELECT MISCELLANEOUS TEST, EGR CONTROL WITH    EGR CONTROL CKT 435
     TECH 1.                                        SHORTED TO GROUND
   • TEST LIGHT STILL CONNECTED BETWEEN EGR         OR
     VALVE HARNESS CONNECTOR "A" AND "E".           FAULTY PCM.
   • TEST LIGHT SHOULD LIGHT AS THE EGR VALVE IS
     CYCLED THROUGH 100%.
     DOES IT?

   NO ──────────────────────── YES

   OPEN IN CKT 435          CHECK FOR A
   OR                       RESTRICTION IN EGR
   OPEN IN CKT 639          TUBE OR PASSAGE, OR
   OR                       A POOR ELECTRICAL
   POOR CONNECTION AT PCM   CONNECTION AT EGR
   OR                       VALVE. IF OK, REPLACE
   FAULTY PCM.              FAULTY EGR VALVE.
```

Fig. 32 Linear EGR system flow check—1994–98 vehicles

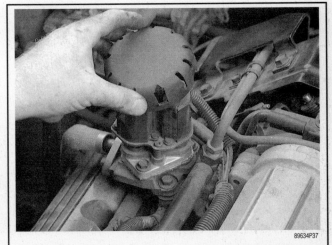

Fig. 33 Twist to unlock, then remove the EGR cover by lifting it straight up

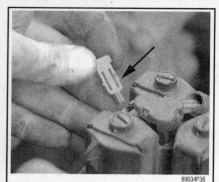

Fig. 34 Remove the EGR valve electrical connector retaining clip . . .

Fig. 35 . . . then detach the electrical connector

Fig. 36 The digital EGR valve is mounted to the flange with 2 bolts (see arrows)

Fig. 37 After removing the bolts, lift the EGR valve from the mounting flange

Fig. 38 Remove and discard the old EGR valve gasket

Fig. 39 Use a scraper to carefully clean the old gasket material from the flange

Fig. 40 Make sure to also clean the EGR valve's gasket mating surface

LINEAR VALVE

▶ See Figures 24, 41 and 42

1. Disconnect the negative battery cable.
2. Detach the EGR valve electrical connector.
3. Unfasten the 2 base-to-flange bolts/nuts, then remove the EGR valve from the vehicle.
4. Remove and discard the gasket from the EGR valve adapter.
5. Installation is the reverse of the removal procedure. Be sure to tighten the EGR valve retaining bolts/nuts to 22 ft. lbs. (30 Nm).

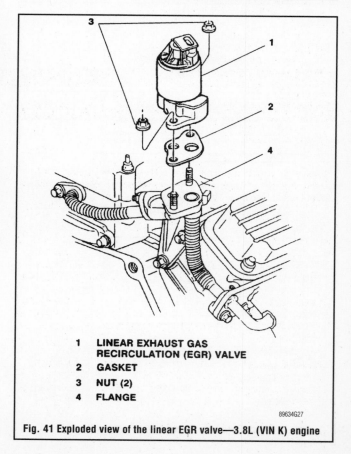

1   LINEAR EXHAUST GAS RECIRCULATION (EGR) VALVE
2   GASKET
3   NUT (2)
4   FLANGE

Fig. 41 Exploded view of the linear EGR valve—3.8L (VIN K) engine

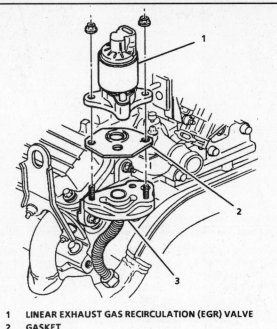

1	LINEAR EXHAUST GAS RECIRCULATION (EGR) VALVE
2	GASKET
3	FLANGE

89634G28

Fig. 42 Location of the EGR valve mounting—3.8L (VIN 1) engine

EGR Solenoid

An EGR solenoid is used to control the EGR valve operation on vehicles without a digital EGR valve.

1. Disconnect the negative battery cable.
2. Remove the air cleaner, as required.
3. Disconnect the electrical connector at the solenoid.
4. Disconnect the vacuum hoses.

ELECTRONIC ENGINE CONTROLS

Electronic Control Module (ECM)

OPERATION

➡**Whenever the term Electronic Control Module (ECM) is used in this manual, it will refer to the engine control computer, whether it is a Powertrain Control Module (PCM) or Electronic Control Module (ECM).**

The heart of the electronic control system, which is found on the vehicles covered by this manual, is a computer control module. The module gathers information from various sensors, then controls fuel supply and engine emission systems. Most early model vehicles are equipped with an Engine Control Module (ECM) which, as its name implies, controls the engine and related emissions systems. Some ECMs may also control the Torque Converter Clutch (TCC) on automatic transaxle vehicles. Later model vehicles may be equipped with a Powertrain Control Module (PCM). This is similar to the original ECMs, but is designed to control additional systems as well. The PCM may control the manual transaxle shift lamp or the shift functions of the electronically controlled automatic transaxle.

Regardless of the name, all computer control modules are serviced in a similar manner. Care must be taken when handling these expensive components in order to protect them from damage. Carefully follow all instructions included with the replacement part. Avoid touching pins or connectors to prevent damage from static electricity.

5. Remove the retaining bolts and the solenoid.
6. Remove the filter, as required.
7. Installation is the reverse of the removal procedure.

Catalytic Converter

OPERATION

The catalytic converter is mounted in the engine exhaust stream ahead of the muffler. Its function is to combine carbon monoxide (CO) and hydrocarbons (HC) with oxygen and break down nitrogen oxide (NOx) compounds. These gasses are converted to mostly CO_2 and water. It heats to operating temperature within about 1–2 minutes, depending on ambient and driving conditions and will operate at temperatures up to about 1500°F (816°C). Inside the converter housing is a single or dual bed ceramic monolith, coated with various combinations of platinum, palladium and rhodium.

The catalytic converter is not serviceable. If tests and visual inspection show the converter to be damaged, it must be replaced. There are 2 types of failures: melting or fracturing. The most common failure is melting, resulting from unburned gasoline contacting the monolith, such as when a cylinder does not fire. Usually when the monolith melts, high backpressure results. When it cracks, it begins to break up into small particles that get blown out the tail pipe.

Poor fuel mileage and/or a lack of power can often be traced to a melted or plugged catalytic converter. The damage may be the result of engine malfunction or the use of leaded gasoline in the vehicle. Proper diagnosis for a restricted exhaust system is essential before any components are replaced. The following procedure that can be used to determine if the exhaust system is restricted.

INSPECTION

1. Raise and safely support the vehicle.
2. Inspect the catalytic converter protector for any damage.

➡**If any part of the protector is dented to the extent that is contacts the converter, replace it.**

3. Check the heat insulator for adequate clearance between the converter and the heat insulator. Repair or replace any damaged components.

All of these computer control modules contain a Programmable Read Only Memory (PROM) chip, MEM-CAL or EEPROM that contains calibration information specific to the vehicle application. For all applications except those equipped with an EEPROM, this chip is not supplied with a replacement module, and must be transferred to the new module before installation. If equipped with an Electronically Erasable Programmable Read Only Memory (EEPROM), it must be reprogrammed after installation. Some later model vehicles have a Knock Sensor (KS) module, mounted in the PCM. The KS module contains the circuitry that allows the PCM to utilize the Knock Sensor signal to diagnose the circuitry.

✳✳ WARNING

To prevent the possibility of permanent control module damage, the ignition switch MUST always be OFF when disconnecting power from or reconnecting power to the module. This includes unplugging the module connector, disconnecting the negative battery cable, removing the module fuse or even attempting to jump start your dead battery using jumper cables.

In the event of an ECM failure, the system will default to a pre-programmed set of values. These are compromise values which allow the engine to operate, although at a reduced efficiency. This is variously known as the default, limp-in or back-up mode. Driveability is almost always affected when the ECM enters this mode.

REMOVAL & INSTALLATION

1986–95 Vehicles

▶ **See Figures 43 and 44**

On these vehicles, the computer control module is located in the engine compartment, in front of the right side shock tower.

1. Make sure the ignition switch is turned **OFF**, then disconnect the negative battery cable.

❊❊ **CAUTION**

To prevent the possibility of permanent control module damage, the ignition switch MUST always be OFF when disconnecting power from or reconnecting power to the module. This includes unplugging the module connector, disconnecting the negative battery cable, removing the module fuse or even attempting to jump your dead battery using jumper cables.

---

2. Locate the computer control module. On these vehicles, the module is mounted inside the passenger compartment, under the dash.
3. Remove the interior access panel/right side hush panel.
4. Carefully detach the harness connectors from the ECM.
5. Remove the ECM-to-bracket retaining screws and remove the ECM, then remove the ECM from its mounting position.

   To install:
6. If the module is being replaced, CAREFULLY replace the PROM chip, MEM-CAL or Knock Sensor (KS) module, as outlined later in this section.
7. Position the ECM in the vehicle and install the ECM-to-bracket retaining screws.

8. Attach the ECM harness connectors.
9. Install the hush panel/interior access panel.
10. Check that the ignition switch is **OFF**, then connect the negative battery cable.
11. If equipped with a computer control module that contains an EEPROM, it must be reprogrammed using a Tech 1® or equivalent scan tool and the latest available software. In all likelihood, the vehicle must be towed to a dealer or repair shop containing the suitable equipment for this service.
12. Perform the functional check, as outlined later in this section.

1996–99 Vehicles

▶ **See Figure 45**

On these vehicles, the computer control module is located in the engine compartment, in front of the right side shock tower, above the EVAP canister.

1. Make sure the ignition switch is turned **OFF**, then disconnect the negative battery cable.

❊❊ **CAUTION**

To prevent the possibility of permanent control module damage, the ignition switch MUST always be OFF when disconnecting power from or reconnecting power to the module. This includes unplugging the module connector, disconnecting the negative battery cable, removing the module fuse or even attempting to jump your dead battery using jumper cables.

---

2. Locate the computer control module. On these vehicles it is located in the engine compartment, in front of the right side shock tower, above the EVAP canister.
3. If equipped with an engine compartment mounted module, one or all of the following steps may be necessary:
   a. Remove the coolant tank reservoir.
   b. Remove the air cleaner intake duct.
   c. Remove the right side splash shield.
   d. Unfasten the retainers and remove the plastic PCM cover/sight shield.
4. Partially lift the PCM up from the mounting bracket, then carefully detach the harness connectors from the PCM.

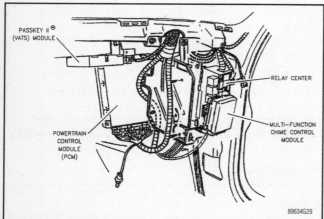

Fig. 43 On 1986–95 vehicles, the control module is located behind the right side of the instrument panel

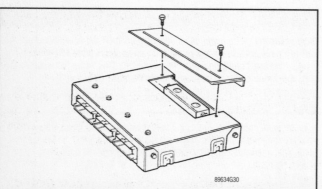

Fig. 44 View of the computer control module and its MEM-CAL or PROM access panel

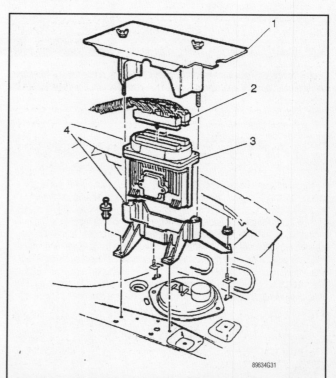

Fig. 45 Exploded view of the PCM sight shield (1), harness connector (2), PCM (3) and mounting bracket (4)

To install:

5. Remove the PCM from the engine compartment. If the PCM is being replaced, CAREFULLY transfer the KS module to the new PCM, as outlined later in this section.

6. Position the PCM in the mounting bracket.

7. Attach the PCM harness connectors.

8. For engine compartment mounted modules, install the following components, as applicable.

    a. Plastic ECM cover/sight shield and secure with the retainers.

    b. Right side splash shield.

    c. Air cleaner intake duct.

    d. Coolant tank reservoir.

9. Check that the ignition switch is **OFF**, then connect the negative battery cable.

10. If equipped with a computer control module that contains an EEPROM, it must be reprogrammed using a Tech 1® or equivalent scan tool and the latest available software. In all likelihood, the vehicle must be towed to a dealer or repair shop containing the suitable equipment for this service.

11. Perform the functional check, as outlined later in this section.

PROM/MEM-CAL/KS Module

REMOVAL & INSTALLATION

▶ See Figures 44, 46 and 47

As stated earlier, all computer control modules contain information regarding the correct parameters for engine and system operation based on vehicle applications. In most modules, this information takes the form of a PROM chip or MEM-CAL, though some modules also store this information in an EEPROM. Some later model vehicles, also include a Knock Sensor (KS) module which is replaced like the PROM and MEM-CAL.

Replacement computers are normally not equipped with this PROM/MEM-CAL/KS module; you must transfer the chip from the old component. The EEPROM is a permanent memory that is physically soldered within the PCM. Unlike the PROM used in some earlier applications or the MEM-CAL, the EEPROM is not serviceable. If the PCM is replaced, the new PCM will have to programmed using a Tech 1® or equivalent scan tool.

✳✳ WARNING

The PROM/MEM-CAL chip, KS module and computer control module are EXTREMELY sensitive to electrical or mechanical damage. NEVER touch the connector pins or soldered components on the circuit board in order to prevent possible electrostatic damage to the components.

1. Make sure the ignition switch is **OFF**, then remove the computer control module from the vehicle.

2. Remove the access panel. Note the position of the MEM-CAL/PROM/KS module for proper installation in the new ECM.

3. If equipped with a MEM-CAL, use 2 fingers to carefully push both retaining clips back away from the MEM-CAL module. At the same time, grasp it at both ends and lift it up out of the socket. Do not remove the cover of the MEM-CAL module.

4. If equipped with a KS module, remove the module cover.

5. If equipped with a PROM or KS module, use 2 fingers to gently squeeze the retaining clips toward each other. At the same time, grasp the module at both ends and carefully lift it up out of the socket. Do not remove the PROM cover.

To install:

6. Fit the replacement MEM-CAL/PROM/KS module into the socket.

➡The small notches in the MEM-CAL/PROM/KS module must be aligned with the small notches in the socket. Press only on the ends of the MEM-CAL/PROM/KS module until the retaining clips snap into the ends of the MEM-CAL/PROM/KS module. Do not press on the middle of the MEM-CAL/PROM/KS module, only the ends.

7. If equipped with a KS module, install the module cover.

8. Install the access cover and retaining screws.

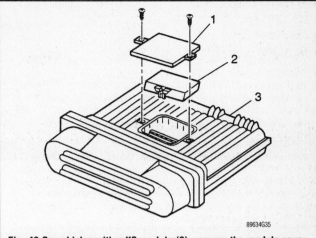

Fig. 46 On vehicles with a KS module (2), remove the module cover (1) from the PCM (3)

Fig. 47 For the KS module, gently squeeze the retaining tabs together, then carefully lift the module from the PCM

9. Make sure the ignition switch is still **OFF**, then install the ECM, as outlined earlier in this section.

FUNCTIONAL CHECK

1988–93 Vehicles

1. Turn the ignition switch **ON**.

2. Enter diagnostics, as outlined later in this section.

    a. Allow Code 12 to flash 4 times to verify that no other codes are present. This indicates the PROM/MEM-CAL is installed properly and the ECM is functioning.

    b. If Trouble Code 42, 43 or 51 occurs, or if the Service Engine Soon light is ON constantly with no codes, the Mem-Cal is not fully seated or is defective.

    c. If it is not fully seated, press firmly on the ends of the PROM/MEM-CAL.

3. If installed backwards, replace the PROM/MEM-CAL.

➡**Anytime the PROM is installed backwards and the ignition switch is turned ON, the PROM is destroyed.**

4. If the pins are bent, remove the PROM/MEM-CAL, straighten the pins and reinstall the PROM/MEM-CAL. If the bent pins break or crack during straightening, discard the PROM/MEM-CAL and replace with a new PROM/MEM-CAL.

➡**To prevent possible electrostatic discharge damage to the PROM or MEM-CAL, do not touch the component leads and do not remove the integrated circuit from the carrier.**

1994–99 Vehicles

1. Using a Tech 1® or equivalent scan tool, perform the on-board diagnostic system check.

2. Start the engine and run for one minute.

3. Scan for DTCs using the Tech 1® or equivalent scan tool, as outlined later in this section.

4. If Trouble Code P0325, P1361, P1350, or P1623 occurs, or if the MIL (Service Engine Soon) is ON constantly with no Diagnostic Trouble Codes (DTCs), the PROM or KS module is not fully seated or is defective.

5. If it is not fully seated, press firmly on the ends of the PROM/KS module.

Oxygen Sensor

OPERATION

♦ **See Figure 48**

There are two types of oxygen sensors used in these vehicles. They are the single wire Oxygen Sensor (02S) and the Heated Oxygen Sensor (H02S). The oxygen sensor is a spark plug shaped device that is screwed into the exhaust manifold. It monitors the oxygen content of the exhaust gases and sends a voltage signal to the Electronic Control Module (ECM). The ECM monitors this voltage and, depending on the value of the signal received, issues a command to adjust for a rich or lean condition.

The heated oxygen sensor has a heating element incorporated into the sensor to aid in the warm up to the proper operating temperature and to maintain that temperature.

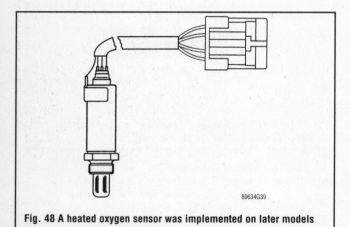

Fig. 48 A heated oxygen sensor was implemented on later models

The proper operation of the oxygen sensor depends upon four basic conditions:

1. Good electrical connections. Since the sensor generates low currents, good clean electrical connections at the sensor are a must.

2. Outside air supply. Air must circulate to the internal portion of the sensor. When servicing the sensor, do not restrict the air passages.

3. Proper operating temperatures. The ECM will not recognize the sensor's signals until the sensor reaches approximately 600°F (316°C).

4. Non-leaded fuel. The use of leaded gasoline will damage the sensor very quickly.

Precautions:

- Careful handling of the oxygen sensor is essential.
- The electrical pigtail and connector are permanently attached and should not be removed from the oxygen sensor.
- The in-line electrical connector and louvered end of the oxygen sensor must be kept free of grease, dirt and other contaminants.
- Avoid using cleaning solvents of any type on the oxygen sensor.
- Do not drop or roughly handle the oxygen sensor.
- The oxygen sensor may be difficult to remove if the engine temperature is below 120°F (48°C). Excessive force may damage the threads in the exhaust manifold or exhaust pipe.

TESTING

Single Wire Sensor

1. Visually inspect the connector to be sure it is connected properly and all of the terminals are on straight, tighten and free of corrosion or other damage.

2. Check the oxygen sensor voltage between the terminals (on 2 wire sensors) of between the sensor terminal and ground (on 1 wire sensors). The voltage should be between 350–500 millivolts. If the voltage is outside of specifications, the sensor is faulty.

3. If the voltage is within specifications, recheck the voltage after heating the engine to normal operating temperature (closed loop status). With the engine running at about 1,200 rpm, the voltage should vary between 100–900 millivolts. If the voltage is not varying or is not within specifications, the sensor is faulty.

4. If the voltage is within specifications, check the circuits back to the ECM for continuity.

5. If the sensor and circuits are functional, the PCM may be bad.

Heated Oxygen Sensor

♦ **See Figure 49**

1. Visually check the connector, making sure it is engaged properly and all of the terminals are straight, tight and free of corrosion.

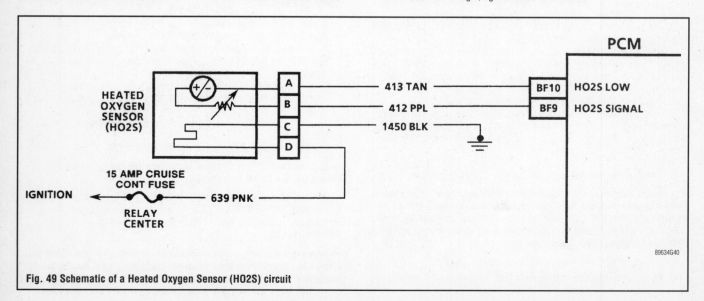

Fig. 49 Schematic of a Heated Oxygen Sensor (HO2S) circuit

2. Detach the sensor electrical connector and check resistance between terminals C and D. Resistance should be 10–15 ohms at 79°F. If resistance is not within specifications, the sensor heater is faulty.

3. If resistance is within specification, check for battery positive (B+) between connector terminals C and D with the ignition **ON**. If battery positive (B+) is not present, check the circuit continuity back to the PCM. If the circuits are functioning properly, the PCM may be faulty.

4. Check the HO2S sensor voltage between terminals A and B with the engine **OFF**. The voltage should be between 350–500 millivolts. If the voltage doesn't fall within that range, the sensor is faulty.

5. If the voltage is within specifications, recheck the voltage after heating the engine to normal operating temperature. With the engine running at 1200 rpm, then voltage should vary between 100–900 millivolts. If the voltage is not varying or not within the range, the sensor is faulty.

6. If the voltage is within specifications, check the circuits back to the PCM for continuity.

7. If the sensor and circuits are functioning properly, the PCM may be faulty.

REMOVAL & INSTALLATION

▶ See Figures 50, 51, 52, 53 and 54

❄❄ WARNING

The sensor uses a permanently attached pigtail and connector. This pigtail should not be removed from the sensor. Damage or removal

of the pigtail or connector could affect the proper operation of the sensor. Keep the electrical connector and louvered end of the sensor clean and free of grease. NEVER use cleaning solvents of any type on the sensor!

1. Disconnect the negative battery cable.
2. Locate the oxygen sensor. It protrudes from the center of the exhaust manifold at the front or rear of the engine compartment; (it looks somewhat like a spark plug).
3. If necessary, raise and safely support the vehicle for access to the oxygen sensor.
4. It may be necessary to tag and disconnect any spark plug wires that obstruct the oxygen sensor.
5. Detach the electrical connector from the oxygen sensor.
6. Spray a commercial heat riser solvent onto the sensor threads and allow it to soak in for at least five minutes.
7. Carefully unscrew and remove the sensor. There are special sockets available that make oxygen sensor removal easier.

To install:

➡**A special anti-seize compound is used on the oxygen sensor threads. The compound consists of a liquid graphite and glass beads. The graphite will burn away, but the glass beads will remain, making the sensor easier to remove.**

8. Coat the new sensor's threads with GM anti-seize compound No. 5613695 or the equivalent. This is not a conventional anti-seize paste. The use

Fig. 50 This spark plug wire may have to be disconnected for access to the O2 sensor

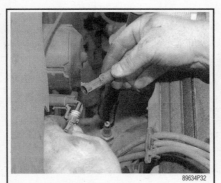

Fig. 51 Unplug the O2 sensor electrical connector

Fig. 52 There is a special socket that, along with a ratchet and extension . . .

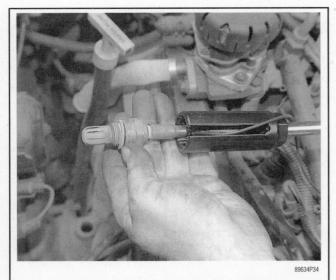

Fig. 53 . . . you can use to remove the O2 sensor from the manifold

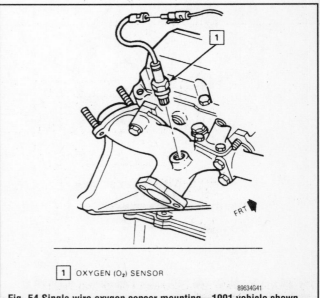

1 OXYGEN (O₂) SENSOR

Fig. 54 Single wire oxygen sensor mounting—1991 vehicle shown

of a regular compound may electrically insulate the sensor, rendering it inoperative. You must coat the threads with an electrically conductive anti-seize compound.

9. Install the sensor and tighten it to 30 ft. lbs. (41 Nm). Do not overtighten.

10. Attach the electrical connector. Be careful not to damage the electrical pigtail. Check the sensor boot for proper fit and installation.

11. If raised, carefully lower the vehicle.

12. Connect the negative battery cable.

Idle Air Control Valve

OPERATION

▶ **See Figures 55 and 56**

Engine idle speeds are controlled by the PCM through the Idle Air Control (IAC) valve mounted on the throttle body. The PCM sends voltage pulses to the IAC motor windings causing the IAC motor shaft and pintle to move in or out a given distance (number of steps) for each pulse (called counts). The movement of the pintle controls the airflow around the throttle plate, which in turn, controls engine idle speed. IAC valve pintle position counts can be observed using a scan tool. Zero counts correspond to a fully closed passage, while 140 counts or more corresponds to full flow.

Idle speed can be categorized in 2 ways: actual (controlled) idle speed and minimum idle speed. Controlled idle speed is obtained by the PCM positioning the IAC valve pintle. Resulting idle speed is determined by total air flow (IAC/passage + PCV + throttle valve + calibrated vacuum leaks). Controlled idle speed is specified at normal operating conditions, which consists of engine coolant at normal operating temperature, air conditioning compressor **OFF**, manual transaxle in neutral or automatic transaxle in **D**.

Minimum idle air speed is set at the factory with a stop screw. This setting allows a certain amount of air to bypass the throttle valves regardless of IAC valve pintle positioning. A combination of this air flow and IAC pintle positioning allows the PCM to control engine idle speed. During normal engine idle operation, the IAC valve pintle is positioned a calibrated number of steps (counts) from the seat. No adjustment is required during routine maintenance. Tampering with the minimum idle speed adjustment may result in premature failure of the IAC valve or improperly controlled engine idle operation.

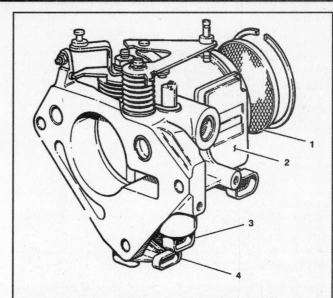

1	THROTTLE BODY AIR INLET SCREEN
2	MAF SENSOR
3	IAC VALVE
4	THROTTLE POSITION SENSOR

89634G43

Fig. 56 Location of the IAC valve—3.8L (VIN 1 and L) shown

TESTING

▶ **See Figures 57, 58 and 59**

1. Visually check the connector, making sure it is connected properly and all of the terminals are straight, tight and free of corrosion.

2. Unplug the IAC connector and check resistance between the IAC terminals. Resistance between terminals A to B and terminals C to D should be 40–80 ohms. If resistance is not within specification, the IAC valve must be replaced.

3. Check resistance between the IAC terminals A to C, A to D, B to C and B to D. Resistance should be infinite. If not, the IAC valve is faulty.

4. If the resistance is within specification, check the IAC circuits back to the PCM for continuity.

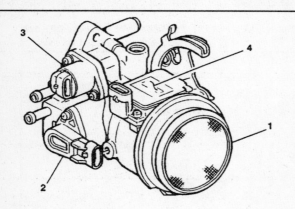

1	THROTTLE BODY AIR INLET SCREEN
2	THROTTLE POSITION SENSOR
3	IAC VALVE
4	MAF SENSOR

89634G42

Fig. 55 The Idle Air Control (IAC) valve is mounted on the throttle body—3.8L (VIN K) engine shown

89634P05

Fig. 57 Attach an ohmmeter to IAC valve terminals A and B and measure the resistance

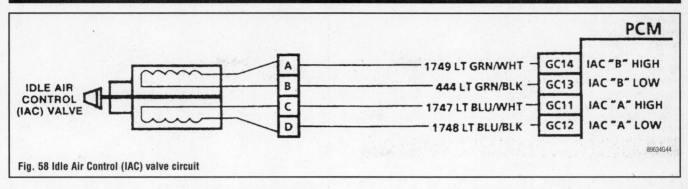

Fig. 58 Idle Air Control (IAC) valve circuit

Fig. 59 When IAC valve terminals B and C are jumpered, the reading should be infinite

5. If the valve and circuits are functional, the computer control module may be faulty.

REMOVAL & INSTALLATION

→On some models, it may be necessary to remove the air inlet assembly.

1. Disconnect the negative battery cable.
2. Detach the IAC valve electrical connector.
3. Remove the IAC valve by performing the following:
   a. On thread-mounted units, use a 1¼ in. (32mm) wrench.
   b. On flange-mounted units, remove the mounting screw assemblies.
4. Remove the IAC valve, then remove the and discard the IAC valve gasket or O-ring.

To install:

5. Clean the mounting surfaces by performing the following:

✳✳ WARNING

NEVER soak the IAC valve in any liquid cleaner or solvent!

   a. If servicing a thread-mounted valve, remove the old gasket material from the surface of the throttle body to ensure proper sealing of the new gasket.
   b. If servicing a flange-mounted valve, clean the IAC valve surfaces on the throttle body to assure proper seal of the new O-ring and contact of the IAC valve flange.
6. If installing a new IAC valve, measure the distance between the tip of the IAC valve pintle and the mounting flange. If the distance is greater than 1.102 in. (28mm), use finger pressure to slowly retract the pintle. The force required to retract the pintle of a new valve will not cause damage to the valve. If reinstalling the original IAC valve, do not attempt to adjust the pintle in this manner.

7. Install the IAC valve into the throttle body by performing the following:
   a. With thread-mounted valves, install with a new gasket. Using a 1¼ in. (32mm) wrench, tighten to 13 ft. lbs. (18 Nm).
   b. With flange-mounted valves, lubricate a new O-ring with transmission fluid and install on the IAC valve. Install the IAC valve to the throttle body. Install the mounting screws using a suitable threadlocking compound. Tighten to 27 inch lbs. (3 Nm).
8. Attach the IAC valve electrical connector.
9. Connect the negative battery cable.
10. The PCM will reset the IAC whenever the ignition switch is turned **ON** and then **OFF**. Start the engine and let it reach normal operating temperatures

Coolant Temperature Sensor

OPERATION

▶ See Figure 60

Most engine functions are affected by the coolant temperature. Determining whether the engine is hot or cold is largely dependent on the temperature of the coolant. An accurate temperature signal to the PCM is supplied by the coolant temperature sensor or Engine Coolant Temperature (ECT) sensor. The coolant temperature sensor is a thermistor mounted in the engine coolant stream. A thermistor is an electrical device that varies its resistance in relation to changes in temperature. Low coolant temperature produces a high resistance, and high coolant temperature produces low resistance. The PCM supplies a signal of 5 volts to the coolant temperature sensor through a resistor in the PCM and measures the voltage. The voltage will be high when the engine is cold and low when the engine is hot.

TESTING

Sensor in Vehicle

▶ See Figures 61, 62, 63, 64 and 65

1. Unfasten the retaining bolts, then remove the bracket.
2. Use a long screwdriver or prytool to lift the ECT sensor locking tab and detach the connector.

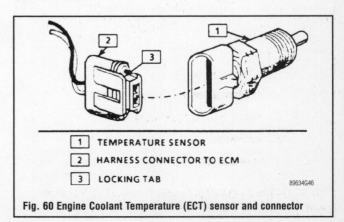

1	TEMPERATURE SENSOR
2	HARNESS CONNECTOR TO ECM
3	LOCKING TAB

Fig. 60 Engine Coolant Temperature (ECT) sensor and connector

Fig. 61 Unfasten the retainers, then remove the throttle bracket for more access to the sensor

Fig. 62 Use a long screwdriver to carefully lift the sensor locking tab, then unplug the connector

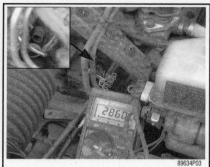

Fig. 63 Use needlenose pliers to attach an ohmmeter to the sensor terminals, then measure resistance (tested at 80°F)

DIAGNOSTIC AID

TEMPERATURE VS. RESISTANCE VALUES (APPROXIMATE)

°C	°F	OHMS
100	212	177
90	194	241
80	176	332
70	158	467
60	140	667
50	122	973
45	113	1188
40	104	1459
35	95	1802
30	86	2238
25	77	2796
20	68	3520
15	59	4450
10	50	5670
5	41	7280
0	32	9420
-5	23	12300
-10	14	16180
-15	5	21450
-20	-4	28680
-30	-22	52700
-40	-40	100700

Fig. 64 Engine Coolant Temperature (ECT) and Intake Air Temperature (IAT) sensor temperature vs. resistance values

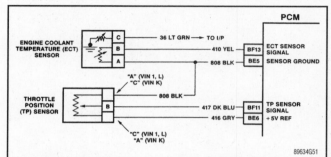

Fig. 65 Engine Coolant Temperature (ECT) and Throttle Position (TP) sensor circuits

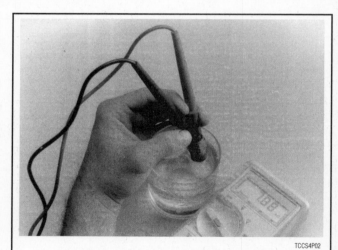

Fig. 66 Submerge the end of the temperature sensor in cold or hot water and check resistance

3. Attach an ohmmeter to the sensor terminals, then measure the resistance and compare with the accompanying chart.

Sensor Removed From Vehicle

▶ See Figures 64, 65 and 66

1. Remove the ECT sensor from the vehicle.
2. Immerse the tip of the sensor in a container of water.
3. Connect a digital ohmmeter to the two terminal of the sensor.
4. Using a calibrated thermometer, compare the resistance of the sensor to the temperature of the water. Refer to the accompanying resistance value chart.
5. Repeat the test at two other temperature points, heating or cooling the water as necessary.
6. If the sensor does not meet specifications, it must be replaced.

REMOVAL & INSTALLATION

▶ See Figures 67, 68 and 69

1. Disconnect the negative battery cable.
2. Drain the radiator into a suitable container, to a level below the sensor.
3. For 1986–91 vehicles, perform the following:
   a. Properly relieve the fuel system pressure, as outlined in Section 5.
   b. Unfasten the 10mm bolt and bracket holding the fuel line to the throttle cable bracket.
   c. Loosen the fuel supply and return lines from the fuel rail and carefully move aside.

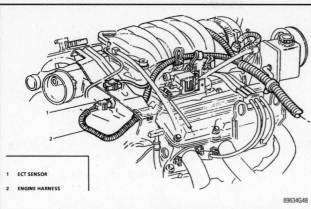

1 ECT SENSOR
2 ENGINE HARNESS

89634G48

Fig. 67 Location of the ECT sensor—3.8L (VIN L) engine shown

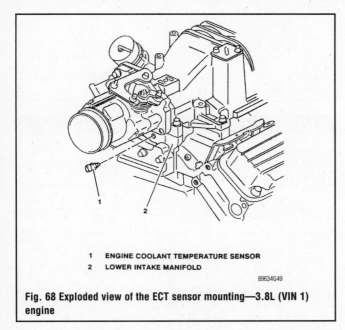

1 **ENGINE COOLANT TEMPERATURE SENSOR**
2 **LOWER INTAKE MANIFOLD**

89634G49

Fig. 68 Exploded view of the ECT sensor mounting—3.8L (VIN 1) engine

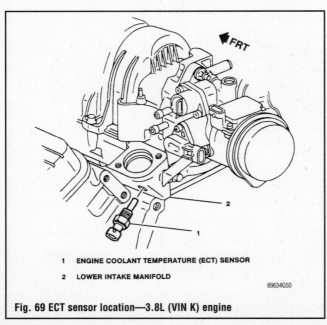

1 **ENGINE COOLANT TEMPERATURE (ECT) SENSOR**
2 **LOWER INTAKE MANIFOLD**

89634G50

Fig. 69 ECT sensor location—3.8L (VIN K) engine

d. Fabricate a loop of wire or use a long prytool to slip under the locking tab of the electrical connector and gently pull on the tab to disengage it.
4. For 1992–99 vehicles, perform the following:
  a. Remove the air induction tube or rear air intake duct, as applicable.
  b. Detach the sensor electrical connector.
5. Using a 19mm deep well socket and extension, remove the sensor.
To install:
6. Coat the ECT sensor threads with a suitable sealant.
7. Install the sensor and tighten to 22 ft. lbs. (30 Nm).
8. Installation is the reverse of the removal procedure.

Intake Air Temperature Sensor

➡️**The Intake Air Temperature (IAT) sensor is the same as the Manifold Air Temperature (MAT) sensor on earlier models.**

The IAT sensor is a thermistor which supplies intake air temperature information to the PCM. The sensor produces high resistance at low temperatures and low resistance at high temperatures. The PCM supplies a 5 volt signal to the sensor and measures the output voltage. The voltage signal will be low when the air is cold and high when the air is hot. The IAT is located in or near the air intake duct.

TESTING

▶ **See Figures 64, 70, 71 and 72**

1. If necessary, remove the Intake Air Temperature (IAT) sensor from the vehicle.
2. Connect a digital ohmmeter to the two terminals of the sensor.
3. Using a calibrated thermometer, compare the resistance of the sensor to the temperature of the ambient air. Refer to the temperature vs. resistance chart.

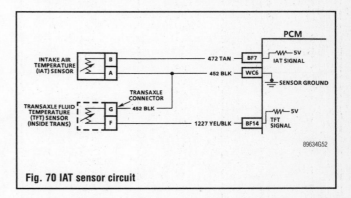

89634G52

Fig. 70 IAT sensor circuit

89634P16

Fig. 71 Testing the IAT/MAT sensor (which is located in the air cleaner housing) at ambient air temperature

Fig. 72 Measure resistance while using a hair dryer to heat the incoming air. Resistance should fall as the temperature rises

4. Repeat the test at two other temperature points, heating or cooling the air as necessary with a hair dryer or other suitable tool.
5. If the sensor does not meet specifications, it must be replaced.

REMOVAL & INSTALLATION

♦ **See Figures 73 and 74**

1. Disconnect the negative battery cable.
2. If necessary, remove the air intake cover and filter element.
3. Detach the IAT sensor electrical connector.
4. Grasp and remove the IAT sensor using a twisting and pulling motion.
5. Installation is the reverse of the removal procedure.

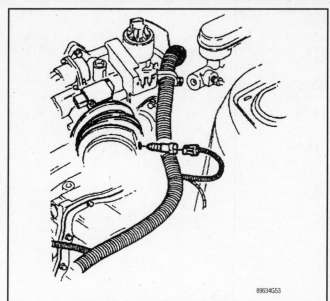

Fig. 74 On 1996–98 vehicles, the IAT sensor is mounted in the rear air intake duct

Mass Air Flow Sensor

OPERATION

♦ **See Figure 75**

The Mass Air Flow (MAF) sensor measures the amount of air which passes through it. The ECM uses this information to determine the operating condition

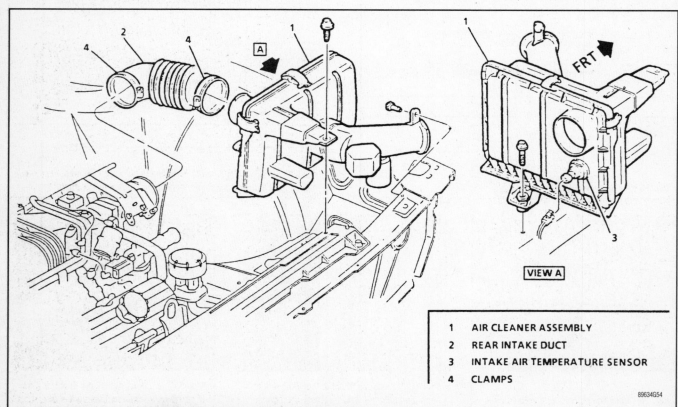

1	AIR CLEANER ASSEMBLY
2	REAR INTAKE DUCT
3	INTAKE AIR TEMPERATURE SENSOR
4	CLAMPS

Fig. 73 The IAT sensor is located in the air cleaner housing on this 1992 vehicle

of the engine, to control fuel delivery. A large quantity of air indicates acceleration, while a small quantity indicates deceleration or idle.

This sensor produces a frequency output between 32 and 150 hertz. A scan tool will display air flow in terms of grams of air per second (gps), with a range from 3gps to 150 gps.

TESTING

▶ **See Figures 76, 77, 78, 79 and 80**

1. Visually check the connector, making sure it is connected properly and all of the terminals are straight, tight and free of corrosion.

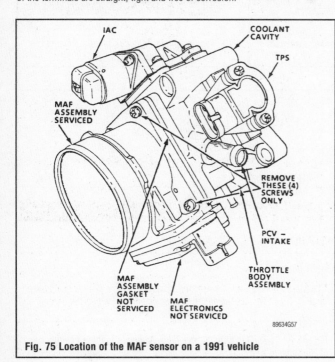

Fig. 75 Location of the MAF sensor on a 1991 vehicle

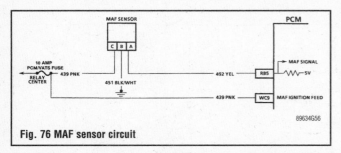

Fig. 76 MAF sensor circuit

2. With the engine running, lightly tap on the MAF sensor and wiggle the wires at the connector, while watching for a change in idle speed. A common problem is MAF sensor wire damage.

3. Backprobe using a DVOM set to the Hertz scale between terminals A and B. Simulate operating conditions by blowing air across the sensor. There should be a frequency swing from the air crossing the wire in the sensor. A normal flow signal will be close to 1200 hertz. If the frequency is not shown, or not proportionate to the air blown across the sensor, the sensor is faulty.

4. Check for battery positive (B+) voltage on terminal C and ground on terminal B. If voltage or ground are not present, check the circuits back to the PCM for continuity.

5. If you receive the proper amount of voltage at the electrical connector and still have a driveability problem, replace the MAF sensor.

6. If the sensor and circuits are functional, the PCM may be faulty.

REMOVAL & INSTALLATION

➡**On 1986–91 vehicles, the MAF sensor is the electronics portion (black) and the aluminum housing to which it is attached. On later models, the MAF sensor just consists of the electronic portion, mounted to the throttle body.**

1986–91 Vehicles

▶ **See Figures 81, 82, 83 and 84**

1. Disconnect the negative battery cable.
2. Loosen the clamps on the ends of the air duct, then remove the duct.
3. Detach the electrical connector from the MAF sensor.
4. Remove the 4 retaining screws holding the MAF sensor to the throttle body.
5. Remove the MAF sensor from the vehicle. Do NOT remove the MAF sensor gasket. It is not removable or serviceable.
6. Installation is the reverse of the removal procedure.

Fig. 77 Attach a DVOM to the MAF sensor electrical connector's top and middle terminals and check for a 5 volt reference signal

Fig. 78 Check the middle and bottom connector terminals for 12 volts

Fig. 79 Connect a DVOM to the MAF sensor and check the air flow's corresponding voltage reading (0.144 volts in this case) . . .

Fig. 80 . . . then use a hair dryer to blow air into the sensor and note the fluctuation in the reading

Fig. 81 Unfasten the clamp retaining screws, then remove the throttle body air duct

Fig. 82 Unplug the MAF sensor electrical connector

Fig. 83 Unfasten the retaining screws, then remove the MAF sensor

Fig. 84 Location of the MAF sensor retainer mounting holes

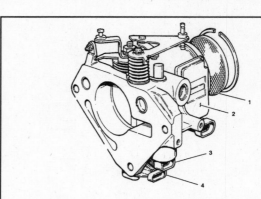

1	THROTTLE BODY AIR INLET SCREEN
2	MAF SENSOR
3	IAC VALVE
4	THROTTLE POSITION SENSOR

Fig. 85 On 1992–95 vehicles, the MAF sensor is mounted to the side of the throttle body

1992–99 Vehicles

▶ **See Figures 85 and 86**

1. Disconnect the negative battery cable.
2. Unplug the MAF sensor electrical connector.
3. Remove the 3 retaining screws, then remove the MAF sensor from the throttle body.
4. Installation is the reverse of the removal procedure.

Manifold Absolute Pressure Sensor

OPERATION

The Manifold Absolute Pressure (MAP) sensor, used on 1996–99 vehicles, measures the changes in intake manifold pressure which result from engine load/speed changes, and converts this information to a voltage output. The MAP sensor reading is the opposite of a vacuum gauge reading: when manifold pressure is high, MAP sensor value is high and vacuum is low. A MAP sensor will produce a low output on engine coast-down with a closed throttle while a wide open throttle will produce a high output. The high output is produced because the pressure inside the manifold is the same as outside the manifold, so 100 percent of the outside air pressure is measured.

The MAP sensor is also used to measure barometric pressure under certain conditions, which allows the PCM to automatically adjust for different altitudes.

The MAP sensor changes the 5 volt signal supplied by the PCM, which reads the change and uses the information to control fuel delivery and ignition timing.

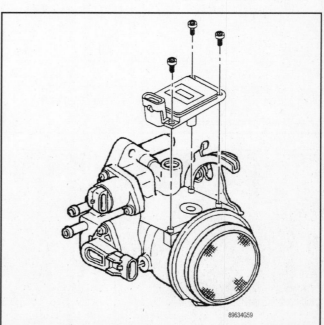

Fig. 86 The MAF sensor is attached to the top of the throttle body on 1996–99 vehicles

TESTING

▶ See Figures 87 and 88

1. Visually check the connector, making sure it is properly connected and that all of its terminals are straight, tight and free of corrosion.

2. With the ignition **ON**, check the voltage between terminals A and B. It should be above 4 volts. Apply 15 in. Hg of vacuum at the MAP vacuum port and check the voltage again. The voltage should be 2 volts now.

➡**When pumping up and releasing the vacuum, check to make sure the voltage readings are smooth. When applying vacuum to the sensor, the change in voltage should happen instantly. A slow change in voltage could point to a faulty sensor.**

3. If the sensor voltage is not within specification, check for a 5 volt reference at terminal C. If the reference signal is found, the sensor is faulty.

4. If the sensor and circuits are functional, the PCM may be faulty.

REMOVAL & INSTALLATION

3.8L (VIN 1) Engine

▶ See Figure 89

1. Disconnect the negative battery cable.
2. Unfasten the two retaining screws.
3. Detach the electrical connector and vacuum hose from the MAP sensor.
4. Remove the MAP sensor from the bracket.
5. Installation is the reverse of the removal procedure.

3.8L (VIN K) Engine

▶ See Figure 90

➡**On these engines, the MAP sensor is mounted to the PCV valve cover.**

1. Disconnect the negative battery cable.
2. Detach the MAP sensor electrical connector.
3. Carefully bend the locking tabs holding the MAP sensor to the PCV valve cover, just enough to remove the MAP sensor.
4. Pull the MAP sensor straight out of the PCV valve cover.

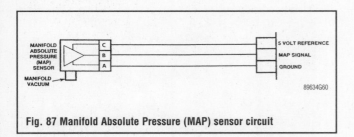

Fig. 87 Manifold Absolute Pressure (MAP) sensor circuit

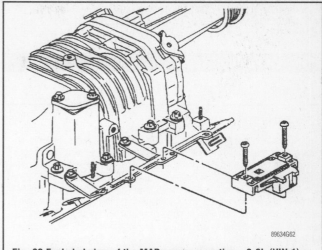

Fig. 89 Exploded view of the MAP sensor mounting—3.8L (VIN 1) engine

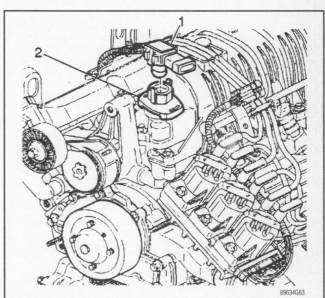

Fig. 90 On the 3.8L (VIN K) engine, the MAP sensor (1) is mounted in the PCV valve cover (2)

Altitude—Meters	Altitude—Feet	Pressure—kPa	Voltage Range
Below 305	Below 1000	100–98	3.8–5.5V
305–610	1000–2000	98–95	3.6–5.3V
610–914	2000–3000	95–92	3.5–5.1V
914–1219	3000–4000	92–89	3.3–5.0V
1219–1524	4000–5000	89–86	3.2–4.8V
1524–1829	5000–6000	86–83	3.0–4.6V
1829–2133	6000–7000	83–80	2.9–4.5V
2133–2438	7000–8000	80–77	2.8–4.3V
2438–2743	8000–9000	77–74	2.6–4.2V
2743–3948	9000–10,000	74–71	2.5–4.0V

Fig. 88 MAP sensor voltage specifications

5. Installation is the reverse of the removal procedure. Make sure that the seal is installed on the MAP sensor and that it is not damaged, and make sure that the MAP sensor-to-PCV valve cover locking tabs are properly engaged.

Throttle Position Sensor

OPERATION

♦ See Figure 91

The Throttle Position (TP) sensor is connected to the throttle shaft and is controlled by the throttle mechanism. A 5 volt reference signal is sent to the TP sensor from the ECM. As the throttle valve angle is changed (accelerator pedal moved), the resistance of the TP sensor also changes. At a closed throttle position, the resistance of the TP sensor is high, so the output voltage to the ECM will be low (approximately 0.5 volt). As the throttle plate opens, the resistance decreases so that, at wide open throttle, the output voltage should be approximately 5 volts. At closed throttle position, the voltage at the TP sensor should be less than 1.25 volts.

By monitoring the output voltage from the TP sensor, the ECM can determine fuel delivery based on throttle valve angle (driver demand). The TP sensor can either be misadjusted, shorted, open or loose. Misadjustment might result in poor idle or poor wide-open throttle performance. An open TP sensor signals the ECM that the throttle is always closed, resulting in poor performance. This usually sets a Code 22. A shorted TP sensor gives the ECM a constant wide-open throttle signal and should set a Code 21. A loose TP sensor indicates to the ECM that the throttle is moving. This causes intermittent bursts of fuel from the injector and an unstable idle. Once the trouble code is set, the ECM will use an artificial default value for the TP sensor, and some vehicle performance will return.

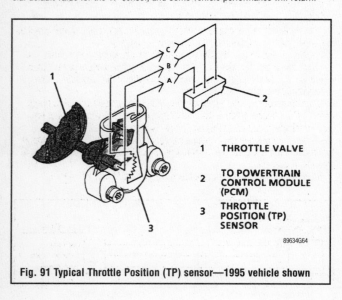

Fig. 91 Typical Throttle Position (TP) sensor—1995 vehicle shown

1 THROTTLE VALVE

2 TO POWERTRAIN CONTROL MODULE (PCM)

3 THROTTLE POSITION (TP) SENSOR

89634G64

TESTING

♦ See Figures 92, 93 and 94

1. Visually check the connector, making sure it is connected properly and all of the terminals are straight, tight and free of corrosion.
2. With the ignition in the **ON** position, check the voltage at terminal B. The voltage should read less that 0.5 volts.
3. Operate the throttle, while watching the voltage. The voltage should increase smoothly to 5 volts as the throttle is opened.
4. If the voltage is not within specification, check the 5 volt reference signal circuit at terminal C and ground the circuit at terminal A for the proper signal. If the correct signal is found, the sensor is faulty. If the proper signal is not found, check the circuits back to the computer control module for continuity.
5. If the circuits are functional, the PCM may be faulty.

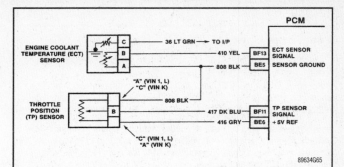

Fig. 92 Throttle Position (TP) sensor circuit—VIN 3, B and C engines have the same terminal identification as do VIN 1 and L

Fig. 93 Attach an ohmmeter (1) to the TP sensor terminals (2) and measure resistance with the throttle closed . . .

Fig. 94 . . . then push the throttle lever back (see arrow), to measure resistance in the Wide Open Throttle (WOT) position

REMOVAL & INSTALLATION

♦ See Figure 95

1. Disconnect the negative battery cable.
2. For 3.0L and 3.8L (VIN 3, B and C) engines, disconnect the PCV vent hose, then detach the TP sensor electrical connector.
3. For 3.8L (VIN 1, L and K) engines, perform the following steps, as necessary:

Fig. 95 Location of the Throttle Position (TP) sensor (1)—1996–99 vehicles shown, others similar

a. Disconnect the manifold vacuum lines from the throttle body and fuel pressure regulator.

b. Detach the IAC, TP sensor, MAF sensor electrical connector.

c. If necessary, detach the EGR valve electrical connector.

4. Unfasten the TP sensor's attaching screws, then remove the TP sensor from the throttle body.

To install:

5. Position the throttle valve in the normal closed idle position, then install the TP sensor on the throttle body assembly, making sure the TP sensor pickup lever is located above the tang on the throttle actuator lever.

6. Apply Loctite® 262 or equivalent threadlocking compound to the TP sensor screws. Install the TP sensor retainer and attaching screws. For 1986–91 vehicles, do not tighten the attaching screw until the TP sensor is adjusted, as outlined later in this section.

7. If not already done, tighten the TP sensor screws securely.

8. Installation is the reverse of the removal procedure.

ADJUSTMENT

1986–91 Vehicles

If a Tech 1® or equivalent scan tool is available, it is advisable to use the scan tool to read the TP sensor voltage. If using a voltmeter, extreme care must be taken to probe the correct terminal carefully. Incorrect testing or probing can damage the TP sensor connector or destroy the ECM.

1. With the TP sensor attaching screws loose, install 3 jumper wires between the TP sensor and harness connector.

2. With the ignition switch **ON**, use a digital voltmeter connected to terminals **B** and **C** and adjust the TP sensor to obtain 0.33–0.46 volts.

3. Tighten the attaching screws, then recheck the reading to insure the adjustment has not changed.

➥If the TP sensor is only being adjusted, remove the screws, add threadlocking compound (Loctite® 262, or equivalent), then reinstall the screws.

4. With the ignition switch **OFF**, remove the jumper wires and connect the harness to the TP sensor.

Camshaft Position Sensor

OPERATION

▶ **See Figure 96**

The PCM uses the Camshaft Position (CMP) sensor to determine the position of the No. 1 piston during its power stroke. This signal is used by the PCM to calculate the fuel injection mode of operation.

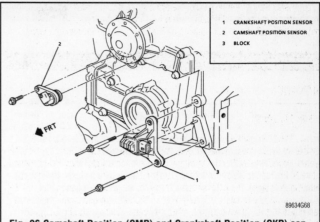

Fig. 96 Camshaft Position (CMP) and Crankshaft Position (CKP) sensor locations—1995 vehicle shown, others similar

If the camshaft signal is lost while the engine is running, the fuel injection system will shift to a calculated fuel injected mode based on the last fuel injection pulse, and the engine will continue to run.

TESTING

▶ **See Figure 97**

➥The best method to test this sensor is with the use of an oscilloscope.

1. Visually check the connector, making sure it is connected properly and all of the terminals are straight, tight and free of corrosion.

2. With the ignition in the **ON** position, check the sensor voltage using an oscilloscope. When the starter is briefly operated, a square wave pattern, alternating from 0–12 volts should be seen at terminal A. If the voltage is within specification, the sensor is functional.

3. If the sensor voltage is not within specifications, use a DVOM to check terminal C for battery positive (B+). If battery positive (B+) voltage is not present, check the circuit continuity and repair as necessary.

4. If battery positive (B+) voltage is present at terminal C, check terminal B for proper ground. If ground is not present, check the circuit for continuity and repair as necessary.

5. If the sensor and circuits are functional, the PCM may be faulty.

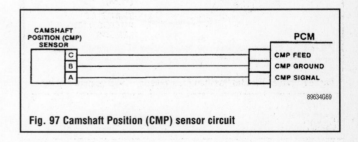

Fig. 97 Camshaft Position (CMP) sensor circuit

REMOVAL & INSTALLATION

1. Disconnect the negative battery cable.

2. Raise and safely support the vehicle. Remove the right front wheel and tire assembly.

3. Remove the right inner fender access cover/splash shield.

4. Detach the electrical connector from the CMP sensor.

5. Unfasten the retaining screw, then remove the CMP sensor.

To install:

6. Install the CMP sensor, and install the retaining screw. Tighten the screw 35–53 inch lbs. (4–6 Nm).

7. Installation is the reverse of the removal procedure.

Crankshaft Position Sensor

OPERATION

▶ **See Figures 96, 98 and 99**

The dual Crankshaft Position (CKP) sensor is mounted to the front of the engine, attached to an aluminum bracket mounted to the left side of the engine at the timing chain cover. A 4-wire connector plugs into the sensor, connecting it to the ignition control module. The CKP sensor contains 2 Hall effect switches with 1 shared magnet mounted between them. The magnet and each Hall effect switch are separated by an air gap. A Hall effect switch reacts like a solid state switch, grounding a low current signal voltage when a magnetic field is present. When the magnetic field is shielded from the switch by a piece of steel placed in the air gap between the magnet and the switch, the voltage signal is not grounded. If the piece of steel (called an interrupter ring) is repeatedly moved in and out of the air gap, the signal voltage will appear to go ON, OFF, ON, OFF, ON, OFF. This ON/OFF signal is similar to the signal that a set of conventional breaker points in a distributor would generate, as the distributor shaft is turned and the points open and close.

In the case of the electronic ignition system, the piece of steel is 2 concentric interrupter rings mounted to the rear of the crankshaft balancer. Each interrupter ring has blades and windows that, in conjunction with the crankshaft revolution, either block the magnetic field or allow it to reach one of the Hall effect switches. The outer Hall effect switch is called the 18X crankshaft position sensor, because the outer interrupter ring has 18 evenly spaced the same width blades and windows. The 18X crankshaft position sensor produces 18 ON/OFF pulses per crankshaft revolution. The Hall effect switch closest to the crankshaft,

the 3X crankshaft position sensor, is called this because the inside interrupter ring has 3 unevenly spaced, different width blades and windows. The 3X crankshaft position sensor produces 3 different length ON/OFF pulses per crankshaft revolution. When a 3X interrupter ring window is between the magnet and the inner switch, the magnetic field will cause the 3X Hall effect switch to ground the 3X signal voltage supplied from the ignition control module. The 18X interrupter ring and Hall effect switch reacts similarly.

The ignition control module interprets the 18X and 3X ON/OFF signals as an indication of crankshaft position, and must have both signals to fire the correct ignition coil. The ignition control module determines crankshaft position for the correct ignition coil sequencing by counting how may 18X signal transitions occur, ON, OFF or OFF, ON during a 3X pulse.

TESTING

▶ **See Figures 100 and 101**

1. Visually check the connector, making sure it is connected properly and all of the terminals are straight, tight and free of corrosion.
2. With the ignition in the **ON** position, check the sensor voltage using an oscilloscope. When the starter is briefly operated a square wave pattern, varying between 0–12 volts and providing 3 pulses per crankshaft revolution should be seen at terminal V. The same signal providing 18 pulses per crankshaft revolution should be seen at terminal A. If voltage is within specification, the sensor is functional.
3. If the voltage falls out of range, use a DVOM to check terminal C for battery positive (B+). If battery positive (B+) voltage is not present, check the circuit continuity and repair as necessary.
4. If battery positive (B+) voltage is found at terminal C, check the terminal D for proper ground. If ground is not present, check the circuit for continuity and repair as necessary.
5. If the sensor and circuits are functional, the PCM may be faulty.

REMOVAL & INSTALLATION

▶ **See Figures 96, 102, 103 and 104**

1. Disconnect the negative battery cable.
2. Remove the serpentine drive belt from the crankshaft pulley.
3. Raise and safely support the vehicle.
4. Remove the right front wheel and tire assembly and the right inner fender access cover/splash shield.
5. Using a 28mm socket, remove the crankshaft harmonic balancer retaining bolt.
6. Remove the crankshaft balancer, using a puller if necessary.
7. For 1992–99 vehicles, remove the CKP sensor shield.
8. Unplug the sensor electrical connector.
9. For 1986–91 vehicles, perform the following:
   a. Remove the sensor and pedestal from the block face.
   b. Remove the sensor from the pedestal.
10. For 1992–99 vehicles, remove the sensor from the block face.

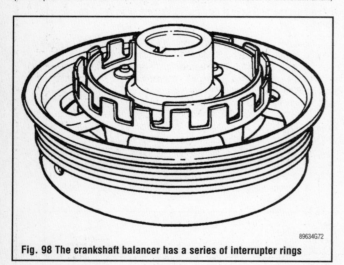

89634G72

Fig. 98 The crankshaft balancer has a series of interrupter rings

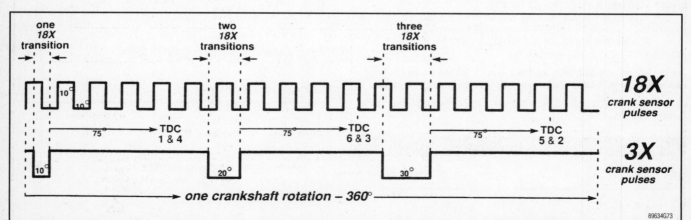

89634G73

Fig. 99 Because of their different blade and window configurations, the two Hall effect switches generate 18 and 3 CKP sensor pulses for each crankshaft revolution

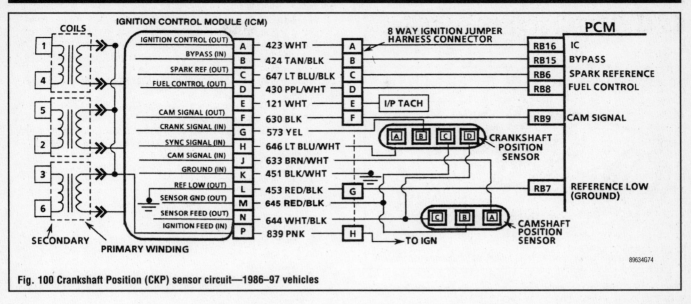

Fig. 100 Crankshaft Position (CKP) sensor circuit—1986–97 vehicles

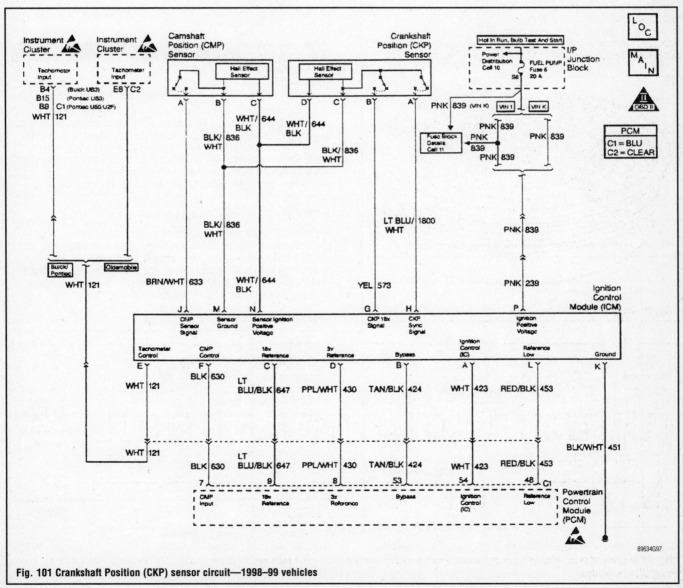

Fig. 101 Crankshaft Position (CKP) sensor circuit—1998–99 vehicles

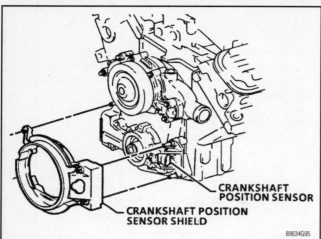

Fig. 102 If so equipped, remove the crankshaft position sensor shield

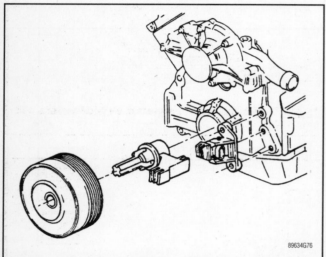

Fig. 103 Position the crankshaft sensor tool on the crankshaft

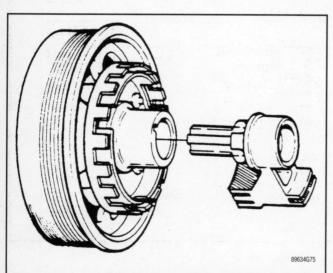

Fig. 104 Insert the crankshaft sensor tool into the harmonic balancer

To install:
   a. For 1986–91 vehicles, perform the following:
   b. Loosely install the crankshaft sensor on the pedestal.
   c. Position the sensor, with the pedestal attached, on crankshaft sensor installation tool J 37089 or equivalent.
   d. Install the bolt to hold the pedestal to the block face, then tighten to 14–28 ft. lbs. (20–40 Nm).
   e. Tighten the pedestal pinch bolt to 30–35 inch lbs. (3–4 Nm).
   f. Remove the special tool.
   g. Place the crankshaft sensor tool on the crankshaft balancer and turn. If any vane on the harmonic balancer touches the tool, replace the balancer.
  11. For 1992–99 vehicles, install the CKP sensor on the block.
   a. Install the retaining bolts and tighten to 14–28 ft. lbs. (20–40 Nm).
   b. Install the crankshaft position sensor shield.
   c. Attach the sensor electrical connector.
  12. Install the balancer on the crankshaft.
  13. Tighten the crankshaft bolt to 200–239 ft. lbs. (270–325 Nm) for 1986–91 vehicles. For 1992–99 vehicles, tighten to 110 ft. lbs. (150 Nm), plus an additional 76° rotation.
  14. Install the inner fender shield and the right tire and wheel assembly.
  15. Carefully lower the vehicle.
  16. Install the serpentine belt.
  17. Connect the negative battery cable.

Knock Sensor

OPERATION

Varying octane levels in today's gasoline engines may cause detonation in some engines. Detonation is caused by an uncontrolled explosion (burn) in the combustion chamber. This uncontrolled explosion can produce a flame front opposite that of a normal flame front produced by the spark plug. The rattling sound normally associated with detonation is the result of 2 or more opposing pressures (flame fronts) colliding within the combustion chamber. Though light detonation is sometimes considered normal, heavy detonation could cause engine damage.

➡The 3.8L (VIN K) engine uses 2 knock sensors.

The Knock Sensor (KS) is mounted in the engine block, where it detects abnormal engine vibration, such as detonation (spark knock). When a knock is detected, the KS produces an AC voltage signal that is sent to the PCM. The system is designed to retard spark 10–15° to counteract the effects of varying levels of octane in gasoline. This allows the engine to use maximum spark advance to improve driveability and fuel economy.

TESTING

▶ **See Figures 105 and 106**

1. Visually check the connector, making sure it is connected properly and that all of the terminals are straight, tight and free of corrosion.
2. Using a DVOM, check for an AC voltage signal between the sensor terminal and ground, while tapping on the engine block near the sensor. If voltage is not detected, check the resistance of the KS sensor between the sensor terminal and sensor body. If the resistance is more than 80–110 kilohms, the sensor is faulty.
3. If voltage is seen, check the circuit continuity back to the PCM.
4. If the sensor and circuits are functional, the PCM may be faulty.

REMOVAL & INSTALLATION

▶ **See Figure 107**

1. Disconnect the negative battery cable.
2. Raise and safely support the vehicle.

3. If necessary, remove the splash shield.

4. Position a suitable drain pan under the vehicle, then drain the engine coolant.

5. If necessary, remove the knock sensor heat shield mounting bolt, located under the freeze plug (or block heater, if equipped).

6. Disconnect the knock sensor wiring harness. On the 3.8L (VIN K) engine, you must detach the connectors from the bank 1 and bank 2 knock sensors.

7. Remove the knock sensor from the engine block.

➡**The knock sensor is mounted in the engine block cooling passage. Engine coolant in the block will drain when the sensor is removed.**

8. Installation is the reverse of removal. Tighten the sensor to 14 ft. lbs. (19 Nm). Do NOT apply any type of sealant to the knock sensor threads.

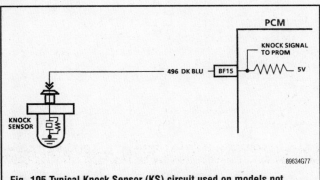

Fig. 105 Typical Knock Sensor (KS) circuit used on models not equipped with the 3.8L (VIN K) engine—1995–97 models with the 3.8L (VIN K) engine are equipped with two sensors

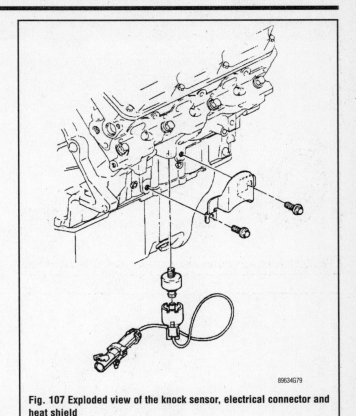

Fig. 107 Exploded view of the knock sensor, electrical connector and heat shield

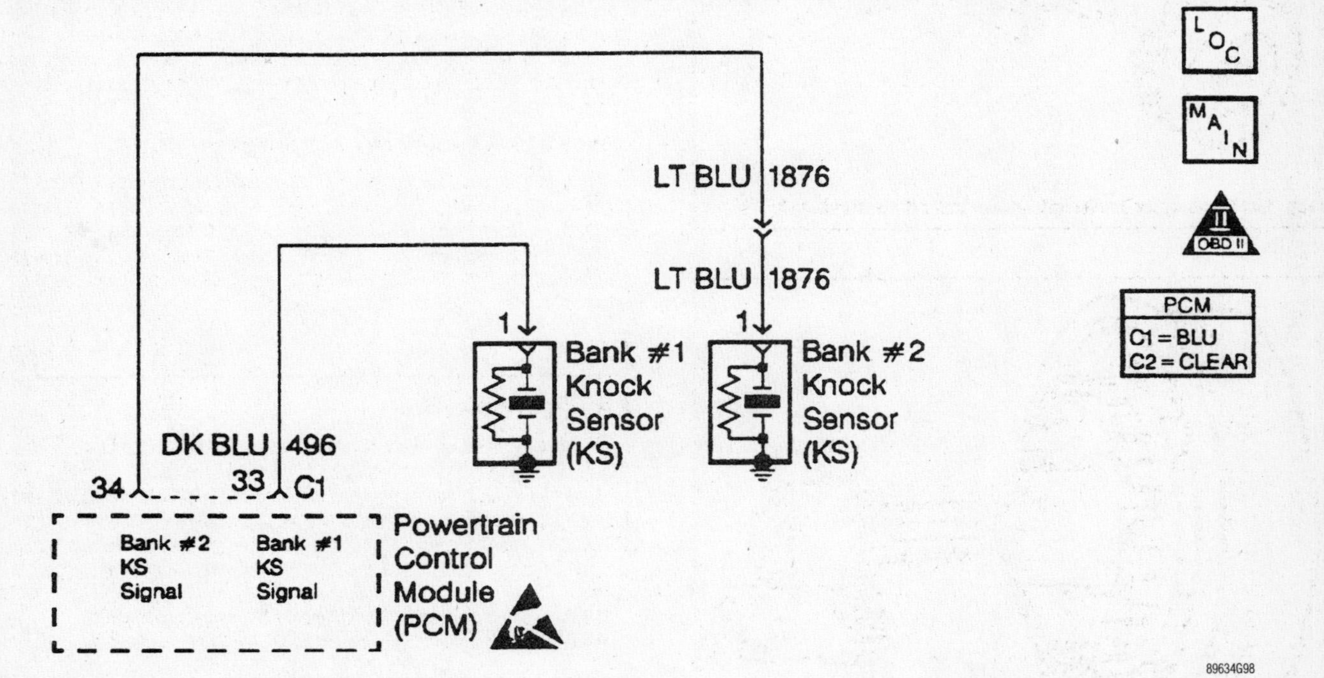

Fig. 106 Knock Sensor (KS) circuits—1998–99 3.8L (VIN K) engine

COMPONENT LOCATIONS

EMISSION CONTROL AND ELECTRONIC ENGINE CONTROL COMPONENT LOCATIONS—3.8L (VIN C) ENGINE

1. Vehicle Emission Control Information (VECI) label
2. Evaporative canister (located under air duct)
3. Mass Air Flow (MAF) sensor
4. Throttle Position (TP) sensor (mounted to side of throttle body)
5. Idle Air Control (IAC) valve (mounted to bottom of throttle body)
6. Engine Coolant Temperature (ECT) sensor (located under throttle bracket)
7. Manifold Air Temperature (MAT) sensor
8. Exhaust Gas Recirculation (EGR) valve
9. Oxygen sensor (mounted in exhaust manifold)
10. PCV valve (mounted in intake manifold)

89634PA1

EMISSION CONTROL AND ELECTRONIC ENGINE CONTROL COMPONENT LOCATIONS—3.8L (VIN K) ENGINE

1. Evaporative emission control solenoid
2. Engine Coolant Temperature (ECT) sensor
3. Evaporative canister (located under PCM)
4. Powertrain Control Module (PCM)
5. Throttle Position (TP) sensor
6. Idle Air Control (IAC) valve
7. Mass Air Flow (MAF) sensor
8. Exhaust Gas Recirculation (EGR) valve
9. Manifold Absolute Pressure (MAP) sensor
10. Positive Crankcase Ventilation (PCV) valve (located under MAP sensor)

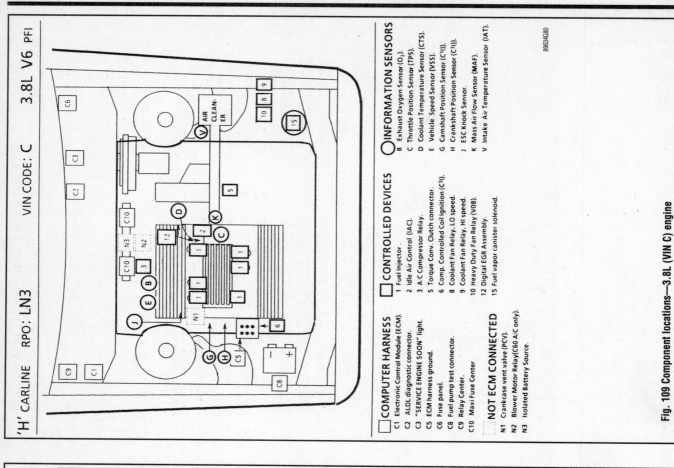

'H' CARLINE   RPO: LN3   VIN CODE: C   3.8L V6 PFI

COMPUTER HARNESS
- C1 Electronic Control Module (ECM).
- C2 ALDL diagnostic connector.
- C3 "SERVICE ENGINE SOON" light.
- C5 ECM harness ground.
- C6 Fuse panel.
- C8 Fuel pump test connector.
- C9 Relay Center.
- C10 Maxi Fuse Center.

NOT ECM CONNECTED
- N1 Crankcase vent valve (PCV).
- N2 Blower Motor Relay(C60 A/C only).
- N3 Isolated Battery Source.

CONTROLLED DEVICES
- 1 Fuel Injector.
- 2 Idle Air Control (IAC).
- 3 A/C Compressor Relay.
- 5 Torque Conv. Clutch connector.
- 6 Comp. Controlled Coil Ignition (C³I).
- 8 Coolant Fan Relay, LO speed.
- 9 Coolant Fan Relay, HI speed.
- 10 Heavy Duty Fan Relay (V08).
- 12 Digital EGR Assembly.
- 15 Fuel vapor canister solenoid.

INFORMATION SENSORS
- B Exhaust Oxygen Sensor (O₂).
- C Throttle Position Sensor (TPS).
- D Coolant Temperature Sensor (CTS).
- E Vehicle Speed Sensor (VSS).
- G Camshaft Position Sensor (C³I).
- H Crankshaft Position Sensor (C³I).
- J ESC Knock Sensor.
- K Mass Air Flow Sensor (MAF).
- V Intake Air Temperature Sensor (IAT).

Fig. 109 Component locations—3.8L (VIN C) engine

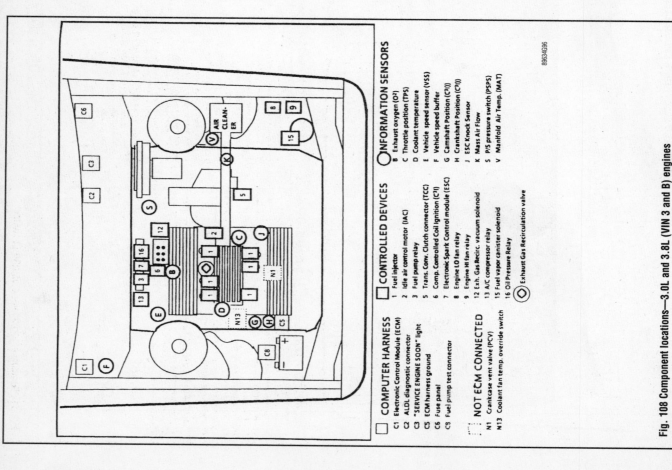

COMPUTER HARNESS
- C1 Electronic Control Module (ECM).
- C2 ALDL diagnostic connector.
- C3 "SERVICE ENGINE SOON" light.
- C5 ECM harness ground.
- C6 Fuse panel.
- C9 Fuel pump test connector.

NOT ECM CONNECTED
- N1 Crankcase vent valve (PCV).
- N13 Coolant fan temp. override switch

CONTROLLED DEVICES
- 1 Fuel injector.
- 2 Idle air control motor (IAC).
- 3 Fuel pump relay.
- 5 Trans. Conv. Clutch connector (TCC).
- 6 Comp. Controlled Coil Ignition (C³I).
- 7 Electronic Spark Control module (ESC).
- 8 Engine LO fan relay.
- 9 Engine HI fan relay.
- 12 Exh. Gas Recirc. vacuum solenoid.
- 13 A/C compressor relay.
- 15 Fuel vapor canister solenoid.
- 16 Oil Pressure Relay.

INFORMATION SENSORS
- B Exhaust oxygen (O²)
- C Throttle position (TPS).
- D Coolant temperature
- E Vehicle speed sensor (VSS)
- F Vehicle speed buffer
- G Camshaft Position (C³I).
- H Crankshaft Position (C³I).
- J ESC Knock Sensor
- K Mass Air Flow
- S P/S pressure switch (PSPS)
- V Manifold Air Temp. (MAT)
- ◇ Exhaust Gas Recirculation valve

Fig. 108 Component locations—3.0L and 3.8L (VIN 3 and B) engines

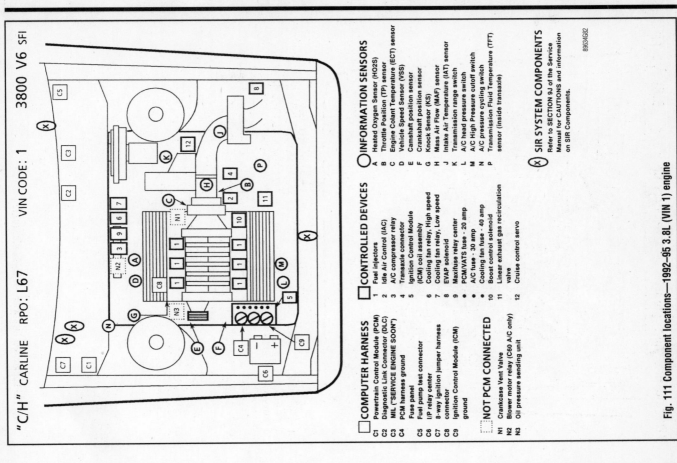

"C/H" CARLINE   RPO: L67   VIN CODE: 1   3800 V6 SFI

☐ **COMPUTER HARNESS**
C1 Powertrain Control Module (PCM)
C2 Diagnostic Link Connector (DLC)
C3 MIL ("SERVICE ENGINE SOON")
C4 PCM harness ground
C5 Fuse panel
C6 Fuel pump test connector
C7 I/P relay center
C8 8-way ignition jumper harness connector
C9 Ignition Control Module (ICM) ground

◻ **NOT PCM CONNECTED**
N1 Crankcase Vent Valve
N2 A/C blower motor relay (C60 A/C only)
N3 Oil pressure sending unit

○ **INFORMATION SENSORS**
A Heated Oxygen Sensor (HO2S)
B Throttle Position (TP) sensor
C Engine Coolant Temperature (ECT) sensor
D Vehicle Speed Sensor (VSS)
E Camshaft position sensor
F Crankshaft position sensor
G Knock Sensor (KS)
H Mass Air Flow (MAF) sensor
J Intake Air Temperature (IAT) sensor
K Transmission range switch
L A/C head pressure switch
M A/C High Pressure cutoff switch
N A/C pressure cycling switch
P Transmission Fluid Temperature (TFT) sensor (inside transaxle)

☐ **CONTROLLED DEVICES**
1 Fuel injectors
2 Idle Air Control (IAC)
3 A/C compressor relay
4 Transaxle connector
5 Ignition Control Module (ICM) coil assembly
6 Cooling fan relay, High speed
7 Cooling fan relay, Low speed
8 EVAP solenoid
9 Maxifuse relay center
● PCM/VATS fuse - 20 amp
● A/C fuse - 30 amp
● Cooling fan fuse - 40 amp
10 Boost control solenoid
11 Linear exhaust gas recirculation valve
12 Cruise control servo

ⓧ **SIR SYSTEM COMPONENTS**
Refer to SECTION 9J of the Service Manual for CAUTIONS and information on SIR Components.

89634G82

Fig. 111 Component locations—1992–95 3.8L (VIN 1) engine

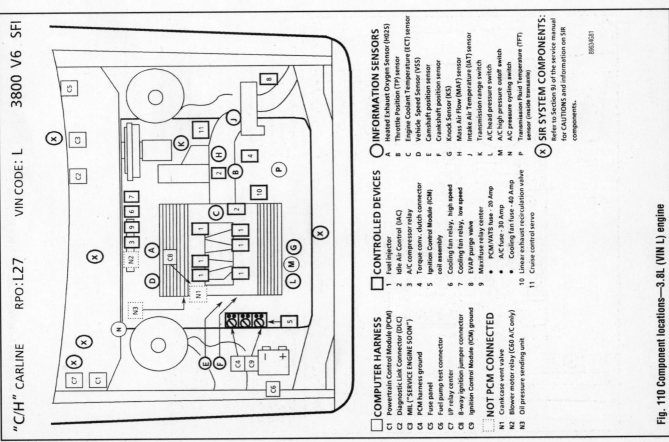

"C/H" CARLINE   RPO: L27   VIN CODE: L   3800 V6 SFI

☐ **COMPUTER HARNESS**
C1 Powertrain Control Module (PCM)
C2 Diagnostic Link Connector (DLC)
C3 MIL ("SERVICE ENGINE SOON")
C4 PCM harness ground
C5 Fuse panel
C6 Fuel pump test connector
C7 I/P relay center
C8 8-way ignition jumper connector
C9 Ignition Control Module (ICM) ground

◻ **NOT PCM CONNECTED**
N1 Crankcase vent valve
N2 Blower motor relay (C60 A/C only)
N3 Oil pressure sending unit

○ **INFORMATION SENSORS**
A Heated Exhaust Oxygen Sensor (HO2S)
B Throttle Position (TP) sensor
C Engine Coolant Temperature (ECT) sensor
D Vehicle Speed Sensor (VSS)
E Camshaft position sensor
F Crankshaft position sensor
G Knock Sensor (KS)
H Mass Air Flow (MAF) sensor
J Intake Air Temperature (IAT) sensor
K Transmission range switch
L A/C head pressure switch
M A/C high pressure cutoff switch
N A/C pressure cycling switch
P Transmission Fluid Temperature (TFT) sensor (inside transaxle)

☐ **CONTROLLED DEVICES**
1 Fuel injector
2 Idle Air Control (IAC)
3 A/C compressor relay
4 Torque conv. clutch connector
5 Ignition Control Module (ICM) coil assembly
6 Cooling fan relay, high speed
7 Cooling fan relay, low speed
8 EVAP purge valve
9 Maxifuse relay center
● PCM/VATS fuse - 20 Amp
● A/C fuse - 30 Amp
● Cooling fan fuse - 40 Amp
10 Linear exhaust recirculation valve
11 Cruise control servo

ⓧ **SIR SYSTEM COMPONENTS:**
Refer to Section 9J of the service manual for CAUTIONS and information on SIR components.

89634G81

Fig. 110 Component locations—3.8L (VIN L) engine

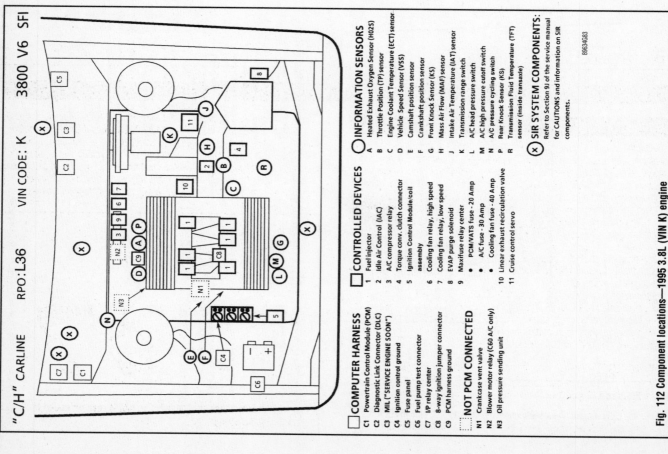

COMPUTER HARNESS

C1 Powertrain Control Module (PCM)
C2 Diagnostic Link Connector (DLC)
C3 MIL ("SERVICE ENGINE SOON")
C4 Ignition control ground
C5 Fuse panel
C6 Fuel pump test connector
C7 I/P relay center
C8 8-way ignition jumper connector
C9 PCM harness ground

NOT PCM CONNECTED

N1 Crankcase vent valve
N2 Blower motor relay (C60 A/C only)
N3 Oil pressure sending unit

CONTROLLED DEVICES

1 Fuel injector
2 Idle Air Control (IAC)
3 A/C compressor relay
4 Torque conv. clutch connector
5 Ignition Control Module/coil assembly
6 Cooling fan relay, high speed
7 Cooling fan relay, low speed
8 EVAP purge solenoid
9 Maxifuse relay center
   • PCM/NATS fuse - 20 Amp
   • A/C fuse - 30 Amp
   • Cooling fan fuse - 40 Amp
10 Linear exhaust recirculation valve
11 Cruise control servo

INFORMATION SENSORS

A Heated Exhaust Oxygen Sensor (HO2S)
B Throttle Position (TP) sensor
C Engine Coolant Temperature (ECT) sensor
D Vehicle Speed Sensor (VSS)
E Camshaft position sensor
F Crankshaft position sensor
G Front Knock Sensor (KS)
H Mass Air Flow (MAF) sensor
J Intake Air Temperature (IAT) sensor
K Transmission range switch
L A/C head pressure switch
M A/C high pressure cutoff switch
N A/C pressure cycling switch
P Rear Knock Sensor (KS)
R Transmission Fluid Temperature (TFT) sensor (inside transaxle)

SIR SYSTEM COMPONENTS:

(X) Refer to Section 9J of the service manual for CAUTIONS and information on SIR components.

89634G63

Fig. 112 Component locations—1995 3.8L (VIN K) engine

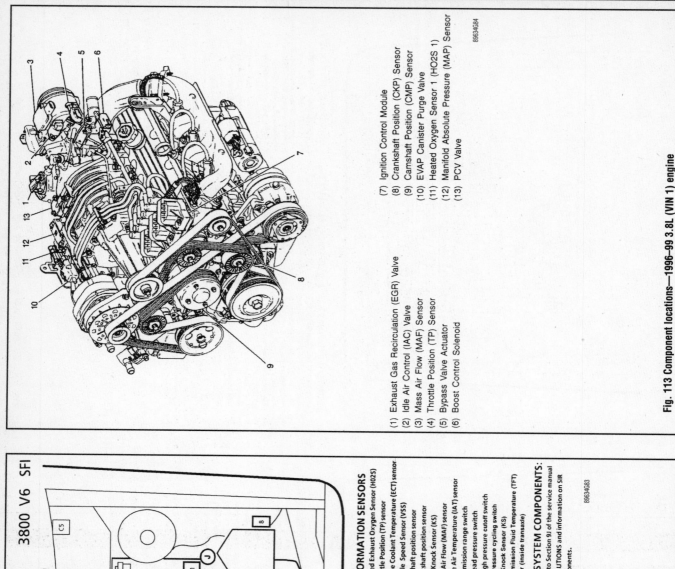

(1) Exhaust Gas Recirculation (EGR) Valve
(2) Idle Air Control (IAC) Valve
(3) Mass Air Flow (MAF) Sensor
(4) Throttle Position (TP) Sensor
(5) Bypass Valve Actuator
(6) Boost Control Solenoid
(7) Ignition Control Module
(8) Crankshaft Position (CKP) Sensor
(9) Camshaft Position (CMP) Sensor
(10) EVAP Canister Purge Valve
(11) Heated Oxygen Sensor 1 (HO2S 1)
(12) Manifold Absolute Pressure (MAP) Sensor
(13) PCV Valve

8963 4G84

Fig. 113 Component locations—1996–99 3.8L (VIN 1) engine

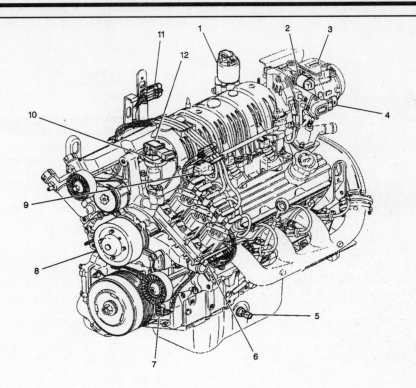

(1) Exhaust Gas Recirculation (EGR) Valve
(2) Idle Air Control (IAC) Valve
(3) Mass Air Flow (MAF) Sensor
(4) Throttle Position (TP) Sensor
(5) Engine Oil Level Switch
(6) Ignition Control Module

(7) Crankshaft Position (CKP) Sensor
(8) Camshaft Position (CMP) Sensor
(9) EVAP Canister Purge Valve
(10) PCV Valve
(11) Heated Oxygen Sensor 1 (HO2S 1)
(12) Manifold Absolute Pressure (MAP) Sensor

89634G85

Fig. 114 Component locations—1996–99 3.8L (VIN K) engine

TROUBLE CODES

General Information

Since the computer control module is programmed to recognize the presence and value of electrical inputs, it will also note the lack of a signal or a radical change in values. It will, for example, react to the loss of signal from the vehicle speed sensor or note that engine coolant temperature has risen beyond acceptable (programmed) limits. Once a fault is recognized, a numeric code is assigned and held in memory. The dashboard warning lamp: CHECK ENGINE or SERVICE ENGINE SOON (SES), will illuminate to advise the operator that the system has detected a fault. This lamp is also known as the Malfunction Indicator Lamp (MIL).

More than one code may be stored. Keep in mind not every engine uses every code. Additionally, the same code may carry different meanings relative to each engine or engine family.

In the event of an computer control module failure, the system will default to a pre-programmed set of values. These are compromise values which allow the engine to operate, although possibly at reduced efficiency. This is variously known as the default, limp-in or back-up mode. Driveability is almost always affected when the ECM enters this mode.

SCAN TOOLS

◆ **See Figures 115 and 116**

On most early models, the stored codes may be read with only the use of a small jumper wire, however the use of a hand-held scan tool such as GM's

TECH-1® or equivalent is recommended. On some 1994 vehicles (equipped with a 16-pin Data Link Connector), and all 1995–99 models, an OBD-II compliant scan tool must be used. There are many manufacturers of these tools; a purchaser must be certain that the tool is proper for the intended use. If you own a scan type tool, it probably came with comprehensive instructions on proper use. Be sure to follow the instructions that came with your unit if they differ from what is given here; this is a general guide with useful information included.

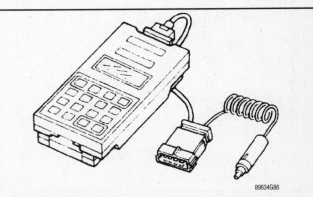

89634G86

Fig. 115 A TECH 1®, or equivalent scan tool is recommended for reading trouble codes

Fig. 116 Inexpensive scan tools, such as this Auto Xray®, are available to interface with your General Motors vehicle

The scan tool allows any stored codes to be read from the ECM or PCM memory. The tool also allows the operator to view the data being sent to the computer control module while the engine is running. This ability has obvious diagnostic advantages; the use of the scan tool is frequently required for component testing. The scan tool makes collecting information easier; the data must be correctly interpreted by an operator familiar with the system.

An example of the usefulness of the scan tool may be seen in the case of a temperature sensor which has changed its electrical characteristics. The ECM is reacting to an apparently warmer engine (causing a driveability problem), but the sensor's voltage has not changed enough to set a fault code. Connecting the scan tool, the voltage signal being sent to the ECM may be viewed; comparison to normal values or a known good vehicle reveals the problem quickly.

ELECTRICAL TOOLS

▶ **See Figure 117**

The most commonly required electrical diagnostic tool is the digital multimeter, allowing voltage, ohmage (resistance) and amperage to be read by one instrument. The multimeter must be a high-impedance unit, with 10 megohms of impedance in the voltmeter. This type of meter will not place an additional load on the circuit it is testing; this is extremely important in low voltage circuits. The multimeter must be of high quality in all respects. It should be han-

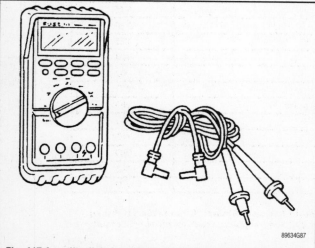

Fig. 117 A quality digital multimeter is an extremely useful piece of diagnostic equipment to have in your tool box

dled carefully and protected from impact or damage. Replace batteries frequently in the unit.

Other necessary tools include an unpowered test light, a quality tachometer with an inductive (clip-on) pick up, and the proper tools for releasing GM's Metri-Pack, Weather Pack and Micro-Pack terminals as necessary. The Micro-Pack connectors are used at the ECM electrical connector. A vacuum pump/gauge may also be required for checking sensors, solenoids and valves.

Diagnosis and Testing

Diagnosis of a driveability and/or emissions problems requires attention to detail and following the diagnostic procedures in the correct order. Resist the temptation to perform any repairs before performing the preliminary diagnostic steps. In many cases this will shorten diagnostic time and often cure the problem without electronic testing.

The proper troubleshooting procedure for these vehicles is as follows:

VISUAL/PHYSICAL INSPECTION

This is possibly the most critical step of diagnosis and should be performed immediately after retrieving any codes. A detailed examination of connectors, wiring and vacuum hoses can often lead to a repair without further diagnosis. Performance of this step relies on the skill of the technician performing it; a careful inspector will check the undersides of hoses as well as the integrity of hard-to-reach hoses blocked by the air cleaner or other component. Wiring should be checked carefully for any sign of strain, burning, crimping, or terminal pull-out from a connector. Checking connectors at components or in harnesses is required; usually, pushing them together will reveal a loose fit.

INTERMITTENTS

If a fault occurs intermittently, such as a loose connector pin breaking contact as the vehicle hits a bump, the ECM will note the fault as it occurs and energize the dash warning lamp. If the problem self-corrects, as with the terminal pin again making contact, the dash lamp will extinguish after 10 seconds but a code will remain stored in the computer control module's memory.

When an unexpected code appears during diagnostics, it may have been set during an intermittent failure that self-corrected; the codes are still useful in diagnosis and should not be discounted.

CIRCUIT/COMPONENT REPAIR

The fault codes and the scan tool data will lead to diagnosis and checking of a particular circuit. It is important to note that the fault code indicates a fault or loss of signal in an ECM-controlled system, not necessarily in the specific component.

Refer to the appropriate Diagnostic Code chart to determine the codes meaning. The component may then be tested following the appropriate component test procedures found in this section. If the component is OK, check the wiring for shorts or opens. Further diagnoses should be left to an experienced driveability technician.

If a code indicates the ECM to be faulty and the ECM is replaced, but does not correct the problem, one of the following may be the reason:

• There is a problem with the ECM terminal connections: The terminals may have to be removed from the connector in order to check them properly.

• The ECM or PROM is not correct for the application: The incorrect ECM or PROM may cause a malfunction and may or may not set a code.

• The problem is intermittent: This means that the problem is not present at the time the system is being checked. In this case, make a careful physical inspection of all portions of the system involved.

• Shorted solenoid, relay coil or harness: Solenoids and relays are turned on and off by the ECM using internal electronic switches called drivers. Each driver is part of a group of four called Quad-Drivers. A shorted solenoid, relay coil or harness may cause an ECM to fail, and a replacement ECM to fail when it is installed. Use a short tester, J34696, BT 8405, or equivalent, as a fast, accurate means of checking for a short circuit.

• The Programmable Read Only Memory (PROM) or MEM-CAL may be faulty: Although the PROM rarely fails, it operates as part of the ECM. Therefore, it could be the cause of the problem. Substitute a known good PROM/MEM-CAL.

- The replacement ECM may be faulty: After the ECM is replaced, the system should be rechecked for proper operation. If the diagnostic code again indicates the ECM is the problem, substitute a known good ECM. Although this is a very rare condition, it could happen.

Reading Codes

1986–94 VEHICLES EXCEPT 1994 MODELS WITH 16-PIN DLC

▶ See Figures 118 and 119

Listings of the trouble for the various engine control system covered in this manual are located in this section. Remember that a code only points to the faulty circuit, NOT necessarily to a faulty component. Loose, damaged or corroded connections may contribute to a fault code on a circuit when the sensor

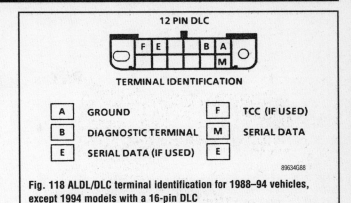

Fig. 118 ALDL/DLC terminal identification for 1988–94 vehicles, except 1994 models with a 16-pin DLC

DTC	DESCRIPTION	ILLUMINATE MIL
13	Oxygen Sensor (O2S) - open circuit	YES
14	Engine Coolant Temperature (ECT) Sensor - high temp. indicated	YES
15	Engine Coolant Temperature (ECT) Sensor - low temp. indicated	YES
16	System Voltage high or low	YES
17	Spark Reference Circuit	NO
18	Cam/Crank Error	YES
21	Throttle Position (TP) Sensor voltage high	YES
22	Throttle Position (TP) Sensor voltage low	YES
23	Intake Air Temperature (IAT) Sensor - low temp. indicated	NO
24	Vehicle Speed Sensor Circuit	YES
25	Intake Air Temperature (IAT) Sensor - high temp. indicated	NO
26	QDM "A" Circuit	YES
31	PRNDL Input Circuit	NO
34	Mass Air Flow (MAF) Sensor - low gm/sec indicated	YES
36	Transaxle Shift Problem	NO
38	Brake Input Circuit	NO
39	Torque Convertor Clutch (TCC) Problem	NO
41	Cam Sensor Circuit	YES
42	Ignition Control (IC) Circuit	YES
43	Knock Sensor (KS)	YES
44	Oxygen Sensor (O2S) - lean exhaust indicated	YES
45	Oxygen Sensor (O2S) - rich exhaust indicated	YES
51	PROM Error	YES
53, 54, 55	EGR Problem	YES
56	QDM "B" Circuit	YES
61	Cruise Vent Solenoid Circuit	NO
62	Cruise Vacuum Solenoid Circuit	NO
63	Cruise System Problem (SPS Indicated Low)	NO
65	Cruise Servo Position Sensor (SPS) Circuit (open/grounded)	NO
66	Excessive A/C Cycling (low refrigerant charge)	NO
67	Cruise Switches Circuit	NO
68	Cruise System Problem (SPS Indicated High)	NO
69	A/C Head Pressure Switch Circuit	NO
99	Power Management	NO

If a DTC not listed above appears on Tech 1, ground DLC Diagnostic Request Terminal "B" and observe flashed codes. If DTC does not reappear, Tech 1 data may be faulty. If DTC does reappear, check for incorrect or faulty PROM.

89634G90

Fig. 119 Engine diagnostic trouble codes—1986–93 vehicles, and 1994 vehicles with a 12-pin DLC connector

or component is operating properly. Be sure that the components are faulty before replacing them, especially the expensive ones.

The Assembly Line Diagnostic Link (ALDL) or Data Link Connector (DLC) may be located under the dashboard, and is sometimes covered with a plastic cover labeled DIAGNOSTIC CONNECTOR.

1. The diagnostic trouble codes can be read by grounding test terminal **B**. The terminal is most easily grounded by connecting it to terminal **A** (internal ECM ground). This is the terminal to the right of terminal **B** on the top row of the ALDL connector.

2. Once the terminals have been connected, the ignition switch must be moved to the **ON** position with the engine not running.

3. The Service Engine Soon or Check Engine light should be flashing. If it isn't, turn the ignition switch **OFF** and remove the jumper wire. Turn the ignition **ON** and confirm that the light is now on. If it is not, replace the bulb and try again. If the bulb still will not light, or if it does not flash with the test terminal grounded, the system should be diagnosed by an experienced driveability technician. If the light is OK, proceed as follows.

4. The code(s) stored in memory may be read through counting the flashes of the dashboard warning lamp. The dash warning lamp should begin to flash Code 12. The code will display as one flash, a pause and two flashes. Code 12 is not a fault code. It is used as a system acknowledgment or handshake code; its presence indicates that the ECM can communicate as requested. Code 12 is used to begin every diagnostic sequence. Some vehicles also use Code 12 after all diagnostic codes have been sent.

5. After Code 12 has been transmitted 3 times, the fault codes, if any, will each be transmitted 3 times. The codes are stored and transmitted in numeric order from lowest to highest.

➡**The order of codes in the memory does not indicate the order of occurrence.**

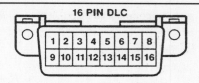

TERMINAL IDENTIFICATION

5   GROUND

9   SERIAL DATA (UART)

16   B +

89634G89

Fig. 120 DLC terminal identification for 1994 vehicles with a 16-pin DLC, as well as all 1995–99 models

DTC	Description	Illuminate MIL
P0101	Mass Air Flow System Performance	Yes
P0102	MAF Sensor Circuit Low Frequency	Yes
P0103	MAF Sensor Circuit High Frequency	Yes
P0107	MAP Sensor Circuit Low Voltage	Yes
P0108	MAP Sensor Circuit High Voltage	Yes
P0112	IAT Sensor Circuit Low Voltage	Yes
P0113	IAT Sensor Circuit High Voltage	Yes
P0117	ECT Sensor Circuit Low Voltage	Yes
P0118	ECT Sensor Circuit High Voltage	Yes
P0121	TP Sensor Performance	Yes
P0122	TP Sensor Circuit Low Voltage	Yes
P0123	TP Sensor Circuit High Voltage	Yes
P0125	ECT Excessive Time to Closed Loop	Yes
P0131	HO2S Circuit Low Voltage Bank 1 Sensor 1	Yes
P0132	HO2S Circuit High Voltage Bank 1 Sensor 1	Yes
P0133	HO2S Circuit Slow Response Bank 1 Sensor 1	Yes
P0134	HO2S CKT Insufficient Activity Bank 1 Sensor 1	Yes
P0135	HO2S Heater Circuit Bank 1 Sensor 1	Yes
P0143	HO2S Circuit Low Voltage Bank 1 Sensor 3 (Post-Converter)	Yes
P0144	HO2S Circuit High Voltage Bank 1 Sensor 3 (Post-Converter)	Yes
P0146	HO2S Circuit Insufficient Activity Bank 1 Sensor 3 (Post-Converter)	Yes
P0147	HO2S Heater Circuit Bank 1 Sensor 3 (Post-Converter)	Yes
P0151	HO2S Circuit Low Voltage Bank 2 Sensor 1	Yes
P0152	HO2S Circuit High Voltage Bank 2 Sensor 1	Yes
P0153	HO2S Circuit Slow Response Bank 2 Sensor 1	Yes
P0154	HO2S Circuit Insufficient Activity Bank 2 Sensor 1	Yes
P0155	HO2S Heater Circuit Bank 2 Sensor 1	Yes
P0171	Fuel Trim System Lean Bank 1	Yes

89634G91

Fig. 121 Engine diagnostic trouble codes (1 of 4)—1994 vehicles with a 16-pin DLC and all 1995–99 vehicles

6. If there are no codes stored, but a driveability or emissions problem is evident, the system should be diagnosed by an experienced driveability technician.

7. If one or more codes are stored, record them. Refer to the applicable Diagnostic Code chart in this section.

8. Switch the ignition **OFF** when finished with code retrieval or scan tool readings.

➡**After making repairs, clear the trouble codes and operate the vehicle to see if it will reset, indicating further problems.**

1994 VEHICLES WITH 16-PIN DLC AND ALL 1995–99 MODELS

▶ **See Figures 120 thru 124**

On 1994–95 3.4L and 3.8L engines, and all 1996 models, an OBD-II compliant scan tool must be used to retrieve the trouble codes. Follow the scan tool manufacturer's instructions on how to connect the scan tool to the vehicle and how to retrieve the codes.

Clearing Codes

Stored fault codes may be erased from memory at any time by using a suitable scan tool, or removing power from the ECM for at least 30 seconds. It may be necessary to clear stored codes during diagnosis to check for any recurrence during a test drive, but the stored codes must be written down when retrieved. The codes may still be required for subsequent troubleshooting. Whenever a repair is complete, the stored codes must be erased and the vehicle test driven to confirm correct operation and repair.

✳✳ WARNING

The ignition switch must be OFF any time power is disconnected or restored to the ECM. Severe damage may result if this precaution is not observed.

When using a scan tool to clear the codes, make sure to follow all of the instructions provided by the manufacturer.

DTC	Description	Illuminate MIL
P0172	Fuel Trim System Rich Bank 1	Yes
P0174	Fuel Trim System Lean Bank 2	Yes
P0175	Fuel Trim System Rich Bank 2	Yes
P0201	Injector 1 Control Circuit	Yes
P0202	Injector 2 Control Circuit	Yes
P0203	Injector 3 Control Circuit	Yes
P0204	Injector 4 Control Circuit	Yes
P0205	Injector 5 Control Circuit	Yes
P0206	Injector 6 Control Circuit	Yes
P0300	Engine Misfire Detected	Yes
P0325	Knock Sensor System	Yes
P0327	Knock Sensor Circuit Bank 1	No
P0332	Knock Sensor Circuit Bank 2	No
P0336	18X Reference Signal Circuit	Yes
P0341	CMP Sensor Circuit Performance	Yes
P0401	EGR System Flow Insufficient	Yes
P0403	EGR Solenoid Control Circuit	Yes
P0404	EGR System Performance	Yes
P0405	EGR Pintle Position Circuit Low Voltage	Yes
P0420	TWC System Low Efficiency	Yes
P0440	EVAP System	Yes
P0442	EVAP Control System Small Leak Detected	Yes
P0446	EVAP Canister Vent Blocked	Yes
P0452	Fuel Tank Pressure Sensor Circuit Low Voltage	Yes
P0453	Fuel Tank Pressure Sensor Circuit High Voltage	Yes
P0500	Vehicle Speed Sensor Circuit	Yes
P0506	Idle Control System Low RPM	Yes
P0507	Idle Control System High RPM	Yes
P0530	A/C Refrigerant Pressure Sensor Circuit	No
P0560	System Voltage	No
P0601	PCM Memory	Yes
P0602	PCM Not Programmed	Yes
P0704	Clutch Anticipate Switch Circuit	No
P0705	Trans Range Switch Circuit	No
P0706	Trans Range Switch Performance	No
P0711	Transaxle Fluid Temperature (TFT) Sensor Circuit	No
P0712	Transaxle Fluid Temperature (TFT) Sensor Circuit - Low Signal.	No
P0713	Transaxle Fluid Temperature (TFT) Sensor Circuit - High Signal Voltage.	No
P0716	Automatic Transmission Input (Shaft) Speed Sensor Circuit Performance.	Yes
P0717	Automatic Transmission Input (Shaft) Speed Sensor No Input. Refer	Yes

89634G92

Fig. 122 Engine diagnostic trouble codes (2 of 4)—1994 vehicles with a 16-pin DLC and all 1995–99 vehicles

DTC	Description	Illuminate MIL
P0719	Brake Switch Circuit Low.	No
P0724	Brake Switch Circuit High.	No
P0730	Incorrect Gear Ratio.	No
P0741	Torque Converter Clutch System Stuck Off.	Yes
P0742	Torque Converter Clutch System Stuck On.	Yes
P0748	Pressure Control Solenoid Valve Circuit Malfunction.	Yes
P0751	Shift Solenoid 1 - Performance/Stuck Off.	Yes
P0753	Shift Solenoid 1 - Electrical.	Yes
P0756	Shift Solenoid 2 - Performance/Stuck Off.	Yes
P0758	Shift Solenoid 2 - Electrical.	Yes
P1106	MAP Sensor CKT Intermittent High Voltage	No
P1107	MAP Sensor CKT Intermittent Low Voltage	No
P1111	IAT Sensor CKT Intermittent High Voltage	No
P1112	IAT Sensor CKT Intermittent Low Voltage	No
P1114	ECT Sensor CKT Intermittent Low Voltage	No
P1115	ECT Sensor CKT Intermittent High Voltage	No
P1121	TP Sensor CKT Intermittent High Voltage	No
P1122	TP Sensor CKT Intermittent Low Voltage	No
P1133	HO2S Insufficient Switching Bank 1 Sensor 1	Yes
P1134	HO2S Transition Time Ratio Bank 1 Sensor 1	Yes
P1153	HO2S Insufficient Switching Bank 2 Sensor 1	Yes
P1154	HO2S Transition Time Ratio Bank 2 Sensor 1	Yes
P1336	CKP System Variation Not Learned	Yes
P1351	IC Circuit Open	Yes
P1352	Bypass Circuit Open	Yes
P1361	IC Circuit Not Toggling	Yes
P1362	Bypass Circuit Shorted	Yes
P1374	3X Reference Circuit	Yes
P1380	EBCM DTC Rough Data Unstable	No
P1381	Misfire Detected No EBCM/PCM Serial Data	No
P1404	EGR Valve Closed Pintle Position	Yes
P1441	EVAP System Flow During Non-Purge	Yes
P1554	Cruise Control Status Circuit	No
P1626	Theft Deterrent System Fuel Enable CKT	No
P1629	Theft Deterrent Crank Signal Malfunction	No
P1635	5 Volt Reference (A) Circuit	Yes
P1639	5 Volt Reference (B) Circuit	Yes

89634G93

Fig. 123 Engine diagnostic trouble codes (3 of 4)—1994 vehicles with a 16-pin DLC and all 1995–99 vehicles

Depending on the electrical distribution of the particular vehicle, power to the ECM may be disconnected by removing the ECM fuse in the fuse box, disconnecting the in-line fuse holder near the positive battery terminal or disconnecting the ECM power lead at the battery terminal. Disconnecting the negative battery cable to clear codes is not recommended as this will also clear other memory data in the vehicle such as radio presets.

DTC	Description	Illuminate MIL
P1641	A/C Relay Control Circuit	No
P1651	Fan 1 Relay Control Circuit	Yes
P1652	Fan 2 Relay Control Circuit	Yes
P1653	Fuel Level Output Control Circuit	No
P1662	Cruise Control Inhibit Control Circuit	No
P1663	Generator Lamp Control Circuit	No
P1665	EVAP Vent Solenoid Control Circuit	Yes
P1671	MIL Control Circuit	No
P1672	Low Engine Oil Level Lamp Control Circuit	No
P1676	EVAP Canister Purge Solenoid Control CKT	Yes
P1810	Automatic Transmission Fluid Pressure Manual Valve Position Switch Malfunction.	Yes
P1811	Maximum Adapt and Long Shift.	No
P1860	Torque Converter Clutch PWM Solenoid Circuit.	Yes
P1887	TCC Release Switch Malfunction.	Yes

89634G94

Fig. 124 Engine diagnostic trouble codes (4 of 4)—1994 vehicles with a 16-pin DLC and all 1995–99 vehicles

VACUUM DIAGRAMS

♦ **See Figures 125 thru 148**

Following are vacuum diagrams for most of the engine and emissions package combinations covered by this manual. Because vacuum circuits will vary based on various engine and vehicle options, always refer first to the vehicle emission control information label, if present. Should the label be missing, or should the vehicle be equipped with a different engine from the vehicle's original equipment, refer to the following diagrams for the same or similar configuration.

If you wish to obtain a replacement emissions label, most manufacturers make the labels available for purchase. The labels can usually be ordered from a local dealer.

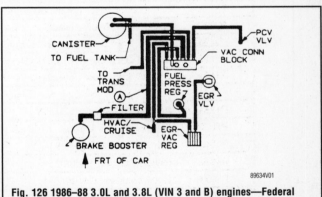

Fig. 126 1986–88 3.0L and 3.8L (VIN 3 and B) engines—Federal and California

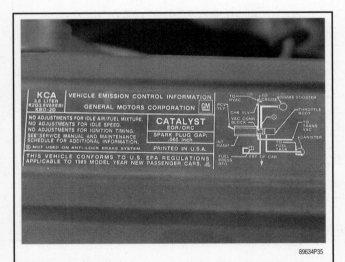

Fig. 125 The VECI sticker, affixed to the radiator panel, includes important emission information regarding your vehicle

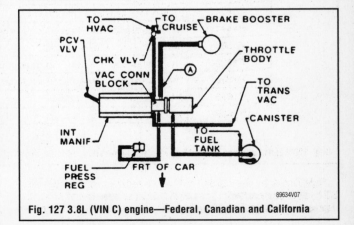

Fig. 127 3.8L (VIN C) engine—Federal, Canadian and California

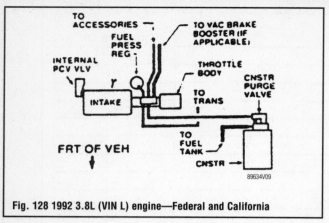

Fig. 128 1992 3.8L (VIN L) engine—Federal and California

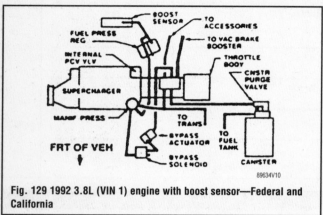

Fig. 129 1992 3.8L (VIN 1) engine with boost sensor—Federal and California

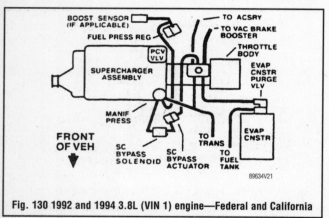

Fig. 130 1992 and 1994 3.8L (VIN 1) engine—Federal and California

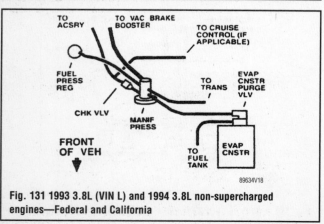

Fig. 131 1993 3.8L (VIN L) and 1994 3.8L non-supercharged engines—Federal and California

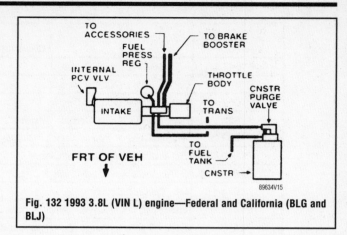

Fig. 132 1993 3.8L (VIN L) engine—Federal and California (BLG and BLJ)

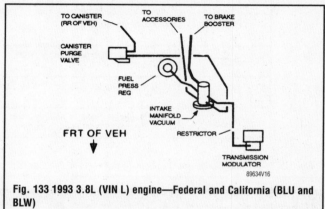

Fig. 133 1993 3.8L (VIN L) engine—Federal and California (BLU and BLW)

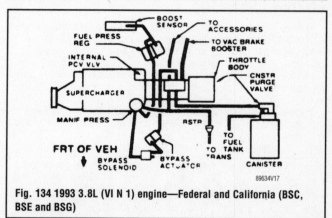

Fig. 134 1993 3.8L (VI N 1) engine—Federal and California (BSC, BSE and BSG)

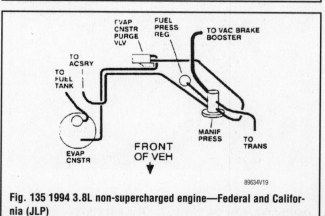

Fig. 135 1994 3.8L non-supercharged engine—Federal and California (JLP)

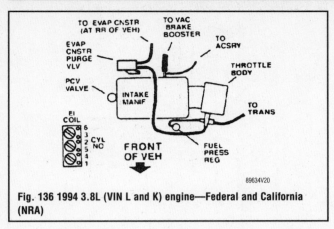

Fig. 136 1994 3.8L (VIN L and K) engine—Federal and California (NRA)

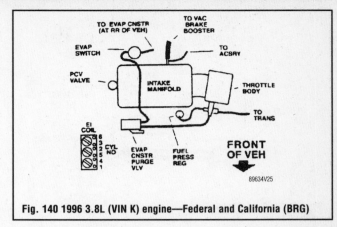

Fig. 140 1996 3.8L (VIN K) engine—Federal and California (BRG)

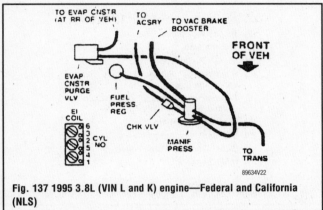

Fig. 137 1995 3.8L (VIN L and K) engine—Federal and California (NLS)

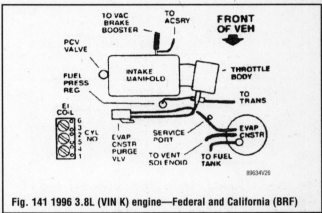

Fig. 141 1996 3.8L (VIN K) engine—Federal and California (BRF)

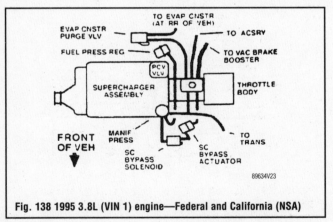

Fig. 138 1995 3.8L (VIN 1) engine—Federal and California (NSA)

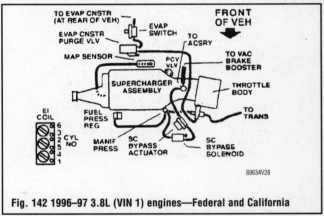

Fig. 142 1996–97 3.8L (VIN 1) engines—Federal and California

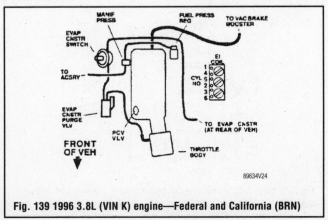

Fig. 139 1996 3.8L (VIN K) engine—Federal and California (BRN)

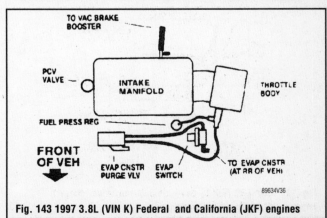

Fig. 143 1997 3.8L (VIN K) Federal and California (JKF) engines

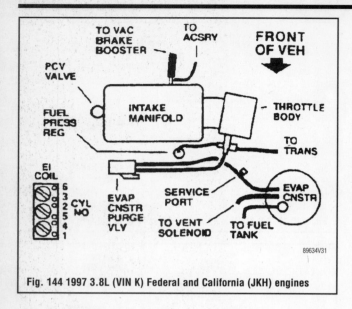

Fig. 144 1997 3.8L (VIN K) Federal and California (JKH) engines

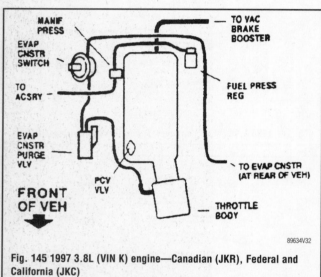

Fig. 145 1997 3.8L (VIN K) engine—Canadian (JKR), Federal and California (JKC)

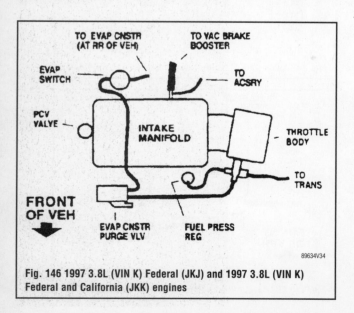

Fig. 146 1997 3.8L (VIN K) Federal (JKJ) and 1997 3.8L (VIN K) Federal and California (JKK) engines

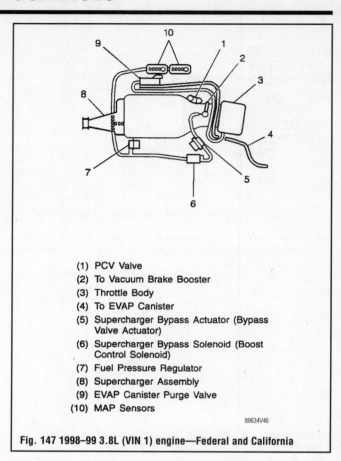

(1) PCV Valve
(2) To Vacuum Brake Booster
(3) Throttle Body
(4) To EVAP Canister
(5) Supercharger Bypass Actuator (Bypass Valve Actuator)
(6) Supercharger Bypass Solenoid (Boost Control Solenoid)
(7) Fuel Pressure Regulator
(8) Supercharger Assembly
(9) EVAP Canister Purge Valve
(10) MAP Sensors

Fig. 147 1998–99 3.8L (VIN 1) engine—Federal and California

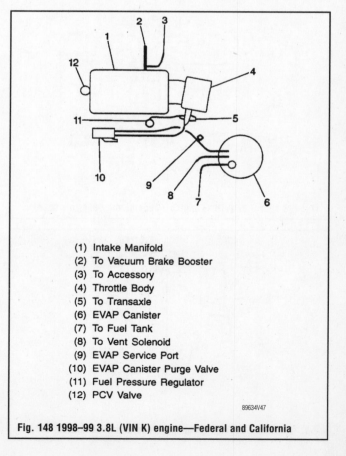

(1) Intake Manifold
(2) To Vacuum Brake Booster
(3) To Accessory
(4) Throttle Body
(5) To Transaxle
(6) EVAP Canister
(7) To Fuel Tank
(8) To Vent Solenoid
(9) EVAP Service Port
(10) EVAP Canister Purge Valve
(11) Fuel Pressure Regulator
(12) PCV Valve

Fig. 148 1998–99 3.8L (VIN K) engine—Federal and California

**BASIC FUEL SYSTEM
  DIAGNOSIS 5-2**
FUEL LINES AND FITTINGS 5-2
QUICK-CONNECT FITTINGS 5-2
  REMOVAL & INSTALLATION 5-2
**GASOLINE FUEL INJECTION
  SYSTEM 5-3**
SYSTEM DESCRIPTION 5-3
SERVICE PRECAUTIONS 5-3
RELIEVING FUEL SYSTEM
  PRESSURE 5-4
    PROCEDURE 5-4
ELECTRIC FUEL PUMP 5-4
  TESTING 5-4
  REMOVAL & INSTALLATION 5-4
THROTTLE BODY 5-5
  REMOVAL & INSTALLATION 5-5
FUEL INJECTOR 5-7
  TESTING 5-7
  REMOVAL & INSTALLATION 5-7
FUEL RAIL ASSEMBLY 5-8
  REMOVAL & INSTALLATION 5-8
FUEL PRESSURE REGULATOR 5-11
  REMOVAL & INSTALLATION 5-11
FUEL TANK 5-13
TANK ASSEMBLY 5-13
  DRAINING 5-13
  REMOVAL & INSTALLATION 5-13
  SENDING UNIT REPLACEMENT 5-14

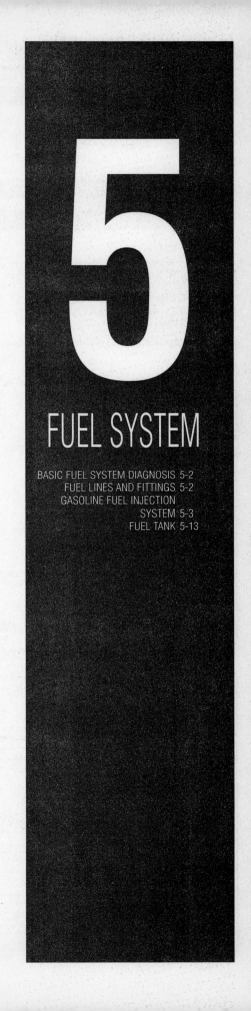

5

FUEL SYSTEM

BASIC FUEL SYSTEM DIAGNOSIS 5-2
FUEL LINES AND FITTINGS 5-2
GASOLINE FUEL INJECTION
SYSTEM 5-3
FUEL TANK 5-13

BASIC FUEL SYSTEM DIAGNOSIS

When there is a problem starting or driving a vehicle, two of the most important checks involve the ignition and the fuel systems. The questions most mechanics attempt to answer first, "is there spark?" and "is there fuel?" will often lead to solving most basic problems. For ignition system diagnosis and testing, please refer to the information on engine electrical components and ignition systems found earlier in this manual. If the ignition system checks out (there is spark), then you must determine if the fuel system is operating properly (is there fuel?).

FUEL LINES AND FITTINGS

Quick-Connect Fittings

REMOVAL & INSTALLATION

▶ **See Figure 1**

Some early model vehicles do not have quick-connect fuel line fittings. On these vehicles, just make sure to use a back-up wrench on the fuel lines when disconnecting them.

➡**This procedure requires Tool Set J37088-A fuel line quick-connect separator, if your vehicle is equipped with metal quick-connect fittings.**

1. Properly relieve the fuel system pressure, as outlined later in this section.
2. If equipped, slide the dust cover back to access the fuel line fitting.
3. Grasp both sides of the fitting. Twist the female connector ¼ turn in each direction to loosen any dirt within the fittings. Using compressed air, blow out the dirt from the quick-connect fittings at the end of the fittings.

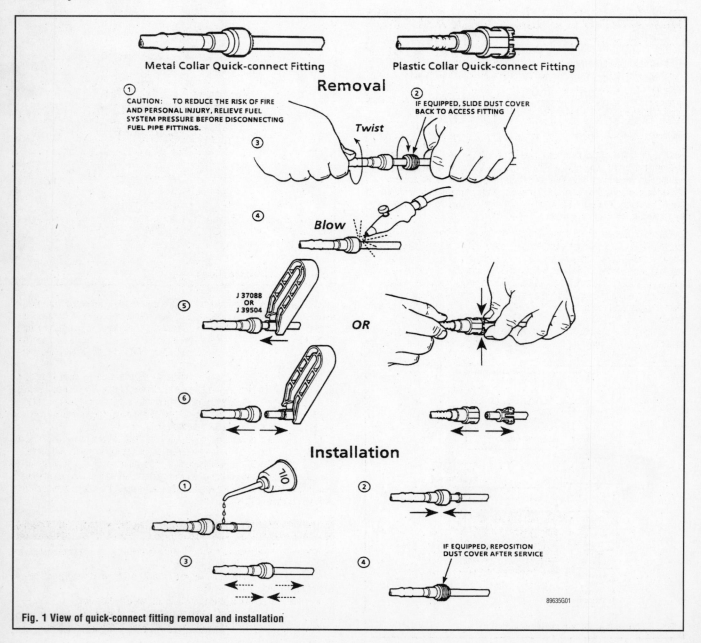

Fig. 1 View of quick-connect fitting removal and installation

✳✳ CAUTION

You MUST wear safety glasses when using compressed air to avoid eye injury due to flying dirt particles!

4. For plastic (hand releasable) fittings, squeeze the plastic retainer release tabs, then pull the connection apart.

5. For metal fittings, choose the correct tool from kit J37088-A for the size of the fitting to be disconnected. Insert the proper tool into the female connector, then push inward to release the locking tabs. Pull the connection apart.

6. If it is necessary to remove rust or burrs from the male tube end of a quick-connect fitting, use emery cloth in a radial motion with the tube end to prevent damage to the O-ring sealing surfaces. Using a clean shop towel, wipe off the male tube ends. Inspect all connectors for dirt and burrs. Clean and/or replace if required.

To install:

✳✳ CAUTION

To reduce the risk of fire or other injury, apply a few drops of clean engine oil to the male fuel pipe end of the fuel fitting. This will ensure proper connection and prevent leakage. If the fitting is not lubricated, the O-rings in the female connector will swell, preventing proper reconnection.

7. Apply a few drops of clean engine oil to the male tube end of the fitting.
8. Push the connectors together to cause the retaining tabs/fingers to snap into place.
9. Once installed, pull on both ends of each connection to make sure they are secure.
10. If equipped, slide the fuel fitting dust cover back into place.

GASOLINE FUEL INJECTION SYSTEM

System Description

▸ **See Figures 2 and 3**

The Sequential Fuel Injection (SFI) system is controlled by an Electronic Control Module (ECM) which monitors engine operations and generates output signals to provide the correct air/fuel mixture, ignition timing and engine idle speed control. Input to the control unit is provided by an oxygen sensor, coolant temperature sensor, detonation sensor, hot film air mass sensor and throttle position sensor. The ECM also receives information concerning engine rpm, road speed, transaxle gear position, power steering and air conditioning.

➡**Although most of the engines covered by this manual have the SFI system, there are two engines, the 3.8L (VIN C and K), which are equipped with a Multi-port Fuel Injection (MFI) system. This system operates basically the same and consists of the same components as the SFI system. The only difference between the systems is the timing by which the injectors are fired.**

With MFI, metered fuel is timed and injected sequentially through the injectors into individual cylinder ports. Each cylinder receives one injection per working cycle (every 2 revolutions), just prior to the opening of the intake valve. In addition, the SFI system incorporates a Computer Controlled Coil Ignition (C$SS3I) system (also called Electronic Ignition), which uses an electronic coil module that replaces the conventional distributor and coil used on most engines. An Electronic Spark Control (ESC) is used to adjust the spark timing.

The injection system uses solenoid-type fuel injectors, 1 at each intake port, rather than the single injector found on the earlier throttle body system. The

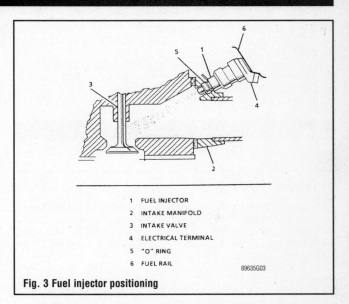

1	FUEL INJECTOR
2	INTAKE MANIFOLD
3	INTAKE VALVE
4	ELECTRICAL TERMINAL
5	"O" RING
6	FUEL RAIL

89635G03

Fig. 3 Fuel injector positioning

injectors are mounted on a fuel rail and are activated by a signal from the electronic control module. The injector is a solenoid-operated valve which remains open depending on the width of the electronic pulses (length of the signal) from the ECM; the longer the open time, the more fuel is injected. In this manner, the air/fuel mixture can be precisely controlled for maximum performance with minimum emissions.

Fuel is pumped from the tank by a high pressure fuel pump, located inside the fuel tank. It is a positive displacement roller vane pump. The impeller serves as a vapor separator and pre-charges the high pressure assembly. A pressure regulator maintains 34–47 psi (240–315 kPa) in the fuel line to the injectors and the excess fuel is fed back to the tank.

Engine idle is controlled by an Idle Air Control (IAC) valve, which provides a bypass channel through which air can flow. It consists of an orifice and pintle, which is controlled by the ECM through a stepper motor. The IAC provides air flow for idle and allows additional air during cold start until the engine reaches operating temperature. As the engine temperature rises, the opening through which air passes is slowly closed.

Service Precautions

When working around any part of the fuel system, take precautionary steps to prevent fire and/or explosion:
• Disconnect negative terminal from battery (except when testing with battery voltage is required).
• When ever possible, use a flashlight instead of a drop light.
• Keep all open flame and smoking material out of the area.
• Use a shop cloth or similar to catch fuel when opening a fuel system.

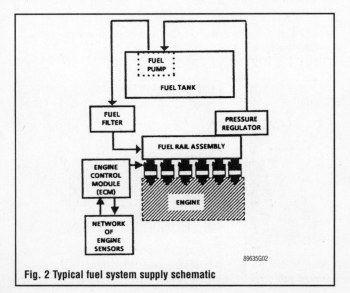

89635G02

Fig. 2 Typical fuel system supply schematic

- Relieve fuel system pressure before servicing.
- Use eye protection.
- Always keep a dry chemical (class B) fire extinguisher near the area.

Relieving Fuel System Pressure

PROCEDURE

♦ **See Figure 4**

➡**To prevent damaging the electrical systems, make sure the ignition key is in the OFF position when disconnecting or reconnecting the negative battery cable.**

1. Disconnect the negative battery cable to avoid possible fuel discharge if an accidental attempt is made to start the engine.
2. Loosen the fuel filler cap to relieve fuel tank vapor pressure.
3. If necessary for access, remove the fuel injector sight shield, then remove the fuel pressure connection cap.
4. Wrap a shop towel around the fuel pressure connection fittings while connecting the gauge to prevent fuel spillage.
5. Connect fuel pressure valve J 34730-1A or equivalent to the fuel pressure relief connection at the fuel rail.
6. Install a bleed hose into an approved container and open the valve to bleed the system pressure. The fuel system is now safe for servicing. Drain any fuel left in pressure gauge into the approved container.
7. Install the fuel filler cap.

Electric Fuel Pump

TESTING

♦ **See Figures 5 and 6**

1. Unscrew the cap from the fuel rail pressure valve on the fuel rail. You may have to remove the fuel injector sight shield for access to the valve.
2. Connect pressure gauge J-34730-1 or equivalent to the fuel pressure test point on the fuel rail. Wrap a rag around the pressure tap to absorb any leakage that may occur when installing the gauge.
3. Turn the ignition **ON**; the fuel pump should run for a few seconds. Check the pump pressure for the following specifications:
   a. 1986–95 vehicles, except 1995 VIN K: 41–47 psi (284–325 kPa).
   b. 1995 VIN K and 1996–99 vehicles: 48–55 psi (333–376 kPa).
4. Start the engine and allow it to idle. The fuel pressure should drop about 3–10 psi (21–69 kPa) due to the lower manifold pressure.

➡**The idle pressure will vary somewhat depending on barometric pressure. Check for a drop in pressure indicating regulator control, rather than specific values.**

5. If the fuel pressure drops more than a few pounds when you shut the engine **OFF**, check the operation of the check valve, the pump coupling connection, fuel pressure regulator valve and the injectors.

6. Before attempting to remove or service any fuel system component, it is necessary to relieve the fuel system pressure.

REMOVAL & INSTALLATION

♦ **See Figures 7 and 8**

The fuel pump is located in the fuel tank. The fuel tank must be removed from the vehicle in order to access the pump.

1. Properly relieve fuel system pressure.
2. If not already done, disconnect the negative battery cable.
3. Raise and safely support the vehicle.
4. Safely drain and remove the fuel tank assembly, as outlined later in this section.
5. If necessary, detach the quick-connect fittings from the fuel sender assembly and remove the fuel lines.
6. Remove the fuel gauge sender and pump assembly by turning the cam locking ring counterclockwise. It may be necessary to use a spanner wrench, such as tool J-24187, to perform this.
7. Carefully lift the assembly from the fuel tank, then remove the fuel pump from the fuel gauge sender unit.
8. Remove the sender O-ring from the top of the sender and discard.
9. Disconnect the pump wires, hose clamps and the clamp from around the pump body.
10. Pull the pump assembly out of the rubber connectors.
11. Inspect the fuel pump attaching hose for any signs of deterioration, and replace as necessary.

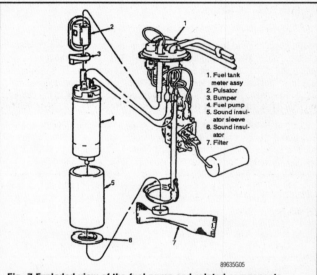

1. Fuel tank meter assy
2. Pulsator
3. Bumper
4. Fuel pump
5. Sound insulator sleeve
6. Sound insulator
7. Filter

89635G05

Fig. 7 Exploded view of the fuel pump and related components—1986–91 vehicles

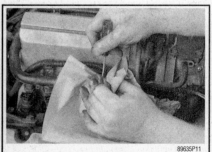

89635P11

Fig. 4 Although a special tool is available, you can use a screwdriver to depress the fuel pressure connection, to relieve fuel pressure

89635P03

Fig. 5 Remove the cap (1) from the fuel rail pressure valve (2) on the fuel rail

89635P04

Fig. 6 Test the fuel system pressure using a suitable gauge attached to the test connection

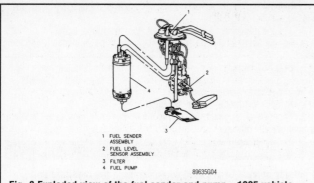

1 FUEL SENDER
  ASSEMBLY
2 FUEL LEVEL
  SENSOR ASSEMBLY
3 FILTER
4 FUEL PUMP

89635G04

Fig. 8 Exploded view of the fuel sender and pump—1995 vehicle shown, later years similar

To install:

12. Push the fuel pump assembly into the attaching hose. Attach the pump electrical wires and fasten the hose clamps to the attaching hose and around the pump body.

13. Place the fuel tank sender and pump assembly into the fuel tank. Use a new O-ring seal during assembly.

14. Place the cam lock over the assembly, then lock by turning clockwise, using a suitable spanner wrench, if necessary.

15. If removed, attach the fuel sender fuel line quick-connect fittings.

➡**When installing the fuel tank, make sure all rubber sound isolators or anti-squeak spacers are replaced in their original locations.**

16. Install the fuel tank, as outlined later in this section.
17. Refill the fuel tank.
18. Connect the negative battery cable.
19. Turn the ignition switch to the **ON** position to pressurize the fuel system and check for leaks.

Throttle Body

The throttle body is located at the front or side of the engine, and is mounted to the intake plenum.

REMOVAL & INSTALLATION

3.0L and 3.8L (VIN 3 and B) Engines

▶ **See Figures 9 and 10**

1. Disconnect the negative battery cable.
2. Drain the coolant into a suitable container, until the level is below the throttle body.
3. Remove the air inlet duct.
4. Tag and disconnect the vacuum hoses and the coolant hoses from the throttle body.

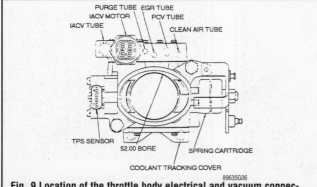

PURGE TUBE   EGR TUBE
IACV MOTOR   PCV TUBE
IACV TUBE   CLEAN AIR TUBE

TPS SENSOR
52.00 BORE   SPRING CARTRIDGE
COOLANT TRACKING COVER

89635G06

Fig. 9 Location of the throttle body electrical and vacuum connections

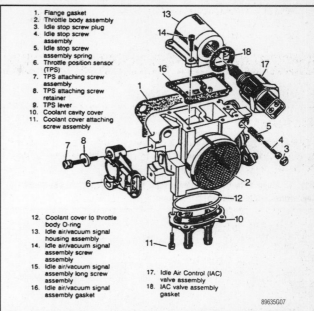

1. Flange gasket
2. Throttle body assembly
3. Idle stop screw plug
4. Idle stop screw assembly
5. Idle stop screw assembly spring
6. Throttle position sensor (TPS)
7. TPS attaching screw assembly
8. TPS attaching screw retainer
9. TPS lever
10. Coolant cavity cover
11. Coolant cover attaching screw assembly
12. Coolant cover to throttle body O-ring
13. Idle air/vacuum signal housing assembly
14. Idle air/vacuum signal assembly screw assembly
15. Idle air/vacuum signal assembly long screw assembly
16. Idle air/vacuum signal assembly gasket
17. Idle Air Control (IAC) valve assembly
18. IAC valve assembly gasket

89635G07

Fig. 10 Exploded view of the throttle body—3.0L and 3.8L (VIN 3 and B) engines shown

5. Detach the Idle Air Control (IAC) valve and the Throttle Position (TP) sensor electrical connectors from the throttle body.
6. Remove the throttle and the cruise control cables.
7. Unfasten the mounting bolts, then remove the throttle body from the vehicle.
8. Remove and discard the throttle body gasket. Thoroughly clean the gasket mating surfaces.

To install:

9. Position a new gasket, then install the throttle body over the gasket. Secure with the mounting bolts.
10. Attach the throttle and cruise control cables to the throttle body.
11. Attach the TP sensor and IAC valve electrical connectors to the throttle body.
12. Connect the coolant hoses, and the vacuum hoses, as tagged during removal.
13. Install the air inlet duct.
14. Fill the cooling system to the proper level.
15. Connect the negative battery cable.

3.8L (VIN C, L, 1 and K) Engines

1988–95 VEHICLES

▶ **See Figures 11 and 12**

1. Disconnect the negative battery cable.
2. Position a suitable drain pan under the radiator, then drain the coolant to a level below the throttle body.

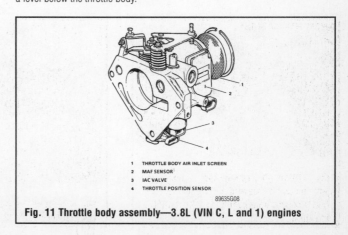

1 THROTTLE BODY AIR INLET SCREEN
2 MAF SENSOR
3 IAC VALVE
4 THROTTLE POSITION SENSOR

89635G08

Fig. 11 Throttle body assembly—3.8L (VIN C, L and 1) engines

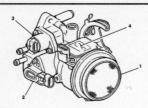

1 THROTTLE BODY AIR INLET SCREEN
2 THROTTLE POSITION SENSOR
3 IAC VALVE
4 MAF SENSOR

89635G09

Fig. 12 Make sure to note the vacuum line and electrical connector locations before disconnecting them

3. Remove the air inlet duct/tube.
4. For 3.8L (VIN 1) engines, remove the accelerator control cable bracket.
5. Disconnect the throttle, throttle valve and cruise control cables.
6. Tag and detach the IAC, TP sensor and MAF sensor electrical connectors from the throttle body.
7. Unfasten the nuts or bolts securing the throttle body to the intake manifold, then remove the throttle body assembly.
8. Remove and discard the throttle body flange gasket. Thoroughly clean the gasket mating surfaces.

To install:

9. Position a new gasket on the intake manifold flange. Position the throttle body over the gasket. Install the retaining bolts and tighten to 11 ft. lbs. (15 Nm).
10. Attach the MAF sensor, TP sensor and IAC valve electrical connectors.

➡Make sure the throttle and cruise control linkage does not hold the throttle open.

11. Connect the throttle, throttle valve and cruise control cables.
12. If removed, install the accelerator control cable bracket.
13. Install the air intake duct/tube.
14. Connect the negative battery cable, then refill the cooling system.

1996–99 VEHICLES

▶ **See Figures 13, 14, 15 and 16**

1. Disconnect the negative battery cable.
2. Position a suitable drain pan under the radiator, then drain the coolant to a level below the throttle body.
3. If necessary, remove the fuel injector sight shield.
4. If equipped, unplug the IAT sensor electrical connector from the IAT sensor. Remove the air inlet duct/tube.
5. Detach the IAC valve, TP sensor and MAF sensor electrical connectors.
6. Remove the accelerator control and cruise control cables from the throttle body lever and bracket.

7. Remove the electrical harness retainer clip from the accelerator control cable bracket.
8. Tag and disconnect the vacuum lines from the throttle body.
9. For the 1996–97 3.8L (VIN K) engine, remove the throttle body support bracket.
10. Unfasten the nuts and bolts holding the throttle body to the intake manifold using a wrench on the manifold side of the inserts to prevent the inserts from rotating in the manifold casting.
11. Remove the throttle body assembly.
12. For 1998–99 engines, if replacing the throttle body, remove the accelerator control cable bracket.

✳ WARNING

Do not use solvent of any kind when cleaning the manifold and throttle body mating surfaces, as this will damage the surfaces. Also, be careful not to gouge the mating surfaces if using a sharp object, such as a gasket scraper to clean the surfaces.

13. Remove and discard the gasket, thoroughly clean the intake manifold and throttle body gasket mating surfaces.

To install:

14. On 1998–99 engines, if installing a new throttle body, install the accelerator control bracket and tighten the retainers to 12 ft. lbs. (16 Nm).
15. Position the new gasket, and new inserts and studs, if necessary.
16. Install the throttle body assembly and secure with the retaining nuts and bolts. Tighten to 7 ft. lbs. (10 Nm).
17. Attach the accelerator control and cruise control cables to the accelerator cable bracket at the throttle body. The throttle should open freely without binding between full closed and wide open throttle.
18. Attach the accelerator control and cruise control cables to the throttle body lever.
19. Check for complete throttle opening and closing positions by operating the accelerator pedal. Also, check for poor carpet fit under the accelerator pedal.

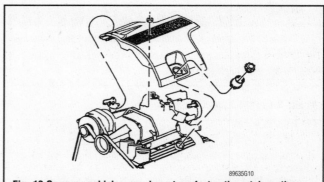

89635G10

Fig. 13 On some vehicles, you have to unfasten the retainer, then remove the fuel injector sight shield

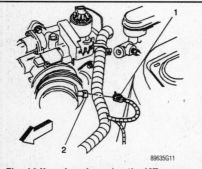

89635G11

Fig. 14 If equipped, unplug the IAT sensor electrical connector (1) from the sensor (2) mounted in the air intake duct

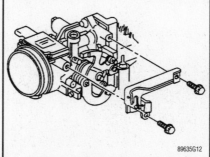

89635G12

Fig. 15 If replacing the throttle body, you must transfer the accelerator control cable bracket to the new throttle body

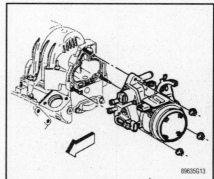

89635G13

Fig. 16 Exploded view of the throttle body mounting

20. Install the electrical harness retainer clip and harness to the accelerator control cable bracket.
21. Connect the vacuum lines to the throttle body, as tagged during removal.
22. Attach the IAC valve, TP sensor and MAF sensor electrical connectors.
23. If removed, install the fuel injector sight shield.
24. Install the air intake tube.
25. Connect the negative battery cable, then refill the cooling system.

Fuel Injector

▶ See Figure 17

Be careful when servicing or removing the fuel injectors to prevent damage to the electrical connector pins on the injector and nozzle. The fuel injector is serviced as a complete assembly only and should never be immersed in any type of cleaner. Support the fuel rail to avoid damaging other components while removing the injector. Be sure to note that different injectors are calibrated for different flow rates. When ordering new fuel injectors, be sure to order the identical part number that is inscribed on the bottom of the old injector.

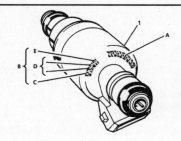

1 INJECTOR ASSEMBLY - FUEL
A PART NUMBER IDENTIFICATION
B BUILD DATE CODE
C MONTH 1-9 (JAN-SEPT) O, N, D (OCT, NOV, DEC)
D DAY
E YEAR
89635G14

Fig. 17 Refer to the part number inscribed on the injector to make sure you get the correct part

TESTING

▶ See Figures 18 and 19

The injectors can be tested by installing a "noid light," (a headlamp bulb may work) into the injector electrical connector, which confirms voltage when the light flashes.

1. Start the engine and listen to each fuel injector individually for a clicking sound.

2. Turn the engine **OFF** and detach the electrical connector from the injector(s) that did not have a clicking sound.
3. Check the injector for continuity across the terminals. Compare the resistance value to a known good injector. The readings should be similar, if so proceed to the next step. If readings differ greatly, replace the injector.
4. Check between each injector terminal and ground. If continuity exists, replace the injector.
5. Detach the fuel injector connector and connect a noid light to the wiring harness connector. Crank the engine, while watching the light. Perform this test on at least two injectors before proceeding. If the light does not flash, check the injector power supply and ground control circuitry. If the light flashes proceed to the next step.
6. If the light flashes, remove the fuel rail from the engine and following the procedure below check the injector operation:
   a. Using mechanic's wire, secure the injector to the fuel rail.
   b. Place a clear plastic container around each injector.

✷✷ CAUTION

Prior to performing this test, all fuel safety precautions must be followed. Make certain the container is approved to handle fuel and is securely positioned around the injector. Do NOT use a glass container. Glass containers can be easily damaged, resulting in a serious fire hazard.

   c. With the help of an assistant or using a remote starter button, crank the engine for 15 seconds while observing the injector operation. The injector should produce a cone shaped spray pattern and all containers should retain equal amounts of fuel.
   d. Once the cranking test is complete, leave the fuel rail pressurized and observe the injectors for leakage.
7. Replace any injector which is leaking or fails to provide a cone shaped spray pattern when energized.

REMOVAL & INSTALLATION

▶ See Figures 20 thru 25

➡The fuel injector is serviced as a complete assembly only. If you find that the fuel injectors are leaking, the engine oil may be contaminated with fuel and require changing.

1. Properly relieve the fuel system pressure.
2. Remove the fuel injector sight shield and/or the air cleaner assembly as necessary.
3. If not already done, disconnect the negative battery cable.
4. Remove the fuel rail from the vehicle, as outlined later in this section.
5. Remove the fuel injector retaining clip(s), then separate the injector from the fuel rail. Discard the injector retaining clips and replace with new ones during installation.
6. Remove and discard the fuel injector upper and lower O-rings, and the lower O-ring back-up.

Fig. 18 Detach the fuel injector electrical connector . . .

Fig. 19 . . . then use an ohmmeter to check injector resistance. Compare with specifications from a known good injector

Fig. 20 After removing the fuel rail, remove the injector retaining clip . . .

Fig. 21 . . . then remove the injector from the fuel rail

Fig. 22 Remove and discard the O-ring from the top of the injector

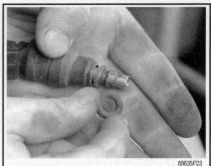

Fig. 23 There is an O-ring and O-ring back-up on the bottom of the injector. Remove and discard the O-ring . . .

Fig. 24 . . . then remove and discard the O-ring back-up. All O-rings should be replaced before installation

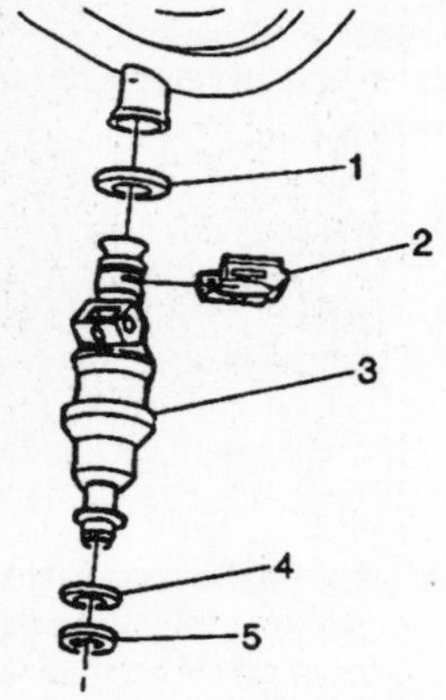

Fig. 25 Fuel injector (3), retaining clip (2), upper O-ring (1), lower O-ring (5) and O-ring back-up (4)

➡Different injectors are calibrated for different flow rates. When ordering new injectors, be sure to order the identical part number that is inscribed on the old injector.

To install:

❊❊ CAUTION

To reduce the risk of fire and personal injury, always install the injector O-rings in the proper position. If the upper and lower O-rings are different colors (black and brown, for example), be sure to install the black O-ring in the upper position and the brown O-ring in the lower position. The O-rings are of the same size, but are made of different materials.

➡The fuel injector lower O-ring uses a nylon collar, called the O-ring back-up, to properly position the O-ring on the injector. Be sure to install the O-ring back-up, or the sealing O-ring may move on the injector when installing the fuel rail. This can result in a vacuum leak and driveability problems will occur.

7. Lubricate the new O-ring seals with clean engine oil and install them on the injector.
8. Assemble a new retainer clip onto the injector.
9. Install the fuel injector into the fuel rail socket with the electrical connections facing outwards.
10. Rotate the injector retaining clip to the locked position.
11. Install the fuel rail assembly.
12. Tighten the fuel filler cap and connect the negative battery cable.
13. With the engine **OFF**, turn the ignition switch to the **ON** position for 2 seconds, then turn it to the **OFF** position for 10 seconds. Again, turn it to the **ON** position and check for fuel leaks.

Fuel Rail Assembly

When servicing the fuel rail assembly, be careful to prevent dirt and other contaminants from entering the fuel passages. Fittings should be capped and holes plugged during servicing. At any time the fuel system is opened for service, the O-ring seals and retainers used with related components should be replaced.

Before removing the fuel rail, the fuel rail assembly may be cleaned with a spray type cleaner, GM-30A or equivalent, following package instructions. Do not immerse fuel rails in liquid cleaning solvent. Be sure to always use new O-rings and seals when reinstalling the fuel rail assemblies.

REMOVAL & INSTALLATION

1986–95 Vehicles

▶ **See Figures 26 thru 41**

1. Disconnect the negative battery cable.
2. Relieve the fuel system pressure, as outlined earlier in this section.
3. Remove the intake manifold plenum, as required.
4. Disconnect the fuel feed and return lines at the fuel rail; be sure to use a back-up wrench on the inlet fitting to prevent turning or refer to the procedure for quick-connect fittings, located earlier in this section.
5. Remove and discard the fuel feed and return line O-rings.
6. Disconnect the vacuum line at the pressure regulator, as required. Remove the return line from the pressure regulator.
7. For 1995 VIN 1 engines, disconnect the vacuum line from the supercharger or the vacuum line for the 1995 VIN K engine.
8. For 1995 VIN K engines, tag and disconnect the ignition coil wires.
9. Either detach the fuel injector electrical connectors or unplug the main injector harness connector.
10. Remove the fuel rail attaching bolts. Remove the fuel rail assembly, pulling up with equal forces on both sides of the rail. Note the location and routing of vacuum hoses around the fuel rail before removing the rail. Cover all openings with masking tape to prevent dirt from entering.

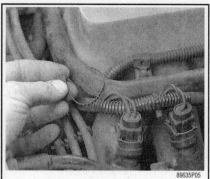

Fig. 26 Remove any necessary wire ties by cutting them off . . .

Fig. 27 . . . in order to free up lines for disconnection

Fig. 28 Remove the bracket for access to the fuel lines

Fig. 29 Unfasten the clamps retaining the fuel lines

Fig. 30 Always use a back-up wrench when disconnecting fuel lines

Fig. 31 Place some paper towels under each fuel line connection to absorb any fuel that leaks out

Fig. 32 Move the fuel lines away from the rail assembly

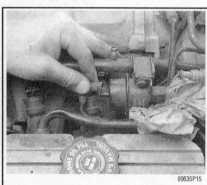

Fig. 33 Disconnect the vacuum line from the fuel pressure regulator

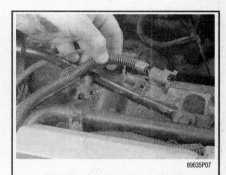

Fig. 34 You can either unplug the entire injector wiring harness, or detach each injector connector as shown here

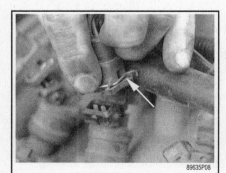

Fig. 35 Each injector connector has a retaining clip, which secures it to the injector

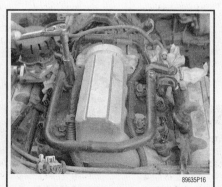

Fig. 36 Unfasten the fuel rail assembly attaching nuts

Fig. 37 Pull the fuel rail assembly up, disengage the injectors, then remove the rail from the vehicle

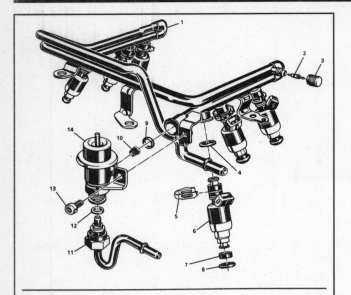

1	RAIL ASSEMBLY - FUEL	8	O-RING - LOWER INJECTOR (BROWN)
2	CORE ASSEMBLY - FUEL PRESSURE CONNECTION	9	O-RING - FUEL OUTLET TUBE
3	CAP - FUEL PRESSURE CONNECTION	10	SCREEN - FILTER
4	O-RING - UPPER INJECTOR (BLACK)	11	TUBE ASSEMBLY - FUEL RETURN
5	CLIP - FUEL INJECTOR RETAINER	12	O-RING - FUEL RETURN TUBE
6	INJECTOR ASSEMBLY - FUEL	13	SCREW - FUEL PRESSURE REGULATOR ATTACHING
7	BACKUP - O-RING	14	REGULATOR ASSEMBLY - FUEL PRESSURE

89635G16

Fig. 38 Exploded view of the fuel rail, regulator and injectors—1995 VIN L engine shown

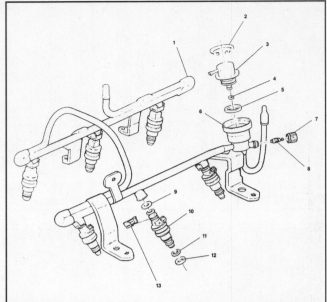

1	RAIL ASSEMBLY, FUEL	8	CORE ASSEMBLY, FUEL PRESSURE CONNECTION
2	SNAP RING, FUEL PRESSURE REGULATOR	9	O-RING, UPPER INJECTOR (BLACK)
3	REGULATOR ASSEMBLY, FUEL PRESSURE	10	INJECTOR ASSEMBLY, FUEL
4	O-RING, FUEL PRESSURE REGULATOR	11	BACKUP O-RING, FUEL INJECTOR
5	BACKUP O-RING, FUEL PRESSURE REGULATOR	12	O-RING, LOWER INJECTOR (BROWN)
6	REGULATOR HOUSING, FUEL PRESSURE	13	RETAINER CLIP, FUEL INJECTOR
7	CAP, FUEL PRESSURE CONNECTION		

89635G18

Fig. 40 Exploded view of the fuel rail, regulator and injectors—1995 VIN K engine shown

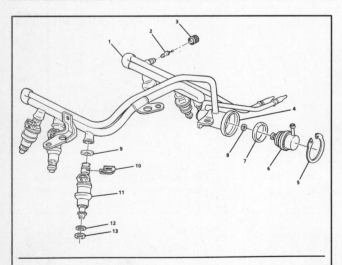

1. RAIL ASSEMBLY - FUEL
2. CORE ASSEMBLY - FUEL PRESSURE CONNECTION
3. CAP - FUEL PRESSURE CONNECTION
4. REGULATOR HOUSING - FUEL PRESSURE
5. SNAP RING, FUEL PRESSURE REGULATOR
6. REGULATOR ASSEMBLY - FUEL PRESSURE
7. BACK-UP O-RING - FUEL PRESSURE REGULATOR
8. O-RING - FUEL PRESSURE REGULATOR
9. O-RING UPPER INJECTOR (BLACK)
10. RETAINER CLIP - FUEL INJECTOR
11. INJECTOR ASSEMBLY - FUEL
12. BACK-UP O-RING - FUEL INJECTOR
13. O-RING - LOWER INJECTOR (BROWN)

89635G17

Fig. 39 Exploded view of the fuel rail assembly—1995 VIN 1 engine shown

89635P18

Fig. 41 You should use a back-up wrench when tightening fuel line fittings

➥If any injectors become separated from the fuel rail and remain in the intake manifold, both O-ring seals and injector retaining clip must be replaced. Use care in removing the fuel rail assembly, to prevent damage to the injector electrical connector terminals and the injector spray tips. When removed, support the fuel rail to avoid damaging its components. The fuel injector is serviced as a complete unit only. Since it is an electrical component, it should not be immersed in any type of cleaner.

11. Remove the injector O-ring seal from the spray tip end of each injector. Discard the O-rings.
   To install:
12. Lubricate new injector O-ring seals with clean engine oil and install on the spray tip end of each injector.

13. Position the fuel rail assembly on the intake manifold. Tilt the rail assembly to install the injectors, seating them by hand. Carefully push the injectors into the cylinder head intake ports until the bolt holes on the fuel rail and manifold are aligned. Install the fuel rail attaching bolts and fuel rail bracket bolts. Tighten the fuel rail attaching bolts, as follows:
   a. 1986–93 vehicles: 7–14 ft. lbs. (10–20 Nm).
   b. 1994 3.8L (VIN L) engines: 8 ft. lbs. (12 Nm).
   c. 1994 3.8L (VIN 1) engines: 22 ft. lbs. (30 Nm).
   d. 1995 3.8L (VIN L) engines: 11 ft. lbs. (15 Nm).
   e. 1995 3.8L (VIN 1) engines: 8 ft. lbs. (11 Nm).
   f. 1995 3.8L (VIN K) engines: 7 ft. lbs. (10 Nm).

14. Attach the injector electrical connectors or main injector wiring harness, as applicable. Rotate the injectors, as required, to prevent stretching the wire harness.

15. For 1995 VIN K engines, connect the ignition coil wires, as tagged during removal.

16. For 1995 VIN 1 engines, connect the vacuum line to the supercharger or connect the vacuum line to the throttle body for the 1995 VIN K engine, as applicable.

17. If disconnected, attach the vacuum line to the pressure regulator.

18. Install new O-rings on the fuel feed and return lines, then connect the fuel lines. Make sure to use a back-up wrench if necessary.

19. Temporarily connect the negative battery cable to check for leaks as follows:
   a. Turn the ignition switch to the **ON** position for 2 seconds, then turn to the **OFF** position for 10 seconds. Again, turn the ignition switch to the **ON** position and check for fuel leaks.

20. Disconnect the negative battery cable.

21. Install the intake manifold plenum.

22. Tighten the fuel filler cap.

23. Connect the negative battery cable.

1996–99 Vehicles

♦ **See Figures 42 and 43**

1. Properly relieve the fuel system pressure.

2. If not already done, disconnect the negative battery cable.

3. Remove the fuel feed and return pipes from the fuel rail tubes by squeezing the tabs and pulling the lines apart.

4. Disconnect the vacuum line from the pressure regulator. Tag and disconnect the vacuum lines from the throttle body.

5. For VIN K engines, tag and disconnect the ignition wires from the ignition coil.

6. For VIN 1 engines, tag and disconnect the ignition wires from the ignition coil and retainers clips on the top of the supercharger.

7. For the VIN 1 engine, remove the alternator and rear alternator mounting bracket.

8. Detach the injector electrical connectors.

9. If equipped, remove the injector electrical harness clips holding the harness to the front of the fuel rail.

➡ **When working on the fuel rail, plug or cap the fuel lines and fuel passage openings to prevent dirt and debris from contaminating the system.**

10. Unfasten the fuel rail hold-down bolts. Remove the fuel rail by pulling it up with equal force on both sides of the rail.

To install:

11. Lubricate new injector O-ring seals with clean engine oil and install on the spray tip end of each injector.

12. Position the fuel rail assembly on the intake manifold. Tilt the rail assembly to install the injectors, seating them by hand. Carefully push the injectors into the cylinder head intake ports until the bolt holes on the fuel rail and manifold are aligned. Install the fuel rail attaching bolts and fuel rail bracket bolts. Tighten the fuel rail attaching bolts to 7 ft. lbs. (10 Nm).

13. For the VIN 1 engine, install the rear alternator mounting bracket and alternator.

14. If equipped, fasten the injector electrical harness clips holding the harness to the front of the fuel rail.

15. Attach the injector electrical connectors.

16. Connect the ignition coil wires to the coil and, if equipped, install the retainer clips on top of the supercharger.

17. Connect the vacuum lines to the throttle body, as tagged during removal, and connect the line to the pressure regulator.

18. Install the fuel feed and return pipes to the fuel rail tubes by squeezing the tabs and pushing the lines on.

19. Temporarily connect the negative battery cable to check for leaks as follows:
   a. Turn the ignition switch to the **ON** position for 2 seconds, then turn to the **OFF** position for 10 seconds. Again, turn the ignition switch to the **ON** position and check for fuel leaks.

20. Disconnect the negative battery cable.

21. Tighten the fuel filler cap.

22. Connect the negative battery cable.

Fuel Pressure Regulator

REMOVAL & INSTALLATION

♦ **See Figures 44 thru 49**

1. Relieve fuel system pressure. Disconnect the negative battery cable.

2. Clean dirt and grease from the regulator retaining ring.

3. If equipped with a bolt on-type pressure regulator, remove the fuel return line from the return tube by squeezing the tab and pulling it off.

4. Disconnect the vacuum line from the regulator.

5. If equipped with a bolt on-type regulator, perform the following:
   a. Remove the regulator attaching bolt(s)/screw(s) from the bracket.

6. If equipped with a snapring-type regulator, perform the following:
   a. Remove the snapring from the regulator.

7. Wrap a towel around the regulator to catch any fuel that may escape. Remove the regulator from the fuel rail using a twisting and pulling motion.

8. If equipped with a bolt on-type pressure regulator, disconnect the fuel return tube assembly from the pressure regulator.

9. Cover all openings with masking tape to prevent dirt entry. If the regulator is being reused, inspect the filter screen, if equipped, for contamination. If contamination exists, replace the filter screen.

10. If further disassembly is necessary, perform the following:

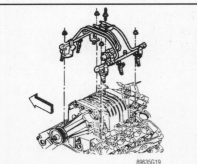

Fig. 42 Exploded view of the fuel rail mounting—1997 3.8L (VIN 1) engine shown

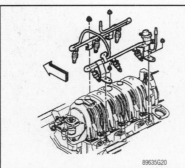

Fig. 43 Exploded view of the fuel rail mounting—1997 3.8L (VIN K) engine shown

Fig. 44 Remove the 2 fuel pressure regulator-to-rail attaching bolts (fuel rail removed from vehicle)

Fig. 45 . . . then remove the regulator by using a twisting and pulling motion

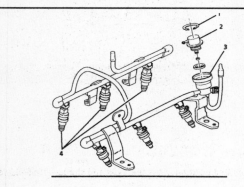

1 SNAP RING
2 FUEL PRESSURE REGULATOR
3 REGULATOR HOSING
4 INJECTORS

Fig. 46 Exploded view of the regulator mounting on the fuel rail—VIN K engine shown

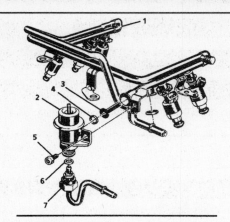

1 RAIL ASSEMBLY - FUEL
2 REGULATOR ASSEMBLY - FUEL PRESSURE
3 SCREEN - FILTER (IF SO EQUIPPED)
4 O-RING - FUEL OUTLET TUBE
5 SCREW - FUEL PRESSURE REGULATOR ATTACHING
6 O-RING - FUEL RETURN TUBE
7 TUBE ASSEMBLY - FUEL RETURN

Fig. 47 Some regulators, such as this 1995 VIN L, are secured with a mounting bolt

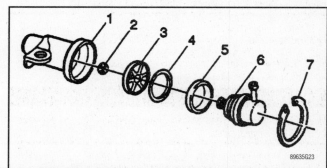

Fig. 48 Exploded view of the regulator housing (1), small O-ring (2), filter screen (3), large O-ring (4), O-ring back-up (5), regulator (6) and snapring (7)

    a. Remove the small regulator O-ring.
    b. Remove the regulator filter screen.
    c. Remove the large regulator O-ring.
    d. Remove the O-ring back-up.

To install:

11. If the regulator was disassembled, perform the following:

➡**Lubricate all O-rings with clean engine oil prior to assembly.**

    a. Install a new regulator O-ring back-up and large O-ring.
    b. Install the regulator filter screen.
    c. Install the small regulator O-ring.

12. If the regulator is not being replaced with a new one, lubricate new O-rings with clean engine oil, then position them on the old regulator.

13. If necessary, connect the fuel return tube to the pressure regulator and secure with the retaining nut. Tighten the nut to 13 ft. lbs. (17 Nm).

14. Install the regulator into the regulator housing and seat with even pressure.

    a. Install the snapring or retaining bolt(s)/screw(s), as applicable.

15. Attach the vacuum line to the regulator.

16. If removed, connect the fuel return tube to the pressure regulator.

17. Connect the negative battery cable.

18. Turn the ignition switch **ON** and **OFF** to allow fuel pressure back into system. Check for leaks.

Fig. 49 If the regulator is not being replaced, remove and discard the old O-rings

FUEL TANK

Tank Assembly

✳✳ CAUTION

NEVER apply battery power to a used fuel pump outside of the fuel tank.

DRAINING

✳✳ CAUTION

Observe all applicable safety precautions when working around fuel. Whenever servicing the fuel system, always work in a well ventilated area. Do not allow fuel spray or vapors to come in contact with a spark or open flame. Keep a dry chemical fire extinguisher near the work area. Always keep fuel in a container specifically designed for fuel storage; also, always properly seal fuel containers to avoid the possibility of fire or explosion.

1. Disconnect the negative battery cable.

✳✳ CAUTION

To reduce the risk of fire and personal injury, always keep a dry chemical (Class B) fire extinguisher near the work area.

2. Remove the fuel cap.
3. Raise and safely support the vehicle with jackstands.
4. Disconnect the filler vent hose from the tank.
5. Use a hand operated pump approved for gasoline to drain as much fuel as possible through the filler vent hose into a suitable container.

✳✳ CAUTION

Never drain or store gasoline in an open container due to the possibility of fire or explosion!

6. Reconnect the filler vent hose and tighten the clamp.
7. Install any removed lines, hoses and cap. Connect the negative battery cable.

REMOVAL & INSTALLATION

✳✳ CAUTION

Observe all applicable safety precautions when working around gasoline. Do not allow fuel spray or fuel vapors to come in contact with a spark or open flame. Keep a dry chemical (Class B) fire extinguisher near the work area. Never drain or store fuel in an open container due to the possibility of fire or explosion.

1. Use a suitable hand operated pump device to drain the fuel through the filler tube into an approved container.

1986–95 Vehicles

▶ See Figures 50 and 51

1. Relieve the fuel system pressure.
2. Disconnect the negative battery cable.
3. Drain all fuel from the tank into a proper container.
4. Detach the sender assembly wires, tank filler and the vent hoses.
5. Disconnect the fuel pipe quick-connectors.
6. Have an assistant support the fuel tank, then disconnect the 2 tank retaining straps.
7. Lower the exhaust by disconnecting at the rear hanger, then carefully

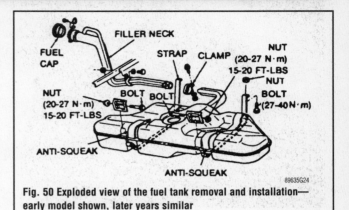

Fig. 50 Exploded view of the fuel tank removal and installation—early model shown, later years similar

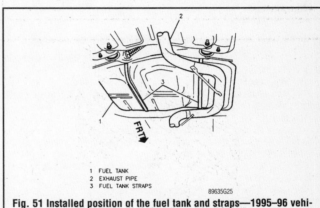

Fig. 51 Installed position of the fuel tank and straps—1995–96 vehicles

remove the fuel tank from the vehicle. Remove the tank from the vehicle slowly, to ensure all connections and hoses have been disconnected.

8. If installing a new tank, transfer the sending unit/pump to the new tank.

To install:
9. Install the fuel tank to the vehicle and install the 2 retaining straps.
10. Raise the exhaust and connect the rear hanger.
11. Connect the fuel pipe quick-connectors.
12. Attach the sender wires, the tank filler and vent hoses.
13. Carefully lower the vehicle.
14. Refill the tank with fuel and connect the negative battery cable.
15. Inspect for any fuel leakage.

1996–99 Vehicles

▶ See Figures 51 and 52

1. Disconnect the negative battery cable.
2. Properly relieve the fuel system pressure, as outlined earlier in this section.
3. Raise and safely support the vehicle.

➡**Before disconnecting any fuel lines from the fuel tank, thoroughly clean around all hose connections.**

4. Disconnect the fuel tank filler pipe EVAP pipe from the fuel tank EVAP pipe.
5. Disconnect the fuel tank filler pipe from the fuel tank.
6. Detach the quick-connect fuel line fittings from the fuel tank.
7. Disconnect the two rear rubber exhaust hangers from the rear of the exhaust system and allow the exhaust system to hang down slightly.

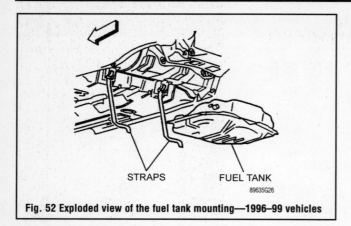

STRAPS   FUEL TANK

89635G26

Fig. 52 Exploded view of the fuel tank mounting—1996–99 vehicles

8. If equipped, unfasten the exhaust shield mounting bolts, then remove the exhaust shield.

9. Support the fuel tank with a suitable jack or assistant.

10. Remove the two bolts securing the fuel tank straps, then swing the straps out of the way.

➡**Do not bend the fuel tank straps, as this may damage the straps.**

11. Lower the fuel tank enough to detach the fuel sender electrical connector and remove the fuel sender retaining clips.

12. Disconnect the EVAP pipe from the rear of the fuel tank.

13. Remove the tank from the vehicle slowly, to ensure all connections and hoses have been disconnected.

To install:

14. Clean all parts well. Inspect the tank for dents, rust or other damage. On high-mileage vehicles, it may be good practice to remove the fuel pump module and replace the flexible strainer on the fuel pump.

15. Position the fuel tank under the vehicle and raise the tank with the help of an assistant or a suitable jack.

16. Connect the EVAP pipe to the rear of the fuel tank.

17. Install the fuel sender retaining clips.

18. Attach the electrical connector to the fuel sender assembly.

19. Raise the tank into position into the vehicle and swing the mounting straps under the tank.

20. Install the front fuel tank strap mounting bolts and tighten to 35 ft. lbs. (47 Nm).

21. Remove the jack.

22. Attach the quick-connect fuel line fittings.

23. Connect the fuel tank filler pipe EVAP pipe to the fuel tank and tighten the hose clamp to 22 inch lbs. (2.5 Nm).

24. Connect the fuel tank filler pipe to the fuel tank and tighten the hose clamp to 22 inch lbs. (2.5 Nm).

25. If equipped, install the exhaust heat shield and the mounting bolts.

26. Position the exhaust system and install the rubber hangers.

27. Carefully lower the vehicle, then refill the fuel system

28. Connect the negative battery cable, then install the fuel filler cap, if not done already.

29. Turn the ignition switch **ON** for 2 seconds, **OFF** for 10 seconds, then **ON** and check for fuel leaks.

SENDING UNIT REPLACEMENT

▶ **See Figure 53**

The fuel gauge sending unit is attached to the fuel pump on cars with an electric in-tank pump. The following procedure is for pump and sending unit removal and installation. Be extremely cautious of sparks or flame when working around the fuel pump. NEVER apply battery power to a used fuel pump out of the fuel tank.

1. Relieve the fuel system pressure, then disconnect the negative battery cable.

2. Raise and support the vehicle safely. Drain the fuel tank.

➡**Before disconnecting any fuel lines from the fuel tank, thoroughly clean around all hose connections.**

3. Remove the fuel tank from the vehicle, and place on a suitable workbench.

4. Remove the fuel gauge/pump retaining ring using a suitable spanner wrench to turn the assembly counterclockwise.

5. Remove the gauge unit and the pump.

To install:

6. Install the gauge unit and the pump.

7. Install the fuel gauge/pump retaining ring using a suitable spanner to turn the assembly clockwise to lock the retaining ring.

8. Install the fuel tank in the vehicle, as outlined in this section.

9. Carefully lower the vehicle.

10. Fill the fuel tank.

11. Turn the ignition switch to the **ON** position for 2 seconds, then turn to the **OFF** position for 10 seconds. Turn the ignition switch back to the **ON** position and check for fuel leaks.

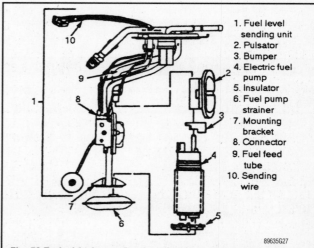

1. Fuel level sending unit
2. Pulsator
3. Bumper
4. Electric fuel pump
5. Insulator
6. Fuel pump strainer
7. Mounting bracket
8. Connector
9. Fuel feed tube
10. Sending wire

89635G27

Fig. 53 Typical fuel pump/level sender assembly—early model shown, later years similar

UNDERSTANDING AND TROUBLESHOOTING ELECTRICAL SYSTEMS 6-2
BASIC ELECTRICAL THEORY 6-2
  HOW DOES ELECTRICITY WORK: THE WATER ANALOGY 6-2
  OHM'S LAW 6-2
ELECTRICAL COMPONENTS 6-2
  POWER SOURCE 6-2
  GROUND 6-3
  PROTECTIVE DEVICES 6-3
  SWITCHES & RELAYS 6-3
  LOAD 6-4
  WIRING & HARNESSES 6-4
  CONNECTORS 6-4
TEST EQUIPMENT 6-5
  JUMPER WIRES 6-5
  TEST LIGHTS 6-5
  MULTIMETERS 6-5
TROUBLESHOOTING ELECTRICAL SYSTEMS 6-6
TESTING 6-6
  OPEN CIRCUITS 6-6
  SHORT CIRCUITS 6-6
  VOLTAGE 6-6
  VOLTAGE DROP 6-7
  RESISTANCE 6-7
WIRE AND CONNECTOR REPAIR 6-7
BATTERY CABLES 6-8
DISCONNECTING THE CABLES 6-8
AIR BAG—GENERATION 1 CORPORATE SYSTEM 6-8
GENERAL DESCRIPTION 6-8
  SYSTEM OPERATION 6-9
  SYSTEM COMPONENTS 6-9
  SERVICE PRECAUTIONS 6-11
  DISARMING THE SIR SYSTEM 6-11
  ENABLING THE SYSTEM 6-11
AIR BAG—OLDSMOBILE INFLATABLE RESTRAINT (IR) SYSTEM 6-12
GENERAL DESCRIPTION 6-12
  SYSTEM COMPONENTS 6-12
  SERVICE PRECAUTIONS 6-12
  DISARMING THE IR SYSTEM 6-13
  ENABLING THE SYSTEM 6-13
HEATING AND AIR CONDITIONING 6-14
BLOWER MOTOR 6-14
  REMOVAL & INSTALLATION 6-14
HEATER CORE 6-14
  REMOVAL & INSTALLATION 6-14
AIR CONDITIONING COMPONENTS 6-16
  REMOVAL & INSTALLATION 6-16
CONTROL CABLES 6-16
  REMOVAL & INSTALLATION 6-16
  ADJUSTMENT 6-16
CONTROL PANEL 6-17
  REMOVAL & INSTALLATION 6-17

CRUISE CONTROL SYSTEMS 6-18
GENERAL DESCRIPTION 6-18
ENTERTAINMENT SYSTEMS 6-19
RADIO 6-19
  REMOVAL & INSTALLATION 6-19
SPEAKERS 6-21
  REMOVAL & INSTALLATION 6-21
POWER ANTENNA 6-22
  REMOVAL & INSTALLATION 6-23
WINDSHIELD WIPERS AND WASHERS 6-23
WINDSHIELD WIPER BLADE AND ARM 6-24
  REMOVAL & INSTALLATION 6-24
WINDSHIELD WIPER MOTOR 6-26
  REMOVAL & INSTALLATION 6-26
WINDSHIELD WASHER MOTOR 6-27
  REMOVAL & INSTALLATION 6-27
INSTRUMENTS AND SWITCHES 6-28
INSTRUMENT CLUSTER 6-28
  REMOVAL & INSTALLATION 6-28
GAUGES 6-32
  REMOVAL & INSTALLATION 6-32
HEADLIGHT SWITCH 6-32
  REMOVAL & INSTALLATION 6-32
REAR DEFOGGER SYSTEM 6-32
  OPERATION 6-32
  TESTING 6-32
  REPAIR 6-32
LIGHTING 6-33
HEADLIGHTS 6-33
  REMOVAL & INSTALLATION 6-33
  AIMING THE HEADLIGHTS 6-34
SIGNAL AND MARKER LIGHTS 6-35
  REMOVAL & INSTALLATION 6-35
FOG LIGHTS 6-38
  REMOVAL & INSTALLATION 6-38
  AIMING 6-38
CIRCUIT PROTECTION 6-39
FUSES 6-39
  REPLACEMENT 6-39
FUSIBLE LINKS 6-40
CIRCUIT BREAKERS 6-41
FLASHERS 6-41
  REPLACEMENT 6-41
WIRING DIAGRAMS 6-42

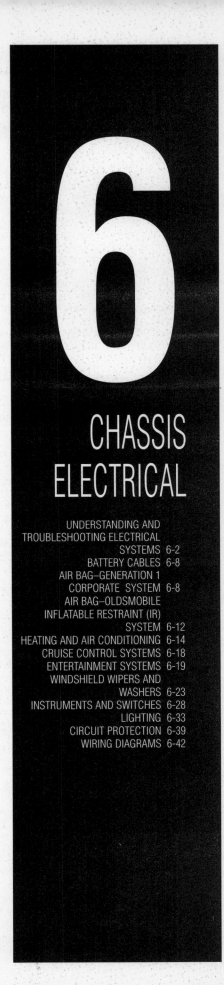

6

CHASSIS ELECTRICAL

UNDERSTANDING AND TROUBLESHOOTING ELECTRICAL SYSTEMS 6-2
BATTERY CABLES 6-8
AIR BAG—GENERATION 1 CORPORATE SYSTEM 6-8
AIR BAG—OLDSMOBILE INFLATABLE RESTRAINT (IR) SYSTEM 6-12
HEATING AND AIR CONDITIONING 6-14
CRUISE CONTROL SYSTEMS 6-18
ENTERTAINMENT SYSTEMS 6-19
WINDSHIELD WIPERS AND WASHERS 6-23
INSTRUMENTS AND SWITCHES 6-28
LIGHTING 6-33
CIRCUIT PROTECTION 6-39
WIRING DIAGRAMS 6-42

UNDERSTANDING AND TROUBLESHOOTING ELECTRICAL SYSTEMS

Basic Electrical Theory

▶ See Figure 1

For any 12 volt, negative ground, electrical system to operate, the electricity must travel in a complete circuit. This simply means that current (power) from the positive (+) terminal of the battery must eventually return to the negative (-) terminal of the battery. Along the way, this current will travel through wires, fuses, switches and components. If, for any reason, the flow of current through the circuit is interrupted, the component fed by that circuit will cease to function properly.

Perhaps the easiest way to visualize a circuit is to think of connecting a light bulb (with two wires attached to it) to the battery—one wire attached to the negative (-) terminal of the battery and the other wire to the positive (+) terminal. With the two wires touching the battery terminals, the circuit would be complete and the light bulb would illuminate. Electricity would follow a path from the battery to the bulb and back to the battery. It's easy to see that with longer wires on our light bulb, it could be mounted anywhere. Further, one wire could be fitted with a switch so that the light could be turned on and off.

The normal automotive circuit differs from this simple example in two ways. First, instead of having a return wire from the bulb to the battery, the current travels through the frame of the vehicle. Since the negative (-) battery cable is attached to the frame (made of electrically conductive metal), the frame of the vehicle can serve as a ground wire to complete the circuit. Secondly, most automotive circuits contain multiple components which receive power from a single circuit. This lessens the amount of wire needed to power components on the vehicle.

HOW DOES ELECTRICITY WORK: THE WATER ANALOGY

Electricity is the flow of electrons—the subatomic particles that constitute the outer shell of an atom. Electrons spin in an orbit around the center core of an atom. The center core is comprised of protons (positive charge) and neutrons (neutral charge). Electrons have a negative charge and balance out the positive charge of the protons. When an outside force causes the number of electrons to unbalance the charge of the protons, the electrons will split off the atom and look for another atom to balance out. If this imbalance is kept up, electrons will continue to move and an electrical flow will exist.

Many people have been taught electrical theory using an analogy with water. In a comparison with water flowing through a pipe, the electrons would be the water and the wire is the pipe.

The flow of electricity can be measured much like the flow of water through a pipe. The unit of measurement used is amperes, frequently abbreviated as amps (a). You can compare amperage to the volume of water flowing through a pipe. When connected to a circuit, an ammeter will measure the actual amount of current flowing through the circuit. When relatively few electrons flow through a circuit, the amperage is low. When many electrons flow, the amperage is high.

Water pressure is measured in units such as pounds per square inch (psi);

The electrical pressure is measured in units called volts (v). When a voltmeter is connected to a circuit, it is measuring the electrical pressure.

The actual flow of electricity depends not only on voltage and amperage, but also on the resistance of the circuit. The higher the resistance, the higher the force necessary to push the current through the circuit. The standard unit for measuring resistance is an ohm. Resistance in a circuit varies depending on the amount and type of components used in the circuit. The main factors which determine resistance are:

- Material—some materials have more resistance than others. Those with high resistance are said to be insulators. Rubber materials (or rubber-like plastics) are some of the most common insulators used in vehicles as they have a very high resistance to electricity. Very low resistance materials are said to be conductors. Copper wire is among the best conductors. Silver is actually a superior conductor to copper and is used in some relay contacts, but its high cost prohibits its use as common wiring. Most automotive wiring is made of copper.
- Size—the larger the wire size being used, the less resistance the wire will have. This is why components which use large amounts of electricity usually have large wires supplying current to them.
- Length—for a given thickness of wire, the longer the wire, the greater the resistance. The shorter the wire, the less the resistance. When determining the proper wire for a circuit, both size and length must be considered to design a circuit that can handle the current needs of the component.
- Temperature—with many materials, the higher the temperature, the greater the resistance (positive temperature coefficient). Some materials exhibit the opposite trait of lower resistance with higher temperatures (negative temperature coefficient). These principles are used in many of the sensors on the engine.

OHM'S LAW

There is a direct relationship between current, voltage and resistance. The relationship between current, voltage and resistance can be summed up by a statement known as Ohm's law.

Voltage (E) is equal to amperage (I) times resistance (R): $E = I \times R$

Other forms of the formula are $R = E/I$ and $I = E/R$

In each of these formulas, E is the voltage in volts, I is the current in amps and R is the resistance in ohms. The basic point to remember is that as the resistance of a circuit goes up, the amount of current that flows in the circuit will go down, if voltage remains the same.

The amount of work that the electricity can perform is expressed as power. The unit of power is the watt (w). The relationship between power, voltage and current is expressed as:

Power (w) is equal to amperage (I) times voltage (E): $W = I \times E$

This is only true for direct current (DC) circuits; The alternating current formula is a tad different, but since the electrical circuits in most vehicles are DC type, we need not get into AC circuit theory.

Electrical Components

POWER SOURCE

Power is supplied to the vehicle by two devices: The battery and the alternator. The battery supplies electrical power during starting or during periods when the current demand of the vehicle's electrical system exceeds the output capacity of the alternator. The alternator supplies electrical current when the engine is running. Just not does the alternator supply the current needs of the vehicle, but it recharges the battery.

The Battery

In most modern vehicles, the battery is a lead/acid electrochemical device consisting of six 2 volt subsections (cells) connected in series, so that the unit is capable of producing approximately 12 volts of electrical pressure. Each subsection consists of a series of positive and negative plates held a short distance apart in a solution of sulfuric acid and water.

The two types of plates are of dissimilar metals. This sets up a chemical reaction, and it is this reaction which produces current flow from the battery when its positive and negative terminals are connected to an electrical load.

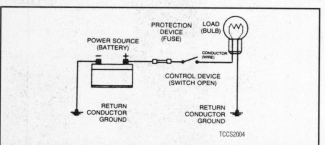

TCCS2004

Fig. 1 This example illustrates a simple circuit. When the switch is closed, power from the positive (+) battery terminal flows through the fuse and the switch, and then to the light bulb. The light illuminates and the circuit is completed through the ground wire back to the negative (-) battery terminal. In reality, the two ground points shown in the illustration are attached to the metal frame of the vehicle, which completes the circuit back to the battery

The power removed from the battery is replaced by the alternator, restoring the battery to its original chemical state.

The Alternator

On some vehicles there isn't an alternator, but a generator. The difference is that an alternator supplies alternating current which is then changed to direct current for use on the vehicle, while a generator produces direct current. Alternators tend to be more efficient and that is why they are used.

Alternators and generators are devices that consist of coils of wires wound together making big electromagnets. One group of coils spins within another set and the interaction of the magnetic fields causes a current to flow. This current is then drawn off the coils and fed into the vehicles electrical system.

GROUND

Two types of grounds are used in automotive electric circuits. Direct ground components are grounded to the frame through their mounting points. All other components use some sort of ground wire which is attached to the frame or chassis of the vehicle. The electrical current runs through the chassis of the vehicle and returns to the battery through the ground (-) cable; if you look, you'll see that the battery ground cable connects between the battery and the frame or chassis of the vehicle.

➡**It should be noted that a good percentage of electrical problems can be traced to bad grounds.**

PROTECTIVE DEVICES

▶ **See Figure 2**

It is possible for large surges of current to pass through the electrical system of your vehicle. If this surge of current were to reach the load in the circuit, the

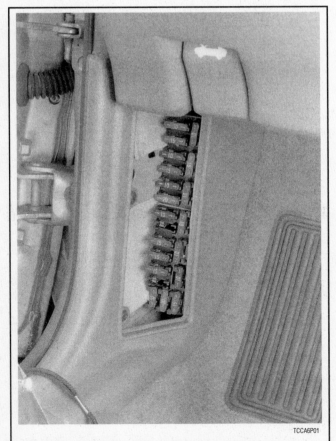

Fig. 2 Most vehicles use one or more fuse panels. This one is located on the driver's side kick panel

surge could burn it out or severely damage it. It can also overload the wiring, causing the harness to get hot and melt the insulation. To prevent this, fuses, circuit breakers and/or fusible links are connected into the supply wires of the electrical system. These items are nothing more than a built-in weak spot in the system. When an abnormal amount of current flows through the system, these protective devices work as follows to protect the circuit:

• Fuse—when an excessive electrical current passes through a fuse, the fuse "blows" (the conductor melts) and opens the circuit, preventing the passage of current.

• Circuit Breaker—a circuit breaker is basically a self-repairing fuse. It will open the circuit in the same fashion as a fuse, but when the surge subsides, the circuit breaker can be reset and does not need replacement.

• Fusible Link—a fusible link (fuse link or main link) is a short length of special, high temperature insulated wire that acts as a fuse. When an excessive electrical current passes through a fusible link, the thin gauge wire inside the link melts, creating an intentional open to protect the circuit. To repair the circuit, the link must be replaced. Some newer type fusible links are housed in plug-in modules, which are simply replaced like a fuse, while older type fusible links must be cut and spliced if they melt. Since this link is very early in the electrical path, it's the first place to look if nothing on the vehicle works, yet the battery seems to be charged and is properly connected.

✳ CAUTION

Always replace fuses, circuit breakers and fusible links with identically rated components. Under no circumstances should a component of higher or lower amperage rating be substituted.

SWITCHES & RELAYS

▶ **See Figures 3 and 4**

Switches are used in electrical circuits to control the passage of current. The most common use is to open and close circuits between the battery and the various electric devices in the system. Switches are rated according to the amount of amperage they can handle. If a sufficient amperage rated switch is not used in a circuit, the switch could overload and cause damage.

Some electrical components which require a large amount of current to operate use a special switch called a relay. Since these circuits carry a large amount of current, the thickness of the wire in the circuit is also greater. If this large wire were connected from the load to the control switch, the switch would have to carry the high amperage load and the fairing or dash would be twice as large to accommodate the increased size of the wiring harness. To prevent these problems, a relay is used.

Relays are composed of a coil and a set of contacts. When the coil has a current passed though it, a magnetic field is formed and this field causes the contacts to move together, completing the circuit. Most relays are normally open, preventing current from passing through the circuit, but they can take any electrical form

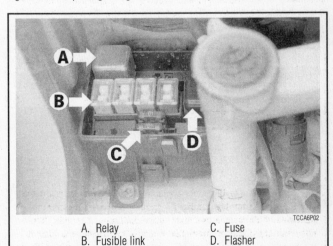

A. Relay   C. Fuse
B. Fusible link   D. Flasher

Fig. 3 The underhood fuse and relay panel usually contains fuses, relays, flashers and fusible links

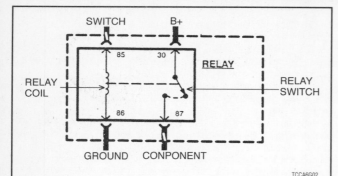

Fig. 4 Relays are composed of a coil and a switch. These two components are linked together so that when one operates, the other operates at the same time. The large wires in the circuit are connected from the battery to one side of the relay switch (B+) and from the opposite side of the relay switch to the load (component). Smaller wires are connected from the relay coil to the control switch for the circuit and from the opposite side of the relay coil to ground

depending on the job they are intended to do. Relays can be considered "remote control switches." They allow a smaller current to operate devices that require higher amperages. When a small current operates the coil, a larger current is allowed to pass by the contacts. Some common circuits which may use relays are the horn, headlights, starter, electric fuel pump and other high draw circuits.

LOAD

Every electrical circuit must include a "load" (something to use the electricity coming from the source). Without this load, the battery would attempt to deliver its entire power supply from one pole to another. This is called a "short circuit." All this electricity would take a short cut to ground and cause a great amount of damage to other components in the circuit by developing a tremendous amount of heat. This condition could develop sufficient heat to melt the insulation on all the surrounding wires and reduce a multiple wire cable to a lump of plastic and copper.

WIRING & HARNESSES

The average vehicle contains meters and meters of wiring, with hundreds of individual connections. To protect the many wires from damage and to keep them from becoming a confusing tangle, they are organized into bundles, enclosed in plastic or taped together and called wiring harnesses. Different harnesses serve different parts of the vehicle. Individual wires are color coded to help trace them through a harness where sections are hidden from view.

Automotive wiring or circuit conductors can be either single strand wire, multi-strand wire or printed circuitry. Single strand wire has a solid metal core and is usually used inside such components as alternators, motors, relays and other devices. Multi-strand wire has a core made of many small strands of wire twisted together into a single conductor. Most of the wiring in an automotive electrical system is made up of multi-strand wire, either as a single conductor or grouped together in a harness. All wiring is color coded on the insulator, either as a solid color or as a colored wire with an identification stripe. A printed circuit is a thin film of copper or other conductor that is printed on an insulator backing. Occasionally, a printed circuit is sandwiched between two sheets of plastic for more protection and flexibility. A complete printed circuit, consisting of conductors, insulating material and connectors for lamps or other components is called a printed circuit board. Printed circuitry is used in place of individual wires or harnesses in places where space is limited, such as behind instrument panels.

Since automotive electrical systems are very sensitive to changes in resistance, the selection of properly sized wires is critical when systems are repaired. A loose or corroded connection or a replacement wire that is too small for the circuit will add extra resistance and an additional voltage drop to the circuit.

The wire gauge number is an expression of the cross-section area of the conductor. Vehicles from countries that use the metric system will typically describe the wire size as its cross-sectional area in square millimeters. In this method, the larger the wire, the greater the number. Another common system for

expressing wire size is the American Wire Gauge (AWG) system. As gauge number increases, area decreases and the wire becomes smaller. An 18 gauge wire is smaller than a 4 gauge wire. A wire with a higher gauge number will carry less current than a wire with a lower gauge number. Gauge wire size refers to the size of the strands of the conductor, not the size of the complete wire with insulator. It is possible, therefore, to have two wires of the same gauge with different diameters because one may have thicker insulation than the other.

It is essential to understand how a circuit works before trying to figure out why it doesn't. An electrical schematic shows the electrical current paths when a circuit is operating properly. Schematics break the entire electrical system down into individual circuits. In a schematic, usually no attempt is made to represent wiring and components as they physically appear on the vehicle; switches and other components are shown as simply as possible. Face views of harness connectors show the cavity or terminal locations in all multi-pin connectors to help locate test points.

CONNECTORS

▶ **See Figures 5 and 6**

Three types of connectors are commonly used in automotive applications—weatherproof, molded and hard shell.

• Weatherproof—these connectors are most commonly used where the connector is exposed to the elements. Terminals are protected against moisture and dirt by sealing rings which provide a weathertight seal. All repairs require the use of a special terminal and the tool required to service it. Unlike standard blade type terminals, these weatherproof terminals cannot be straightened once they are bent. Make certain that the connectors are properly seated and all of the sealing rings are in place when connecting leads.

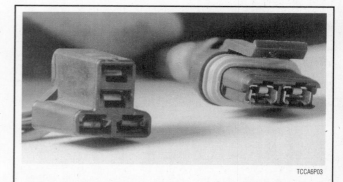

Fig. 5 Hard shell (left) and weatherproof (right) connectors have replaceable terminals

Fig. 6 Weatherproof connectors are most commonly used in the engine compartment or where the connector is exposed to the elements

• Molded—these connectors require complete replacement of the connector if found to be defective. This means splicing a new connector assembly into the harness. All splices should be soldered to insure proper contact. Use care when probing the connections or replacing terminals in them, as it is possible to create a short circuit between opposite terminals. If this happens to the wrong terminal pair, it is possible to damage certain components. Always use jumper wires between connectors for circuit checking and NEVER probe through weatherproof seals.

• Hard Shell—unlike molded connectors, the terminal contacts in hard-shell connectors can be replaced. Replacement usually involves the use of a special terminal removal tool that depresses the locking tangs (barbs) on the connector terminal and allows the connector to be removed from the rear of the shell. The connector shell should be replaced if it shows any evidence of burning, melting, cracks, or breaks. Replace individual terminals that are burnt, corroded, distorted or loose.

Test Equipment

Pinpointing the exact cause of trouble in an electrical circuit is most times accomplished by the use of special test equipment. The following describes different types of commonly used test equipment and briefly explains how to use them in diagnosis. In addition to the information covered below, the tool manufacturer's instructions booklet (provided with the tester) should be read and clearly understood before attempting any test procedures.

JUMPER WIRES

Never use jumper wires made from a thinner gauge wire than the circuit being tested. If the jumper wire is of too small a gauge, it may overheat and possibly melt. Never use jumpers to bypass high resistance loads in a circuit. Bypassing resistances, in effect, creates a short circuit. This may, in turn, cause damage and fire. Jumper wires should only be used to bypass lengths of wire or to simulate switches.

Jumper wires are simple, yet extremely valuable, pieces of test equipment. They are basically test wires which are used to bypass sections of a circuit. Although jumper wires can be purchased, they are usually fabricated from lengths of standard automotive wire and whatever type of connector (alligator clip, spade connector or pin connector) that is required for the particular application being tested. In cramped, hard-to-reach areas, it is advisable to have insulated boots over the jumper wire terminals in order to prevent accidental grounding. It is also advisable to include a standard automotive fuse in any jumper wire. This is commonly referred to as a "fused jumper". By inserting an in-line fuse holder between a set of test leads, a fused jumper wire can be used for bypassing open circuits. Use a 5 amp fuse to provide protection against voltage spikes.

Jumper wires are used primarily to locate open electrical circuits, on either the ground (-) side of the circuit or on the power (+) side. If an electrical component fails to operate, connect the jumper wire between the component and a good ground. If the component operates only with the jumper installed, the ground circuit is open. If the ground circuit is good, but the component does not operate, the circuit between the power feed and component may be open. By moving the jumper wire successively back from the component toward the power source, you can isolate the area of the circuit where the open is located. When the component stops functioning, or the power is cut off, the open is in the segment of wire between the jumper and the point previously tested.

You can sometimes connect the jumper wire directly from the battery to the "hot" terminal of the component, but first make sure the component uses 12 volts in operation. Some electrical components, such as fuel injectors or sensors, are designed to operate on about 4 to 5 volts, and running 12 volts directly to these components will cause damage.

TEST LIGHTS

▶ **See Figure 7**

The test light is used to check circuits and components while electrical current is flowing through them. It is used for voltage and ground tests. To use a 12 volt test light, connect the ground clip to a good ground and probe wherever

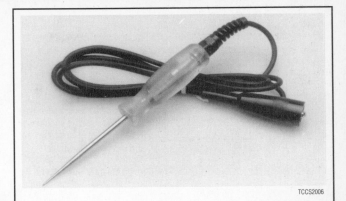

TCCS2006

Fig. 7 A 12 volt test light is used to detect the presence of voltage in a circuit

necessary with the pick. The test light will illuminate when voltage is detected. This does not necessarily mean that 12 volts (or any particular amount of voltage) is present; it only means that some voltage is present. It is advisable before using the test light to touch its ground clip and probe across the battery posts or terminals to make sure the light is operating properly.

Do not use a test light to probe electronic ignition, spark plug or coil wires. Never use a pick-type test light to probe wiring on computer controlled systems unless specifically instructed to do so. Any wire insulation that is pierced by the test light probe should be taped and sealed with silicone after testing.

Like the jumper wire, the 12 volt test light is used to isolate opens in circuits. But, whereas the jumper wire is used to bypass the open to operate the load, the 12 volt test light is used to locate the presence of voltage in a circuit. If the test light illuminates, there is power up to that point in the circuit; if the test light does not illuminate, there is an open circuit (no power). Move the test light in successive steps back toward the power source until the light in the handle illuminates. The open is between the probe and a point which was previously probed.

The self-powered test light is similar in design to the 12 volt test light, but contains a 1.5 volt penlight battery in the handle. It is most often used in place of a multimeter to check for open or short circuits when power is isolated from the circuit (continuity test).

The battery in a self-powered test light does not provide much current. A weak battery may not provide enough power to illuminate the test light even when a complete circuit is made (especially if there is high resistance in the circuit). Always make sure that the test battery is strong. To check the battery, briefly touch the ground clip to the probe; if the light glows brightly, the battery is strong enough for testing.

➡ **A self-powered test light should not be used on any computer controlled system or component. The small amount of electricity transmitted by the test light is enough to damage many electronic automotive components.**

MULTIMETERS

Multimeters are an extremely useful tool for troubleshooting electrical problems. They can be purchased in either analog or digital form and have a price range to suit any budget. A multimeter is a voltmeter, ammeter and ohmmeter (along with other features) combined into one instrument. It is often used when testing solid state circuits because of its high input impedance (usually 10 megaohms or more). A brief description of the multimeter main test functions follows:

• Voltmeter—the voltmeter is used to measure voltage at any point in a circuit, or to measure the voltage drop across any part of a circuit. Voltmeters usually have various scales and a selector switch to allow the reading of different voltage ranges. The voltmeter has a positive and a negative lead. To avoid damage to the meter, always connect the negative lead to the negative (-) side of the circuit (to ground or nearest the ground side of the circuit) and connect the positive lead to the positive (+) side of the circuit (to the power source or the nearest power source). Note that the negative voltmeter lead will always be black and that the positive voltmeter will always be some color other than black (usually red).

• Ohmmeter—the ohmmeter is designed to read resistance (measured in ohms) in a circuit or component. Most ohmmeters will have a selector switch which permits the measurement of different ranges of resistance (usually the selector switch allows the multiplication of the meter reading by 10, 100, 1,000 and 10,000). Some ohmmeters are "auto-ranging" which means the meter itself will determine which scale to use. Since the meters are powered by an internal battery, the ohmmeter can be used like a self-powered test light. When the ohmmeter is connected, current from the ohmmeter flows through the circuit or component being tested. Since the ohmmeter's internal resistance and voltage are known values, the amount of current flow through the meter depends on the resistance of the circuit or component being tested. The ohmmeter can also be used to perform a continuity test for suspected open circuits. In using the meter for making continuity checks, do not be concerned with the actual resistance readings. Zero resistance, or any ohm reading, indicates continuity in the circuit. Infinite resistance indicates an opening in the circuit. A high resistance reading where there should be none indicates a problem in the circuit. Checks for short circuits are made in the same manner as checks for open circuits, except that the circuit must be isolated from both power and normal ground. Infinite resistance indicates no continuity, while zero resistance indicates a dead short.

✳✳ WARNING

Never use an ohmmeter to check the resistance of a component or wire while there is voltage applied to the circuit.

• Ammeter—an ammeter measures the amount of current flowing through a circuit in units called amperes or amps. At normal operating voltage, most circuits have a characteristic amount of amperes, called "current draw" which can be measured using an ammeter. By referring to a specified current draw rating, then measuring the amperes and comparing the two values, one can determine what is happening within the circuit to aid in diagnosis. An open circuit, for example, will not allow any current to flow, so the ammeter reading will be zero. A damaged component or circuit will have an increased current draw, so the reading will be high. The ammeter is always connected in series with the circuit being tested. All of the current that normally flows through the circuit must also flow through the ammeter; if there is any other path for the current to follow, the ammeter reading will not be accurate. The ammeter itself has very little resistance to current flow and, therefore, will not affect the circuit, but it will measure current draw only when the circuit is closed and electricity is flowing. Excessive current draw can blow fuses and drain the battery, while a reduced current draw can cause motors to run slowly, lights to dim and other components to not operate properly.

Troubleshooting Electrical Systems

When diagnosing a specific problem, organized troubleshooting is a must. The complexity of a modern automotive vehicle demands that you approach any problem in a logical, organized manner. There are certain troubleshooting techniques, however, which are standard:

• Establish when the problem occurs. Does the problem appear only under certain conditions? Were there any noises, odors or other unusual symptoms? Isolate the problem area. To do this, make some simple tests and observations, then eliminate the systems that are working properly. Check for obvious problems, such as broken wires and loose or dirty connections. Always check the obvious before assuming something complicated is the cause.

• Test for problems systematically to determine the cause once the problem area is isolated. Are all the components functioning properly? Is there power going to electrical switches and motors? Performing careful, systematic checks will often turn up most causes on the first inspection, without wasting time checking components that have little or no relationship to the problem.

• Test all repairs after the work is done to make sure that the problem is fixed. Some causes can be traced to more than one component, so a careful verification of repair work is important in order to pick up additional malfunctions that may cause a problem to reappear or a different problem to arise. A blown fuse, for example, is a simple problem that may require more than another fuse to repair. If you don't look for a problem that caused a fuse to blow, a shorted wire (for example) may go undetected.

Experience has shown that most problems tend to be the result of a fairly simple and obvious cause, such as loose or corroded connectors, bad grounds or damaged wire insulation which causes a short. This makes careful visual inspection of components during testing essential to quick and accurate troubleshooting.

Testing

OPEN CIRCUITS

▶ **See Figure 8**

This test already assumes the existence of an open in the circuit and it is used to help locate the open portion.

1. Isolate the circuit from power and ground.
2. Connect the self-powered test light or ohmmeter ground clip to the ground side of the circuit and probe sections of the circuit sequentially.
3. If the light is out or there is infinite resistance, the open is between the probe and the circuit ground.
4. If the light is on or the meter shows continuity, the open is between the probe and the end of the circuit toward the power source.

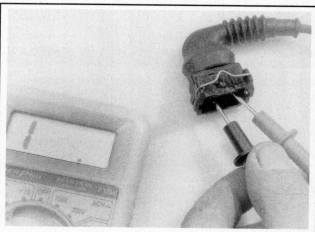

TCCA6P10

Fig. 8 The infinite reading on this multimeter indicates that the circuit is open

SHORT CIRCUITS

➡**Never use a self-powered test light to perform checks for opens or shorts when power is applied to the circuit under test. The test light can be damaged by outside power.**

1. Isolate the circuit from power and ground.
2. Connect the self-powered test light or ohmmeter ground clip to a good ground and probe any easy-to-reach point in the circuit.
3. If the light comes on or there is continuity, there is a short somewhere in the circuit.
4. To isolate the short, probe a test point at either end of the isolated circuit (the light should be on or the meter should indicate continuity).
5. Leave the test light probe engaged and sequentially open connectors or switches, remove parts, etc. until the light goes out or continuity is broken.
6. When the light goes out, the short is between the last two circuit components which were opened.

VOLTAGE

This test determines voltage available from the battery and should be the first step in any electrical troubleshooting procedure after visual inspection. Many electrical problems, especially on computer controlled systems, can be caused by a low state of charge in the battery. Excessive corrosion at the battery cable terminals can cause poor contact that will prevent proper charging and full battery current flow.

1. Set the voltmeter selector switch to the 20V position.
2. Connect the multimeter negative lead to the battery's negative (-) post or terminal and the positive lead to the battery's positive (+) post or terminal.
3. Turn the ignition switch **ON** to provide a load.
4. A well charged battery should register over 12 volts. If the meter reads below 11.5 volts, the battery power may be insufficient to operate the electrical system properly.

VOLTAGE DROP

▶ **See Figure 9**

When current flows through a load, the voltage beyond the load drops. This voltage drop is due to the resistance created by the load and also by small resistances created by corrosion at the connectors and damaged insulation on the wires. The maximum allowable voltage drop under load is critical, especially if there is more than one load in the circuit, since all voltage drops are cumulative.

1. Set the voltmeter selector switch to the 20 volt position.
2. Connect the multimeter negative lead to a good ground.
3. Operate the circuit and check the voltage prior to the first component (load).
4. There should be little or no voltage drop in the circuit prior to the first component. If a voltage drop exists, the wire or connectors in the circuit are suspect.
5. While operating the first component in the circuit, probe the ground side of the component with the positive meter lead and observe the voltage readings. A small voltage drop should be noticed. This voltage drop is caused by the resistance of the component. Repeat the test for each component (load) down the circuit.
6. Repeat the test for each component (load) down the circuit.
7. If a large voltage drop is noticed, the preceding component, wire or connector is suspect.

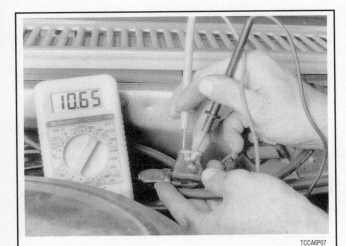

TCCA6P07

Fig. 9 This voltage drop test revealed high resistance (low voltage) in the circuit

RESISTANCE

▶ **See Figures 10 and 11**

❊❊ WARNING

Never use an ohmmeter with power applied to the circuit. The ohmmeter is designed to operate on its own power supply. The normal 12 volt electrical system voltage could damage the meter!

1. Isolate the circuit from the vehicle's power source.
2. Ensure that the ignition key is **OFF** when disconnecting any components or the battery.

TCCA6P08

Fig. 10 Checking the resistance of a coolant temperature sensor with an ohmmeter. Reading is 1.04 kilohms

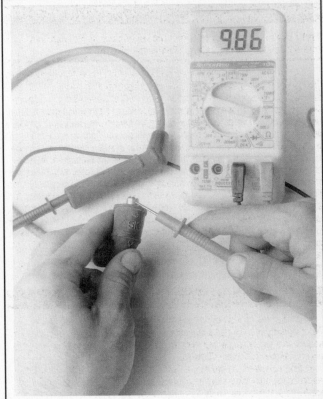

TCCA6P09

Fig. 11 Spark plug wires can be checked for excessive resistance using an ohmmeter

3. Where necessary, also isolate at least one side of the circuit to be checked, in order to avoid reading parallel resistances. Parallel circuit resistances will always give a lower reading than the actual resistance of either of the branches.
4. Connect the meter leads to both sides of the circuit (wire or component) and read the actual measured ohms on the meter scale. Make sure the selector switch is set to the proper ohm scale for the circuit being tested, to avoid misreading the ohmmeter test value.

Wire and Connector Repair

Almost anyone can replace damaged wires, as long as the proper tools and parts are available. Wire and terminals are available to fit almost any need. Even the specialized weatherproof, molded and hard shell connectors are now available from aftermarket suppliers.

Be sure the ends of all the wires are fitted with the proper terminal hardware and connectors. Wrapping a wire around a stud is never a permanent solution and will only cause trouble later. Replace wires one at a time to avoid confusion. Always route wires exactly the same as the factory.

➡**If connector repair is necessary, only attempt it if you have the proper tools. Weatherproof and hard shell connectors require special tools to release the pins inside the connector. Attempting to repair these connectors with conventional hand tools will damage them.**

BATTERY CABLES

Disconnecting the Cables

When working on any electrical component on the vehicle, it is always a good idea to disconnect the negative (-) battery cable. This will prevent potential damage to many sensitive electrical components such as the Engine Control Module (ECM), radio, alternator, etc.

➡**Any time you disengage the battery cables, it is recommended that you disconnect the negative (-) battery cable first. This will prevent your accidentally grounding the positive (+) terminal to the body of the vehicle when disconnecting it, thereby preventing damage to the above mentioned components.**

Before you disconnect the cable(s), first turn the ignition to the **OFF** position. This will prevent a draw on the battery which could cause arcing (electricity trying to ground itself to the body of a vehicle, just like a spark plug jumping the gap) and, of course, damaging some components such as the alternator diodes.

When the battery cable(s) are reconnected (negative cable last), be sure to check that your lights, windshield wipers and other electrically operated safety components are all working correctly. If your vehicle contains an Electronically Tuned Radio (ETR), don't forget to also reset your radio stations. Ditto for the clock.

AIR BAG—GENERATION 1 CORPORATE SYSTEM

General Description

◆ **See Figures 12 and 13**

➡**If your vehicle is a pre-1992 Oldsmobile Delta 88/Eighty Eight equipped with an air bag, turn to the following section on the Oldsmobile Inflatable Restraint (IR) Air Bag System for information.**

The air bag system used on most vehicles covered by this manual is referred to as the Supplemental Inflatable Restraint (SIR) system. The air bag is designed to deploy when the vehicle is involved in a front end collision of sufficient force, up to 30 degrees off center line of the vehicle. The steering column still continues to be collapsible, the same as on vehicles without an air bag.

1992–99 Bonneville, Eighty Eight, and LeSabre models use GM's Generation 1 Corporate (GEN 1) Supplemental Inflatable Restraint system, also simply referred to as the SIR system. This system has an energy reserve, which can store a large enough electrical charge to deploy the air bag for 10 minutes after the battery has been disconnected or damaged. This system must be disabled if any service is to be performed on the SIR system or steering wheel assembly.

➡**Throughout this manual, you may find air bag systems referred to as Supplemental Inflatable Restraint (SIR), Inflatable Restraint (IR) system, or even Supplemental Restraint System (SRS). In this book, SIR is the Generation 1 system and IR is the Oldsmobile developed Inflatable Restraint system.**

Many later model vehicles may be equipped with a driver and a passenger side air bag. When a frontal crash occurs of sufficient force, up to 30° off the centerline of the vehicle, a bag is deployed from both the center of the steering wheel and from above the instrument panel compartment on the passenger's side.

The system has an energy reserve, which can store a large enough electrical charge to deploy the air bag(s) for up to ten minutes after the battery has been disconnected or damaged. The system **MUST** be disabled before any service is performed on or around SIR components or SIR wiring.

The GEN 1 system requires the replacement of all sensors and inflator module after a deployment. This system has self-diagnostic ability. Although some diagnostic codes can be obtained by counting flashes of the INFLATABLE RESTRAINT lamp, other codes can only be obtained or cleared by using a scan tool.

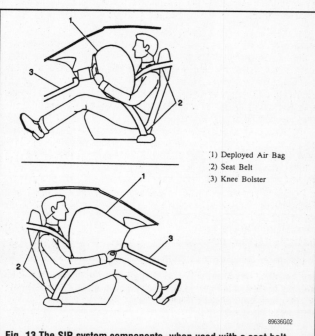

:1) Deployed Air Bag
:2) Seat Belt
:3) Knee Bolster

Fig. 13 The SIR system components, when used with a seat belt, can provide additional protection during an accident

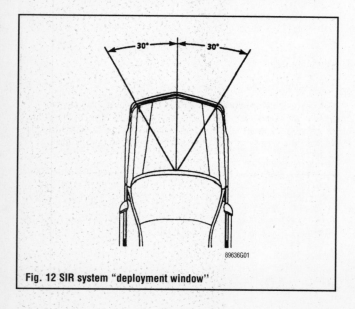

Fig. 12 SIR system "deployment window"

SYSTEM OPERATION

Except Vehicles With Dual Air Bags

The SIR system contains a deployment loop and a Diagnostic Energy Reserve Module (DERM). The function of the deployment loop is to supply current through the inflator module in the steering wheel, which will cause air bag deployment during a severe accident. The DERM supplies the necessary power, even if the battery has been damaged.

The deployment loop is made up of the arming sensors, coil assembly, inflator module and the discriminating sensors. The inflator module is only supplied sufficient current to deploy the air bag, when the arming sensors and at least one of the discriminating sensors close simultaneously. The function of the DERM is to supply the deployment loop a 36 Volt Loop Reserve (36VLR) to assure air bag deployment for seconds after ignition voltage is lost during an accident.

The DERM in conjunction with the resistors make it possible to detect circuit and component faults within the deployment loop. If the voltages monitored by the DERM fall outside expected limits, the DERM will indicate a fault code through the storage of a malfunction code and turning ON the INFLATABLE RESTRAINT lamp.

Vehicles With Dual Air Bags

The DERM along with both the driver and passenger deployment loops are the main portion of the SIR system. Each deployment loop's main function is to supply current through its inflator module, allowing air bag deployment in the event of a frontal crash severe enough to warrant deployment.

A dual pole arming sensor, coil assembly (driver's side only), inflator module and 2 discriminating sensors make up each deployment loop. The dual pole arming sensor switches power to the inflator module on each deployment loop's high side. Either discriminating sensor can supply ground to the inflator modules on the loops' low side. The inflator modules are supplied with sufficient current to deploy only when the dual pole arming sensor and at least 1 discriminating sensor close simultaneously.

SYSTEM COMPONENTS

▶ See Figure 14

Diagnostic Energy Reserve Module (DERM)

➡**The DERM is also called the Sensing and Diagnostic Module (SDM) on later vehicles; however it serves the same purpose.**

The DERM is designed to perform 5 main functions. It maintains an energy reserve of 36 volts for several seconds. The DERM performs diagnostic monitoring of the SIR system and records malfunction codes, which can be obtained from a hand scan tool or the INFLATABLE RESTRAINT lamp. It warns the driver of a malfunction by controlling the INFLATABLE RESTRAINT lamp and keeps a record of the SIR system during a vehicle accident. Air bag deployment can still take place without the DERM connected, if adequate voltage is present at the arming sensor or dual pole sensor.

The DERM is connected to the system with a 24-way connector. This harness has a shorting bar across certain terminals in the contact areas. The shorting bar connects the INFLATABLE RESTRAINT lamp input to ground when the DERM is disconnected causing the lamp to light when the ignition switch is **ON**.

The DERM does not need to be replaced after each air bag deployment. After 4 deployments the DERM will register a Code 52. The Code 52 informs that the accident memory is full and the DERM must be replaced.

Inflatable Restraint Indicator

The INFLATABLE RESTRAINT or AIR BAG indicator lamp is used to verify the DERM operation by flashing 7–9 times when the ignition is first turned **ON**. It is also used to warn the driver of a SIR malfunction. For certain tests it can provide diagnostic information by flashing the fault code when the fault code diagnostic mode is enabled.

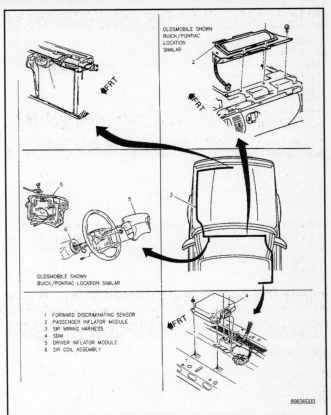

1 FORWARD DISCRIMINATING SENSOR
2 PASSENGER INFLATOR MODULE
3 SIR WIRING HARNESS
4 SDM
5 DRIVER INFLATOR MODULE
6 SIR COIL ASSEMBLY

Fig. 14 Typical SIR component locations—1996 vehicle shown, others similar

Discriminating Sensor

There can be 2, 3 or 4 discriminating sensors. The forward, left or right sensors are located in the engine compartment. The passenger sensor, if equipped, is located behind the right side of the instrument panel or the center of the console. These sensors are calibrated to close with velocity changes which are severe enough to warrant air bag deployment.

The sensors consist of a sensing element, a normally open switch and a diagnostic resistor. The diagnostic resistor is wired in parallel with the switch within each sensor. They provide a ground for current to pass during normal non-deployment operation. The DERM measures this current to determine component faults.

When the arming sensor is located in the same housing as the passenger compartment discriminating sensor, the assembly is referred known as a dual sensor.

Arming Sensor

This sensor is found on vehicles with a single air bag.

➡**All sensors are specifically calibrated to each series vehicle and keyed to the mounting brackets. Great care must be taken to mount the correct sensors on the vehicle being serviced. The sensors, mounting brackets and wiring harness must never be modified from original design.**

The arming sensor is a protective switch in the power feed side of the deployment loop. It is calibrated to close at low level velocity changes. This insures that the inflator module is connected to the 36VLR output of the DERM or ignition 1 voltage.

The sensor consists of a sensing element, normally open switch a diagnostic resistor and 2 steering diodes. The resistor is connected in parallel with the switch and allows a small amount of current to flow through the deployment loop during normal non-deployment operation. The DERM monitors this voltage to determine component faults.

The arming sensor is located in the same housing as the passenger compartment discriminating sensor. The assembly is referred to as the dual sensor and is located behind the right side of the instrument panel.

Passenger Compartment Discriminating Sensor

This sensor can either be part of the dual sensor or can be a separate sensor altogether.

Dual Sensor

On single air bag vehicles so equipped, the dual sensor is a sensor that combines the arming sensor and the passenger compartment discriminating sensor into the same unit.

Dual Pole Arming Sensor

This sensor is on vehicles with dual air bags. It is located behind the left side of the instrument panel above the steering column.

The dual pole arming sensor is a dual pole switch located in the driver/passenger deployment loop's power feed side (high side). It consists of a sensing element that closes the normally open dual switch contacts when the vehicle velocity changes at a rate indicating potential need for deployment.

SIR Coil Assembly

▶ **See Figure 15**

The coil assembly consists of 2 current carrying coils. They are attached to the steering column and allow rotation of the steering wheel, while maintaining continuous contact of the deployment loop through the inflator module.

There is a shorting bar on the lower steering column connector, which connects the SIR coil to the SIR harness. The shorting bar shorts the circuit when the connector is disconnected. The circuit to the module is shorted in this way to help prevent unwanted deployment of the air bag, while performing service.

Inflator Module

SINGLE AIR BAG

▶ **See Figures 16 and 17**

The inflator module is located in the steering wheel hub under the vinyl trim. It includes the air bag, inflator and initiator. When the vehicle is in an accident, current is passed through the deployment loop. This current passing through the deployment loop ignites the squib in the inflator module. The gas produced rapidly inflates the air bag.

There is a shorting bar on the lower steering column connector, which connects the SIR coil to the SIR harness. The shorting bar shorts the circuit when the connector is disconnected. The circuit to the module is shorted in this way to help prevent unwanted deployment of the air bag, while performing service.

DUAL AIR BAGS

▶ **See Figures 14, 18 and 19**

The 1993 Bonneville SSE and SSEi, and all 1994–99 vehicles are equipped with a driver/passenger SIR system which has 2 inflator modules. The driver inflator module is located on the steering wheel, while the passenger inflator module is mounted in the instrument panel above the instrument panel compartment. Each module includes the air bag, inflator and initiator. When the vehicle is in a frontal crash of sufficient force to close the dual pole arming sensor and at least one discriminating sensor simultaneously, current flows through both deployment loops. The current passing through the initiators ignites the material in the inflator modules and the air bags are inflated.

There is a shorting bar on the driver inflator module side of the upper steering column connector, which connects the SIR coil to the driver inflator module. The shorting bar shorts the driver inflator module circuit when the SIR coil connector is disconnected. The circuit to the module is shorted in this way

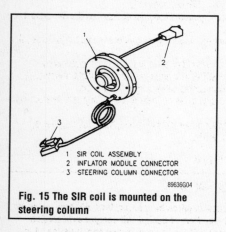

1 SIR COIL ASSEMBLY
2 INFLATOR MODULE CONNECTOR
3 STEERING COLUMN CONNECTOR

89636G04

Fig. 15 The SIR coil is mounted on the steering column

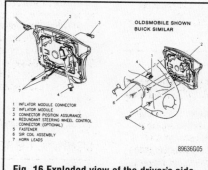

OLDSMOBILE SHOWN
BUICK SIMILAR

1 INFLATOR MODULE CONNECTOR
2 INFLATOR MODULE
3 CONNECTOR POSITION ASSURANCE
4 REDUNDANT STEERING WHEEL CONTROL CONNECTOR (OPTIONAL)
5 FASTENER
6 SIR COIL ASSEMBLY
7 HORN LEADS

89636G05

Fig. 16 Exploded view of the driver's side SIR inflator module—Oldsmobile and Buick shown

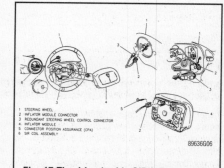

1 STEERING WHEEL
2 INFLATOR MODULE CONNECTOR
3 REDUNDANT STEERING WHEEL CONTROL CONNECTOR
4 INFLATOR MODULE
5 CONNECTOR POSITION ASSURANCE (CPA)
6 SIR COIL ASSEMBLY

89636G06

Fig. 17 The driver's side SIR inflator module is mounted to the steering wheel—Pontiac shown

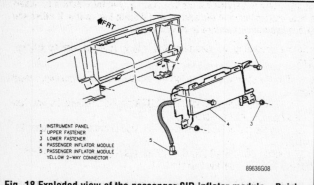

1 INSTRUMENT PANEL
2 UPPER FASTENER
3 LOWER FASTENER
4 PASSENGER INFLATOR MODULE
5 PASSENGER INFLATOR MODULE YELLOW 2-WAY CONNECTOR

89636G08

Fig. 18 Exploded view of the passenger SIR inflator module—Buick shown

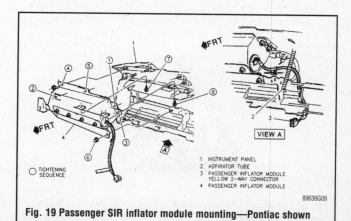

VIEW A

1 INSTRUMENT PANEL
2 ASPIRATOR TUBE
3 PASSENGER INFLATOR MODULE YELLOW 2-WAY CONNECTOR
4 PASSENGER INFLATOR MODULE

TIGHTENING SEQUENCE

89636G09

Fig. 19 Passenger SIR inflator module mounting—Pontiac shown

to help prevent unwanted deployment of the air bag while performing service.

There is also a shorting bar on the passenger inflator module connector, which connects the SIR wiring harness to the passenger inflator module. The shorting bar shorts the passenger inflator module circuit whenever this connector is disconnected. The circuit to the module is shorted in this way to help prevent unwanted deployment of the air bag while performing service.

Resistor Module

This component is found on vehicles with a single air bag. The resistor module is in the SIR harness between the inflator module and DERM. This allows the DERM to monitor the deployment loop for faults and also allows the DERM to detect if the air bag has been deployed.

The resistors in the resistor module are balanced with the resistors in the arming and discriminating sensors to allow the DERM to monitor voltage drops across the circuits. These resistors also help reduce the possibility of unwanted deployment in the case of wiring harness damage.

Knee Bolster

The knee bolster is used to absorb energy and control the driver's forward movement during an accident by limiting leg movement.

Fuse Panel

Vehicles with dual air bags have a specific fuse panel located in the lower instrument panel trim pad. It is hinged to swing out for easy access.

➡**When closing the swing out fuse panel, the lever that was pulled to open it must also be pulled when closing it. Failure to do so may damage the latch mechanism and prevent the fuse panel from staying closed.**

Wiring Harness and Connectors

The wiring harness and connectors for the SIR system are of special design. Any wiring repairs should be done using tool kit J-38125, or equivalent. Always use the crimp and seal splice sleeves contained in this wiring repair kit. If damage is done to a component pigtail the component must be replaced.

SERVICE PRECAUTIONS

▶ **See Figure 20**

❊❊ CAUTION

To avoid personal injury when servicing the SIR system or components in the immediate area, do not use electrical test equipment such as battery or AC powered voltmeter, ohmmeter, etc. or any type of tester other than specified. Do not use a non-powered probe tester. Instructions must be followed in detail to avoid deployment.

• When performing service around the SIR system components or wiring, the SIR system **MUST** be disabled. Failure to do so could result in possible air bag deployment, personal injury or unneeded SIR system repairs.
• When carrying a live inflator module, make sure that the bag and trim cover are pointed away from you. Never carry the inflator module by the wires or

89636G11

Fig. 20 This symbol indicates that a component is sensitive to Electrostatic Discharge (ESD)

connector on the underside of the module. In case of accidental deployment, the bag will then deploy with minimal chance of injury.

• When placing a live inflator module on a bench or other surface, always face the bag and trim cover up, away from the surface.
• Never disconnect any electrical connection with the ignition switch **ON** unless instructed to do so in a test.
• Always wear a grounded wrist static strap when servicing any control module or component labeled with a Electrostatic Discharge (ESD) sensitive device symbol.
• Avoid touching module connector pins.
• Leave new components and modules in the shipping package until ready to install them.
• Always touch a vehicle ground after sliding across a vehicle seat or walking across vinyl or carpeted floors to avoid static charge damage.
• The DERM can maintain sufficient voltage to cause a deployment for up to 10 minute, even if the battery is disconnected.
• Sensor mounting and wiring must never be modified.
• Never strike or jar a sensor, or deployment could occur.
• Never power up the SIR system when any sensor is not rigidly attached to the vehicle.
• The inflator module is to be stored and shipped under DOT E-8236 flammable solid regulations.
• The inflator module must be deployed before it is discarded.
• After deployment the air bag surface may contain sodium hydroxide dust. Always wear gloves and safety glasses when handling the assembly. Wash hands with mild soap and water afterwards.
• A Code 51 requires, at minimum, replacement of the arming sensor, passenger compartment discriminating sensor, forward discriminating sensor and the inflator module.
• Any visible damage to sensors requires component replacement.
• Wire and connector repair must be performed using kit J-38125-A, or equivalent. Use special crimping tools, a heat torch and seals.
• Absolutely no wire connector, or terminal repair is to be attempted on the arming sensor, passenger compartment discriminating sensor, forward discriminating sensor, inflator module or SIR coil assembly
• Never use a battery or AC powered test light or tester on the SIR system or deployment could occur.
• Never use an ohmmeter on the SIR system, unless instructed to do so, or deployment could occur.
• Never bake dry paint on vehicle or allow to exceed temperatures over 300°F, without disabling the SIR system and removing the inflator module.
• Sensors are not interchangeable between models or years.
• Never allow welding cables to lay on, near or across any vehicle electrical wiring.
• Avoid extension cords for power tools or droplights to lay on, near or across any vehicle electrical wiring.

DISARMING THE SIR SYSTEM

▶ **See Figures 21, 22, 23 and 24**

➡**Proper and safe operation requires the sensor, brackets and wiring to be installed in the exact locations of design. All components service must be exactly aligned and tighten to exact torque specification. It is not advisable to service the air bag system. The information provided is to help you understand the system and disarm the system if other non-air bag system service are to be performed.**

➡**Before beginning the disarming procedure, read all service precautions.**

1. Turn the steering wheel so that the vehicle's wheels are pointing straight ahead.
   a. Turn the ignition switch to the **LOCK** position, remove the key, then disconnect the negative battery cable.
2. Wrap the end of the battery cable with tape to avoid possible terminal contact.
3. Remove the AIRBAG fuse (fuse #7 for 1992–93 vehicles, or #1C for 1994–99 vehicles) from the fuse block.

➡**With the AIRBAG fuse removed and the ignition in the RUN position, the AIR BAG warning lamp illuminates. This is a normal operation and does not indicate a system malfunction.**

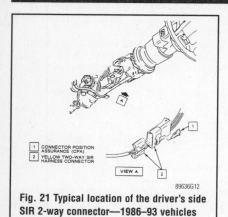

Fig. 21 Typical location of the driver's side SIR 2-way connector—1986–93 vehicles

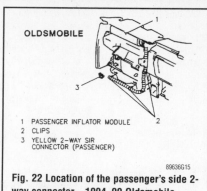

OLDSMOBILE

1 PASSENGER INFLATOR MODULE
2 CLIPS
3 YELLOW 2-WAY SIR CONNECTOR (PASSENGER)

89636G15

Fig. 22 Location of the passenger's side 2-way connector—1994–99 Oldsmobile shown

BUICK

1 PASSENGER INFLATOR MODULE
2 YELLOW 2-WAY SIR CONNECTOR (PASSENGER)

89636G16

Fig. 23 Passenger's side SIR connector location—1994–99 Buick shown

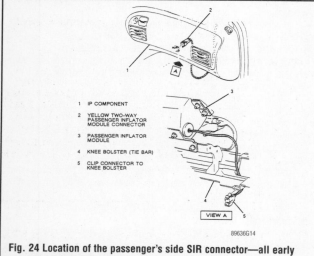

1 IP COMPONENT
2 YELLOW TWO-WAY PASSENGER INFLATOR MODULE CONNECTOR
3 PASSENGER INFLATOR MODULE
4 KNEE BOLSTER (TIE BAR)
5 CLIP CONNECTOR TO KNEE BOLSTER

VIEW A

89636G14

Fig. 24 Location of the passenger's side SIR connector—all early and 1994–99 Pontiac models

4. Remove the left side sound insulator/steering column filler panel and courtesy lamp, as needed.
5. Remove the Connector Positive Assurance (CPA) lockpin on the yellow 2-way connector at the base of the steering column.
6. Unplug the yellow 2-way SIR connector, located near the base of the steering column.

7. If equipped with a passenger side air bag, remove the right side instrument panel sound insulator to access the connector. Remove the CPA lockpin, then unplug the yellow 2-way passenger inflator module connector. The connector is located at the base of the right side instrument panel, clipped to the knee bolster (tie bar and steering column filler).
8. If necessary, connect the negative battery cable. The system can now be safely serviced.

ENABLING THE SYSTEM

→Before beginning the enabling procedure, read all service precautions.

1. Make sure the ignition switch is in the **LOCK** position, then remove the key from the ignition.
2. If not already done, disconnect the negative battery cable and tape the end of cable to avoid possible terminal contact.
3. If equipped with a passenger's side air bag, attach the yellow 2-way connector and the CA to the inflatable restraint instrument panel module pigtail. Install the right side instrument panel sound insulator.
4. Reconnect the SIR 2-way yellow connector at the base of the steering column. Reinstall the CPA lockpin on the yellow connector.
5. Install the left side sound insulator/steering column filler panel and lamp, if removed.
6. Install the SIR fuse in the fuse panel.
7. Connect the battery cable.
8. Staying well away from both air bags, turn the ignition switch to the **RUN** position and check that the INFLATABLE RESTRAINT/AIR BAG lamp flashes 7–9 times and then goes out.

AIR BAG—OLDSMOBILE INFLATABLE RESTRAINT (IR) SYSTEM

General Description

→Throughout this manual, you may find air bag systems referred to as Supplemental Inflatable Restraint (SIR), Inflatable Restraint (IR) system, or even Supplemental Restraint System (SRS). In this book, SIR is the Generation 1 system and IR is the Oldsmobile developed Inflatable Restraint system.

This air bag system, referred to as the Inflatable Restraint (IR) system, was only used on pre-1992 Oldsmobile Delta 88/Eighty Eight models. The air bag is designed to deploy when the vehicle is involved in a front end collision of sufficient force, up to 30 degrees off center line of the vehicle. The steering column still continues to be collapsible, the same as vehicle without an air bag.

This system has an energy reserve, which can store a large enough electrical charge to deploy the air bag for a period of 15 seconds after the battery has been disconnected or damaged. This system must be disabled if any service is to be performed on the IR system or steering wheel assembly.

The system consists of a control module known as the Passenger Compartment Sensor/Diagnostic Module (PCSDM), a power supply module, Energy Reserve Module (ERM), steering wheel or inflator module, a coil assembly that assures electrical continuity to the inflator module as the steering wheel is turned, forward sensor, arming sensor, and an indicator lamp. Diagnostics are carried out by the Passenger Compartment Sensor/Diagnostic Module (PCSDM).

SYSTEM COMPONENTS

♦ See Figures 25 and 26

Passenger Compartment Sensor/Diagnostic Module (PCSDM)

The PCSDM contains the passenger compartment sensor and the diagnostic module. The diagnostic module processes the vehicle deceleration and forward sensor signal to determine if deployment is necessary. A deployment signal is sent to the inflator module when the forward sensor or when passenger compartment sensor closes and the arming sensor closes at the same time. This module also controls the indicator lamp.

This system can store codes, but they must be read with tester J-36884, or equivalent. This system utilizes the indicator lamp to warn of a problem, but flash code diagnostics are not possible.

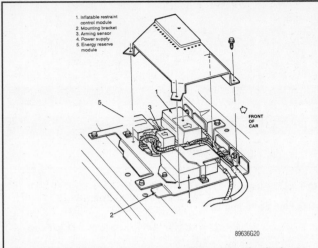

1. Inflatable restraint control module
2. Mounting bracket
3. Arming sensor
4. Power supply
5. Energy reserve module

89636G20

Fig. 25 Oldsmobile IR system components located under the front seat

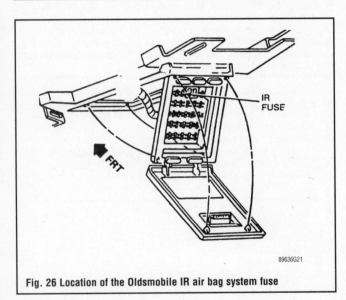

IR FUSE

FRT

89636G21

Fig. 26 Location of the Oldsmobile IR air bag system fuse

Arming and Forward Sensors

All sensors are specifically calibrated to each series vehicle and keyed to the mounting brackets. Great care must be taken to mount the correct sensors on the vehicle being serviced. The sensors, mounting brackets and wiring harness must never be modified from original design.

The forward sensor is a normally open switch. In an accident, the sensor closes and the electrical circuit is complete. If the forward sensor and the arming sensor close at the same time the air bag will deploy.

The arming sensor is a normally open switch that closes during deceleration encountered in an accident. The arming sensor is wired in series with the steering module. A resistor is connected in parallel with the switch and allows a small amount of current to flow through the circuit for diagnostic purposes.

Power Supply Module

The power supply module provides a boosted voltage to the IR system to ensure deployment during low voltage conditions, perform limited internal diagnostics and monitor the integrity of the IR wiring and 8-terminal connector.

Energy Reserve Module

The reserve module provides sufficient electrical power to deploy the air bag even if the vehicle battery is damaged or disconnected.

Inflator Module

The inflator module, consists of the air bag, electrical initiator and inflator assembly. If an accident occurs, the inflatable bag is deployed by a gas producing generator. The trim cover opens at the seam as the bag is deployed.

Indicator Lamp

The red INFLATABLE RESTRAINT lamp will light for 5–15 seconds when the ignition is turned **ON**. This informs the driver that the system is functioning properly. If the lamp does not operate correctly, this indicates an IR system fault and the system should be checked.

Fuse Panel

Some vehicles with have a specific fuse panel located in the lower instrument panel trim pad. It is hinged to swing out for easy access. On other models the IR fuse is located with the other fuses.

Knee Bolster

The knee bolster is used to absorb energy and control the driver's forward movement during an accident by limiting leg movement.

Wiring Harness and Connectors

The wiring harness and connectors for the IR system are of special design. Any wiring repairs should be done using tool kit J-38125, or equivalent. Always use the crimp and seal splice sleeves contained in this wiring repair kit. If damage is done to a component pigtail the component must be replaced.

The Initiator circuit has a special yellow shorting bar connectors that help prevent accidental deployment during service. The IR wire harness components are part of the body wiring harness assembly. Sections of harness which include more than a 1 IR wire are wrapped in yellow tape.

SERVICE PRECAUTIONS

♦ See Figure 20

Please refer to the Generation 1 Corporate Air Bag System text, earlier in this section, for all applicable precautions other than the following:
• If the vehicle is equipped with an optional passenger power, do not connect the seat power feed harness to the IR diagnostic module terminal connector, since damage to the IR diagnostic module may result.
• Follow repair and removal and installation procedures in the correct order to avoid unnecessary repairs. Tighten fasteners to specifications.

DISARMING THE IR SYSTEM

♦ See Figure 26

➡**Proper and safe operation requires the sensor, brackets and wiring to be installed in the exact locations of design. The information provided is to help you understand the system and disarm the system if other non-air bag system service are to be performed. Before beginning the disabling procedure, read all service precautions.**

1. Turn the steering wheel so wheels are facing straight ahead and turn the ignition switch to the **LOCK** position. Remove the key from the ignition.
2. Disconnect the negative battery cable and tape the end of cable to avoid possible terminal contact.

✵✵ CAUTION

To avoid personal injury, wait at least 30 minutes after disconnecting the battery cable before servicing the IR system on 1986–91 Delta 88/Eighty Eight models. Servicing the IR system during that period of time may result in personal injury.

3. Remove the IR fuse from the fuse block.
4. Remove the left side sound insulator and lamp.
5. Disconnect the IR inflator connector from the base of the steering column.
6. If necessary, connect the negative battery cable. The system is now safe for servicing.

ENABLING THE SYSTEM

➡**Before beginning the enabling procedure, read all service precautions.**

1. Disconnect the negative battery cable and tape the end of cable to avoid possible terminal contact. Remove the IR fuse.

HEATING AND AIR CONDITIONING

Refer to Section 1 for discharging and charging of the air conditioning system.

The heating system provides heating, ventilation and defrosting for the windshield and side windows. The heater core is a heat exchanger supplied with coolant from the engine cooling system. Temperature is controlled by the temperature valve which moves an air door that directs air flow through the heater core for more heat or bypasses the heater core for less heat.

Vacuum actuators control the mode doors which direct air flow to the outlet ducts. The mode selector on the control panel directs engine vacuum to the actuators. The position of the mode doors determines whether air flows from the floor, panel, defrost or panel and defrost ducts (bi-level mode).

Blower Motor

REMOVAL & INSTALLATION

▶ **See Figure 27**

1. Disconnect the negative battery cable.
2. If necessary, tag and disconnect the number 2, 4 and 6 spark plug wires from the ignition coil and move the coil out of the way.
3. For 1993–99 vehicles, remove the nuts and cross brace bar.
4. Detach the electrical connections from the blower motor.
5. Disconnect the cooling tube from the blower motor.
6. Unfasten the screws securing the blower motor to the blower module assembly.
7. Remove the blower motor and fan assembly from the module.
8. If necessary, unfasten the nut attaching the fan to the blower motor shaft, then pull the fan from the blower motor.

To install:

9. If the fan was removed from the motor, position the fan on the shaft, then install the retaining nut. Tighten the nut to 12 inch lbs. (1.4 Nm).
10. Position the blower motor and fan assembly to the module, then install the retaining screws. Tighten to 5 inch lbs. (0.6 Nm).
11. Connect the cooling tube to the blower motor.
12. Attach the electrical connector to the blower motor.
13. On 1993–98 vehicles, install the cross brace bar and retaining nuts. Tighten the nuts to 18 ft. lbs. (25 Nm).
14. If removed, install the coil and connect the spark plug wires, as tagged during removal.
15. Connect the negative battery cable.

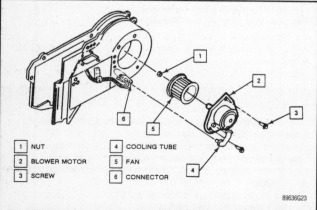

1	NUT	4	COOLING TUBE
2	BLOWER MOTOR	5	FAN
3	SCREW	6	CONNECTOR

89636G23

Fig. 27 The blower motor and fan assembly is mounted in the heater and A/C module, and is accessible from the engine compartment

2. Reconnect the IR inflator connector at the base of the steering column, if disconnected.
3. Install the sound insulator and lamp, if removed.
4. Install the IR fuse and connect the battery cable.

Heater Core

REMOVAL & INSTALLATION

1986–91 Vehicles

▶ **See Figures 28 and 29**

1. Disconnect the negative battery cable. Drain the coolant into a clean container for reuse.

✳✳ CAUTION

When draining the coolant, keep in mind that cats and dogs are attracted by ethylene glycol antifreeze, and are quite likely to drink any that is left in an uncovered container or in puddles on the ground. This will prove fatal in sufficient quantity. Always drain the coolant into a sealable container. Coolant should be reused unless it is contaminated or several years old.

2. Remove the right side sound insulator. Remove the underdash and splash cover covering the heater hoses in the engine compartment.
   a. Remove the center and lower instrument panel trim plates.
3. Disconnect the heater hoses from the heater core. You may need tool J-37097 or equivalent hose clamp removal pliers in order to remove the hoses.
4. If equipped with electronic climate control, perform the following steps:
   a. Disconnect the wires and the hose from the programmer.
   b. Remove the programmer linkage cover and linkage.

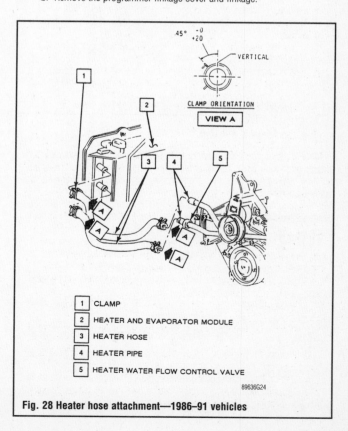

1	CLAMP
2	HEATER AND EVAPORATOR MODULE
3	HEATER HOSE
4	HEATER PIPE
5	HEATER WATER FLOW CONTROL VALVE

89636G24

Fig. 28 Heater hose attachment—1986–91 vehicles

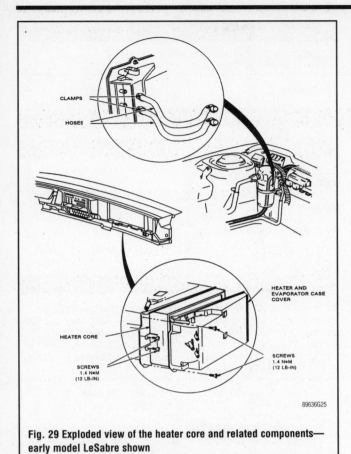

Fig. 29 Exploded view of the heater core and related components—early model LeSabre shown

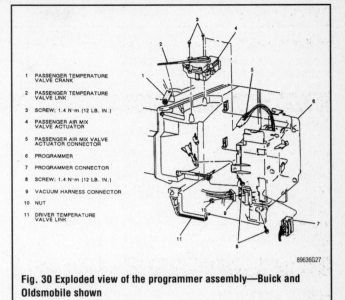

Fig. 30 Exploded view of the programmer assembly—Buick and Oldsmobile shown

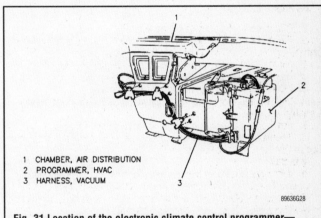

1 CHAMBER, AIR DISTRIBUTION
2 PROGRAMMER, HVAC
3 HARNESS, VACUUM

89636G28

Fig. 31 Location of the electronic climate control programmer—Pontiac shown

c. Remove the programmer mounting bolts and the programmer.

5. Remove the heater core cover screws, then remove the cover.

6. Unfasten the heater core retainers, then remove the heater core assembly.

To install:

7. Install the heater core assembly and heater core cover, securing with the retainers. Tighten to 12 inch lbs. (1.4 Nm).

8. If equipped with electronic climate control, perform the following:

a. Install the programmer and secure with the mounting bolts.

b. Install the programmer linkage and linkage cover.

c. Connect the wires and the hose to the programmer.

9. Attach the heater hoses.

10. Install the center and lower instrument panel trim plates.

11. Connect the negative battery cable.

12. Fill cooling system and check for leaks. Start the engine and allow to come to normal operating temperature. Recheck for leaks. Top-up the coolant.

13. Install the right side sound insulator and any trim panels that were removed and the splash shields.

1992–99 Vehicles

▶ **See Figures 30 and 31**

1. Properly disable the SIR system, as outlined in this section.

2. Drain the cooling system into a suitable container.

3. Using a suitable pair of hose clamp pliers, unfasten the clamps, then disconnect the heater hoses from the heater core.

4. If equipped with manual climate control, remove the A/C temperature valve actuator as follows:

a. Remove the instrument panel assembly, as outlined in Section 10 of this manual.

b. Remove the temperature valve link rod from the temperature valve by snapping it out.

c. Detach the electrical connector from the A/C temperature valve actuator.

d. Unfasten the retaining screws, then remove the A/C temperature valve actuator (passenger air mix valve actuator).

5. If equipped with electronic climate control, remove the programmer as outlined in the following steps.

6. For Buick and Oldsmobile, remove the programmer as follows:

a. Open the glove compartment, disengage the stops and swing the door down.

b. Detach the electrical and vacuum connectors.

c. Remove the driver temperature valve link rod.

d. Unfasten the screws and remove the programmer from the vehicle.

7. For Pontiac, remove the programmer as follows:

a. Unbolt the PCM from its attaching bracket and allow to hang by its wires.

b. Detach the vacuum and side electrical connector from the programmer.

c. Remove the temperature valve link rod by reaching up through the PCM bracket to get to the rod.

d. Unfasten the programmer attaching screws.

e. Remove the temperature valve actuator connector by reaching up through the PCM bracket to get to the connector.

f. Remove the programmer from the vehicle.

8. Remove the heater core cover screws, then remove the cover.

9. Unfasten the heater core retainers, then remove the heater core assembly.

To install:

10. Position the heater core in the vehicle and install the retaining screws. Tighten the screws 12 inch lbs. (1.4 Nm).

11. Install the heater core cover and attaching screws. Tighten the screws to 12 inch lbs. (1.4 Nm).

12. For Buick and Oldsmobile, if equipped with electronic climate control, perform the following:

a. Place the programmer in position and secure with the retaining screws. Tighten the screws to 12 inch lbs. (1.4 Nm).

b. Attach the electrical and vacuum connectors.

c. Adjust the valve link rod by starting the vehicle, setting the temperature to 90° F (32°C). Allow at least 45 seconds for the programmer motor to move the output crank to its full hot position. Move the temperature valve to the full hot position and snap the valve link into the retainer on the output crank.

d. Install the glove compartment door by inserting and pushing forward.

e. For Pontiac, if equipped with electronic climate control, perform the following:

f. Place the programmer in position.

g. Reach up through the PCM bracket and attach the temperature valve actuator connector.

h. Install the programmer attaching screws and tighten to 12 inch lbs. (1.4 Nm).

i. Attach the electrical and vacuum connectors.

j. Attach the temperature valve link rod to the air mix valve.

k. Adjust the valve link rod by starting the vehicle, setting the temperature to 90°F (32°C). Allow at least 45 seconds for the programmer motor to move the output crank to its full hot position. Move the temperature valve to the full hot position and snap the valve link into the retainer on the output crank.

l. Position the PCM to the bracket and secure with the mounting bolts.

13. If equipped with manual climate control, install the A/C temperature valve actuator as follows:

a. Position the actuator and secure with the retaining screws. Tighten the screws to 12 inch lbs. (1.4 Nm).

b. Attach the electrical connector to the actuator.

➡**Before connecting the temperature valve link rod during installation, you must adjust the rod.**

c. Adjust the temperature valve link rod by starting the vehicle, setting the fan to HIGH and the temperature to full hot. Allow at least 45 seconds for the A/C temperature valve actuator to move to the full hot position. Move the temperature valve to the full hot position, then snap the temperature valve link rod into the temperature valve.

d. Install the instrument panel assembly, as outlined in Section 10 of this manual.

14. Connect the heater hoses to the core, making sure the clamps are in the proper position.

15. If equipped enable the SIR system.

16. Connect the negative battery cable.

17. Fill cooling system and check for leaks. Start the engine and allow to come to normal operating temperature. Recheck for leaks and top off the coolant.

Air Conditioning Components

REMOVAL & INSTALLATION

Repair or service of air conditioning components is not covered by this manual, because of the risk of personal injury or death, and because of the legal ramifications of servicing these components without the proper EPA certification and experience. Cost, personal injury or death, environmental damage, and legal considerations (such as the fact that it is a federal crime to vent refrigerant into the atmosphere), dictate that the A/C components on your vehicle should be serviced only by a Motor Vehicle Air Conditioning (MVAC) trained, and EPA certified automotive technician.

➡**If your vehicle's A/C system uses R-12 refrigerant and is in need of recharging, the A/C system can be converted over to R-134a refrigerant (less environmentally harmful and expensive). Refer to Section 1 for additional information on R-12 to R-134a conversions, and for additional considerations dealing with your vehicle's A/C system.**

Control Cables

REMOVAL & INSTALLATION

▶ **See Figure 32**

1. Disconnect the negative battery cable.
2. Remove the heater and A/C control panel.
3. Lower the glove compartment to gain access to the control cable turnbuckle.
4. Remove the right sound insulator.
5. If necessary, unsnap the retainers from the ashtray and instrument panel brace.
6. Remove the push-on retainer, then disconnect temperature control cable from the heater and A/C control module.

To install:

7. Install the control cable and the push-on retainer.
8. Snap the cable into the connect brace.
9. Adjust the cable.
10. Install the sound insulator and glove compartment.

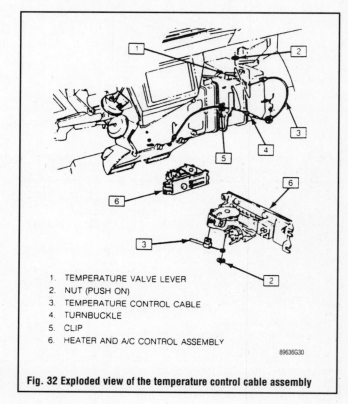

1. TEMPERATURE VALVE LEVER
2. NUT (PUSH ON)
3. TEMPERATURE CONTROL CABLE
4. TURNBUCKLE
5. CLIP
6. HEATER AND A/C CONTROL ASSEMBLY

89636G30

Fig. 32 Exploded view of the temperature control cable assembly

ADJUSTMENT

▶ **See Figure 32**

1. Disconnect the negative battery cable.
2. Remove the right sound insulator.
3. Lower the glove compartment to gain access to the control cable turnbuckle.
4. Move the control to full cold position. Adjust the turnbuckle until the temperature valve just comes to a stop on the left.
5. Move the control to full hot and check that valve is held against the right side. If not, re-adjust the turnbuckle until the valve just stops against the right side.
6. Always recheck full cold to make sure the valve is tight against the stop on the left.
7. Install the sound insulator and glove compartment.

Control Panel

REMOVAL & INSTALLATION

❊❊ CAUTION

Some vehicles are equipped with the Supplemental Inflatable Restraint (SIR) or air bag system. The SIR system must be disabled before performing service on or around SIR system components, steering column, instrument panel components, wiring and sensors. Failure to follow safety and disabling procedures could result in accidental air bag deployment, possible personal injury and unnecessary SIR system repairs.

1986–93 Vehicles

▶ See Figures 33, 34 and 35

1. If equipped with air bags, disable the SIR system.
2. Disconnect the negative battery cable.
3. Remove the center trim panel by carefully prying it off.
4. Remove the control panel retaining screws/bolts.
5. Pull the assembly out slightly in order to access the rear of the unit.
6. Detach the electrical and vacuum connectors and the temperature cable from the rear of the control assembly.
7. Remove the heater and A/C control assembly from the vehicle.

To install:
8. Connect the temperature cable to the control assembly.
9. Attach the electrical connectors and vacuum lines to the control assembly.
10. Place the assembly in position and secure with the retaining screws.
11. Install the center instrument panel trim.

12. Connect the negative battery cable.
13. If equipped with air bags, enable the SIR system.

1994–99 Vehicles

BUICK

▶ See Figure 36

1. Disconnect the negative battery cable.
2. Remove the instrument panel lower trim plates.
3. Remove the air vent deflectors.
4. Unfasten the instrument panel accessory trim plate screws and trim plate.
5. Unfasten the HVAC control assembly screws, then pull the control out enough to access the connectors.
6. Detach the electrical and vacuum connectors from the rear of the control assembly.
7. Remove the control assembly from the vehicle.

To install:
8. Attach the connectors to the rear of the control assembly, then position the assembly in the vehicle.
9. Install the control retaining screws and tighten to 17 inch lbs. (1.9 Nm).
10. Position the instrument panel trim plate and secure with the retaining screws.
11. Install the air vent deflectors and lower trim plates.
12. Connect the negative battery cable and check for proper HVAC control operation.

OLDSMOBLE

▶ See Figure 37

1. Disconnect the negative battery cable.
2. Remove the instrument panel closet panel.

Fig. 33 Unfasten the 4 climate control panel bolts. They can be removed either with a ratchet or Torx® driver

Fig. 34 Pull the control panel partially out, in order to detach the electrical connector

Fig. 35 Unplug the electrical connection(s), then remove the assembly from the vehicle

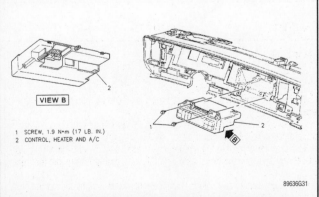

Fig. 36 Heater and A/C control panel mounting—Buick with automatic climate control shown, manual system similar

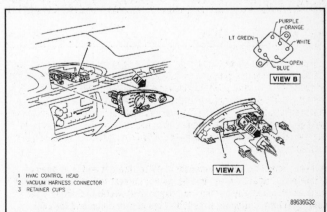

Fig. 37 Exploded view of the HVAC control assembly and connectors—Oldsmobile

3. Remove the HVAC control from the closet, detach the electrical and vacuum connectors, then remove the control from the vehicle.

To install:

4. Attach the electrical and vacuum connectors to the HVAC control.

5. Position the HVAC control to the closet and press the control it to engage the retainer clips.

6. Install the instrument panel closet panel.

7. Connect the negative battery cable and check for proper HVAC control operation.

PONTIAC

1. If equipped with air bags, disable the SIR system.
2. Disconnect the negative battery cable.
3. Remove the instrument panel trim plate by carefully prying it off.

4. Remove the control panel retaining screws/bolts.

5. Pull assembly out slightly in order to access the rear of the unit.

6. Detach the electrical and vacuum connectors from the rear of the control assembly.

7. Remove the heater and A/C control assembly from the vehicle.

To install:

8. Attach the electrical connectors and vacuum lines to the control assembly.

9. Place the assembly in position and secure with the retaining screws. Tighten the screws to 17 inch lbs. (1.9 Nm).

10. Install the instrument panel trim plate.

11. If equipped with air bags, enable the SIR system.

12. Connect the negative battery cable and check for proper HVAC control operation.

CRUISE CONTROL SYSTEMS

General Description

▶ See Figure 38

Cruise control is a speed control system that maintains a desired vehicle speed under normal driving conditions. However, steep grades up or down may cause variations in the selected speeds. The electronic cruise control system has the capability to cruise, coast, resume speed, accelerate and "tap up" and "tap down."

➡**To keep the vehicle under control and to prevent possible personal injury and vehicle damage, the cruise control should not be used on slippery or winding roads or in traffic of heavy or varying volume. When traveling down a steeply graded hill, the cruise control should be disengaged by depressing the brake pedal lightly. The transmission can then be shifted into a lower gear range to help control vehicle speed.**

The main parts of the cruise control system are the functional control switches, cruise control module, speed sensor and brake/clutch release switches.

There are two basic systems used on the vehicles covered in this manual, vacuum controlled and electronically controlled. Also, some models have a cruise control module and some use the engine control computer. With the introduction of Powertrain Control Modules (PCM) which computerize the control of a number of different systems, there are several different ways of handling cruise control functions. These systems may work the same way. The only difference being if the selected cruise is maintained by vacuum or electricity or a cruise control module or the engine control module.

The main parts of the cruise control system are the mode control switches, cruise control module or PCM, depending on the vehicle, the servo, vehicle speed sensor, vacuum supply, and electrical and vacuum release switches.

The vacuum operated cruise control system uses vacuum to operate a servo. The servo has a diaphragm which is connected directly to the throttle cable. The

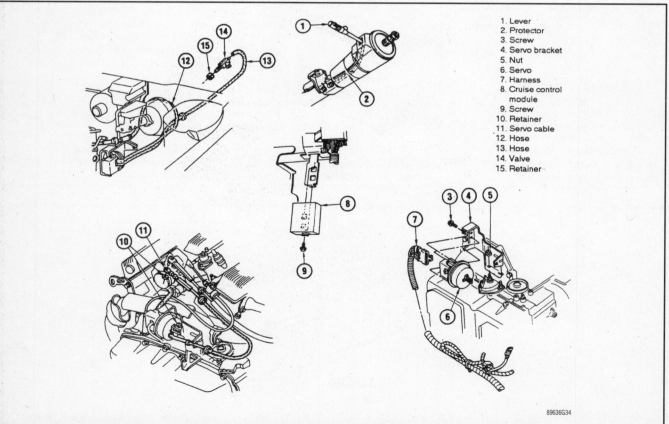

1. Lever
2. Protector
3. Screw
4. Servo bracket
5. Nut
6. Servo
7. Harness
8. Cruise control module
9. Screw
10. Retainer
11. Servo cable
12. Hose
13. Hose
14. Valve
15. Retainer

89636G34

Fig. 38 Cruise control system components—vacuum operated system shown, electronic stepper shares some components

throttle then moves with changes in vacuum. The servo maintains a desired vehicle speed by trapping vacuum in the servo at the proper servo position. The cruise control module (or PCM, depending on vehicle) monitors vehicle speed and controls the servo vacuum and vent valves to maintain desired speed. The control module/PCM contains a low speed limiter which will prevent system engagement below a minimum speed, about 25 mph (40km/h). The operation of the cruise system is controlled by switches, usually located in a multi-function turn signal lever. The system may be disengaged by turning off the switch or by pressing the brake or clutch pedal slightly. An electrical switch, mounted on the brake and clutch pedal bracket, disengages the system electrically when the brake pedal is depressed. A vacuum release valve, mounted on the brake pedal bracket, vents the trapped vacuum in the servo to the atmosphere when the brake pedal is depressed, allowing the servo to quickly return the throttle to idle position.

The electronic stepper cruise control system uses a cruise control module to reach the desired vehicle cruise operation. There are 2 components in the module which help do this. This first is an electronic controller and the other is an electric stepper motor. The controller monitors vehicle speed and operates the electric stepper motor. The motor moves a band and throttle linkage, in response to the controller, to maintain the desired cruising speed. The cruise control module has a low speed limit which prevents system engagement at speeds below 25 mph (40km/h). Operation of the controller is controlled by functional switches located on the multi-function turn signal lever. Cruise control release switch and stop lamp switch assemblies are provided to disengage the cruise system. The switches are mounted on the brake pedal bracket. When the brake pedal is depressed, the cruise control system is electrically disengaged and the throttle returned to the idle position.

ENTERTAINMENT SYSTEMS

Radio

REMOVAL & INSTALLATION

➡**Before beginning the radio removal procedure, be sure to note your radio presets, as these will be erased when you disconnect the negative battery cable.**

✳ WARNING

When installing the radio, do not pinch the wires, or a short circuit to ground may happen and damage the radio.

Buick

◗ See Figure 39

1. Disconnect the negative battery cable.
2. Remove the lower instrument panel trim plate by carefully prying it out.
3. Remove the air vent deflectors.
4. Remove the glove compartment retaining bolts, then remove the compartment.
5. Unfasten the retainers, then remove the instrument panel accessory trim plate.
6. Remove the radio mounting bolts. Slide the radio out partially, then detach the electrical connector and speaker lead from the rear of the radio.
7. If installing a new radio, transfer the top and bottom brackets to the new radio.

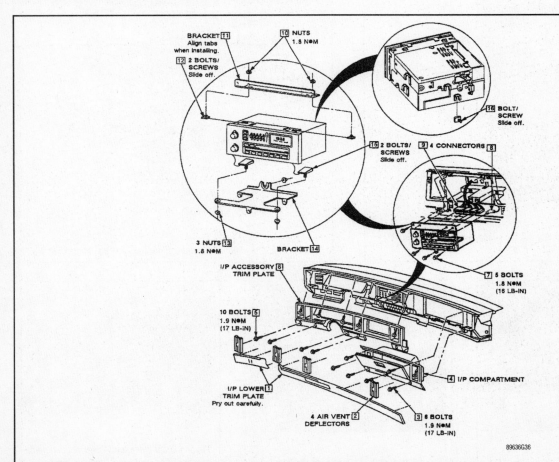

89636G36

Fig. 39 Exploded view of the radio mounting and fastener tightening specifications—1986–94 Buick shown

To install:

8. Attach the radio electrical connector and speaker lead, then position in the vehicle.

9. Install the radio mounting bolts and tighten to 16 inch lbs. (1.8 Nm).

10. The remainder of installation is the reverse of the removal procedure. Make sure to tighten the retainers to the specifications shown in the accompanying figure.

Oldsmobile

1986–91 VEHICLES

▶ See Figures 40 and 41

1. Disconnect the negative battery cable.
2. Remove the center and lower trim plates.
3. Remove the mounting screws; there are usually four screws.
4. Slide the radio rearward and disconnect the wiring and antenna lead.
5. Remove the radio from the vehicle.

To install:

6. Raise the radio into position, then connect the wiring.
7. Install the radio mounting screws.
8. Install the trim plates.
9. Connect the negative battery cable.

1992–99 VEHICLES

1. Disconnect the negative battery cable.
2. For 1992–93 vehicles, perform the following:
   a. Unfasten the instrument panel-to-cluster trim panel screws. Tilt the trim plate rearward.

b. If equipped, detach the driver information display and rear defogger switch connectors.
   c. Remove the trim plate.
3. For 1994–99 vehicles, perform the following:
   a. Open the instrument panel compartment door.
   b. Remove the center trim plate assembly by remove the two fasteners and carefully pulling rearward.
4. Remove the radio fasteners, then pull the radio rearward.
5. Detach the connectors and the antenna lead, then remove the radio from the vehicle.
6. If replacing the radio, make sure to transfer the mounting brackets to the new radio
7. Installation is the reverse of the removal procedure. Tighten the radio retainers to 17 inch lbs. (1.9 Nm).

Pontiac

1986–91 VEHICLES

▶ See Figures 42 thru 48

1. Disconnect the negative battery cable.
2. Remove the instrument panel trim plate by carefully prying around the perimeter with a suitable tool.
3. Detach the 2 wires from the cigar lighter.
4. Remove the ashtray.
5. Remove the screws from the upper radio mounting bracket.
6. Unfasten the ashtray bracket and rear support bracket retainers.
7. Use your fingers to depress the 2 instrument panel engagement tabs up through the access holes.

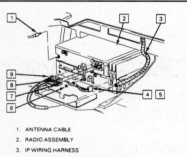

1. ANTENNA CABLE
2. RADIO ASSEMBLY
3. IP WIRING HARNESS
4. STRG WHEEL CONTROL CONN (C60 A/C)
5. A/C CONTROL HARNESS (C68 A/C)
6. 2.8 N•M (25 LB-IN)
7. FRONT SPEAKER CONN (WHITE)
8. IGNITION/GROUND CONN (BLACK)
9. REAR SPEAKER CONN (BLUE)

89636G37

Fig. 40 Slide the radio partially out to detach the connectors from the rear of the radio

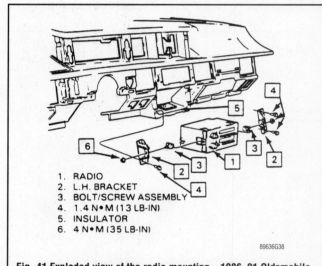

1. RADIO
2. L.H. BRACKET
3. BOLT/SCREW ASSEMBLY
4. 1.4 N•M (13 LB-IN)
5. INSULATOR
6. 4 N•M (35 LB-IN)

89636G38

Fig. 41 Exploded view of the radio mounting—1986–91 Oldsmobile

89636P50

Fig. 42 Remove the trim plate by carefully prying around the edges

89636P51

Fig. 43 Unfasten the 2 retaining screws from the upper radio bracket

89636P56

Fig. 44 Once the ashtray bracket retainers are removed, unfasten the rear radio bracket bolt

Fig. 45 You must depress the two tabs (1) from under the access holes (2) in order to remove the radio

Fig. 46 Pull the radio partially out to access the connectors at the rear of the radio

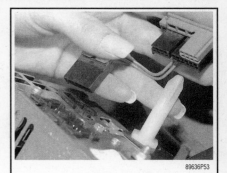

Fig. 47 Once the radio is out far enough, detach the electrical connectors . . .

Fig. 48 . . . and the antenna lead from the rear of the radio

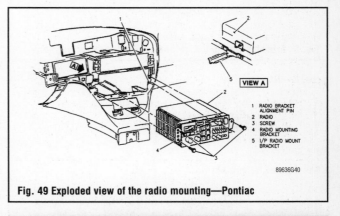

Fig. 49 Exploded view of the radio mounting—Pontiac

1 RADIO BRACKET ALIGNMENT PIN
2 RADIO
3 SCREW
4 RADIO MOUNTING BRACKET
5 I/P RADIO MOUNT BRACKET

8. Slide the radio partially out and detach the electrical connectors and antenna lead.
9. Remove the radio from the vehicle.

To install:
10. Attach the wiring and antenna lead to the back of the radio.
11. Push the radio into the instrument panel until the tangs engage.
12. Install the retainers to the rear support brackets and ashtray brackets. Tighten to 35 inch lbs. (4 Nm).
13. Install the radio upper mounting bracket retaining bolts/screws and tighten to 12 inch lbs. (1.4 Nm).
14. Install the ashtray, then attach the 2 wires to the lighter.
15. Place the trim plate in position, then push firmly to seat it in place.
16. Connect the negative battery cable.

1992–99 VEHICLES

▶ **See Figure 49**

1. Disconnect the negative battery cable.
2. Remove the instrument panel trim plate by carefully prying it up. Pull the trim plate up, then rearward.
3. Unfasten the radio-to-instrument panel retainers.
4. Pull the radio rearward and detach the electrical connector and antenna lead.
5. Remove the radio from the vehicle. If the radio is being replaced, make sure to transfer the rear mounting bracket to the new radio.

To install:
6. Attach the radio lead and connectors to the rear of the radio.
7. Position the radio in the instrument panel.
8. Install the retaining fasteners and tighten to 17 inch lbs. (1.9 Nm).
9. Install the trim plate, then connect the negative battery cable.

Speakers

REMOVAL & INSTALLATION

Front Speakers

▶ **See Figures 50 and 51**

➡ Depending upon the model, your vehicle may have front speakers mounted in the doors and/or on the instrument panel.

1. Disconnect the negative battery cable.
2. Remove the retaining screws from the speaker covers.
3. Remove the speaker cover/grille.
4. Lift the speaker up, detach the electrical connector, then remove the speaker from the vehicle.

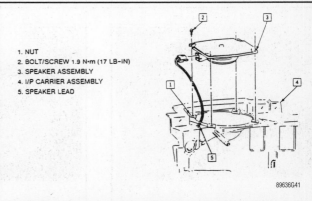

1. NUT
2. BOLT/SCREW 1.9 N·m (17 LB-IN)
3. SPEAKER ASSEMBLY
4. I/P CARRIER ASSEMBLY
5. SPEAKER LEAD

Fig. 50 Exploded view of a front speaker mounted in the instrument panel

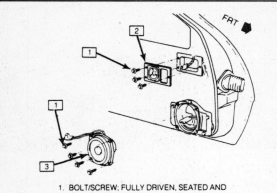

1. BOLT/SCREW; FULLY DRIVEN, SEATED AND NOT STRIPPED
2. UPPER FRONT DOOR SPEAKER (UW6 OPTION)
3. LOWER FRONT DOOR SPEAKER

89636G42

Fig. 51 Exploded view of a door mounted front speaker assembly

To install:

5. Attach the speaker electrical connector.
6. Place the speaker in its mounting position, then install the grille.
7. Install the retaining screws.
8. Connect the negative battery cable.

Rear Speakers

▶ See Figures 52 thru 58

1. Disconnect the negative battery cable.
2. For vehicles equipped with power boosters, perform the following:

a. Remove the rear seat and the undershelf cover.
b. If necessary, remove the speaker grille(s).
c. Detach the speaker electrical connector.
d. Remove the optional speaker from its mounting position.
e. Unfasten the main speaker mounting bolts, then remove the speaker from its bracket.
3. For vehicles without a power booster, perform the following:
a. Open the trunk lid.
b. Unscrew the plastic retaining wingnuts.
c. Remove the speaker housing.
4. Remove the bolts and sealing strip.
5. Remove the speaker.
6. If equipped with Bose amplified speakers, unfasten the 12 or so screws, then remove the speaker and amplifier assembly.
7. Detach the electrical connector.

To install:

8. Attach the speaker electrical connector.
9. Install the speaker and speaker retainers.
10. For vehicles not equipped with a power booster, install the sealing strip, speaker housing and retaining nuts.
11. If equipped with a power booster, install the optional speaker, speaker grille(s), undershelf cover and seat.
12. Connect the negative battery cable.

Power Antenna

The power antenna is designed to raise automatically when the radio is turned **ON**, with the ignition switch in **RUN** or **ACCY**. If the radio or ignition switch is turned to the **OFF** position, the antenna will automatically retract to its down position. The antenna is connected to the radio by a coaxial cable.

When the ignition switch and radio is turned **ON**, power is supplied to the antenna relay. The relay contacts closes and the antenna motor runs. After the antenna is at its full height, the UP switch opens and the motor stops.

When the ignition switch or radio is turned **OFF**, the circuit through the relay is opened and the antenna automatically retracts to its DOWN position.

89636P41

Fig. 52 On vehicles with a power booster, you have to remove the rear seat, unfasten the retaining clips . . .

89636P42

Fig. 53 . . . unclip the seat belt retainers and remove the undershelf cover for access to the speakers

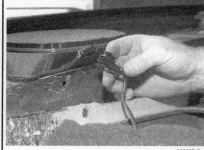

89636P43

Fig. 54 Unplug the speaker electrical connector . . .

89636P44

Fig. 55 . . . then remove the optional speaker from its mounting

89636P45

Fig. 56 Remove the main speaker retaining bolts . . .

89636P46

Fig. 57 . . . then remove the speaker from its mounting bracket

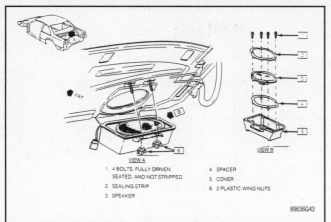

Fig. 58 For vehicles not equipped with a power booster, you must remove the speaker through the trunk of the vehicle

➥Always switch the radio OFF when entering a car wash. If the radio is not switched OFF, the antenna mast can be damaged when the ignition switch is turned to the ON position.

REMOVAL & INSTALLATION

Because of the varied applications of power antennas, the following general power antenna removal and installation procedures are outlined. These removal steps can be altered as necessary.

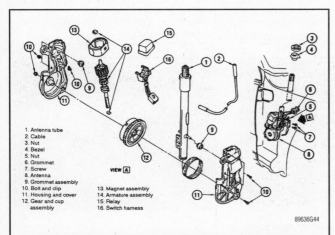

Fig. 59 Exploded view of the front mounted power antenna assembly —early model Oldsmobile shown

Front Mounted Type

▶ See Figure 59

1. Disconnect the negative battery cable.
2. Remove the instrument panel sound absorber pad.
3. Disconnect the antenna lead-in and harness connector from the relay assembly.
4. Apply masking tape to the edge of the fender and door.
5. If required, remove the inner to outer fender retaining screws.
6. If required, raise the vehicle and support it safely; then remove the necessary front wheel and tire assembly.
7. Remove the lower rocker panel retaining screws, lower fender to body retaining bolt and remove the lower rocker panel, as required.
8. Remove the inner splash shield from the fender, as required.
9. Remove the upper antenna retaining nut, using an appropriate tool.
10. Remove the antenna-to-bracket retaining bolts, then remove the antenna assembly from the vehicle.

To install:

11. Fit the antenna into position, then loosely install the antenna gasket and upper nut.
12. Loosely install the antenna-to-bracket retaining bolts.
13. Tighten the upper antenna retaining nut, using the appropriate tool, then tighten the antenna to bracket retaining bolts.
14. Complete installation in the reverse order of the removal procedure.
15. Apply silicone grease to the harness connector before reconnecting.
16. Check the operation of the antenna mast. Reset the clock, if required.

Rear Mounted Type

▶ See Figures 60 thru 71

1. Disconnect the negative battery cable. Open the trunk
2. From inside the trunk, remove the trim panel from either the right or left rear wheel area.
3. Depending upon on which side the antenna is mounted, it may be necessary to remove the jack and jack case from the side of the trunk.
4. Remove the antenna mounting bracket retaining screws.
5. Remove the upper antenna nut and bezel from the antenna, using an appropriate tool.
6. Remove the lead-in cable and wiring connector. If equipped, disconnect the drain hose.
7. Unfasten the mounting bolts, then remove the antenna assembly from the vehicle.

To install:

8. Position the antenna in the vehicle, then connect the lead-in cable.
9. Install the nut and bezel to the antenna and mounting bracket retaining screws.
10. Apply silicone grease to the harness connector, then attach it.
11. If removed, install the jack case and jack.
12. Connect the negative battery cable, turn the ignition **ON**, then check for proper operation of the antenna.
13. Install the trim panel, making sure to install the retainers in the proper positions.
14. Reset the clock and other memory components as required.

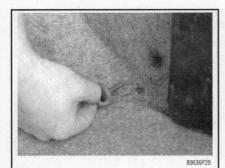

Fig. 60 To remove the trunk trim panels, there are a few different types of retainers. Unscrew this wingnut type

Fig. 61 Use a trim panel removal tool to unfasten this type of retainer

Fig. 62 Make sure to note where each retainer goes, as they are not marked

Fig. 63 If necessary, open the jack storage case, remove the jack and the case retainers, then remove the case

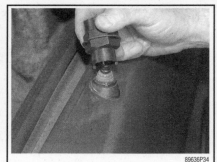

Fig. 64 There is a special tool available for loosening the upper antenna nut and bezel . . .

Fig. 65 . . . however, a pair of needlenose pliers also gets the job done

Fig. 66 Remove the nut from the upper mount

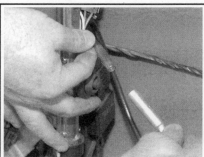

Fig. 67 Disconnect the radio-to-antenna lead-in cable . . .

Fig. 68 . . . and unplug the antenna electrical connector

Fig. 69 On some vehicles, there is a drain hose which must be disconnected

Fig. 70 Remove the power antenna mounting bolts (see arrows) . . .

Fig. 71 . . . then remove the antenna assembly from the vehicle

WINDSHIELD WIPERS AND WASHERS

Windshield Wiper Blade and Arm

REMOVAL & INSTALLATION

▶ **See Figures 72, 73 and 74**

Wiper element replacement procedures are detailed in Section 1.

1. With the wipers ON, turn the ignition **OFF** when the wiper arm is at the mid-wipe position.
2. Lift the wiper arm off the windshield, then disengage the retaining latch with a screwdriver or equivalent tool.
3. Pull the wiper blade arm assembly from the transmission drive shaft.
4. If necessary, lift the blade retaining latch and remove the blade from the arm.

To install:

➡The blade must be installed with the blade retaining latch pointed toward the passenger side of the vehicle.

5. If removed, install the wiper blade on the arm.
6. With the ignition **ON**, turn the wiper/washer switch ON, and then OFF to return the transmission assembly to the park position.
7. Position the wiper arm and blade assembly slightly below the stop surface of the park ramp, then press the arm head casting fully onto the transmission drive shaft.
8. Push the wiper arm retaining latch in.
9. Lift the replaced arm assembly over the park ramp.

➡The correct park position and outwipe dimension are determined with the wipers operating at low speed on wet glass.

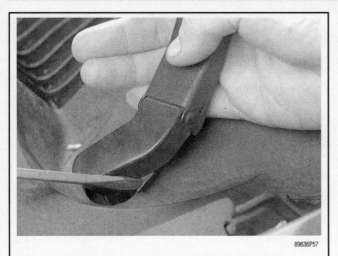

Fig. 72 Use a suitable tool to pull the wiper arm retaining tab out . . .

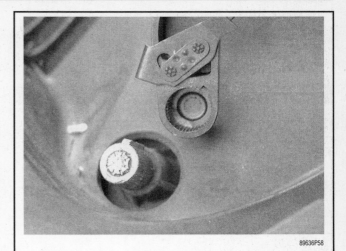

Fig. 73 . . . then you can pull the arm off the shaft. Note the splines on the arm and linkage

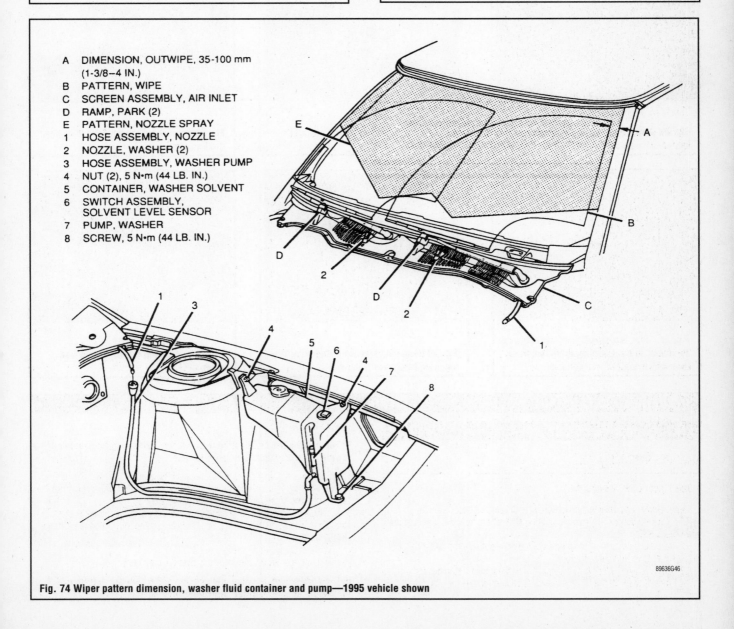

A   DIMENSION, OUTWIPE, 35-100 mm
    (1-3/8–4 IN.)
B   PATTERN, WIPE
C   SCREEN ASSEMBLY, AIR INLET
D   RAMP, PARK (2)
E   PATTERN, NOZZLE SPRAY
1   HOSE ASSEMBLY, NOZZLE
2   NOZZLE, WASHER (2)
3   HOSE ASSEMBLY, WASHER PUMP
4   NUT (2), 5 N•m (44 LB. IN.)
5   CONTAINER, WASHER SOLVENT
6   SWITCH ASSEMBLY,
    SOLVENT LEVEL SENSOR
7   PUMP, WASHER
8   SCREW, 5 N•m (44 LB. IN.)

Fig. 74 Wiper pattern dimension, washer fluid container and pump—1995 vehicle shown

10. Inspect the wiper pattern. Dimension A (in the accompanying figure) should be $1\frac{3}{8}$–$1\frac{3}{4}$ in. (35–100mm) from the top of the driver's blade assembly on the outwipe edge of the glass.

11. Check the park position. Both wiper arms must be against the park ramps.

Windshield Wiper Motor

REMOVAL & INSTALLATION

See Figures 75 thru 87

1. Remove the wiper blade and arm assemblies, as outlined earlier in this section.
2. Turn the ignition **ON** and the wiper switch **OFF** so the wiper motor returns to the park position.
3. Disconnect the negative battery cable.
4. Unfasten any necessary retainers and remove the air inlet screen assembly. Disconnect the washer hoses.
5. Disconnect the wiper arm transmission drive link from the crank arm using a suitable wiper transmission separator tool.
6. On some vehicles, it may be necessary to remove the nut from the ball crank and remove the crank arm.
7. Detach the electrical connectors from the wiper motor. Remove the wiper motor mounting bolts/screws.
8. Guide the crank arm through the hole in the dash/shroud upper panel, then remove the motor.

To install:

9. Guide the crank arm through the hole in the dash/shroud upper panel, then place the motor into position.
10. Install the wiper motor mounting bolts/screws. Tighten to 71 inch lbs. (8 Nm).
11. Attach the electrical connectors to the motor.

89636P76

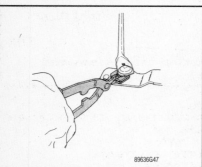

Fig. 75 Remove the air inlet screen retaining bolts/screws . . .

89636P77

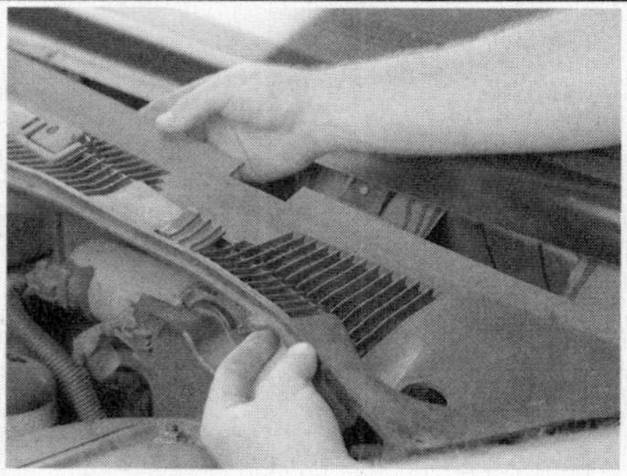

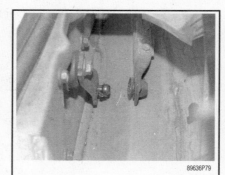

Fig. 76 . . . then remove the air inlet screen

89636P78

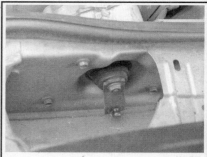

Fig. 77 Disconnect the windshield washer fluid hose(s)

89636G47

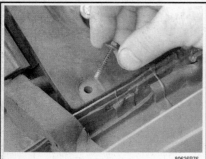

Fig. 78 There is a special tool available to separate the transmission drive link from the crank arm

89636P79

Fig. 79 View of the transmission drive link separated from the crank arm

89636P82

Fig. 80 Location of the wiper arm ball crank

89636P83

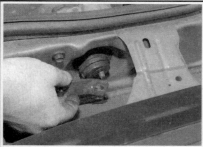

Fig. 81 If necessary, unfasten the ball crank retaining nut, then remove the crank arm

89636P80

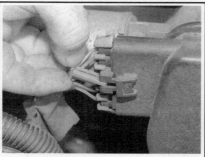

Fig. 82 Remove the wiper motor connector CPA clip . . .

89636P81

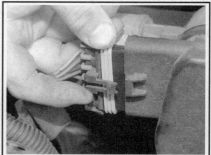

Fig. 83 . . . then unplug the wiper motor electrical connector

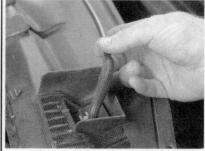

Fig. 84 After removing the retaining bolts, turn the motor vertically . . .

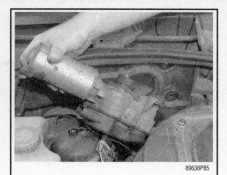

Fig. 85 . . . then remove the motor from the vehicle

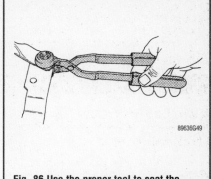

Fig. 86 Use the proper tool to seat the drive link socket on the crank arm ball

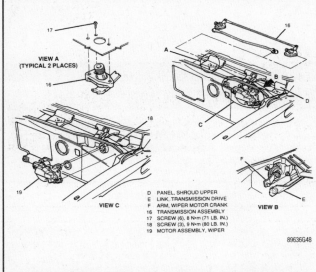

Fig. 87 Exploded view of the wiper motor and transmission assemblies

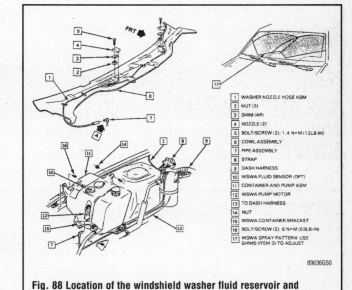

Fig. 88 Location of the windshield washer fluid reservoir and pump—1986–91 vehicles

12. Connect the wiper arm drive link socket to the crank arm ball using a suitable wiper transmission installation tool. Make sure the socket is fully seated on the ball.

13. Install the air inlet screen assembly.

14. Install the wiper arms, then connect the washer hoses.

15. Connect the negative battery cable, then check the wiper motor operation.

Windshield Washer Motor

REMOVAL & INSTALLATION

1986–95 Vehicles

▸ **See Figures 74 and 88**

1. Disconnect the negative battery cable.
2. Drain or siphon the washer solvent from the reservoir.
3. For 1986–91 vehicles, remove the brace.
4. Unfasten the reservoir screws.
5. Detach the electrical connectors and washer hose.
6. If necessary, remove the reservoir from the vehicle.
7. Remove the washer pump motor from the reservoir.

To install:

8. Install the washer pump motor on the reservoir. Make sure the pump is fully seated in the reservoir gasket.
9. Position the reservoir in the vehicle.
10. Attach the electrical connectors and washer hose.
11. Install the reservoir retaining screws.
12. Install the brace.
13. Fill the reservoir with washer solvent.
14. Connect the negative battery cable, then check for proper washer pump operation.

1996–99 Vehicles

▸ **See Figure 89**

1. Disconnect the negative battery cable.
2. Drain or siphon the washer solvent from the reservoir.
3. Detach the electrical connectors from the washer.
4. Disconnect the hose from the washer pump.
5. Loosen the nut at the bottom of the washer reservoir.
6. Unfasten the 2 nuts, then remove the washer solvent reservoir.
7. Remove the washer pump from the container.
8. If necessary, remove the solvent lever sensor switch from the washer solvent container.

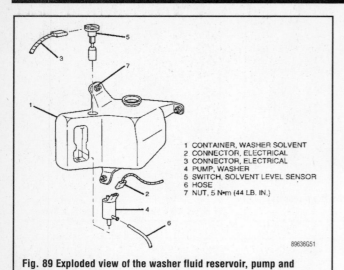

1 CONTAINER, WASHER SOLVENT
2 CONNECTOR, ELECTRICAL
3 CONNECTOR, ELECTRICAL
4 PUMP, WASHER
5 SWITCH, SOLVENT LEVEL SENSOR
6 HOSE
7 NUT, 5 N•m (44 LB. IN.)

89636G51

Fig. 89 Exploded view of the washer fluid reservoir, pump and level sensor

To install:

9. Install the solvent level sensor switch in the washer solvent container. The tab on the solvent level sender switch must be lined up with the slot in the hole.

10. Install the washer pump into the reservoir, making sure the pump is pushed all the way into the container seal.

11. Install the washer solvent reservoir and secure with the 3 nuts. Tighten the nuts to 44 inch lbs. (5 Nm).

12. Attach the electrical connectors to the solvent level sensor and washer pump.

13. Connect the hose to the washer pump.

14. Fill the reservoir with washer solvent.

15. Connect the negative battery cable, then check for proper washer pump operation.

INSTRUMENTS AND SWITCHES

※※ CAUTION

Many vehicles are equipped with SIR or air bag systems. Before performing any diagnosis or repair procedures, you must follow all safety and disarming procedures. Failure to safely disable the system may result in air bag deployment, possible injury or unnecessary repairs.

Instrument Cluster

REMOVAL & INSTALLATION

There are several different interior trim packages and instrument cluster options. The procedures listed here may be alter as you find necessary to accommodate the specific needs of the option packages you have on your car. Also refer to Section 10 for additional information on the instrument panel or console.

Individual gauges may not be replaceable on these clusters. If one has failed, cluster assembly replacement may be necessary, depending on application and parts availability.

1986–90 Vehicles

◗ **See Figures 90 thru 98**

1. Disconnect the negative battery cable. If equipped with SIR, disable the SIR system, as outlined earlier in this section.

※※ CAUTION

Some models covered by this manual may be equipped with a Supplemental Inflatable Restraint (SIR) system, which uses an air bag. Whenever working near any of the SIR components, such as the impact sensors, the air bag module, steering column and instrument panel, disable the SIR, as described in this section.

2. Remove the instrument panel trim plate as follows:

a. If equipped with tilt wheel, move the steering wheel to its lowest position.

b. For vehicles with column shift, move the shift lever to the **1** position.

c. Use a suitable tool to pry lightly around the edge of the trim plate, then remove the plate. Be careful not to crack or damage the plate.

3. Remove the instrument panel top cover/pad, as follows:

a. Remove the speaker, side defogger and defroster grilles by carefully prying them out.

b. Remove the speaker (if equipped), by unfasten the screws and detaching the electrical connector.

c. If equipped with a twilight sentinel, pop up the photocell retainer and turn the photocell counterclockwise in the retainer and pull it down-and-out.

d. Remove the instrument panel top cover-to-instrument panel screws.

e. Slide the instrument panel top cover out far enough to disconnect the aspirator hose and the electrical connector, if equipped.

f. Remove the instrument panel top cover from the instrument panel.

4. If equipped with quartz electronic speedometer clusters, remove the steering column trim cover, so the shift indicator can be removed.

89636P67

Fig. 90 Carefully pry around the perimeter, then remove the instrument panel trim plate

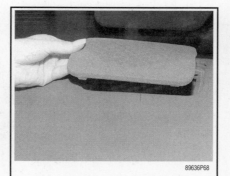

89636P68

Fig. 91 Remove the instrument panel top cover speaker grilles

89636P69

Fig. 92 Pry the defroster grille out, then turn the twilight sentinel photocell to unlock it and pull it from the grille

Fig. 93 Unfasten the top cover-to-instrument panel retaining bolts/screws

Fig. 94 Lift the instrument panel top cover off for access to the cluster retainers

Fig. 95 On this vehicle, there are three retainers on the top and two on the bottom securing the instrument cluster

Fig. 96 After all of the retainers are removed, pull the cluster housing assembly straight back

Fig. 97 Unplug any necessary instrument cluster electrical connectors, then remove the cluster

Fig. 98 Once the cluster is removed, you can replace the gauge bulbs located on the back of the cluster

5. If necessary, remove the steering column filler panel.

6. Remove the instrument cluster-to-instrument panel carrier screws. Pull the cluster housing assembly straight out; this will separate the electrical connectors from the cluster.

➡ **If not already done, it may be helpful to tilt the wheel all the way down and pull the gear select lever to low, when removing the cluster.**

7. Disconnect the non-volatile memory chip, if equipped.

To install:

8. Reconnect the non-volatile memory chip, if equipped.

9. Attach the electrical connectors, then position the instrument cluster and install the retaining screws.

10. If equipped, install the steering column filler panel.

11. Install the instrument panel top cover and the shift indicator, if equipped.

12. Connect the aspirator hose and the electrical connections.

13. Install the photo cell and retainer, if equipped with a twilight sentinel.

14. Install the speaker, defogger and defroster grilles.

15. Position the instrument panel trim plate, then push it firmly in place.

16. Connect the negative battery cable and enable the SIR system.

1991–99 Vehicles

BUICK

▶ **See Figure 99**

1. Disable the SIR system. If not already done, disconnect the negative battery cable.

2. Carefully pry the lower trim plate out with a suitable tool.

3. Pry the air deflectors out carefully.

4. Unfasten the instrument panel trim plate fasteners, then remove the trim plate.

5. If equipped with column shift, disconnect the PRNDL cable.

6. Unfasten the dimmer switch fasteners, then remove the dimmer switch.

7. Remove the instrument cluster fasteners, then remove the cluster.

To install:

8. Position the instrument cluster and install the fasteners. Tighten to 15 inch lbs. (1.6 Nm).

9. Install the dimmer switch and fasteners. Tighten to 17 inch lbs. (1.9 Nm).

10. If equipped, attach the PRNDL cable.

11. Install the instrument panel trim plate and secure with the retaining fasteners. Tighten to 17 inch lbs. (1.9 Nm).

12. Snap the air deflector into place.

13. Install the instrument panel lower trim panel.

14. Enable the SIR system and connect the negative battery cable.

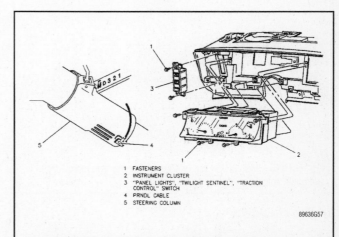

1 FASTENERS
2 INSTRUMENT CLUSTER
3 "PANEL LIGHTS", "TWILIGHT SENTINEL", "TRACTION CONTROL" SWITCH
4 PRNDL CABLE
5 STEERING COLUMN

Fig. 99 Exploded view of the instrument cluster and related components—1995 Buick shown

1991–93 OLDSMOBILE

▶ **See Figures 100 and 101**

1. Disconnect the negative battery cable. Disable the SIR system.
2. Remove the steering column filler panel retaining screws, then remove the panel.
3. Disconnect the PRNDL cable.
4. Remove the instrument panel trim plate by removing the air outlet deflectors, the screws, then gently prying outward.
5. Remove the cluster to instrument panel screws and pull right end of cluster rearward.
6. Disconnect the cluster connector by reaching around cluster and depressing the locking tab on the connector.
7. Pull the bottom of the cluster rearward and rotate the assembly so it is facing up.
8. Remove the cluster assembly by sliding toward the center of the vehicle.

To install:

9. Attach the cluster connector, being careful not to damage the connector.
10. Install the cluster to the vehicle and rotate into the proper position.
11. Install the cluster-to-instrument panel screws and tighten to 14 inch lbs. (1.6 Nm).
12. Install the instrument panel cluster trim plate, retaining screws and air deflectors.
13. Connect the PRNDL cable.
14. Position the steering column filler panel, then install the retaining screws.
15. Enable the SIR system and connect the negative battery cable.

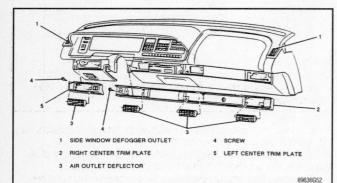

1	SIDE WINDOW DEFOGGER OUTLET	4	SCREW
2	RIGHT CENTER TRIM PLATE	5	LEFT CENTER TRIM PLATE
3	AIR OUTLET DEFLECTOR		

89636G52

Fig. 100 Exploded view of the instrument panel trim plate and air deflectors—1993 Oldsmobile shown

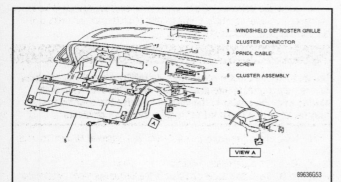

1	WINDSHIELD DEFROSTER GRILLE
2	CLUSTER CONNECTOR
3	PRNDL CABLE
4	SCREW
5	CLUSTER ASSEMBLY

89636G53

Fig. 101 Exploded view of the instrument cluster mounting—1993 Oldsmobile shown

1994–99 OLDSMOBILE

▶ **See Figures 102, 103 and 104**

1. Disconnect the negative battery cable.
2. Remove the instrument panel molding fasteners, then carefully pull the molding rearward. Carefully pry the windshield defroster grille upwards.

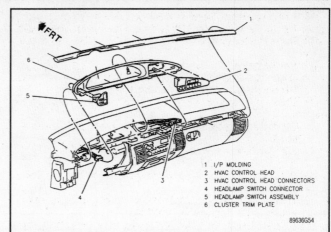

1	I/P MOLDING
2	HVAC CONTROL HEAD
3	HVAC CONTROL HEAD CONNECTORS
4	HEADLAMP SWITCH CONNECTOR
5	HEADLAMP SWITCH ASSEMBLY
6	CLUSTER TRIM PLATE

89636G54

Fig. 102 Exploded view of the instrument cluster trim plate—1995 Oldsmobile shown

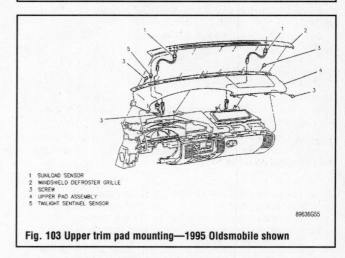

1	SUNLOAD SENSOR
2	WINDSHIELD DEFROSTER GRILLE
3	SCREW
4	UPPER PAD ASSEMBLY
5	TWILIGHT SENTINEL SENSOR

89636G55

Fig. 103 Upper trim pad mounting—1995 Oldsmobile shown

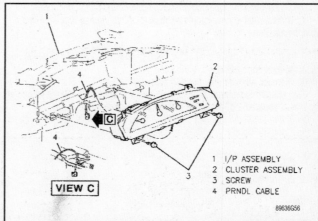

1	I/P ASSEMBLY
2	CLUSTER ASSEMBLY
3	SCREW
4	PRNDL CABLE

VIEW C

89636G56

Fig. 104 Exploded view of the instrument cluster—1995 Oldsmobile shown

3. If equipped, remove the sunload and twilight sentinel sensor, turning the sensors ¼ turn to release.
4. Remove the windshield defroster grille.
5. Unfasten the cluster trim plate-to-instrument panel fasteners.
6. Tilt the top of the trim plate rearward, then pull the bottom of the trim plate rearward.
7. Remove the HVAC control head and head/park lamp switch from the connectors.

8. If necessary, detach the HVAC control head vacuum harness connector.

9. Remove the HVAC control head by carefully pushing one side outward.

10. Remove the head/park lamp switch by carefully pushing one side outward.

11. Remove the trim plate.

12. Unfasten the upper trim pad fasteners, then remove the upper trim pad.

13. If equipped, with column shift, disconnect the PRNDL cable.

14. Unfasten the instrument cluster-to-panel fasteners, then pull the cluster rearward.

15. Detach the cluster connector, then remove it from the vehicle.

To install:

16. Attach the instrument cluster connector to the cluster.

17. If equipped, connect the PRNDL cable.

18. Position the cluster in the vehicle and secure with the fasteners. Tighten to 14 inch lbs. (1.6 Nm).

19. Position the upper trim pad and install the fasteners. Place the windshield defroster grill at the base of the windshield.

20. If equipped, install the sunload and twilight sentinel sensors, turning ¼ turn to secure.

21. Install the windshield defroster grille by carefully pressing into place.

22. Route the connectors through the holes in the cluster trim plate.

23. Position the trim plate to the instrument panel and secure with the fasteners. Tighten to 17 inch lbs. (1.9 Nm).

24. Attach the HVAC control head to the connector, then install the control head to the trim plate.

25. Attach the head/park lamp switch to the connector, then install the switch to the trim plate.

26. Install the instrument panel molding by carefully pushing forward to secure the clips.

27. Install the molding fasteners (in the instrument panel compartment).

28. Enable the SIR system and connect the negative battery cable.

PONTIAC

▶ **See Figures 105, 106 and 107**

1. Disable the SIR system and disconnect the negative battery cable.

2. Remove the instrument panel trim plate by carefully prying it out. Pull the plate up, then rearward.

3. If equipped, detach the sub-woofer gain control switch connector.

4. Unfasten the steering column filler fasteners, then remove the filler.

5. Lower the steering column.

6. Cover the top of the steering column to prevent damage.

7. Remove the cluster upper trim plate-to-instrument panel fasteners.

8. Remove the interior lamp dimmer and twilight sentinel control knob from the head/parking lamp switch.

➡**Be careful not the loose the interior lamps dimmer knob retainer!**

9. Detach the cigar lighter connector.

10. Remove the instrument cluster trim plate.

11. Unfasten the instrument cluster-to-panel fasteners. Pull the eight end of the cluster rearward and rotate the cluster to face upward.

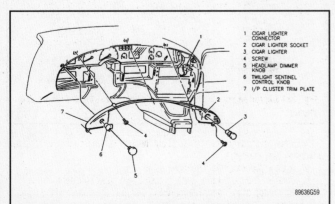

Fig. 105 Exploded view of the instrument panel cluster trim plate— 1995 Pontiac shown

1 CIGAR LIGHTER CONNECTOR
2 CIGAR LIGHTER SOCKET
3 CIGAR LIGHTER
4 SCREW
5 HEADLAMP DIMMER KNOB
6 TWILIGHT SENTINEL CONTROL KNOB
7 I/P CLUSTER TRIM PLATE

89636G59

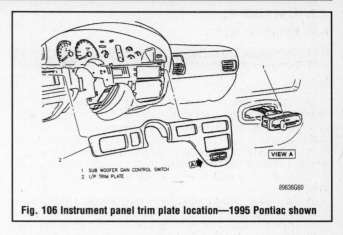

Fig. 106 Instrument panel trim plate location—1995 Pontiac shown

1 SUB WOOFER GAIN CONTROL SWITCH
2 I/P TRIM PLATE

89636G60

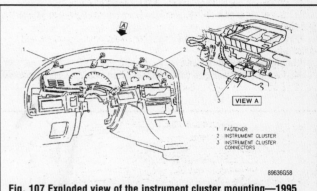

Fig. 107 Exploded view of the instrument cluster mounting—1995 Pontiac shown

1 FASTENER
2 INSTRUMENT CLUSTER
3 INSTRUMENT CLUSTER CONNECTORS

89636G58

12. Detach the cluster connector by reaching around the top or bottom right side of the cluster and depressing the locking tab.

13. On vehicles with 2 connectors, reach around the top or bottom of the cluster assembly and depress the locking tab to detach the connector.

14. Remove the instrument cluster by sliding it toward the center of the vehicle.

To install:

15. Position the instrument cluster to the panel, facing upward. Slide the cluster in from the center of the vehicle, then rotate to the proper position.

16. Attach the instrument cluster connector(s) by reaching around the top or bottom of the cluster assembly. Check for proper attachment and make sure there are not bent or damaged pins.

✳✳ WARNING

Do not force the cluster connectors. Carefully align the connectors before pushing them into place. Look down the back side of the cluster from the center of the vehicle to guide the connector(s). It may be helpful to use a mirror to help align the connector.

17. Install the instrument cluster fasteners, and tighten to 14 inch lbs. (1.6 Nm).

18. Attach the cigar lighter connector.

19. Install the cluster upper trim plate to the instrument panel by carefully inserting the tab.

20. Install the interior lamp dimmer and twilight sentinel control knob to the head/park lamp switch. Properly align the retainer in the knob before installation to ensure retention.

21. Install the cluster trim plate fasteners and tighten to 17 inch lbs. (1.9 Nm).

22. Remove the protective cover from the steering column, then raise the column.

23. Install the steering column filler and install the attaching screws. Tighten to 17 inch lbs. (1.9 Nm).

24. If equipped, attach the sub-woofer gain control switch connector.

25. Install the trim plate by pushing it into place.
26. Enable the SIR system, then connect the negative battery cable.

Gauges

REMOVAL & INSTALLATION

The gauges are an integral part of the instrument cluster assembly. If one of the gauges is faulty, the entire cluster must be replaced.

The speedometer removal procedure is the same as the instrument cluster procedure. If your car has an electronic display the speedometer can't be serviced separately. Before servicing or replacing an instrument cluster or display you should make certain the problem is with the display and not an input sensor. If the odometers work properly and speedometer doesn't, the speedometer is probably defective. If the odometers don't function and the speedometer does then the odometer is most likely bad. But, if both the speedometer and odometers don't work the problem is probably the speed sensor. The problem could also be and circuits between the display and battery, ignition, engine control computer or grounds. Since these devices are extremely expensive it is advisable to have them diagnosed by a professional repair shop before replacement.

Headlight Switch

REMOVAL & INSTALLATION

▶ **See Figures 108, 109, 110 and 111**

1. Disconnect the negative battery cable. Remove the steering column lower cover or the instrument panel trim plate covering the headlight switch, if equipped with a rocker-type headlight switch.
2. Disconnect the electrical harness retainer below headlight switch assembly. The switch connector is integral to the instrument panel. Pull the switch outward to disconnect it.
3. Remove the screw with the ground wire at the bottom of the switch housing, as well as all other mounting screws.
4. Pull assembly down and rearward, detach wiring harness connectors, bulb(s) and remove assembly.

To install:

5. Connect wiring harness connectors, bulb(s) and install the assembly.
6. Install the screw with ground wire at the bottom of switch housing and all other mounting screws.
7. Connect the electrical harness retainer below headlight switch assembly. Push the switch inward to connect it.
8. Install the steering column lower cover or the instrument panel trim plate covering the headlight switch, if equipped with a rocker-type headlight switch.
9. Connect the negative battery cable.

Rear Defogger System

OPERATION

A grid type heating element is affixed to the rear window, and an instrument panel mounted switch with an integral indicator lamp is used to turn the system ON. When the system is turned ON, a small electric current passes through the grid and its circuit, generating heat to clear the window. All rear defogger systems operate on 12 volts.

Certain conditions, such as outside temperature, vehicle speed, atmospheric pressure and even the number of passengers inside the vehicle, affect the length of time required to remove fog from the glass.

The defogger is designed to turn OFF after approximately 10 minutes of operation. If the defogger is turned ON again, it will only operate for approximately 5 minutes. You can, however, turn the system OFF before the time is up by turning the defogger switch or ignition switch OFF.

TESTING

▶ **See Figure 112**

1. Start the engine and pull out the defogger switch knob.
2. Using a test lamp, ground the end and touch the probe to each grid line. The test lamp should operate as indicated.
3. If the test lamp remains bright at both ends of the grid lines, check for a loose ground.

➡**The range zones may vary slightly from one glass to another, but the test lamp brilliance will decrease proportionately as it is moved from left to right on the grid line.**

4. If an abnormal reading is observed by the test lamp on any grid line, place the test lamp probe on the left of that bus bar and move the probe toward the right until the test lamp goes out. This will indicate a break in the continuity on that grid line.

REPAIR

1. Locate the break(s) on the grid line(s) and mark the outside of the glass, using a grease pencil.
2. Disconnect the negative battery cable.
3. Clean the area to be repaired. Buff with steel wool and wipe clean with a damped cloth with alcohol.
4. Position a strip of tape above and below the grid line area to be repair.
5. Repair the grid line break using defogger repair kit (Part 1052858 or equivalent) and follow the manufacturer's instructions.
6. After the grid line has been repaired, carefully remove the strips of tape.
7. Apply heat, using a heat gun, to the repaired area for approximately 1–2 minutes. A minimum temperature of 300°F (149°C) is required.

Fig. 108 Carefully pry off the instrument panel lower trim plate

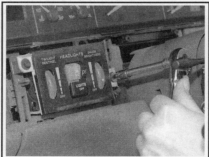

Fig. 109 Unfasten the headlight switch-to-instrument panel retaining bolts

Fig. 110 Pull the headlight switch assembly away from the panel

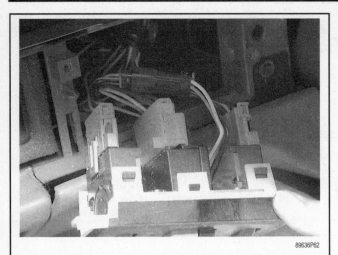

Fig. 111 Unplug the electrical connectors from the back of the switch, then remove the switch from the panel

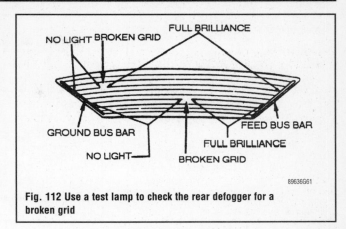

Fig. 112 Use a test lamp to check the rear defogger for a broken grid

➡To avoid damage to the interior trim, protect the trim near the area to be repair. Allow the repair materials to cure for at least 24 hours. Do not operate the unit until such time.

8. Test the rear defogger operation to verify proper operation.

LIGHTING

Headlights

REMOVAL & INSTALLATION

♦ See Figures 113, 114, 115 and 116

❊❊ CAUTION

Halogen bulbs contain gas under pressure. Handling the bulbs incorrectly could cause it to shatter into flying glass fragments. Do NOT leave the light switch ON. Always allow the bulb to cool before removal. Handle the bulb only by the base; avoid touching the glass itself.

1. Open the vehicle's hood and secure it in an upright position.
2. Remove headlight assembly or headlight assembly covers, as necessary for access to the bulbs at the rear of the headlight assembly.
3. If assembly is removed from car, place on towel to protect the lens surface. If you can reach the back of the bulb assembly you don't need to remove the lens assembly. Some headlamp bulbs use a lockring. If your car has a lockring around the bulb, unfasten the locking ring which secures the bulb and socket assembly, then withdraw the assembly rearward.

4. Grasp the connector assembly, turn to align tabs and remove the bulb assembly.
5. Remove the wire connector from the light bulb and turn the bulb out of the headlight assembly.
   To install:
6. Before installing a light bulb into the socket, ensure that all electrical contact surfaces are free of corrosion or dirt.
7. Line up the replacement headlight bulb with the socket. Firmly push the bulb onto the socket until the spring clip latches over the bulb's projection.

❊❊ WARNING

Do not touch the glass bulb with your fingers. Oil from your fingers can severely shorten the life of the bulb. If necessary, wipe off any dirt or oil from the bulb with rubbing alcohol before completing installation.

8. To ensure that the replacement bulb functions properly, activate the applicable switch to illuminate the bulb which was just replaced. (If this is a combination low and high beam bulb, be sure to check both intensities.) If the replacement light bulb does not illuminate, either it too is faulty or there is a problem in the bulb circuit or switch. Correct if necessary.

Fig. 113 You must turn the bulb assembly to align the tabs, then pull the bulb and connector rearward

Fig. 114 Pull the bulb and connector assembly rearward, holding it by the base, NOT by the glass

Fig. 115 Holding the bulb by its base, unplug it from the electrical connector

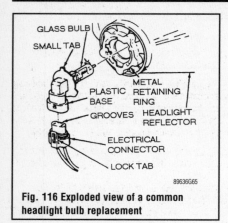

Fig. 116 Exploded view of a common headlight bulb replacement

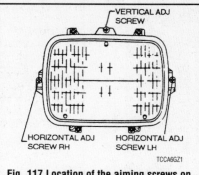

Fig. 117 Location of the aiming screws on most vehicles with sealed beam headlights

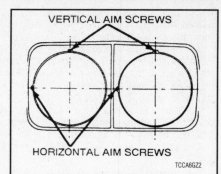

Fig. 118 Dual headlight adjustment screw locations—one side shown here (other side should be mirror image)

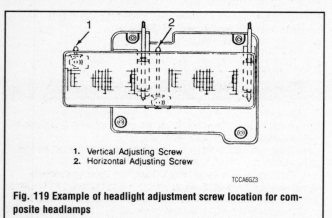

1. Vertical Adjusting Screw
2. Horizontal Adjusting Screw

Fig. 119 Example of headlight adjustment screw location for composite headlamps

AIMING THE HEADLIGHTS

▶ See Figures 117, 118, 119, 120 and 121

The headlights must be properly aimed to provide the best, safest road illumination. The lights should be checked for proper aim and adjusted as necessary. Certain state and local authorities have requirements for headlight aiming; these should be checked before adjustment is made.

❊❊ CAUTION

About once a year, when the headlights are replaced or any time front end work is performed on your vehicle, the headlight should be accurately aimed by a reputable repair shop using the proper equipment. Headlights not properly aimed can make it virtually impossible to see and may blind other drivers on the road, possibly causing an accident. Note that the following procedure is a temporary fix, until you can take your vehicle to a repair shop for a proper adjustment.

Headlight adjustment may be temporarily made using a wall, as described below, or on the rear of another vehicle. When adjusted, the lights should not glare in oncoming car or truck windshields, nor should they illuminate the passenger compartment of vehicles driving in front of you. These adjustments are rough and should always be fine-tuned by a repair shop which is equipped with headlight aiming tools. Improper adjustments may be both dangerous and illegal.

For most of the vehicles covered by this manual, horizontal and vertical aiming of each sealed beam unit is provided by two adjusting screws which move the retaining ring and adjusting plate against the tension of a coil spring. There is no adjustment for focus; this is done during headlight manufacturing.

➡Because the composite headlight assembly is bolted into position, no adjustment should be necessary or possible. Some applications, however, may be bolted to an adjuster plate or may be retained by adjusting screws. If so, follow this procedure when adjusting the lights, BUT always have the adjustment checked by a reputable shop.

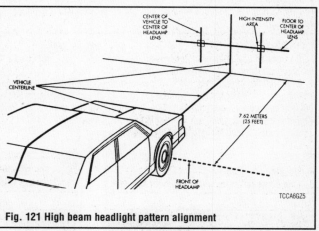

Fig. 120 Low beam headlight pattern alignment

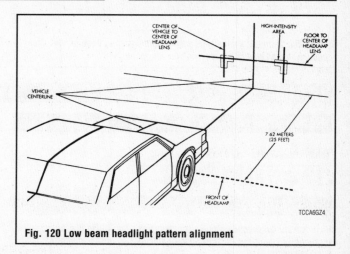

Fig. 121 High beam headlight pattern alignment

Before removing the headlight bulb or disturbing the headlamp in any way, note the current settings in order to ease headlight adjustment upon reassembly. If the high or low beam setting of the old lamp still works, this can be done using the wall of a garage or a building:

1. Park the vehicle on a level surface, with the fuel tank about ½ full and with the vehicle empty of all extra cargo (unless normally carried). The vehicle should be facing a wall which is no less than 6 feet (1.8m) high and 12 feet (3.7m) wide. The front of the vehicle should be about 25 feet (7.6m) from the wall.

2. If aiming is to be performed outdoors, it is advisable to wait until dusk in order to properly see the headlight beams on the wall. If done in a garage, darken the area around the wall as much as possible by closing shades or hanging cloth over the windows.

3. Turn the headlights **ON** and mark the wall at the center of each light's low beam, then switch on the brights and mark the center of each light's high beam.

A short length of masking tape which is visible from the front of the vehicle may be used. Although marking all four positions is advisable, marking one position from each light should be sufficient.

4. If neither beam on one side is working, and if another like-sized vehicle is available, park the second one in the exact spot where the vehicle was and mark the beams using the same-side light. Then switch the vehicles so the one to be aimed is back in the original spot. It must be parked no closer to or farther away from the wall than the second vehicle.

5. Perform any necessary repairs, but make sure the vehicle is not moved, or is returned to the exact spot from which the lights were marked. Turn the headlights **ON** and adjust the beams to match the marks on the wall.

6. Have the headlight adjustment checked as soon as possible by a reputable repair shop.

Signal and Marker Lights

REMOVAL & INSTALLATION

The replacement of all the light bulbs is straightforward. First look for the easiest way to access the connector. If you can reach under the car to the connector with your hand, then you won't need to remove the lens assembly. If there is no way to reach the bulb or the connector, you must check for an access cover or see if the lens cover has screws. If the lens is secured by screws, removing the lens would be best access to the bulb. If the lens has no screws showing on the outside of the vehicle, then access is from the back side. Once you have access to the bulb, simply grasp the connector and turn counterclockwise to align the slots, then remove the bulb from the lens housing.

Front Turn Signal and Parking Lights

▶ See Figures 122, 123, 124 and 125

1. Depending on the vehicle and bulb application, either unscrew and remove the lens, or disengage the bulb and socket assembly from the rear of the lens housing.

2. To remove a light bulb with retaining pins from its socket, grasp the bulb, then gently depress and twist it ⅛ turn counterclockwise, and pull it from the socket.

To install:

3. Before installing a light bulb into the socket, ensure that all electrical contact surfaces are free of corrosion or dirt.

➡**Before installing the light bulb, note the positions of the two retaining pins on the bulb. They will likely be at different heights on the bulb, to ensure that the bulb is installed correctly. If, when installing the bulb, it does not turn easily, do not force it. Remove the bulb and rotate it 180 degrees from its former position, then reinsert it into the bulb socket.**

4. Insert the light bulb into the socket and, while depressing the bulb, twist it ⅛ turn clockwise until the two pins on the light bulb are properly engaged in the socket.

5. To ensure that the replacement bulb functions properly, activate the applicable switch to illuminate the bulb which was just replaced. If the replacement light bulb does not illuminate, either it too is faulty or there is a problem in the bulb circuit or switch. Correct if necessary.

6. If applicable, install the socket and bulb assembly into the rear of the lens housing; otherwise, install the lens over the bulb.

Side Marker Light

▶ See Figures 126, 127 and 128

1. Disengage the bulb and socket assembly from the lens housing.
2. Gently grasp the light bulb and pull it straight out of the socket.

To install:

3. Before installing the light bulb into the socket, ensure that all electrical contact surfaces are free of corrosion or dirt.

4. Line up the base of the light bulb with the socket, then insert the light bulb into the socket until it is fully seated.

5. To ensure that the replacement bulb functions properly, activate the applicable switch to illuminate the bulb which was just replaced. If the replacement light bulb does not illuminate, either it too is faulty or there is a problem in the bulb circuit or switch. Correct as necessary.

6. Install the socket and bulb assembly into the lens housing.

Fig. 122 The front turn signal/parking light bulb can usually be accessed from behind

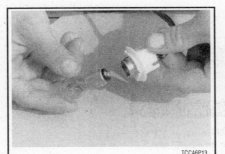

Fig. 123 Depress and twist this type of bulb counterclockwise, then pull the bulb straight from its socket

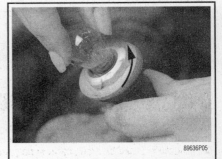

Fig. 124 For the turn signal/parking light bulb, carefully push the bulb in and turn it counterclockwise in order to unlock it . . .

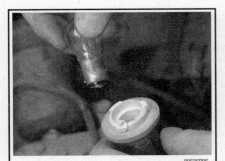

Fig. 125 . . . then carefully remove the bulb from the socket

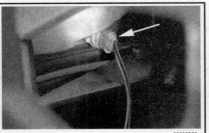

Fig. 126 The driver's side marker light can be accessed through the engine compartment. On the passenger's side (shown), you may have to reach under the vehicle

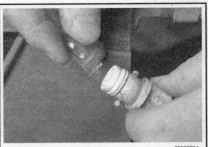

Fig. 127 Twist the light bulb and socket to unlock it, remove the assembly and pull the bulb from the socket

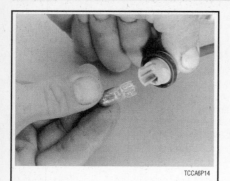

Fig. 128 Simply pull this side marker light bulb straight from its socket

Fig. 129 Once the carpet is pulled down, you can see the retaining wingnuts which must be removed to access the rear bulbs

Fig. 130 Carefully pull the rear light assembly away from the vehicle for access to the bulbs

Fig. 131 Depress the bulb and socket retaining tabs, turn the socket . . .

Fig. 132 . . . then pull the bulb and socket from the rear of the lens

Fig. 133 Carefully press the bulb in and twist it approximately ⅛ turn counterclockwise to remove it from the socket

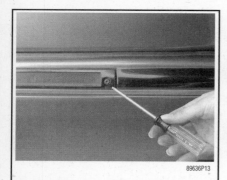

Fig. 134 Use a Torx® driver to unfasten the rear side marker lens retaining screws

Fig. 135 Pull the lamp assembly out in order to access the bulb and connector

Fig. 136 The pins (1) have to be disengaged from the lens retainers (2) in order to remove the bulb and socket assembly

Rear Turn Signal, Brake and Parking Lights

▶ See Figures 129, 130, 131, 132 and 133

1. Most rear lamps can be accessed from inside the trunk. Open trunk and look for access past the carpet.

2. By pulling back the carpet or removing the large plastic carpet retaining nuts, you can see the back of the light assembly.

3. If you can reach the bulb from inside the trunk, you don't need to remove the lens assembly to replace the bulbs. But, if you can't reach the bulb and connector assembly, you may need to remove the lens assembly.

4. If necessary, remove the tail light panel screws and the lens assembly.

5. You can now simply turn the bulb connector assembly counterclockwise and remove it from the lens housing.

➡ To remove the bulb, turn the twist lock socket (at the rear of the housing) counterclockwise ¼ turn, then remove the socket with the bulb; replace the bulb if defective.

To install:

6. Install the bulb in the socket.

7. Check that the connector is properly connected to the bulb and try the lights. Don't assemble everything until you are certain the bulb works. If the bulb doesn't work, check the grounds and use a 12 volt test light to make certain you have power to the bulb.

8. When you're sure the lights work, install the bulb into the lens housing.

9. If removed, install the lens housing and carpeting.

Rear Side Marker Light Bulb

▶ See Figures 134, 135, 136 and 137

1. If equipped, remove the side marker lens assembly retaining screws. The lens may be secured with Torx® screws, depending upon the year of your vehicle.

2. If there are no lens retaining screws, use a flat-bladed tool wrapped in cloth to carefully pry the lens off, to access the bulbs.

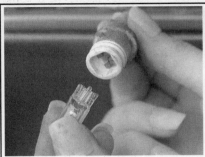

Fig. 137 Remove the bulb by pulling it straight out of the socket

Fig. 138 Use a screwdriver to unfasten the center high-mount lens retaining screws . . .

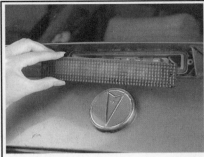

Fig. 139 . . . then remove the lens for access to the bulbs

Fig. 140 Pull the light bulb from the retaining clips

Fig. 141 Unfasten the license plate light retaining screws

Fig. 142 Lower the assembly, then twist and unlock the bulb and socket from the lens

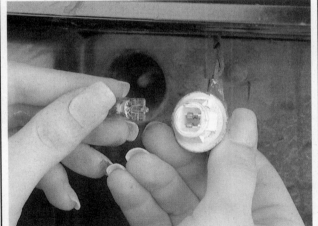

Fig. 143 Remove the bulb by pulling it straight out of the socket

3. Pull the lamp assembly away from the side of the vehicle to access the light bulb and connector.
4. Turn the bulb and socket to disengage the lens retainers, then remove the bulb and socket from the lamp.
5. Pull the bulb straight out of the socket and replace if necessary.
6. Installation is the reverse of the removal procedure.

High-Mount Brake Light

▶ See Figures 138, 139 and 140

➡ Depending upon the vehicle, the center high-mount brake light may be accessed from outside the vehicle, through the trunk, or through the passenger compartment.

1. Remove the center high-mount bracket light lens retaining screws.
2. Remove the lens in order to get to the bulbs.
3. Carefully pull the bulb away from its retaining clip contacts.
4. Installation is the reverse of the removal procedure. Before installing the lens, make sure the brake light operates properly by having an assistant depress the brake pedal.

License Plate Lights

▶ See Figures 141, 142 and 143

1. Remove the license plate light retaining screws.
2. Carefully lower the license plate light assembly. Disengage the bulb and socket from the lens.
3. Carefully pull the bulb straight out of the socket.
4. Installation is the reverse of the removal procedure. Before raising the assembly into position, turn on the headlights, and check that the license plate bulb(s) illuminate.

Trunk Lights

▶ See Figure 144

The trunk, or cargo area, bulb is replaced simply by pulling it straight out of the socket.

Fig. 144 To remove the trunk light, depress the bulb, rotate it ⅛ turn, then remove it from the socket

Fog Lights

REMOVAL & INSTALLATION

▶ **See Figures 145, 146, 147 and 148**

1. Disconnect the negative battery cable.
2. Remove the fog lamp-to-bumper assembly retaining screws. Be careful not to disturb the adjusting screw.
3. Squeeze the bulb and socket assembly retaining clip prongs inward, and pull the bulb and socket from the rear of the fog lamp.
4. Unplug the fog lamp electrical connector.
5. Install the assembly, retaining bolts and connect the negative battery cable.

AIMING

1. Park the car on a level surface, at least 25 ft. (7.6m) from a wall that is perpendicular to the ground surface. Make sure there is no excess weight in the trunk, unless you normally travel with that amount of weight in the car. Bounce the car a few times to settle the suspension.
2. Measure and record the distance from the ground to the center of each fog light lens.
3. Turn the fog lights on and adjust so the hot-spots (lit area of most concentrated intensity) are 4 in. (10cm) below the height of the lenses. The ADJUSTING screw is located at the top right corner of the fog light.

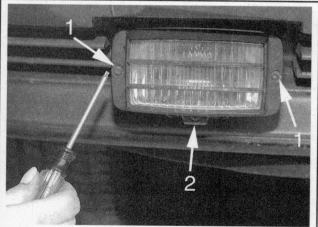

Fig. 145 Unfasten the 2 Torx® fog light retaining screws (1), making sure not to disturb the adjusting screw (2)

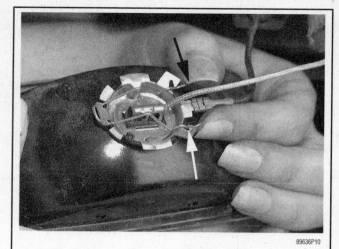

Fig. 146 Squeeze the bulb and socket retaining clip prongs inward . . .

Fig. 147 . . . then pull the bulb from the rear of the fog lamp

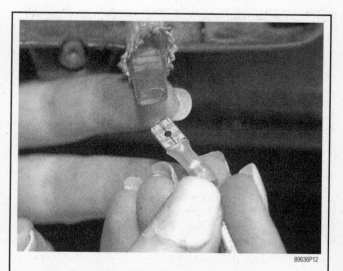

Fig. 148 Unfasten the fog lamp electrical connector

LIGHT BULB APPLICATIONS

BULB USAGE	TRADE NO.
INSTRUMENT CLUSTER, INDICATOR WARNING LAMPS	
Illumination	PC195
Telltales	PC118
INTERIOR LIGHTING	
Ashtray	161
CHMSL	1156
Console Shift Lamp	558
Courtesy and Reading Lamps	563
Door Courtesy	194
Glove Box	194
Hush Panel	168
Rail Courtesy Lamps	A3173B
Visor Vanity	564
EXTERIOR LIGHTING	
Backup	1141
Combination Tail	194
Fog	885
Front Sidemarkers	194
Headlamp	
High Beam	9005
Low Beam	9006
License	194
Front Park/Turn	2057NA
Rear Sidemarkers	194
Rear Tail/Stop Signal	2057
Rear Turn	1156
Trunk	93
Underhood	561

89636C01

CIRCUIT PROTECTION

Fuses

Fuses (located on a swing down unit near the steering column or in the glove box) protect all the major electrical systems in the car. In case of an electrical overload, the fuse melts, breaking the circuit and stopping the flow of electricity.

If a fuse blows, the cause should be investigated and corrected before the installation of a new fuse. This, however, is easier to say than to do. Because each fuse protects a limited number of components, your job is narrowed down somewhat. Begin your investigation by looking for obvious fraying, loose connections, breaks in insulation, etc. Use the techniques outlined at the beginning of this section. Electrical problems are almost always a real headache to solve, but if you are patient and persistent, and approach the problem logically (that is, don't start replacing electrical components randomly), you will eventually find the solution.

Each fuse block uses miniature fuses (normally plug-in blade terminal-type for these vehicles) which are designed for increased circuit protection and greater reliability. The compact plug-in or blade terminal design allows for fingertip removal and replacement.

Although most fuses are interchangeable in size, the amperage values are not. Should you install a fuse with too high a value, damaging current could be allowed to destroy the component you were attempting to protect by using a fuse in the first place. The plug-in type fuses have a volt number molded on them and are color coded for easy identification. Be sure to only replace a fuse with the proper amperage rated substitute.

A blown fuse can easily be checked by visual inspection or by continuity checking.

The amperage of each fuse and the circuit it protects are marked on the fuse box, which is located under the left side (driver's side) of the instrument panel and pulls down for easy access.

REPLACEMENT

▶ **See Figures 149 thru 154**

1. Remove the trim panels or covers necessary for access to the fuses.
2. Locate the fuse for the circuit in question.

➡**When replacing the fuse, DO NOT use one with a higher amperage rating.**

3. Check the fuse by pulling it from the fuse block and observing the element. If it is broken, install a replacement fuse the same amperage rating. If the fuse blows again, check the circuit for a short to ground or faulty device in the circuit protected by the fuse.

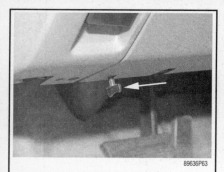

Fig. 149 To access the fuse block, unfasten the plastic panel retaining wingnuts . . .

Fig. 150 . . . then pull the lower steering column trim panel away

Fig. 151 Your vehicle may come with a fuse puller which allows you to easily grip the fuse . . .

Fig. 152 . . . and pull it from the block to check if it's blown and in need of replacement

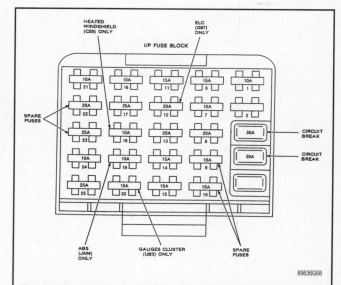

Fig. 154 Typical fuse block identification—fuse locations will vary depending upon the vehicle and option packages

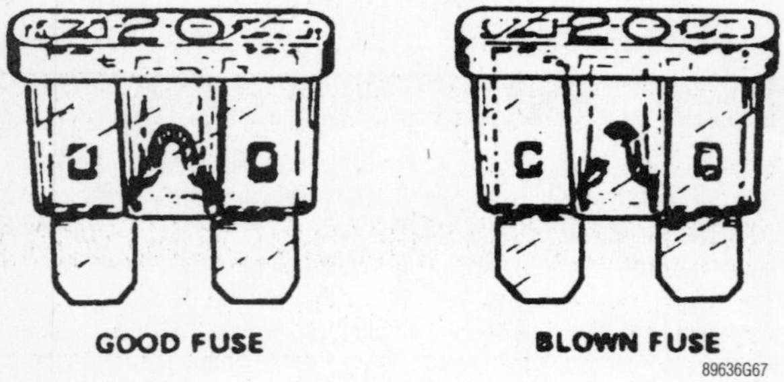

4. Continuity can also be checked with the fuse installed in the fuse block with the use of a test light connected across the 2 test points on the end of the fuse. If the test light lights, replace the fuse. Check the circuit for a short to ground or faulty device in the circuit protected by the fuse.

Fusible Links

▶ See Figures 155 and 156

The fusible link is a short length of special Hypalon (high temperature) insulated wire, integral with the engine compartment wiring harness and should not be confused with standard wire. It is several wire gauges smaller than the circuit which it protects. Under no circumstances should a fuse link replacement repair be made using a length of standard wire cut from bulk stock or from another wiring harness.

GOOD FUSE   **BLOWN FUSE**

Fig. 153 Visual examination will reveal a blown fuse, but it should not be replaced until repairs are made

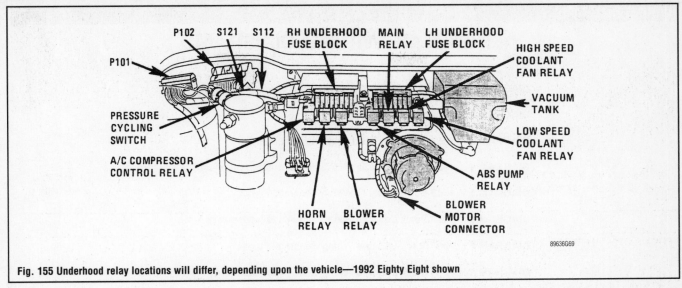

Fig. 155 Underhood relay locations will differ, depending upon the vehicle—1992 Eighty Eight shown

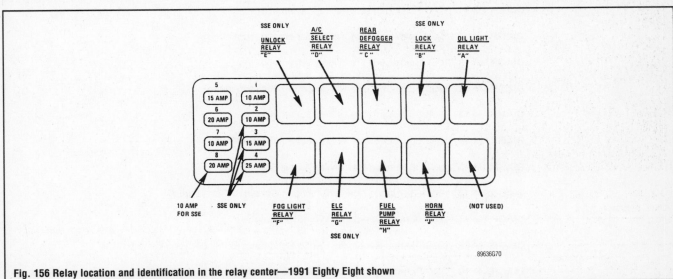

Fig. 156 Relay location and identification in the relay center—1991 Eighty Eight shown

Most newer cars have replaced fusible links with very large plug-in fuses. Sometimes these fuses are referred to as Fusible Links or Maxi-fuses. These new plug in type fusible link no longer require repair; simply replacement like a fuse.

Circuit Breakers

The headlights are protected by a circuit breaker in the headlamp switch. If the circuit breaker trips, the headlights will either flash on and off, or stay off altogether. The circuit breaker rests automatically after the overload is removed.

The windshield wipers are also protected by a circuit breaker. If the motor overheats, the circuit breaker will trip, remaining off until the motor cools or the overload is removed. One common cause of overheating is operation of the wipers in heavy snow.

The circuit breakers for the power door locks and power windows are located in the fuse box.

Flashers

REPLACEMENT

The turn signal flasher is under the instrument panel to the left of the steering column brace. On the Bonneville, it may be on the left side on the shroud. The hazard flasher is under the instrument panel to the right of the steering column.

The turn signal flasher is installed in a clamp attached to the base of the steering column support inside the car. In all cases, replacement is made by unplugging the old unit and plugging in a new one.

WIRING DIAGRAMS

INDEX OF WIRING DIAGRAMS

DIAGRAM 1   Sample Diagram: How To Read & Interpret Wiring Diagrams

DIAGRAM 2   Wiring Diagram Symbols

DIAGRAM 3   1987-88 Buick LeSabre Wiring Schematic

DIAGRAM 4   1987-88 Buick LeSabre Wiring Schematic (continued)

DIAGRAM 5   1989 Buick LeSabre Wiring Schematic

DIAGRAM 6   1989 Buick LeSabre Wiring Schematic (continued)

DIAGRAM 7   1990 Buick LeSabre Wiring Schematic

DIAGRAM 8   1990 Buick LeSabre Wiring Schematic (continued)

DIAGRAM 9   1991 Buick LeSabre Wiring Schematic

DIAGRAM 10 1991 Buick LeSabre Wiring Schematic (continued)

DIAGRAM 11 1992 Buick LeSabre Wiring Schematic

DIAGRAM 12 1992 Buick LeSabre Wiring Schematic (continued)

DIAGRAM 13 1993 Buick LeSabre Wiring Schematic

DIAGRAM 14 1993 Buick LeSabre Wiring Schematic (continued)

DIAGRAM 15 1987-88 Pontiac Bonneville Wiring Schematic

DIAGRAM 16 1987-88 Pontiac Bonneville Wiring Schematic (continued)

DIAGRAM 17 1989 Pontiac Bonneville Wiring Schematic

DIAGRAM 18 1989 Pontiac Bonneville Wiring Schematic (continued)

DIAGRAM 19 1990 Pontiac Bonneville Wiring Schematic

DIAGRAM 20 1990 Pontiac Bonneville Wiring Schematic (continued)

DIAGRAM 21 1991 Pontiac Bonneville Wiring Schematic

DIAGRAM 22 1991 Pontiac Bonneville Wiring Schematic (continued)

DIAGRAM 23 1992 Pontiac Bonneville Wiring Schematic

DIAGRAM 24 1992 Pontiac Bonneville Wiring Schematic (continued)

DIAGRAM 25 1993 Pontiac Bonneville Wiring Schematic

DIAGRAM 26 1993 Pontiac Bonneville Wiring Schematic (continued)

DIAGRAM 27 1987-88 Oldsmobile Eighty Eight Wiring Schematic

DIAGRAM 28 1987-88 Oldsmobile Eighty Eight Wiring Schematic (continued)

DIAGRAM 29 1989 Oldsmobile Eighty Eight Wiring Schematic

DIAGRAM 30 1989 Oldsmobile Eighty Eight Wiring Schematic (continued)

89636W0A

INDEX OF WIRING DIAGRAMS

DIAGRAM 31 1990 Oldsmobile Eighty Eight Wiring Schematic

DIAGRAM 32 1990 Oldsmobile Eighty Eight Wiring Schematic (continued)

DIAGRAM 33 1991 Oldsmobile Eighty Eight Wiring Schematic

DIAGRAM 34 1991 Oldsmobile Eighty Eight Wiring Schematic (continued)

DIAGRAM 35 1992 Oldsmobile Eighty Eight Wiring Schematic

DIAGRAM 36 1992 Oldsmobile Eighty Eight Wiring Schematic (continued)

DIAGRAM 37 1993 Oldsmobile Eighty Eight Wiring Schematic

DIAGRAM 38 1993 Oldsmobile Eighty Eight Wiring Schematic (continued)

DIAGRAM 39 1994-95 Buick, Oldsmobile and Pontiac Engine Schematic

DIAGRAM 40 1996-97 Buick, Oldsmobile and Pontiac Engine Schematic

DIAGRAM 41 1998 Buick, Oldsmobile and Pontiac Engine Schematic

DIAGRAM 42 1994-98 Buick, Oldsmobile, Pontiac Starting, Charging, Cooling Chassis Schematics

DIAGRAM 43 1994-96 Buick Headlights Chassis Schematic

DIAGRAM 44 1997-98 Buick Headlights Chassis Schematic

DIAGRAM 45 1994-98 Oldsmobile, Pontiac Headlights w/o DRL Chassis Schematic

DIAGRAM 46 1994-98 Oldsmobile, Pontiac Headlights w/ Twilight Sentinel/DRL Chassis Schematic

DIAGRAM 47 1994-98 Buick Parking/Marker Lights Chassis Schematic

DIAGRAM 48 1994 Oldsmobile Parking/Marker w/o Adaptive Light Monitor Chassis Schematic

DIAGRAM 49 1994 Oldsmobile Parking/Marker w/ Adaptive Light Monitor Chassis Schematic

DIAGRAM 50 1995-98 Oldsmobile Parking/Marker Chassis Schematic

DIAGRAM 51 1994-98 Pontiac Parking/Marker Lights w/o Adaptive Light Monitor Chassis Schematic

DIAGRAM 52 1994-98 Pontiac Parking/Marker Lights w/ Adaptive Light Monitor Chassis Schematic

DIAGRAM 53 1994-98 Buick, Oldsmobile Turn/Hazard/Stop w/o Adaptive Light Monitor Chassis Schematic

DIAGRAM 54 1994-98 Buick, Oldsmobile Turn/Hazard/Stop w/ Adaptive Light Monitor Chassis Schematic

DIAGRAM 55 1994-98 Buick, Oldsmobile Cornering Lights Chassis Schematics

DIAGRAM 56 1994-98 Buick, Oldsmobile, Pontiac Turn/Hazard w/o Adaptive Light Monitor Chassis Schematic

DIAGRAM 57 1994-98 Pontiac Turn/Hazard w/ Adaptive Light Monitor Chassis Schematic

DIAGRAM 58 1994-98 Buick, Oldsmobile, Pontiac Fuel Pump, Back-up, Horns Chassis Schematics

89636W0B

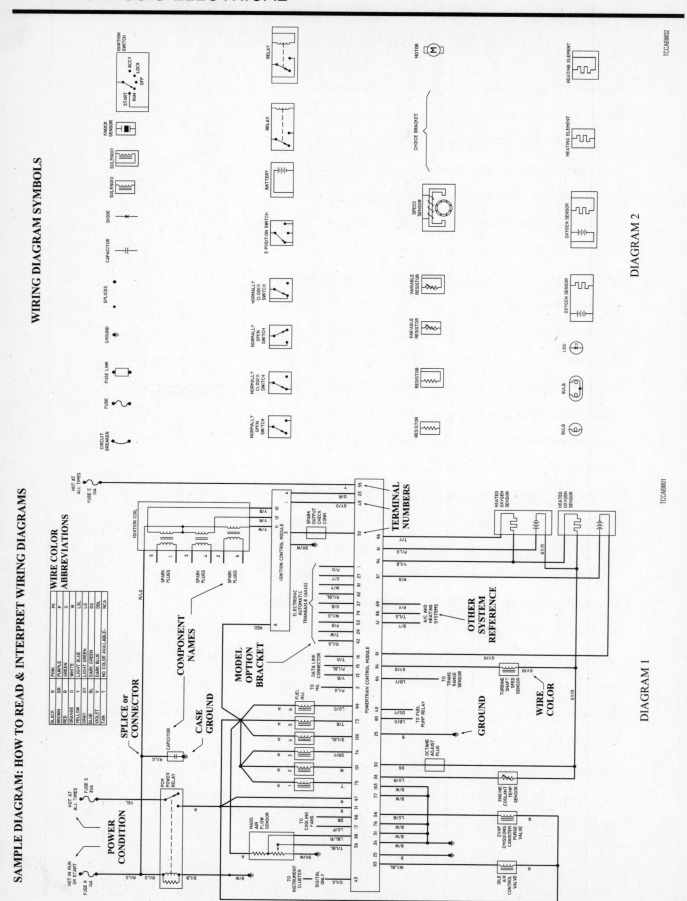

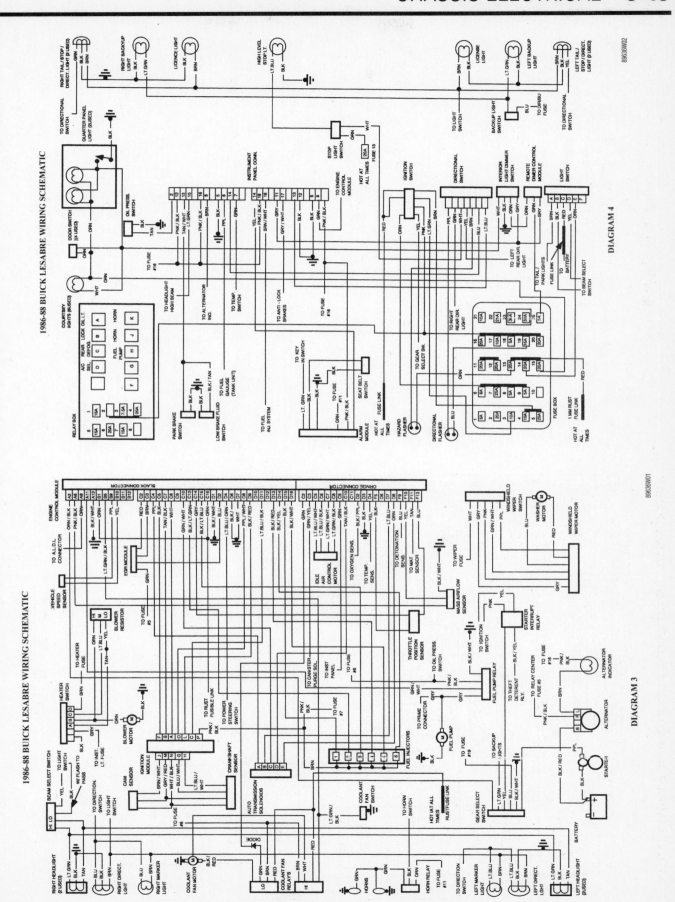

DIAGRAM 4

DIAGRAM 3

1986-88 BUICK LESABRE WIRING SCHEMATIC

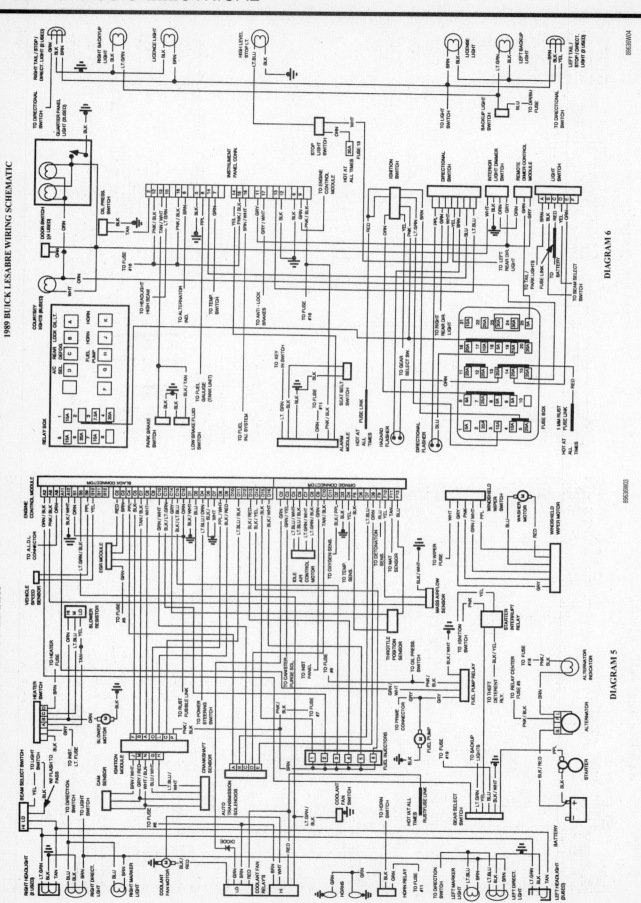

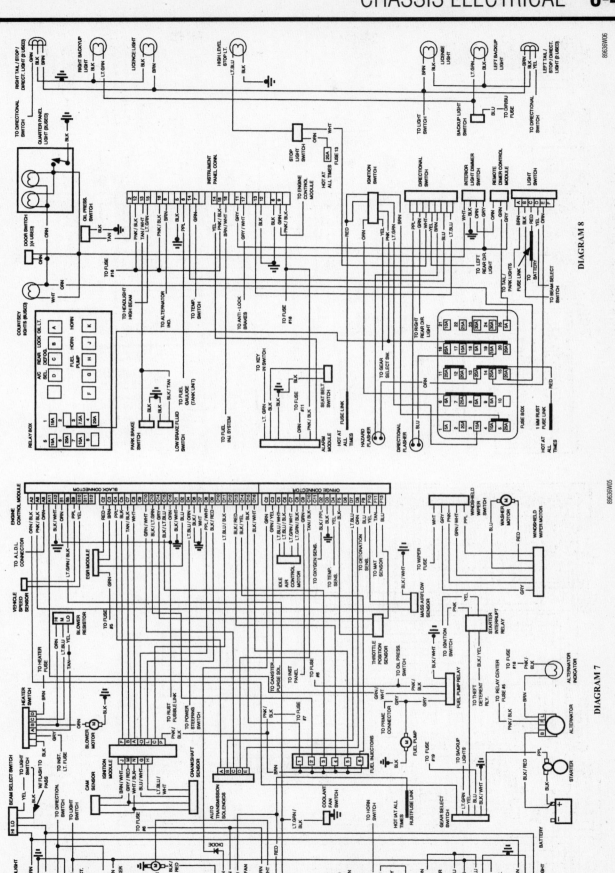

1990 BUICK LESABRE WIRING SCHEMATIC

DIAGRAM 8

DIAGRAM 7

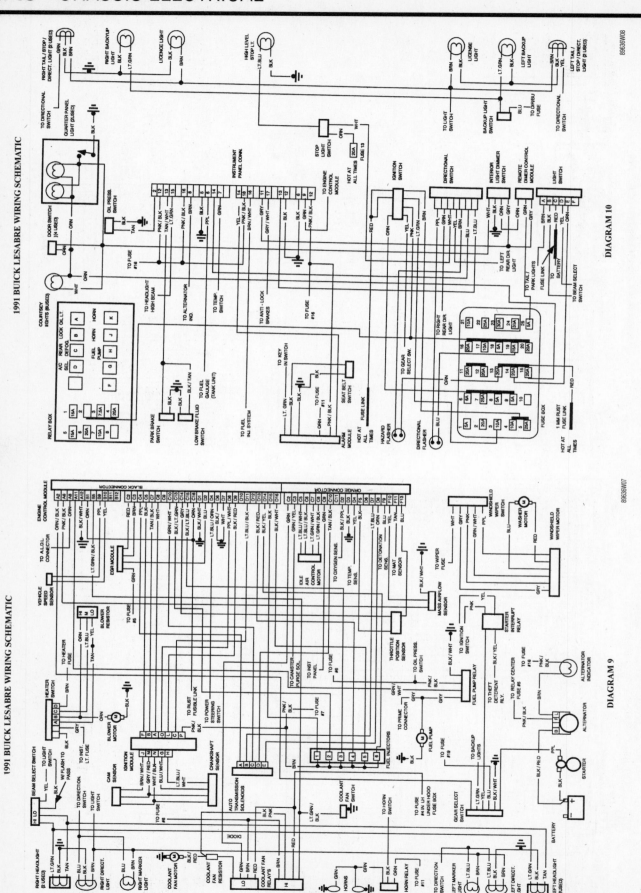

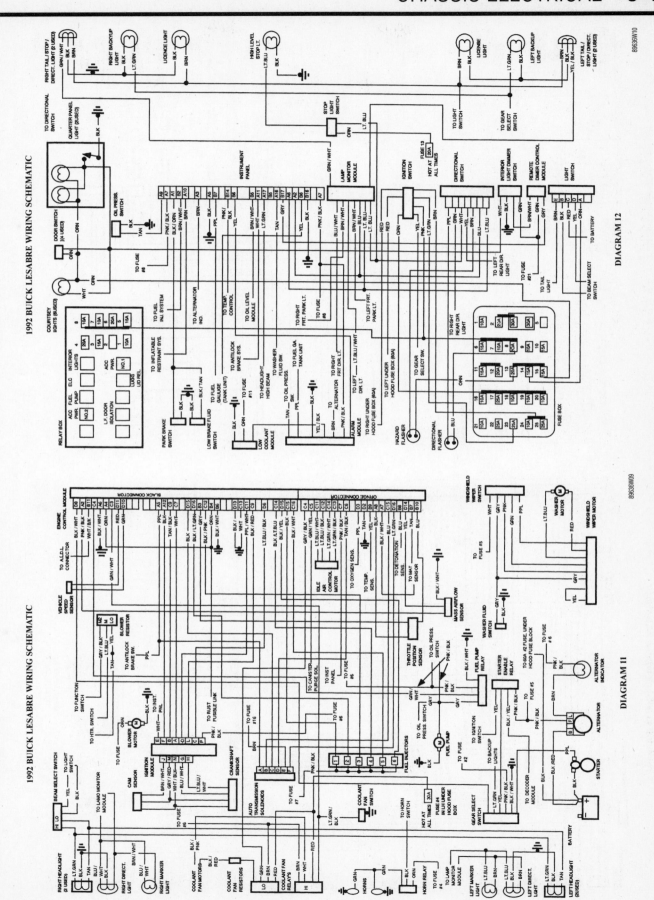

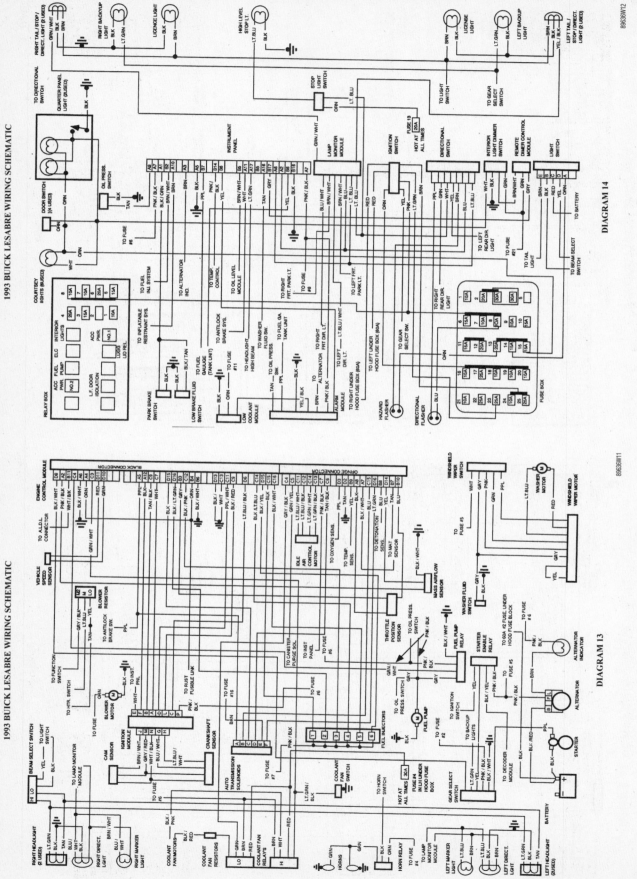

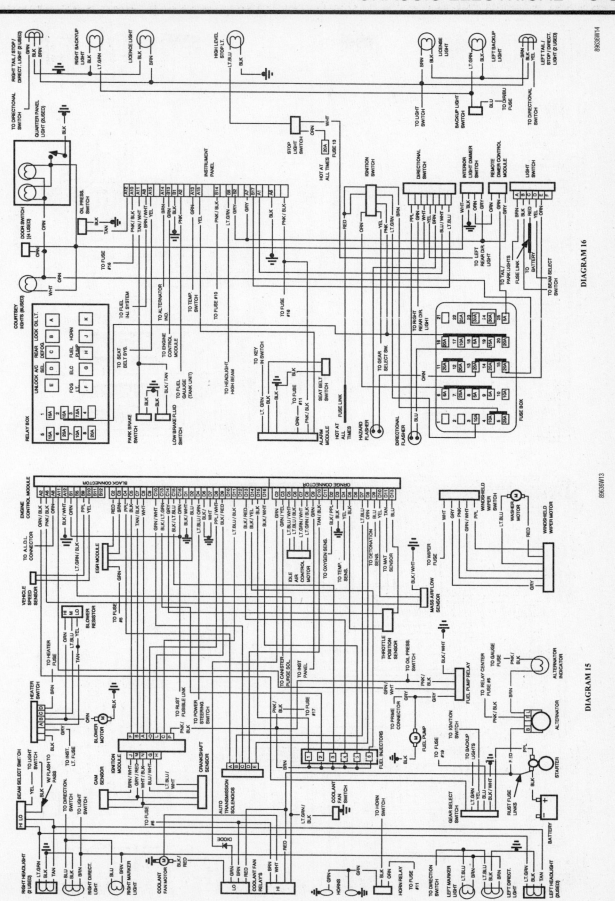

1989 PONTIAC BONNEVILLE WIRING SCHEMATIC

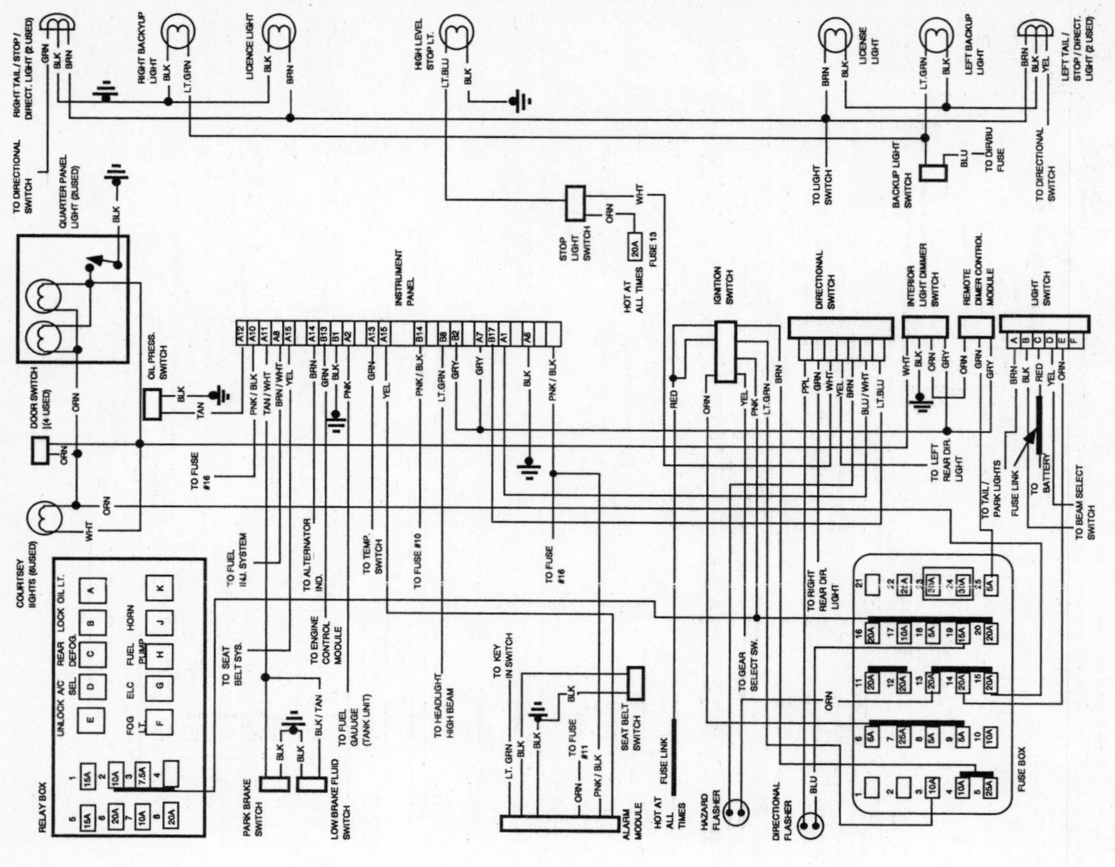

DIAGRAM 18

1989 PONTIAC BONNEVILLE WIRING SCHEMATIC

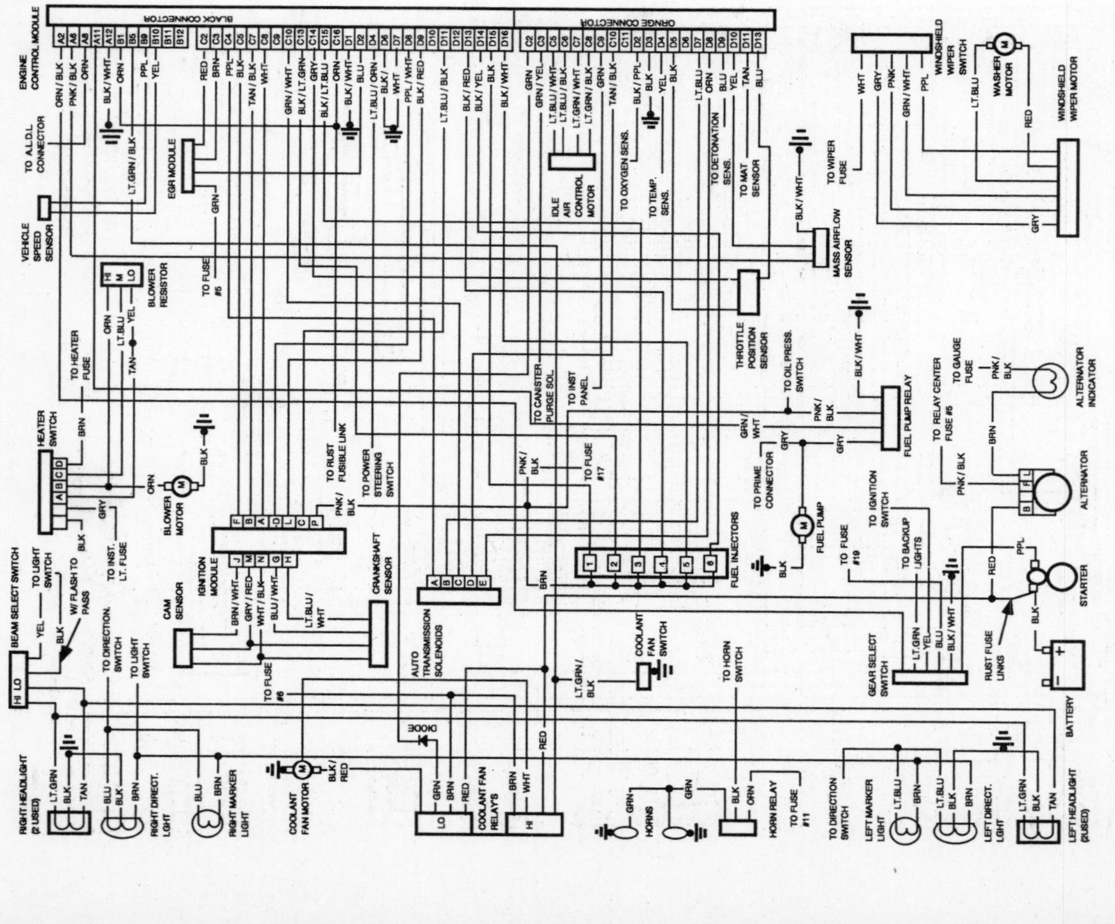

DIAGRAM 17

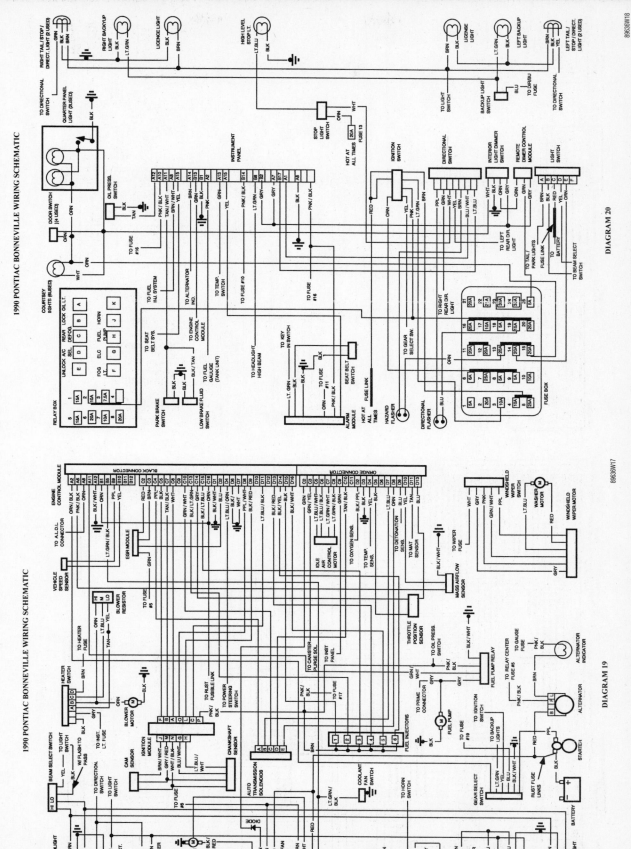

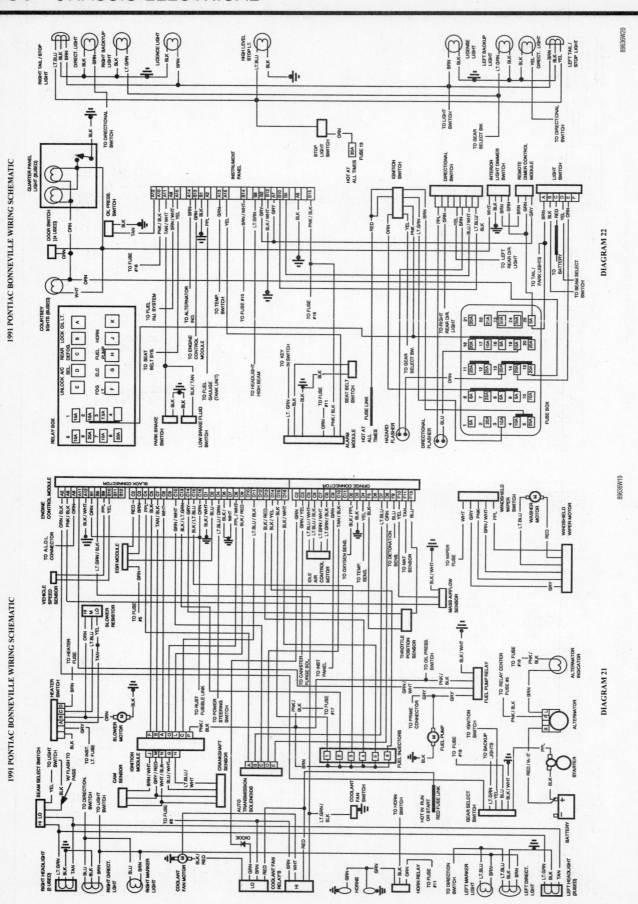

1991 PONTIAC BONNEVILLE WIRING SCHEMATIC

DIAGRAM 22

1991 PONTIAC BONNEVILLE WIRING SCHEMATIC

DIAGRAM 21

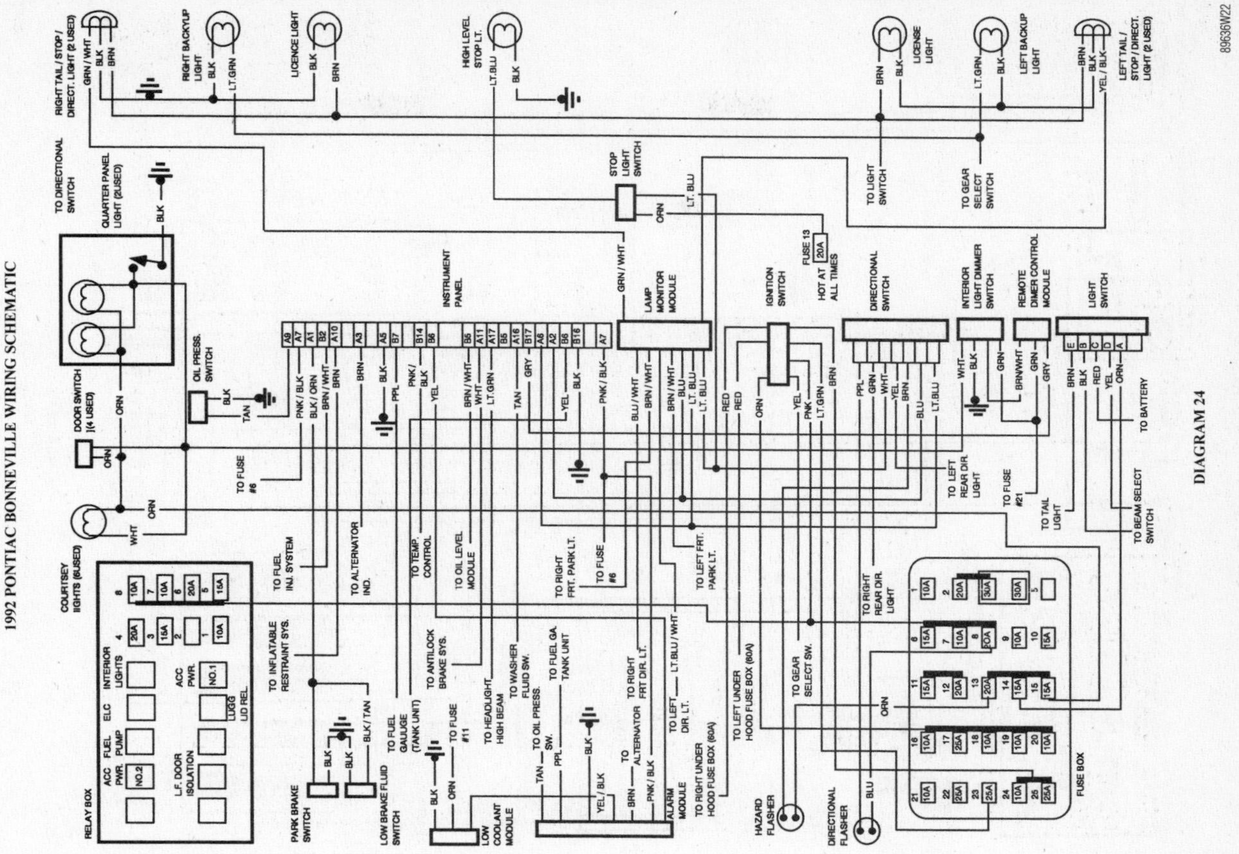

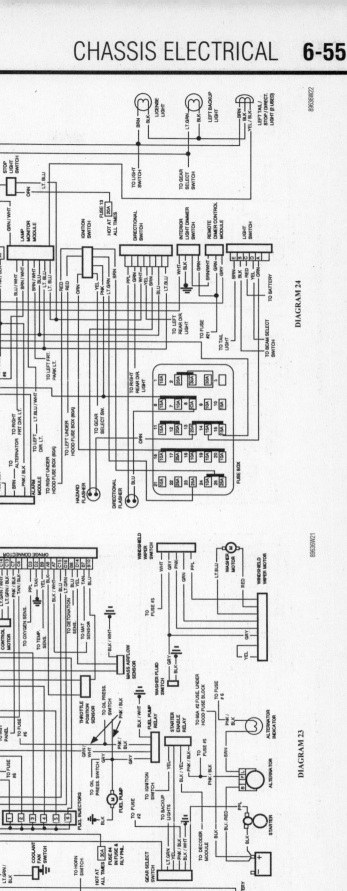

1992 PONTIAC BONNEVILLE WIRING SCHEMATIC

DIAGRAM 24

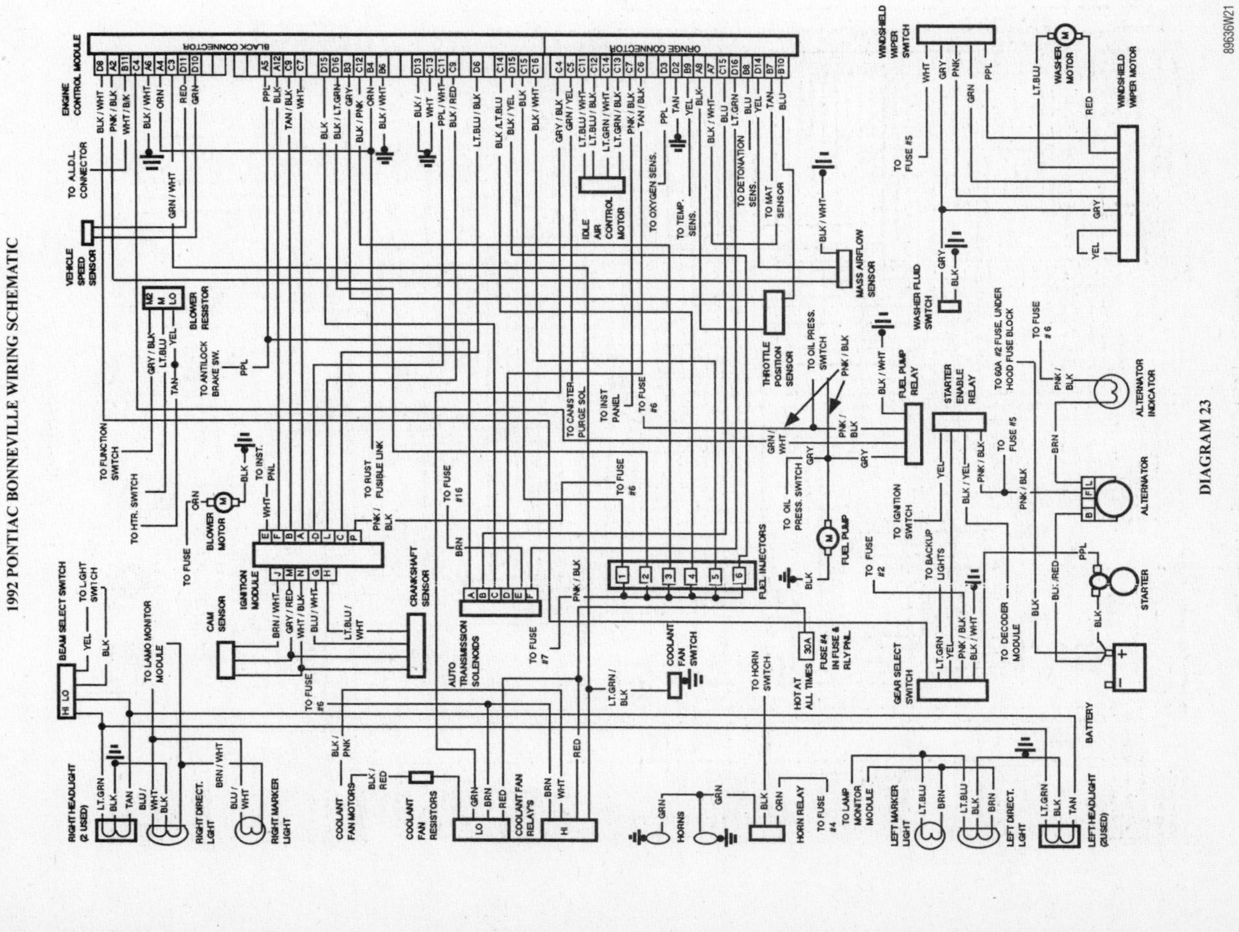

1992 PONTIAC BONNEVILLE WIRING SCHEMATIC

DIAGRAM 23

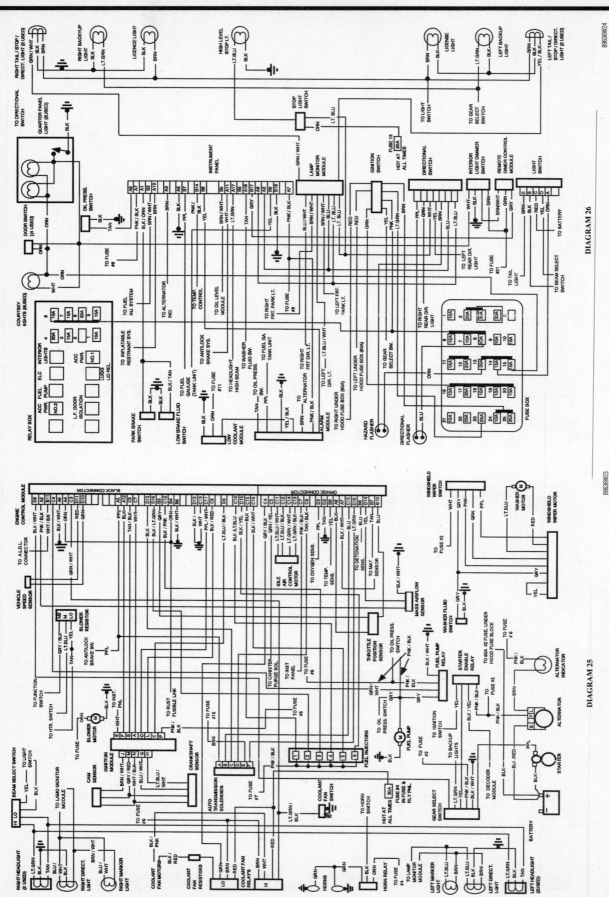

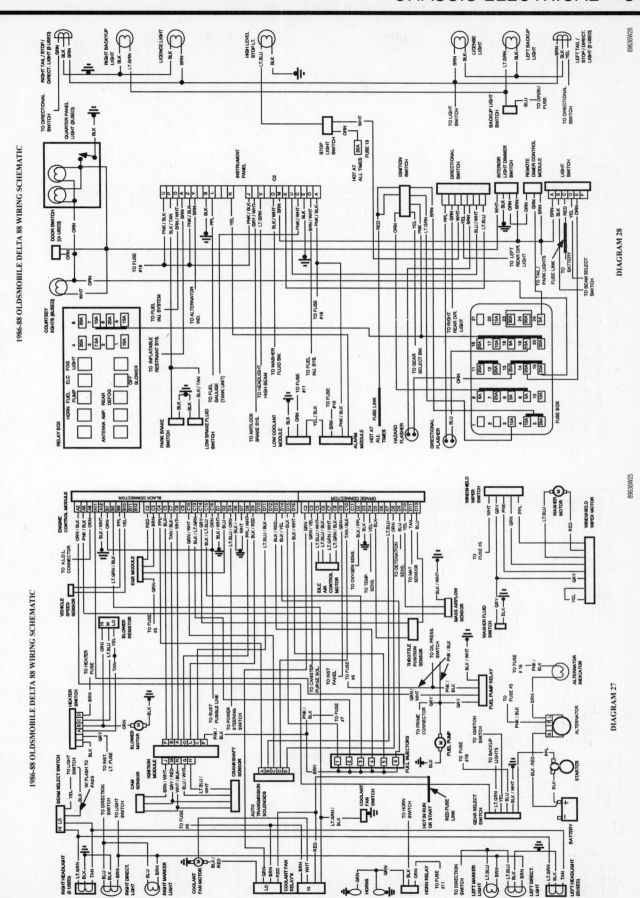

1986-88 OLDSMOBILE DELTA 88 WIRING SCHEMATIC

DIAGRAM 28

1986-88 OLDSMOBILE DELTA 88 WIRING SCHEMATIC

DIAGRAM 27

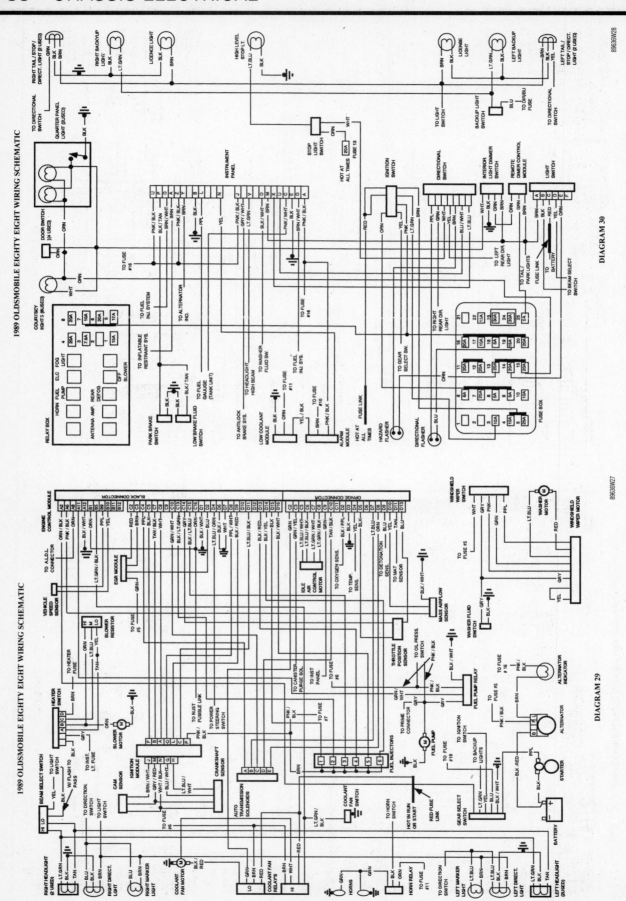

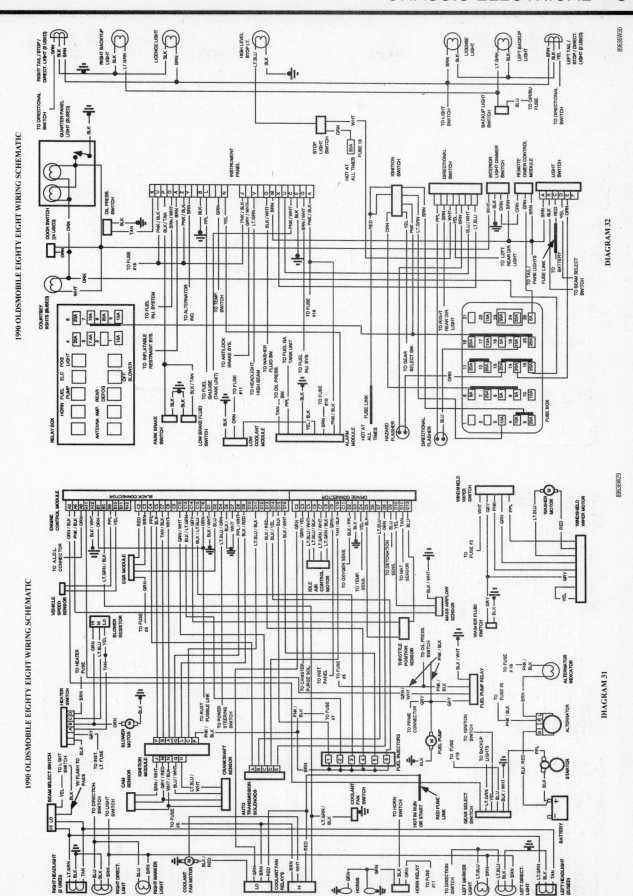

1990 OLDSMOBILE EIGHTY EIGHT WIRING SCHEMATIC

DIAGRAM 32

1990 OLDSMOBILE EIGHTY EIGHT WIRING SCHEMATIC

DIAGRAM 31

1991 OLDSMOBILE EIGHTY EIGHT WIRING SCHEMATIC

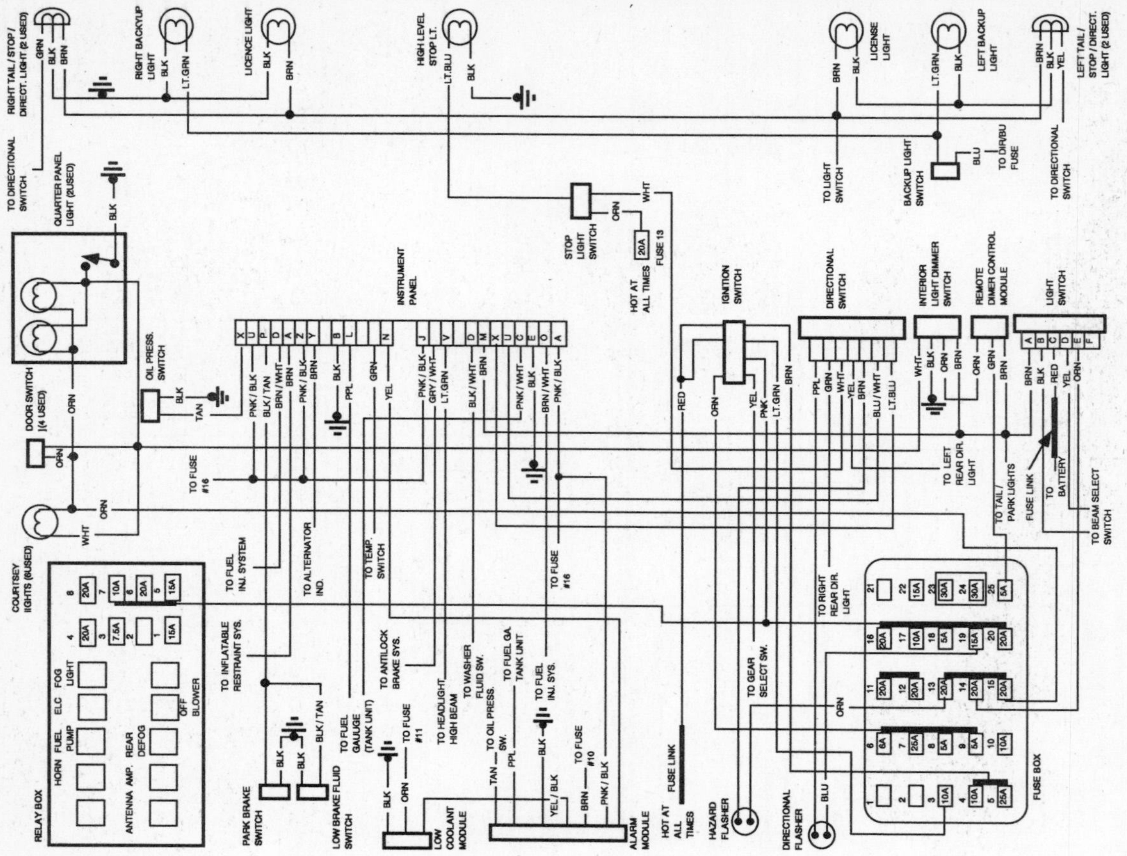

89636W32

DIAGRAM 34

1991 OLDSMOBILE EIGHTY EIGHT WIRING SCHEMATIC

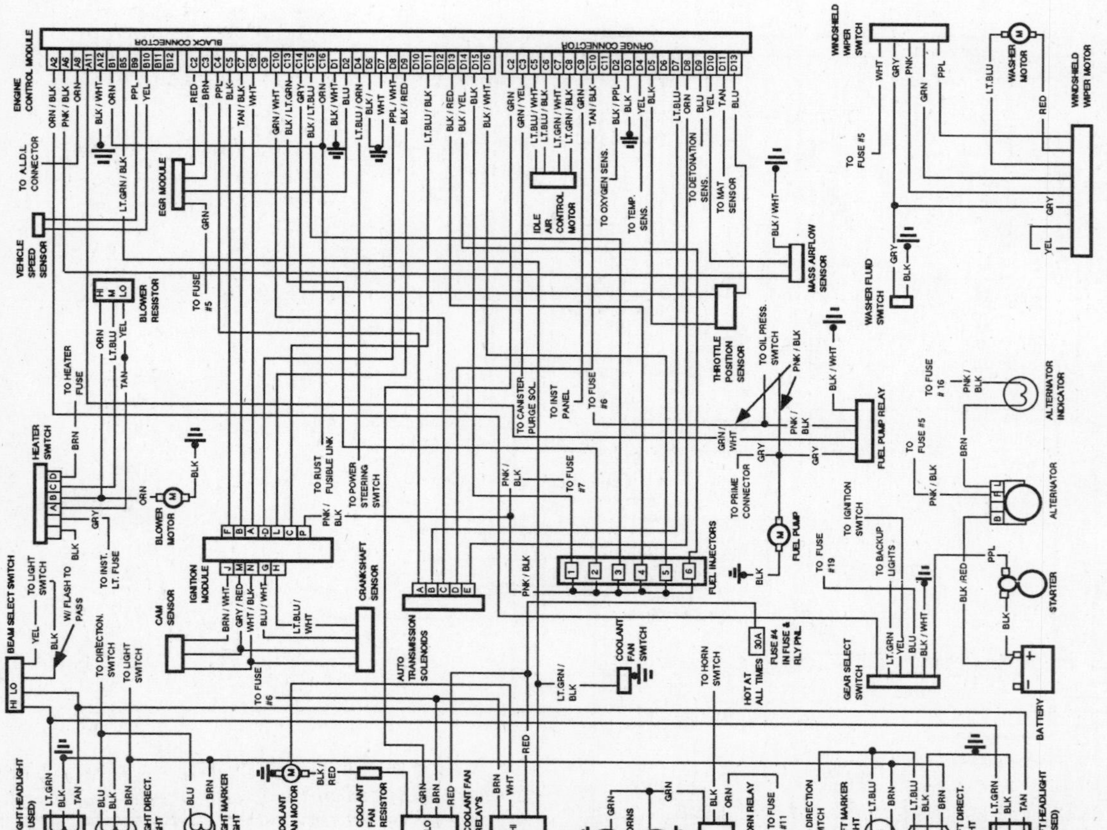

89636W31

DIAGRAM 33

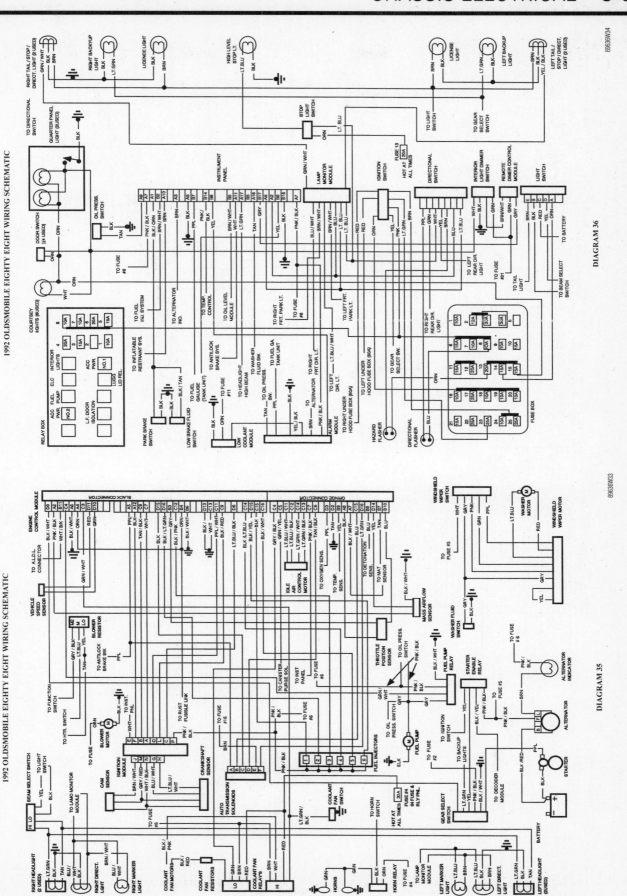

1992 OLDSMOBILE EIGHTY EIGHT WIRING SCHEMATIC

DIAGRAM 36

1992 OLDSMOBILE EIGHTY EIGHT WIRING SCHEMATIC

DIAGRAM 35

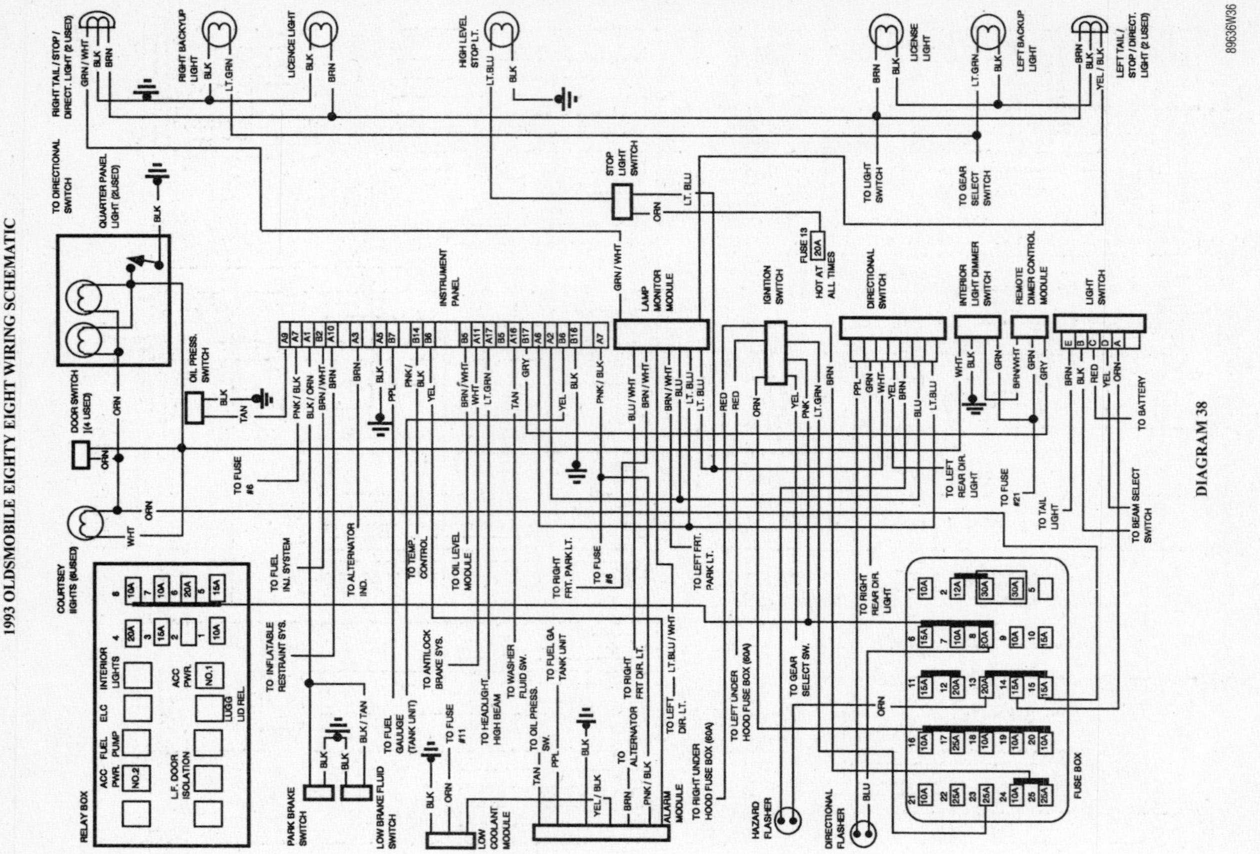
1993 OLDSMOBILE EIGHTY EIGHT WIRING SCHEMATIC
89636W36
INSTRUMENT PANEL
LAMP MONITOR MODULE
IGNITION SWITCH
DIRECTIONAL SWITCH
INTERIOR LIGHT DIMMER SWITCH
REMOTE DIMER CONTROL MODULE
LIGHT SWITCH
STOP LIGHT SWITCH
RELAY BOX
COURTSEY LIGHTS (6 USED)
FUSE BOX
HAZARD FLASHER
DIRECTIONAL FLASHER
PARK BRAKE SWITCH
LOW BRAKE FLUID SWITCH
LOW COOLANT MODULE
ALARM MODULE
DIAGRAM 38

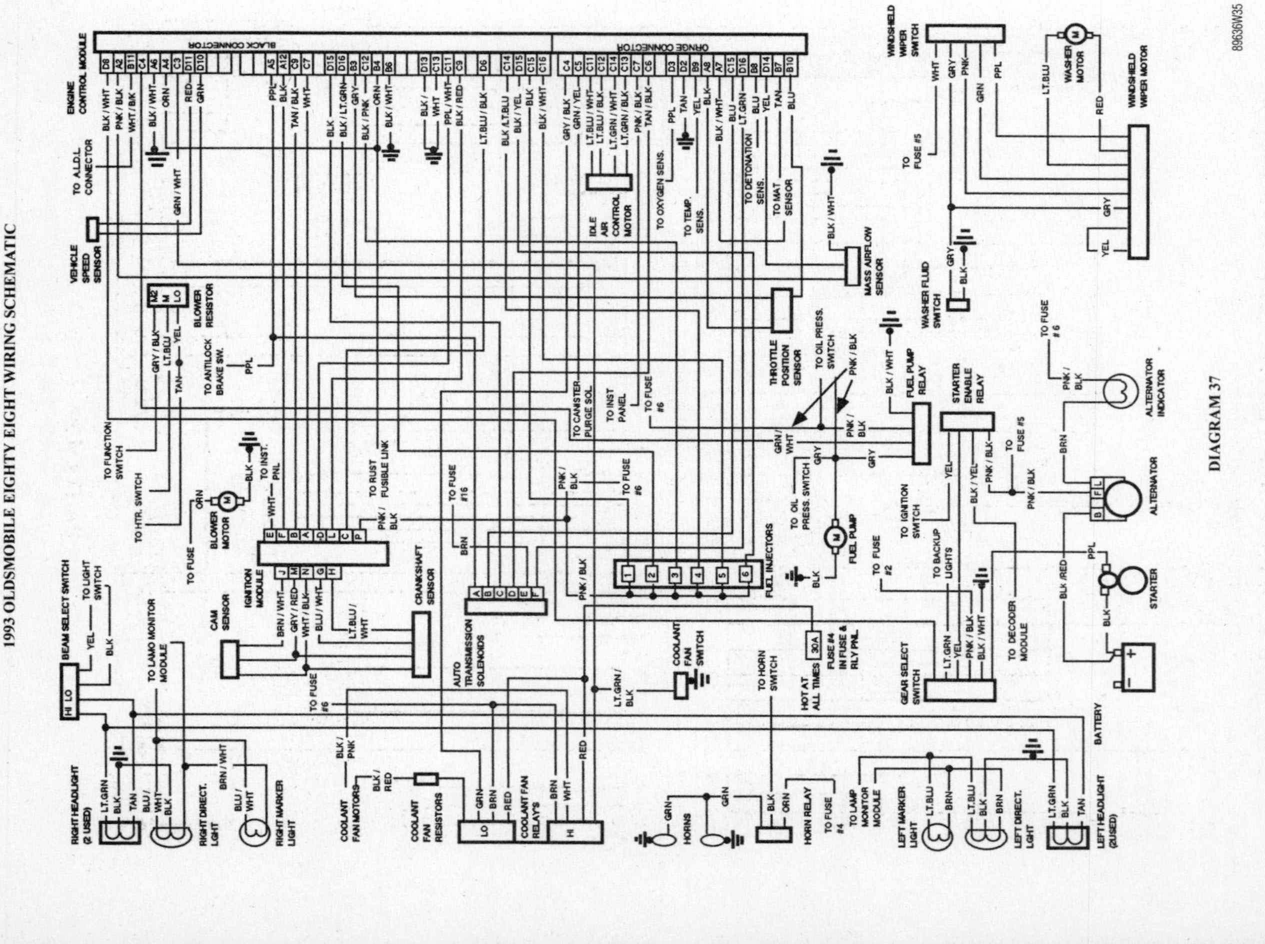
1993 OLDSMOBILE EIGHTY EIGHT WIRING SCHEMATIC
89636W35
ENGINE CONTROL MODULE
BLACK CONNECTOR
ORNGE CONNECTOR
VEHICLE SPEED SENSOR
BLOWER RESISTOR
IGNITION MODULE
CAM SENSOR
CRANKSHAFT SENSOR
AUTO TRANSMISSION SOLENOIDS
IDLE AIR CONTROL MOTOR
MASS AIRFLOW SENSOR
THROTTLE POSITION SENSOR
FUEL PUMP RELAY
STARTER ENABLE RELAY
FUEL INJECTORS
FUEL PUMP
GEAR SELECT SWITCH
WINDSHIELD WIPER SWITCH
WINDSHIELD WIPER MOTOR
WASHER MOTOR
WASHER FLUID SWITCH
ALTERNATOR INDICATOR
ALTERNATOR
STARTER
BATTERY
HORNS
HORN RELAY
COOLANT FAN MOTORS
COOLANT FAN RESISTORS
COOLANT FAN RELAYS
COOLANT FAN SWITCH
BEAM SELECT SWITCH
DIAGRAM 37

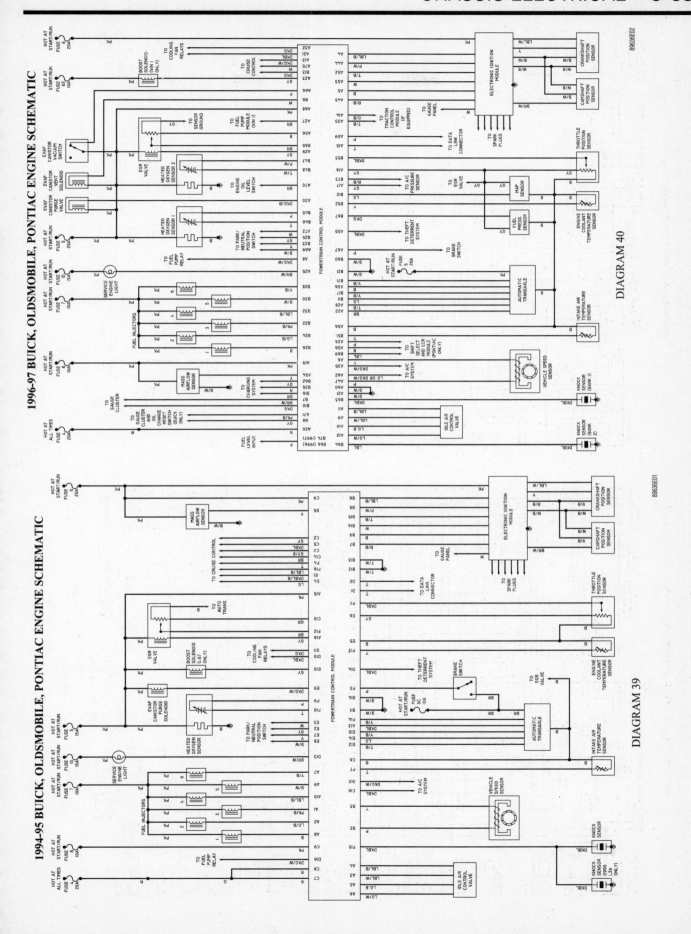

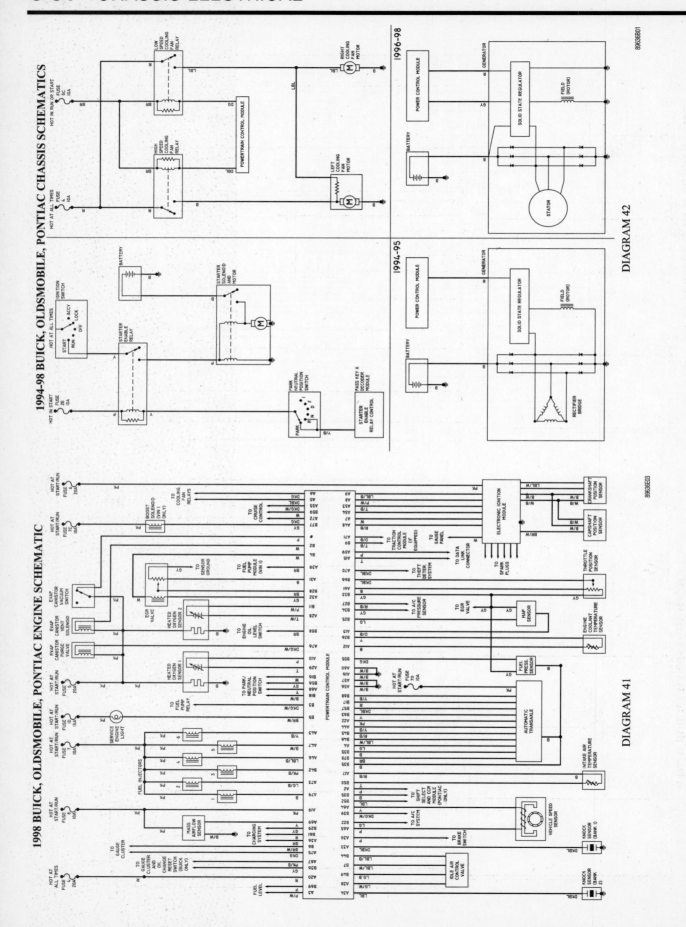

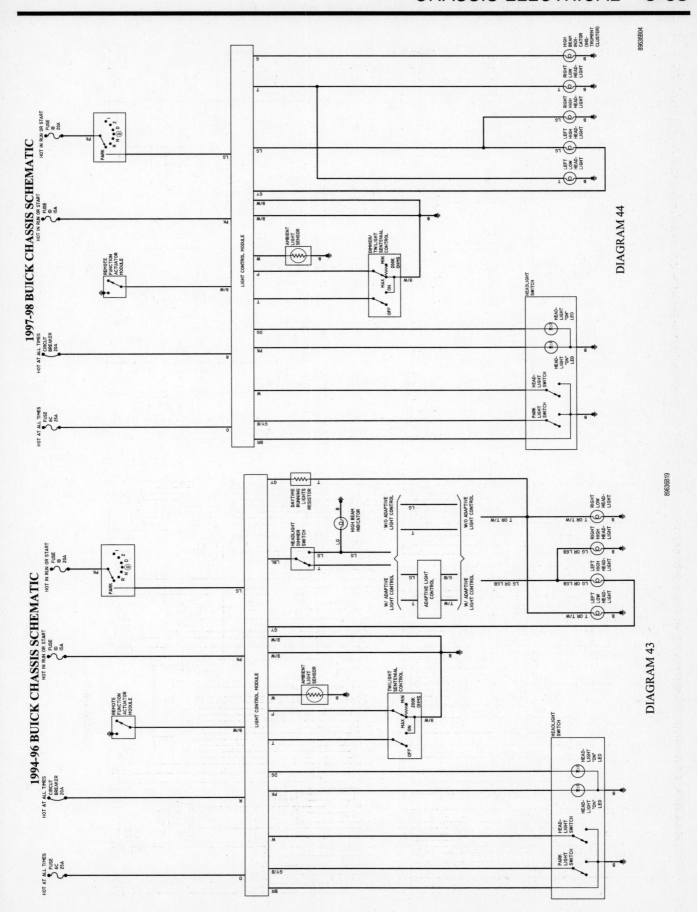

1997-98 BUICK CHASSIS SCHEMATIC

DIAGRAM 44

1994-96 BUICK CHASSIS SCHEMATIC

DIAGRAM 43

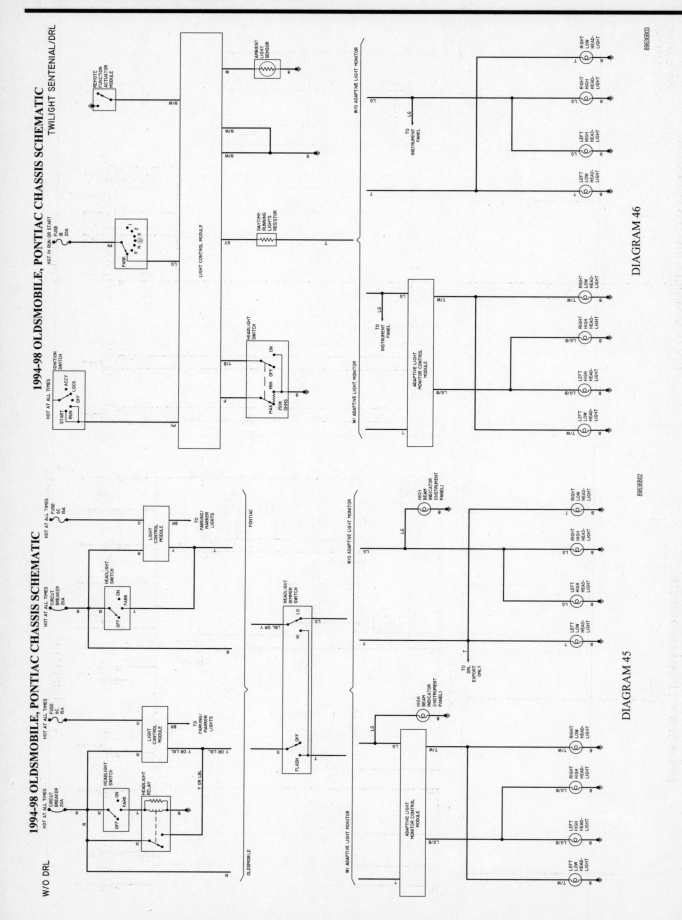

1994-98 OLDSMOBILE, PONTIAC CHASSIS SCHEMATIC

TWILIGHT SENTENIAL/DRL

DIAGRAM 46

1994-98 OLDSMOBILE, PONTIAC CHASSIS SCHEMATIC

W/O DRL

DIAGRAM 45

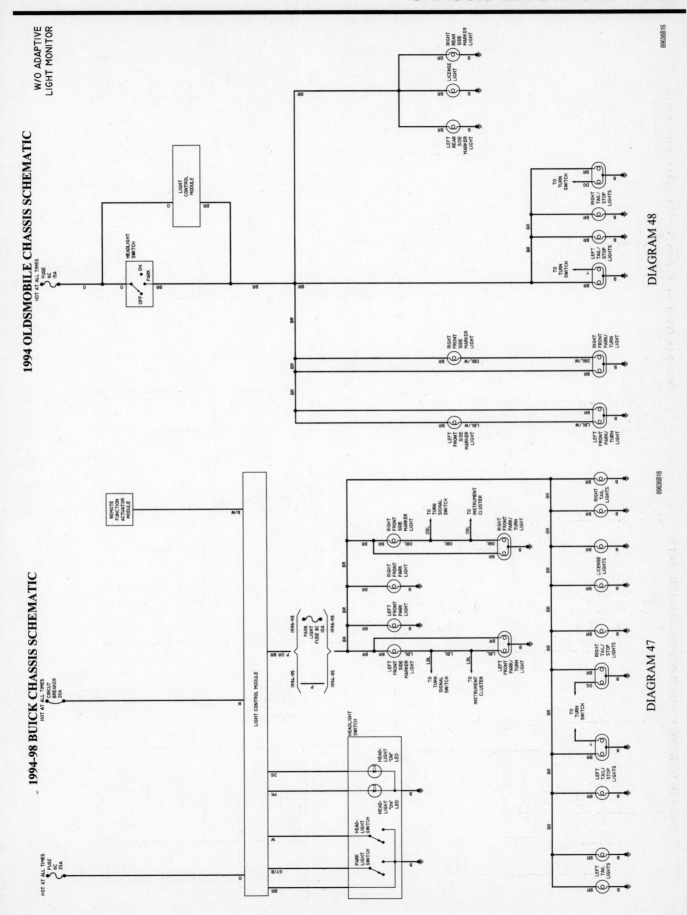

W/O ADAPTIVE LIGHT MONITOR

1994 OLDSMOBILE CHASSIS SCHEMATIC

DIAGRAM 48

1994-98 BUICK CHASSIS SCHEMATIC

DIAGRAM 47

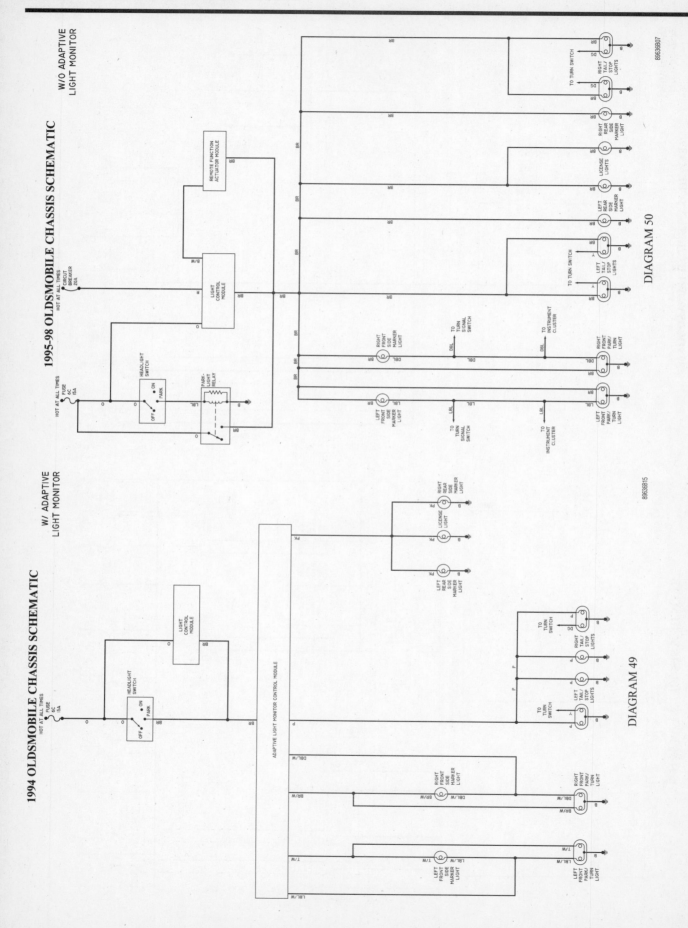

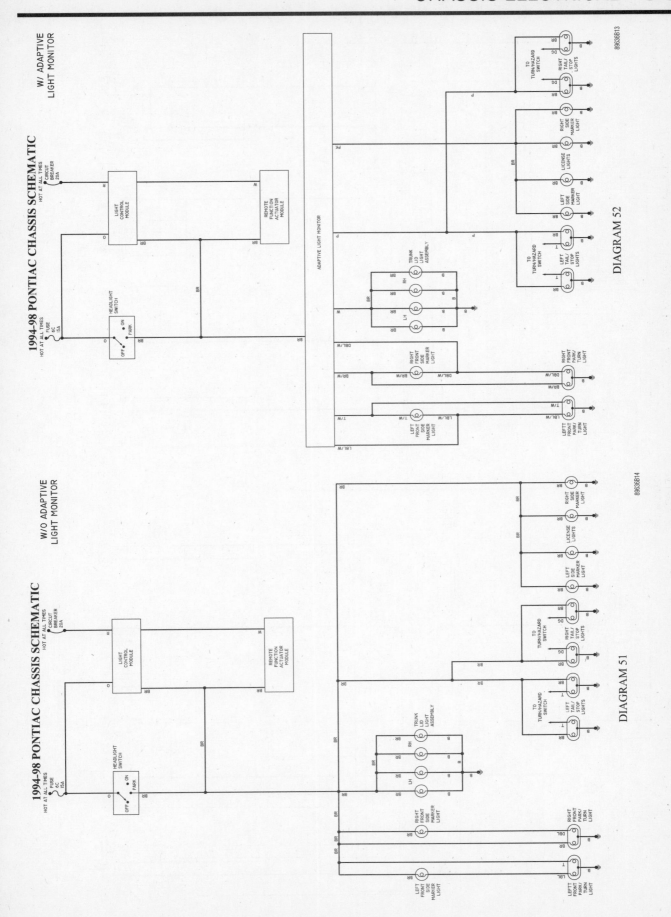

W/ ADAPTIVE LIGHT MONITOR

1994-98 PONTIAC CHASSIS SCHEMATIC

DIAGRAM 52

W/O ADAPTIVE LIGHT MONITOR

1994-98 PONTIAC CHASSIS SCHEMATIC

DIAGRAM 51

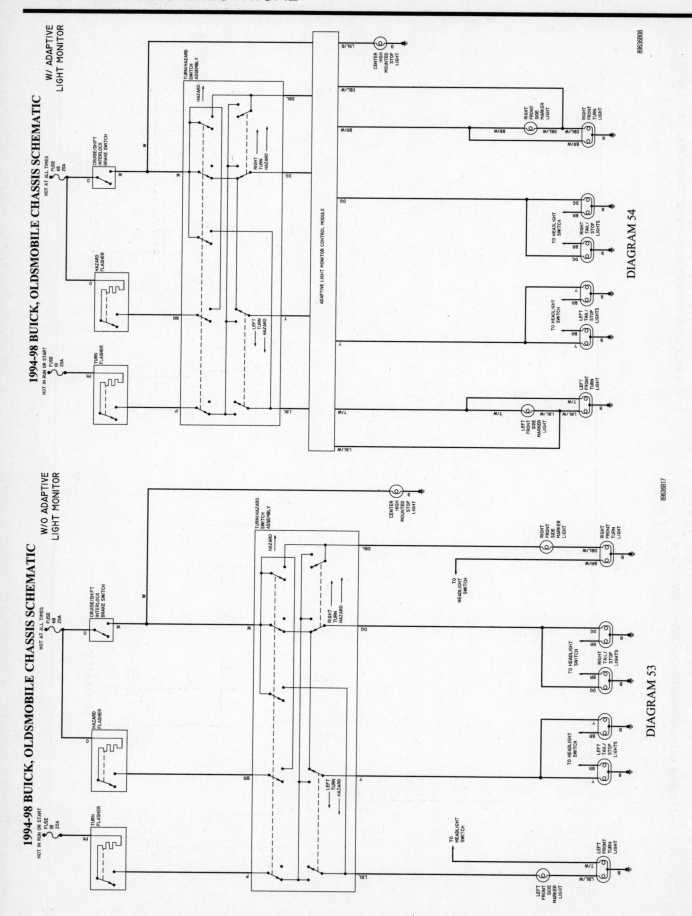

1994-98 BUICK, OLDSMOBILE CHASSIS SCHEMATIC

W/ ADAPTIVE LIGHT MONITOR

DIAGRAM 54

1994-98 BUICK, OLDSMOBILE CHASSIS SCHEMATIC

W/O ADAPTIVE LIGHT MONITOR

DIAGRAM 53

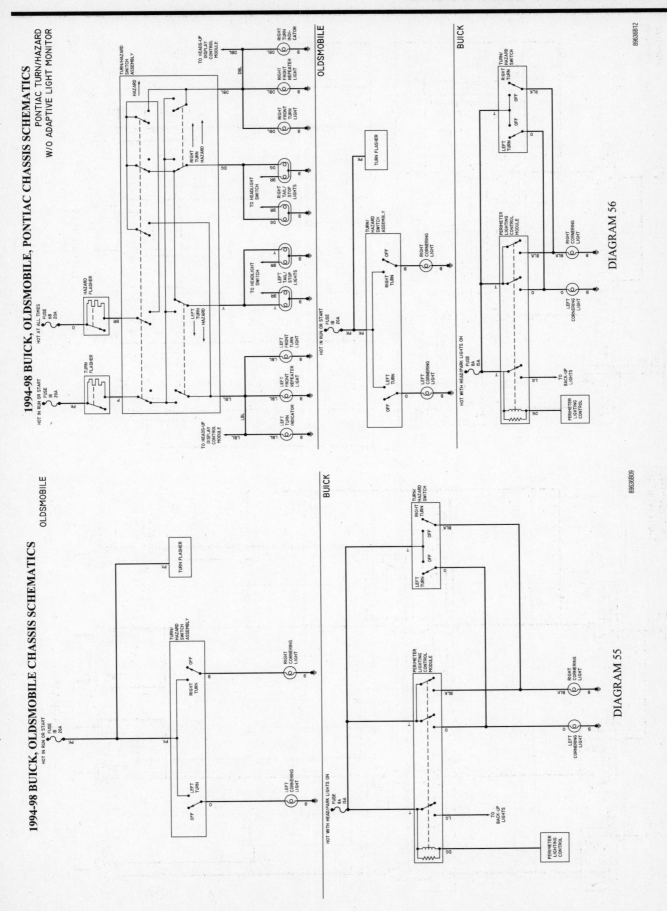

1994-98 BUICK, OLDSMOBILE, PONTIAC CHASSIS SCHEMATICS

PONTIAC TURN/HAZARD
W/O ADAPTIVE LIGHT MONITOR

OLDSMOBILE

BUICK

DIAGRAM 56

1994-98 BUICK, OLDSMOBILE CHASSIS SCHEMATICS

OLDSMOBILE

BUICK

DIAGRAM 55

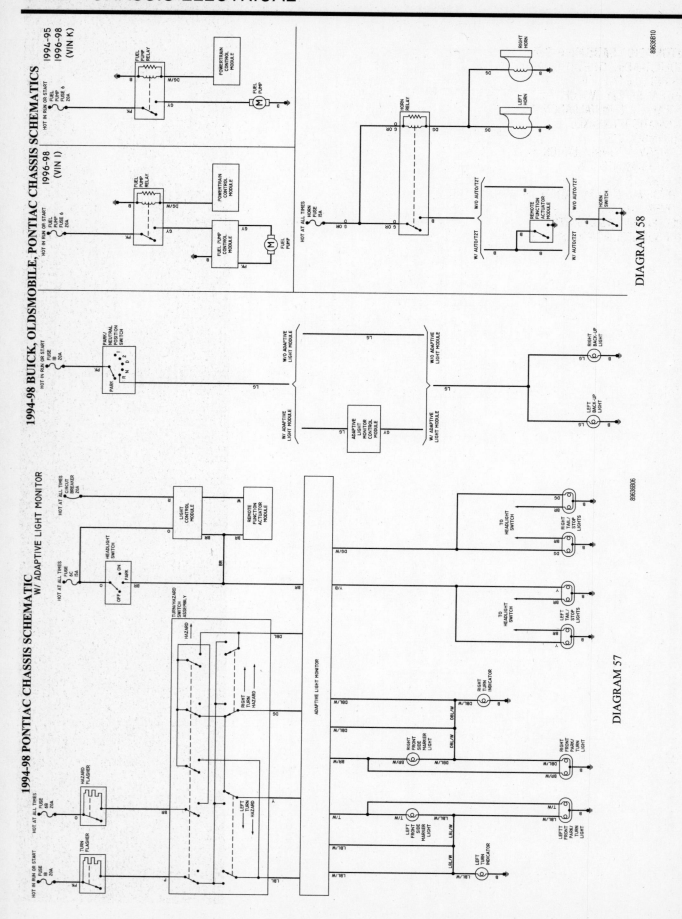

AUTOMATIC TRANSAXLE 7-2
UNDERSTANDING THE AUTOMATIC
  TRANSAXLE 7-2
NEUTRAL SAFETY SWITCH 7-2
  REMOVAL & INSTALLATION 7-2
AUTOMATIC TRANSAXLE
  ASSEMBLY 7-3
  REMOVAL & INSTALLATION 7-3
    ADJUSTMENTS 7-5
HALFSHAFTS 7-6
  REMOVAL & INSTALLATION 7-6
    OVERHAUL 7-9
SPECIFICATIONS CHARTS
  TORQUE SPECIFCATIONS 7-13

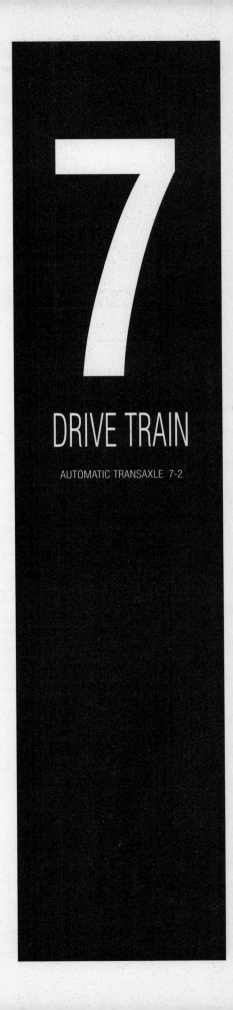

7

DRIVE TRAIN

AUTOMATIC TRANSAXLE 7-2

AUTOMATIC TRANSAXLE

Understanding the Automatic Transaxle

The automatic transaxle allows engine torque and power to be transmitted to the front wheels within a narrow range of engine operating speeds. It will allow the engine to turn fast enough to produce plenty of power and torque at very low speeds, while keeping it at a sensible rpm at high vehicle speeds (and it does this job without driver assistance). The transaxle uses a light fluid as the medium for the transmission of power. This fluid also works in the operation of various hydraulic control circuits and as a lubricant. Because the transaxle fluid performs all of these functions, trouble within the unit can easily travel from one part to another. For this reason, and because of the complexity and unusual operating principles of the transaxle, a very sound understanding of the basic principles of operation will simplify troubleshooting.

Neutral Safety Switch

REMOVAL & INSTALLATION

➡The neutral safety switch, sometimes called the park/neutral position switch, also contains the back-up light switch.

1986–90 Vehicles

▸ **See Figure 1**

1. Disconnect the negative battery cable.
2. Disconnect the shift linkage.
3. Detach the electrical connector.
4. Unfasten the mounting bolts, then remove the switch.
To install:
5. If you are reinstalling the old switch, perform the following:
   a. Place the shift shaft in NEUTRAL.
   b. Align the flats of the shift shaft with the switch.
   c. Loosely assemble the mounting bolts to the case.
   d. Insert a gauge pin or ³⁄₃₂ in. drill bit in the service slots.
   e. Tighten the bolts to 20 ft. lbs. (27 Nm).
   f. Remove the gauge pin.
6. If installing a new switch, perform the following:
   a. Place the shift shaft in NEUTRAL.
   b. Align the flats of the shift shaft to the flats in the switch.

➡If the switch has been rotated and the pin broken, the switch can be adjusted using the old switch installation procedure.

   c. Install the mounting bolts and tighten to 20 ft. lbs. (27 Nm). If the bolt holes do not align with the mounting boss on the transaxle, make sure the shift shaft is in the NEUTRAL position, do not rotate the switch. The switch is pinned in the NEUTRAL position.
7. Adjust the switch as follows:
   a. Place the transaxle control shifter assembly in the NEUTRAL notch in the detent plate.
   b. Loosen the switch attaching bolts.

   c. Rotate the switch on the shifter assembly to align the service adjustment slots.
   d. Insert a gauge pin or ³⁄₃₂ in. drill bit in the service slots.
   e. Tighten the attaching screws to 20 ft. lbs. (27 Nm). Remove the gauge pin.
8. Attach the electrical connector and shift linkage.
9. Connect the negative battery cable.

1991–95 Vehicles

▸ **See Figure 2**

1. Set the parking brake and place the gear shift selector to **N**.
2. Remove the manual shaft nut.
3. Disconnect the cable/bracket from the transmission shaft.
4. Remove the switch retaining bolts.
5. Detach the electrical connector.
6. Remove the nut from the starter.
7. Disconnect the cable.
8. Remove the park/neutral position switch.
To install:
9. Connect the cable.
10. Install the nut and tighten to 35 inch lbs. (4 Nm).
11. Attach the electrical connector.
12. Make sure the transaxle shaft is still in NEUTRAL. If it has been moved, rotate the shaft clockwise from PARK through REVERSE, into NEUTRAL, being careful not to damage the shaft flats, corners or threads.
13. Install the park/neutral position switch, as follows:
   a. Align the flats in the park/neutral position switch with the transaxle manual shaft flats.
   b. Press the park/neutral position switch onto the shaft and fully seat against the transaxle.
14. When installing the original switch, insert a gauge pin or ³⁄₃₂ in. drill bit into the service slots. New replacement park/neutral position switches are already pinned into the NEUTRAL position.
15. Install the retaining switch retaining bolts, and tighten to 20 ft. lbs. (27 Nm).
16. Remove the gauge pin or drill bit, if installed previously.
17. Place the linkage cable/bracket onto the manual shaft.
18. Install the nuts.

➡After adjusting the park/neutral position switch, make sure the engine starts only in PARK or NEUTRAL. If the engine starts in any other position, readjust the switch.

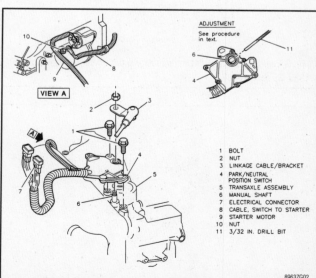

Fig. 2 Exploded view of the park/neutral position switch—1995 vehicle shown

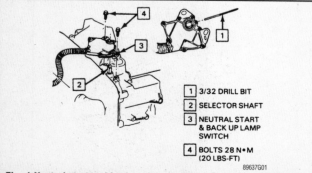

1	3/32 DRILL BIT
2	SELECTOR SHAFT
3	NEUTRAL START & BACK UP LAMP SWITCH
4	BOLTS 28 N•M (20 LBS-FT)

Fig. 1 Neutral start and back-up lamp switch installation—1986–90 vehicles

19. Adjust the switch as follows:
    a. Place the transaxle control shifter assembly in the NEUTRAL notch in the detent plate.
    b. Loosen the switch attaching bolts.
    c. Rotate the switch on the shifter assembly to align the service adjustment slots.
    d. Insert a gauge pin or ³⁄₃₂ in. drill bit in the service slots.
    e. Tighten the attaching screws to 20 ft. lbs. (27 Nm). Remove the gauge pin.
20. Check for proper operation, readjust as needed.

1996–99 Vehicles

▶ **See Figures 3 and 4**

1. Set the parking brake and place the gear shift selector to **N**.
2. Detach the electrical connector(s).
3. Unfasten the linkage retaining nut.
4. Remove the cable and lever.
5. Remove the park/neutral position switch.
   To install:
6. Make sure the transaxle shaft is still in NEUTRAL. If it has been moved, rotate the shaft clockwise from PARK, through REVERSE, into NEUTRAL, being careful not to damage the shaft flats, corners or threads.
7. Adjust the switch as follows (if reinstalling the old switch):

➡**New replacement park/neutral position switches are already pinned in the NEUTRAL position.**

   a. When installing a switch with a sheared pin, insert the alignment tool into the two slots on the switch in the area of the transaxle shaft. Rotate the

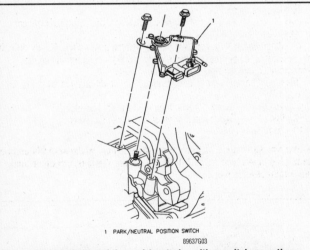

Fig. 3 Exploded view of the park/neutral position switch mounting—1996–99 vehicles

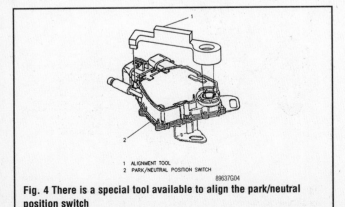

Fig. 4 There is a special tool available to align the park/neutral position switch

tool until the rear leg on the tool falls into the slot on the switch near the hose. Make sure the tool is properly seated in all three slots. Remove the tool.
8. Check for a cracked carrier if the pin is sheared or if installing the original switch.
9. Install the park/neutral position switch:
   a. Align the flats in the park/neutral position switch with the transaxle manual shaft flats.
   b. Press the park/neutral position switch onto the shaft and fully seat against the transaxle.
10. Install the bolts loosely. Check the alignment of the switch with the alignment tool, then tighten the bolts to 18 ft. lbs. (25 Nm).
11. Remove the alignment tool.
12. Install the cable and lever.
13. Install the linkage retaining nut and tighten to 15 ft. lbs. (20 Nm).
14. Attach the electrical connectors.
15. Set the parking brake. After switch installation, make sure that the engine starts only in PARK or NEUTRAL. If the engine starts in any other position, the switch must be readjusted.
16. Check the shifter for normal freedom of movement and proper shift control cable adjustment.

Automatic Transaxle Assembly

REMOVAL & INSTALLATION

▶ **See Figures 5 thru 16**

1. Disconnect the negative terminal from the battery. Detach the wire connector at the Mass Air Flow sensor.
2. If equipped, remove the cross brace to strut towers, as follows:
   a. Loosen the bar assembly through-bolts.
   b. Remove the inboard strut nuts.
   c. Remove the brace assembly.

Fig. 5 The automatic transaxle fluid level sensor is mounted in the top of the transaxle case

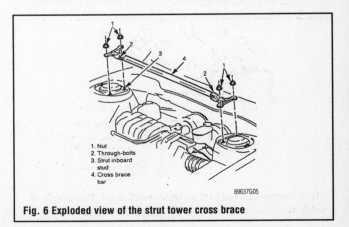

1. Nut
2. Through-bolts
3. Strut inboard stud
4. Cross brace bar

Fig. 6 Exploded view of the strut tower cross brace

d. Reinstall the inboard strut nuts.
3. Remove the air intake duct.
4. Disconnect the cruise control cable from the throttle body.
5. Remove the shift control linkage from the mounting bracket at the transaxle and the lever at the manual shaft.
6. Label and detach the connectors from the following:
   a. Park/neutral/backup lamp switch.
   b. Transaxle electrical connector.
   c. Vehicle speed sensor and fuel pipe retainers.
7. Remove the fuel pipe retainers.
8. Disconnect the vacuum modulator hose from the modulator.

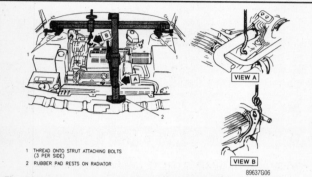

1 THREAD ONTO STRUT ATTACHING BOLTS (3 PER SIDE)
2 RUBBER PAD RESTS ON RADIATOR

89637G06

Fig. 7 You have to use a suitable holding fixture to support the engine. If necessary, one can usually be rented

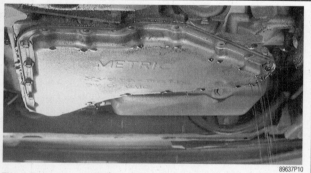

89637P10

Fig. 8 Drain the automatic transaxle fluid into a suitable drain pan, but be careful, as this can be messy

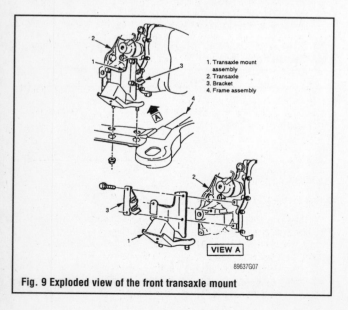

1. Transaxle mount assembly
2. Transaxle
3. Bracket
4. Frame assembly

89637G07

Fig. 9 Exploded view of the front transaxle mount

✳✳ WARNING

You must support or remove the engine. If the engine is not support you may damage the engine, transaxle, halfshafts or many other components.

9. Remove the three top transaxle-to-engine block bolts and install a suitable engine support fixture. Load the support fixture by tightening the wingnuts several turns in order to relieve the tension on the frame and the mounts.
10. Turn the steering wheel to the full left position.
11. Raise and safely support the vehicle. Remove both front tire and wheel assemblies.
12. Drain the automatic transaxle fluid into a suitable container.
13. Remove the right and left front ball joint nuts, then separate both control arms from the steering knuckle.
14. Remove the right halfshaft from the transaxle only. Do not remove the halfshaft from the hub/bearing assembly.

➡**Carefully guide the output shaft past the lip seal. Do not allow the halfshaft splines to contact any portion of the lip seal.**

15. Remove the left halfshaft from the transaxle and hub/knuckle assembly. Be careful not to damage the pan.
16. Support the transaxle with a suitable stand.
17. Remove the bolts at the transaxle and the nuts at the cradle member. Remove the left front transaxle mount.
18. Remove the right front mount-to-cradle nuts. Remove the left rear transaxle mount-to-transaxle bolts.
19. Remove the torque strut bracket from the transaxle.
20. Remove the right transaxle mount-to-transaxle bolts.

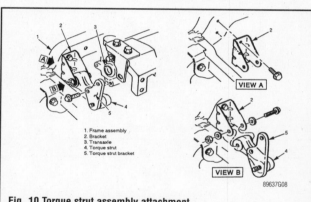

1. Frame assembly
2. Bracket
3. Transaxle
4. Torque strut
5. Torque strut bracket

89637G08

Fig. 10 Torque strut assembly attachment

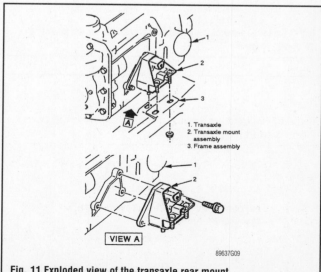

1. Transaxle
2. Transaxle mount assembly
3. Frame assembly

89637G09

Fig. 11 Exploded view of the transaxle rear mount

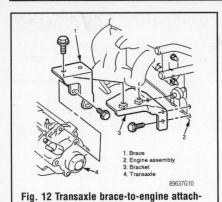

Fig. 12 Transaxle brace-to-engine attachment

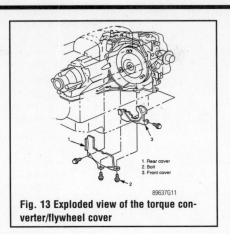

Fig. 13 Exploded view of the torque converter/flywheel cover

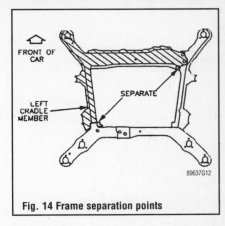

Fig. 14 Frame separation points

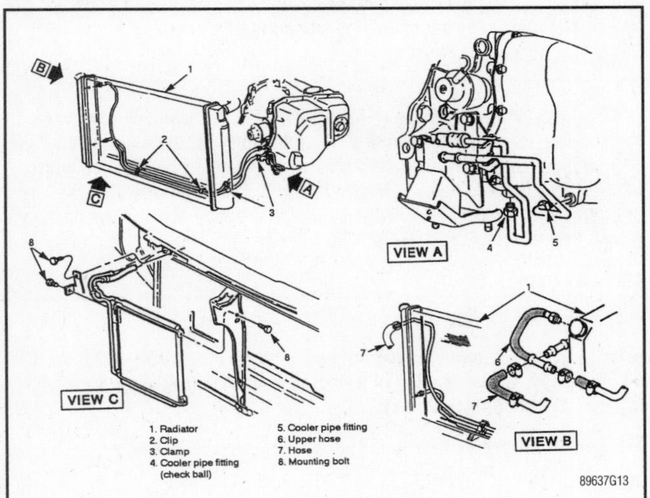

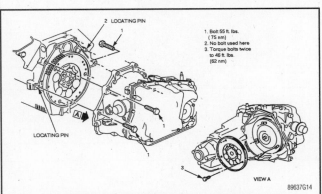

Fig. 15 Typical oil cooler line attachment

Fig. 16 Transaxle-to-engine mounting. Notice that one bolt mounts in the opposite direction

21. Remove the left rear transaxle mount. Remove the transaxle brace from the engine bracket.

22. Remove the stabilizer shaft link-to-control arm bolt.

➡ **Be sure to matchmark the flywheel-to-converter relationship for proper alignment upon reassembly.**

23. Unfasten the flywheel cover bolts, then remove the cover. Matchmark the flywheel-to-torque converter installed position, then remove the flywheel-to-converter bolts.

24. Remove the bolts attaching the rear frame member to the front frame.

25. Remove the front left cradle-to-body bolt and the front cradle dog leg-to-right cradle member bolts.

26. Remove the frame/cradle assembly by swinging it aside and supporting it with a jackstand.

27. Disconnect the oil cooler lines from the transaxle, then plug the lines to avoid contamination.

➡ **One bolt located between the transaxle and the engine block is installed in the opposite direction.**

28. Remove the remaining lower transaxle-to-engine bolts and lower the transaxle from the vehicle. Be careful when removing the transaxle to avoid damaging the right-hand output shaft, shaft seal, hoses, lines and wiring.

To install:

29. Install the transaxle into the vehicle using the dowel pin as guide. Tighten the bolts to the specifications shown in the chart at the end of this section.

30. The installation is the reverse of the removal procedure. Keep the following important points in mind when installing the transaxle:

➡ **Be careful when installing the right side halfshaft into the transaxle case. The splined shaft can easily cause damage to the seal.**

  a. Before installing the right side halfshaft, install a suitable axle seal protector.

  b. Tighten the retainers to the specifications given in the chart at the end of this section.

  c. Align the flywheel-to-torque converter marks made during removal. The torque converter-to-flywheel bolts should always be tightened twice.

  d. Check adjustment of the shift cables, as outlined later in this section.

  e. After installing the front wheels and tires, make sure to tighten the lug nuts to specification.

  f. When installing the cross brace to the struts, perform the following:
  • Place the assembly on the inboard strut studs.
  • Install the strut stud nuts and tighten to 18 ft. lbs. (24 Nm).
  • Tighten the torque bar assembly through-bolts to 21 ft. lbs. (28 Nm).

  g. Check and adjust the fluid level as necessary, making sure to use the proper type of fluid.

  h. When installing the transaxle-to-engine block brace, tighten the brace-to-engine bolts first and the brace-to-transaxle case last to avoid pulling the transaxle case out of line.

31. After the installation is complete, road test the vehicle and check for proper operation and leaks.

ADJUSTMENTS

Shift Linkage/Control Cable

♦ See Figures 17, 18, 19 and 20

1. Raise the adjustment lock tab so that the tab is fully raised and allows free movement of the cable in the adjustment assembly.

2. Position the shift lever in the **N** position. This is found by rotation the selector shaft clockwise from **P** through **R** to **N**.

3. Place the shift control assembly in **N**.

4. With the lock tab fully raised, push the tab down to fully seat in the cable adjuster to adjust the cable in the mounting bracket.

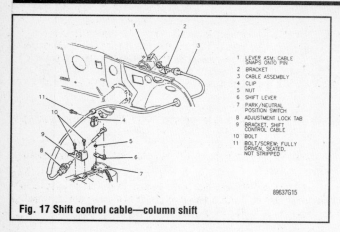

Fig. 17 Shift control cable—column shift

1 LEVER ASM: CABLE SNAPS ONTO PIN
2 BRACKET
3 CABLE ASSEMBLY
4 CLIP
5 NUT
6 SHIFT LEVER
7 PARK/NEUTRAL POSITION SWITCH
8 ADJUSTMENT LOCK TAB
9 BRACKET, SHIFT CONTROL CABLE
10 BOLT
11 BOLT/SCREW; FULLY DRIVEN, SEATED, NOT STRIPPED

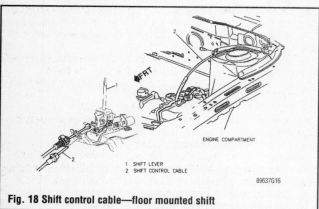

Fig. 18 Shift control cable—floor mounted shift

1 SHIFT LEVER
2 SHIFT CONTROL CABLE

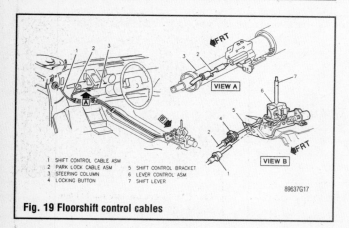

Fig. 19 Floorshift control cables

1 SHIFT CONTROL CABLE ASM
2 PARK LOCK CABLE ASM
3 STEERING COLUMN
4 LOCKING BUTTON
5 SHIFT CONTROL BRACKET
6 LEVER CONTROL ASM.
7 SHIFT LEVER

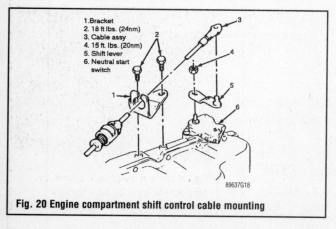

1. Bracket
2. 18 ft lbs. (24nm)
3. Cable assy
4. 15 ft. lbs. (20nm)
5. Shift lever
6. Neutral start switch

Fig. 20 Engine compartment shift control cable mounting

Throttle Valve Cable

▶ See Figures 21, 22 and 23

1. Stop the engine.

➡Check the throttle body for full travel prior to any adjustments by fully depressing the accelerator pedal and having an assistant check the throttle body for wide open throttle. If full throttle is not achieved, the accelerator system must be repaired before adjusting the TV cable.

2. Depress and hold down the metal readjustment tab at the engine end of the TV cable.
3. Move the slider until it stops against the fitting.
4. Release the adjustment tab.
5. Rotate the throttle lever, by hand, to its full travel position.
6. The slider must move (ratchet) toward the lever when the lever is rotated to its full travel position.

Halfshafts

REMOVAL & INSTALLATION

➡When removing the halfshaft for any reason, the transaxle sealing surface (the male/female shank of the halfshaft) should be inspected for corrosion. If corrosion is present, the surface should be cleaned with 320 grit cloth or equivalent. Transmission fluid can be used to clean off any remaining debris. The surface should be wiped dry and the halfshaft reinstalled free of any build-up.

1986–92 Vehicles

▶ See Figures 24 thru 37

➡Use care when removing the halfshaft. When either end of the shaft is disconnected, overextension of the joint could result in separation of internal components and possible joint failure.

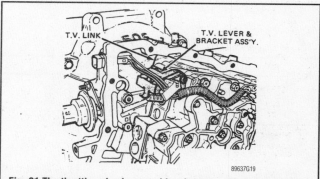

Fig. 21 The throttle valve lever and bracket assembly is mounted on the throttle body

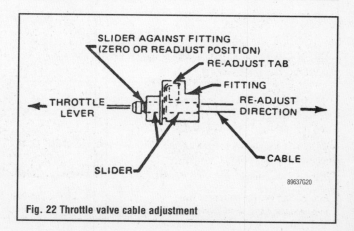

Fig. 22 Throttle valve cable adjustment

1. Disconnect the negative battery cable.
2. Raise and safely support the vehicle. Remove the tire and wheel assembly.
3. Install a modified inner drive joint seal protector on the outer joint.
4. Insert a drift into the rotor and caliper to prevent the rotor from turning.

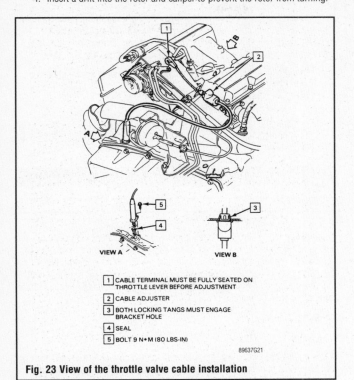

1 CABLE TERMINAL MUST BE FULLY SEATED ON THROTTLE LEVER BEFORE ADJUSTMENT
2 CABLE ADJUSTER
3 BOTH LOCKING TANGS MUST ENGAGE BRACKET HOLE
4 SEAL
5 BOLT 9 N•M (80 LBS-IN)

89637G21

Fig. 23 View of the throttle valve cable installation

5. Remove the hub nut and washer using a hub nut socket tool.
6. Remove the lower ball joint cotter pin and nut, then loosen the joint using a ball joint separator tool. Discard the cotter pin and replace with a new one during installation. If removing the right halfshaft, turn the wheel to the left; if removing the left halfshaft, turn the wheel to the right.
7. With a prybar between the suspension support and the lower control arm, separate the joint.
8. Pull out on the lower knuckle area and with a plastic or rubber mallet strike the end of the axle shaft to disengage the axle from the hub and bearing. The shaft nut can be partially installed to protect the threads.
9. Separate the hub and bearing assembly from the halfshaft and move the strut and knuckle assembly rearward. Remove the inner joint from the transaxle using the proper tool.

➡If equipped with the anti-lock brake system, care must be used to prevent damage to the toothed sensor ring on the halfshaft and the wheel speed sensor on the steering knuckle.

To install:

10. On 1992 vehicles, if installing the right side halfshaft, install a suitable axle seal protector, tool J 37292-A or equivalent. Install the tool in a position so it can be pulled out after the halfshaft is installed (T-handle between the 5 and 7 o'clock positions).
11. Seat the halfshaft into the transaxle by placing a screwdriver or equivalent tool into the groove on the joint housing and tapping until seated.
12. Verify the halfshaft is seated into the transaxle by grasping on the housing and pulling outboard. Do not pull on the halfshaft.
13. Install the halfshaft into the hub and bearing assembly.
14. Install the lower ball joint to the knuckle. Tighten the nut in 2 steps as follows:
    a. Step 1: Tighten to 88 inch lbs. (10 Nm).
    b. Step 2: Tighten two additional flats, to a value of 41 ft. lbs. (56 Nm).
15. Install a new cotter pin. If necessary, you can TIGHTEN the nut up to one additional flat to install the cotter pin. NEVER loosen the nut to install the pin.
16. Install the washer and new shaft nut.
17. Insert drift into rotor and caliper to prevent rotor from turning.

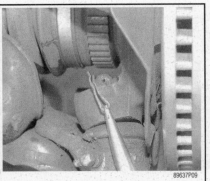

1 REMOVE TABS
2 J 34754 DRIVE AXLE SEAL PROTECTOR

89637G27

Fig. 24 Fabricate a modified seal protector to install on the outer joint

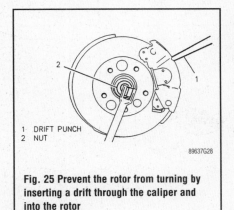

1 DRIFT PUNCH
2 NUT

89637G28

Fig. 25 Prevent the rotor from turning by inserting a drift through the caliper and into the rotor

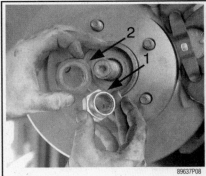

89637P08

Fig. 26 Remove the hub nut (1) and washer (2)

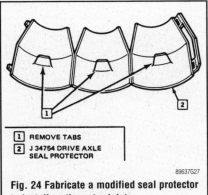

89637P09

Fig. 27 Remove the cotter pin with needlenose pliers, then discard the pin

89637P07

Fig. 28 Pull the hub, bearing and knuckle assembly away from the halfshaft

89637P02

Fig. 29 Use a large prytool to carefully separate the inner CV-joint from the transaxle case

Fig. 30 Be very careful when prying the halfshaft from the transaxle

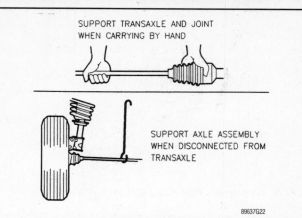

Fig. 31 You must handle the halfshaft very carefully to avoid damaging it

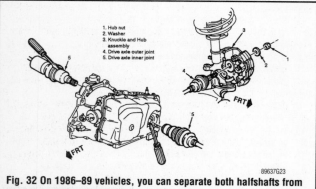

Fig. 32 On 1986–89 vehicles, you can separate both halfshafts from the transaxle with a prybar

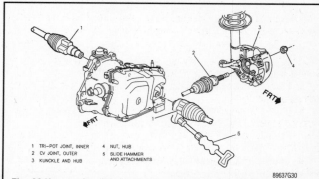

Fig. 33 You need a slide hammer to remove the halfshafts from the transaxle on 1990–99 vehicles

Fig. 34 Carefully remove the halfshaft from the vehicle

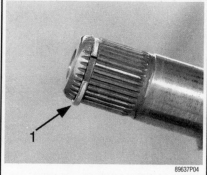

Fig. 35 The end of the halfshaft is grooved, with a retaining circlip (1)

Fig. 36 While the halfshaft is removed, be sure not to get any dirt or other debris in the transaxle case

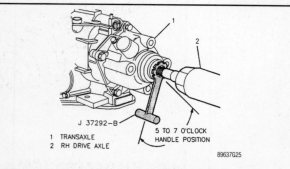

Fig. 37 If necessary, install a suitable axle seal protector tool

18. Tighten the shaft nut to the following specifications:
  a. 1986–88 vehicles: 190 ft. lbs. (270 Nm).
  b. 1989–90 vehicles: 185 ft. lbs. (260 Nm).
  c. 1991–92 vehicles: 107 ft. lbs. (145 Nm).
19. Remove the boot protector.
20. Install the tire and wheel assembly.
21. Carefully lower the vehicle. Tighten the lug nuts to 100 ft. lbs. (135 Nm).
22. Connect the negative battery cable.

1993–99 Vehicles

◆ See Figures 25, 31, 33, 37 and 38

➡Use care when removing the halfshaft. When either end of the shaft is disconnected, overextension of the joint could result in separation of internal components and possible joint failure.

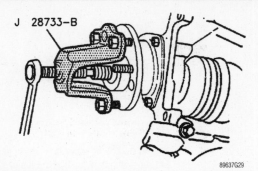

Fig. 38 Use a suitable puller to separate the halfshaft from the hub and bearing assembly

1. Disconnect the negative battery cable.
2. Raise and safely support the vehicle. Remove the tire and wheel assembly.
3. If necessary, loosen or remove the stabilizer shaft link.

➡**Make sure to use the proper tools when separating the ball joint. Failure to use the proper tools can damage the ball joint and seal.**

4. Remove the lower ball joint cotter pin and nut, then loosen the joint using a suitable ball joint separator tool. If removing the right halfshaft, turn the wheel to the left, if removing the left halfshaft turn the wheel to the right.
5. Place a prybar between the suspension support and lower control arm, then separate the joint.
6. Insert drift into rotor and caliper to prevent rotor from turning, then remove the hub nut and washer using a hub nut socket tool.
7. Separate the axle from the hub using a suitable puller; the hub nut can be partially installed to protect the threads. Move the strut and knuckle rearward.
8. Remove the inner joint from the transaxle using a suitable slide hammer and axle shaft remover tool.

➡**If equipped with the anti-lock brake system, care must be taken to prevent damage to the toothed sensor ring on the halfshaft and the wheel speed sensor on the steering knuckle.**

To install:

9. If installing the right side halfshaft, install a suitable axle seal protector, tool J 37292-A or equivalent. Install the tool in a position so it can be pulled out after the halfshaft is installed (T-handle between 5 and 7 o'clock position).
10. Seat the halfshaft into the transaxle by placing a suitable screwdriver into the groove on the joint housing and tapping until seated. Make sure the halfshaft is seated into the transaxle by grasping the housing and pulling outboard. Do not pull on the halfshaft.
11. Install the halfshaft into the hub and bearing assembly. Install a new hub nut. Insert a drift into the caliper and rotor to prevent the rotor from turning. Tighten the hub nut to 107 ft. lbs. (145 Nm).
12. Install the lower ball joint to the knuckle, and tighten the ball joint nut as follows:
    a. Step 1: Tighten the nut to 88 inch lbs. (10 Nm).

b. Step 2: Tighten the nut an additional 120° (2 flats on the nut), during which a torque of 41 ft. lbs. (55 Nm) must be obtained.
13. Install a new cotter pin. If necessary to align the slot into the nut, tighten the nut up to one more flat. Never loosen the nut to install the cotter pin!
14. Install the stabilizer shaft link assembly and tighten the nut to 13 ft. lbs. (17 Nm).
15. If a boot protector was installed, remove it by pulling in line with the handle.
16. Install the tire and wheel assembly, then carefully lower the vehicle. Tighten the lug nuts to 100 ft. lbs. (135 Nm).

OVERHAUL

Outer CV-Joint and Seal

◗ **See Figures 39 thru 48**

1. Remove the halfshaft from the vehicle and mount in a suitable vise.
2. Remove the large seal retaining clamp from the CV-joint with side cutters. Discard the clamp.
3. Remove the small seal retaining clamp with side cutters or, for swage ring removal, use a hand grinder to cut through the ring (being careful not to damage the halfshaft).
4. Separate the joint seal from the CV-joint race at the large diameter end and slide the seal away from the joint along the axle shaft.
5. Wipe off the grease from the face of the CV inner race.
6. Spread the ears on the race retaining ring with J-8059 or equivalent snapring pliers and remove the CV-joint from the axle shaft.
7. Remove the joint seal from the axle shaft.
8. Use a brass drift and hammer to gently tap on the CV-joint cage until it is tilted enough to remove the first ball.
9. Tilt the cage in the opposing direction and remove the opposing ball.
10. Repeat until all the ball are removed. There are usually 6 balls.
11. Position cage and inner race 90° to centerline of the outer race, and align cage windows with the lands of the outer race.
12. Remove the cage and inner race from the outer race.
13. Rotate the inner race 90° to centerline of the cage so that the lands of the inner race are aligned with the windows of the cage.
14. Pivot the inner race into cage window and remove the inner race.
15. Clean the inner and outer race assemblies, cage and balls thoroughly with a suitable solvent. All traces of old grease and contaminants must be removed. Thoroughly dry all parts.

To install:

16. If equipped, install a new swage ring on the neck of the seal. Do not swage.
17. Slide the seal onto the axle shaft on position the neck of the seal in the seal groove on the axle shaft.
18. For the swage ring, mount the swage clamp tool, J 41048 or equivalent, in a vise and proceed as follows:
    a. Position the outboard end of the halfshaft in the tool.
    b. Align the top of the seal neck on the bottom die using the indicator line.
    c. Place the top half of the tool on the lower half of the tool.

Fig. 39 Check the CV-boot for wear

Fig. 40 Clean the CV-joint housing prior to removing the boot

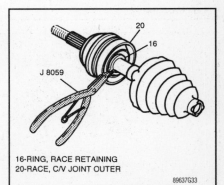

16-RING, RACE RETAINING
20-RACE, C/V JOINT OUTER

Fig. 41 Use a pair of snapring pliers to spread the ears on the race retaining ring

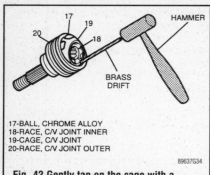

17-BALL, CHROME ALLOY
18-RACE, C/V JOINT INNER
19-CAGE, C/V JOINT
20-RACE, C/V JOINT OUTER

89637G34

Fig. 42 Gently tap on the cage with a brass drift and hammer, until it is tilted enough to remove the first ball

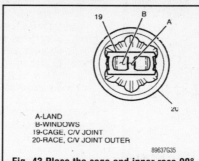

A-LAND
B-WINDOWS
19-CAGE, C/V JOINT
20-RACE, C/V JOINT OUTER

89637G35

Fig. 43 Place the cage and inner race 90° to centerline of the outer race, and align the cage windows with the lands of the outer race

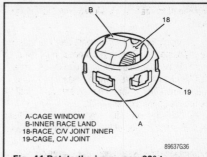

A-CAGE WINDOW
B-INNER RACE LAND
18-RACE, C/V JOINT INNER
19-CAGE, C/V JOINT

89637G36

Fig. 44 Rotate the inner race 90° to centerline of the cage, so that the lands of the inner race are aligned with the windows of the cage

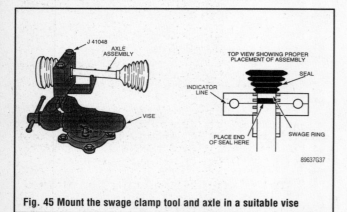

89637G37

Fig. 45 Mount the swage clamp tool and axle in a suitable vise

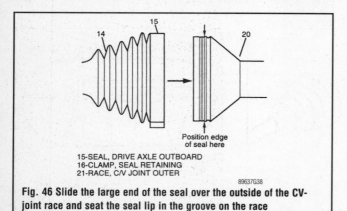

15-SEAL, DRIVE AXLE OUTBOARD
16-CLAMP, SEAL RETAINING
21-RACE, C/V JOINT OUTER

89637G38

Fig. 46 Slide the large end of the seal over the outside of the CV-joint race and seat the seal lip in the groove on the race

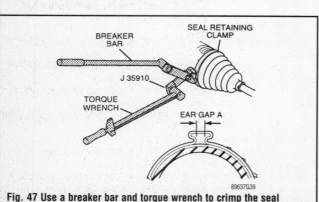

89637G39

Fig. 47 Use a breaker bar and torque wrench to crimp the seal retaining clamp to the proper specifications

d. Make sure there are no pinch points on the seal before continuing. Any pinching could damage the seal.

e. Install the bolts and tighten by hand until snug.

f. Make sure that the seal, housing and swage ring all stay in alignment. Continue to tighten each bolt 180°, alternating until both sides are bottomed.

19. Put a light coat of grease from the service kit on the ball grooves of the inner race and outer race.

20. Hold the inner race 90° to centerline of the cage with the lands of the inner race aligned with the windows of the cage and insert the inner race into the cage.

21. Hold the cage and inner race 90° to centerline of the outer race and align the cage windows with the lands of the outer race.

22. Install the cage and inner race into the outer race.

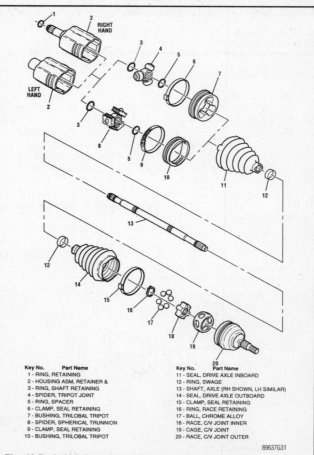

Key No.	Part Name
1 - RING, RETAINING
2 - HOUSING ASM, RETAINER &
3 - RING, SHAFT RETAINING
4 - SPIDER, TRIPOT JOINT
5 - RING, SPACER
6 - CLAMP, SEAL RETAINING
7 - BUSHING, TRILOBAL TRIPOT
8 - SPIDER, SPHERICAL TRUNNION
9 - CLAMP, SEAL RETAINING
10 - BUSHING, TRILOBAL TRIPOT

Key No.	Part Name
11 - SEAL, DRIVE AXLE INBOARD
12 - RING, SWAGE
13 - SHAFT, AXLE (RH SHOWN, LH SIMILAR)
14 - SEAL, DRIVE AXLE OUTBOARD
15 - CLAMP, SEAL RETAINING
16 - RING, RACE RETAINING
17 - BALL, CHROME ALLOY
18 - RACE, C/V JOINT INNER
19 - CAGE, C/V JOINT
20 - RACE, C/V JOINT OUTER

89637G31

Fig. 48 Exploded view of the left and right halfshaft assemblies—1995 vehicle shown, others similar

→Make sure that the retaining ring side of the inner race faces the axle shaft.

23. Insert the first ball, then tilt the cage in the opposite direction to install the opposing ball. Repeat this process until the remaining balls are installed.

24. Place about half the grease from the service kit inside the seal and pack the CV-joint with the remaining grease.

25. Push the CV joint onto the axle shaft until the retaining ring is seated in the groove on the axle shaft.

26. Slide the large diameter of the seal with the large seal retaining clamp in place over the outside of the CV joint race and locate the seal lip in the groove on the race.

✳✴✳ WARNING

The seal must not be dimpled, stretched or out of shape in any way. IF the seal is NOT shaped correctly, equalize pressure in seal and shape seal properly by hand or replace.

27. Crimp the retaining clamp to 130 ft. lbs. (176 Nm).
28. Install the halfshaft into the vehicle.

Inner Tri-Pot Joint and Seal

SPIDER/TRI-POT BALL ASSEMBLY

▶ See Figures 45, 47 and 49 thru 52

1. Remove the halfshaft from the vehicle and mount in a suitable vise.
2. If equipped, remove the swage ring from the axle shaft using a hand grinder to cut through the ring (being careful not to damage the halfshaft).
3. Remove the large retaining clamp from tri-pot joint with side cutter, and discard.

✳✴✳ WARNING

Do not cut through the seal and damage the sealing surface of tri-pot housing and trilobal tri-pot bushing.

4. If necessary, remove the small seal retaining clamp using side cutters.
5. Separate the seal from the trilobal tri-pot bushing at large diameter and slide seal away from the joint.
6. Remove the tri-pot housing from the spider and shaft. Remove the trilobal tri-pot bushing from the housing.
7. Spread the spacer ring with J-8059 snapring pliers and slide space ring and tri-pot spider back on axle shaft.
8. Remove the shaft retaining ring from the groove on the axle shaft, then slide the spider from the shaft. Clean the tri-pot balls, needle rollers and housing thoroughly with suitable solvent. All traces of old grease and contaminants must be removed. Thoroughly dry all parts.
9. Remove the spacer rung and seal from the axle shaft.
10. Inspect the joint balls and needle rollers for damage or wear. Handle with care, and don't reuse them if there is any sign of damage.
    To install:
11. Install a new small seal retaining clamp, or swage, as applicable. Do NOT crimp/swage.
12. Slide the seal onto the axle shaft and position neck of seal in groove on the axle shaft.
13. For the swage ring, mount the swage clamp tool, J 41048 or equivalent, in a vise and proceed as follows:
    a. Position the outboard end of the halfshaft in the tool.
    b. Align the top of the seal neck on the bottom die using the indicator line.
    c. Place the top half of the tool on the lower half of the tool.
    d. Make sure there are no pinch points on the seal before continuing. Any pinching could damage the seal.
    e. Install the bolts and tighten by hand until snug.
    f. Make sure that the seal, housing and swage ring all stay in alignment. Continue to tighten each bolt 180°, alternating until both sides are bottomed.
14. If equipped, crimp the seal using tool J-35910 to 100 ft. lbs. (136 Nm).
15. Install the spacer ring onto the axle shaft and beyond the second groove.
16. Slide the tri-pot spider toward the spacer ring as far as it will go on the shaft.
17. Make sure the counterbored face of the tri-pot spider faces the end of the axle shaft.

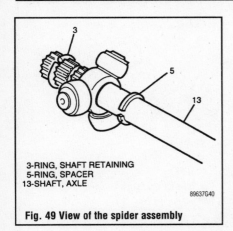

3-RING, SHAFT RETAINING
5-RING, SPACER
13-SHAFT, AXLE

89637G40

Fig. 49 View of the spider assembly

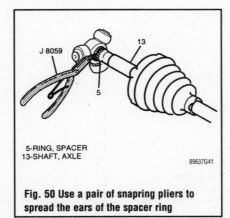

5-RING, SPACER
13-SHAFT, AXLE

89637G41

Fig. 50 Use a pair of snapring pliers to spread the ears of the spacer ring

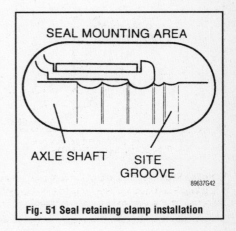

SEAL MOUNTING AREA

AXLE SHAFT   SITE GROOVE

89637G42

Fig. 51 Seal retaining clamp installation

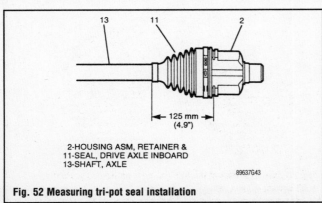

2-HOUSING ASM, RETAINER &
11-SEAL, DRIVE AXLE INBOARD
13-SHAFT, AXLE

89637G43

Fig. 52 Measuring tri-pot seal installation

18. Use snapring pliers to install the shaft retaining ring in the groove of the axle shaft.
19. Slide the tri-pot spider towards the end of the axle shaft and reseat the spacer ring in the groove on shaft.
20. Place about half the grease provided with the repair kit into the seal and use the remainder to repack the tri-pot housing.
21. Install the trilobal tri-pot bushing to the housing. Make sure the bushing is flush with the face of the housing.
22. Position the new large clamp on the seal.
23. Slide tri-pot housing over the tri-pot spider on axle shaft and remove the slotted sheet metal plate.
24. Slide large diameter end of seal with large clamp in place, over the outside of the trilobal bushing, and locate the lip of seal in the bushing groove.
25. Position the tri-pot at the proper vehicle dimension, 4.9 inches (125mm).

❋❋ WARNING

The seal must not be dimpled, stretched or out of shape in any way. If the seal is NOT shaped correctly, carefully insert a thin, flat, blunt tool (no sharp edges) into the between the large seal opening and trilobal tri-pot bushing to equalize pressure. Shape the seal properly by hand and remove the tool.

26. Use a breaker bar and torque wrench to crimp retaining clamp to 130 ft. lbs. (176 Nm).
27. Make certain the seal, housing and large clamp all remain in alignment while crimping.
28. Install the halfshaft in the vehicle.

SPIDER/BEARING BLOCK ASSEMBLY

▶ See Figures 52 and 53 thru 57

1. Remove the halfshaft from the vehicle and mount in a suitable vise.
2. If equipped, remove the swage ring from the axle shaft using a hand grinder to cut through the ring (being careful not to damage the halfshaft).
3. Remove the large retaining clamp from the tri-pot joint with a side cutter, and discard.

❋❋ WARNING

Do not cut through the seal and damage the sealing surface of tri-pot housing and trilobal tri-pot bushing.

4. Remove the swage ring from the axle shaft using a hand grinder to cut through the ring (being careful not to damage the halfshaft).
5. Separate the seal from the trilobal tri-pot bushing at the large diameter and slide the seal away from the joint, along the axle shaft.
6. Remove the housing from the spider and shaft.
7. Use snapring pliers to spread the spacer ring, then slide the ring and spider back on the axle shaft.

8. Remove the shaft retaining ring from the groove on the axle shaft and slide the spider assembly off of the shaft.
9. Clean the bearing blocks, spider and housing thoroughly with suitable solvent. All traces of the old grease and any contaminants must be removed. Dry all components.
10. Remove the trilobal tri-pot bushing from the housing.
11. Remove the spacer ring and seal from the axle shaft.
12. Inspect the joint seal, spider, housing and trilobal tri-pot bushing for damage and/or wear.

To install:

13. Install a new swage ring on the neck of the seal. Do NOT swage.
14. Slide the seal onto the shaft and position the neck of the seal in the seal groove on the axle shaft.
15. For the swage ring, mount the swage clamp tool, J 41048 or equivalent, in a vise and proceed as follows:
    a. Position the outboard end of the halfshaft in the tool.
    b. Align the top of the seal neck on the bottom die using the indicator line.
    c. Place the top half of the tool on the lower half of the tool.
    d. Make sure there are no pinch points on the seal before continuing. Any pinching could damage the seal.
    e. Install the bolts and tighten by hand until snug.
    f. Make sure that the seal, housing and swage ring all stay in alignment. Continue to tighten each bolt 180°, alternating until both sides are bottomed.
16. Install the spacer ring on the axle shaft, and position beyond the 2nd groove.
17. Attach the bearing blocks to the spider trunnions as follows:
    a. Apply a small amount of grease to the inside of the bearing blocks.
    b. Align the flats on the opening in the bearing block with the flats on the spider trunnion.
    c. Attach the bearing block to the spider trunnion.
    d. Rotate 90° to secure the block to the spider.
18. Slide the spider assembly against the spacer ring on the shaft. Be sure that the counterbored face of the spider faces the end of the shaft.
19. Install the shaft retaining ring in the groove of the axle shaft with snapring pliers.

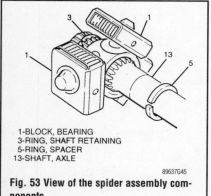

1-BLOCK, BEARING
3-RING, SHAFT RETAINING
5-RING, SPACER
13-SHAFT, AXLE

89637G45

Fig. 53 View of the spider assembly components

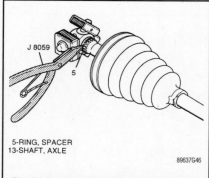

5-RING, SPACER
13-SHAFT, AXLE

89637G46

Fig. 54 Use snapring pliers to spread the ears, then remove the spacer ring

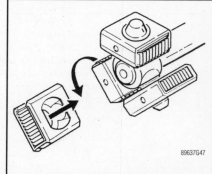

89637G47

Fig. 55 Bearing block-to-spider installation

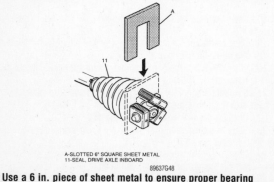

A-SLOTTED 6" SQUARE SHEET METAL
11-SEAL, DRIVE AXLE INBOARD

89637G48

Fig. 56 Use a 6 in. piece of sheet metal to ensure proper bearing block alignment

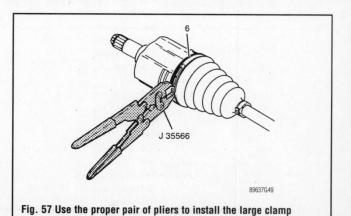

J 35566

89637G49

Fig. 57 Use the proper pair of pliers to install the large clamp

20. Slide the spider toward the end of the shaft and reseat the spacer ring in the groove on the shaft.
21. Place about half the grease from the service kit in the seal, then use the remaining grease to pack the housing.
22. Place a slotted, 6 inch square piece of sheet metal between the seal and bearing blocks, to maintain proper alignment during assembly.
23. Install the trilobal tri-pot bushing to the housing.
24. Position the larger clamp on the seal.
25. Slide the housing over the spider assembly on the shaft and remove the slotted sheet metal plate.
26. Slide the large diameter of the seal, with the larger clamp, in place over the outside of the trilobal tri-pot bushing and place the lip of the seal in the groove.
27. Position the tri-pot at the proper vehicle dimension, 4.9 inches (125mm).

✳✳ WARNING

The seal must not be dimpled, stretched or out of shape in any way. If the seal is NOT shaped correctly, carefully insert a thin, flat, blunt tool (no sharp edges) into the between the large seal opening and trilobal tri-pot bushing to equalize pressure. Shape the seal properly by hand and remove the tool.

28. Latch the seal retaining clamp with an earless seal clamp tool, J 35566, or equivalent. Make sure that the seal, housing and large clamp stay in alignment while latching.
29. Install the halfshaft in the vehicle.

TORQUE SPECIFICATIONS

Component	ft. lbs.	inch lbs.	Nm
Automatic Transaxle			
Converter cover bolt		115	13
Filler tube bracket bolt	15		20
Flywheel-to-torque converter bolts (in 2 steps)	46		62
Frame-to-body bolt	83		112
Oil cooler hose clamp			
1986-94 Vehicles		16	1.8
Oil cooler pipe and tube nut			
1986-91 vehicles	30		41
1992-99 vehicles	24-33		32-44
Oil cooler pipe-to-radiator fitting			
1986-95 vehicles	20		27
Oil cooler pipe ballcheck fitting at transaxle			
1992-95 vehicles	34-43		46-58
1996-99 vehicles	43		58
Park/neutral safety switch shift lever nut	15		20
Park/neutral safety switch-to-transaxle bolt			
1986-95 vehicles	20		27
1996-99 vehicles	18		25
Shift control assembly-to-floor console bracket nut			
1986-91 vehicles	18		25
Shift control cable bracket-to-transaxle	18		25
Shift lever-to-park/neutral position switch nut	15		20
Transaxle-to-engine bolts	55		75
Transaxle brace-to-engine assembly			
Brace-to-engine bolt			
1986-91 vehicles	21		28
Brace-to-engine bracket bolt			
1992-93 vehicles	37		50
1994 vehicles	46		63
1995-99 vehicles	70		95
Brace-to-transaxle bolt			
1986-91 vehicles	37		50
1992-93 vehicles	33		45
1994-99 vehicles	46		63
Engine bracket-to-engine bolt			
1992-94 vehicles	70		95
1995-99 vehicles	46		63
Transaxle mounts			
Frame bracket-to-frame bolt			
1986-93 vehicles	38		52
1994 vehicles	46		63
Frame nut			
1986-93 vehicles	30		41
1994 vehicles	37		50
Mount assembly-to-transaxle bolt			
1986-93 vehicles	38-40		52-54
1994 vehicles	46		63

89637C01

TORQUE SPECIFICATIONS

Component	ft. lbs.	inch lbs.	Nm
Automatic Transaxle (cont.)			
Transaxle bracket-to-mount nut			
1986-91 vehicles	30		41
Transaxle strut bracket-to-transaxle bolt			
1992-93 vehicles	38		52
1994 vehicles	46		63
Torque strut-to-frame bracket bolt			
1992-93 vehicles	39		53
1994 vehicles	46		63
Front mount frame bracket-to-frame bolts			
1995 vehicles	63		85
Front mount bracket-to-transaxle bolts			
1995-99 vehicles	43		58
Rear mount-to-transaxle bolts			
1995-99 vehicles	42		58
Rear mount bolt and nut to frame			
1995-99 vehicles	53		72
Rear mount through bolt and nut			
1995-99 vehicles	75		105
Left side mount-to-frame bolts			
1995-99 vehicles	37		50
Left side mount-to-mount bracket nuts			
1995-99 vehicles	29		40
Left side mount bracket bolts			
1995-99 vehicles	55		75
TV cable-to-transaxle bolt			
1986-91 vehicles		80	9
CV-Joints			
Ball joint-to-steering knuckle nut			
1986-91 vehicles	41-50		55-65
Hub nut			
1986-91 vehicles	192		260
1992-99 vehicles	107		145
Seal retaining clamp			
1986-92 vehicles			
Small joint seal clamp	100		136
Large joint seal clamp	75		100
1993-99 vehicles			
Outer joint seal			
Small joint seal clamp	100		136
Large joint seal clamp	130		176
Inner joint seal			
Small joint seal clamp	100		136
Large joint seal clamp	130		176

89637C02

WHEELS 8-2
WHEELS 8-2
    REMOVAL & INSTALLATION 8-2
    INSPECTION 8-3
WHEEL LUG STUDS 8-3
    REMOVAL & INSTALLATION 8-3
FRONT SUSPENSION 8-4
STRUT AND KNUCKLE SCRIBING 8-5
    PROCEDURE 8-5
MACPHERSON STRUT 8-5
    TESTING 8-5
    REMOVAL & INSTALLATION 8-5
    OVERHAUL 8-6
LOWER BALL JOINTS 8-7
    INSPECTION 8-7
    REMOVAL & INSTALLATION 8-7
STABILIZER SHAFT 8-8
    REMOVAL & INSTALLATION 8-8
LOWER CONTROL ARMS 8-8
    REMOVAL & INSTALLATION 8-8
FRONT HUB, BEARING AND STEERING
  KNUCKLE 8-9
    REMOVAL & INSTALLATION 8-9
WHEEL ALIGNMENT 8-10
    CASTER 8-10
    CAMBER 8-10
    TOE 8-10
REAR SUSPENSION 8-11
COIL SPRINGS 8-12
    REMOVAL & INSTALLATION 8-12
STRUT 8-12
    REMOVAL & INSTALLATION 8-12
REAR CONTROL ARMS 8-14
    REMOVAL & INSTALLATION 8-14
STABILIZER SHAFT AND
  INSULATORS 8-15
    REMOVAL & INSTALLATION 8-15
STABILIZER SHAFT MOUNTING
  BRACKET 8-15
    REMOVAL & INSTALLATION 8-15
ADJUSTING LINK 8-15
    REMOVAL & INSTALLATION 8-15
REAR BALL JOINT 8-15
    INSPECTION 8-15
    REMOVAL & INSTALLATION 8-16
HUB AND BEARINGS 8-16
    REMOVAL & INSTALLATION 8-16
WHEEL ALIGNMENT 8-16
STEERING 8-17
STEERING WHEEL 8-17
    REMOVAL & INSTALLATION 8-17
WINDSHIELD WIPER SWITCH 8-18
    REMOVAL & INSTALLATION 8-18
TURN SIGNAL SWITCH 8-19
    REMOVAL & INSTALLATION 8-19
IGNITION SWITCH 8-20
    REMOVAL & INSTALLATION 8-20
IGNITION LOCK CYLINDER 8-20
    REMOVAL & INSTALLATION 8-20

COMBINATION SWITCH 8-20
    REMOVAL & INSTALLATION 8-20
STEERING LINKAGE 8-21
    REMOVAL & INSTALLATION 8-21
POWER STEERING GEAR 8-22
    REMOVAL & INSTALLATION 8-22
POWER STEERING PUMP 8-23
    REMOVAL & INSTALLATION 8-23
    SYSTEM BLEEDING 8-24
COMPONENT LOCATIONS
  FRONT SUSPENSION COMPONENT
    LOCATIONS 8-4
  REAR SUSPENSION COMPONENT
    LOCATIONS 8-11
SPECIFICATIONS CHARTS
  TORQUE SPECIFICATIONS 8-25

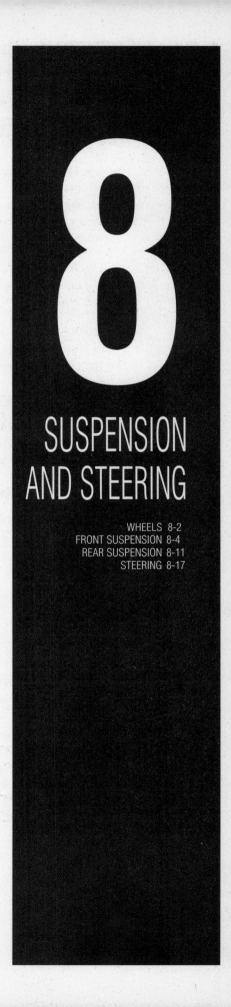

8

SUSPENSION AND STEERING

WHEELS 8-2
FRONT SUSPENSION 8-4
REAR SUSPENSION 8-11
STEERING 8-17

WHEELS

Wheels

REMOVAL & INSTALLATION

▶ **See Figures 1 thru 7**

➡ **On these vehicles, you will need a 19mm socket to loosen and remove the wheel lug nuts.**

1. Park the vehicle on a level surface.
2. Remove the jack, tire iron and, if necessary, the spare tire from their storage compartments.
3. Check the owner's manual or refer to Section 1 of this manual for the jacking points on your vehicle. Then, place the jack in the proper position.
4. If equipped with lug nut trim caps, remove them by either unscrewing or pulling them off the lug nuts, as appropriate. Consult the owner's manual, if necessary.

Fig. 1 Place the jack at the proper lifting point on your vehicle

5. If equipped with a wheel cover or hub cap, insert the tapered end of the tire iron in the groove and pry off the cover.
6. Apply the parking brake and block the diagonally opposite wheel with a wheel chock or two.

➡ **Wheel chocks may be purchased at your local auto parts store, or a block of wood cut into wedges may be used. If possible, keep one or two of the chocks in your tire storage compartment, in case any of the tires has to be removed on the side of the road.**

7. If equipped with an automatic transaxle, place the selector lever in **P** or Park; with a manual transmission/transaxle, place the shifter in Reverse.
8. With the tires still on the ground, use the tire iron/wrench to break the lug nuts loose.

➡ **If a nut is stuck, never use heat to loosen it or damage to the wheel and bearings may occur. If the nuts are seized, one or two heavy hammer blows directly on the end of the bolt usually loosens the rust. Be careful, as continued pounding will likely damage the brake drum or rotor.**

9. Using the jack, raise the vehicle until the tire is clear of the ground. Support the vehicle safely using jackstands.
10. Remove the lug nuts, then remove the tire and wheel assembly.
To install:
11. Make sure the wheel and hub mating surfaces, as well as the wheel lug studs, are clean and free of all foreign material. Always remove rust from the wheel mounting surface and the brake rotor or drum. Failure to do so may cause the lug nuts to loosen in service.
12. Install the tire and wheel assembly and hand-tighten the lug nuts.
13. Using the tire wrench, tighten all the lug nuts, in a crisscross pattern, until they are snug.
14. Raise the vehicle and withdraw the jackstand, then lower the vehicle.
15. Using a torque wrench, tighten the lug nuts in a crisscross pattern to 100 ft. lbs. (136 Nm). Check your owner's manual or refer to Section 1 of this manual for the proper tightening sequence.

Fig. 2 Before jacking the vehicle, block the diagonally opposite wheel with one or, preferably, two chocks

Fig. 3 With the vehicle still on the ground, break the lug nuts loose using the wrench end of the tire iron

Fig. 4 After the lug nuts have been loosened, raise the vehicle using the jack until the tire is clear of the ground

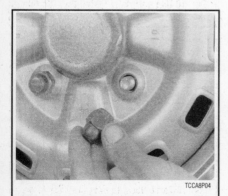

Fig. 5 Remove the lug nuts from the studs

Fig. 6 Remove the wheel and tire assembly from the vehicle

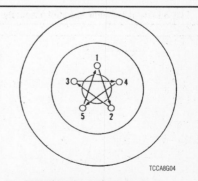

Fig. 7 Typical wheel lug tightening sequence

❊❊❊ WARNING

Do not overtighten the lug nuts, as this may cause the wheel studs to stretch or the brake disc (rotor) to warp.

16. If so equipped, install the wheel cover or hub cap. Make sure the valve stem protrudes through the proper opening before tapping the wheel cover into position.

17. If equipped, install the lug nut trim caps by pushing them or screwing them on, as applicable.

18. Remove the jack from under the vehicle, and place the jack and tire iron/wrench in their storage compartments. Remove the wheel chock(s).

19. If you have removed a flat or damaged tire, place it in the storage compartment of the vehicle and take it to your local repair station to have it fixed or replaced as soon as possible.

INSPECTION

Inspect the tires for lacerations, puncture marks, nails and other sharp objects. Repair or replace as necessary. Also check the tires for treadwear and air pressure as outlined in Section 1 of this manual.

Check the wheel assemblies for dents, cracks, rust and metal fatigue. Repair or replace as necessary.

Wheel Lug Studs

REMOVAL & INSTALLATION

With Disc Brakes

▶ **See Figures 8, 9 and 10**

1. Raise and support the appropriate end of the vehicle safely using jackstands, then remove the wheel.

2. Remove the brake pads and caliper. Support the caliper aside using wire or a coat hanger. For details, please refer to Section 9 of this manual.

3. Remove the outer wheel bearing and lift off the rotor. For details on wheel bearing removal, installation and adjustment, please refer to Section 1 of this manual.

4. Properly support the rotor using press bars, then drive the stud out using an arbor press.

➡ If a press is not available, CAREFULLY drive the old stud out using a blunt drift. MAKE SURE the rotor is properly and evenly supported or it may be damaged.

To install:

5. Clean the stud hole with a wire brush and start the new stud with a hammer and drift pin. Do not use any lubricant or thread sealer.

6. Finish installing the stud with the press.

➡ If a press is not available, start the lug stud through the bore in the hub, then position about 4 flat washers over the stud and thread the lug nut. Hold the hub/rotor while tightening the lug nut, and the stud should be drawn into position. MAKE SURE THE STUD IS FULLY SEATED, then remove the lug nut and washers.

7. Install the rotor and adjust the wheel bearings.

8. Install the brake caliper and pads.

9. Install the wheel, then remove the jackstands and carefully lower the vehicle.

10. Tighten the lug nuts to the proper torque.

With Drum Brakes

▶ **See Figures 11, 12 and 13**

1. Raise the vehicle and safely support it with jackstands, then remove the wheel.

2. Remove the brake drum.

3. If necessary to provide clearance, remove the brake shoes, as outlined in Section 9 of this manual.

4. Using a large C-clamp and socket, press the stud from the axle flange.

5. Coat the serrated part of the stud with liquid soap and place it into the hole.

To install:

6. Position about 4 flat washers over the stud and thread the lug nut. Hold the flange while tightening the lug nut, and the stud should be drawn into position. MAKE SURE THE STUD IS FULLY SEATED, then remove the lug nut and washers.

7. If applicable, install the brake shoes.

8. Install the brake drum.

9. Install the wheel, then remove the jackstands and carefully lower the vehicle.

10. Tighten the lug nuts to the proper torque.

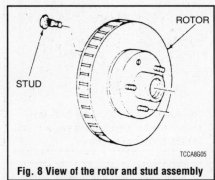

Fig. 8 View of the rotor and stud assembly

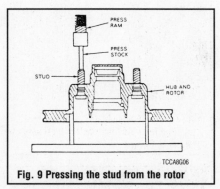

Fig. 9 Pressing the stud from the rotor

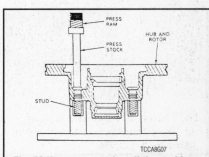

Fig. 10 Use a press to install the stud into the rotor

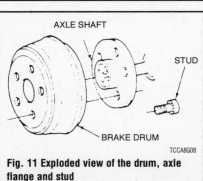

Fig. 11 Exploded view of the drum, axle flange and stud

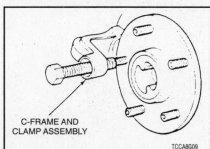

Fig. 12 Use a C-clamp and socket to press out the stud

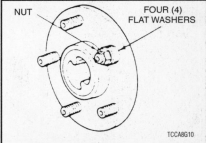

Fig. 13 Force the stud onto the axle flange using washers and a lug nut

FRONT SUSPENSION

FRONT SUSPENSION COMPONENT LOCATIONS

1. Lower control arm
2. Ball joint
3. Stabilizer link
4. Strut
5. Tie rod ends
6. Power steering gear
7. Stabilizer shaft

These cars use a MacPherson strut front suspension design. A MacPherson strut combines the functions of a shock absorber and an upper suspension member (upper arm) into one unit. The strut is surrounded by a coil spring, which provides normal front suspension functions.

The strut bolts to the body shell at its upper end, and to the steering knuckle at the lower end. The strut pivots with the steering knuckle by means of a sealed mounting assembly at the upper end which contains a preloaded, non-adjustable bearing.

The steering knuckle is connected to the chassis at the lower end by a conventional lower control arm, and pivots in the arm in a preloaded ball joint of standard design. The knuckle is fastened to the ball joint stud by means of a slotted nut and cotter pin.

Advantages of the MacPherson strut design, aside from its relative simplicity, include reduced weight and friction, minimal intrusion into the engine and passenger compartments, and ease of service.

Strut and Knuckle Scribing

PROCEDURE

♦ See Figure 14

Before servicing the following components, perform the scribing procedure, outlined below:
- Strut mount
- Strut bumper
- Strut shield
- Spring seat
- Spring insulator

This procedure will allow the components to be installed with the original camber setting. Then, only the toe must be inspected and adjusted.

1. Use a chisel in order to place a mark across the strut/knuckle interface (1).
2. Scribe the strut flange on the inboard side along the curve of the knuckle (2).
3. Using a sharp tool, scribe the knuckle along the lower outboard strut radius (3).
4. During assembly, carefully match the marks to the components.

Do not use the scribing procedure when replacing the following components:
- Front spring
- Strut
- Knuckle
- Control arm

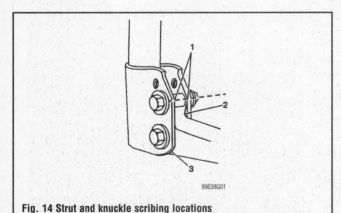

Fig. 14 Strut and knuckle scribing locations

MacPherson Strut

TESTING

The function of the shock absorber is to dampen harsh spring movement and provide a means of dissipating the motion of the wheels so that the shocks

encountered by the wheels are not totally transmitted to the body and, therefore, to you and your passengers. As the wheel moves up and down, the shock absorber shortens and lengthens, thereby imposing a restraint on movement by its hydraulic action.

A good way to see if your shock absorbers are functioning correctly is to push one corner of the car until it is moving up and down for almost the full suspension travel, then release it and watch its recovery. If the car bounces slightly about one more time and comes to a rest, the shock is all right. If the car continues to bounce excessively, the shocks will probably require replacement.

REMOVAL & INSTALLATION

♦ See Figure 15

1. Loosen the strut housing tie bar through-bolts on both ends of the tie bar.
2. If equipped with Computer Command Ride (CCR), detach the CCR electrical connector.
3. Unfasten the 3 strut-to-body mounting nuts from the top of the strut assembly.
4. Raise and safely support the vehicle. Position a jackstand under the engine cradle and carefully lower the vehicle so the weight of the vehicle rests on the jackstand and not the control arms. The control arms must hang free.
5. Remove the tire and wheel assembly.
6. If equipped with ABS, detach the front wheel speed sensor connector. If necessary, remove the speed sensor bracket from the strut.
7. Disconnect the brake line bracket from the strut assembly.

➡**The knuckle must be retained after the strut-to-knuckle bolts have been removed. Failure to observe this may cause ball joint and/or half-shaft damage.**

8. Remove the strut-to-steering knuckle bolts.
9. Carefully remove the strut assembly from the vehicle. When removing the strut, be careful to avoid chipping or cracking the spring coating when handling the front suspension coil spring.

To install:
10. Place the strut assembly in position.
11. Install the washer and tie bar.
12. Install the three strut-to-steering knuckle bolts/nuts. Tighten the upper strut mount nuts to 18 ft. lbs. (24 Nm). Tighten the tie bar through-bolts (outboard first) to 27 ft. lbs. (37 Nm).
13. If equipped with CCR, attach the electrical connector.
14. Install the strut-to-knuckle bolts.

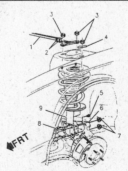

1 STRUT HOUSING TIE BAR
2 THROUGH-BOLTS, 37 N·m (27 LB. FT.)
3 NUT, STRUT MOUNT, 24 N·m (18 LB.FT.)
4 WASHER
5 BOLT, FRONT WHEEL SPEED SENSOR BRACKET, 17 N·m (13 LB. FT.)
6 RETAIN KNUCKLE ONCE STRUT IS REMOVED
7 NUT, STRUT TO KNUCKLE, 190 N·m (140 LB. FT.)
8 BOLT, BRAKE LINE BRACKET, 17 N·m (13 LB. FT.)
9 STRUT

Fig. 15 Exploded view of the strut-to-body mounting—1995 vehicle shown, other years similar

15. Connect the brake line bracket to the strut assembly.

16. If equipped with ABS, install the speed sensor bracket to the strut and attach the speed sensor connector.

17. Tighten the strut-to-knuckle nuts, as follows:
    a. 1986–90 vehicles: 144 ft. lbs. (195 Nm).
    b. 1991 vehicles: 180 ft. lbs. (244 Nm).
    c. 1992–99 vehicles: 140 ft. lbs. (190 Nm).

18. Tighten the bracket line and speed sensor bracket bolts to 13 ft. lbs. (17 Nm).

19. Install the tire and wheel assembly.

20. Remove the jackstand, then carefully lower the vehicle.

21. Tighten the wheel lugs to 100 ft. lbs. (136 Nm).

22. Take the vehicle to a reputable repair shop to have the front end alignment checked and adjusted, as necessary.

OVERHAUL

▶ **See Figures 16, 17, 18 and 19**

※※ CAUTION

Strut overhaul is a dangerous procedure and requires the use of a special spring compressor. If not certain of this procedure or if the proper tools aren't available, it is recommended you not perform this operation.

1. Remove the strut assembly from the car.

※※ WARNING

When removing the strut from the vehicle, be careful not to chip or crack the spring coating.

2. Install the strut in strut compressor J-34013, or equivalent.

3. Turn the compressor forcing screw until the spring compresses slightly.

4. Hold the strut shaft from turning using a using a socket, then remove the 24mm strut shaft nut.

5. Install rod tool J-34013-38, or equivalent, to help guide the strut shaft out of the assembly.

6. Loosen the compressor screw while guiding the strut shaft out of the assembly. Continue loosening the compressor screw until the strut and spring can be removed. Be careful to avoid chipping or cracking the spring coating when handling the coil spring.

To assemble:

7. Install the strut in strut compressor tool with clamp J-34013-20 clamped on the dampener shaft.

8. Position the strut in the compressor with the damper rod clamp clamped on the strut shaft in the compressor.

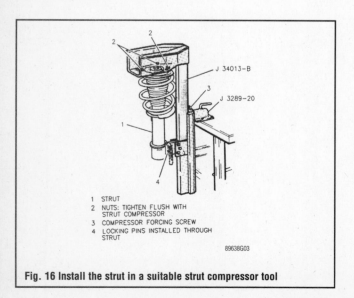

1 STRUT
2 NUTS: TIGHTEN FLUSH WITH STRUT COMPRESSOR
3 COMPRESSOR FORCING SCREW
4 LOCKING PINS INSTALLED THROUGH STRUT

89638G03

Fig. 16 Install the strut in a suitable strut compressor tool

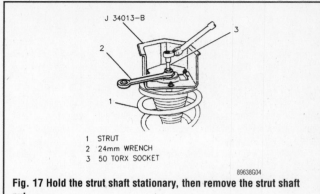

1 STRUT
2 24mm WRENCH
3 50 TORX SOCKET

89638G04

Fig. 17 Hold the strut shaft stationary, then remove the strut shaft nut

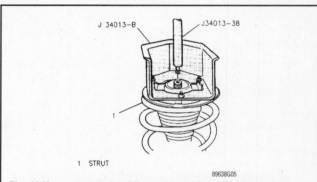

1 STRUT

89638G05

Fig. 18 Use a strut shaft guiding rod to guide the shaft out of the assembly

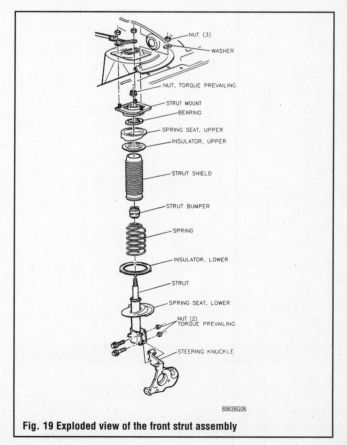

NUT (3)
WASHER
NUT, TORQUE PREVAILING
STRUT MOUNT
BEARING
SPRING SEAT, UPPER
INSULATOR, UPPER
STRUT SHIELD
STRUT BUMPER
SPRING
INSULATOR, LOWER
STRUT
SPRING SEAT, LOWER
NUT (2) TORQUE PREVAILING
STEERING KNUCKLE

89638G06

Fig. 19 Exploded view of the front strut assembly

9. Install the spring over the strut in the proper position, then move the assembly upright in the strut compressor. Install the upper locking pin.

➡ **The flat on the upper spring seat must face out from the centerline of vehicle or, when mounted in the strut compressor, the spring seat must face the same direction as the steering knuckle mounting flange. If the bearing had been removed from the upper spring seat, the bearing must be installed into the upper spring seat in the same orientation as it was previously. Also, the bearing must be installed in the spring seat before attaching to the strut mount.**

10. Install rod tool J-34013-38, or equivalent, into the strut assembly to guide the strut shaft.

11. Start turning the compressor screw clockwise on J-34013-B, while guiding the rod tool to center the strut shaft in the assembly.

12. Continue turning the compressor forcing screw on the strut compressor until the strut shaft threads can be seen through the top of the strut assembly.

13. Install the washer and nut.

14. Remove clamp J-34013-20, or equivalent, from the strut shaft.

15. Tighten the mounting nut to 55 ft. lbs. (75 Nm),while holding the strut shaft with a socket. You'll probably need a 24mm crow's foot wrench for this task.

16. Remove the 3 retaining nuts holding the strut to the compressor assembly.

17. Remove the 2 locking pins at the bottom of the strut.

18. Remove the strut assembly from the strut spring compressor tool.

19. Install the strut in the vehicle, as outlined earlier in this section.

Lower Ball Joints

INSPECTION

1. Raise and safely support the vehicle. Position a jackstand under the engine cradle, then lower the vehicle so the weight of the vehicle rests on the a jackstand and not the control arms.

2. Grasp the wheel at the top and the bottom and shake the wheel in and out.

3. If you see any movement at the ball joint or movement of the steering knuckle in relation the control arm, the ball joints are defective and should be replaced.

REMOVAL & INSTALLATION

♦ **See Figures 20, 21 and 22**

➡ **Use only the proper tools for separating the ball joint from the steering knuckle. If you don't use the correct tools, you could damage the ball joint and seal.**

1. Raise and safely support the vehicle. Position a jackstand under the engine cradle and lower the vehicle so the weight of the vehicle rests on the jackstand and not the control arms.

2. Remove the tire and wheel assembly.

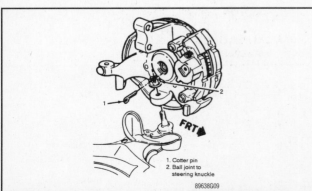

1. Cotter pin
2. Ball joint to steering knuckle

89638G09

Fig. 20 Remove the cotter pin, then loosen the ball stud's castellated nut

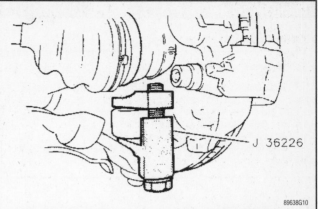

J 36226

89638G10

Fig. 21 Removing the ball joint from the knuckle using ball joint separator tool J-36226

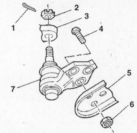

1 PIN
2 NUT BALL JOINT TO KNUCKLE; TIGHTEN TO 10 N-m (88 LB. IN) THEN TIGHTEN 2 FLATS TO 55 N-m (41 LB. FT.), MIN.
3 KNUCKLE
4 BALL JOINT MOUNTING BOLTS MUST FACE DOWN
5 CONTROL ARM
6 BALL JOINT MOUNTING NUTS 68 N-m (50 LB. FT.)
7 SERVICE BALL JOINT

89638G12

Fig. 22 Installation of a replacement ball joint

3. Remove and discard the cotter pin, then loosen the castellated nut from the ball stud.

4. Disconnect the ball joint from the steering knuckle, using tool J-36226, or equivalent suitable ball joint separator tool.

5. Loosen the stabilizer shaft link nut.

✳✳ WARNING

Be careful not to damage the halfshaft seals when drilling out the ball joint rivets.

6. Drill out the three rivets retaining the ball joint, then remove the ball joint from the steering knuckle and the control arm.

To install:

7. Position the ball joint to the steering knuckle, aligning with the holes in the control arm.

8. Install the 3 ball joint bolts, facing down, and the nuts. Tighten the ball joint-to-control arm nuts to 50 ft. lbs. (68 Nm).

9. Install the stabilizer shaft link nut and tighten to 13 ft. lbs. (17 Nm).

10. Install the ball joint slotted nut and tighten to 88 inch lbs. (10 Nm). Then, tighten the nut an additional 120° (2 flats on the nut) during which a torque of 41 ft. lbs. (55 Nm) must be achieved.

11. Install a new cotter pin. To align the slot, if necessary, tighten the nut up to one more flat. NEVER loosen the nut to install the pin.

12. Install the tire and wheel assembly.

13. Carefully lower the vehicle, then tighten the lug nuts to 100 ft. lbs. (136 Nm).

Stabilizer Shaft

REMOVAL & INSTALLATION

▶ See Figures 23 and 24

1. Raise and safely support the vehicle. Position a jackstand under the engine cradle and lower the vehicle so the weight of the vehicle rests on the jackstand and not the control arms. The control arms must hang free.
2. Remove the front wheel and tire assemblies.
3. Remove the left and right stabilizer link bolts.
4. If equipped, remove the left and right side stabilizer shaft mounting bolts and brackets.

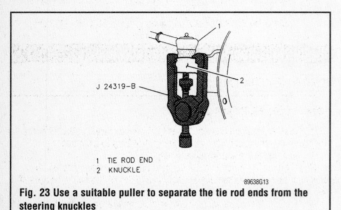

1 TIE ROD END
2 KNUCKLE

89638G13

Fig. 23 Use a suitable puller to separate the tie rod ends from the steering knuckles

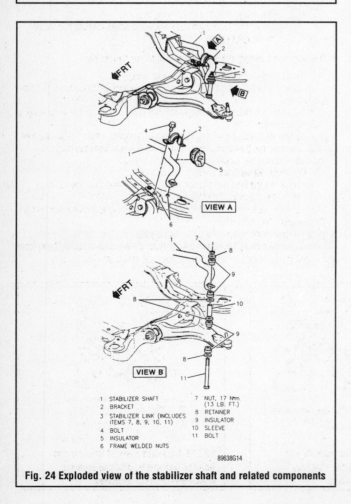

VIEW A

VIEW B

1 STABILIZER SHAFT	7 NUT, 17 N•m
2 BRACKET	(13 LB. FT.)
3 STABILIZER LINK (INCLUDES	8 RETAINER
ITEMS 7, 8, 9, 10, 11)	9 INSULATOR
4 BOLT	10 SLEEVE
5 INSULATOR	11 BOLT
6 FRAME WELDED NUTS	

89638G14

Fig. 24 Exploded view of the stabilizer shaft and related components

5. Matchmark the tie rod position, then, using a suitable puller, disconnect the tie rod ends from the steering knuckles.
6. Disconnect the exhaust pipe from the exhaust manifold and turn the passenger side strut assembly completely to the right.
7. Slide the stabilizer shaft over the steering knuckle, then pull down until the stabilizer bar clears the frame.
8. Remove the stabilizer shaft from the vehicle.

To install:

9. Position the stabilizer shaft in the vehicle, over the steering knuckle. Raise the stabilizer bar over the frame and slide into position.
10. Loosely install the stabilizer bar mount bushings/insulators, brackets and bolts.
11. Loosely install the stabilizer link/bushing components.
12. Install the tie rod ends to the steering knuckles.
13. Install the stabilizer shaft mounting bracket bolts and tighten as follows:
    a. 1986–92 vehicles: 37 ft. lbs. (50 Nm).
    b. 1993–99 vehicles: 35 ft. lbs. (47 Nm).
14. Install the stabilizer link/bushing nut and tighten to 13 ft. lbs. (17 Nm).
15. Install the tie rod end-to-knuckle nuts and tighten to 35 ft. lbs. (47 Nm). Install a new cotter pin. The nuts can be tightened up to 52 ft. lbs. (70 Nm) for cotter pin alignment. Never loosen the nut to insert the cotter pin.
16. Connect the exhaust pipe to the exhaust manifold and tighten the bolts to 18 ft. lbs. (25 Nm).
17. Install the tire and wheel assemblies.
18. Raise the vehicle and remove the jackstands.
19. Carefully lower the vehicle, then tighten the wheel lug nuts to 100 ft. lbs. (136 Nm).

Lower Control Arms

REMOVAL & INSTALLATION

▶ See Figures 21, 25 and 26

➡**Use only the proper tools for separating the ball joint from the steering knuckle. If you don't use the correct tools, you could damage the ball joint and seal.**

1. Raise and safely support the vehicle. Position a jackstand under the engine cradle/frame and lower the vehicle so the weight of the vehicle rests on the jackstand and not the control arms. The control arms must hang free.
2. Remove the tire and wheel assembly.
3. Disconnect the stabilizer shaft-to-control arm bolt.
4. Separate the ball joint from the steering knuckle and the control arm, as outlined earlier in this section.
5. Unfasten the control arm mounting bolts, then remove the control arm from the engine cradle/frame.

To install:

6. Position the control arm to the engine cradle. Install the bolts, washers nuts as shown in the accompanying figure, but do not tighten the control arm

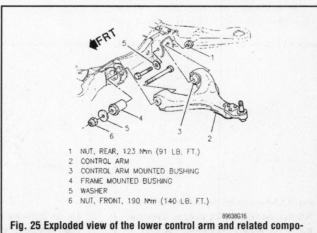

| 1 NUT, REAR, 123 N•m (91 LB. FT.) |
| 2 CONTROL ARM |
| 3 CONTROL ARM MOUNTED BUSHING |
| 4 FRAME MOUNTED BUSHING |
| 5 WASHER |
| 6 NUT, FRONT, 190 N•m (140 LB. FT.) |

89638G16

Fig. 25 Exploded view of the lower control arm and related components

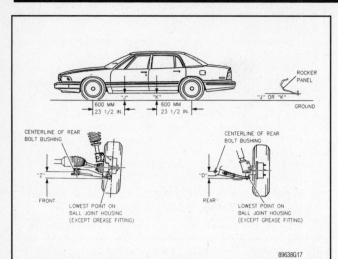

Fig. 26 On 1993–99 vehicles, you MUST measure the vehicle height (as shown) before tightening the control arm retainer

bolts at this time. The weight of the vehicle must be supported by the control arms so the vehicle design trim heights are obtained before tightening the control arm mounting nuts.

7. Install the stabilizer shaft to the control arm.

8. Connect the ball joint to the steering knuckle.

9. Tighten the stabilizer shaft link nut to 13 ft. lbs. (17 Nm). Install the ball joint slotted nut and tighten to 88 inch lbs. (10 Nm). Then tighten the nut an additional 120° (2 flats on the nut) during which a torque of 41 ft. lbs. (55 Nm) must be achieved.

10. Install a new cotter pin. To align the slot, if necessary, tighten the nut up to one more flat. NEVER loosen the nut to install the pin.

11. For 1986–92 vehicles, perform the following steps:

a. Raise the vehicle so the weight of the vehicle is supported by the control arm.

➡ **The weight of the vehicle must be supported by the control arms when tightening the control arm mounting nuts.**

b. Tighten the rear control arm mounting nut to 88 ft. lbs. (120 Nm) and the front mounting nut to 144 ft. lbs. (195 Nm).

c. Raise the vehicle and remove the jackstand.

12. Replace the tire and wheel assembly.

13. Carefully lower the vehicle, then tighten the wheel lug nuts to 100 ft. lbs. (136 Nm).

14. For 1993–99 vehicles, perform the following steps to check the trim height and tighten the control arm retainers.

a. Make sure the vehicle is parked on level ground, check the tire pressure and the fuel level. The fuel tank should be full.

b. There should be no extra weight in the passenger compartment or trunk; the trunk must be empty except for the spare tire and jack.

c. If equipped with Electronic Level Control (ELC), make sure it is operating properly.

d. Place the front seat to the rear position.

e. Bounce the vehicle 3 times at the front and rear of normalize the suspension.

f. Make measurements D, Z, J and K, as shown on the accompanying illustration.

g. Compare the measurements taken with those listed below. Maximum variation side-to-side and front-to-rear is ¾ in. (19mm).

- D—2 $\frac{11}{16}$–3 $\frac{7}{16}$ in. (68–88mm)
- Z—1 $\frac{15}{16}$–2 $\frac{3}{7}$ in. (50–70mm)
- J—9–9 $\frac{13}{16}$ in. (229–249mm)
- K—9 $\frac{9}{32}$–10 $\frac{1}{16}$ in. (236–256mm)

h. Tighten the FRONT control arm mounting nut to 140 ft. lbs. (190 Nm).

i. Tighten the REAR control arm mounting nut to 91 ft. lbs. (123 Nm).

Front Hub, Bearing and Steering Knuckle

REMOVAL & INSTALLATION

♦ **See Figures 27, 28 and 29**

1. Raise and support the vehicle safely. Place jackstands under the frame, then lower the vehicle slightly to allow the control arms to hang free.

2. Remove the tire and wheel assembly.

3. Insert a drift punch into the caliper and rotor vanes to prevent the rotor from turning, then remove the hub/drive axle nut. Clean the threads of the nut.

4. Unfasten the caliper mounting bolts, then remove and support the caliper aside with a suitable piece of wire.

5. Remove the rotor by sliding it from the hub.

6. If equipped with ABS, detach the front wheel speed sensor connector and unclip it from the dust shield.

➡ **The hub and bearing are replaced only as an assembly.**

7. For 1986–92 vehicles, perform the following:

a. Using a suitable front hub spindle removal tool, separate the hub from the halfshaft.

b. Remove the hub and bearing retaining bolts, shield, hub and bearing assembly and the O-ring.

c. Separate the ball joint from the steering knuckle, using the proper tool.

d. Remove the halfshaft assembly and tap the seal from the steering knuckle. Remove the steering knuckle from the hub.

8. For 1993–99 vehicles, perform the following:

a. Unfasten the hub and bearing retaining bolts and dust shield.

b. Place the transaxle in PARK.

c. Using a suitable front hub spindle removal tool, separate the hub and bearing from the drive axle.

d. If necessary, remove the steering knuckle.

9. Clean the rust and foreign material from the knuckle mounting face, bore and chamfer to allow the bearing to properly seat in the knuckle.

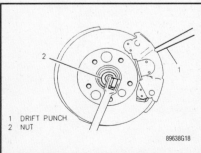

Fig. 27 Before removing and installing the hub nut, immobilize the rotor by inserting a drift pin through the caliper, into the rotor

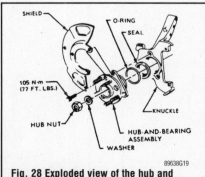

Fig. 28 Exploded view of the hub and bearing assembly, and the steering knuckle—1986–92 vehicles

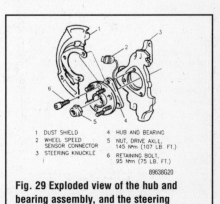

Fig. 29 Exploded view of the hub and bearing assembly, and the steering knuckle—1993–99 vehicles

To install:

10. For 1993–99 vehicles, perform the following:

   a. If removed, install the steering knuckle.

   b. Position the hub and bearing assembly to the drive axle. Apply a light coating of grease to the knuckle bore. If the new hub and bearing has a protective plastic cover, remove it before installation. Also, do not handle the knuckle or hub assembly by the ABS sensor wire.

   c. Install a new drive axle nut and draw the hub and bearing onto the axle.

   d. Place the transaxle in NEUTRAL.

   e. Install the dust shield, being careful not to damage the bearing outboard lip seal.

   f. Install the hub and bearing bolts, then tighten to 70 ft. lbs. (95 Nm).

11. For 1986–92 vehicles, perform the following:

   a. Install a new hub and bearing seal in the steering knuckle with a suitable seal installation tool. Install the steering knuckle to the strut.

   b. Lubricate the hub and bearing with grease. Fill the cavity between the seal and bearing completely.

   c. Install the halfshaft.

   d. Connect the ball joint to the steering knuckle and insert a new O-ring around the hub and bearing assembly.

   e. Install the hub and bearing, and shield into the steering knuckle. Tighten the bolts to 70 ft. lbs. (90 Nm).

12. If equipped, attach the ABS front wheel speed sensor connector, then clip the wire to the dust shield.

13. Install the rotor and caliper assembly. Tighten the caliper bolts to 38 ft. lbs. (52 Nm).

14. Insert a drift punch into the caliper and rotor vanes to prevent the rotor from turning. If not already done, install the shaft washer and nut (if equipped). Tighten the nut to the following specifications:

   • 1986–88 vehicles: 190 ft. lbs. (270 Nm).
   • 1989–90 vehicles: 185 ft. lbs. (260 Nm).
   • 1991–99 vehicles: 107 ft. lbs. (145 Nm).

15. Install the tire and wheel assembly.

16. Carefully lower the vehicle, then tighten the lug nuts to 100 ft. lbs. (136 Nm).

Wheel Alignment

If the tires are worn unevenly, if the vehicle is not stable on the highway or if the handling seems uneven in spirited driving, the wheel alignment should be checked. If an alignment problem is suspected, first check for improper tire inflation and other possible causes. These can be worn suspension or steering components, accident damage or even unmatched tires. If any worn or damaged components are found, they must be replaced before the wheels can be properly aligned. Wheel alignment requires very expensive equipment and involves minute adjustments which must be accurate; it should only be performed by a trained technician. Take your vehicle to a properly equipped shop.

Following is a description of the alignment angles which are adjustable on most vehicles and how they affect vehicle handling. Although these angles can apply to both the front and rear wheels, usually only the front suspension is adjustable.

CASTER

▶ See Figure 30

Looking at a vehicle from the side, caster angle describes the steering axis rather than a wheel angle. The steering knuckle is attached to a control arm or strut at the top and a control arm at the bottom. The wheel pivots around the line between these points to steer the vehicle. When the upper point is tilted back, this is described as positive caster. Having a positive caster tends to make the wheels self-centering, increasing directional stability. Excessive positive caster makes the wheels hard to steer, while an uneven caster will cause a pull to one side. Overloading the vehicle or sagging rear springs will affect caster, as will raising the rear of the vehicle. If the rear of the vehicle is lower than normal, the caster becomes more positive.

CAMBER

▶ See Figure 31

Looking from the front of the vehicle, camber is the inward or outward tilt of the top of wheels. When the tops of the wheels are tilted in, this is negative

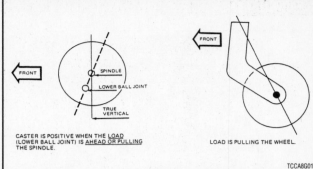

CASTER IS POSITIVE WHEN THE LOAD (LOWER BALL JOINT) IS AHEAD OR PULLING THE SPINDLE.

LOAD IS PULLING THE WHEEL.

TCCA8G01

Fig. 30 Caster affects straight-line stability. Caster wheels used on shopping carts, for example, employ positive caster

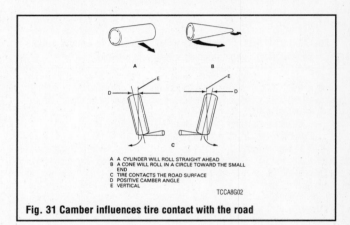

A A CYLINDER WILL ROLL STRAIGHT AHEAD
B A CONE WILL ROLL IN A CIRCLE TOWARD THE SMALL END
C TIRE CONTACTS THE ROAD SURFACE
D POSITIVE CAMBER ANGLE
E VERTICAL

TCCA8G02

Fig. 31 Camber influences tire contact with the road

camber; if they are tilted out, it is positive. In a turn, a slight amount of negative camber helps maximize contact of the tire with the road. However, too much negative camber compromises straight-line stability, increases bump steer and torque steer.

TOE

▶ See Figure 32

Looking down at the wheels from above the vehicle, toe angle is the distance between the front of the wheels, relative to the distance between the back of the wheels. If the wheels are closer at the front, they are said to be toed-in or to have negative toe. A small amount of negative toe enhances directional stability and provides a smoother ride on the highway.

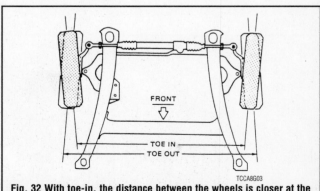

FRONT

TOE IN
TOE OUT

TCCA8G03

Fig. 32 With toe-in, the distance between the wheels is closer at the front than at the rear

REAR SUSPENSION

REAR SUSPENSION COMPONENT LOCATIONS

1. Spring
2. Strut
3. Lower control arm
4. Adjustment link
5. Ball joint
6. Stabilizer shaft and bushings

The rear suspension on these vehicles features control arms, springs and struts for each wheel. An option that is available is Electronic Level Control (ELC). This system includes auto-leveling components which use air struts for suspension control in the rear.

Coil Springs

REMOVAL & INSTALLATION

▶ See Figures 33, 34 and 35

✳✳ CAUTION

The coil spring replacement is a dangerous procedure and requires the use of a special tools and cautions. If not certain of this procedure or if the proper tools aren't available, it is recommend you not perform this operation.

1. Raise and support the vehicle safely. Support the vehicle so the control arms hang free.
2. Remove rear wheel and tire assemblies.
3. If equipped with ELC, disconnect the ELC height sensor on the right control arm and/or the parking brake cable retaining clip on the left control arm.
4. Unfasten the rear stabilizer shaft from the bracket on the knuckle.

✳✳ CAUTION

The coil spring removal tool MUST be secured to the jack or personal injury could occur!

5. Place a proper coil spring removal tool securely on a transmission jack and position it to cradle the control arm bushings.
6. Place a chain around the spring and through the control arm as a safety measure, then raise the jack to remove the tension from the control arm pivot bolts.
7. Remove the pivot bolt and nut from the rear of the control arm.

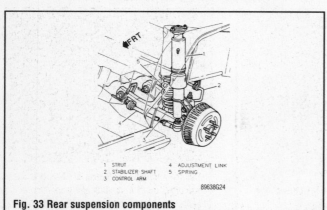

1 STRUT   4 ADJUSTMENT LINK
2 STABILIZER SHAFT 5 SPRING
3 CONTROL ARM
89638G24

Fig. 33 Rear suspension components

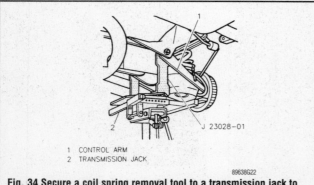

1 CONTROL ARM
2 TRANSMISSION JACK
89638G22

Fig. 34 Secure a coil spring removal tool to a transmission jack to cradle the control arm, in order to remove the spring

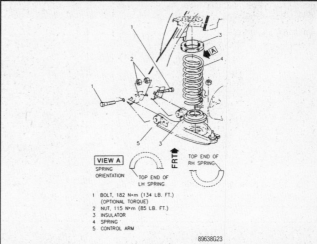

VIEW A
SPRING ORIENTATION   TOP END OF LH SPRING   TOP END OF RH SPRING

1 BOLT, 182 N•m (134 LB. FT.) (OPTIONAL TORQUE)
2 NUT, 115 N•m (85 LB. FT.)
3 INSULATOR
4 SPRING
5 CONTROL ARM
89638G23

Fig. 35 Exploded view of the spring mounting and proper installation position

8. Slowly, maneuver the jack to relieve tension from the front control arm pivot bolt.
9. Lower the jack to allow the control arm to pivot downward.

➡ **Do not apply force to the control arm and/or ball joint to remove the spring. Proper maneuvering of the spring will allow for easy removal.**

10. When all the compression is removed from the spring, remove the safety chain, spring and the insulators.
11. Inspect the insulators carefully and replace them if they are cut or worn. If the vehicle has over 50,000 miles (80,450 km).
To install:
12. Snap the upper insulator on the spring prior to installation.
13. Position the lower insulator and spring in the vehicle. Install the coil springs so the upper end of the springs are positioned properly, as shown in the accompanying figure.
14. Raise the control arm into position, using the coil spring tool mounted on a transmission jack.
15. Slowly maneuver the jack to allow the installation of the front and rear control arm pivot bolts and nuts.
16. Attach the rear stabilizer shaft to the knuckle bracket.
17. If equipped, connect the ELC height sensor link on the right control arm and/or the parking brake cable retaining clip on the left control arm.
18. Install the tire and wheel assemblies.
19. Remove the jack from under the vehicle, then carefully lower the vehicle.

➡ **The control arm retainers must be tightened with the vehicle unsupported and resting on its wheels at the normal trim height. Failure to do this can adversely affect ride and handling.**

20. Tighten the control arm pivot nuts to 85 ft. lbs. (115 Nm).
21. Tighten the control arm pivot bolts to the following specifications:
    a. 1986–90 vehicles: 125 ft. lbs. (170 Nm)
    b. 1991–93 vehicles: 138 ft. lbs. (187 Nm)
    c. 1994 vehicles: 118 ft. lbs. (160 Nm)
    d. 1995–99 vehicles: 134 ft. lbs. (182 Nm)
22. Tighten the stabilizer support bolt to 13–14 ft. lbs. (17–18 Nm).

Strut

REMOVAL & INSTALLATION

▶ See Figures 36 thru 49

1. For 1986–94 vehicles, remove the trunk side cover for access to the strut upper mounting nuts. You may have to remove the rear seat to access the front nut. For 1995–99 vehicles, remove the rear seat cushion and seat back to get to the strut upper nuts. Remove any necessary cover(s) from the strut upper retainers.

Fig. 36 From inside the trunk, unfasten the retaining clips . . .

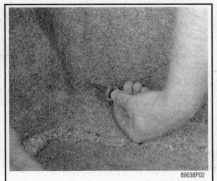

Fig. 37 . . . and the trim cover retaining wingnuts

Fig. 38 Remove the plastic upper trim cover retainers . . .

Fig. 39 . . . then lower the plastic trim cover

Fig. 40 After the cover is removed, you can access the upper strut mounting nuts

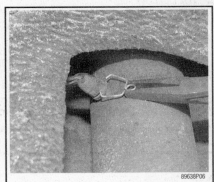

Fig. 41 Use pliers to unfasten the ELC air tube retaining clip

Fig. 42 Unplug the ELC air tube (1) from the nipple (2) on the strut

Fig. 43 Matchmark the installed position of the strut-to-knuckle flange

Fig. 44 Unfasten the lower strut-to-knuckle mounting nuts. Note that there are two bolts

Fig. 45 The lower strut mounting bolt hole is oval, to allow for camber adjustment

Fig. 46 Remove the bolt, washer and nut

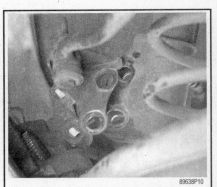

Fig. 47 Separate the strut from the steering knuckle . . .

Fig. 48 . . . then remove the strut from the vehicle

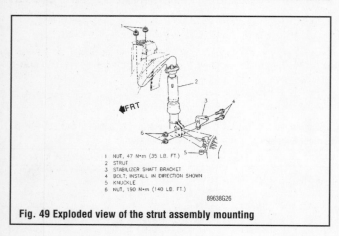

1 NUT, 47 N•m (35 LB. FT.)
2 STRUT
3 STABILIZER SHAFT BRACKET
4 BOLT; INSTALL IN DIRECTION SHOWN
5 KNUCKLE
6 NUT, 190 N•m (140 LB. FT.)

89638G26

Fig. 49 Exploded view of the strut assembly mounting

2. Raise and safely support the vehicle.
3. Remove the tire and wheel assembly.
4. If equipped with Electronic Level Control (ELC), unfasten the tube clip, then disconnect the air tube from the strut.
5. Support the control arm with a suitable jack.
6. Unfasten the strut-to-knuckle bolts.
7. Remove the strut tower mounting nuts through the trunk or the body slot behind the rear seat back.
8. Separate the strut from the knuckle.
9. If equipped with Computer Control Ride (CCR), lower the strut, then detach the electrical connector.
10. Remove the strut assembly from the vehicle.
To install:
11. If equipped with CCR, attach the electrical connector to the strut.
12. Position the strut assembly in the vehicle, then install the upper strut mounting nuts.
13. Install the strut to the stabilizer shaft bracket and knuckle. Insert the bolts in the direction shown in the accompanying figure.
14. If equipped, attach the ELC air tube.
15. Tighten the strut upper mount nuts to 35 ft. lbs. (47 Nm) and the strut-to-knuckle nuts to 140 ft. lbs. (190 Nm).
16. Install the tire and wheel assembly. Remove the jack from under the vehicle.
17. Carefully lower the vehicle, then tighten the wheel lug nuts to 100 ft. lbs. (136 Nm).
18. Replace the trunk side cover and/or rear seat back and cushion, as applicable.
19. Take your vehicle to a reputable repair shop to have the rear alignment checked and adjusted, as necessary.

REMOVAL & INSTALLATION

▶ **See Figure 50**

1. Raise and support the vehicle safely. Remove the tire and wheel assembly.
2. If equipped, disconnect the ELC height sensor on the right control arm and/or the parking brake cable retaining clip on the left control arm.
3. Remove the cotter pin, then unfasten the suspension adjustment link retaining nut and separate the link assembly from the control arm. For more information, refer to the procedure located later in this section.
4. Remove the spring, as outlined earlier in this section.
5. Remove the cotter pin and slotted nut from the ball joint. Turn the nut over and install it with the flat portion facing up. Do NOT tighten the nut.
6. Use a suitable tool to separate the ball joint from the steering knuckle.
7. Remove the control arm from the vehicle.

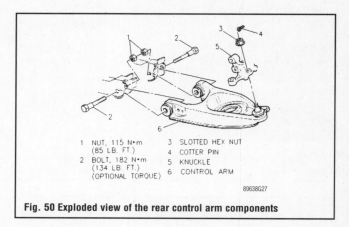

1 NUT, 115 N•m (85 LB. FT.)	3 SLOTTED HEX NUT
	4 COTTER PIN
2 BOLT, 182 N•m (134 LB. FT.) (OPTIONAL TORQUE)	5 KNUCKLE
	6 CONTROL ARM

89638G27

Fig. 50 Exploded view of the rear control arm components

To install:
8. Position the control arm ball joint stud in the steering knuckle. Install a new slotted nut and tighten as follows:
    a. Tighten the nut to 88 inch lbs. (10 Nm).
    b. Tighten the nut an additional 4 flats; the torque should be 40 ft. lbs. (55 Nm), minimum. It may be necessary to partially load the joint to keep the ball stud from rotating while the nut is being tightened.
    c. Tighten the nut up to one more flat to align the slot with the cotter pin hole.
9. Install a new cotter pin.
10. Install the spring, as outlined earlier in this section.
11. Connect the adjustment link assembly to the control arm and secure with the retaining nut. Tighten the nut to 63 ft. lbs. (85 Nm).
12. If equipped, connect the ELC height sensor on the right control arm and/or the parking brake cable retaining clip on the left control arm.
13. Install the tire and wheel assembly.
14. Lower the vehicle, then tighten the wheel lug nuts to 100 ft. lbs. (136 Nm).

➡**The control arm retainers must be tightened with the vehicle unsupported and resting on its wheels at the normal trim height. Failure to do this can adversely affect ride and handling.**

15. Tighten the control arm pivot nuts to 85 ft. lbs. (115 Nm).
16. Tighten the control arm pivot bolts to the following specifications:
    a. 1986–90 vehicles: 125 ft. lbs. (170 Nm)
    b. 1991–93 vehicles: 138 ft. lbs. (187 Nm)
    c. 1994 vehicles: 118 ft. lbs. (160 Nm)
    d. 1995–99 vehicles: 134 ft. lbs. (182 Nm)
17. Tighten the stabilizer support bolt to 13–14 ft. lbs. (17–18 Nm).

Stabilizer Shaft and Insulators

REMOVAL & INSTALLATION

▶ **See Figure 51**

1. Raise and safely support the vehicle.
2. Remove the rear tire and wheel assemblies.
3. Remove the stabilizer shaft link bolts, nut, retainer and insulator from the stabilizer shaft bracket.
4. Remove the link bolt, then bend the open end of the link downward.
5. Remove the stabilizer shaft and insulators.

To install:

6. Install the stabilizer shaft and insulators. Install the insulator into link with slit rearward.
7. Install the link by bending upward to close around insulator, then install the install the link bolt.
8. Install the link insulator, retainers, support bolt and nut.
9. Install the wheel and tire assemblies, then carefully lower the vehicle. Tighten the wheel lug nuts to 100 ft. lbs. (136 Nm).
10. Tighten the link nut to 13 ft. lbs. (17 Nm) and the link bolt to 17 ft. lbs. (23 Nm).

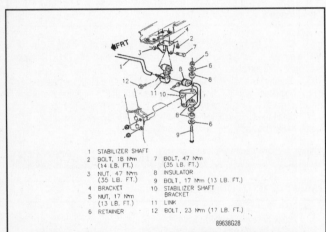

1	STABILIZER SHAFT	7	BOLT, 47 Nm
2	BOLT, 18 Nm (14 LB. FT.)		(35 LB. FT.)
3	NUT, 47 Nm (35 LB. FT.)	8	INSULATOR
		9	BOLT, 17 Nm (13 LB. FT.)
4	BRACKET	10	STABILIZER SHAFT BRACKET
5	NUT, 17 Nm (13 LB. FT.)	11	LINK
6	RETAINER	12	BOLT, 23 Nm (17 LB. FT.)

89638G28

Fig. 51 Exploded view of the stabilizer shaft and insulators (bushings)

Stabilizer Shaft Mounting Bracket

REMOVAL & INSTALLATION

▶ **See Figure 51**

1. Unfasten the retaining bolt and nut.
2. Remove the stabilizer shaft mounting bracket bolts and bracket.

To install:

3. Install the bracket and bolts.
4. Install the bolt and nut.
5. Tighten the bracket bolts to 14 ft. lbs. (18 Nm) and the nut to 35 ft. lbs. (47 Nm).

Adjusting Link

REMOVAL & INSTALLATION

▶ **See Figure 52**

1. Raise and support the vehicle safely. Support the vehicle with a suitable jack under the frame, so the control arms hang free.
2. Remove and discard the cotter pin. Loosen the slotted nut so that a few

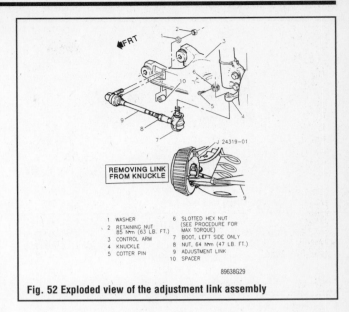

REMOVING LINK FROM KNUCKLE

1	WASHER	6	SLOTTED HEX NUT (SEE PROCEDURE FOR MAX TORQUE)
2	RETAINING NUT 85 Nm (63 LB. FT.)	7	BOOT, LEFT SIDE ONLY
3	CONTROL ARM	8	NUT, 64 Nm (47 LB. FT.)
4	KNUCKLE	9	ADJUSTMENT LINK
5	COTTER PIN	10	SPACER

89638G29

Fig. 52 Exploded view of the adjustment link assembly

threads are showing between the bottom of the nut and the knuckle. The purpose of this is to retain the arm when you break the stud taper loose.

➡ **When separating a linkage joint, do NOT try to disengage the joint by driving a wedge between the joint and the attached part. This will damage the seal.**

3. Use a suitable ball joint separator tool to separate the adjustment link from the knuckle.
4. Unfasten the link retaining nut, then remove the link from the control arm.

To install:

5. Position the link to the control arm and secure with the retaining nut.
6. Attach the link to the knuckle. Position the boot toward the front of the vehicle.
7. Tighten the retaining nut to 63 ft. lbs. (85 Nm) and the new slotted hex nut to 33 ft. lbs. (45 Nm).
8. Install a new cotter pin. After tightening the slotted nut, align the slot in the nut to the cotter hole by tightening up to one additional flat. Do not loosen the nut to install the cotter pin.
9. Lubricate the adjustment link joint.
10. Install the tire and wheel assembly.
11. Lower the vehicle, then tighten the wheel lug nuts to 100 ft. lbs. (136 Nm).
12. Take your vehicle to a reputable repair shop to have the alignment checked and adjusted, if necessary.

Rear Ball Joint

INSPECTION

▶ **See Figure 53**

The ball joint has a visual wear indicator. Checking the condition of the ball joint is a simple procedure. The vehicle must be supported by the wheels during ball joint inspection to insure that the vehicle weight is properly loading the ball joints. Wear is indicated by a 0.50 in. (13mm) diameter nipple retracting into the ball joint cover (the ball joint grease fitting is threaded into this nipple). The nipple protrudes 0.050 in. (1.27mm) beyond the ball joint cover surface on a new, unworn joint. The ball joint should be replaced if the nipple for the grease fitting is flush or below the cover surface.

As part of the inspection, check the ball stud tightness in the knuckle boss. Check it by shaking the wheel and feeling for movement of the stud end or castellated nut at the knuckle boss. Checking the fastener tightness at the castellated nut is an alternate method of inspecting. A loose nut can indicate a bent stud or an "opened up" hole in the knuckle boss. If worn, the ball joint and knuckle must be replaced.

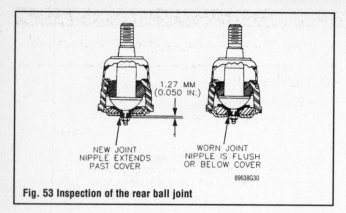

Fig. 53 Inspection of the rear ball joint

If, during suspension service, the ball joint is separated from the knuckle, inspect the ball joint seal for damage. A damaged seal will cause joint failure. If you find seal damage, you must replace the ball joint.

REMOVAL & INSTALLATION

▸ See Figure 54

✳✳ CAUTION

The ball joint replacement is a dangerous procedure and requires the use of a special tools and cautions. If not certain of this procedure or if the proper tools aren't available, it is recommend you not perform this operation. Place a chain through the spring to help protect uncontrolled expansion.

1. Raise and support the vehicle safely. Remove the tire and wheel assembly.
2. If equipped with ELC, remove the height sensor link from the right control arm.
3. If necessary, remove the parking brake cable retaining clip.
4. Remove the cotter pin and nut from the outer suspension adjustment link. Use a suitable puller to separate the outer suspension adjustment link from the knuckle

✳✳ CAUTION

The control arm MUST be supported to prevent the coil spring from forcing the control arm downward.

5. Support the control arm with a suitable jack.
6. Remove the ball joint cotter pin and slotted nut. Discard the cotter pin. Turn the nut over and reinstall with the flat portion facing upward, but do NOT tighten the nut.

➡ **Make sure to have the proper separating tool, because using the wrong tool will damage the ball joint or seal.**

7. Install ball joint separator J-34505, or equivalent tool, and separate the knuckle from the stud by backing off inverted nut against the tool. Remove the slotted hex nut.
8. Install the tools on the ball joint and control arm, as shown in the accompanying illustration, and press the ball joint out of the control arm.
To install:
9. Install the tools all the ball joint and control arm, as shown in accompanying figure, and press the new ball joint into control arm.
10. Position the knuckle on the ball joint. Install a new slotted nut and tighten as follows:
   a. Step 1: Tighten the nut to 88 inch lbs. (10 Nm)
   b. Tighten the nut an additional four flats; the torque should be 40 ft. lbs. (55 Nm) minimum. It may be necessary to partially load the joint to keep the ball joint from rotating while the nut is being tightened.
   c. Tighten the nut up to one more flat to align the slot with the cotter pin hole.
11. Align slot and install a NEW cotter pin. Never back nut off to align holes.
12. Install the adjustment link in the vehicle. Position the boot toward front of the vehicle. Tighten the slotted hex nut to 33 ft. lbs. (45 Nm).

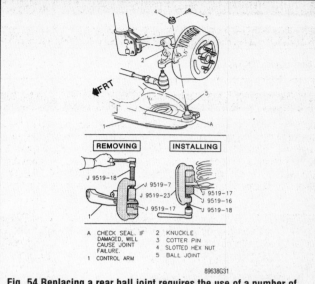

Fig. 54 Replacing a rear ball joint requires the use of a number of special tools

13. After tightening the nut to specifications, align the slot in the nut to the cotter pin hole, by tightening ONLY, and install a new cotter pin. Do NOT loosen the nut to install the cotter pin.
14. Lubricate the ball joint and adjustment link with a suitable grease.
15. If equipped with ELC, install the height sensor link to the right control arm.
16. If removed, install the parking brake retaining clip to the left control arm.
17. Install the tire and wheel assembly, then carefully lower the vehicle. Tighten the wheel lug nuts to 100 ft. lbs. (136 Nm).

Hub and Bearings

REMOVAL & INSTALLATION

1. Raise and safely support the vehicle.
2. Remove the tire and wheel assembly.

✳✳ WARNING

Never hammer on the brake drum, as this could damage the brake drum.

3. Remove the brake drum from the vehicle. It may be necessary to remove the ABS sensor wiring connector, if equipped.

➡ **The bolts that attach the hub and bearing assembly also support the brake assembly. When removing these bolts, support the brake components with a suitable piece of wire. Do NOT let the brake line or ABS electrical wire support the brake assembly.**

4. Unfasten the four retaining bolts, then remove the hub and bearing assembly from the axle.
To install:
5. Install the hub and bearing assembly to the axle and secure with the four retaining bolts. Tighten the bolts to 52 ft. lbs. (70 Nm).
6. Install the brake drum. If necessary, attach the ABS sensor wiring connector.
7. Install the tire and wheel assembly.
8. Carefully lower the vehicle. Tighten the wheel lug nuts to 100 ft. lbs. (136 Nm).

Wheel Alignment

Refer to Wheel Alignment in the Front Suspension portion of this section for precautions and explanations of important alignment angles, which also pertain to the rear wheels.

STEERING

Steering Wheel

REMOVAL & INSTALLATION

✷✷ CAUTION

Some vehicles are equipped with the Supplemental Inflatable Restraint (SIR) system, which uses an air bag. Whenever working near any of the SIR components, such as the impact sensors, the air bag module, steering column and instrument panel, disable the SIR system, as described in Section 6. Failure to follow safety and disabling procedures could result in accidental air bag deployment, unnecessary SIR system repairs, and above all, possible personal injury.

Vehicles Without SIR

▶ See Figures 55 thru 63

1. Disconnect the negative battery cable.
2. For vehicles equipped with a standard steering wheel, perform the following:
   a. Remove the screws holding the steering pad.
   b. Remove the steering pad and disconnect the horn lead.
3. For vehicles equipped with a steering wheel control pad, perform the following.

Fig. 55 Carefully pry out the steering wheel control pad and horn pads

Fig. 56 Push down on the horn lead, twist it out of the cam tower, then disconnect it from the steering wheel

Fig. 57 Slide a suitable tool down to unlatch the electrical connector retaining tab . . .

Fig. 58 . . . then unplug the connector. Note the location of the tab

Fig. 59 You must use a Torx® driver to unfasten the screw retaining the wire

Fig. 60 Use a suitable pair of pliers to remove the retaining circlip

Fig. 61 Use a ratchet and extension combination to unfasten the steering wheel retaining nut

Fig. 62 Assemble a suitable steering wheel puller on the steering wheel, then turn the puller's threaded rod . . .

Fig. 63 . . . to press and remove the steering wheel from the shaft

a. Use a thin, flat-bladed tool to pry the control button assembly out, along the top edge of the assembly.

b. Pry out the horn control pads.

c. Disconnect the horn lead by pushing down on it, then twisting it out of the cam tower.

d. Detach the steering wheel control connector.

e. If necessary, unfasten the Torx® screw and remove the remaining wire from the steering wheel.

4. Use a pair of snapring pliers to remove the retainer.

5. Unfasten the steering wheel retaining nut.

6. Matchmark the steering shaft and steering wheel to ensure proper alignment during installation.

7. Install an approved steering wheel puller, then remove the steering wheel from the shaft.

To install:

8. Install the steering wheel, aligning it with the mark made on the shaft during removal. Install the steering shaft retaining nut and tighten to 30 ft. lbs. (41 Nm).

9. Install the retaining clip with a pair of snapring pliers.

10. Connect the horn lead and install the steering pad, using the reverse of the removal procedure.

11. If necessary, install the screws holding the steering pad.

12. Connect the negative battery cable.

Vehicles With SIR

▶ See Figure 64

1. Properly disable the SIR system, as outlined in Section 6 of this manual.

2. If not already done, disconnect the negative battery cable.

☀ CAUTION

When carrying a live air bag, make sure the bag and trim cover and pointed away from the body. In the unlikely event of an accidental deployment, the bag will then deploy with minimal chance of injury. In addition, when placing a live air bag on a bench or other surface, always face the bag and trim cover up, away from the surface. This will reduce the chance of personal injury if it is accidentally deployed.

3. Remove the SIR inflator module by performing the following steps:

a. Unfasten the 2 inflator module attaching screws from the back of the steering wheel.

b. Carefully lift the inflator module from the steering wheel to access the wire connectors.

c. Push down and rotate the horn contact lead counterclockwise, and remove from the steering column tower.

d. Remove the horn contact lead.

e. Remove the CPA retaining clip from the SIR wiring connector. Detach the SIR wiring connector from the inflator module.

f. If equipped, detach the steering wheel control switch connector.

g. Remove the inflator module from the vehicle and position on a suitable workbench.

4. Remove the steering wheel locknut.

5. Matchmark the steering shaft and steering wheel to ensure proper alignment during installation.

6. Install tools J 1859-03 and J 38720, or other suitable puller and side screws to the steering wheel, then remove the steering wheel from the vehicle.

To install:

7. Feed the wiring through the slot in the steering wheel.

8. Position the steering wheel on the shaft, aligning the mark on the steering wheel with the mark on the shaft.

9. Install the steering wheel locknut and tighten to 30 ft. lbs. (41 Nm).

10. Install the SIR inflator module by performing the following steps:

a. If equipped, attach the steering wheel control switch connector.

b. Install the CPA retainer to the SIR wiring connector.

c. Feed the horn contact lead to the steering column horn tower; push the lead into the horn tower and rotate it clockwise to the locked position.

d. Connect the horn ground lead.

e. Attach the SIR connector and CPA.

f. Position the inflator module to the steering wheel. Install the top surface of the module first to ease assembly and fit. Ensure that the inflator module is properly aligned with the steering wheel and that the wires behind the module are not pinched during installation.

g. Install the inflator module attaching screws through the back of the steering wheel. Tighten the screws to 27 inch lbs. (3 Nm).

11. Properly enable the SIR system, as outlined in Section 6 of this manual.

12. If not already done, disconnect the negative battery cable.

Windshield Wiper Switch

REMOVAL & INSTALLATION

1. Disconnect the negative battery cable.

2. Remove the steering wheel, the cover and the lock plate assembly.

☀ CAUTION

Some vehicles are equipped with the Supplemental Inflatable Restraint (SIR) or air bag system. The SIR system must be disabled before performing service on or around SIR system components, steering column, instrument panel components, wiring and sensors. Failure to follow safety and disabling procedures could result in accidental air bag deployment, possible personal injury and unnecessary SIR system repairs.

3. Remove the turn signal actuator arm, the lever and the hazard flasher button.

4. Remove the turn signal switch screws, the lower steering column trim panel and the steering column bracket bolts.

5. Disconnect the turn signal switch and the wiper switch connectors.

6. Pull the turn signal switch rearward 6–8 inches (15–20cm), remove the key buzzer switch and cylinder lock assembly.

7. Remove and pull the steering column housing rearward. Remove the housing cover screw.

8. Remove the wiper switch pivot and the switch assembly.

To install:

9. Install the pivot and switch assembly.

10. Reposition and reinstall the steering column. Replace the housing cover screw.

11. Install the cylinder lock and key buzzer assembly. Reposition the turn signal switch.

12. Connect the turn signal switch and wiper switch connectors.

13. Install the steering column bracket bolts and the column trim panel.

14. Replace the turn signal switch screws.

15. Install the hazard flasher button, turn signal actuator arm and lever.

16. Install the lock plate assembly, cover and the steering wheel.

17. Connect the negative battery cable.

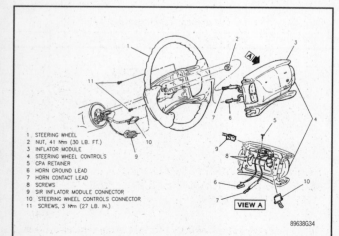

1 STEERING WHEEL
2 NUT, 41 Nm (30 LB. FT.)
3 INFLATOR MODULE
4 STEERING WHEEL CONTROLS
5 CPA RETAINER
6 HORN GROUND LEAD
7 HORN CONTACT LEAD
8 SCREWS
9 SIR INFLATOR MODULE CONNECTOR
10 STEERING WHEEL CONTROLS CONNECTOR
11 SCREWS, 3 Nm (27 LB. IN.)

VIEW A

89638G34

Fig. 64 Exploded view of the steering wheel and SIR inflator module mounting

Turn Signal Switch

REMOVAL & INSTALLATION

▶ **See Figures 65, 66, 67, 68 and 69**

➡**If the vehicle is not equipped with the SIR system (air bags), skip Step 1 and simply disconnect the negative battery cable. Also, disregard all instructions below related to air bags.**

1. If equipped, disable the SIR system, as outlined in Section 6 of this manual.
2. If not already done, disconnect the negative battery cable.
3. Remove the steering wheel and the shroud.
4. Remove the inflation restraint (air bag module) coil assembly-to-steering shaft lock screw (home boss) and retaining ring. Remove the coil assembly from the shaft and allow it to hang freely.
5. Position a suitable lock plate compression tool on the end of the steering shaft and compress the lock plate by turning the shaft nut clockwise. Pry the wire snapping out of the shaft groove.
6. Remove the tool, then lift the lock plate from the shaft.
7. Remove the canceling cam, upper bearing preload spring, bearing seat and inner race from the shaft.
8. Position the turn signal switch in the right turn position. Remove the turn signal lever screw, then remove the lever.
9. Remove the turn signal switch by performing the following steps:
   a. Remove the switch-to-steering column screws, then pull the switch out and allow it to hang freely.
   b. From under the dash, remove the retainer spring and wiring protector.
   c. Remove the hazard knob.
   d. Detach the electrical connector from the lower steering column, then gently pull the wiring connector through the gear shift lever bowl, the column housing and the lock housing cover. Remove the switch.

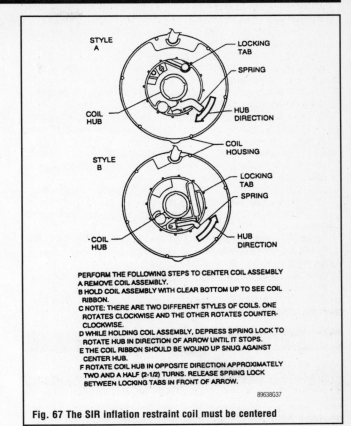

PERFORM THE FOLLOWING STEPS TO CENTER COIL ASSEMBLY
A REMOVE COIL ASSEMBLY.
B HOLD COIL ASSEMBLY WITH CLEAR BOTTOM UP TO SEE COIL RIBBON.
C NOTE: THERE ARE TWO DIFFERENT STYLES OF COILS. ONE ROTATES CLOCKWISE AND THE OTHER ROTATES COUNTER-CLOCKWISE.
D WHILE HOLDING COIL ASSEMBLY, DEPRESS SPRING LOCK TO ROTATE HUB IN DIRECTION OF ARROW UNTIL IT STOPS.
E THE COIL RIBBON SHOULD BE WOUND UP SNUG AGAINST CENTER HUB.
F ROTATE COIL HUB IN OPPOSITE DIRECTION APPROXIMATELY TWO AND A HALF (2-1/2) TURNS. RELEASE SPRING LOCK BETWEEN LOCKING TABS IN FRONT OF ARROW.

89638G37

Fig. 67 The SIR inflation restraint coil must be centered

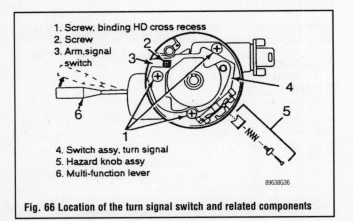

89638G35

Fig. 65 If equipped with air bags, remove the inflator restraint coil from the steering column

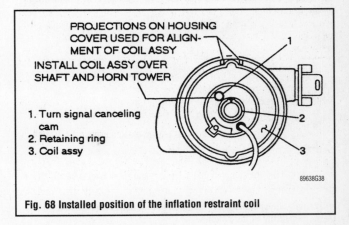

89638G38

Fig. 68 Installed position of the inflation restraint coil

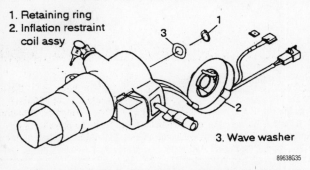

89638G36

Fig. 66 Location of the turn signal switch and related components

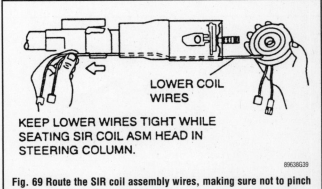

89638G39

Fig. 69 Route the SIR coil assembly wires, making sure not to pinch them

To install:

10. Route the turn signal switch harness through the steering column housing, then connect the switch and install the screw.

11. Install the switch actuator arm and screw.

12. Install the inner race, bearing seat and the bearing preload spring. Replace the turn signal canceling cam.

13. Use lock plate compression tool to install the lock plate, compress the lock plate, then install the shaft lock retaining ring.

14. To install the SIR inflation restraint coil, perform the following steps:

    a. Install the home boss-to-steering column lock screw, allowing the hub to rotate.

    b. While holding the coil assembly (in one hand) with the steering wheel connector facing upwards, rotate the coil hub in the appropriate direction until it stops; the coil ribbon is now wound snug.

    c. Rotate the coil hub 2½ turns in the opposite direction until the center lock hole is even with the notch in the coil housing.

    d. While holding the hub in position, install the lock screw into the center lock hole.

    e. Install the coil assembly using the horn tower on the inner ring canceling cam and outer ring projections for alignment purposes.

15. Install the steering wheel and the shroud.

16. If equipped with the SIR system, properly enable the system, as outlined in Section 6 of this section.

17. If not already done, connect the negative battery cable, then check the turn signals for proper operation.

Ignition Switch

REMOVAL & INSTALLATION

▶ **See Figure 70**

➡**If the vehicle is not equipped with an air bag, skip Step 1 and simply disconnect the negative battery cable. Also, disregard all instructions below related to air bags.**

1. If equipped, disable the SIR system, as outlined in Section 6 of this manual.

2. If not already done, disconnect the negative battery cable.

3. Lower the steering column; be sure to properly support it.

4. Position the switch in the **OFF-UNLOCKED** position. With the lock cylinder removed, the rod is in **LOCK** when it is in the next to the uppermost detent; **OFF-UNLOCKED** is 2 detents from the top.

5. Remove both switch screws, then remove the switch assembly.

To install:

6. Place the new switch in the **OFF-UNLOCKED** position. Ensure the lock cylinder and actuating rod are in **OFF-UNLOCKED** position (3rd detent from the top).

7. Install the actuating rod into the switch and assemble the switch on the column. Tighten the mounting screws.

➡**Use only the specified screws since over-length screws could impair the collapsibility of the column.**

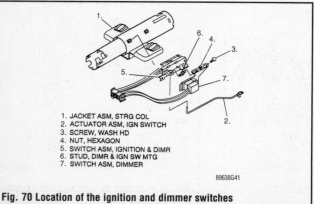

1. JACKET ASM, STRG COL
2. ACTUATOR ASM, IGN SWITCH
3. SCREW, WASH HD
4. NUT, HEXAGON
5. SWITCH ASM, IGNITION & DIMR
6. STUD, DIMR & IGN SW MTG
7. SWITCH ASM, DIMMER

89638G41

Fig. 70 Location of the ignition and dimmer switches

8. Install the steering column.

9. If equipped with the SIR system, properly enable the system, as outlined in Section 6 of this section.

10. If not already done, connect the negative battery cable, then check the turn signals for proper operation.

Ignition Lock Cylinder

REMOVAL & INSTALLATION

▶ **See Figure 71**

➡**If the vehicle is not equipped with an air bag, skip Step 1 and simply disconnect the negative battery cable. Also, disregard all instructions below related to air bags.**

1. If equipped, disable the SIR system, as outlined in Section 6 of this manual.

2. If not already done, disconnect the negative battery cable.

3. Remove the turn signal switch assembly.

4. Remove the key from the lock cylinder. Remove the buzzer switch and clip.

5. Reinsert the key into the lock cylinder and turn it to the **LOCK** position.

6. Remove the cylinder lock-to-steering column screw, then remove the lock set.

7. If equipped, detach the pass key connector.

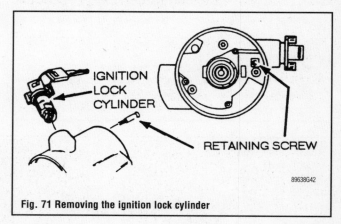

IGNITION LOCK CYLINDER

RETAINING SCREW

89638G42

Fig. 71 Removing the ignition lock cylinder

To install:

8. Install the lock cylinder, attach the pass key connector (if equipped), then tighten the lock-to-steering column screw to 22 inch lbs. (2.5 Nm).

9. Position the key in the **RUN** position and reverse the removal procedures.

10. Install the turn signal switch.

11. If equipped with the SIR system, properly enable the system, as outlined in Section 6 of this section.

12. If not already done, connect the negative battery cable, then check the turn signals for proper operation.

Combination Switch

The combination switch is attached to the upper portion of the steering column and is part of the turn signal lever.

REMOVAL & INSTALLATION

➡**If the vehicle is not equipped with an air bag, skip Step 1 and simply disconnect the negative battery cable. Also, disregard all instructions below related to air bags.**

1. If equipped, disable the SIR system, as outlined in Section 6.

2. If not already done, disconnect the negative battery cable.

3. Remove the left side sound insulator.

4. Lower the steering column trim plate.

5. Remove the steering column-to-dash screws and lower the steering column.

6. Remove the inflation restraint (air bag module) and the combination switch assembly.

7. Position the ignition switch in the **OFF-UNLOCKED** position. With the cylinder removed, the rod is in **LOCK** when it is in the next to the uppermost detent; **OFF-UNLOCKED** is 2 detents from the top.

8. Remove the mounting screws and disconnect the electrical connectors. Remove the ignition switch assembly along with the dimmer switch.

To install:

9. Adjust the dimmer switch.

10. Install the dimmer switch and attach the mounting screws. Put the ignition switch in **OFF-UNLOCKED** position; make sure the lock cylinder and actuating rod are in **OFF-UNLOCKED** (third detent from the top) position.

11. Install the activating rod into the switch and assemble the switch on the column. Tighten the mounting screws.

12. Connect the electrical connections at the dimmer switch.

13. Install the combination switch and replace the air bag module.

14. Position the steering column in place and install the column mounting screws.

15. Install the column trim plate and replace the sound insulator.

16. If equipped with the SIR system, properly enable the system, as outlined in Section 6 of this section.

17. If not already done, connect the negative battery cable, then check the turn signals for proper operation.

Steering Linkage

REMOVAL & INSTALLATION

Tie Rod Ends (Outer)

▶ See Figures 72 thru 78

1. Raise and safely support the vehicle.
2. Use a suitable marker to matchmark the tie rod end installation position.

This is to ensure proper installation and will lessen the chance that the toe setting will require adjustment.

3. Remove and discard the cotter pin, then back off the jam nut from the tie rod end.

4. Attach a universal steering linkage puller to the tie rod end. Tighten the puller's threaded rod to separate the tie rod end from the steering knuckle.

5. Remove the castellated nut, then lift the tie rod end from the steering knuckle.

6. Unscrew the tie rod end from the tie rod, counting the number of turns for alignment purposes during installation.

To install:

7. Thread the tie rod end onto the tie rod until the matchmarks align. Do not tighten the jam nut.

8. Connect the tie rod end to the steering knuckle, then install the castellated nut to the tie rod end stud. Tighten the nut to 35 ft. lbs. (47 Nm). Tighten the nut up to ⅙ additional turn, or 52 ft. lbs. (70 Nm) maximum, to align the cotter pin slot. Never loosen the nut to install the cotter pin.

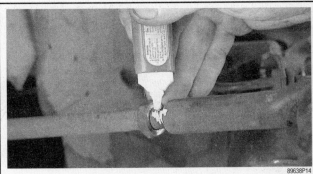

Fig. 72 Use correction fluid or equivalent to matchmark the installed position of the tie rod end

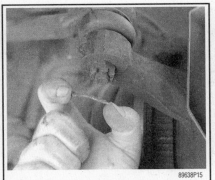

Fig. 73 Remove and discard the cotter pin from the tie rod end

Fig. 74 Loosen, but do not remove, the castellated nut, then install a suitable puller to separate the tie rod end

Fig. 75 Remove the castellated nut, then lift the tie rod end from the steering knuckle

Fig. 76 Unscrew the tie rod end from the tie rod, counting the number of turns for installation

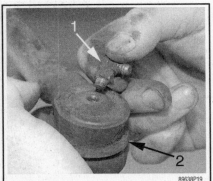

Fig. 77 If necessary, you can unscrew the grease fitting (1) from the tie rod end (2)

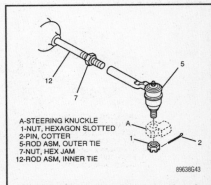

A-STEERING KNUCKLE
1-NUT, HEXAGON SLOTTED
2-PIN, COTTER
5-ROD ASM, OUTER TIE
7-NUT, HEX JAM
12-ROD ASM, INNER TIE

Fig. 78 Exploded view of the outer tie rod end assembly

9. Install a new cotter pin into the hole in the tie rod stud.
10. Tighten the jam nut against the tie rod end to 50 ft. lbs. (68 Nm).
11. Carefully lower the vehicle.
12. Take the vehicle to reputable repair shop and have the toe professionally checked and/or set. If it is out of adjustment enough, a tire can wear out in only a few miles. It is advisable to have a front end alignment professionally done after replacing steering or suspension components to avoid costly tire wear.

Tie Rods (Inner)

▶ See Figures 79, 80, 81 and 82

➡ Disassembly of the rack and pinion assembly requires special tools and skills. Before attempting this time consuming and difficult procedure, check on the availability of already rebuilt rack and pinion assemblies. You may find it more cost effective to purchase a rebuilt assembly from your local parts jobber.

1. Raise and safely support the vehicle.
2. Remove the rack and pinion assembly from the vehicle, as outlined later in this section.
3. Remove the tie rod end.
4. Remove the hexagonal jam nut from the tie rod.
5. Remove the tie rod end clamp.
6. Remove the boot clamp with side cutters.

➡ Mark the location of the breather tube on the housing before removing the rack and pinion boot and breather tube.

7. Remove the rack and pinion boot and breather tube.
8. Remove the shock dampener from the tie rod and slide it back on the rack.
9. Remove the inner rod from the rack. Place a wrench on the flat of rack. Place a wrench on the flat of the tie rod housing and rotate the housing counterclockwise until the tie rod separates from the rack.

To install:
10. Hold the rack during tie rod installation to prevent internal gear damage.
11. Install the shock dampener onto the rack.

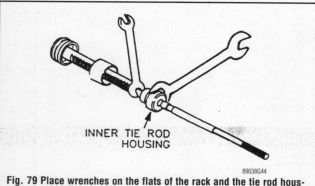

Fig. 79 Place wrenches on the flats of the rack and the tie rod housing, then rotate the housing counterclockwise

12. Install the tie rod to the rack, and tighten the tie rod to 70 ft. lbs. (95 Nm).

➡ Make certain the tie rod rocks freely in the housing before staking the inner rod to the rack.

13. Support the rack and housing of the tie rod.
14. Stake both sides of the tie rod housing to the flats on the rack.
15. Check both stakes by inserting a 0.010 inch (0.25mm) feeler gauge between the rack and tie rod housing. The feeler gauge must not pass between the rack and housing stake.
16. Slide the shock dampener over the housing until it engages.
17. Install the new boot.
18. Apply grease to the tie rod in the illustrated areas.
19. Install the boot onto the tie rod and up to the housing.
20. Align the breather tube with the mark made during removal, elbow of boot to the breather tube.
21. Install the boot onto the housing until seated in the housing groove. After installation, the boot must NOT be twisted.
22. Position the boot clamp on the boot and crimp securely.
23. Install the hexagonal jam nut on the tie rod.
24. Attach the tie rod ends, then install the rack and pinion assembly into the car, as outlined later in this section.
25. Carefully lower the vehicle.
26. Take the vehicle to reputable repair shop and have the toe professionally set. If it is out of adjustment enough, a tire can wear out in only a few miles. It is advisable to have a front end alignment professional done after replacing steering or suspension components to avoid costly tire wear.

Power Steering Gear

REMOVAL & INSTALLATION

▶ See Figures 83, 84 and 85

1. Raise and safely support the vehicle, allowing the front suspension to hang freely.
2. Remove both front tire and wheel assemblies.

✳✳ CAUTION

Failure to disconnect the intermediate shaft from the rack and pinion stub shaft can result in damage to the steering gear and/or intermediate shaft. This damage may cause a loss of steering control and possibly, personal injury.

➡ The wheels of the vehicle must be straight ahead and the steering column in the LOCK position before disconnecting the steering column or intermediate shaft from the steering gear. Failure to do so will cause the SIR coil assembly to become uncentered, which will damage the coil.

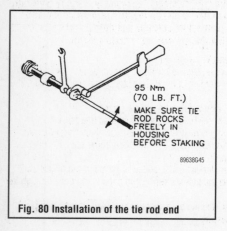

Fig. 80 Installation of the tie rod end

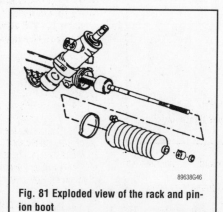

Fig. 81 Exploded view of the rack and pinion boot

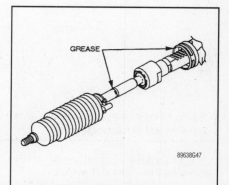

Fig. 82 Apply grease to the areas shown when installing the boot seal

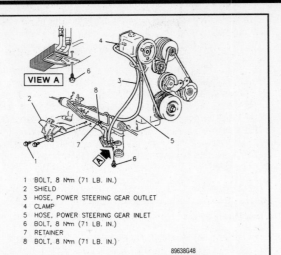

1 BOLT, 8 N•m (71 LB. IN.)
2 SHIELD
3 HOSE, POWER STEERING GEAR OUTLET
4 CLAMP
5 HOSE, POWER STEERING GEAR INLET
6 BOLT, 8 N•m (71 LB. IN.)
7 RETAINER
8 BOLT, 8 N•m (71 LB. IN.)

89638G48

Fig. 83 Power steering fluid line routing—non-supercharged engine shown

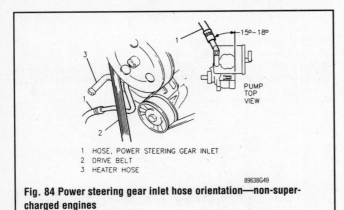

1 HOSE, POWER STEERING GEAR INLET
2 DRIVE BELT
3 HEATER HOSE

89638G49

Fig. 84 Power steering gear inlet hose orientation—non-supercharged engines

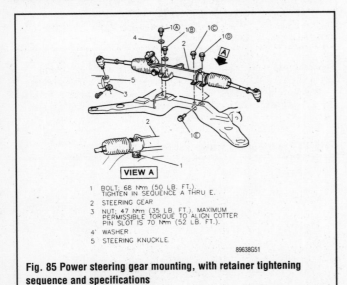

1 BOLT; 68 N•m (50 LB. FT.)
  TIGHTEN IN SEQUENCE A THRU E.
2 STEERING GEAR
3 NUT; 47 N•m (35 LB. FT.) MAXIMUM
  PERMISSIBLE TORQUE TO ALIGN COTTER
  PIN SLOT IS 70 N•m (52 LB. FT.).
4 WASHER
5 STEERING KNUCKLE

89638G51

Fig. 85 Power steering gear mounting, with retainer tightening sequence and specifications

3. If equipped, move the intermediate shaft cover upward, then unfasten the intermediate shaft-to-stub shaft pinch bolt.

4. Using a suitable puller, separate both tie rod ends from the steering knuckles.

5. Position a suitable drain pan under the power steering fluid lines. Remove the power steering fluid line retainer, then disconnect the outlet and inlet hoses from the steering gear. Allow the fluid to drain, then plug the lines to avoid contaminating the system.

6. Remove the steering gear assembly-to-chassis mounting bolts.

7. Support the body with suitable jackstands to allow for the lowering of the frame.

8. Loosen the front frame mounting bolts.

9. Remove the rear frame bolts, then lower the rear of the frame about 3 inches (76mm).

❋❋ WARNING

Do not lower the frame too far, or you could damage the engine components nearest the cowl.

10. Remove the steering gear assembly by maneuvering it through the left wheel well opening.

To install:

11. Install the rack and pinion assembly into the vehicle, maneuvering it through the left wheel well opening.

12. Raise the rear of the frame, then install the frame bolts and tighten to 76 ft. lbs. (103 Nm).

13. Install the rack and pinion assembly-to-chassis bolts. Tighten the rack mounting bolts to 50 ft. lbs. (68 Nm).

14. Remove the jackstands.

15. Apply Loctite® thread locking kit 1052624, or equivalent thread locking compound to the steering gear mounting bolts.

16. Install the steering gear mounting bolts, and washers, then tighten the retainers to 50 ft. lbs. (68 Nm) in the sequence shown in the accompanying figure.

17. Unplug and attach the power steering gear outlet and inlet hoses, then tighten the fittings to 20 ft. lbs. (27 Nm).

18. Install the power steering fluid line retainer.

19. Connect the tie rod ends to the steering knuckles. Tighten the nuts to 35 ft. lbs. (47 Nm). Install a new cotter pin. Tighten the nut up to an additional ⅙ turn, or to 52 ft. lbs. (70 Nm) to align the cotter pin slot. Do not loosen the nut to install the cotter pin.

20. Install the intermediate shaft-to-stub shaft pinch bolt and tighten to 35 ft. lbs. (47 Nm). If equipped, move the intermediate shaft cover upward into position.

21. Install both front tire and wheel assemblies, then carefully lower the vehicle.

22. Refill the power steering pump reservoir, then bleed the power steering system and check for leaks.

23. Take the vehicle to a reputable repair shop and have the front end alignment checked and adjusted as necessary.

Power Steering Pump

REMOVAL & INSTALLATION

▶ **See Figures 83, 84, 86 and 87**

➡**On Two Flow Electronic (TFE) systems, if the pump is being replaced, make sure to replace the pump with one that is specified for the TFE system. The TFE pump (without its actuator and fitting) looks identical to the non-TFE pumps, but the two are not interchangeable.**

1. Disconnect the negative battery cable.

2. If necessary for access, remove the strut housing upper tie bar.

3. Remove the power steering pump drive belt(s) or serpentine drive belt, as applicable.

4. On the TFE pump, detach the electrical connector.

5. If necessary, remove the lower bolt from the mounting bracket.

6. Disconnect the power steering pump inlet and outlet hoses from the pump. On supercharged engines, also disconnect the remove reservoir hose from the pump reservoir, if necessary.

7. Position the power steering pump pulley so the bolts can be accessed through the holes. Remove the power steering pump mounting bolts through the holes.

8. Remove the power steering pump assembly. If replacing the pump, transfer the pulley as necessary.

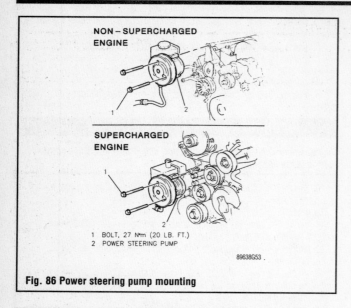

NON – SUPERCHARGED ENGINE

SUPERCHARGED ENGINE

1 BOLT, 27 N·m (20 LB. FT.)
2 POWER STEERING PUMP

89638G53

Fig. 86 Power steering pump mounting

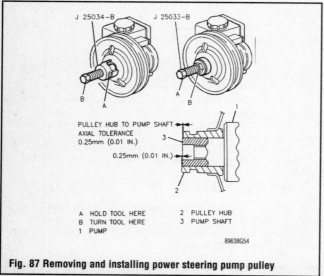

J 25034–B   J 25033–B

PULLEY HUB TO PUMP SHAFT
AXIAL TOLERANCE
0.25mm (0.01 IN.)

0.25mm (0.01 IN.)

A HOLD TOOL HERE   2 PULLEY HUB
B TURN TOOL HERE   3 PUMP SHAFT
1 PUMP

89638G54

Fig. 87 Removing and installing power steering pump pulley

To install:

9. Hand-start the power steering gear inlet hose connection to the pump. Orient the hose as shown in the accompanying figures.

10. Install the pump and pulley assembly. On non-supercharged engines, install and tighten the lower bolt first, then check that a clearance of 0.080–0.200 in. (2–5mm) exists between the hose and heater pipes as the contact may cause noise after installation.

11. Attach the power steering gear outlet hose to the pump. The hose must be routed outboard and under the engine harness and heater hoses.

12. On supercharged engines, if necessary, reconnect the hose from the remove reservoir to the pump reservoir.

13. Tighten the power steering gear inlet hose-to-pump fitting to 20 ft. lbs. (27 Nm) and the hose clamp at the pump to 15 inch lbs. (1.7 Nm). Tighten the pump mounting bolts to 20 ft. lbs. (27 Nm).

14. If equipped with a TFE pump, attach the connector.

15. Install the power steering belt(s) or serpentine belt, as applicable.

16. If removed, install the strut housing upper tie bar and tighten the nuts to 18 ft. lbs. (25 Nm).

17. Connect the negative battery cable. Bleed the power steering system and check for leaks.

SYSTEM BLEEDING

♦ See Figure 88

1. Fill the power steering pump reservoir with power steering fluid.

2. With the engine **OFF** and the wheels off the ground. Turn the steering wheel all the way to the left, add steering fluid to the **COLD** mark on the level indicator.

3. Bleed the system by turning the wheels from side to side. Keep the fluid level at the **COLD** mark.

4. Start the engine and add fluid if necessary. Turn the wheels from right to left and add fluid if necessary.

5. Return the wheels to the center position and lower the vehicle.

6. Allow the engine to warn up, road test the vehicle and recheck the fluid level.

7. Check the system for leaks, road test and recheck the fluid level.

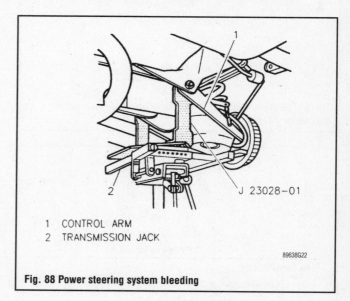

1 CONTROL ARM
2 TRANSMISSION JACK

J 23028–01

89638G22

Fig. 88 Power steering system bleeding

TORQUE SPECIFICATIONS

Component	ft. lbs.	inch lbs.	Nm
Wheels			
Lug nuts	100		136
Front Suspension			
MacPherson Struts			
Upper strut mount nuts	18		24
Tie bar through bolts (outboard first)	27		37
Strut-to-knuckle nuts			
1986-90 vehicles	144		195
1991 vehicles	180		244
1992-99 vehicles	140		190
Brake line and speed sensor bracket bolts	13		17
Lower Ball Joint			
Ball joint-to-control arm nuts	50		68
Stabilizer shaft link nut	13		17
Ball joint slotted nut			
Step 1		88	10
Step 2 (an additional 120°, 2 flats on the nut)	41		55
Stabilizer Shaft			
Stabilizer shaft mounting bracket bolts			
1986-92 vehicles	37		50
1993-99 vehicles	35		47
Stabilizer link/bushing nut	13		17
Lower Control Arm			
Rear mounting nut			
1986-92 vehicles	88		120
1993-99 vehicles	91		123
Front mounting nut			
1986-92 vehicles	144		195
1993-99 vehicles	140		190
Rear mounting nut	91		123
Front Hub and Bearing, and Knuckle			
Hub and bearing-to-knuckle bolts 70 ft. lbs. (95 Nm).			
Hub nut			
1986-88 vehicles	190		270
1989-90 vehicles	185		260
1991-99 vehicles	108		145
Rear Suspension			
Coil Springs			
Control arm pivot nuts	85		115
Control arm pivot bolts			
1986-90 vehicles	125		170
1991-93 vehicles	138		187
1994 vehicles	118		160
1995-99 vehicles	134		182
Stabilizer support bolt	13-14		17-18
Struts			
Strut upper mount nuts	35		47
Strut-to-knuckle nuts	140		190

89638C01

TORQUE SPECIFICATIONS

Component	ft. lbs.	inch lbs.	Nm
Rear Suspension (cont.)			
Control Arms			
Control arm pivot nuts	85		115
Control arm pivot bolts			
1986-90 vehicles	125		170
1991-93 vehicles	138		187
1994 vehicles	118		160
1995-99 vehicles	135		182
Stabilizer Bar			
Stabilizer shaft link			
link retaining nut	13		17
link mounting bolt	17		23
Stabilizer shaft bracket			
bracket bolts	14		18
bracket nut	35		47
Stabilizer support bolt	13-14		17-18
Adjustment link			
retaining nut	63		85
slotted hex nut	33		45
Ball joint slotted nut			
Step 1		88	10
Step 2 (tighten an additional 120°)	41		55
Rear Hub and Bearing bolts	52		70
Steering			
Steering wheel locknut			
locknut	30		41
inflator module retaining screws		27	3
Lock cylinder-to-steering column screw		22	2.5
Outer tie rod end			
hex slotted nut			
Step 1	35		47
Step 2: (tighten an additional 60°)	52		70
Jam nut	50		68
Inner tie rod end retainer	70		95
Power Steering Gear			
Frame bolts	76		103
Rack and pinion assembly-to-chassis bolts	50		68
Steering gear mounting retainers	50		68
Power steering gear outlet and inlet hose fittings	20		27
Intermediate shaft-to-stub shaft pinch bolts	35		47
Power Steering Pump			
Power steering gear inlet hose-to-pump fitting	20		27
Pump hose clamp fitting		5	1.7
Pump mounting bolts	20		27
Strut housing upper tie bar nuts	18		25

89638C02

BRAKE OPERATING SYSTEM 9-2
BASIC OPERATING PRINCIPLES 9-2
    DISC BRAKES 9-2
    DRUM BRAKES 9-2
BRAKE LIGHT SWITCH 9-3
    REMOVAL & INSTALLATION 9-3
    ADJUSTMENT 9-3
MASTER CYLINDER 9-4
    REMOVAL & INSTALLATION 9-4
POWER BRAKE BOOSTER 9-4
    REMOVAL & INSTALLATION 9-4
PROPORTIONING VALVES 9-5
BLEEDING THE BRAKE SYSTEM 9-7
    MANUAL BLEEDING 9-7
    PRESSURE BLEEDING 9-8
    BENCH BLEEDING THE MASTER
    CYLINDER 9-9
DISC BRAKES 9-9
BRAKE PADS 9-9
    REMOVAL & INSTALLATION 9-9
    INSPECTION 9-10
BRAKE CALIPER 9-10
    REMOVAL & INSTALLATION 9-10
    OVERHAUL 9-11
BRAKE DISC (ROTOR) 9-13
    REMOVAL & INSTALLATION 9-13
    INSPECTION 9-13
DRUM BRAKES 9-13
BRAKE DRUMS 9-14
    REMOVAL & INSTALLATION 9-15
    INSPECTION 9-15
BRAKE SHOES 9-15
    INSPECTION 9-15
    REMOVAL & INSTALLATION 9-15
    ADJUSTMENTS 9-19
WHEEL CYLINDERS 9-20
    REMOVAL & INSTALLATION 9-20
    OVERHAUL 9-20
PARKING BRAKE 9-22
CABLES 9-22
    REMOVAL & INSTALLATION 9-22
    ADJUSTMENT 9-23
TEVES II ANTI-LOCK BRAKE SYSTEM 9-23
GENERAL DESCRIPTION 9-23
    SYSTEM COMPONENTS 9-24
SYSTEM TESTING 9-25
    SERVICE PRECAUTIONS 9-25
    DEPRESSURIZING THE HYDRAULIC
    UNIT 9-25
    VISUAL INSPECTION 9-25
    FUNCTIONAL CHECK 9-25
    DISPLAYING ABS TROUBLE CODES 9-25
    INTERMITTENTS 9-26
    CLEARING TROUBLE CODES 9-26
HYDRAULIC UNIT 9-26
    REMOVAL & INSTALLATION 9-26
WHEEL SPEED SENSORS 9-27
    REMOVAL & INSTALLATION 9-27
VALVE BLOCK ASSEMBLY 9-27
    REMOVAL & INSTALLATION 9-27
PRESSURE WARNING SWITCH 9-28
    REMOVAL & INSTALLATION 9-28
HYDRAULIC ACCUMULATOR 9-28
    REMOVAL & INSTALLATION 9-28
BRAKE FLUID RESERVOIR AND SEAL 9-28
    REMOVAL & INSTALLATION 9-28
PUMP AND MOTOR ASSEMBLY 9-28
    REMOVAL & INSTALLATION 9-28
FILLING AND BLEEDING 9-29

SYSTEM FILLING 9-29
SYSTEM BLEEDING 9-29
**TEVES MARK IV ANTI-LOCK BRAKE
SYSTEM 9-29**
GENERAL DESCRIPTION 9-29
    SYSTEM OPERATION 9-30
    SYSTEM COMPONENTS 9-30
SYSTEM TESTING 9-31
    SERVICE PRECAUTIONS 9-31
    DIAGNOSTIC PROCEDURE 9-31
ELECTRONIC BRAKE CONTROL MODULE
(EBCM) 9-32
    REMOVAL & INSTALLATION 9-32
ANTI-LOCK DIODE 9-33
    LOCATION 9-33
WHEEL SPEED SENSORS 9-33
    REMOVAL & INSTALLATION 9-33
WHEEL SPEED SENSORS RELUCTOR RING 9-34
    REMOVAL & INSTALLATION 9-34
PRESSURE MODULATOR VALVE (PMV)
    ASSEMBLY 9-34
    REMOVAL & INSTALLATION 9-34
PMV FLUID LEVEL SENSOR 9-35
    REMOVAL & INSTALLATION 9-35
PMV RESERVOIR 9-35
    REMOVAL & INSTALLATION 9-35
BLEEDING THE ABS SYSTEM 9-35
**DELCO VI AND DELCO BOSCH V ANTI-
LOCK BRAKING SYSTEMS (ABS) 9-35**
GENERAL INFORMATION 9-35
    BASIC KNOWLEDGE REQUIRED 9-36
    ON-BOARD DIAGNOSTICS 9-36
    ENHANCED DIAGNOSTICS 9-36
DIAGNOSTIC PROCEDURES 9-36
    INTERMITTENT FAILURES 9-37
    INTERMITTENTS AND POOR
    CONNECTIONS 9-37
READING CODES 9-37
CLEARING CODES 9-38
ABS SERVICE 9-38
    PRECAUTIONS 9-38
ELECTRONIC BRAKE CONTROL MODULE
(EBCM) 9-38
    REMOVAL & INSTALLATION 9-38
ELECTRONIC BRAKE LAMP DRIVER MODULE
(LDM) 9-39
    REMOVAL & INSTALLATION 9-39
ABS PUMP RELAY 9-39
    LOCATION 9-39
ANTI-LOCK DIODE 9-39
    LOCATION 9-39
WHEEL SPEED SENSORS 9-39
    REMOVAL & INSTALLATION 9-39
WHEEL SPEED SENSORS RELUCTOR RING 9-40
    REMOVAL & INSTALLATION 9-40
PRESSURE MODULATOR VALVE (PMV)
    ASSEMBLY 9-40
    REMOVAL & INSTALLATION 9-40
PMV FLUID LEVEL SENSOR 9-41
FILLING AND BLEEDING 9-41
    SYSTEM FILLING 9-41
    SYSTEM BLEEDING 9-41
SPECIFICATIONS CHART
    BRAKE SPECIFICATIONS 9-42

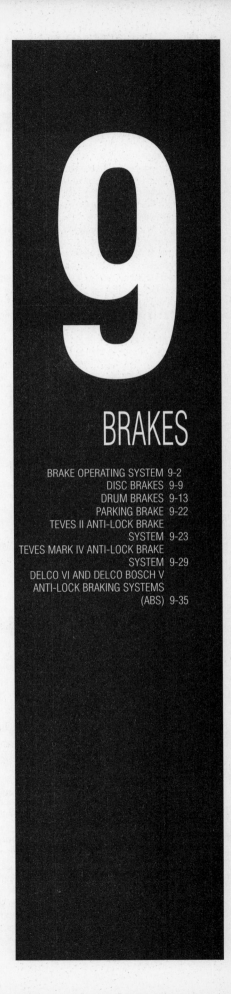

9

BRAKES

BRAKE OPERATING SYSTEM 9-2
DISC BRAKES 9-9
DRUM BRAKES 9-13
PARKING BRAKE 9-22
TEVES II ANTI-LOCK BRAKE
SYSTEM 9-23
TEVES MARK IV ANTI-LOCK BRAKE
SYSTEM 9-29
DELCO VI AND DELCO BOSCH V
ANTI-LOCK BRAKING SYSTEMS
(ABS) 9-35

BRAKE OPERATING SYSTEM

Basic Operating Principles

Hydraulic systems are used to actuate the brakes of all modern automobiles. The system transports the power required to force the frictional surfaces of the braking system together from the pedal to the individual brake units at each wheel. A hydraulic system is used for two reasons.

First, fluid under pressure can be carried to all parts of an automobile by small pipes and flexible hoses without taking up a significant amount of room or posing routing problems.

Second, a great mechanical advantage can be given to the brake pedal end of the system, and the foot pressure required to actuate the brakes can be reduced by making the surface area of the master cylinder pistons smaller than that of any of the pistons in the wheel cylinders or calipers.

The master cylinder consists of a fluid reservoir along with a double cylinder and piston assembly. Double type master cylinders are designed to separate the front and rear braking systems hydraulically in case of a leak. The master cylinder coverts mechanical motion from the pedal into hydraulic pressure within the lines. This pressure is translated back into mechanical motion at the wheels by either the wheel cylinder (drum brakes) or the caliper (disc brakes).

Steel lines carry the brake fluid to a point on the vehicle's frame near each of the vehicle's wheels. The fluid is then carried to the calipers and wheel cylinders by flexible tubes in order to allow for suspension and steering movements.

In drum brake systems, each wheel cylinder contains two pistons, one at either end, which push outward in opposite directions and force the brake shoe into contact with the drum.

In disc brake systems, the cylinders are part of the calipers. At least one cylinder in each caliper is used to force the brake pads against the disc.

All pistons employ some type of seal, usually made of rubber, to minimize fluid leakage. A rubber dust boot seals the outer end of the cylinder against dust and dirt. The boot fits around the outer end of the piston on disc brake calipers, and around the brake actuating rod on wheel cylinders.

The hydraulic system operates as follows: When at rest, the entire system, from the piston(s) in the master cylinder to those in the wheel cylinders or calipers, is full of brake fluid. Upon application of the brake pedal, fluid trapped in front of the master cylinder piston(s) is forced through the lines to the wheel cylinders. Here, it forces the pistons outward, in the case of drum brakes, and inward toward the disc, in the case of disc brakes. The motion of the pistons is opposed by return springs mounted outside the cylinders in drum brakes, and by spring seals, in disc brakes.

Upon release of the brake pedal, a spring located inside the master cylinder immediately returns the master cylinder pistons to the normal position. The pistons contain check valves and the master cylinder has compensating ports drilled in it. These are uncovered as the pistons reach their normal position. The piston check valves allow fluid to flow toward the wheel cylinders or calipers as the pistons withdraw. Then, as the return springs force the brake pads or shoes into the released position, the excess fluid reservoir through the compensating ports. It is during the time the pedal is in the released position that any fluid that has leaked out of the system will be replaced through the compensating ports.

Dual circuit master cylinders employ two pistons, located one behind the other, in the same cylinder. The primary piston is actuated directly by mechanical linkage from the brake pedal through the power booster. The secondary piston is actuated by fluid trapped between the two pistons. If a leak develops in front of the secondary piston, it moves forward until it bottoms against the front of the master cylinder, and the fluid trapped between the pistons will operate the rear brakes. If the rear brakes develop a leak, the primary piston will move forward until direct contact with the secondary piston takes place, and it will force the secondary piston to actuate the front brakes. In either case, the brake pedal moves farther when the brakes are applied, and less braking power is available.

All dual circuit systems use a switch to warn the driver when only half of the brake system is operational. This switch is usually located in a valve body which is mounted on the firewall or the frame below the master cylinder. A hydraulic piston receives pressure from both circuits, each circuit's pressure being applied to one end of the piston. When the pressures are in balance, the piston remains stationary. When one circuit has a leak, however, the greater pressure in that circuit during application of the brakes will push the piston to one side, closing the switch and activating the brake warning light.

In disc brake systems, this valve body also contains a metering valve and, in some cases, a proportioning valve. The metering valve keeps pressure from traveling to the disc brakes on the front wheels until the brake shoes on the rear wheels have contacted the drums, ensuring that the front brakes will never be used alone. The proportioning valve controls the pressure to the rear brakes to lessen the chance of rear wheel lock-up during very hard braking.

Warning lights may be tested by depressing the brake pedal and holding it while opening one of the wheel cylinder bleeder screws. If this does not cause the light to go on, substitute a new lamp, make continuity checks, and, finally, replace the switch as necessary.

The hydraulic system may be checked for leaks by applying pressure to the pedal gradually and steadily. If the pedal sinks very slowly to the floor, the system has a leak. This is not to be confused with a springy or spongy feel due to the compression of air within the lines. If the system leaks, there will be a gradual change in the position of the pedal with a constant pressure.

Check for leaks along all lines and at wheel cylinders. If no external leaks are apparent, the problem is inside the master cylinder.

DISC BRAKES

Instead of the traditional expanding brakes that press outward against a circular drum, disc brake systems utilize a disc (rotor) with brake pads positioned on either side of it. An easily-seen analogy is the hand brake arrangement on a bicycle. The pads squeeze onto the rim of the bike wheel, slowing its motion. Automobile disc brakes use the identical principle but apply the braking effort to a separate disc instead of the wheel.

The disc (rotor) is a casting, usually equipped with cooling fins between the two braking surfaces. This enables air to circulate between the braking surfaces making them less sensitive to heat buildup and more resistant to fade. Dirt and water do not drastically affect braking action since contaminants are thrown off by the centrifugal action of the rotor or scraped off the by the pads. Also, the equal clamping action of the two brake pads tends to ensure uniform, straight line stops. Disc brakes are inherently self-adjusting. There are three general types of disc brake:

1. A fixed caliper.
2. A floating caliper.
3. A sliding caliper.

The fixed caliper design uses two pistons mounted on either side of the rotor (in each side of the caliper). The caliper is mounted rigidly and does not move.

The sliding and floating designs are quite similar. In fact, these two types are often lumped together. In both designs, the pad on the inside of the rotor is moved into contact with the rotor by hydraulic force. The caliper, which is not held in a fixed position, moves slightly, bringing the outside pad into contact with the rotor. There are various methods of attaching floating calipers. Some pivot at the bottom or top, and some slide on mounting bolts. In any event, the end result is the same.

DRUM BRAKES

Drum brakes employ two brake shoes mounted on a stationary backing plate. These shoes are positioned inside a circular drum which rotates with the wheel assembly. The shoes are held in place by springs. This allows them to slide toward the drums (when they are applied) while keeping the linings and drums in alignment. The shoes are actuated by a wheel cylinder which is mounted at the top of the backing plate. When the brakes are applied, hydraulic pressure forces the wheel cylinder's actuating links outward. Since these links bear directly against the top of the brake shoes, the tops of the shoes are then forced against the inner side of the drum. This action forces the bottoms of the two shoes to contact the brake drum by rotating the entire assembly slightly (known as servo action). When pressure within the wheel cylinder is relaxed, return springs pull the shoes back away from the drum.

Most modern drum brakes are designed to self-adjust themselves during application when the vehicle is moving in reverse. This motion causes both shoes to rotate very slightly with the drum, rocking an adjusting lever, thereby causing rotation of the adjusting screw. Some drum brake systems are designed to self-adjust during application whenever the brakes are applied. This on-board adjustment system reduces the need for maintenance adjustments and keeps both the brake function and pedal feel satisfactory.

Brake Light Switch

REMOVAL & INSTALLATION

1986–95 Vehicles

▶ See Figure 1

1. Disconnect the negative battery cable.
2. If necessary for access, remove the instrument panel sound insulator(s).
3. If equipped, loosen the tubular clip from the stoplight switch assembly.
4. Detach the electrical connector from the rear of the switch assembly.
5. On 1991–95 vehicles, disconnect the vacuum hose from the switch.
6. Remove the stoplight switch from the vehicle.

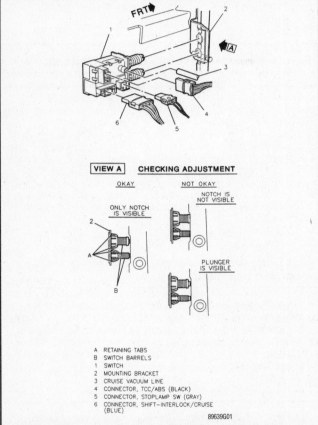

	CHECKING ADJUSTMENT

A RETAINING TABS
B SWITCH BARRELS
1 SWITCH
2 MOUNTING BRACKET
3 CRUISE VACUUM LINE
4 CONNECTOR, TCC/ABS (BLACK)
5 CONNECTOR, STOPLAMP SW (GRAY)
6 CONNECTOR, SHIFT–INTERLOCK/CRUISE
  (BLUE)

89639G01

Fig. 1 Exploded view of the brake light switch mounting, and proper installed position

To install:

7. Connect the switch and install it, as shown in the accompanying figure. Make all of the connections, including the vacuum hose, before installing the switch. Make sure the connectors are fully seated.
8. Fully depress the brake pedal, then hold it in that position.

➡When pressing the switch into the mounting bracket, do NOT use more than 25 lbs. (111 Nm) of side load pressure to the 2 terminal housing connectors.

9. Install the switch, with all of the connections already made, into the mounting bracket. Press the switch in until you can't hear any more clicks, and all retaining tabs are seated.
10. Adjust the switch as outlined later in this section.
11. If removed, tighten the tubular clip to the stoplight switch assembly.
12. Install the instrument panel sound insulator.
13. Connect the negative battery cable.

1996–99 Vehicles

▶ See Figure 2

➡These vehicle utilize 2 switches with different retainers. The TCC/ABS switch and the stop lamp/BTSI switch retainers are two different sizes. The TCC/ABS switch retainer (upper) is larger (⅝ in. diameter), and the stop lamp/BTSI switch retainer (lower) is smaller (½ in. diameter). The brake pedal switch retainer has locating tabs in which the pointer tab of the retainer must point to the locating mark on the brake pedal switch bracket. Both retainers have locating marks that face the 12 o'clock position when they are installed.

1. Disconnect the negative battery cable.
2. Remove the instrument panel sound insulator(s), as necessary for access to the switch.
3. Twist the upper or lower switch, as applicable, counterclockwise to unlock it, then pull it out of the retainer.
4. Detach the electrical connectors from the switch and remove it from the vehicle.

To install:

➡When installing the brake pedal switches, it is very important that the brake pedal remain in the full up or at rest position, or damage to the brake system and/or switch misadjustment will occur.

5. Attach the electrical connectors to the switch.
6. Slide the upper or lower switch (with all of the connections made) into the retainer. Press the switch in until the switch plunder if fully depressed into the switch barrel. Twist the switch clockwise until travel stop has been reached (about 60°). With the switch fully locked, the electrical connector will be in the 3 o'clock position.
7. Install the instrument panel sound insulator(s).
8. Connect the negative battery cable.

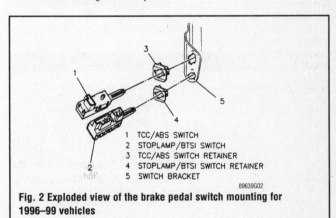

1 TCC/ABS SWITCH
2 STOPLAMP/BTSI SWITCH
3 TCC/ABS SWITCH RETAINER
4 STOPLAMP/BTSI SWITCH RETAINER
5 SWITCH BRACKET

89639G02

Fig. 2 Exploded view of the brake pedal switch mounting for 1996–99 vehicles

ADJUSTMENT

1986–95 Vehicles

▶ See Figure 1

1. Pull the brake pedal rearward, until no clicks are heard. Then release the pedal. Repeat this step to make sure no audible clicks remain.
2. Check the adjustment of the switch. Compare the installation with the accompanying figure. Only the notch should be visible. If the plunger is visible or the notch is not, repeat the adjustment procedure.
3. The proper switch adjustment is achieved when no clicks are heard when the pedal is pulled upward and the brake lights stay OFF when the brake pedal is released.

1996–99 Vehicles

▶ See Figure 2

The switches are self-adjusting when they are installed properly in the fully locked position. The twist lock switches do not require any further adjustment.

Master Cylinder

※※ WARNING

For 1986–91 vehicles equipped with ABS, the entire Hydraulic Assembly must be removed along with the master cylinder. Please refer to the procedure, located under the Teves Mark II ABS system in this section. For 1992–99 vehicles, the master cylinder can be removed independently of the ABS components.

※※ WARNING

For 1994–99 vehicles with ABS, after bleeding the brake system you must perform an "Auto Bleed" sequence, using a Tech 1® or equivalent scan tool. If you do not have access to a suitable scan tool, your vehicle will probably have to be towed to a shop with the proper diagnostic equipment to have the procedure performed.

REMOVAL & INSTALLATION

▶ See Figures 3, 4 and 5

※※ CAUTION

Brake fluid contains polyglycol ethers and polyglycols. Avoid contact with the eyes and wash your hands thoroughly after handling brake fluid. If you do get brake fluid in your eyes, flush your eyes with clean, running water for 15 minutes. If eye irritation persists, or if you have taken brake fluid internally, IMMEDIATELY seek medical assistance.

1. Disconnect the negative battery cable.
2. Use a turkey baster or equivalent tool to siphon the brake fluid from the master cylinder into a suitable container.

※※ WARNING

Clean, high quality brake fluid is essential to the safe and proper operation of the brake system. You should always buy the highest quality brake fluid that is available. If the brake fluid becomes contaminated, drain and flush the system, then refill the master cylinder with new fluid. Never reuse any brake fluid. Any brake fluid that is removed from the system should be discarded. Also, do not allow any brake fluid to come in contact with a painted surface; it will damage the paint.

3. If equipped, unfasten the retainer and detach the electrical connector from the fluid level sensor.
4. For 1991–99 vehicles with ABS, disconnect the reservoir hose and plug it to avoid contamination and fluid loss.
5. Use a flare nut wrench to disconnect the hydraulic lines from the master cylinder. Plug or cap the lines to avoid contaminating the system.

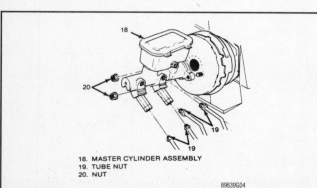

18. MASTER CYLINDER ASSEMBLY
19. TUBE NUT
20. NUT

89639G04

Fig. 3 Exploded view of the master cylinder-to-power booster attachment—1986–90 vehicles without ABS

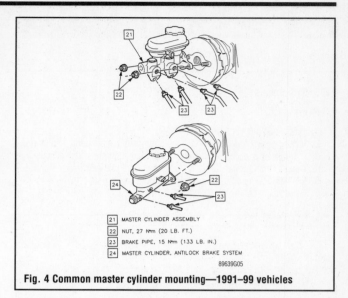

21 MASTER CYLINDER ASSEMBLY
22 NUT, 27 Nm (20 LB. FT.)
23 BRAKE PIPE, 15 Nm (133 LB. IN.)
24 MASTER CYLINDER, ANTILOCK BRAKE SYSTEM

89639G05

Fig. 4 Common master cylinder mounting—1991–99 vehicles

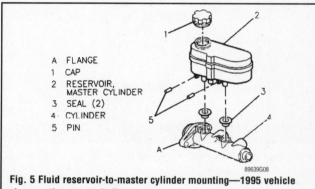

A   FLANGE
1   CAP
2   RESERVOIR, MASTER CYLINDER
3   SEAL (2)
4   CYLINDER
5   PIN

89639G08

Fig. 5 Fluid reservoir-to-master cylinder mounting—1995 vehicle shown, other years similar

6. Unfasten the master cylinder-to-power booster mounting bolts/nuts, then remove the master cylinder assembly.
7. On 1991–99 ABS equipped vehicles, if replacing the master cylinder, transfer the reservoir to the new master cylinder.
   To install:
8. Install the master cylinder assembly to the power booster and secure with the mounting bolts/nuts. Tighten to 20 ft. lbs. (27 Nm).
9. Unplug and connect the hydraulic lines to the master cylinder. Tighten the lines to 11 ft. lbs. (15 Nm), using a flare nut wrench.
10. For 1991–99 ABS equipped vehicles, unplug and connect the reservoir hose assembly.
11. If equipped, attach the electrical connector to the fluid level sensor and secure with the retainer, if applicable.
12. Connect the negative battery cable.
13. Refill the master cylinder with clean brake fluid from a fresh, sealed container. Bleed the brake system as outlined in this section, then recheck the fluid level.

Power Brake Booster

REMOVAL & INSTALLATION

1986–90 Vehicles

▶ See Figure 6

1. Unfasten the retaining nuts, then remove the master cylinder from the booster. It is not necessary to disconnect the lines from the master cylinder. Just move the cylinder aside for access to the power booster. Be careful not to flex or distort the brake lines.

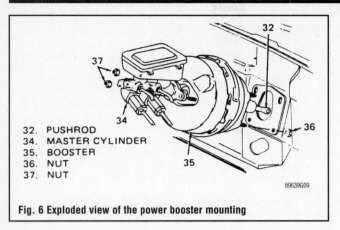

32. PUSHROD
34. MASTER CYLINDER
35. BOOSTER
36. NUT
37. NUT

89639G09

Fig. 6 Exploded view of the power booster mounting

2. Disconnect the vacuum booster pushrod from the brake pedal inside the car. It is retained by a bolt. A spring washer lies under the bolt head, and a flat washer goes on the other side of the pushrod eye, next to the pedal arm.

3. Remove the four attaching nuts from inside the vehicle, then remove the booster from its mounting position on the firewall.

To install:

4. Position the booster on the firewall. Tighten the mounting nuts to 15 ft. lbs. (21 Nm).

5. Connect the booster pushrod to the brake pedal.

6. Install the master cylinder and secure with the retaining nuts. Tighten the nuts to 20 ft. lbs. (27 Nm).

1991–99 Vehicles

▶ **See Figure 7**

> ❊❊ **WARNING**
>
> **For 1994–99 vehicles with ABS, after bleeding the brake system you must perform an "Auto Bleed" sequence, using a Tech 1® or equivalent scan tool. If you do not have access to a suitable scan tool, your vehicle will probably have to be towed to a shop with the proper diagnostic equipment to have the procedure performed.**

➡ **The booster can be removed from the vehicle without removing or disconnecting the master cylinder. However, if both the booster and master cylinder are to be removed, remove the master cylinder first.**

1. Disconnect the negative battery cable.
2. Detach the booster vacuum hose from the vacuum check valve.

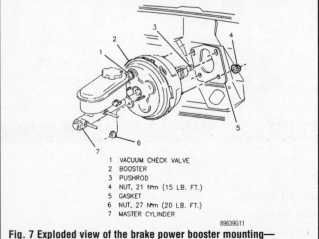

1 VACUUM CHECK VALVE
2 BOOSTER
3 PUSHROD
4 NUT, 21 N·m (15 LB. FT.)
5 GASKET
6 NUT, 27 N·m (20 LB. FT.)
7 MASTER CYLINDER

89639G11

Fig. 7 Exploded view of the brake power booster mounting— 1991–99 vehicles

3. Unfasten the master cylinder attaching nuts. Separate the master cylinder from the booster. Move the master cylinder forward just enough to clear the booster studs. This will flex the brake pipes slightly, so be very careful not to bend or distort the pipes.

4. Remove the acoustical barrier from the booster studs, located inside the passenger compartment, under the instrument panel.

5. Unfasten the booster attaching nuts, from inside the vehicle.

6. Remove the booster from the brake pedal. Tilt the entire booster slightly to work the pushrod off the pedal clevis pin without putting undue side pressure on the pushrod.

7. Remove the booster from the vehicle, then remove the gasket.

To install:

8. Place the gasket on the booster. Position the booster in the vehicle.

9. Attach the booster pushrod to the brake pedal. Tilt the entire booster slightly to work the pushrod onto the pedal clevis pin without putting undue side pressure on the pushrod.

10. Install the booster attaching nuts and tighten to 15 ft. lbs. (21 Nm).

11. Install the acoustical barrier to the booster studs, located under the instrument panel.

12. Position the master cylinder to the booster and secure with the retaining nuts. Tighten the nuts to 20 ft. lbs. (27 Nm).

13. Attach the booster vacuum hose to the vacuum check valve.

14. Connect the negative battery cable.

Proportioning Valves

1986–90 Vehicles

▶ **See Figure 8**

On non-ABS vehicles, these parts are installed in the master cylinder body. On ABS equipped vehicles, the proportioning valve is usually located near the fuel filter under the car on the right side.

➡ **If equipped with Anti-lock Brake System (ABS), ensure that the hydraulic accumulator is fully depressurized before disconnecting any hydraulic lines, hoses or fittings.**

1. If equipped with ABS, raise and safely support the vehicle.
2. Disconnect and plug the brake lines from the proportioning valves.
3. Remove the proportioner valve(s) and O-ring assembly.

To install:

4. Lubricate new O-rings and the external proportioner valve threads with clean brake fluid. Install new O-rings on the proportioner valve(s).

5. On non-ABS vehicles, install the new valve(s) into the master cylinder and tighten to 24 ft. lbs. (31 Nm).

6. On vehicles with ABS, install the new valve(s) to the brake line.

7. Connect the brake pipes to the proportioning valve(s), then tighten to 11 ft. lbs. (15 Nm).

8. If raised, carefully lower the vehicle.

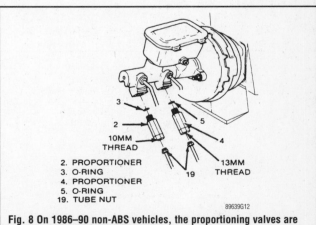

2. PROPORTIONER
3. O-RING
4. PROPORTIONER
5. O-RING
19. TUBE NUT

10MM THREAD
13MM THREAD

89639G12

Fig. 8 On 1986–90 non-ABS vehicles, the proportioning valves are mounted in the master cylinder

9. Refill the master cylinder and bleed the brake system.
10. Connect the negative battery cable.

1991–99 Vehicles

NON-ABS VEHICLES

▶ See Figures 9 and 10

1. Disconnect the negative battery cable.
2. Remove the master cylinder fluid reservoir, as follows:

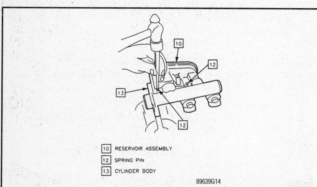

10	RESERVOIR ASSEMBLY
12	SPRING PIN
13	CYLINDER BODY

89639G14

Fig. 9 Use a hammer and drift pin to carefully drive the spring pins out

a. Remove the master cylinder from the vehicle, and clamp the flange of the master cylinder body in a suitable vise. Clamp only on the flange, NOT on the master cylinder body.

b. Use a ⅛ in. punch to carefully drive out the spring pins, being careful not to damage the when driving out the pins.

c. Remove the reservoir by pulling straight up, away from the cylinder body.

d. Remove the O-rings from the grooves in the reservoir. Discard the O-rings and replace with new ones during installation.

3. Remove the proportioner valve cap, then remove the O-rings and springs.

4. Remove the proportioner valve pistons. Use needle nose pliers to remove the pistons, but be careful not the scratch or damage the piston stems.

5. Remove the proportioner valve seals from the pistons.

6. Inspect the pistons for corrosion or deformation and replace if found.

To install:

7. Lubricate new O-rings and proportioner valve seals with the silicone grease in the repair kit. Also, lubricate the stems of the proportioner valve pistons.

8. Install new seals on the proportioner valve pistons with the seal lips facing upward toward the cap assembly.

9. Install the proportioner valve pistons and seals into the master cylinder body.

10. Place the springs in the master cylinder body.

11. Install new O-rings in the groove in the proportioning valve cap assemblies.

12. Install the proportioning valve caps in the master cylinder body, then tighten the caps to 20 ft. lbs. (27 Nm).

13. Install the master cylinder fluid reservoir, as follows:

a. Lubricate new O-rings and reservoir bayonets with clean brake fluid, then install the O-rings in the grooves in the reservoir. Make sure the O-rings are properly seated.

b. Install the reservoir to the master cylinder body by pressing it straight down by hand into the body.

c. Drive the spring pins in to secure the reservoir, being careful not to damage the reservoir or cylinder body.

d. Remove the master cylinder from the vise, then install in the vehicle.

VEHICLES WITH ABS

▶ See Figures 11 and 12

1. Raise and safely support the vehicle.

2. Clean the proportioning valve and brake pipe connections with denatured alcohol or equivalent to be sure no contaminants enter the brake system during servicing.

3. Use a flare nut wrench to disconnect the brake lines from the proportioning valve, then remove the proportioning valve from the vehicle.

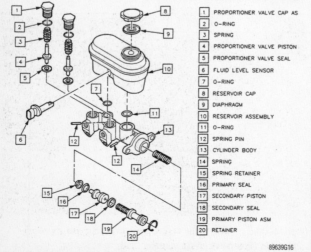

1	PROPORTIONER VALVE CAP AS
2	O-RING
3	SPRING
4	PROPORTIONER VALVE PISTON
5	PROPORTIONER VALVE SEAL
6	FLUID LEVEL SENSOR
7	O-RING
8	RESERVOIR CAP
9	DIAPHRAGM
10	RESERVOIR ASSEMBLY
11	O-RING
12	SPRING PIN
13	CYLINDER BODY
14	SPRING
15	SPRING RETAINER
16	PRIMARY SEAL
17	SECONDARY PISTON
18	SECONDARY SEAL
19	PRIMARY PISTON ASM
20	RETAINER

89639G16

Fig. 10 Exploded view of the master cylinder components, including the proportioning valves—non-ABS vehicles

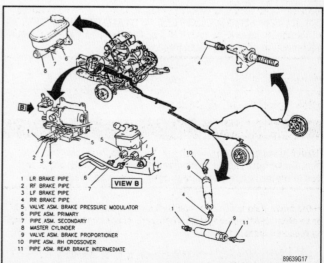

1	LR BRAKE PIPE
2	RF BRAKE PIPE
3	LF BRAKE PIPE
4	RR BRAKE PIPE
5	VALVE ASM. BRAKE PRESSURE MODULATOR
6	PIPE ASM. PRIMARY
7	PIPE ASM. SECONDARY
8	MASTER CYLINDER
9	VALVE ASM. BRAKE PROPORTIONER
10	PIPE ASM. RH CROSSOVER
11	PIPE ASM. REAR BRAKE INTERMEDIATE

VIEW B

89639G17

Fig. 11 Exploded view of the proportioner valve location—1995 vehicle shown

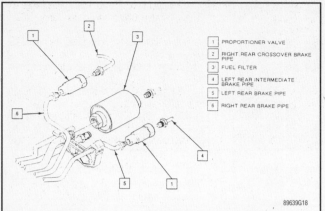

1	PROPORTIONER VALVE
2	RIGHT REAR CROSSOVER BRAKE PIPE
3	FUEL FILTER
4	LEFT REAR INTERMEDIATE BRAKE PIPE
5	LEFT REAR BRAKE PIPE
6	RIGHT REAR BRAKE PIPE

89639G18

Fig. 12 On vehicles such as this 1991 model, the proportioning valves are located near the fuel filter

To install:

4. Install the proportioner valve in the vehicle, then connect the brake line, using a flare nut wrench. Tighten the proportioner valve fittings to 11 ft. lbs. (15 Nm).

5. Carefully lower the vehicle.

Bleeding the Brake System

The purpose of bleeding the brakes is to expel air trapped in the hydraulic system. The system must be bled whenever the pedal feels spongy, indicating that compressible air has entered the system. It must also be bled whenever the system has been opened or repaired. You will need a helper for this job. You may need to bleed the hydraulic system at all 4 wheel positions if air has entered the system due to low fluid level, or from brake lines having been disconnected from the master cylinder. If a brake line is disconnected from one wheel, only that wheel caliper/cylinder needs to be bled. If lines are disconnected at any fitting located between the master cylinder and the wheels, then the brake system served by the disconnected line must be bled.

✳✳ WARNING

For 1986–90 ABS equipped vehicles, the procedure for bleeding the brake system is different than the procedure below. Please refer to the procedure for your vehicle, under the applicable ABS portion of this section. For 1991–99 vehicles, the procedure is the same, regardless if the vehicle has ABS or not. However, for 1994–99 vehicles with ABS, after bleeding the brake system you must perform an "Auto Bleed" sequence, using a Tech 1® or equivalent scan tool. If you do not have access to a suitable scan tool, your vehicle will probably have to be towed to a shop with the proper diagnostic equipment to have the procedure performed.

MANUAL BLEEDING

◆ See Figures 13, 14, 15, 16 and 17

✳✳ CAUTION

Never reuse brake fluid which has been bled from the brake system. Brake fluid should be changed every few years. It wears out due to moisture being absorbed, which lowers the boiling point.

➡Old brake fluid is often the cause of spongy brakes returning a week or so after bleeding the system. If all parts check good. Change the fluid by repeated bleeding.

1. Deplete the booster reserve by applying the brakes a few times with the engine **OFF** until all reserve is depleted.

2. Fill the master cylinder reservoir to the full level mark with brake fluid from a fresh, sealed container. You must maintain the fluid level during the bleeding procedure.

✳✳ WARNING

Clean, high quality brake fluid is essential to the safe and proper operation of the brake system. You should always buy the highest quality brake fluid that is available. If the brake fluid becomes contaminated, drain and flush the system, then refill the master cylinder with new fluid. Never reuse any brake fluid. Any brake fluid that is removed from the system should be discarded. Also, do not allow any brake fluid to come in contact with a painted surface; it will damage the paint.

3. If the master cylinder is known or suspected to have air in the bore, bleed it as follows before bleeding any of the wheel cylinders or calipers:
   a. Loosen the forward brake line connection and the master cylinder.
   b. Fill the master cylinder until fluid begins to flow from the front pipe connector port, maintaining the fluid level.
   c. Tighten the front brake pipe on the master cylinder securely.

✳✳ WARNING

Make sure the master cylinder reservoir cap is installed before the brake pedal is pressed. This prevents brake fluid from spraying out of the reservoir.

89639P19

Fig. 13 To bleed the rear brakes, remove the cap from the wheel cylinder bleeder screw (see arrow)

89639P20

Fig. 14 Attach a hose to the bleeder valve with the other end submerged in a container of clean brake fluid

Fig. 15 If necessary, you can remove the bleeder valve from the wheel cylinder by unscrewing it

Fig. 16 To bleed the front brakes, remove the protective cap covering the bleeder valve/screw

Fig. 17 Attach the brake bleeder line, with the other end submerged in a container full of clean brake fluid, then open the valve

d. Have an assistant depress the brake pedal slowly one time, and hold. Loosen the forward brake pipe connection again to purge air from the bore. Tighten the connection and then slowly released the brake pedal. Wait 15 seconds. Repeat the sequence, including the 15 second wait, until all air is removed from the bore.

e. Tighten the brake pipe connection to 11 ft. lbs. (15 Nm).

4. After all the air has been removed from the front connection, repeat the same procedure at the rear connection of the master cylinder.

5. Individual wheel cylinders and calipers are bled only after all the air has been removed from the master cylinder.

> **✳✳ WARNING**
>
> **Make sure the master cylinder reservoir cap is installed before the brake pedal is pressed. This prevents brake fluid from spraying out of the reservoir.**

6. If all of the wheel circuits must be bled, use one of the following two sequences, depending upon the year of your vehicle:

a. 1986–90 vehicles: right rear, left front, left rear, then right front.

b. 1991–99 vehicles: right rear, left rear, right front, then left front.

7. Fill the master cylinder reservoir with brake fluid. Keep the level at least ½ full during the bleeding operation.

8. Raise and support the vehicle safely.

9. Remove the bleeder valve cap, and place a proper size box end wrench, or suitable bleeder wrench, over the bleeder valve.

10. Attach a transparent tube to the bleeder valve, and submerge the other end of the tube in a clear container, partially filled with clean brake fluid.

11. Have an assistant slowly depress the brake pedal one time, and hold.

12. Loosen the bleeder valve to purge the air from the cylinder.

13. Tighten the bleeder screw, then slowly release the brake pedal. Wait 15 seconds.

14. Repeat this sequence until all the air is removed. Depending upon the amount of air in the system, you may have to repeat the sequence at least 10 times to remove all of the air from the system.

15. Lower the vehicle and refill the master cylinder.

16. Check the brake pedal for sponginess. If the pedal is spongy, repeat the entire bleeding procedure.

17. For 1994–99 vehicles, use a Tech 1® or equivalent scan tool to pressure bleed the brake system, using the "Auto Bleed" sequence. Then, repeat the wheel cylinder and caliper bleeding sequence.

PRESSURE BLEEDING

▶ **See Figures 18 and 19**

The pressure bleeding equipment you use MUST be of the diaphragm type. It must have a rubber diaphragm between the air supply and the brake fluid to prevent air, moisture, oil and all other contaminants from entering the system.

1. Fill the master cylinder reservoir to the full mark with the proper type of brake fluid from a fresh, sealed container.

2. Install bleeder adapter tool J 29567, J 35589 or equivalent, to the master cylinder. The proper adapter must be installed on the master cylinder to avoid damaging the reservoir.

3. Charge the bleeder ball to 20–25 psi (140–172 kPa).

4. Connect the line/hose to the adapter, then open the line valve. The bleeder adapter has a bleed valve on top of the adapter to help eliminate air from the adapter.

5. Raise and safely support the vehicle.

6. Use one of the following two bleeding sequences, depending upon the year of your vehicle:

a. 1986–90 vehicles: right rear, left front, left rear, then right front.

b. 1991–99 vehicles: right rear, left rear, right front, then left front.

7. Remove the bleeder valve cap, and place a proper size box end wrench, or suitable bleeder wrench, over the bleeder valve.

8. Attach a transparent bleeder hose to the bleeder valve, and submerge the other end of the of the hose in a clean container partially filled with clean brake fluid.

9. Open the bleeder valve ½ to ¾ of a turn, then allow the fluid to flow until no air is seen in the fluid.

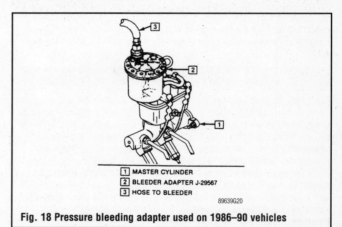

1	MASTER CYLINDER
2	BLEEDER ADAPTER J-29567
3	HOSE TO BLEEDER

Fig. 18 Pressure bleeding adapter used on 1986–90 vehicles

Fig. 19 Later model vehicles use a different type of pressure bleeding adapter

10. Tighten the wheel cylinder bleeder valve to 88 inch lbs. (10 Nm) or the caliper bleeder valve to 115 inch lbs. (13 Nm).

11. Repeat the bleeding steps until all of the calipers/cylinders have been bled. Then, install the bleeder valve caps.

12. Carefully lower the vehicle. Check the brake pedal for sponginess. If the pedal is spongy, repeat the entire bleeding procedure.

13. Remove the bleeder ball and adapter.

14. Fill the master cylinder reservoir to the full mark.

15. For 1994–99 vehicles, use a Tech 1® or equivalent scan tool to pressure bleed the brake system, using the "Auto Bleed" sequence. Then, repeat the wheel cylinder and caliper bleeding sequence.

BENCH BLEEDING THE MASTER CYLINDER

✳✳ WARNING

All new master cylinders should be bench bled prior to installation. Bleeding a new master cylinder on the vehicle is not a good idea. With air trapped inside, the master cylinder piston may bottom in the bore and possibly cause internal damage.

DISC BRAKES

✳✳ CAUTION

Older brake pads or shoes may contain asbestos, which has been determined to be a cancer causing agent. Never clean the brake surfaces with compressed air! Avoid inhaling any dust from any brake surface! When cleaning the brake surfaces, use a commercially available brake cleaning fluid.

Brake Pads

➡**Always replace all pads on both front wheels at the same time. Failure to do so will result in uneven braking action and premature wear.**

REMOVAL & INSTALLATION

◆ **See Figures 20 thru 29**

1. Disconnect the negative battery cable.

2. Remove ⅔ of the brake fluid from the master cylinder reservoir using a clean syringe or equivalent. Install the reservoir cap.

3. Raise and safely support the vehicle with jackstands.

4. Mark the relationship of the wheel to the hub and bearing assembly.

5. Remove the tire and wheel assembly.

6. Remove the caliper, as outlined later, and suspend from the strut with a wire hook or suitable piece of wire. Do NOT disconnect the brake hose or allow the caliper to hang from the brake line!

1. Remove the master cylinder from the vehicle, and plug the outlet ports.

2. Secure the master cylinder in a soft jawed bench vise, with the front end slightly down.

3. Remove the master cylinder reservoir cap.

4. Fill the master cylinder reservoir with clean, fresh brake fluid.

5. Use a blunt tipped rod (a long socket extension works well) to slowly depress the master cylinder primary piston about 1 in. (25mm). Make sure the piston travels full its full stroke. As air bleeds from the master cylinder, the primary piston will not travel the full inch.

6. Reposition the master cylinder in the vise with the front end tilted slightly up.

7. Stroke the primary piston about 1 in. (25mm) several times again.

8. Reposition the master cylinder in the vise, so it is level.

9. Loosen the plugs in the outlet ports on at a time. Then push the piston into the bore in order to force the air from the cylinder.

10. Tighten the plugs before allowing the piston to return to its original position. This prevents air from being drawn back into the cylinder.

11. Fill the master cylinder reservoir with clean brake fluid, then install the master cylinder reservoir cap.

12. Install the master cylinder on the vehicle, then follow normal bleeding procedures.

7. Remove the outboard shoe and lining (pad) by using a prytool to disengage the buttons on the shoe from the holes in the caliper housing.

8. Remove the inboard shoe and lining (pad) from the caliper.

9. Before installing new pads, clean the outside surface of the caliper boot with denatured alcohol, or equivalent.

To install:

10. On 1986–90 vehicles, install new sleeves and bushings. Lubricate the sleeves with a light coating of silicone grease before installation. These parts must always be replaced when the pads are replaced. The parts are usually included in the pad replacement kits.

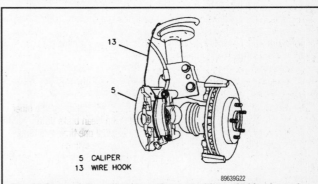

5 CALIPER
13 WIRE HOOK

89639G22

Fig. 20 Suspend the caliper from the strut with a suitable piece of wire. Do NOT allow the caliper to hang by the brake line

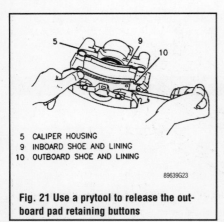

5 CALIPER HOUSING
9 INBOARD SHOE AND LINING
10 OUTBOARD SHOE AND LINING

89639G23

Fig. 21 Use a prytool to release the outboard pad retaining buttons

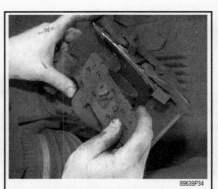

89639P34

Fig. 22 Remove the outboard brake pad from the caliper

89639P35

Fig. 23 Slide the inboard pad out, disengaging the retaining clip ears . . .

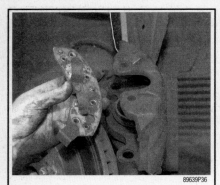
Fig. 24 . . . and remove the inboard pad from the caliper

Fig. 25 There is a special tool available to compress the caliper piston into its bore (inboard pad installed)

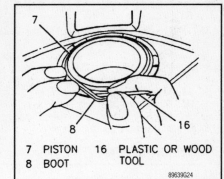
7 PISTON   16 PLASTIC OR WOOD
8 BOOT   TOOL

Fig. 26 Carefully lift the edge of the piston boot to release any trapped air

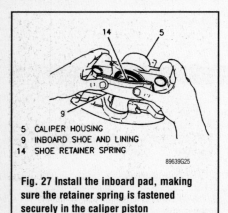
5 CALIPER HOUSING
9 INBOARD SHOE AND LINING
14 SHOE RETAINER SPRING

Fig. 27 Install the inboard pad, making sure the retainer spring is fastened securely in the caliper piston

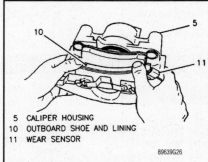
5 CALIPER HOUSING
10 OUTBOARD SHOE AND LINING
11 WEAR SENSOR

Fig. 28 The outboard pad must be installed with the wear sensor at the trailing edge of the pad

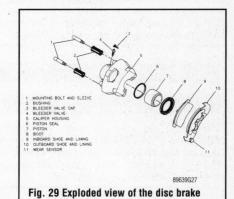
1 MOUNTING BOLT AND SLEEVE
2 BUSHING
3 BLEEDER VALVE CAP
4 BLEEDER VALVE
5 CALIPER HOUSING
6 PISTON SEAL
7 PISTON
8 BOOT
9 INBOARD SHOE AND LINING
10 OUTBOARD SHOE AND LINING
11 WEAR SENSOR

Fig. 29 Exploded view of the disc brake pads and caliper

11. Bottom the piston into the caliper bore, using a C-clamp, adjustable pliers, or a tool specifically designed for that purpose. Position the tool over the caliper and piston, tightening it slowly to press the piston into the bore. Be careful not to damage the piston or piston boot.

12. After bottoming the piston, use a small plastic or wooden tool to lift the inner edge of the boot next to the piston, and press out any trapped air. Make sure the boot lies flat and that the convolutions are tucked back into place.

13. Install the inboard pad by snapping the pad retainer spring into the caliper piston. The shoe portion must lay flat against the piston. After installing the shoe and lining (pad), check that the boot is not touching the shoe. If it is, remove the pad and reseat or reposition the boot.

14. Install the outboard pad with the wear sensor at the trailing edge of the pad during forward wheel rotation. The back of the shoe must lay flat against the caliper.

15. Install the caliper, as outlined later in this section.

16. Install the wheel and tire assembly, then carefully lower the vehicle. Tighten the wheel lug nuts to 100 ft. lbs. (136 Nm).

17. Fill the master cylinder with the proper amount of brake fluid from a fresh, sealed container. Install the reservoir cap.

18. Apply about 175 lbs. (778 N) of force to the brake pedal, three times, to seat the pads.

INSPECTION

▶ See Figure 30

The pad thickness should be inspected every time that the tires are removed for rotation. The outer pad has a wear sensor which will make a squealing noise when the pads wear to the point required replacement.

When the pad thickness is worn to within $FR1/32 in. (0.76mm) of the shoe or rivet, at either end of the pad, replace the pads in axle sets. This is the factory recommended measurement; however, your state's automobile inspection laws may not agree with this.

When checking the disc brakes, check both ends of the outer pads by looking in at each end of the caliper. These are the points at which the highest rate

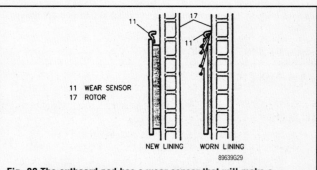
11 WEAR SENSOR
17 ROTOR

NEW LINING   WORN LINING

Fig. 30 The outboard pad has a wear sensor that will make a screeching noise against the rotor when the pad is worn to a certain limit

of wear occurs. The inner pad can be checked for premature wear by looking down through the inspection hole in the top of the caliper. Some inboard pads have a thermal layer against the shoe, integrally molded with the lining. Do not confuse this extra layer with uneven inboard/outboard pad wear.

Brake Caliper

REMOVAL & INSTALLATION

▶ See Figures 29, 30 thru 36

1. Disconnect the negative battery cable.
2. Remove the master cylinder reservoir cap, then remove the ⅔ of the fluid from the reservoir with a clean syringe and place it in a suitable container. Install the reservoir cap.
3. Raise and safely support the vehicle with jackstands.

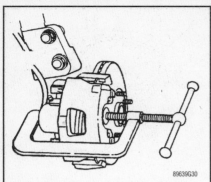

Fig. 31 Bottom the caliper piston in its bore using a large C-clamp

Fig. 32 You can also use a large pair of channel type slip joint pliers to compress the caliper piston into its bore

Fig. 33 Use a Torx® driver to unfasten the 2 caliper mounting bolts

Fig. 34 Pull the caliper mounting bolts from their sleeves

Fig. 35 Lift the caliper up and off the rotor

Fig. 36 Lubricate the caliper mounting bolts with a suitable grease

4. Mark the relationship of the wheel to the hub and bearing assembly.

5. Remove the tire and wheel assembly.

6. Reinstall two of the lug nuts to retain the rotor.

7. Push the pistons into the caliper bore to provide clearance between the linings and the rotor, as follows:

a. Install a large C-clamp over the top of the caliper housing and against the back of the outboard shoe.

➡If the C-clamp is tightening too far, the outboard shoe retaining spring will be deformed and require replacement.

b. Slowly tighten the C-clamp until the pistons are pushed into the caliper bore enough to slide the caliper assembly off the rotor.

8. If the caliper is going to be replaced or removed for overhaul, disconnect and plug the brake hose.

❋❋ WARNING

Do NOT allow the caliper to hang from the brake hose!

9. Unfasten the caliper mounting bolts and sleeves, then pull the caliper from the mounting bracket and rotor. Support the caliper with a suitable piece wire from the strut, if not removing.

10. Inspect the mounting bolts and sleeves for corrosion and the support bushings for cuts or damage; replace if necessary.

To install:

11. Liberally coat the inside diameter of the bushings with silicone grease.

12. Position the caliper and brake pad assembly over the rotor.

13. Install the mounting bolts and sleeves. The bolts and sleeves should slide through the bushings with only hand pressure. If greater force or mechanical assistance is necessary, perform the following:

a. Remove the bolts and sleeves, along with the bushings.

b. Inspect the mounting bores for corrosion. If the bores are corroded, remove it using a 1 in. (25mm) wheel cylinder honing brush.

c. Clean the bores with denatured alcohol.

d. Install the bushings and relubricate.

14. Tighten the caliper mounting bolts to 38 ft. lbs. (51 Nm).

15. If removed, unplug and connect the brake hose, using new copper washers and a new inlet fitting bolt. Tighten the fitting bolt to 24 ft. lbs. (32 Nm).

16. Remove the two wheel lugs, and install the wheel and tire assembly.

17. Carefully lower the vehicle.

18. Fill the master cylinder. If the brake line was disconnected, bleed the brake system as outlined in this section.

19. Check for hydraulic leaks. Pump the brake pedal a few times before moving the vehicle.

OVERHAUL

▶ See Figures 37 thru 44

➡Some vehicles may be equipped dual piston calipers. The procedure to overhaul the caliper is essentially the same with the exception of multiple pistons, O-rings and dust boots.

1. Remove the caliper from the vehicle and place on a clean workbench.

❋❋ CAUTION

NEVER place your fingers in front of the pistons in an attempt to catch or protect the pistons when applying compressed air. This could result in personal injury!

Fig. 37 For some types of calipers, use compressed air to drive the piston out of the caliper, but make sure to keep your fingers clear

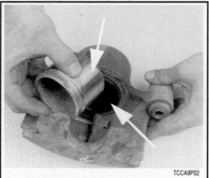

Fig. 38 Withdraw the piston from the caliper bore

Fig. 39 On some vehicles, you must remove the anti-rattle clip

Fig. 40 Use a prytool to carefully pry around the edge of the boot . . .

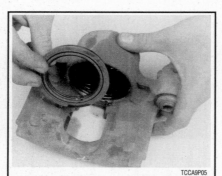

Fig. 41 . . . then remove the boot from the caliper housing, taking care not to score or damage the bore

Fig. 42 Use extreme caution when removing the piston seal; DO NOT scratch the caliper bore

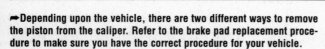

Fig. 43 Use the proper size driving tool and a mallet to properly seal the boots in the caliper housing

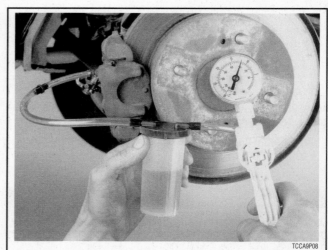

Fig. 44 There are tools, such as this Mighty-Vac, available to assist in proper brake system bleeding

➡Depending upon the vehicle, there are two different ways to remove the piston from the caliper. Refer to the brake pad replacement procedure to make sure you have the correct procedure for your vehicle.

2. The first method is as follows:

a. Stuff a shop towel or a block of wood into the caliper to catch the piston.

b. Remove the caliper piston using compressed air applied into the caliper inlet hole. Inspect the piston for scoring, nicks, corrosion and/or worn or damaged chrome plating. The piston must be replaced if any of these conditions are found.

3. For the second method, you must rotate the piston to retract it from the caliper.

4. If equipped, remove the anti-rattle clip.

5. Use a prytool to remove the caliper boot, being careful not to scratch the housing bore.

6. Remove the piston seals from the groove in the caliper bore.

7. Carefully loosen the brake bleeder valve cap and valve from the caliper housing.

8. Inspect the caliper bores, pistons and mounting threads for scoring or excessive wear.

9. Use crocus cloth to polish out light corrosion from the piston and bore.

10. Clean all parts with denatured alcohol and dry with compressed air.

To assemble:

11. Lubricate and install the bleeder valve and cap.

12. Install the new seals into the caliper bore grooves, making sure they are not twisted.

13. Lubricate the piston bore.

14. Install the pistons and boots into the bores of the calipers and push to the bottom of the bores.

15. Use a suitable driving tool to seat the boots in the housing.

16. Install the caliper in the vehicle.

17. Install the wheel and tire assembly, then carefully lower the vehicle.

18. Properly bleed the brake system.

Brake Disc (Rotor)

REMOVAL & INSTALLATION

▶ **See Figure 45**

1. Disconnect the negative battery cable.

2. Remove ⅔ of the brake fluid from the brake reservoir using a clean syringe or equivalent.

3. Raise and safely support the vehicle with jackstands.

4. Mark the relationship of the wheel to the hub and bearing assembly.

5. Remove the tire and wheel assembly.

6. Remove the caliper and suspend it from the strut with a wire hook or suitable piece of wire. Do NOT disconnect the brake hose or allow the caliper to hang from the brake line!

Fig. 45 The rotor can be removed by sliding it straight off the lug studs

Fig. 46 A rotor with grooves this deep will have to be resurfaced or, more likely, replaced

➡ **If the original rotor is still on the vehicle, it may be retained with star washers, so you must remove and discard these retaining washers.**

7. Remove the rotor assembly by sliding it off the hub. If it is stuck on, use penetrating oil and tap lightly until free.

To install:

8. Install the brake rotor over the hub assembly.

9. Install the brake caliper as outlined in this section.

10. Install the wheel and tire assembly.

11. Carefully lower the vehicle. Tighten the wheel lug nuts to 100 ft. lbs. (136 Nm). If the lug nuts aren't tightened properly, the rotor will warp from heat, causing premature wear and noise.

12. Fill the master cylinder reservoir to the FULL level with the correct type of DOT 3 brake fluid from a clean, unsealed container.

13. Firmly depress the brake pedal three times before moving the vehicle.

INSPECTION

▶ **See Figure 46**

Check the rotor surface for wear or scoring. Deep scoring, grooves or rust pitting can be removed by refacing, a job to be referred to your local machine shop or garage. All rotors have a minimum thickness dimension cast into them. This dimension is the minimum wear specification, and NOT a refinish dimension.

Do not use a rotor, that after refinishing, will not meet the specifications stamped into the rotor.

Check the rotor parallelism; it must vary less than 0.0005 in. (0.0127mm) measured at four or more points around the circumference. Make all measurements at the same distance in from the edge of the rotor. Refinish the rotor if it fails to meet this specification.

1. Measure the disc run-out with a dial indicator. If run-out exceeds 0.004 in. (0.10mm) for 1986–93 vehicles, or 0.002 in. (0.060mm) for 1994–99 vehicles, the rotor must be refaced or replaced as necessary.

DRUM BRAKES

✳✳ CAUTION

Older brake pads or shoes may contain asbestos, which has been determined to be a cancer causing agent. Never clean the brake surfaces with compressed air! Avoid inhaling any dust from any brake surface! When cleaning the brake surfaces, use a commercially available brake cleaning fluid.

Brake Drums

REMOVAL & INSTALLATION

▶ **See Figures 47 and 48**

1. Mark the relationship of the wheel to the axle flange to help maintain wheel balance after assembly.

1. Adjuster shoe and lining
2. Spring connecting link
3. Adjuster actuator
4. Adjuster screw and socket
5. Upper return spring
6. Actuator spring
7. Hold-down springs
8. Hold-down pins
9. Lower return spring
10. Shoe and lining
11. Parking brake lever
12. Parking brake cable
13. Wheel cylinder
14. Brake backing plate

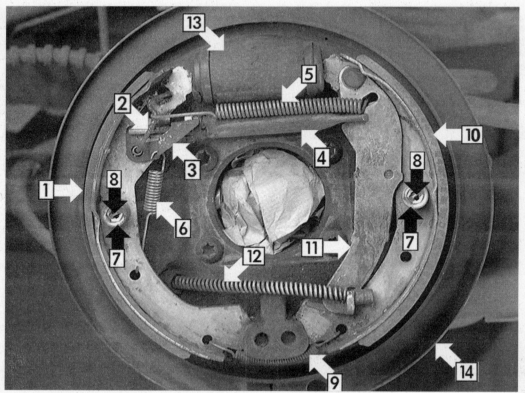

89639P14

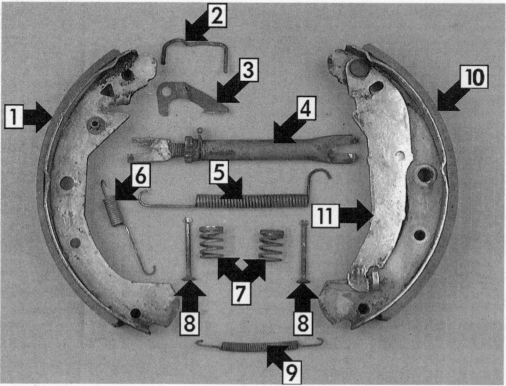

89639P04

2. Remove the tire and wheel assembly.

3. Mark the relationship of the brake drum to the axle flange.

➡**Do not pry against the splash shield that surrounds the backing plate in an attempt to free the drum. This will bend the splash shield.**

4. If difficulty is encountered in removing the brake drum, the following steps may be of assistance.

    a. Make sure the parking brake is released.

    b. Back off the parking brake cable adjustment.

    c. Remove the access hole plug from the backing plate.

    d. Using a screwdriver, back off the adjusting screw.

    e. Reinstall the access hole plug to prevent dirt or contamination from entering the drum brake assembly.

    f. Use a small amount of penetrating oil applied around the brake drum pilot hole.

    g. Carefully remove the brake drum from the vehicle.

5. After removing the brake drum it should be checked for the following:

    a. Inspecting for cracks and deep grooves.

    b. Inspect for out of round and taper.

    c. Inspecting for hot spots (black in color).

To install:

6. Install the brake drum onto the vehicle aligning the reference marks on the axle flange.

7. Install the tire and wheel assembly and hand-tighten the lug nuts.

8. Carefully lower the vehicle, then tighten the lug nuts to 100 ft. lbs. (136 Nm).

9. Road test the vehicle for proper brake operation.

INSPECTION

▶ **See Figure 49**

1. After removing the brake drum, wipe out the accumulated dust with a damp cloth.

✳✳ WARNING

Do not blow the brake dust out of the drums with compressed air or lung-power. Brake linings contain asbestos, a known cancer causing substance. Dispose of the cloth used to clean the parts after use.

2. Inspect the drums for cracks, deep grooves, roughness, scoring, or out-of-roundness. Replace any drum which is cracked; do not try to weld it up.

3. Smooth any slight scores by polishing the friction surface with fine emery cloth. Heavy or extensive scoring will cause excessive lining wear and should be removed from the drum through resurfacing, a job to be referred to your local machine shop or garage. The maximum refinished diameter of the

drums is 8.880 in. (225.5mm). The drum must be replaced if the diameter is 8.909 in. (226.30mm).

Brake Shoes

INSPECTION

After removing the brake drum, inspect the brake shoes. If the lining is worn down to within $FR1/32 in. (0.8mm) above the rivet, the shoes must be replaced.

➡**This figure may disagree with your state's automobile inspection laws. If the brake lining is soaked with brake fluid or grease, it must be replaced. If this is the case, the brake drum should be sanded with crocus cloth to remove all traces of brake fluid, and the wheel cylinders should be rebuilt. Clean all grit from the friction surface of the drum before replacing it.**

If the lining is chipped, cracked or otherwise damaged, it must be replaced with a new lining.

➡**Always replace the brake linings in sets of two on both ends of the axle. Never replace just one shoe or both shoes on one side.**

Check the condition of the shoes, retracting springs and hold-down springs for signs of overheating. If the shoes or springs have a slight blue color, this indicates overheating, then replacement of the shoes and springs is recommended. The wheel cylinders should be rebuilt as a precaution against future problems.

REMOVAL & INSTALLATION

1986–90 Vehicles

▶ **See Figures 50 thru 62**

1. Raise and safely support the vehicle. Mark the relation ship of wheel to studs in the bearing flange, for reference during assembly. Remove the tire and wheel.

2. Mark the relationship of drum to the bearing flange, for reference during assembly. Remove the brake drum assembly. Clean the brake surfaces, using a commercially available brake cleaning fluid.

3. For additional clearance, you can remove the hub and bearing, prior to brake component removal, as follows:

    a. Unfasten the hub and bearing Torx ® retaining bolts, then carefully remove the hub and bearing.

    b. Reinstall the hub retaining bolts to hold the brake backing plates and brake components in place.

4. Remove the actuator and the upper return spring with the proper tools.

89639P02

Fig. 47 The brake drum can usually be pulled straight off the lug studs

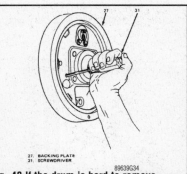

27. BACKING PLATE
31. SCREWDRIVER

89639G34

Fig. 48 If the drum is hard to remove, remove the access plug, then back off the adjusting screw

89639P01

Fig. 49 Most vehicles will have their maximum wear specification stamped into the brake drum

Fig. 50 Unfasten the Torx® bolts securing the hub and bearing to the backing plate . . .

Fig. 51 . . . and remove the hub and bearing, but make sure to reinstall the bolts in the backing plate

Fig. 52 Use a pair of pliers to unhook the actuator spring

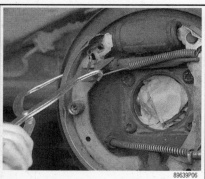

Fig. 53 There are special pliers available to unhook the upper return spring

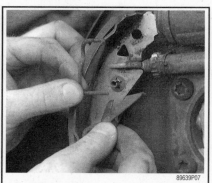

Fig. 54 Remove the spring connecting link and adjuster actuator

Fig. 55 Although there are special tools available, you can also use pliers to remove the hold-down springs and pins

Fig. 56 Remove the adjuster screw assembly

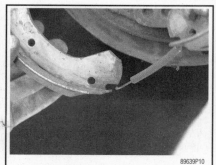

Fig. 57 Remove the left (adjuster) shoe and lining, unhooking it from the lower return spring

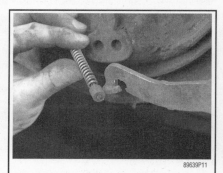

Fig. 58 Unhook the parking brake cable from the right brake shoe and parking brake lever assembly

Fig. 59 Clean the areas on the backing plate which are to be lubricated . . .

Fig. 60 . . . then lubricate the areas with a suitable grease as shown

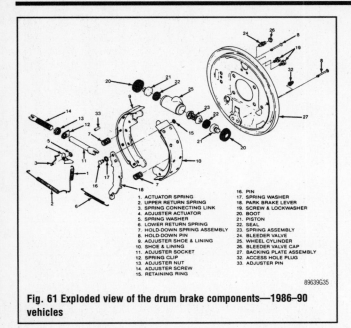

1. ACTUATOR SPRING
2. UPPER RETURN SPRING
3. SPRING CONNECTING LINK
4. ADJUSTER ACTUATOR
5. SPRING WASHER
6. LOWER RETURN SPRING
7. HOLD-DOWN SPRING ASSEMBLY
8. HOLD-DOWN PIN
9. ADJUSTER SHOE & LINING
10. SHOE & LINING
11. ADJUSTER SOCKET
12. SPRING CLIP
13. ADJUSTER NUT
14. ADJUSTER SCREW
15. RETAINING RING
16. PIN
17. SPRING WASHER
18. PARK BRAKE LEVER
19. SCREW & LOCKWASHER
20. BOOT
21. PISTON
22. SEAL
23. SPRING ASSEMBLY
24. BLEEDER VALVE
25. WHEEL CYLINDER
26. BLEEDER VALVE CAP
27. BACKING PLATE ASSEMBLY
32. ACCESS HOLE PLUG
33. ADJUSTER PIN

89639G35

Fig. 61 Exploded view of the drum brake components—1986–90 vehicles

5. Disconnect the spring connecting link, adjuster actuator and, if replacing the shoe and linings, the hold-down washer.

6. Remove the hold-down springs and the pins, using pliers or a special tool for that purpose.

7. Remove the adjuster screw assembly.

8. Unhook the left (adjuster) shoe and lining from the lower return spring.

9. Unhook the parking brake cable from the lever and the right shoe and lining, then remove the right shoe and lining from the vehicle.

10. If necessary, remove the retaining ring, pin and spring washer securing the parking brake lever to the shoe and lining.

11. Clean off the brake backing plate, then lubricate the backing plate as shown in the accompanying figure.

12. Inspect all of the brake components. If any of them are of doubtful strength or quality, due to discoloration from heat, overstress or wear, the parts should be replaced.

To install:

13. Install the parking brake lever on the shoe and lining and retain with the spring washer, pin and retaining ring. Install the spring washer with the concave side against the parking brake lever.

14. Install the adjuster pin in the shoe and lining so that the pin projects 0.275–0.283 in. (7.0–7.2mm) from the side of the shoe web where the adjuster actuator is installed.

15. Disassemble, clean and reassemble the adjusting screw, as follows:

   a. Disassembly the adjusting screw.

   b. Clean the adjusting screw threads with a wire brush, then wash all components with clean denatured alcohol.

   c. Apply a suitable brake lubricant to the adjuster screw threads, the inside diameter of the socket and socket face.

   d. You have achieved sufficient lubrication when a continuous bead of lubricant is on the end of the adjuster nut and the socket when the threads are fully engaged. Check the threads of the adjuster screw for smooth rotation over the full length.

16. Install the spring clip in the same position from which it was removed.

➡**Do not stretch the lower return spring. The spring will be damaged if the extended length is greater than 3.88 in. (98.6mm).**

17. Install the lower return spring between the shoe and linings.

18. Install the adjuster shoe and lining and shoe and lining (after connecting the parking brake cable) with the hold-down pins and springs.

19. The lower return spring should be positioned under the anchor plate. For cable adjustment, refer to the procedure located in this section.

20. The adjuster shoe and lining is the one in which the adjuster pin was installed in the shoe web. Install the adjuster shoe and lining to the front of the

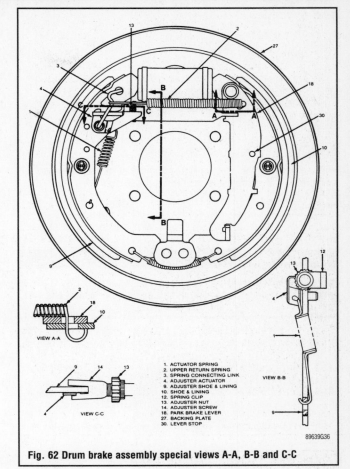

1. ACTUATOR SPRING
2. UPPER RETURN SPRING
3. SPRING CONNECTING LINK
4. ADJUSTER ACTUATOR
9. ADJUSTER SHOE & LINING
10. SHOE & LINING
12. SPRING CLIP
13. ADJUSTER NUT
14. ADJUSTER SCREW
18. PARK BRAKE LEVER
27. BACKING PLATE
30. LEVER STOP

VIEW A-A

VIEW B-B

VIEW C-C

89639G36

Fig. 62 Drum brake assembly special views A-A, B-B and C-C

car on the left side brake assembly or to the rear of the car on the right side brake assembly.

21. Install the adjusting screw assembly between the adjuster shoe and lining and the other shoe and lining on the backing plate. Proper assembly of the adjusting screw is with the adjuster screw engaging the notch in the adjuster shoe and lining and the spring clip pointing toward the backing plate.

22. Install the spring washer with the concave side against the web of the adjuster shoe and lining.

23. Position the adjuster actuator so that its top leg engages the notch in the adjuster screw (view C-C in the accompanying figure).

24. Install the spring connecting link and hold in place.

➡**Do not overstretch the upper return spring. The spring will be damaged if it is extended past 5.5 in. (140mm).**

25. Install the upper return spring. Insert the angled hook end of the spring through the parking brake lever and shoe/lining assembly (view A-A in the accompanying figure).

26. Grasp the long, straight section of the spring with suitable brake spring pliers. Pull the spring straight across and then down to hook into the crook on the spring connecting link.

➡**Do not overstretch the actuator spring. The spring will be damaged if it is stretched more than 3.27 in. (8.80mm).**

27. Install the actuator spring with suitable pliers. Position as shown in view B-B of the accompanying figure.

28. Check to make sure the parking brake lever is at its stop and that the brake shoes are properly centered on the wheel cylinder pistons.

29. Install the brake drum, then adjust the brakes, as outlined later in this section.

30. Install the wheel and tire assembly, then carefully lower the vehicle.

31. Tighten the wheel lug nuts to 100 ft. lbs. (136 Nm).

1991–99 Vehicles

♦ **See Figures 63 thru 69**

1. Loosen the wheel lug nuts.
2. Raise and safely support the vehicle.
3. Matchmark the installed relationship of the wheel to the lug studs in the bearing flange, then remove the wheel and tire assembly.
4. Matchmark the position of the drum to the lug studs, then remove the brake drum.
5. Remove the actuator spring. Use a suitable brake spanner and removal tool to pry the loop end of the spring from the adjuster actuator, then disconnect from the web of the parking brake shoe.

➥When removing the retractor spring from either shoe or lining, do not overstretch it. Overstretching reduces the spring's effectiveness.

6. Lift the end of the retractor spring from the adjuster shoe and lining. Insert the hood end of the spanner tool between the retractor spring and the adjuster shoe web, and pry or twist to lift the end of the spring out of the shoe web hole.

> ✳✳ **CAUTION**
>
> **Make sure to keep your fingers clear of the retractor spring to avoid pinching them between the spring and shoe web or spring and backing plate.**

7. Pry the end of the retractor spring toward the axle with the flat edge of the spanner tool until the spring snaps down off the shoe web onto the backing plate.
8. Remove the adjuster shoe and lining, adjuster actuator and adjusting screw assembly.
9. Disconnect the parking brake lever from the parking brake shoe and lining. Do not remove the parking brake cable from the lever, unless the lever is being replaced.
10. Lift the end of the retractor spring from the parking brake shoe and lin-

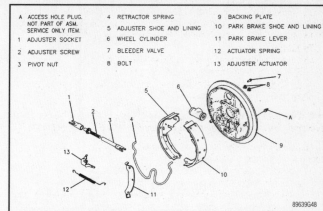

	A	ACCESS HOLE PLUG. NOT PART OF ASM. SERVICE ONLY ITEM.	4	RETRACTOR SPRING	9	BACKING PLATE
	1	ADJUSTER SOCKET	5	ADJUSTER SHOE AND LINING	10	PARK BRAKE SHOE AND LINING
	2	ADJUSTER SCREW	6	WHEEL CYLINDER	11	PARK BRAKE LEVER
	3	PIVOT NUT	7	BLEEDER VALVE	12	ACTUATOR SPRING
			8	BOLT	13	ADJUSTER ACTUATOR

Fig. 65 Exploded view of the drum brake components—1991–99 vehicles

ing. Insert the hook end of the spanner tool between the retractor spring and parking brake shoe web, and pry or twist to lift the end of the spring out of the shoe web hole.

> ✳✳ **CAUTION**
>
> **Keep your fingers clear of the spring to avoid pinching them between the spring and shoe web or spring and backing plate.**

11. Pry the end of the retractor spring toward the axle with the flat edge of the spanner tool until the spring snaps down off the shoe web onto the backing plate.
12. Remove the parking brake shoe and lining. If only the shoes and linings are being replaced, the retractor spring does not have to be removed. Otherwise, remove the retractor spring from the anchor plate.

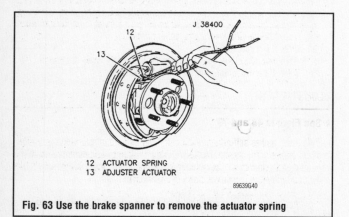

12 ACTUATOR SPRING
13 ADJUSTER ACTUATOR

Fig. 63 Use the brake spanner to remove the actuator spring

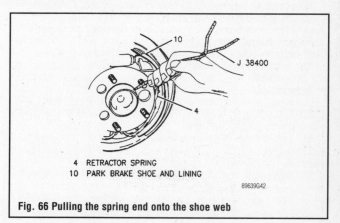

4 RETRACTOR SPRING
10 PARK BRAKE SHOE AND LINING

Fig. 66 Pulling the spring end onto the shoe web

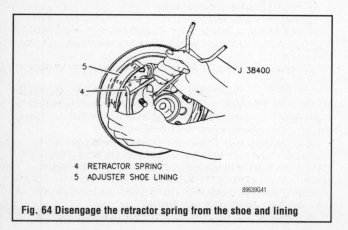

4 RETRACTOR SPRING
5 ADJUSTER SHOE LINING

Fig. 64 Disengage the retractor spring from the shoe and lining

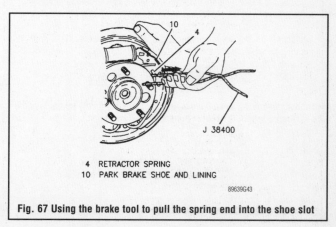

4 RETRACTOR SPRING
10 PARK BRAKE SHOE AND LINING

Fig. 67 Using the brake tool to pull the spring end into the shoe slot

13. Clean all parts with denatured alcohol. Replace all parts that are questionable in strength or quality due to discoloration from heat, over-stress or wear.

14. Inspect the wheel cylinder for leakage, and cut or damaged boots.

To install:

15. Lubricate the following with suitable brake lubricant:

a. Six raised shoe pads on the backing plate.

b. Anchor surfaces on the backing plate that contact the lower ends of the brake shoes.

➡ **When installing the retractor spring into either shoe and lining, do not overstretch it. Overstretching will reduce the spring's effectiveness.**

16. If the retractor spring was removed, reinstall it, hooking the center spring section under the tab on the anchor.

17. Install the parking brake shoe and lining, as follows:

a. Position the shoe and lining on the backing plate.

b. Using brake spanner tool, pull the end of the retractor spring up to rest on the web of the brake shoe.

c. Using the spanner tool, pull the end of the retractor spring over, until it snaps into the slot in the brake shoe.

18. Install the parking brake lever to the parking brake shoe and lining.

19. If disconnected, connect the parking brake cable to the lever.

20. Disassemble, clean and reassemble the adjusting screw, as follows:

a. Disassembly adjusting screw.

b. Clean the adjusting screw threads with a wire brush, then wash all components with clean denatured alcohol.

c. Apply a suitable brake lubricant to the adjuster screw threads, the inside diameter of the socket and socket face.

d. You have achieved sufficient lubrication when a continuous bead of lubricant is on the end of the adjuster nut and the socket when the threads are fully engaged. Check the threads of the adjuster screw for smooth rotation over the full length.

21. Install the adjusting screw assembly and adjuster shoe lining, as follows:

a. Engage the pivot nut with the web of the parking brake shoe and lining in the parking brake lever, view A-A in the accompanying figure.

b. Position the adjuster shoe and lining so the shoe web engages the deep slot in the adjuster socket (view B-B in the accompanying figure).

22. Install the retractor spring into the adjuster shoe and lining. Use the spanner tool to pull the end of the retractor spring up to seat on the web of the brake shoe, then pull the end of the retractor spring over until it snaps into the slot in the brake shoe.

23. Install the adjuster actuator, as follows:

a. Lubricate the tab and pivot point on the adjuster actuator with suitable brake lubricant.

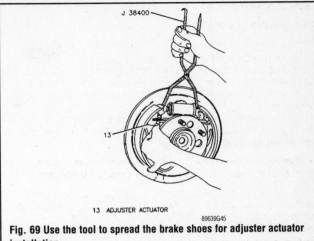

Fig. 69 Use the tool to spread the brake shoes for adjuster actuator installation

b. Using the spanner tool, spread the brake shoes while working the adjuster actuator into position.

24. Install the actuator spring, as follows:

a. Engage the U-shaped end of the spring in the hole in the web of the parking brake shoe.

b. Use the spanner tool to stretch the spring and engage the loop end over the tab on the adjuster actuator.

25. Check the following to be sure of proper positioning and function of the adjuster actuator:

a. The adjuster actuator pivot in the shoe web slot.

b. The notch in the adjuster actuator on step in the adjusting screw notch.

c. Arm of the adjuster actuator resting freely on the star wheel under the teeth of the adjuster screw, not trapped under the teeth in a downward angle.

d. Install the spanner tool between the upper ends of the shoe and lining assemblies. Spread the shoes and watch for proper rotation of the star wheel.

26. Adjust the service brakes and parking brakes.

27. Install the brake drum.

28. Install the wheel and tire assembly, then carefully lower the vehicle.

29. Tighten the wheel lug nuts to 100 ft. lbs. (136 Nm).

ADJUSTMENTS

◆ **See Figures 48 and 70**

The drum brakes self-adjust anytime the brakes are applied, with no vehicle motion required. This system works well and no manual adjustment is usually necessary. Adjustment will be required when new brake shoes are installed. The following procedure is with the brake drum removed.

1. Raise and support the car safely.

2. Mark the relation of wheel to studs, so you install it in the same location.

3. Remove the wheel and tire assembly.

4. Remove the brake drum.

5. Make certain the parking brake is off and the brake shoes are sitting against the stops. If not readjust the parking brake, as outlined later in this section.

6. Measure the drum inside diameter using a suitable drum-to-brake shoe clearance gauge.

7. Turning the adjuster nut (star wheel on the adjuster), adjust the shoe and lining diameter to be 0.050 in. (1.27mm) less than the inside drum diameter for each rear wheel. Go slowly and don't overtighten or force the drum on. It's very difficult to remove the drum on an overadjusted system.

8. If you've over-adjusted or the drum is hard to remove; remove the access hole plug from the backing plate. Insert a flat tool though the hole and press in to push the park brake lever off its stop. This allows the lining to retract. You must not remove the drum and reassemble the brakes. Don't pry on the backing plate. If necessary, insert a punch through the hole at the bottom of the splash shield and tap gently to loosen drum.

9. After adjustment, install the drum and the tire and wheel assembly.

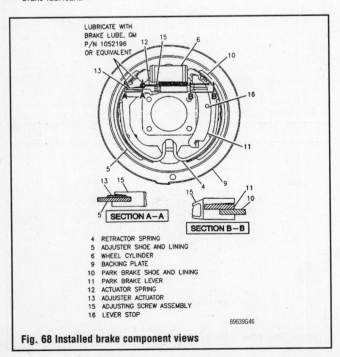

LUBRICATE WITH
BRAKE LUBE, GM
P/N 1052196
OR EQUIVALENT

SECTION A-A

SECTION B-B

4 RETRACTOR SPRING
5 ADJUSTER SHOE AND LINING
6 WHEEL CYLINDER
9 BACKING PLATE
10 PARK BRAKE SHOE AND LINING
11 PARK BRAKE LEVER
12 ACTUATOR SPRING
13 ADJUSTER ACTUATOR
15 ADJUSTING SCREW ASSEMBLY
16 LEVER STOP

Fig. 68 Installed brake component views

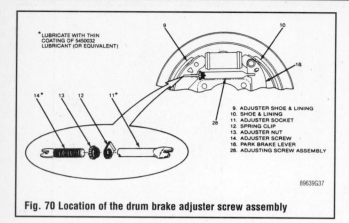

Fig. 70 Location of the drum brake adjuster screw assembly

9. ADJUSTER SHOE & LINING
10. SHOE & LINING
11. ADJUSTER SOCKET
12. SPRING CLIP
13. ADJUSTER NUT
14. ADJUSTER SCREW
18. PARK BRAKE LEVER
28. ADJUSTING SCREW ASSEMBLY

*LUBRICATE WITH THIN COATING OF 5450032 LUBRICANT (OR EQUIVALENT)

10. Perform the adjustment procedure at the other rear wheel and tire assembly.

11. Carefully lower the vehicle, then tighten the lug nuts to 100 ft. lbs. (136 Nm).

12. Apply and release the brakes about 30–35 times with normal pedal force, pausing about one second between pedal applications.

Wheel Cylinders

REMOVAL & INSTALLATION

▶ **See Figures 71, 72, 73 and 74**

1. Raise and safely support the vehicle. Remove the rear wheel and tire assembly.

2. Clean the area around the wheel cylinder assembly inlet and pilot.

3. Remove the brake drum assembly.

4. Remove any brake components, necessary for access to the wheel cylinder.

5. Disconnect and plug the inlet brake line.

6. Remove the wheel cylinder-to-backing plate mounting screws and/or lockwashers, then remove the wheel cylinder assembly.

To install:

7. Apply Loctite® Master Gasket, or equivalent to the wheel cylinder shoulder face that contact the backing plate.

8. Position the wheel cylinder assembly to the backing plate, then install the retaining screws/bolts and/or lockwashers. Tighten the retainers to 106 inch lbs. (12 Nm).

9. Unplug and connect the inlet brake line. Tighten the line nut to 12 ft. lbs. (17 Nm), using a flare nut wrench.

10. Install any brake components that were removed for access to the wheel cylinder.

11. Install the brake drum and the wheel and tire assembly.

12. Carefully lower the vehicle, then properly bleed the brake system, as outlined in this section.

OVERHAUL

▶ **See Figures 76 thru 85**

Wheel cylinder overhaul kits may be available, but often at little or no savings over a reconditioned wheel cylinder. It often makes sense with these components to substitute a new or reconditioned part instead of attempting an overhaul.

If no replacement is available, or you would prefer to overhaul your wheel cylinders, the following procedure may be used. When rebuilding and installing wheel cylinders, avoid getting any contaminants into the system. Always use clean, new, high quality brake fluid. If dirty or improper fluid has been used, it will be necessary to drain the entire system, flush the system with proper brake fluid, replace all rubber components, then refill and bleed the system.

1. Remove the wheel cylinder from the vehicle and place on a clean workbench.

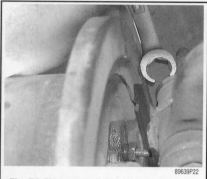

Fig. 71 Always use a flare nut wrench when disconnecting brake lines

Fig. 72 Pull the brake line from the rear of the backing plate

Fig. 73 Use a box end wrench to remove the 2 wheel cylinder mounting bolts . . .

Fig. 74 . . . then remove the wheel cylinder from the brake backing plate

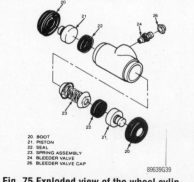

20. BOOT
21. PISTON
22. SEAL
23. SPRING ASSEMBLY
24. BLEEDER VALVE
26. BLEEDER VALVE CAP

Fig. 75 Exploded view of the wheel cylinder components—1986–90 vehicles

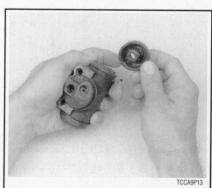

Fig. 76 Remove the outer boots from the wheel cylinder

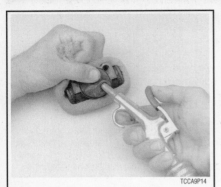

Fig. 77 Compressed air can be used to remove the pistons and seals

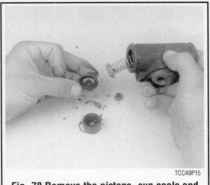

Fig. 78 Remove the pistons, cup seals and spring from the cylinder

Fig. 79 Use brake fluid and a soft brush to clean the pistons . . .

Fig. 80 . . . and the bore of the wheel cylinder

Fig. 81 Once cleaned and inspected, the wheel cylinder is ready for assembly

Fig. 82 Lubricate the cup seals with brake fluid

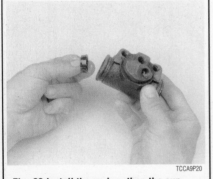

Fig. 83 Install the spring, then the cup seals in the bore

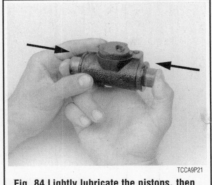

Fig. 84 Lightly lubricate the pistons, then install them

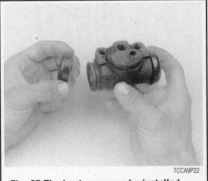

Fig. 85 The boots can now be installed over the wheel cylinder ends

2. First remove and discard the old rubber boots, then withdraw the pistons. Piston cylinders are equipped with seals and a spring assembly, all located behind the pistons in the cylinder bore.

3. Remove the remaining inner components, seals and spring assembly. Compressed air may be useful in removing these components. If no compressed air is available, be VERY careful not to score the wheel cylinder bore when removing parts from it. Discard all components for which replacements were supplied in the rebuild kit.

4. Wash the cylinder and metal parts in denatured alcohol or clean brake fluid.

5. Allow the parts to air dry or use compressed air. Do not use rags for cleaning, since lint will remain in the cylinder bore.

6. Inspect the piston and replace it if it shows scratches.

7. Lubricate the cylinder bore and seals using clean brake fluid.

8. Position the spring assembly.

9. Install the inner seals, then the pistons.

10. Insert the new boots into the counterbores by hand. Do not lubricate the boots.

11. Install the wheel cylinder.

✳✳ WARNING

Never use a mineral-based solvent such as gasoline, kerosene or paint thinner for cleaning purposes. These solvents will swell rubber components and quickly deteriorate them.

PARKING BRAKE

Cables

REMOVAL & INSTALLATION

Front Cable

▶ **See Figure 86**

1. Raise and safely support the vehicle.
2. Loosen the equalizer/adjuster assembly at the front parking brake cable.
3. Remove the front parking brake cable from the equalizer assembly.
4. Disconnect the cable retaining nut from the underbody.
5. Carefully lower the vehicle.
6. Remove the cable from the control lever assembly.

To install:

7. Install the cable to the control lever assembly.
8. Install the cable casing retaining nut to the underbody and tighten the nut to 22 ft. lbs. (30 Nm).
9. Attach the front parking brake cable to the equalizer assembly. Tighten the equalizer assembly at the front parking brake cable.
10. Adjust the parking brake cable, as outlined later in this section.
11. Lower the vehicle.

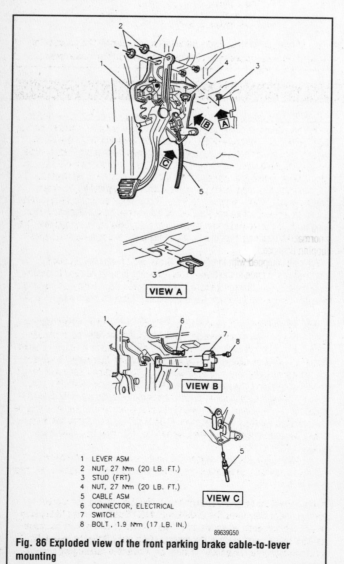

1 LEVER ASM
2 NUT, 27 N·m (20 LB. FT.)
3 STUD (FRT)
4 NUT, 27 N·m (20 LB. FT.)
5 CABLE ASM
6 CONNECTOR, ELECTRICAL
7 SWITCH
8 BOLT, 1.9 N·m (17 LB. IN.)

89639G50

Fig. 86 Exploded view of the front parking brake cable-to-lever mounting

Intermediate Cable

1. Raise and safely support the vehicle.
2. Disconnect the intermediate brake cable from the adjuster.
3. Remove the clip from the brake pipe retainer and cable, then remove the cable from the rear equalizer.
4. Remove the cable from the bracket and brake pipe retainers.

To install:

5. Route and install the cable into the brake pipe retainers, then snap the cable into the bracket.
6. Install the cable through the top support hole in the underbody.
7. Connect the left and right rear cables to the intermediate cable, utilizing the equalizer.
8. Install the clip around the cable and the brake pipe retainer, then tighten the retaining bolts to 53 inch lbs. (6 Nm).
9. Connect the cable to the adjuster.
10. Adjust the parking brake, as outlined later in this section.
11. Carefully lower the vehicle.

Rear Cable

▶ **See Figures 87 and 88**

1. Raise and safely support the vehicle.
2. Back off the adjuster nut to release the cable tension.
3. Remove the tire and wheel assembly.
4. Remove the brake drum and insert the proper tool between the brake shoe and the top part of the actuator bracket.
5. Push the bracket to the front and release the top adjuster bracket rod.
6. Remove the rear hold-down spring, actuator lever and the lever return spring.
7. Disconnect the adjuster screw spring and remove the top rear brake shoe return spring.
8. Disconnect the parking brake cable from the parking brake lever.

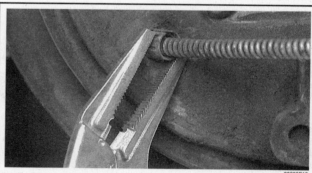

89639P12

Fig. 87 Use pliers, or a special tool, to depress the parking brake cable conduit fitting's retaining tangs . . .

89639P13

Fig. 88 . . . then remove the parking brake cable conduit fitting from the brake backing plate (components removed for clarity)

9. Depress the conduit fitting retaining tangs and remove the conduit fitting from the backing plate.

10. Remove the left rear cable by backing off the equalizer nut and disconnecting the conduit from the under body bracket.

11. Remove the right rear cable by disconnecting the cable end button from the connector and remove the conduit fitting from the axle bracket.

To install:

12. Install the right rear cable by connecting the conduit fitting to the axle bracket and cable end button to the connector.

13. Install the left rear cable by connecting the conduit fitting to the axle bracket and the left cable to the equalizer nut. Connect the conduit fitting the underbody bracket.

14. Install the conduit fitting to the backing plate and connect the parking brake cable to the parking brake lever.

15. Install the top brake shoe return spring and the adjuster screw spring.

16. Replace the lever return spring, actuator lever and the rear hold-down spring.

17. Install the top adjuster bracket rod. Replace the brake drum assembly.

18. Install the tire and wheel assembly. Adjust the parking brake cable.

19. Carefully lower the vehicle.

ADJUSTMENT

▶ **See Figure 89**

1. Adjust the rear brakes, as outlined in this section.

2. Apply and release the parking brake 6 times to 10 clicks, for 1986–90 vehicles. For 1991–99 vehicles, apply and release the parking brake 5 times, to 6 clicks. Release the park brake pedal.

3. Check the parking brake pedal for full release by turning the ignition to the **ON** position and checking the BRAKE warning lamp. The lamp should be off. If the lamp is on, make sure the pedal is in the fully release position ad pull downward on the front parking brake cable to remove the slack.

4. Raise and safely support the vehicle. Remove the access hole plug from the rear brake backing plates.

5. Adjust the parking brake cable until a ⅛ in. drill bit can be inserted through the access hole into the space between the shoe web and the parking brake lever. Satisfactory cable adjustment is achieved when a ⅛ in. bit will fit into the space, but a ¼ in. bit will not.

6. Apply the parking brake one click, and check the rear wheel rotation. When you try to rotate the wheels by hand in a forward direction, they should not move; in a rearward direction, they should either drag, or not move.

7. Release the parking brake and check for free wheel rotation.

8. Reinstall the access hole plugs, then carefully lower the vehicle.

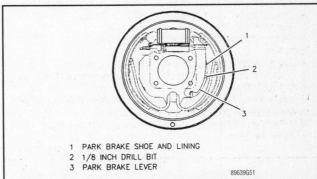

1 PARK BRAKE SHOE AND LINING
2 1/8 INCH DRILL BIT
3 PARK BRAKE LEVER

89639G51

Fig. 89 Proper parking brake adjustment will permit the passage of a ⅛ in. drill bit between the brake shoe and parking brake lever

TEVES II ANTI-LOCK BRAKE SYSTEM

General Description

The Teves Mark II Anti-lock Brake System (ABS), used on 1986–90 vehicles covered by this manual, is manufactured by Alfred Teves Technologies of West Germany. The 4-wheel system uses a combination of wheel speed sensors and a microprocessor to determine impending wheel lock-up and adjust the brake pressure to maintain the best braking. This system helps the driver maintain the control of the vehicle under heavy braking conditions.

✳✳ CAUTION

Some procedures in this section require that hydraulic lines, hoses and fitting be disconnected for inspection or testing purposes. Before disconnecting any hydraulic lines, hoses or fittings, be sure that the accumulator is fully depressurized. Failure to depressurize the hydraulic accumulator may result in personal injury.

➡**The use of rubber hoses or parts other than those specified for the ABS system may lead to functional problems and/or impaired braking or ABS function. Install all components included in repair kits for this system. Lubricate rubber pats with clean fresh brake fluid to ease assembly. Do not use lubricated shop air to clean or dry components; damage to rubber parts may result.**

Under normal driving conditions the Anti-lock braking system functions the same as a standard brake system. The primary difference is that the power assist for normal braking is provided by the booster portion of the hydraulic unit through the use of pressurized brake fluid.

If a wheel locking tendency is noted during a brake application, the ABS system will modulate hydraulic pressure in the individual wheel circuits to prevent any wheel from locking. A separate hydraulic line and 2 specific solenoid valves are provided for each front wheel; both rear wheels share a set of solenoid valves and a single pipe from the master cylinder to the proportioner valve or tee. The proportioner valve splits the right and left rear brake circuits to the wheels.

The ABS system can increase, decrease or hold pressure in each hydraulic circuit depending on signals from the wheel speed sensors and the electronic brake control module.

During an ABS stop, a slight bump or a kick-back will be felt in the brake pedal. This bump will be followed by a series of short pulsations which occur in rapid succession. The brake pedal pulsations will continue until there is no longer a need for the anti-lock function or until the vehicle is stopped. A slight ticking or popping noise may be heard during brake applications with anti-lock. This noise is normal and indicates that the anti-lock system is being used.

During anti-lock stops on dry pavement, the tires may make intermittent chirping noises as they approach lock-up. These noises are considered normal as long as the wheel does not truly lock or skid. When the anti-lock system is being used, the brake pedal may rise even as the brakes are being applied. This is normal. Maintaining a constant force on the pedal will provide the shortest stopping distance.

Vehicles equipped with the Anti-lock Brake System may be stopped by applying normal force to the brake pedal. Although there is no need to push the brake pedal beyond the point where it stops or holds the vehicle, applying more force causes the pedal to travel toward the floor. This extra brake travel is normal.

Vehicles equipped with the Anti-lock Brake System have an amber warning light in the instrument panel marked ANTI-LOCK. Additionally, some models using this system will flash other ABS related messages on the Graphic Control Center or other message panels. The warning light will illuminate if a malfunction in the anti-lock brake system is detected by the electronic controller. In case of an electronic malfunction, the controller will turn on the ANTI-LOCK warning light and disable some or all of the anti-lock system. If only the ANTI-LOCK light is on, normal braking with full assist is operational but there may be reduced or no anti-lock function. If the ANTI-LOCK warning light and the red BRAKE warning light come on at the same time, there may be a fault in the hydraulic brake system.

The ANTI-LOCK light will turn on during the starting of the engine and will usually stay on for approximately 3 seconds after the ignition switch is returned to the RUN position.

➡**Due to system de-pressurization over time, a vehicle not started in several hours may have the BRAKE and ANTI-LOCK warning lights stay on up to 30 seconds when started. This is normal and occurs because the ABS pump must restore the correct pressure within the hydraulic accumulator; both lamps will remain on while this recharging is completed.**

The Anti-lock Brake System uses a 2 circuit design so that some braking capacity is still available if hydraulic pressure is lost in 1 circuit. A BRAKE warning light is located on the instrument cluster and is designed to alert the driver of conditions that could result in reduced braking ability. Certain models may display brake related messages on screens or other panels; these messages supplement the brake warning light.

The BRAKE warning light should turn on briefly during engine starting and should remain on whenever the parking brake is not fully released. Additionally, the BRAKE warning lamp will illuminate if a sensor detects low brake fluid, if the pressure switch detects low accumulator pressure or if certain on-board computers run a self-check of the dashboard and instruments.

If the BRAKE warning light stays on longer than 30 seconds after starting the engine, or comes on and stays on while driving, there may be a malfunction in the brake hydraulic system.

SYSTEM COMPONENTS

Electronic Brake Control Module (EBCM)

The EBCM monitors the speed of each wheel and the electrical status of the hydraulic unit. The EBCM's primary functions are to detect wheel lock-up, control the brake system while in anti-lock mode and monitor the system for proper electrical operation. When one or more wheels approach lock-up during a stop, the EBCM will command appropriate valve positions to modulate brake fluid pressure and provide optimum braking. It will continue to command pressure changes in the system until a locking tendency is no longer noted.

The EBCM is a separate computer used exclusively for control of the anti-lock brake system. The unit also controls the retention and display of the ABS trouble codes when in the diagnostic mode. As the EBCM monitors the system or performs a self-check, it can react to a fault by disabling all or part of the ABS system and illuminating the amber ANTI-LOCK warning light. The EBCM is located on the right side of the dashboard, generally behind the glove box.

Wheel Speed Sensors

▶ See Figure 90

A wheel speed sensor at each wheel transmits speed information to the EBCM by generating a small AC voltage relative to the wheel speed. The voltage is generated by magnetic induction caused by passing a toothed sensor ring past a stationary sensor. The signals are transmitted through a pair of wires which are shielded against interference. The EBCM then calculates wheel speed for each wheel based on the frequency of the AC voltage received from the sensor.

Hydraulic Components

The ABS uses an integrated hydraulic unit mounted on the firewall or cowl. This unit functions as a brake master cylinder and brake booster. Additionally, the hydraulic unit provides brake fluid pressure modulation for each of the individual wheel circuits as required during braking. The hydraulic unit consists of several individual components.

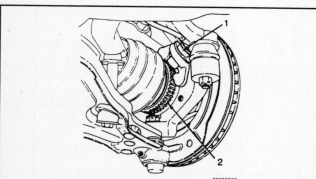

Fig. 90 Location of the Teves Mark II ABS front wheel speed sensor (1) and toothed wheel (2)

MASTER CYLINDER/BOOSTER ASSEMBLY

This portion of the hydraulic unit contains the valves and pistons necessary to develop hydraulic pressure within the brake lines. Pressure in the booster servo circuit is controlled by a spool valve which opens in response to the amount of force applied to the brake pedal. The rate at which the vehicle decelerates depends on the type of road surface and the pressure applied to the brake pedal.

The master cylinder portion uses a 3-circuit configuration during normal braking; individual circuits are provided for each front wheel while a shared circuit is used for the rear wheels. The 3 circuits are isolated so that a leak or malfunction in one will allow continued braking on the others.

The master cylinder/booster is a non-serviceable component and should never be disassembled.

VALVE BLOCK

The valve block is attached to the right side of the hydraulic unit and includes the 6 solenoid valves used to modulate pressures in the 3 circuits during anti-lock braking. Each circuit is equipped with an inlet and outlet valve.

During normal braking, the inlet valves are open and the outlet valves are closed. When anti-lock control begins, the EBCM switches 12 volts to the appropriate valve circuit. This allows the fluid pressure in each circuit to be increased, decreased or held constant as the situation dictates. The position of the valves can be changed as quickly as 15 times per second when ABS is engaged.

The valve block may be serviced separately from the master cylinder/booster assembly but should never be disassembled.

MAIN VALVE

The main valve is a 2-position valve controlled by the EBCM. Except for testing, the valve is open only during ABS stops. When open, the valve allows pressurized brake fluid from the booster servo into the master cylinder front brake circuits to prevent excessive pedal travel.

The main valve is not serviceable as a component; the master cylinder/booster assembly must be replaced.

ACCUMULATOR

The hydraulic accumulator is used to store brake fluid at high pressure so that a supply of pressurized fluid is available for ABS operation and to provide power assist. The accumulator uses a rubber diaphragm to separate high pressure nitrogen gas from the brake fluid.

Nitrogen in the accumulator is pre-charged to approximately 870 psi. During normal operation, the pump and motor assembly charges the accumulator with brake fluid to an operation range of 2000–2600 psi.

Because of the high pressures in the system, it is extremely important to observe all safety and pressure reduction precautions before performing repairs or diagnosis.

PUMP/MOTOR ASSEMBLY

The ABS system uses a pump and motor assembly located on the left side of the hydraulic unit to pressurize fluid from the reservoir and store it in the accumulator. When pressure within the system drops, the pressure switch on the hydraulic unit grounds the pump motor relay which energizes the pump motor and pump.

The pump/motor assembly is serviceable only as an assembly; the pump must never be disconnected from the motor.

FLUID LEVEL SENSOR

Found in the fluid reservoir, this sensor is a float which operates 2 reed switches when low fluid level is detected. One switch will cause the red BRAKE warning light to illuminate; the other signals the EBCM and possibly other computers of the low fluid situation. Depending on model and equipment, other messages may be displayed to the driver. The EBCM will engage the amber ANTI-LOCK warning light and disable the ABS function.

PRESSURE SWITCH

The pressure switch is mounted on the pump/motor assembly and serves 2 major functions, controlling the pump/motor and providing low pressure warning to the EBCM.

The switch will allow the pump/motor to run when system pressure drops below approximately 2030 psi and will shut the pump/motor off when pressure in the accumulator is approximately 2610 psi. Should pressure within the accumulator drop below approximately 1500 psi, internal switches will both signal the EBCM and turn on the red BRAKE warning lamp. If the system re-pressurizes and reaches at least 1900 psi, the switches will reset.

PROPORTIONER VALVE

Included in the rear brake circuit is a proportioner valve or tee assembly which limits brake pressure build-up at the rear brake calipers. Since the front brakes do the majority of the braking, less pressure is required for the rear brakes under certain conditions. The proportioner valve improves front-to-rear brake balance during normal braking.

System Testing

SERVICE PRECAUTIONS

> ※※ **CAUTION**
>
> **This brake system uses a hydraulic accumulator which, when fully charged, contains brake fluid at very high pressure. Before disconnecting any hydraulic lines, hoses or fittings be certain that the accumulator pressure is completely relieved. Failure to depressurize the accumulator may result in personal injury and/or vehicle damage.**

- If the vehicle is equipped with air bag (SIR) system, always properly disable the system before commencing work on the ABS system.
- Certain components within the ABS system are not intended to be serviced or repaired individually. Only those components with removal and installation procedures should be serviced.
- Do not use rubber hoses or other parts not specifically specified for the Teves ABS system. When using repair kits, replace all parts included in the kit. Partial or incorrect repair may lead to functional problems and require the replacement of the hydraulic unit.
- Lubricate rubber parts with clean, fresh brake fluid to ease assembly. Do not use lubricated shop air to clean parts; damage to rubber components may result.
- Use only brake fluid from an unopened container. Use of suspect or contaminated brake fluid can reduce system performance and/or durability.
- When any hydraulic component or line is removed or replaced, it may be necessary to bleed the entire system.
- A clean repair area is essential. Perform repairs after components have been thoroughly cleaned; use only denatured alcohol to clean components. Do not allow ABS components to come into contact with any substance containing mineral oil; this includes used shop rags.
- Remove the lock pin before disconnecting Connector Position Assurance (CPA) connectors in the harnesses.
- The EBCM is a microprocessor similar to other computer units in the vehicle. Insure that the ignition switch is **OFF** before removing or installing controller harnesses. Avoid static electricity discharge at or near the Controller.
- Never disconnect any electrical connection with the ignition switch **ON** unless instructed to do so in a test.
- Always wear a grounded wrist strap when servicing any control module or component labeled with a Electrostatic Discharge (ESD) symbol.
- Avoid touching module connector pins.
- Leave new components and modules in the shipping package until ready to install them.
- To avoid static discharge, always touch a vehicle ground after sliding across a vehicle seat or walking across carpeted or vinyl floors.
- Never allow welding cables to lie on, near or across any vehicle electrical wiring.
- Do not allow extension cords for power tools or droplights to lie on, near or across any vehicle electrical wiring.

DEPRESSURIZING THE HYDRAULIC UNIT

> ※※ **CAUTION**
>
> **On these vehicles, the ABS hydraulic unit accumulator MUST be depressurized before performing any procedures which include disconnecting the fluid lines!**

The ABS pump/motor assembly will keep the accumulator charged to a pressure between approximately 2000 and 2600 psi any time the ignition is in the **ON** or **RUN** position. The pump/motor cannot operate if the ignition is **OFF** or if a battery cable is disconnected.

1. With the ignition **OFF** or the negative battery cable disconnected, pump the brake pedal a minimum of 25 times using at least 50 lbs. of pedal force each time.
2. A definite increase in pedal effort will be felt as the accumulator becomes discharged.
3. After the increased pedal effort occurs, continue with 5–10 additional brake applications to release any remaining pressure.

VISUAL INSPECTION

Before any system diagnosis is begun, the brake system should be inspected visually for common faults which could disable the ABS or cause a code to set. Check the vehicle carefully for any sign of: binding parking brake or faulty parking brake switch, low brake fluid, system fluid leaks including pump/motor area, failed fuses or fusible links, failed ABS relay, loose or damaged wiring including connectors, harnesses, and insulation wear. Check the mounting and function of the brake calipers at each wheel. Carefully inspect the multi-pin connectors at the EBCM for pushouts or poor connections.

FUNCTIONAL CHECK

Once the visual check has been performed, perform the functional check to determine if the problem is truly ABS related or arises from common faults.

DISPLAYING ABS TROUBLE CODES

♦ **See Figures 91 and 92**

Only certain ABS malfunctions will cause the EBCM to store diagnostic trouble codes. Failures causing a code will generally involve wheel speed sensors, main valve or the inlet and outlet valves. Conditions affecting the pump/motor assembly, the accumulator, pressure switch or fluid level sensor usually do not cause a code to set. Some early 1988 vehicles may not have the ability to store trouble codes. The system functions the same way and the diagnosis and testing works about the same too. The only difference is the controller does not have code storing ability.

The EBCM will store trouble codes in a non-volatile memory. These codes remain in memory until erased through use of the correct procedure. The codes are NOT erased by disconnecting the EBCM, disconnecting the battery cable or turning off the ignition. Always be sure to clear the codes from the memory after repairs are made. To read stored ABS trouble codes:

1. Turn ignition switch to **ON**. Allow the pump to charge the accumulator; if fully discharged, dash warning lights may stay on up to 30 seconds. If ANTI-LOCK warning light does not go off within 30 seconds, note it.
2. Turn ignition switch to **OFF**.
3. Remove the cover from the ALDL connector. Enter the diagnostic mode by using a jumper wire to connect pins H and A or to connect pin H to body ground.

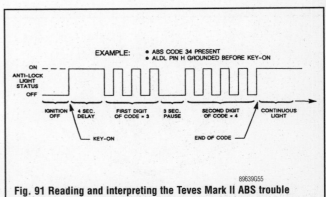

Fig. 91 Reading and interpreting the Teves Mark II ABS trouble codes

4. Turn the ignition switch to **ON** and count the light flashes for the first digit of the first code. The ANTI-LOCK light should illuminate for 4 seconds before beginning to flash. If, after 4 seconds, the
light turns off and stays off, no codes are stored.

5. The light will pause for 3 seconds between the first and second digits of the first code and then continue flashing. When counting flashes, count only the ON pulses.

6. When the EBCM is finished transmitting the second digit of the first code, the ANTI-LOCK light will remain on. This last, constant ON should not be counted as a flash. Record the 2-digit code.

7. Without turning the ignition switch **OFF**, disconnect the jumper from pin H and reconnect it. If an additional code is present, it will be displayed in similar fashion to the first. Record the second code.

8. Repeat the disconnection and reconnection of pin H without changing the ignition switch until no more codes are displayed. The system is capable of storing and displaying 7 codes; the ANTI-LOCK warning light will stay on continuously when all codes have been displayed.

9. After recording each code, remove the jumper from the ALDL, replace the cover and proceed.

➡**The ABS trouble codes are not specifically designated current or history codes. If the ANTI-LOCK light is on before entering the ABS diagnostic mode, at least one of the stored codes is current. It is impossible to tell which code is current. If the ANTI-LOCK light is off before entering the diagnostic mode, none of the codes are current.**

ABS CODE	SYSTEM	ABS CODE	SYSTEM
11	EBCM	45	2 SENSOR (LF)
12	EBCM	46	2 SENSORS (RF)
21	MAIN VALVE	47	2 SENSORS (REAR)
22	LF INLET VALVE	48	3 SENSORS
23	LF OUTLET VALVE	51	LF OUTLET VALVE
24	RF INLET VALVE	52	RF OUTLET VALVE
25	RF OUTLET VALVE	53	REAR OUTLET VALVE
26	REAR INLET VALVE	54	REAR OUTLET VALVE
27	REAR OUTLET VALVE	55	LF WSS
31	LF WSS	56	RF WSS
32	RF WSS	57	RR WSS
33	RR WSS	58	LR WSS
34	LR WSS	61	EBCM LOOP CKT
35	LF WSS	71	LF OUTLET VALVE
36	RF WSS	72	RF OUTLET VALVE
37	RR WSS	73	REAR OUTLET VALVE
38	LR WSS	74	REAR OUTLET VALVE
41	LF WSS	75	LF WSS
42	RF WSS	76	RF WSS
43	RR WSS	77	RR WSS
44	LR WSS	78	LR WSS

89639G56

Fig. 92 Teves Mark II ABS diagnostic trouble code chart

INTERMITTENTS

Although the ABS trouble codes stored by the EBCM are not identified as current or history codes, these codes may still be useful in diagnosing intermittent conditions.

If an intermittent condition is being diagnosed:

1. Obtain an accurate description of the circumstances in which the failure occurs.

2. Display and clear any ABS trouble codes which may be present in the EBCM.

3. Test drive the vehicle, attempting to duplicate the failure condition exactly.

4. After duplicating the condition(s), stop the vehicle and display any ABS codes which have set.

Most intermittent problems are caused by faulty electrical connections or wiring. Always check for poor mating of connector halves or terminals not fully seated in connector bodies, deformed or damaged terminals and poor terminal to wire connections.

Most failures within the ABS will disable the anti-lock function for the entire ignition cycle, even if the fault clears before the next key off occurrence. There are 3 situations which will allow the ABS to re-engage if the condition is corrected during the ignition cycle. Each of these will illuminate 1 or both dash warning lights.

• Low system voltage: If the EBCM detects low voltage, the ANTI-LOCK warning lamp is illuminated. If the correct minimum voltage is restored to the EBCM, normal ABS function will resume.

• Low brake fluid level: Once detected by the fluid level sensor, this condition illuminates both the BRAKE and ANTI-LOCK warning lights; when the sensor indicates acceptable fluid level, the normal ABS function will resume.

• Low accumulator pressure: Should the accumulator lose or not develop correct pressure, both the BRAKE and ANTI-LOCK warning lights will illuminate. Full function is restored when the correct pressure is achieved.

• Any condition interrupting power to either the EBCM or hydraulic unit may cause the warning lights to come on intermittently. These circuits include the main relay, main relay fuse, EBCM fuse, pump motor relay and all related wiring.

CLEARING TROUBLE CODES

Stored ABS trouble codes should not be cleared until all repairs are completed. The control module will not allow any codes to be cleared until all have been read. After reading each stored code, drive the vehicle at a speed over 18 mph.

Re-read the system; if codes are still present, not all codes were read previously or additional repair is needed.

➡**In the following diagnostic charts, certain special tools may be required. Use of the J-35592 Pinout box or equivalent is required to avoid damage to the connectors at the EBCM; use of J-35604 pressure gauge and J-35604-88 adapter (or equivalents) will be required to measure accumulator pressure. The use of a high-impedance multimeter (DVM or DVOM) is required at all times.**

Hydraulic Unit

REMOVAL & INSTALLATION

♦ **See Figure 93**

1. Disconnect the negative battery cable.

2. Depressurize the hydraulic accumulator by applying and releasing the brake pedal a minimum of 20–25 times, using 50 lbs. of pedal force. A noticeable change in pedal feel will occur when the pressure is released.

3. Detach the electrical connectors from the ABS hydraulic unit.

4. Unfasten the pump mounting bolts, then move the energy unit to gain access to the brake lines.

5. Disconnect and plug the brake lines from the valve block.

6. Remove the sound insulators, if necessary.

7. Disconnect the pushrod from the brake pedal and push the dust boot forward past the hex on the pushrod.

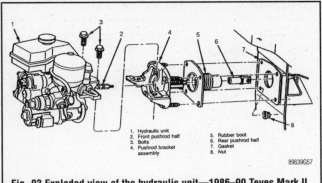

Fig. 93 Exploded view of the hydraulic unit—1986–90 Teves Mark II
ABS system

8. Separate the pushrod halves by unscrewing the 2 pieces.

9. From under the hood, remove the hydraulic unit-to-pushrod mounting
bolts.

10. Remove the hydraulic unit from the vehicle; the front part of the pushrod
will remain locked into the hydraulic unit.

To install:

11. Install the hydraulic unit to the pushrod bracket. Tighten the support
bolts to 37 ft. lbs. (50 Nm).

12. Install the pushrod halves by threading the 2 pieces together.

13. Install the pushrod to the brake pedal and reposition the dust boot.

14. Install the sound insulators that were removed.

15. Connect the brake lines to the valve block and tighten to 11 ft. lbs. (15
Nm).

16. Reposition the energy unit and replace the pump mounting bolts.
Tighten to 71 inch lbs. (8 Nm).

17. Connect the electrical connections at the hydraulic unit.

18. Connect the negative battery cable and bleed the brake system.

Wheel Speed Sensors

REMOVAL & INSTALLATION

Front

▶ **See Figure 94**

1. Disconnect the negative battery cable.

2. Unplug the sensor connector from the wiring harness.

3. Raise and safely support the vehicle. Remove the tire and wheel assembly.

4. Remove the sensor mounting screw, then remove the sensor.

To install:

5. Install the sensor and secure with the sensor mounting screw.

6. Install the tire and wheel assembly. Lower the vehicle.

7. Attach the sensor connector to the wiring harness.

8. Connect the negative battery cable.

Rear

▶ **See Figure 95**

1. Disconnect the negative battery cable.

2. Unplug the sensor connector, which is located in the trunk.

3. Raise and safely support the vehicle. Remove the tire and wheel assembly.

4. Unfasten the grommet retaining screws.

5. Remove the sensor mounting bolts, then remove the sensor.

To install:

6. Install the sensor and secure with the sensor mounting bolts.

7. Install the grommet retaining screws.

8. Install the tire and wheel assembly, then carefully lower the vehicle.

9. Attach the sensor connector, located in the trunk.

10. Connect the negative battery cable.

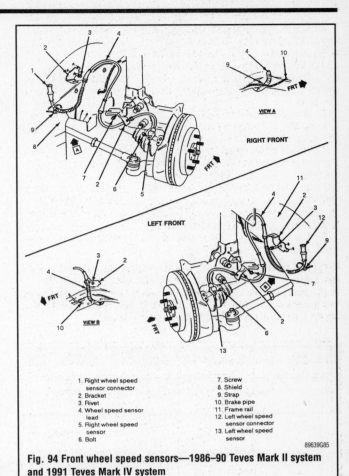

1. Right wheel speed	7. Screw
sensor connector	8. Shield
2. Bracket	9. Strap
3. Rivet	10. Brake pipe
4. Wheel speed sensor	11. Frame rail
lead	12. Left wheel speed
5. Right wheel speed	sensor connector
sensor	13. Left wheel speed
6. Bolt	sensor

Fig. 94 Front wheel speed sensors—1986–90 Teves Mark II system
and 1991 Teves Mark IV system

Fig. 95 The rear ABS wheel speed sensor is visible once the hub
and bearing assembly is removed

Valve Block Assembly

REMOVAL & INSTALLATION

▶ **See Figure 96**

1. With the ignition **OFF** disconnect the negative battery cable.

2. Depressurize the accumulator, as outlined earlier in this section.

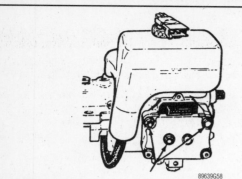

Fig. 96 Remove the fasteners from the positions shown by arrows only; the other fasteners must NOT be disturbed

3. Drain or remove the brake fluid from the reservoir.
4. Disconnect the electrical harness running to the valve block.
5. It may be necessary on some models to disconnect the brake lines from the bottom of the valve block.
6. At the valve block, remove the 3 nuts or 2 nuts and 1 bolt with hex faces only. Remove the valve block assembly and O-rings by sliding the valve block off of the studs. Recover any O-rings or gaskets from the mounting points and/or the fluid line ports.

✳✳ WARNING

Do not attempt to disassemble the valve block by removing the bolts with the recessed drive heads; the unit cannot be overhauled or repaired.

To install:
7. Lubricate the O-rings with clean brake fluid.
8. Install the valve block and O-rings onto the master cylinder body.
9. Install the 3 nuts or 2 nuts and 1 bolt, then tighten to 18 ft. lbs. (25 Nm).
10. If removed, connect the brake lines to the bottom of the valve block.
11. Reinstall the hydraulic unit if it was removed.
12. Connect the wiring harnesses.
13. Refill the system or reservoir to the correct level.
14. Connect the negative battery cable.
15. Properly bleed the brake system, as outlined in this section.

Pressure Warning Switch

REMOVAL & INSTALLATION

▶ See Figure 97

1. Disconnect the negative battery cable.
2. Depressurize the accumulator, as outlined earlier in this section.

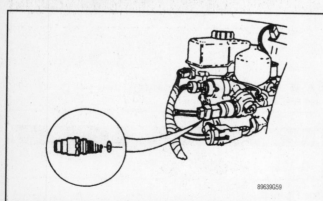

Fig. 97 Typical location of the pressure warning switch

3. Detach the electrical connector from the pressure/warning switch.
4. Remove the pressure/warning switch using special tool J-35804 or equivalent.
5. Remove the O-ring from the switch, then discard the O-ring.
To install:
6. Lubricate a new O-ring with clean brake fluid.
7. Install the O-ring on the pressure/warning switch.
8. Install the switch and tighten to 17 ft. lbs. (23 Nm), using the special tool.
9. Attach the electrical connector to the pressure/warning switch.
10. Connect the negative battery cable.
11. Turn the ignition to the **ON** position. The BRAKE light should go out within 60 seconds.
12. Check for leakage around the switch.

Hydraulic Accumulator

REMOVAL & INSTALLATION

1. Disconnect the negative battery cable.
2. Depressurize the accumulator. Make certain the system is completely relieved of all hydraulic pressure.
3. Unscrew the hydraulic accumulator from the hydraulic unit.
4. Remove the O-ring from the accumulator.
To install:
5. Lubricate a new O-ring with clean brake fluid and install it on the accumulator.
6. Install the accumulator and tighten to 32 ft. lbs. (43 Nm).
7. Connect the negative battery cable.
8. Turn the ignition switch to the **ON** position. The BRAKE light should go out within 60 seconds.
9. Check for leakage around the accumulator.

Brake Fluid Reservoir and Seal

REMOVAL & INSTALLATION

1. Disconnect the negative battery cable.
2. Depressurize the accumulator. Make certain the system is completely relieved of all hydraulic pressure.
3. Remove the return hose and drain the brake fluid into a container. Discard the fluid properly.
4. Detach the 2 wire connectors from the fluid level sensor assembly.
5. Remove the reservoir-to-block mounting bolt.
6. Remove the reservoir by carefully prying between the reservoir and the master cylinder.
To install:
7. Lubricate the seals with clean brake fluid.
8. Install the seals and O-ring into the master cylinder body.
9. Push the reservoir into the master cylinder until it is fully seated.
10. Install the reservoir to valve block mounting bracket bolt.
11. Attach the 2 wire connectors to the reservoir cap.
12. Connect the sump hose to the reservoir.
13. Refill the reservoir with clean brake fluid.
14. Connect the negative battery cable.

Pump and Motor Assembly

REMOVAL & INSTALLATION

1. Disconnect the negative battery cable.
2. Depressurize the accumulator. Make certain the system is completely relieved of all hydraulic pressure.
3. Detach the electrical connector from the pressure switch and the electric motor. Remove the fluid from the reservoir.

➡ **Do not remove brake fluid from the reservoir using a syringe or other instrument which is contaminated with water, petroleum based fluids or any other foreign material. Contamination of the brake fluid may result in impaired system operation, property damage or personal injury.**

4. Remove the hydraulic accumulator and O-ring.
5. Disconnect the high pressure hose fitting connected to the pump.
6. Remove the pressure hose assembly and O-rings.
7. Disconnect the wire clip then, pull the return hose fitting out of the pump body.
8. Remove the bolt attaching the pump and motor assembly to the main body.
9. Remove the pump and motor assembly by sliding it off of the locating pin.

➡ **Replace the insulators if damaged or deteriorated.**

To install:
10. Position the pump and motor assembly to the main body.
11. Install the bolt attaching the pump and motor assembly to the main body.
12. Connect the pressure hose assembly.
13. Connect the return hose and fitting into the pump body. Install the wire clip.
14. Install the bolt, O-rings and fitting of the high pressure hose to the pump assembly.
15. Attach the electrical connector to the pump motor.
16. Connect the negative battery cable.

Filling and Bleeding

SYSTEM FILLING

➡ **Do not allow the pump to run more than 60 seconds at one time. If the pump must run longer, allow the pump to cool several minutes between 60 second runs.**

With the ignition **OFF** and the negative battery cable disconnected, discharge the pressure within the accumulator. Remove the cap from the reservoir; fill the reservoir to the correct level with DOT 3 fluid.

➡ **Use only DOT 3 brake fluid from a clean, sealed container. Use of DOT 4 fluid or DOT 5 silicone fluid is not recommended. Internal damage to the pump components may result.**

SYSTEM BLEEDING

Front and/or rear brake circuits should be bled using pressure bleeding equipment. The pressure bleeder must be of the diaphragm type and must have a rubber diaphragm between the air supply and brake fluid. If necessary, the front brakes may be bled manually; manual bleeding is not recommended for the rear brakes.

Front Brake Circuit

❋ CAUTION

Do not move vehicle until a firm brake pedal is achieved. Failure to obtain firm brake pedal may result in personal injury and/or property damage.

1. With the ignition switch **OFF**, disconnect the negative battery cable.
2. Depressurize the accumulator.
3. Remove the reservoir cap or disconnect the wiring sensor from the fluid level sensor and remove the sensor.
4. Install the special tool No. J-35798 in place of the cap or sensor.
5. Attach the brake bleeder to the adapter tool No. J-35798 and charge to 20 psi (138 kPa).
6. Attach a bleeder hose to 1 front bleeder valve and submerge the other end in a container of clean brake fluid.
7. Open the bleeder valve.
8. Allow the fluid to flow from the bleeder until no air bubbles are seen in the brake fluid.
9. Close the bleeder valve.
10. Repeat Steps 4–7 on the other front bleeder valve.
11. Check the fluid level and adjust as necessary.
12. Remove the brake bleeding equipment and adapters, install the cap or sensor.

Rear Brake Circuit

❋ CAUTION

Do not move vehicle until a firm brake pedal is achieved. Failure to obtain firm brake pedal may result in personal injury and/or property damage.

1. With the ignition switch **OFF**, disconnect the negative battery cable.
2. Depressurize the accumulator.
3. Check the fluid level in the reservoir and fill as necessary.
4. Turn the ignition switch **ON** and allow the system to charge. (Listen for the pump motor; it will stop when the system is charged.)
5. Attach a bleeder hose to 1 of the rear bleeder valves and submerge the other end in a container of clean brake fluid.
6. Open the bleeder valve.
7. With the ignition **ON**, slightly depress the brake pedal for at least 10 seconds.
8. Allow the fluid to flow from the bleeder until no air bubbles are seen in the brake fluid. Repeat the above step if necessary.
9. Close the bleeder valve.
10. Repeat Steps 2–6 on the other rear bleeder valve.
11. Depressurize the system. Inspect the reservoir fluid level and adjust as necessary.

TEVES MARK IV ANTI-LOCK BRAKE SYSTEM

General Description

▶ **See Figure 98**

The Teves Mark IV ABS system is used on 1991–93 vehicles covered by this manual. The system allows individual modulation of braking force at each wheel as well as providing traction control at the drive wheels if the vehicle is so equipped. The ABS system employs a conventional diagonally-split braking system and additional ABS components. The system allows the operator to maintain directional control during heavy braking situations by preventing locked-wheel skidding.

On vehicles equipped with the Traction Control System (TCS), wheel spin at the drive wheels is reduced by selective application of the wheel brakes if vehicle speed is below 25 mph (40 km/h). The TCS system is designed to improve traction on loose or wet surfaces and aid in getting the vehicle moving from rest.

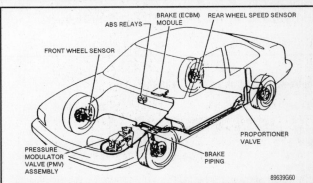

Fig. 98 Teves Mark IV Anti-lock Brake System (ABS) components—1991–93 vehicles

SYSTEM OPERATION

Braking is performed by the conventional brake system until the Electronic Brake Control Module (EBCM) detects a wheel beginning to lock, or the brake pedal has traveled beyond a specified limit. The EBCM will then command the system into anti-lock mode.

Electric signals are received by the EBCM from each wheel speed sensor. By comparing these signals to each other and to pre-programmed values, the EBCM can determine that one or more wheels is approaching lock-up. The EBCM activates the Pressure Modulator Valve (PMV) to control fluid pressure to the wheels. The PMV assembly has 2 valves per hydraulic circuit; the EBCM operates these valves electrically to control brake pressure. The valves may be placed into 3 modes: pressure increase, pressure reduce or pressure hold. By switching rapidly between these 3 modes, the EBCM can reduce pressure at the locking wheel, slow the most rapid wheel to the average or maintain the wheels just below the point of lock-up.

During the pressure increase mode, the inlet valve within the PMV is open, allowed to enter the particular hydraulic circuit. As this mode cycles, pressure and fluid is reduced within the master cylinder, causing the brake pedal to drop nearer to the floor. When the pedal travel exceeds a pre-determined level, the EBCM will activate the PMV pump motor. Pump pressure is applied to the wheel circuit(s) in need and/or the master cylinder hydraulic circuits. With pressure applied to the master cylinder hydraulic circuits, the pedal will rise until the brake travel switch is de-activated, switching the pump off.

During vehicle operation, the EBCM performs a series of self-tests, checking both electronic and hydraulic systems for vaults. If detectable problems exist, the EBCM will set a fault code and/or illuminate the ANTI-LOCK dash warning lamp. The ANTI-LOCK warning lamp is in addition to the normal BRAKE warning lamp which warns of problems in the conventional brake system.

Traction Control System (TCS)

The traction control system is additional to the ABS system and is not found on all vehicles with ABS. With traction control, brake pressure is increased to reduce wheel spin; with ABS, line pressure is reduced to allow greater wheel spin. The EBCM monitors the speed of the drive wheels through the wheel speed sensors; if wheel slip is detected below 25 mph with the brakes not applied, the EBCM enters the traction control mode.

Once in traction control mode, the EBCM commands two isolation valves in the PMV into operation. The isolation valves close to separate the non-driven wheels and the master cylinder circuits from the drive wheels. Once isolated, brake fluid pressure may be applied to the drive wheels without affecting the other circuits. The EBCM turns on the PMV pump motor and begins cycling the inlet and outlet valves to slow the slipping wheel(s).

Since the pump motor supplies more fluid than required, two pressure relief valves allow excess fluid to return to the master cylinder reservoir. If the brakes are manually applied by the operator during traction control operation, the PMV pressure switch and the brake pedal switch signal the EBCM to disable traction control and allow manual braking. Additionally, manual braking can override the traction control system at any time; the isolation valves act as one-way check valves, allowing manually-applied brake fluid pressure to enter the system.

Vehicles equipped with TCS are also be equipped with a manual switch to disable the traction system. When the switch is engaged, canceling system operation, a TRACTION OFF dashboard warning lamp will be illuminated. Some vehicles also have indicators showing that the TCS is engaged, either by lighting a dashboard lamp or displaying a TRACTION ENGAGED message.

SYSTEM COMPONENTS

Electronic Brake Control Module (EBCM)

Located on the inner firewall, the EBCM is a solid-state computer which monitors the speed of each wheel as well as the electrical status of the PMV assembly. Once wheel lock or wheel slip (with TCS) is detected, the EBCM operates the inlet and outlet valves in the PMV to control wheel speed. The valves can be cycled very rapidly, allowing control to be maintained in all operating situations.

The EBCM will disable either the TCS or ABS if a fault is detected. In most cases, the system will remain disabled for the remainder of the driving cycle, even if the fault self-corrects before the next key-on cycle. If either low system

voltage is detected at the EBCM or low brake fluid level is detected at the PMV, the systems(s) will be disabled until the condition is corrected. Once the sensors indicate normal voltage or fluid level, the system(s) are enabled, even if the vehicle has not been shut off and restarted.

If the control unit detects an electrical fault, it will disable the TCS and/or ABS system immediately and illuminate the appropriate dash warning lamp to advise the operator. A fault code will usually be set in memory. Although it is possible for just the TCS system to be disabled, any fault in the ABS system will also cause the TCS system to be disabled.

The fault codes may be retrieved when the EBCM is placed into the diagnostic mode. A bi-directional hand scanner is required to retrieve or clear stored codes; no warning lamp flash outputs are used.

Wheel Speed Sensors

A wheel speed sensor at each wheel transmits speed information to the EBCM by generating a small AC voltage relative to the wheel speed. The voltage is generated by magnetic induction caused by passing a toothed sensor ring past a stationary sensor. the signals are transmitted through a pair of wires which are shielded against interference. The EBCM then calculates wheel speed for each wheel based on the frequency of the AC signal received from the sensor.

Warning Lamps

▶ See Figure 99

➡Certain models equipped with traction control may cause a pilot lamp to light or a message to be displayed when the system is engaged. These signals are a convenience to the operator but are not system warning lamps.

BRAKE

The red BRAKE warning lamp in the instrument panel illuminates to alert the operator of conditions in the conventional braking system which may affect braking or vehicle operation. The lamp will illuminate when the parking brake is applied, the brake fluid in the master cylinder reservoir is low or when the ignition is switched to **START**, allowing the function of the bulb to be confirmed. Illumination of this lamp during vehicle operation signals a potentially hazardous condition within the brake system.

ANTI-LOCK

The amber ANTI-LOCK dashboard warning lamp is lit when the EBCM detects a fault within the ABS system. When this lamp is lit, the ABS system is disabled. If only the ANTI-LOCK lamp is lit, full power-assisted braking is available without the added benefit of the anti-lock system.

TRACTION/TRACTION OFF

This warning lamp applies specifically to the traction control system. It will light if the EBCM detects a problem specific to the TCS or if the operator has switched the system off manually.

On vehicles equipped with traction control, the EBCM is programmed to prevent brake overheating. During heavy braking conditions, if traction control mode is entered and the controller determines that the brakes are too hot to

ACTION	NORMAL RESULT
Ignition Switch: RUN Traction Control System: ON	ANTILOCK Indicator lights for approximately 2 to 4 seconds, then turns off. TRACTION Indicator lights for approximately 2 to 4 seconds, then turns off.
Park brake: applied	BRAKE Indicator lights, chime sounds.
Park brake: released	BRAKE Indicator does not light, chime does not sound.
Ignition Switch: START	ANTILOCK and BRAKE Indicators light, TRACTION Indicator lights briefly.
Release Ignition Switch to RUN when engine starts	ANTILOCK Indicator lights for approximately 2 to 4 seconds, then turns off. BRAKE Indicator turns off when Ignition Switch is released. TRACTION Indicator lights for approximately 2 to 4 seconds, then turns off.
Traction Control System: OFF	TRACTION Indicator lights.

89639G63

Fig. 99 Normal functions of the ABS/TCS dashboard warning lamps

function properly, the TCS is disabled and the warning lamp is lit. After a period of time, usually 15–20 minutes, the system is enabled and the warning lamp extinguished. This protective behavior is normal operation and should not be mistaken for an intermittent system failure.

Additionally, the EBCM monitors the signal from the transaxle temperature switch. If transaxle temperature exceeds approximately 320°F (160°C), the controller will disable the traction system, allowing both the brakes and the transaxle to cool. When the temperature switch closes again, at approximately 300°F (140°C), the EBCM will keep the system disabled for an additional 3–5 minutes to allow further cooling. The dash warning lamp will be illuminated during the period of disablement.

TCC/ABS Brake Switch

This normally closed switch is integral to the normal electrical/vacuum-release brake switch. It monitors position of the brake pedal, opening when the pedal exceeds 40 percent of total travel. The EBCM then turns on the pump in the pressure modulator valve assembly, circulating fluid and forcing the pedal upward until the switch closes.

Fluid Level Sensors

The brake fluid reservoirs on both the master cylinder and pressure modulator valve contain fluid level sensors. If the master cylinder reservoir becomes low on fluid, the red BRAKE warning lamp will be lit, signaling a potential system hazard. If the fluid level in the PMV reservoir becomes too low, the amber ANTI-LOCK warning lamp is lit and the ABS/TCS system disabled until the level returns to minimum.

Pressure Modulator Valve (PMV) Assembly

The assembly consists of the pump and motor, the valve body and the fluid reservoir. The reservoir provides fluid to the pump while the pump circulates the fluid to the master cylinder and maintains pedal height. The valve block contains the inlet and outlet valves for each wheel circuit.

When equipped with traction control, the PMV contains the isolation valves used to block pressure in the master cylinder and rear wheel circuits. A pressure switch within the PMV detects operator application of the brakes during TCS operation; when this signal is received, the EBCM immediately disables TCS function and allows manual braking.

The PMV is not serviceable except for replacement of the reservoir.

Proportioner Valves

Each rear wheel circuit contains a proportioning valve to limit brake pressure to the non-driven wheels. These valves improve front-to-rear brake balance during normal braking.

System Testing

SERVICE PRECAUTIONS

• Some vehicles are equipped with a Supplemental Inflatable Restraint (SIR) or air bag system. The air bag (SIR) system must be disabled before performing service on or around SIR components or wiring. Failure to follow safety and disabling procedures could result in possible air bag deployment, personal injury or unnecessary SIR system repairs.
• The use of rubber hoses or parts other than those specified for the ABS system may lead to functional problems and/or impaired braking or ABS function. Install all components included in repair kits for this system. Lubricate rubber parts with clean fresh brake fluid to ease assembly. Do not use lubricated shop air to clean or dry components; damage to rubber parts may result.
• Certain components in the ABS/TCS system are not intended to be serviced or disassembled. Only those components with removal and installation procedures should be serviced.
• Always disconnect the EBCM and PMV connectors before any welding is done on the vehicle.
• Never connect or disconnect the EBCM or PMV connectors with the ignition **ON**.
• Use only brake fluid from an unopened container. Use of suspect or contaminated brake fluid can reduce system performance and/or durability.

• When any hydraulic component or line is removed or replaced, it may be necessary to bleed the entire system.
• A clean repair area is essential. Perform repairs after components have been thoroughly cleaned.
• The EBCM is a microprocessor similar to other computer units in the vehicle. Insure that the ignition switch is **OFF** before removing or installing controller harnesses. Avoid static electricity discharge at or near the controller.
• Never disconnect any electrical connection with the ignition switch **ON** unless instructed to do so in a test.
• Always wear a grounded wrist strap when servicing any control module or component labeled with a Electrostatic Discharge (ESD) symbol.
• Avoid touching module connector pins.
• Leave new components and modules in the shipping package until ready to install them.
• To avoid static discharge, always touch a vehicle ground after sliding across a vehicle seat or walking across carpeted or vinyl floors.
• Never allow welding cables to lie on, near or across any vehicle electrical wiring.
• Do not allow extension cords for power tools or droplights to lie on, near or across any vehicle electrical wiring.

DIAGNOSTIC PROCEDURE

Diagnosis of the anti-lock and/or traction control system consists of 3 steps which must be performed in order.
1. Visual inspection
2. Functional check
3. Additional testing as specified by the functional check.

Some diagnostic procedures require that the ignition be left **ON** for an extended period of time while testing. Low battery voltage may result, causing incorrect readings or impaired system function. It is recommended that a battery charger be connected and a slow charge applied during testing.

Visual Inspection

The initial visual inspection requires a thorough external check of both the conventional and ABS/TCS systems. Many faults are caused by items such as loose connectors, corroded grounds, failed fuses or low fluid levels. The visual inspection, when properly performed, will reveal these faults. Check the parking brake lever and cables for full release. Check the hydraulic system for leakage, line damage or restriction. System connectors should be tested for tightness; if a connector is suspect or has been exposed to moisture, separate the halves and check for corrosion on the terminal pins. Check connector shells for pin separation or push-out. Fuses in both the underdash and underhood panels should be checked. Correct the fluid level in the reservoirs if necessary.

Functional Check/Displaying Codes

▶ See Figures 100 and 101

If no problem is found during the Visual Inspection, the functional check must be performed. This test requires the use of a bi-directional hand-scanner, such as the General Motors Tech 1® or its equivalent. The scan tool is used to recover and/or clear stored fault codes during testing. The procedure also includes test driving the vehicle if necessary. Once fault codes or symptoms are determined, the test chart directs the use of the appropriate supplementary chart.

➡If multiple codes are stored, diagnose the code which first appears on the hand scanner.

Intermittent Faults

Faults which occur intermittently are difficult to diagnose. When diagnosing such problems, keep an overall view of system function in mind. Faults may result from low system voltage, low brake fluid in the PMV reservoir or any interruption of the signal(s) from the wheel speed sensor(s). Any condition interrupting the power supply to the EBCM or hydraulic unit will also cause the dash warning lamp to illuminate. Most intermittent or random faults relate to loose connectors or faulty terminals. Again, the visual inspection is of prime importance.

The diagnostic codes can be helpful in tracking intermittent faults. While not

ABS CODE DIAGNOSIS GUIDE

CODE	DESCRIPTION	CAUSE		CODE	DESCRIPTION	CAUSE
21	RF speed sensor circuit open	B		45	LF inlet valve circuit	A
22	RF speed sensor signal erratic	C		46	LF outlet valve circuit	A
23	RF wheel speed is 0 mph	D		47	LF speed sensor noisy	I
25	LF speed sensor circuit open	B		51	RR inlet valve circuit	A
26	LF speed sensor signal erratic	C		52	RR outlet valve circuit	A
27	LF wheel speed is 0 mph	D		53	RR speed sensor noisy	I
31	RR speed sensor circuit open	B		55	LR inlet valve circuit	A
32	RR speed sensor signal is erratic	C		56	LR outlet valve circuit	A
33	RR wheel speed is 0 mph	D		57	LR speed sensor noisy	I
35	LR speed sensor circuit open	B		61	Pump motor test fault	G
36	LR speed sensor signal erratic	C		62	Pump motor fault in ABS stop	H
37	LR wheel speed is 0 mph	D		71	EBCM problem	J
41	RF inlet valve circuit	A		72	VCC/antilock brake switch sircuit	F
42	RF outlet valve circuit	A		73	Fluid level switch circuit	E
43	RF speed sensor noisy	I				

CAUSE "A" • Inlet or outlet valve circuit open or shorted to ground.
CAUSE "B" • Wheel speed sensor circuit open or shorted.
CAUSE "C" • Wheel speed sensor circuit open or shorted intermittently.
CAUSE "D" • Wheel speed sensor signal missing.
CAUSE "E" • Fluid level switch circuit.
CAUSE "F" • VCC/antilock brake switch circuit open or shorted.
CAUSE "G" • Malfunctioning pump motor, electrical or mechanical failure.
CAUSE "H" • Pump pressure is too low, defective pump motor or pump motor run sensor circuit, or air in hydraulic system.
CAUSE "I" • Electrical noise or excessive vibration detected in wheel speed sensor circuit above 40 km/h (25 mph).
CAUSE "J" • Internal electronic brake control module (EBCM) fault.

HISTORY CODES:

"History" codes indicate intermittent problems. Do not use trouble code diagnosis for intermittent problems until you have done the following:

• Check all connectors for good contact. Repair/replace as necessary.
• Test drive vehicle.
  The purpose of test drive is to:
  1) Observe an abnormal condition that does not cause ANTILOCK and BRAKE indicators to light; and
  2) To determine exact conditions which cause one of the indicators to light.

CLEARING CODES:

• To clear codes use a scan tool.
• After codes have been cleared, test drive vehicle

89639G61

Fig. 100 Teves Mark IV ABS trouble codes—1991 vehicles

DIAGNOSTIC TROUBLE CODE (DTC) GUIDE

PERFORM ABS/TCS FUNCTIONAL CHECK BEFORE PROCEEDING WITH ANY DIAGNOSIS.

INTERMITTENT "HISTORY" DIAGNOSTIC TROUBLE CODES:

STORED DIAGNOSTIC TROUBLE CODES THAT DO NOT LIGHT THE AMBER "ANTILOCK" INDICATOR ARE INTERMITTENT PROBLEMS OR HISTORY CODES THAT WERE NOT CLEARED DURING PRIOR SERVICE. DO NOT USE DIAGNOSTIC TROUBLE CODE DIAGNOSIS FOR INTERMITTENT PROBLEMS UNTIL REFERRING TO "INTERMITTENTS AND POOR CONNECTIONS" IN THIS SECTION.

MULTIPLE DIAGNOSTIC TROUBLE CODES: DIAGNOSE FIRST DIAGNOSTIC TROUBLE CODE THAT APPEARS ON BI-DIRECTIONAL SCAN TOOL SCREEN.

CLEARING DIAGNOSTIC TROUBLE CODES:

• CLEAR DIAGNOSTIC TROUBLE CODES USING A BI-DIRECTIONAL SCAN TOOL.
• CYCLE IGNITION SWITCH.
• AFTER DIAGNOSTIC TROUBLE CODES HAVE BEEN CLEARED, REFER TO "ABS/TCS FUNCTIONAL CHECK" CHART IN THIS SECTION TO ASSURE ALL PROBLEMS HAVE BEEN REPAIRED.

DTC	DESCRIPTION		DTC	DESCRIPTION
21	RF speed sensor circuit open		44	LF isolation valve circuit
22	RF speed sensor signal erratic		45	LF inlet valve circuit
23	RF wheel speed is 0 mph		46	LF outlet valve circuit
25	LF speed sensor circuit open		48	RF isolation valve circuit
26	LF speed sensor signal erratic		51	RR inlet valve circuit
27	LF wheel speed is 0 mph		52	RR outlet valve circuit
31	RR speed sensor circuit open		55	LR inlet valve circuit
32	RR speed sensor signal is erratic		56	LR outlet valve circuit
33	RR wheel speed is 0 mph		61	Pump motor test fault
35	LR speed sensor circuit open		62	Pump motor fault in ABS stop
36	LR speed sensor signal erratic		71	EBCM problem
37	LR wheel speed is 0 mph		72	TCC/antilock brake switch circuit
41	RF inlet valve circuit		73	Fluid level switch circuit
42	RF outlet valve circuit		74	PMV pressure switch circuit

89639G62

Fig. 101 Teves Mark IV ABS trouble codes—1992–93 vehicles

designated History or Current, certain combinations can point to fault status. Stored codes which do not light the ANTI-LOCK warning lamp are intermittent or history codes. If the ANTI-LOCK lamp is lit and one or more codes are stored, at least one (or more) of the codes is current.

Additionally, when diagnosing intermittent faults, keep the following system basics in mind:

• It is possible to feel the system self-test at very low speed if the brake pedal is barely applied. Both the sound (fluid returning to the master cylinder) and the slight vibration (valves cycling through test mode) are normal conditions.

• Any fault in the anti-lock system will light the TRACTION light. When both lamps are lit, diagnose the ABS system.

• The systems will disable if either the EBCM senses overheating in the brakes or transaxle. Once cooled, the ABS/TCS becomes available and the dash lamp(s) extinguish. This self-protective operation is completely normal but may become a source of operator concern.

• When diagnosing an apparent TCS fault, make certain the TCS OFF switch is not engaged.

• If a faulty wheel speed signal is suspected, check tires and wheels for matching sizes and tire pressures.

• If necessary, the vehicle must be test driven to recreate circumstances causing the fault.

➡ **The operator of the vehicle is the best source of information about fault occurrences. An accurate description of driving conditions will allow the fault to be duplicated during the test drive.**

1. Display, record and clear all fault codes in the EBCM.
2. Test drive the vehicle, attempting to recreate the failure conditions.
3. Safely stop the vehicle. Display and record the stored codes, if any.
4. If codes were stored, refer to the appropriate diagnostic chart. If no codes were stored, refer to the symptom chart.

Clearing Codes

Stored fault codes must be cleared using the bi-directional hand scanner. After repairs are completed, clear all stored codes and test drive the vehicle. Recheck for any newly-stored codes after the test drive.

Electronic Brake Control Module (EBCM)

The electronic brake control module is located on the right side of the vehicle and positioned under the right sound insulator panel. In order to gain access to electronic brake control module, it will be necessary to first remove the trim panel.

REMOVAL & INSTALLATION

▶ **See Figures 102 and 103**

➡ **On vehicles with the Traction Control System (TCS), the EBCM is referred to as the EBTCM.**

1. Make sure the ignition is in the **OFF** position.
2. Disconnect the negative battery cable.
3. Remove the sound insulators necessary for access to the module.

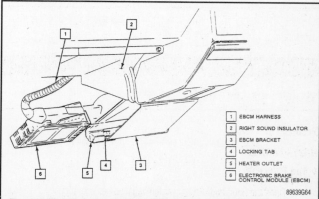

1	EBCM HARNESS
2	RIGHT SOUND INSULATOR
3	EBCM BRACKET
4	LOCKING TAB
5	HEATER OUTLET
6	ELECTRONIC BRAKE CONTROL MODULE (EBCM)

89639G64

Fig. 102 Exploded view of the EBCM mounting—1991 vehicles

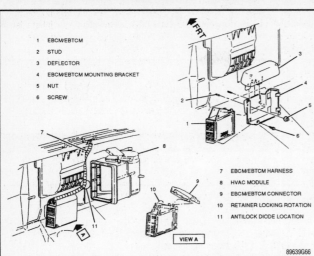

1 EBCM/EBTCM
2 STUD
3 DEFLECTOR
4 EBCM/EBTCM MOUNTING BRACKET
5 NUT
6 SCREW

7 EBCM/EBTCM HARNESS
8 HVAC MODULE
9 EBCM/EBTCM CONNECTOR
10 RETAINER LOCKING ROTATION
11 ANTILOCK DIODE LOCATION

VIEW A

89639G66

Fig. 103 Exploded view of the EBCM/EBTCM and mounting bracket—1992–93 vehicles

4. If necessary, remove the floor outlet.
5. If equipped, unfasten the EBCM/EBTCM retaining bolt.
6. Slide the EBCM from the mounting bracket, toward the accelerator pedal.
7. Detach the EBCM electrical connector, then remove the module from the vehicle.
8. For 1991 vehicles, to remove the EBCM bracket, perform the following:
   a. Unfasten the screws and remove the ALDL.
   b. Remove the bracket by lifting upward.
9. For 1992–93 vehicles, to remove the EBCM/EBTCM bracket, perform the following:
   a. Unfasten the retaining nuts, remove the deflector, then remove the bracket.
   To install:
10. For 1992–93 vehicles, to install the EBCM/EBTCM bracket, perform the following:
    a. Position the bracket, install the deflector and secure with the retaining nuts. Tighten the nuts to 89 inch lbs. (10 Nm).
11. On 1991 vehicles, if the bracket was removed, perform the following:
    a. Position the bracket to the heater outlet.
    b. Install the ALDL.
    c. Install the retaining screws and tighten to 13 inch lbs. (1.5 Nm).
12. Attach the EBCM electrical connector, then slide the module assembly into the bracket.
13. If equipped, install the retaining bolt and tighten to 42 inch lbs. (4.7 Nm).
14. Install any sound insulators that were removed.
15. Connect the negative battery cable.

Anti-lock Diode

LOCATION

The anti-lock diode is taped to the wiring harness near the EBCM, under the dashboard.

Wheel Speed Sensors

REMOVAL & INSTALLATION

Front

1991 VEHICLES

▶ **See Figure 96**

1. Open the hood and disconnect the negative battery cable.
2. Detach the wheel speed sensor electrical connector.

3. Cut the strap retaining the sensor lead.
4. Raise and safely support the vehicle.
5. Remove the sensor lead from the brackets.
6. Unfasten the retaining bolt, then remove the sensor. Inspect the sensor face for metal particles, dirt or grease and clean off as required. The face of the sensor should show no evidence of contact with the toothed ring or other damage. If damage is noted, determine the cause and correct. The sensor should be replaced if the damage interferes with proper operation.
   To install:

✳✳ WARNING

Make sure you install the wheel speed sensor cables properly, as correct installation is crucial to the ABS operation. Make sure the cables are routed through the retainers. If the cables are not clipped securely, they may rub against moving components, causing circuit and system damaged.

7. Route the sensor cable, then install the retainers.

➡If the wheel speed sensor is removed or replaced, the sensor body must be coated with a suitable anti-corrosion compound, where the sensor contacts the knuckle.

8. Position the sensor in the knuckle. Install the retaining bolt and tighten to 84 inch lbs. (9.5 Nm).
9. Carefully lower the vehicle.
10. Attach the wheel speed sensor connector.
11. Install a new strap securing the sensor lead to the harness.
12. Connect the negative battery cable, then close the hood.

1992–93 VEHICLES

▶ **See Figures 104 and 105**

1. Disconnect the negative battery cable.
2. Raise and safely support the vehicle. Remove the tire and wheel assembly.
3. Detach the wheel speed sensor electrical connector.
4. Remove the front hub and bearing assembly.
5. Gently pry the wheel speed sensor slinger off, using a suitable prytool. Discard the old slinger.
6. Remove the sensor by gently prying the bearing assembly off with a suitable prytool.
7. Do not let debris get into the bearing while the sensor is removed. Do not add lubricant to the bearing through the sensor housing opening. The bearing is lubricated for the life of the vehicle. Do not clean the grease from the toothed sensor ring. The grease won't affect the sensor operation.
8. Inspect the bearing and sensor cap for any indication of water or debris entry. If you find any water or debris, you must replace the hub and bearing assembly.
   To install:
9. Apply Loctite® 262, or equivalent locking fixative to the groove in the outer diameter of the bearing hub, per the directions in the service kit.

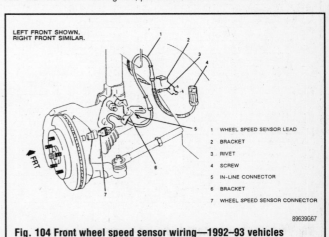

LEFT FRONT SHOWN,
RIGHT FRONT SIMILAR.

1 WHEEL SPEED SENSOR LEAD
2 BRACKET
3 RIVET
4 SCREW
5 IN-LINE CONNECTOR
6 BRACKET
7 WHEEL SPEED SENSOR CONNECTOR

89639G67

Fig. 104 Front wheel speed sensor wiring—1992–93 vehicles

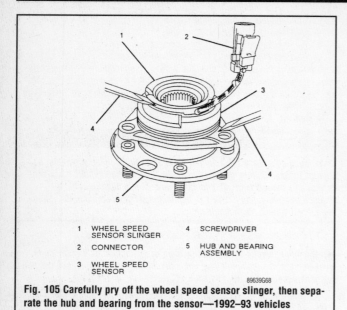

1. WHEEL SPEED SENSOR SLINGER
2. CONNECTOR
3. WHEEL SPEED SENSOR
4. SCREWDRIVER
5. HUB AND BEARING ASSEMBLY

89639G68

Fig. 105 Carefully pry off the wheel speed sensor slinger, then separate the hub and bearing from the sensor—1992–93 vehicles

10. Using tool J-38764 or equivalent and a press, install the sensor.
11. Install the hub and bearing assembly and attach the sensor connector.
12. Install the tire and wheel assembly, then carefully lower the vehicle.
13. Connect the negative battery cable.

Rear

▶ **See Figure 106**

1. Disconnect the negative battery cable.
2. Raise and safely support the vehicle. Remove the tire and wheel assembly.
3. Disconnect the wheel speed sensor electrical connector.
4. Remove the rear hub and bearing assembly.
5. Unfasten the Torx® screws, then remove the sensor.
To install:
6. Install the sensor with O-ring intact.
7. Install the Torx screws and tighten to 33 inch lbs. (3.7 Nm).
8. Install the hub and bearing assembly.
9. Connect the wheel speed sensor electrical connector.
10. Install the tire and wheel assembly and lower the vehicle.
11. Connect the negative battery cable.

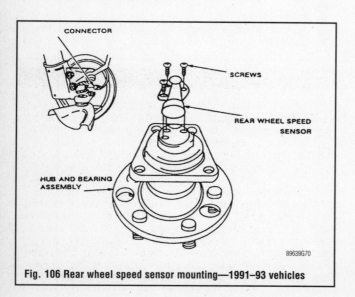

89639G70

Fig. 106 Rear wheel speed sensor mounting—1991–93 vehicles

Wheel Speed Sensors Reluctor Ring

REMOVAL & INSTALLATION

The toothed wheels which rotate past the speed sensors are integral parts of their respective assemblies. If the front ring is damaged, the drive axle must be replaced. If a rear ring is damaged, the hub and bearing assembly must be replaced.

Pressure Modulator Valve (PMV) Assembly

REMOVAL & INSTALLATION

▶ **See Figures 107 and 108**

1. Remove the air cleaner assembly.
2. Disconnect the negative battery cable.
3. Label and disconnect the following wiring connectors from the PMV assembly:
   a. Fluid level switch
   b. Pump motor
   c. Valve block
4. Loosen or reposition the clamp on the hose at the PMV reservoir.

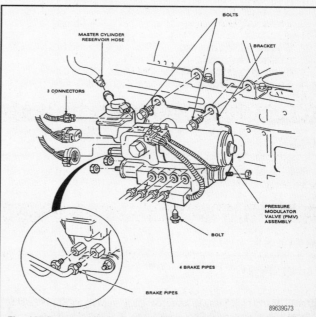

89639G73

Fig. 107 Pressure Modulator Valve (PMV) and related components

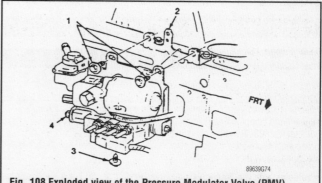

89639G74

Fig. 108 Exploded view of the Pressure Modulator Valve (PMV) mounting

5. Disconnect the hose from the reservoir. Catch escaping fluid in a clean container, then plug the hose with a ⅝ inch (15.5mm) diameter plug.

6. Disconnect the primary and secondary brake lines at the PMV.

7. Disconnect the 4 brake lines from the PMV assembly.

8. Raise and safely support the vehicle.

9. Remove the lower PMV assembly retaining bolt.

10. Carefully lower the vehicle.

11. Remove the harness strap.

12. Support the PMV assembly, then remove the upper retaining bolts. Remove the assembly from the vehicle. If the unit is being replaced with another, the reservoir and bracket(s) must be transferred to the new assembly.

➡**The PMV assembly is not serviceable. Do not attempt to disassemble any part of the unit.**

To install:

13. Position the PMV assembly and install the upper retaining bolts. Tighten the bolts to 20 ft. lbs. (27 Nm).

14. Install the harness.

15. Raise and safely support the vehicle. Install the lower retaining bolt and tighten it to 20 ft. lbs. (27 Nm). Lower the vehicle.

16. Connect the 4 brake lines to the PMV. Tighten each line to 11 ft. lbs. (15 Nm).

17. Install the primary and secondary brake lines, tightening each to 11 ft. lbs. (15 Nm).

18. Connect the hose to the PMV reservoir and secure the clamp.

19. Attach the electrical connectors to the PMV assembly; make certain each connector is squarely seated and firmly retained.

20. Connect the negative battery cable.

21. Install the air cleaner assembly.

22. Fill the brake fluid reservoir.

23. Bleed the brake system.

24. Clean any spilled brake fluid from the PMV assembly and surrounding area to prevent damage to other components or paint work.

PMV Fluid Level Sensor

REMOVAL & INSTALLATION

The fluid level sensor is integrated with the PMV reservoir. If the sensor fails, the reservoir must be replaced.

PMV Reservoir

REMOVAL & INSTALLATION

♦ **See Figure 109**

The reservoir with the fluid level sensor is the only replaceable component on the PMV assembly. It may be replaced without removing the PMV assembly from the vehicle.

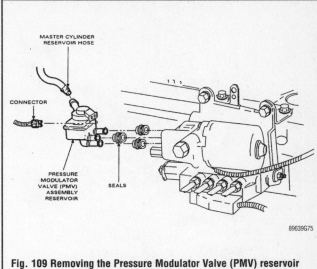

Fig. 109 Removing the Pressure Modulator Valve (PMV) reservoir

1. Disconnect the electrical connector from the reservoir.

2. Loosen or reposition the clamp on the hose at the PMV reservoir.

3. Disconnect the hose from the reservoir. Catch escaping fluid in a clean container; plug the hose with a ⅝ inch (15.5mm) diameter plug.

4. Carefully pry or force the reservoir free of its rubber mounts on the PMV assembly.

5. Remove and discard the rubber seals from the PMV; taking care to note the orientation or placement of the seals.

To install:

6. Lubricate new seals with clean brake fluid, then fit the seals to the PMV assembly. Make certain the seals are correctly installed.

7. Clean the reservoir and ports with denatured alcohol. Install the reservoir onto the PMV assembly.

8. Connect the hose to the reservoir and secure the clamp.

9. Attach the reservoir wiring connector.

10. Fill the reservoir with clean, fresh brake fluid.

11. Bleed the brake system.

12. Clean any spilled brake fluid from the PMV assembly and surrounding area to prevent damage to other components or paint work.

Bleeding the ABS System

On these vehicles, the bleeding procedure is the same as for those vehicles not equipped with ABS. Please refer to the bleeding procedure, located earlier in this section.

DELCO VI AND DELCO BOSCH V ANTI-LOCK BRAKING SYSTEMS (ABS)

General Information

♦ **See Figure 110**

The Delco VI Anti-lock Braking System (ABS) was first introduced on these vehicles in 1994. In 1996, the standard ABS system was the Delco Bosch V system. ABS provides the driver with 3 important benefits over standard braking systems: increased vehicle stability, improved vehicle steerability, and potentially reduced stopping distances during braking. It should be noted that although the ABS-VI system offers definite advantages, the system cannot increase brake pressure above master cylinder pressure applied by the driver and cannot apply the brakes itself.

➡**Vehicles with the Traction Control System (TCS), utilize a Electronic Brake and Traction Control Module (EBTCM).**

These Anti-lock Braking Systems consist of a conventional braking system with vacuum power booster, compact master cylinder, front disc brakes, rear drum brakes and interconnecting hydraulic brake lines augmented with the ABS components. The ABS-VI system includes a pressure modulator valve, Electronic Brake Control Module (EBCM or EBTCM), a system relay, 4 wheel speed sensors, interconnecting wiring and an amber ABS warning light.

The EBCM monitors inputs from the individual wheel speed sensors and determines when a wheel or wheels is/are about to lock up. The EBCM controls the motors on the hydraulic modulator assembly to reduce brake pressure to the wheel about to lock up. When the wheel regains traction, the brake pressure is increased until the wheel again approaches lock-up. The cycle repeats until either the vehicle comes to a stop, the brake pedal is released, or no wheels are about to lock up. The EBCM also has the ability to monitor itself and can store

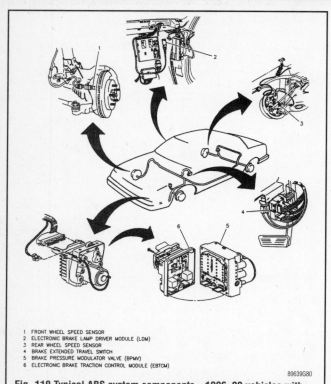

1 FRONT WHEEL SPEED SENSOR
2 ELECTRONIC BRAKE LAMP DRIVER MODULE (LDM)
3 REAR WHEEL SPEED SENSOR
4 BRAKE EXTENDED TRAVEL SWITCH
5 BRAKE PRESSURE MODULATOR VALVE (BPMV)
6 ELECTRONIC BRAKE TRACTION CONTROL MODULE (EBTCM)

89639G80

Fig. 110 Typical ABS system components—1996–99 vehicles with TCS shown, others similar

diagnostic codes in a non-volatile (will not be erased if the battery is disconnected) memory. The EBCM is serviced as an assembly.

The Anti-lock braking system employs 2 modes: base (conventional) braking and anti-lock braking. Under normal braking, the conventional part of the system stops the vehicle. When in the ABS mode, the Electromagnetic Brakes (EMB) action of the ABS system controls the two front wheels individually and the rear wheels together. If the one rear wheel is about to lock up, the hydraulic pressure to both wheels is reduced, controlling both wheels together.

BASIC KNOWLEDGE REQUIRED

Before using this section, it is important that you have a basic knowledge of the following items. Without this basic knowledge, it will be difficult to use the diagnostic procedures contained in this section.

Basic Electrical Circuits—You should understand the basic theory of electricity and know the meaning of voltage, current (amps) and resistance (ohms). You should understand what happens in a circuit with an open or shorted wire. You should be able to read and understand a wiring diagram.

Use Of Circuit Testing Tools—You should know how to use a test light and how to use jumper wires to bypass components to test circuits. You should be familiar with the High Impedance Multimeter (DVM) such as J 34029-A. You should be able to measure voltage, resistance and current and be familiar with the meter controls and how to use them correctly.

ON-BOARD DIAGNOSTICS

These anti-lock braking systems contain sophisticated onboard diagnostics that, when accessed with a bi-directional scan tool, are designed to identify the source of any system fault as specifically as possible, including whether or not the fault is intermittent. There are over 58 diagnostic fault codes to assist with diagnosis.

The last diagnostic fault code to occur is identified, specific ABS data is stored at the time of this fault, and the first five codes set are stored. Additionally, using a bi-directional scan tool, each input and output can be monitored, thus enabling fault confirmation and repair verification. Manual control of components and automated functional tests are also available when using a GM

approved scan tool. Details of many of these functions are contained in the following sections.

ENHANCED DIAGNOSTICS

Enhanced Diagnostic Information, found in the CODE HISTORY function of the bi-directional scan tool, is designed to provide specific fault occurrence information. For each of the first five (5) and the very last diagnostic fault codes stored, data is stored to identify the specific fault code number, the number of failure occurrences, and the number of drive cycles since the failure first and last occurred (a drive cycle occurs when the ignition is turned **ON** and the vehicle is driven faster than 10 mph). However, if a fault is present, the drive cycle counter will increment by turning the ignition **ON** and **OFF**. These first five (5) diagnostic fault codes are also stored in the order of occurrence. The order in which the first 5 faults occurred can be useful in determining if a previous fault is linked to the most recent faults, such as an intermittent wheel speed sensor which later becomes completely open.

During difficult diagnosis situations, this information can be used to identify fault occurrence trends. Does the fault occur more frequently now than it did during the last time when it only failed 1 out of 35 drive cycles? Did the fault only occur once over a large number of drive cycles, indication an unusual condition present when the fault occurred? Does the fault occur infrequently over a large number of drive cycles, indication special diagnosis techniques may be required to identify the source of the fault?

If a fault occurred 1 out of 20 drive cycles, the fault is intermittent and has not reoccurred for 19 drive cycles. This fault may be difficult or impossible to duplicate and may have been caused by a severe vehicle impact (large pot hole, speed bump at high speed, etc.) that momentarily opened an electrical connector or caused unusual vehicle suspension movement. Problem resolution is unlikely, and the problem may never reoccur (check diagnostic aids proved for that code). If the fault occurred 3 out of 15 drive cycles, the odds of finding the cause are still not good, but you know how often it occurs and you can determine whether or not the fault is becoming more frequent based on an additional or past occurrences visit if the source of the problem cannot or could not be found. If the fault occurred 10 out of 20 drive cycles, the odds of finding the cause are very good, as the fault may be easily reproduced.

By using the additional fault data, you can also determine if a failure is randomly intermittent or if it has not reoccurred for long periods of time due to weather changes or a repair prior to this visit. Say a diagnostic fault code occurred 10 of 20 drive cycles but has not reoccurred for 10 drive cycles. This means the failure occurred 10 of 10 drive cycles but has not reoccurred since. A significant environmental change or a repair occurred 10 drive cycles ago. A repair may not be necessary if a recent repair can be confirmed. If no repair was made, the service can focus on diagnosis techniques used to locate difficult to recreate problems.

Diagnostic Procedures

When servicing the anti-lock braking system, the following steps should be followed in order. Failure to follow these steps may result in the loss of important diagnostic data and may lead to difficult and time consuming diagnosis procedures.

1. Connect a bi-directional scan tool, as instructed by the tool manufacturer, then read all current and historical diagnostic codes. Be certain to note which codes are current diagnostic code failures. DO NOT CLEAR CODES unless directed to do so.

2. Using a bi-directional scan tool, read the CODE HISTORY data. Note the diagnostic fault codes stored and their frequency of failure. Specifically note the last failure that occurred and the conditions present when this failure occurred. This last failure should be the starting point for diagnosis and repair.

3. Perform a vehicle preliminary diagnosis inspection. This should include:

a. Inspection of the compact master cylinder for proper brake fluid level.

b. Inspection of the ABS hydraulic modulator for any leaks or wiring damage.

c. Inspection of brake components at all four (4) wheels. Verify no drag exists. Also verify proper brake apply operation.

d. Inspection for worn or damaged wheel bearings that allow a wheel to wobble.

e. Inspection of the wheel speed sensors and their wiring. Verify correct air gap range, solid sensor attachment, undamaged sensor toothed ring, and undamaged wiring, especially at vehicle attachment points.

f. Verify proper outer CV-joint alignment and operation.

g. Verify tires meet legal tread depth requirements.

4. If no codes are present, or mechanical component failure codes are present, perform the automated modulator test using the Tech 1® or T-100® to isolate the cause of the problem. If the failure is intermittent and not reproducible, test drive the vehicle while using the automatic snapshot feature of the bi-directional scan tool.

Perform normal acceleration, stopping, and turning maneuvers. If this does not reproduce the failure, perform an ABS stop, on a low coefficient surface such as gravel, from approximately 30–50 mph (48–80 km/h) while triggering any ABS code. If the failure is still not reproducible, use the enhanced diagnostic information found in CODE HISTORY to determine whether or not this failure should be further diagnosed.

5. Once all system failures have been corrected, clear the ABS codes. The Tech 1® and T-100®, when plugged into the ALDL connector, becomes part of the vehicle's electronic system. The Tech 1® and T-100® can also perform the following functions on components linked by the Serial Data Link (SDL):

- Display ABS data
- Display and clear ABS trouble codes
- Control ABS components
- Perform extensive ABS diagnosis
- Provide diagnostic testing for intermittent ABS conditions

Each test mode has specific diagnosis capabilities which depend upon various keystrokes. In general, five (5) keys control sequencing: YES, NO, EXIT, UP arrow and DOWN arrow. The F0 through F9 keys select operating modes, perform functions within an operating mode, or enter trouble code or model year designations.

In general, the Tech 1® has five (5) test modes for diagnosing the anti-lock brake system. The five (5) test modes are as follows:

MODE F0: DATA LIST—In this test mode, the Tech 1® continuously monitors wheel speed data, brake switch status and other inputs and outputs.

MODE F1: CODE HISTORY—In this mode, fault code history data is displayed. This data includes how many ignition cycles since the fault code occurred, along with other ABS information. The first five (5) and last fault codes set are included in the ABS history data.

MODE F2: TROUBLE CODES—In this test mode, trouble codes stored by the EBCM, both current ignition cycle and history, may be displayed or cleared.

MODE F3: ABS SNAPSHOT—In this test mode, the Tech 1® captures ABS data before and after a fault occurrence or a forced manual trigger.

MODE F4: ABS TESTS—In this test mode, the Tech 1® performs hydraulic modulator functional tests to assist in problem isolation during troubleshooting. Included here is manual control of the motors which is used prior to bleeding the brake system.

Press F7 to covert from English to metric.

INTERMITTENT FAILURES

As with most electronic systems, intermittent failures may be difficult to accurately diagnose. The following is a method to try to isolate an intermittent failure especially wheel speed circuitry failures.

If an ABS fault occurs, the ABS warning light indicator will be on during the ignition cycle in which the fault was detected. If it is an intermittent problem which seems to have corrected itself (ABS warning light off), a history trouble code will be stored. Also stored will be the history data of the code at the time the fault occurred. The Tech 1® must be used to read ABS history data.

INTERMITTENTS AND POOR CONNECTIONS

Most intermittents are caused by faulty electrical connections or wiring, although occasionally a sticking relay or solenoid can be a problem. Some items to check are:

1. Poor mating of connector halves, or terminals not fully seated in the connector body (backed out).

2. Dirt or corrosion on the terminals. The terminals must be clean and free of any foreign material which could impede proper terminal contact.

3. Damaged connector body, exposing the terminals to moisture and dirt, as well as not maintaining proper terminal orientation with the component or mating connector.

4. Improperly formed or damaged terminals. All connector terminals in problem circuits should be checked carefully to ensure good contact tension. Use a corresponding mating terminal to check for proper tension. Refer to "Checking Terminal Contact" later in this section for the specific procedure.

5. The J 35616-A Connector Test Adapter Kit must be used whenever a diagnostic procedure requests checking or probing a terminal. Using the adapter will ensure that no damage to the terminal will occur, as well as giving an idea of whether contact tension is sufficient. If contact tension seems incorrect, refer to "Checking Terminal Contact" later in this section for specifics.

6. Poor terminal-to-wire connection. Checking this requires removing the terminal from the connector body. Some conditions which fall under this description are poor crimps, poor solder joints, crimping over wire insulation rather than the wire itself, corrosion in the wire-to-terminal contact area, etc.

7. Wire insulation which is rubbed through, causing an intermittent short as the bare area touches other wiring or parts of the vehicle.

8. Wiring broken inside the insulation. This condition could cause a continuity check to show a good circuit, but if only 1 or 2 strands of a multi-strand type wire are intact, resistance could be far too high.

Checking Terminal Contact

When diagnosing an electrical system that uses Metri-Pack 150/280/480/630 series terminals (refer to Terminal Repair Kit J 38125-A for terminal identification), it is important to check terminal contact between a connector and component, or between inline connectors, before replacing a suspect component.

Mating terminals must be inspected to ensure good terminal contact. A poor connection between the male and female terminal at a connector may be the result of contamination or deformation.

Contamination is caused by the connector halves being improperly connected, a missing or damaged connector seal, or damage to the connector itself, exposing the terminals to moisture and dirt. Contamination, usually in underhood or underbody connectors, leads to terminal corrosion, causing an open circuit or an intermittently open circuit.

Deformation is caused by probing the mating side of a connector terminal without the proper adapter, improperly joining the connector halves or repeatedly separating and joining the connector halves. Deformation, usually to the female terminal contact tang, can result in poor terminal contact causing an open or intermittently open circuit.

Follow the procedure below to check terminal contact.

1. Separate the connector halves. Refer to Terminal Repair Kit J 38125-A, if available.

2. Inspect the connector halves for contamination. Contamination will result in a white or green buildup within the connector body or between terminals, causing high terminal resistance, intermittent contact or an open circuit. An underhood or underbody connector that shows signs of contamination should be replaced in its entirety: terminals, seals, and connector body.

3. Using an equivalent male terminal from the Terminal Repair Kit J 38125-A, check the retention force of the female terminal in question by inserting and removing the male terminal to the female terminal in the connector body. Good terminal contact will require a certain amount of force to separate the terminals.

4. Using an equivalent female terminal from the Terminal Repair Kit J 38125-A, compare the retention force of this terminal to the female terminal in question by joining and separating the male terminal to the female terminal in question. If the retention force is significantly different between the two female terminals, replace the female terminal in question, using a terminal from Terminal Repair Kit J 38125-A.

Reading Codes

♦ **See Figures 111 and 112**

Diagnostic fault codes can only be read through the use of a bi-directional scan tool, such as GM's Tech 1® or equivalent. There are no provisions for "Flash Code" diagnostics. Follow the scan tool manufacturer's instructions.

DTC	DESCRIPTION	
21	RF Wheel Speed Sensor circuit open or shorted	
22	RF Wheel Speed Sensor signal erratic	
23	RF Wheel Speed Sensor signal missing	
25	LF Wheel Speed Sensor circuit open or shorted	
26	LF Wheel Speed Sensor signal erratic	
27	LF Wheel Speed Sensor signal missing	
31	RR Wheel Speed Sensor circuit open or shorted	
32	RR Wheel Speed Sensor signal erratic	
33	RR Wheel Speed Sensor signal missing	
35	LR Wheel Speed Sensor circuit open or shorted	
36	LR Wheel Speed Sensor signal erratic	
37	LR Wheel Speed Sensor signal missing	
41	RF Inlet Valve circuit open or shorted	
42	RF Outlet Valve circuit open or shorted	
44	LF Isolation Valve circuit open or shorted	
45	Power Interruption Fault	
46	LF Outlet Valve circuit open or shorted	
48	RF Isolation Valve circuit open or shorted	
51	RR Inlet Valve circuit open or shorted	
52	RR Outlet Valve circuit open or shorted	
55	LR Inlet Valve circuit open or shorted	
56	LR Outlet Valve circuit open or shorted	
61	Pump Motor Circuit Test	
62	Low Brake Pedal during an ABS stop	
71	EBCM/EBTCM internal failure	
72	Brake Switch circuit open or shorted	
73	Fluid Level Switch circuit open or shorted	
74	Pressure Switch circuit open or shorted	
75	PCM requested TCS to be disabled	
76	UART SDL circuit or signal malfunction	
77	Delivered Torque Circuit open or shorted	

89639G76

Fig. 111 ABS Diagnostic Trouble Codes—1994–95 vehicles

DTC	DESCRIPTION
C1211	ABS Indicator Lamp Circuit Malfunction
C1214	Solenoid Valve Relay Contact Circuit Open
C1216	Solenoid Valve Relay Coil Circuit Open
C1217	BPMV Pump Motor Relay Contact Circuit Open
C1221	LF Wheel Speed Sensor Input Signal = 0
C1222	RF Wheel Speed Sensor Input Signal = 0
C1223	LR Wheel Speed Sensor Input Signal = 0
C1224	RR Wheel Speed Sensor Input Signal = 0
C1225	LF WSS - Excessive Wheel Speed Variation
C1226	RF WSS - Excessive Wheel Speed Variation
C1227	LR WSS - Excessive Wheel Speed Variation
C1228	RR WSS - Excessive Wheel Speed Variation
C1232	LF Wheel Speed Sensor Circuit Open Or Shorted
C1233	RF Wheel Speed Sensor Circuit Open Or Shorted
C1234	LR Wheel Speed Sensor Circuit Open Or Shorted
C1235	RR Wheel Speed Sensor Circuit Open Or Shorted
C1236	Low System Voltage
C1237	High System Voltage
C1238	Brake Thermal Model Exceeded
C1241	MAGNASTEER Circuit Malfunction
C1242	BPMV Pump Motor Ground Circuit Open
C1243	BPMV Pump Motor Stalled
C1255	EBTCM Internal Malfunction (ABS/TCS Disabled)
C1256	EBTCM Internal Malfunction
C1261	LF Hold Valve Solenoid Malfunction
C1262	LF Release Valve Solenoid Malfunction
C1263	RF Hold Valve Solenoid Malfunction
C1264	RF Release Valve Solenoid Malfunction
C1265	LR Hold Valve Solenoid Malfunction
C1266	LR Release Valve Solenoid Malfunction
C1267	RR Hold Valve Solenoid Malfunction
C1268	RR Release Valve Solenoid Malfunction
C1271	LF TCS Master Cylinder Isolation Valve Malfunction
C1272	LF TCS Prime Valve Malfunction
C1273	RF TCS Master Cylinder Isolation Valve Malfunction
C1274	RF TCS Prime Valve Malfunction
C1275	PCM Serial Data Malfunction
C1276	Delivered Torque Signal Malfunction
C1277	Requested Torque Signal Malfunction
C1278	TCS Temporarily Inhibited By PCM
C1291	Open Brake Lamp Switch During Deceleration
C1293	DTC C1291 Set In Current Or Previous Ignition Cycle
C1294	Brake Lamp Switch Circuit Always Closed
C1295	Brake Lamp Switch Circuit Open

89639G81

Fig. 112 ABS Diagnostic Trouble Codes—1996–99 vehicles

Clearing Codes

The trouble codes in EBCM memory are erased with a Tech 1® or equivalent scan tool, using the "Clear DTCs" function. Make sure to check for proper system operation and absence of DTCs when the clearing procedure is completed. The DTCs cannot be cleared by unplugging the EBCM, disconnecting the battery cables, or turning the ignition **OFF**.

ABS Service

PRECAUTIONS

Failure to observe the following precautions may result in system damage.
• Performing diagnostic work on the ABS-VI requires the use of a Tech 1® Scan diagnostic tool or equivalent. If unavailable, please refer diagnostic work to a qualified technician.
• Before performing electric arc welding on the vehicle, disconnect the Electronic Brake Control Module (EBCM) and the hydraulic modulator connectors.
• When performing painting work on the vehicle, do not expose the Electronic Brake Control Module (EBCM) to temperatures in excess of 185°F (85°C) for longer than 2 hours. The system may be exposed to temperatures up to 200°F (95°C) for less than 15 minutes.
• Never disconnect or connect the Electronic Brake Control Module (EBCM) or hydraulic modulator connectors with the ignition switch **ON** or damage to the system will occur.
• Never disassemble any component of the Anti-Lock Brake System (ABS) which is designated non-serviceable; the component must be replaced as an assembly.
• When filling the master cylinder, always use Delco Supreme 11 brake fluid or equivalent, which meets DOT 3 specifications; petroleum-base fluid will destroy the rubber parts.

Electronic Brake Control Module (EBCM)

REMOVAL & INSTALLATION

➡**Vehicles with the Traction Control System (TCS) are equipped with an Electronic Brake and Traction Control Module (EBTCM).**

1994–95 Vehicles

◆ **See Figure 113**

1. Make sure the ignition switch is in the **OFF** position. Disconnect the negative battery cable.
2. Detach the EBCM (or EBTCM) electrical connector by rotating the locking clip forward.
3. Unfasten the module retaining nuts.
4. Remove the EBCM/EBTCM by sliding it up and away from the strut tower.
To install:
5. Position the EBCM/EBTCM into the lower locating slot, then slide it downward.

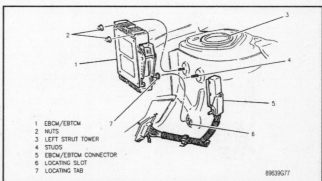

1 EBCM/EBTCM
2 NUTS
3 LEFT STRUT TOWER
4 STUDS
5 EBCM/EBTCM CONNECTOR
6 LOCATING SLOT
7 LOCATING TAB

89639G77

Fig. 113 The EBCM/EBTCM is mounted to the left strut tower on 1994–95 vehicles

6. Install the retaining nuts and tighten to 96 inch lbs. (11 Nm).
7. Attach the EBCM/EBTCM electrical connector.
8. Connect the negative battery cable.

1996–99 Vehicles

1. Make sure the ignition switch is in the **OFF** position, then disconnect the negative battery cable.
2. Remove the air cleaner assembly and the Powertrain Control Module (PCM) cover.
3. Detach the EBCM/EBTCM electrical connector and motor ground cable connector.
4. Remove the EBCM/EBTCM bracket from the vehicle.

➡ On 1996–99 vehicles, the PMV is referred to as the Brake Pressure Modulator Valve (BPMV), and is attached to the EBCM/EBTCM.

5. Unfasten the 4 EBCM/EBTCM-to-Brake Pressure Modulator Valve (BPMV) bolts.
6. Remove the EBCM/EBTCM by pulling it rearward, until the internal connector disengages. Do NOT twist the unit.

❊❊ WARNING

Do NOT pry the EBCM/EBTCM. Be careful not to damage the seal, if reusing the module. If the seal gets damaged during removal, repair with a suitable silicone sealer or replace the module.

To install:

7. Clean the EBCM/EBTCM seal and BPMV gasket with alcohol. Position the EBCM/EBTCM to the BPMV and install the 4 retaining bolts. Tighten the bolts to 40 inch lbs. (4.5 Nm).
8. Install the EBCM/EBTCM bracket and tighten the center bracket mounting bolt to 10 ft. lbs. (14 Nm).
9. Attach the EBCM/EBTCM harness connector and the motor ground cable connector. Make sure the lock tab is securely fastened.
10. Install the PCM cover and air cleaner assembly.
11. Connect the negative battery cable.

Electronic Brake Lamp Driver Module (LDM)

REMOVAL & INSTALLATION

▶ **See Figure 114**

➡ Only 1996–99 vehicles are equipped with the Electronic Brake Lamp Driver Module (LDM).

1. Disconnect the negative battery cable.
2. Remove the instrument panel glove compartment.
3. Unsnap the LDM from the mall bracket.
4. Open the LDM endcap and remove the circuit board by pulling it straight out.

To install:

5. Position the circuit board into the LDM case and close the endcap. Be careful not to damage the circuit board.
6. Snap the LDM into the mall bracket clip.
7. Install the glove compartment.
8. Connect the negative battery cable.

ABS Pump Relay

LOCATION

The ABS pump relay is located at the center rear of the engine compartment, below the left side underhood fuse block (behind the maxifuse/relay center cover).

Anti-lock Diode

LOCATION

The anti-lock diode is taped to the wiring harness near the EBCM/EBTCM.

Wheel Speed Sensors

REMOVAL & INSTALLATION

Front

1994–95 VEHICLES

▶ **See Figure 115**

1. Disconnect the negative battery cable.
2. Raise and safely support the vehicle. Remove the tire and wheel assembly.
3. Detach the wheel speed sensor electrical connector.
4. Remove the front hub and bearing assembly. Clean the dirt from the sensor housing and sensor interface area.
5. Gently pry the wheel speed sensor slinger off, using a suitable prytool. Discard the old slinger.
6. Remove the sensor by gently prying the bearing assembly off with a suitable prytool.
7. Do not let debris get into the bearing while the sensor is removed. Do not add lubricant to the bearing through the sensor housing opening. The bearing is lubricated for the life of the vehicle. Do not clean the grease from the toothed sensor ring. The grease won't affect the sensor operation.
8. Inspect the bearing and sensor cap for any indication of water or debris entry. If you find any water or debris, you must replace the hub and bearing assembly.

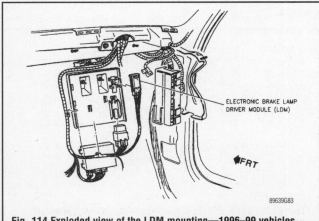

Fig. 114 Exploded view of the LDM mounting—1996–99 vehicles

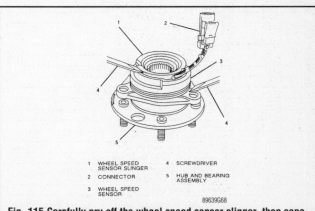

Fig. 115 Carefully pry off the wheel speed sensor slinger, then separate the hub and bearing from the sensor—1994–95 vehicles

To install:

9. Clean the sealant from the outer diameter of the bearing hub using a clean, lint free cloth.

10. Apply Loctite® 262, or equivalent locking fixative to the groove in the outer diameter of the
bearing hub, per the directions in the service kit.

11. Using tool J-38764 or equivalent and a press, install the sensor.

12. Install the hub and bearing assembly and attach the sensor connector.

13. Install the tire and wheel assembly, then carefully lower the vehicle.

14. Connect the negative battery cable.

1996–99 VEHICLES

1. Disconnect the negative battery cable.

2. Raise and safely support the vehicle. Remove the wheel and tire assembly.

3. Detach the wheel speed sensor electrical connector.

4. Remove the front hub and bearing assembly. Clean the dirt from the sensor housing and sensor interface area.

5. Using a split plate puller, tool J 22912-01 or equivalent, remove the sensor from the bearing assembly.

6. Do not let debris get into the bearing while the sensor is removed. Do not add lubricant to the bearing through the sensor housing opening. The bearing is lubricated for the life of the vehicle. Do not clean the grease from the toothed sensor ring. The grease won't affect the sensor operation.

7. Inspect the bearing and sensor cap for any indication of water or debris entry. If you find any water or debris, you must replace the hub and bearing assembly.

To install:

8. Apply Loctite® 620 to the groove in the outer diameter of the bearing hub, as instructed in the service kit.

9. Place the hub and bearing on a suitable stud protector ring.

10. Install the sensor, using a front wheel speed sensor installation tool, to press the sensor into place.

11. Install the hub and bearing assembly.

12. Attach the wheel speed sensor electrical connector.

13. Install the wheel and tire assembly, then carefully lower the vehicle.

14. Connect the negative battery cable.

Rear

▶ See Figure 116

1. Disconnect the negative battery cable.

2. Raise and safely support the vehicle. Remove the wheel and tire assembly.

3. Detach the wheel speed sensor electrical connector.

4. Unfasten the lower strut attaching nut and bolt.

5. Clean the dirt from the sensor housing and interface area.

6. Unfasten the sensor Torx® mounting screws using a T15 bit, then remove the sensor.

7. Do not let debris get into the bearing while the sensor is removed. Do not add lubricant to the bearing through the sensor housing opening. The bearing is lubricated for the life of the vehicle. Do not clean the grease from the toothed sensor ring. The grease won't affect the sensor operation.

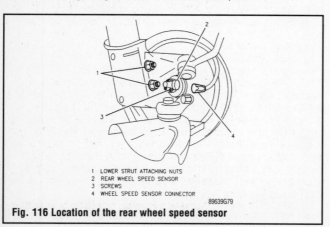

1   LOWER STRUT ATTACHING NUTS
2   REAR WHEEL SPEED SENSOR
3   SCREWS
4   WHEEL SPEED SENSOR CONNECTOR

89639G79

Fig. 116 Location of the rear wheel speed sensor

8. Inspect the bearing and sensor cap for any indication of water or debris entry. If you find any water or debris, you must replace the hub and bearing assembly.

9. Check the sensor ring and sensor for contact. If contact is found, the complete hub and bearing nut be replaced.

To install:

10. Lubricate a new sensor O-ring, then install the sensor to the housing.

11. Install the Torx® screws in a spiral pattern and tighten to 25 inch lbs. (2.8 Nm).

12. Install the lower strut attaching bolt and tighten to 140 ft. lbs. (190 Nm).

13. Attach the wheel speed sensor electrical connector.

14. Install the tire and wheel assembly, then carefully lower the vehicle.

15. Tighten the lug nuts to 100 ft. lbs. (136 Nm). Connect the negative battery cable.

Wheel Speed Sensors Reluctor Ring

REMOVAL & INSTALLATION

The toothed wheels which rotate past the speed sensors are integral parts of their respective assemblies. If the front ring is damaged, the drive axle must be replaced. If a rear ring is damaged, the hub and bearing assembly must be replaced.

Pressure Modulator Valve (PMV) Assembly

REMOVAL & INSTALLATION

1994–95 Vehicles

▶ See Figures 107 and 108

1. Remove the air cleaner assembly.

2. Disconnect the negative battery cable.

3. Label and disconnect the following wiring connectors from the PMV assembly:

   a. Fluid level switch

   b. Pump motor

   c. Valve block

4. Loosen or reposition the clamp on the hose at the PMV reservoir.

5. Disconnect the hose from the reservoir. Catch escaping fluid in a clean container, then plug the hose with a 5⁄8 inch (15.5mm) diameter plug.

6. Disconnect the primary and secondary brake lines at the PMV.

7. Disconnect the 4 brake lines from the PMV assembly.

8. Raise and safely support the vehicle.

9. Remove the lower PMV assembly retaining bolt.

10. Carefully lower the vehicle.

11. Remove the harness strap.

12. Support the PMV assembly, then remove the upper retaining bolts. Remove the assembly from the vehicle. If the unit is being replaced with another, the reservoir and bracket(s) must be transferred to the new assembly.

➡The PMV assembly is not serviceable. Do not attempt to disassemble any part of the unit.

To install:

13. Position the PMV assembly and install the upper retaining bolts. Tighten the bolts to 20 ft. lbs. (27 Nm).

14. Install the harness.

15. Raise and safely support the vehicle. Install the lower retaining bolt and tighten it to 20 ft. lbs. (27 Nm). Lower the vehicle.

16. Connect the 4 brake lines to the PMV. Tighten each line to 11 ft. lbs. (15 Nm).

17. Install the primary and secondary brake lines, tightening each to 11 ft. lbs. (15 Nm).

18. Connect the hose to the PMV reservoir and secure the clamp.

19. Attach the electrical connectors to the PMV assembly; make certain each connector is squarely seated and firmly retained.

20. Connect the negative battery cable.

21. Install the air cleaner assembly.

22. Fill the brake fluid reservoir.
23. Fill and bleed the hydraulic brake system, then perform the "Auto Bleed Procedure" as outlined in this section.
24. Clean any spilled brake fluid from the PMV assembly and surrounding area to prevent damage to other components or paint work.

1996–99 Vehicles

➡On 1996–99 vehicles, the PMV is referred to as the Brake Pressure Modulator Valve (BPMV), and is attached to the EBCM/EBTCM.

✳✳ CAUTION

Due to safety reasons, the BPMV must be repaired or disassembled, the complete unit must be replaced. With the exception of the EBCM/EBTCM, no screws may be loosened. If the screws are loosened, it will not be possible to get the brake circuits leak-tight and personal injury may result.

1. Make sure the ignition switch is in the **OFF** position, then disconnect the negative battery cable.
2. Remove the air cleaner assembly and the PCM cover.
3. Detach the EBCM/EBTCM electrical connector and motor ground cable connector.
4. Disconnect the brake pipe fittings, using a flare nut wrench. Note the location of the pipes for installation purposes.

✳✳ WARNING

When removing the BPMV, protect the vehicle's painted surfaces from possible brake fluid spillage. Do not allow any brake fluid to come in contact with a painted surface; it will damage the paint.

5. Remove the EBCM/EBTCM bracket and mounting bolt.

➡Reposition the brake pipes as necessary to remove the BPMV. Excessive bending may damage the pipes.

6. Remove the upper BPMV bracket from the frame rail.
7. Remove the EBCM/BPMV assembly from the vehicle.
8. Unfasten the 4 EBCM-to-BPMV bolts, then separate the EBCM from the BPMV, pulling rearward until separated.

✳✳ WARNING

Do NOT pry the EBCM/EBTCM. Be careful not to damage the seal, if reusing the module. If the seal gets damaged during removal, repair with a suitable silicone sealer or replace the module.

9. Clean the EBCM seal and BPMV gasket surface with alcohol.
To install:
10. Position the EBCM to the BPMV. Tighten the 4 mounting bolts to 40 inch lbs. (4.5 Nm), and the center bolt with the bracket to 10 ft. lbs. (14 Nm).
11. Position the BPMV bracket to the BPMV. If a new BPMV is being installed, remove the shipping plugs from the valve openings.
12. Place the EBCM/BPMV assembly into the vehicle. Tighten the frame rail bracket bolts to 106 inch lbs. (12 Nm).

✳✳ CAUTION

Make sure the brake pipes are correctly connected to the BPMV. If the pipes are accidentally switched, wheel lock-up will occur, causing possible personal injury. The only 2 ways this condition can be detected are with a scan tool, or performing an "anti-lock" stop.

13. Connect the brake pipe fittings, in the locations noted during removal. Tighten the fittings to 13 ft. lbs. (18 Nm).
14. Attach the EBCM harness connector and the motor ground cable connector. Make sure the lock tab is securely fastened.
15. Install the PCM cover and air cleaner assembly.
16. Connect the negative battery cable.
17. Fill and bleed the hydraulic brake system, then perform the "Auto Bleed Procedure" as outlined in this section.

PMV Fluid Level Sensor

The fluid level sensor is integrated with the PMV reservoir. If the sensor fails, the reservoir must be replaced.

Filling and Bleeding

✳✳ WARNING

Do NOT allow brake fluid to spill on or come in contact with the vehicle's finish as it will remove the paint. In case of a spill, immediately flush the area with water.

SYSTEM FILLING

The master cylinder reservoirs must be kept properly filled to prevent air from entering the system. No special filling procedures are required because of the anti-lock system.

When adding fluid, use only DOT 3 fluid; the use of DOT 5 or silicone fluids is specifically prohibited. Use of improper or contaminated fluid may cause the fluid to boil or cause the rubber components in the system to deteriorate. Never use any fluid with a petroleum base or any fluid which has been exposed to water or moisture.

SYSTEM BLEEDING

Auto Bleed Procedure

1994–99 VEHICLES

The auto-bleed procedure is used to provide a complete brake system bleed on vehicles with ABS. The procedure cycles the system valves and runs the pump to purge air from secondary circuits normally closed off during non-ABS/TCS mode operation and bleeding. It is to be used when it is suspected that air has been ingested into the systems secondary circuits, or when the BPMV has been replaced.

To successfully perform this procedure, you will need the following equipment:

- Scan tool
- Pressure brake bleeder that can produce at least 30 psi
- Jack and stands to safely support the vehicle.
- Clean plastic bleeder bottle with a hose that fits snugly on the bleeder valves. The other end of the hose should protrude into the bottle, with its end immersed in brake fluid.
- Assistant to pump the brake pedal during the procedure.
- Suitable safety apparel, including goggles.

1. Raise and safely support the vehicle.
2. Remove all 4 wheel and tire assemblies.
3. Check the brake system for leaks and/or component damage. If any if found, they must be fixed before performing the procedure.
4. Make sure the vehicle's battery is in a full state of charge.
5. Connect a Tech 1® or equivalent scan tool to the DLC.
6. Turn the ignition to the **RUN** position, but do NOT start the engine.
7. Establish communications with the scan tool and select ABS/TCS features.
8. Select "Special Tests".
9. Select "Automated Bleed Procedure".
10. Bleed the base brakes as outlined earlier in this section.
11. Follow the scan tool menu driven instructions until the proper brake pedal height is achieved. If any malfunctions are found, the bleed procedure will be aborted. If DTCs are present, the scan tool will display "DTCs PRESENT" or list the DTCs depending on when the DTCs were set. The DTCs can be displayed or cleared as appropriate in the "Trouble Codes" mode. Refer to the code list earlier in this section for ABS codes. If the test is aborted, but no codes are found, check and correct all system malfunctions before attempting the bleed procedure again. If a road test is necessary for diagnosis, and the brake pedal feels spongy, perform a conventional brake bleed, making sure to achieve a firm brake pedal before driving the vehicle.
12. When the Auto Bleed Procedure is complete, depress the brake pedal. It

should be high and firm. If not, re-inspect the brake system thoroughly for any conditions which could cause excess brake pedal travel. If the brake system is OK, but the excessive brake pedal travel exists, repeat the Auto Bleed Procedure.

13. Disconnect the scan tool. Reinstall the wheel and tire assemblies, then carefully lower the vehicle. Check the fluid level in the reservoir and add if necessary. Road test the vehicle, making several ABS and Traction Control actuations in a suitable area. The brake pedal should stay high and firm after the road test.

BRAKE SPECIFICATIONS
All measurements in inches unless noted

Year	Model	Master Cylinder Bore	Brake Disc			Brake Drum Diameter			Wheel Cylinder or Caliper Bore	
			Original Thickness	Minimum Thickness	Maximum Runout	Original Inside Diameter	Max. Wear Limit	Maximum Machine Diameter	Front	Rear
1986	LeSabre	0.937	1.043	0.972	0.004	8.860	8.909	8.880	2.52	0.937
	Delta 88	0.937	1.043	0.972	0.004	8.860	8.909	8.880	2.52	0.937
1987	Bonneville	0.937	1.043	0.972	0.004	8.860	8.909	8.880	2.52	0.937
	LeSabre	0.937	1.043	0.972	0.004	8.860	8.909	8.880	2.52	0.937
	Delta 88	0.937	1.043	0.972	0.004	8.860	8.909	8.880	2.52	0.937
1988	Bonneville	0.937	1.043	0.972	0.004	8.860	8.909	8.880	2.52	0.937
	LeSabre	0.937	1.043	0.972	0.004	8.860	8.909	8.880	2.52	0.937
	Delta 88	0.937	1.043	0.972	0.004	8.860	8.909	8.880	2.52	0.937
1989	Bonneville	0.937	1.043	0.972	0.004	8.860	8.909	8.880	2.52	0.937
	LeSabre	0.937	1.043	0.972	0.004	8.860	8.909	8.880	2.52	0.937
	Delta 88	0.937	1.043	0.972	0.004	8.860	8.909	8.880	2.52	0.937
1990	Bonneville	0.937	1.043	0.972	0.004	8.860	8.909	8.880	2.52	0.937
	LeSabre	0.937	1.043	0.972	0.004	8.860	8.909	8.880	2.52	0.937
	Delta 88	0.937	1.043	0.972	0.004	8.860	8.909	8.880	2.52	0.937
1991	Bonneville	1.000	1.043	0.972	0.004	8.860	8.909	8.880	2.52	0.937
	LeSabre	1.000	1.043	0.972	0.004	8.860	8.809	8.880	2.52	0.937
	Delta 88	1.000	1.043	0.972	0.004	8.860	8.909	8.880	2.52	0.937
1992	Bonneville	1.000	1.276	1.224	0.004	8.860	8.909	8.880	2.52	0.937
	LeSabre	1.000	1.276	1.224	0.004	8.860	8.809	8.880	2.52	0.937
	Delta 88	1.000	1.276	1.224	0.004	8.860	8.909	8.880	2.52	0.937
1993	Bonneville	1.000	1.276	1.224	0.004	8.860	8.909	8.880	2.52	0.937
	LeSabre	1.000	1.276	1.224	0.004	8.860	8.809	8.880	2.52	0.937
	Delta 88	1.000	1.276	1.224	0.004	8.860	8.909	8.880	2.52	0.937
1994	Bonneville	1.000	1.260	1.224	0.002	8.863	8.909	8.920	2.50	0.937
	LeSabre	1.000	1.260	1.244	0.002	8.863	8.809	8.920	2.50	0.937
	Delta 88	1.000	1.260	1.244	0.002	8.863	8.909	8.920	2.50	0.937
1995	Bonneville	1.000	1.260	1.224	0.002	8.863	8.909	8.920	2.50	0.937
	LeSabre	1.000	1.260	1.244	0.002	8.863	8.809	8.920	2.50	0.937
	Delta 88	1.000	1.260	1.244	0.002	8.863	8.909	8.920	2.50	0.937
1996	Bonneville	1.000	1.260	1.224	0.002	8.863	8.909	8.920	2.50	0.937
	LeSabre	1.000	1.260	1.244	0.002	8.863	8.809	8.920	2.50	0.937
	Delta 88	1.000	1.260	1.244	0.002	8.863	8.909	8.920	2.50	0.937
1997	Bonneville	1.000	1.260	1.224	0.002	8.863	8.909	8.920	2.50	0.937
	LeSabre	1.000	1.260	1.244	0.002	8.863	8.809	8.920	2.50	0.937
	Delta 88	1.000	1.260	1.244	0.002	8.863	8.909	8.920	2.50	0.937
1998	Bonneville	1.000	1.260	1.224	0.002	8.863	8.909	8.920	2.50	0.937
	LeSabre	1.000	1.260	1.244	0.002	8.863	8.809	8.920	2.50	0.937
	Delta 88	1.000	1.260	1.244	0.002	8.863	8.909	8.920	2.50	0.937
1999	Bonneville	1.000	1.260	1.224	0.002	8.863	8.909	8.920	2.50	0.937
	LeSabre	1.000	1.260	1.244	0.002	8.863	8.809	8.920	2.50	0.937
	Eighty Eight	1.000	1.260	1.244	0.002	8.863	8.909	8.920	2.50	0.937

89639C01

EXTERIOR 10-2
DOORS 10-2
  ADJUSTMENT 10-2
HOOD 10-2
  REMOVAL & INSTALLATION 10-2
  ALIGNMENT 10-3
TRUNK LID 10-4
  REMOVAL & INSTALLATION 10-4
  ALIGNMENT 10-4
GRILLE 10-4
  REMOVAL & INSTALLATION 10-4
OUTSIDE MIRRORS 10-5
  REMOVAL & INSTALLATION 10-5
  MIRROR FACE REPLACEMENT 10-5
SUNROOF 10-5
  REMOVAL & INSTALLATION 10-5
  MOTOR SYNCHRONIZATION 10-6
  TRACK ASSEMBLY
    SYNCHRONIZATION 10-6
INTERIOR 10-8
INSTRUMENT PANEL AND PAD 10-8
  REMOVAL & INSTALLATION 10-8
CONSOLE 10-12
  REMOVAL & INSTALLATION 10-12
DOOR PANELS 10-14
  REMOVAL & INSTALLATION 10-14
DOOR LOCKS 10-17
  REMOVAL & INSTALLATION 10-17
DOOR LOCK CYLINDER 10-17
  REMOVAL & INSTALLATION 10-17
DOOR GLASS AND REGULATOR 10-18
  REMOVAL & INSTALLATION 10-18
WINDOW ACTUATOR 10-19
  REMOVAL & INSTALLATION 10-20
WINDSHIELD AND FIXED GLASS 10-20
  REMOVAL & INSTALLATION 10-20
  WINDSHIELD CHIP REPAIR 10-20
INSIDE REAR VIEW MIRROR 10-20
  REMOVAL & INSTALLATION 10-20
POWER SEAT MOTOR 10-21
  REMOVAL & INSTALLATION 10-21
  ADJUSTMENT 10-21
SPECIFICATIONS CHART
  TORQUE SPECIFICATIONS 10-22

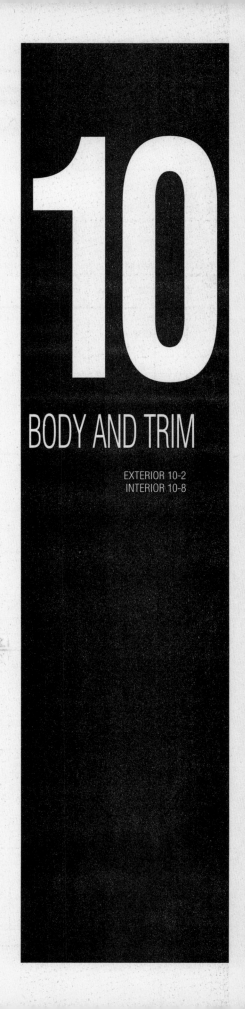

10

BODY AND TRIM

EXTERIOR 10-2
INTERIOR 10-8

EXTERIOR

Doors

ADJUSTMENT

Striker

▶ **See Figures 1, 2 and 3**

1. Loosen the door striker. On some models, the striker itself is turned with a Torx® head tool while others use 2 bolts to retain the striker.
2. Tighten the bolts finger-tight, so you can move striker with light force.
3. Hold the outside handle and gently push door against body to ensure a proper fit.
4. Unlatch and open the door.

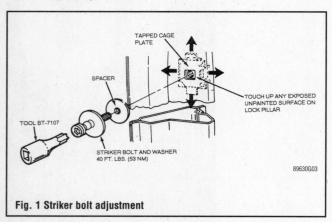

Fig. 1 Striker bolt adjustment

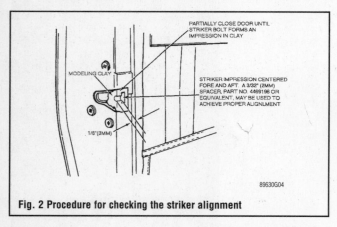

Fig. 2 Procedure for checking the striker alignment

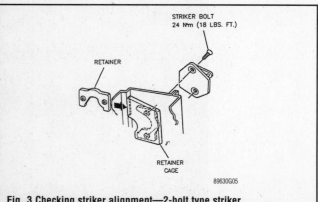

Fig. 3 Checking striker alignment—2-bolt type striker

5. Tighten the striker.
6. Check the alignment, repeat as steps as necessary.
7. Touch up the painted area so that unprotected metal doesn't show, in order to avoid rust.

Door

▶ **See Figure 4**

➡ **Adjust the door fore-aft or up-down as follows with the following procedure.**

1. Loosen nuts and move door to front or rear as necessary.
2. Loosen bolts and move door in, out, up or down as necessary.

✳✳ WARNING

Take care not to damage the body or painted surfaces by closing a misaligned door too hard.

3. Adjust the door hinges until the door and body edges are parallel and the door is flush-to-1/16 inch (1.6mm) out from the fender. It may be necessary to repeat the steps a few times to obtain the best alignment.

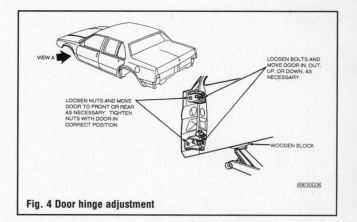

Fig. 4 Door hinge adjustment

Hood

REMOVAL & INSTALLATION

▶ **See Figures 5 thru 10**

1. Raise the hood. Install protective coverings over the fenders, to prevent damage to the paint and moldings when removing or installing the hood.
2. Disconnect the underhood lamp wire.
3. Mark the position of the hinge on the hood to lid in alignment when hood is reinstalled.
4. Use extreme care and remove the spring from hinge, if equipped.
5. With the hood supported, loosen the ball socket retainers, then pry off the assist rods.
6. With an assistant's help supporting the hood, remove the hinge-to-hood screws and bolts on each side of the hood.
7. With the help of an assistant, carefully remove the hood.
To install:
8. With an assistant's help, align the hood with the marks made during removal.
9. Install the hood to hinge screws on each side of the hood and hand-tighten.
10. Install the hood hinge spring, if equipped.
11. Align the hood and tighten the retaining bolts to 21–24 ft. lbs. (29–33 Nm).
12. If equipped, install the open assist rods.
13. Connect the underhood lamp wire.

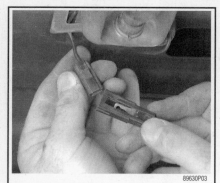

Fig. 5 If equipped, unplug the underhood lamp wiring

Fig. 6 Use a suitable paint marker or equivalent to matchmark the hood hinges

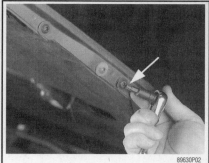

Fig. 7 On some vehicles, you must use a ratchet with a Torx® socket to remove the hood retainers

Fig. 8 Check under the hood insulation for any hidden hood mounting bolts . . .

Fig. 9 . . . then, with someone supporting the hood, remove the retaining bolts

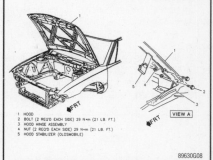

Fig. 10 Exploded view of the hood and retainers—1998 vehicle shown, others similar

ALIGNMENT

Hood

▸ See Figure 11

Fore and aft adjustment may be made at the hinge-to-hood attaching screws. Vertical adjustment at the front may be made by adjusting the rubber bumpers up or down. These adjustment may require several steps. Take care to lower the hood slowly each time. If the hood is closed hard when it is not aligned, you can damage the body or painted surface.

Hood Primary Latch

1. Loosen the bolts and set the hood primary latch so that the top edge of the latch is 2.4 in. (61mm) from the top of the radiator support. This will be the starting point for up/down latch adjustment. The bolts should be snugged to hold the latch in position.

2. Carefully lower the hood, but do not allow the striker to engage with the latch. Check the side-to-side adjustment of the latch to the striker. Raise the hood and tighten the primary latch bolts to 84 inch lbs. (9 Nm).

3. You must perform a drop test to determine if an up/down latch adjustment is necessary. The hood drop test will determine the amount of drop force required for the striker to fully engage with the latch.

　a. Place a millimeter and inch ruler, between the hood and fender.

　b. Raise the hood so the front upper edge is 3⅛ in. (80mm) above the top surface of the fender. This part of the test will determine if the latch is set too high.

　c. Drop the hood. The striker should not engage with the latch.

　d. Repeat the test by increasing the measurement to 3¾ in. (95mm). If the striker engages with the latch below a 4¼ in. (110mm) test height, the latch is too high.

　e. Repeat the test at 4¼ in. (110mm) and 6⅜ in. (160mm). The striker should engage in this range. If the striker does not engage at 6⅜ in. (160mm), the latch is too low.

　f. Adjust the latch as necessary, then tighten the bolts to 84 inch lbs. (9.5 Nm).

　g. Check the latch for proper operation.

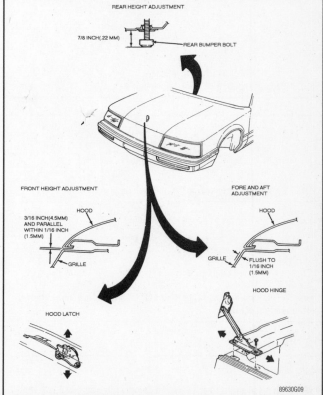

Fig. 11 Hood and latch adjustment and alignment specifications— LeSabre shown, other models similar

Trunk Lid

REMOVAL & INSTALLATION

▶ **See Figures 12 and 13**

1. Prop the lid open and place protective covering along the edges of the rear compartment opening to prevent damage to the painted areas.
2. If equipped, remove the lid trim panel by unfastening the push-in retainers, then remove the trim panel.
3. If necessary, disconnect the wiring harness from the lid. Connect a piece of string to the end of the wiring connector, then pull the wiring through.
4. Mark the location of the hinge strap-to-lid attaching bolts.

➡**Before removing the trunk lid bolts, loosen all of them evenly.**

5. While a helper supports the lid, loosen all of the hinge-to-lid bolts, then remove the bolts and carefully remove the lid.

To install:

6. Have an assistant help you maneuver the trunk lid in position, aligning the marks made during removal.
7. With the help of an assistant, align the lid, then install and hand-tighten all the bolts.
8. Realign the lid as necessary, and tighten the hinge-to-lid attaching bolts to 18–24 ft. lbs. (25–33 Nm).
9. Using the string, pull the wiring back through the trunk lid.
10. If equipped, install the lid trim panel by inserting the push-in retainers.

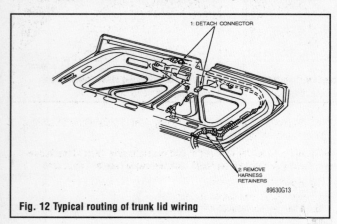

Fig. 12 Typical routing of trunk lid wiring

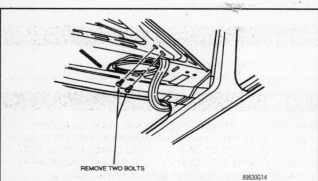

Fig. 13 Trunk lid-to-hinge retaining bolt locations—LeSabre shown, other models similar

ALIGNMENT

▶ **See Figure 14**

➡**Make sure that the rubber overslam bumpers are screwed into the trunk lid completely. Do NOT loosen the overslam bumpers to make an adjustment.**

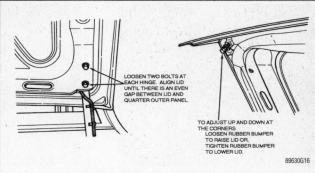

Fig. 14 Trunk lid adjustments—LeSabre shown, other vehicles similar

Fore/Aft Adjustment and Flushness

1. With the lid closed, check the fore/aft adjustment of the trunk lid at the rear corners of the lid. Also, check the flushness of the lid to the quarters. If adjustment is necessary, loosen the trunk lid-to-hinge bolts and adjust the lid.
2. Tighten the hinge bolts to 18–24 ft. lbs. (25–33 Nm).
3. If the trunk lid is not flush at the rear, loosen the inner latch striker mounting nut, then close the trunk.
4. From beneath the rear bumper fascia, mark the vertical location of the outer latch striker mounting nuts.
5. Loosen the outer latch striker mounting nuts. The latch should move upward. If the latch striker does not move, it's probably at the top of its adjustment range. This will require that an adjustment be made to the latch assembly.
6. Check that the trunk lid remains flush to the quarter panels, then tighten the outer latch striker mounting nuts to 80 inch lbs. (9 Nm).
7. Tighten the inner latch striker mounting nuts to 80 inch lbs. (9 Nm).

Lid-to-Quarter Gaps

1. With the trunk lid closed, inspect the trunk lid-to-quarter panel gaps, $^3\!/_{32}$–$^1\!/_8$ in. (3–4mm) at the front and rear corners of the lid. If the proper gaps are present, latch striker adjustments may be necessary. If the proper gaps are not present, the trunk lid will have to be adjusted, as follows:
   a. Remove the rear shelf speaker covers.
   b. Loosen the lid hinge-to-rear shelf attachments.
   c. Position the trunk in the opening to get the proper gaps.
2. Loosen the latch mounting bolts.
3. With an assistant in the trunk, gently close the lid until the latch contacts the latch striker. Hold the lid down and have the assistant snug the latch mounting bolts.
4. Raise the trunk lid, then tighten the latch mounting bolts to 93 inch lbs. (10.5 Nm).
5. Tighten the hinge-to-shelf bolts to 13 ft. lbs. (18 Nm).
6. Check the trunk lid for proper adjustment and gaps.

Grille

REMOVAL & INSTALLATION

▶ **See Figure 15**

1. Disconnect the negative battery cable.
2. Disconnect any electrical connectors to accessories, if necessary.
3. Remove the grille retaining screws. The screws may be located on the fascia, on the hood, behind the center bracket or in front of the grille, depending upon the vehicle.
4. Remove the grille assembly from the vehicle.

To install:

5. Position the grille into proper position, then install the retaining screws.
6. Attach any electrical connectors, then connect the negative battery cable.

Fig. 15 Unfasten the grille-to-fascia retaining screws

Fig. 16 Unfasten the retaining screw . . .

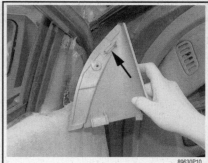

Fig. 17 . . . then remove the mirror finish panel. Note the panel retaining clip (see arrow)

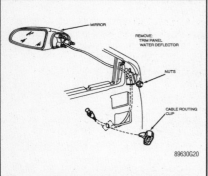

Fig. 18 Exploded view of the outside mirror cable routing

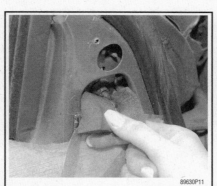

Fig. 19 Pull the sound absorber filler pad out of the door

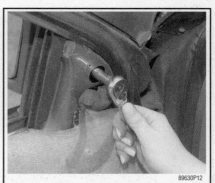

Fig. 20 Unfasten the side view mirror retaining nuts and bolts

Outside Mirrors

REMOVAL & INSTALLATION

▶ **See Figures 16, 17, 18, 19 and 20**

1. Disconnect the negative battery cable.

➡**This procedure is for power mirrors. The procedure for a manual mirror is the same with the exception of the lack of electrical wiring.**

2. Remove the door trim panel, plastic fasteners from the sound insulator and water deflector, as required.
3. Unfasten the retainer, then remove the mirror trim panel.
4. Disconnect the wiring connector and remove the wiring from the door retaining tabs.
5. Remove the mirror retaining nuts/screws, then remove the mirror with insulator and wiring.

To install:

6. Refit the mirror with insulator and wiring into position.
7. Install the mirror retaining nuts/screws.
8. Route the wiring through the door retaining tabs and reconnect the electrical connector. Make certain the wiring harness does not interfere with the window glass operation.
9. Install the water deflector, sound insulator and door trim panel, as required.
10. Connect the negative battery cable.

MIRROR FACE REPLACEMENT

1. Disconnect the negative battery cable.
2. Cover mirror surface with tape. Pull the mirror and backing plate from the mirror housing.
3. Remove the jackscrews from the mirror head backing, if equipped.

4. If mirror is the glued on type, you may need to break mirror surface and remove from backing. Wear eye protection!

➡**The left side mirror face is flat and the right side mirror face is convex. Each side must be replaced with the same type of mirror face.**

To install:

5. Align the screw retainers and reinstall.
6. If the type not retained with screws, glue the replacement assembly into place.
7. Connect the negative battery cable.

Sunroof

REMOVAL & INSTALLATION

✳✳ CAUTION

When working on, or operating the sunroof, leave the ignition switch OFF whenever possible. A momentary actuation of the sunroof switch can cause the sunroof to move directly from the VENT position to the fully CLOSED position, resulting in personal injury. Keep hands, clothing, etc. away from the sunroof opening.

Motor and Express Module

1986–91 VEHICLES

1. Disconnect the negative battery cable.
2. Remove the windshield header courtesy/reading lamp and housing.
3. Remove the lace.
4. Partially lower the headlining in order to access the motor.
5. Drill out the 2 retaining rivets, then remove the bracket.
6. Pull the relay from the mounting tab.

✳✳ WARNING

Whenever the motor is removed from the vehicle, it must be checked for synchronization before installation.

7. Detach the motor electrical connector, then remove the motor.

To install:

8. Reassemble the bracket to the motor using rivets, if removed.
9. Install the retaining screws.
10. Install the relay to the mounting tab.
11. Attach the motor electrical connector.
12. Install the headliner to its original position.
13. Install the headlining material to the sunroof opening.
14. Install the lace.
15. Install the windshield header courtesy/reading lamp.
16. Connect the negative battery cable.

1992–99 VEHICLES

▶ **See Figure 21**

1. Disconnect the negative battery cable.
2. Remove the weatherstrip lace around the sunroof opening (inside the vehicle).
3. Remove or lower the formed headlining, as necessary.
4. Unfasten the attaching screws.
5. Remove the motor from roof by pulling it off of the transmission.

➡**If motor is removed from vehicle, it must be synchronized before installation.**

6. If equipped, remove the express module by sliding it out of the slots in the bracket toward the center of the vehicle.
7. Detach the electrical connector.

To install:

8. Connect the electrical connectors and slide the express module into place.
9. Reverse the removal procedures for installation. Install the motor assembly to the transmission.
10. Install the retaining bolts.
11. Install the headliner and weatherstrip.

MOTOR SYNCHRONIZATION

▶ **See Figure 22**

1. Remove the motor from sunroof, but do not disengage the wiring.
2. Inspect the motor to see that the notch on the larger wheel is oriented toward the connector, and that a line drawn through the axle of the larger wheel and the hole near it align with the axle of the smaller wheel.
3. If necessary, activate the power switch to align them. The motor is now synchronized.
4. When installing the synchronized motor onto the transmission and into the sunroof, visually align the mounting screw holes in the motor with the corresponding holes in the roof. Failure to do so will require twisting the motor to align the holes, and this will desynchronize the motor.

TRACK ASSEMBLY SYNCHRONIZATION

▶ **See Figure 23**

1. Remove the formed headlining.
2. Cycle the glass panel to the flush position.
3. Remove the screws at the front opening and slide through and shield assembly to the rear.
4. Remove the motor.
5. Mark the fourth rib from front on lift arm on either side of vehicle. Use a china marker or something that won't wipe off when handling.
6. The vertical line make by the forth rib should continue through the center of the pin on the trolley lift arm.
7. If not, use locking pliers with padded jaws or a window regulator handle on transmission to move lift arm to alignment.
8. Synchronize motor.
9. Install the motor.
10. Slide trough and shield assembly to forward position.
11. Install the screws in the shield and trough.
12. Install the headlining and weatherstrip.

Sunshade and Glass Panel

1986–91 VEHICLES

1. Slide the sunshade fully rearward.
2. Slide the halo rearward.
3. Pop the deflector arms off the bracket.
4. Remove the screws by partially opening the glass to access the front screws, then raise the glass to the vent position to get to the rear screws.
5. Remove the glass panel.
6. Position the halo and sunshade halfway across the sunroof opening.
7. Lift the halo to clear the sunshade, then push the halo fully rearward.
8. Push the sunshade fully forward. Flex the center rear of the sunshade upward to disengage the guides. Rotate the sunshade sideways, then pull it out of the vehicle.

To install:

9. Install the sunshade, by positioning the shade so that both guides on one side and the gear guide on the opposite rear corner are properly located in the track slide. Flex the shade upward in the center, and engage with the remaining guide with the track. Check that all guides are properly engaged.
10. Slide the halo forward of the shade, then slide the shade and halo fully rearward.
11. Install the sliding glass panel and retaining screws to the lifter arms.
12. Adjust the sliding glass panel height and fit.
13. Install the deflector arms.
14. Be careful not to disengage the plastic slide on the forward portion of the lifter arm from the track slot.
15. If the plastic slide disengages from the track slot, it may be inserted as follows:

   a. Place a 2.5mm hex wrench next to the track and under the plastic slide. Using the wrench as a platform, squeeze the slide downward and fit it back into the track slot.

16. Slide the halo fully forward, then install the 3 screws.

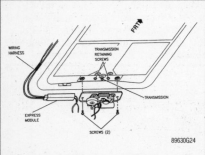

Fig. 21 Motor and express module replacement—1992 Bonneville SSE shown, other models similar

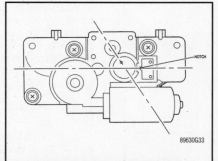

Fig. 22 Anytime the sunroof motor is removed, it must be synchronized prior to installation

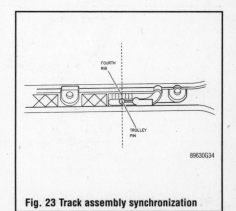

Fig. 23 Track assembly synchronization

1992–99 VEHICLES

▶ **See Figures 24 thru 31**

1. Remove the glass panel/module, as follows:
   a. Remove the headlining.
   b. Cycle the glass to the rear.
   c. Remove the retaining screws. Start with rear on both sides. Leave the second from the rear screw in place. They can be identified from the inside of the vehicle, in that they are a machine thread type.
   d. Remove the third and fourth screws on from rear on both sides.
   e. Remove the remaining screw in any order.
   f. Cycle the glass to the flushed or closed position.
   g. Remove the motor.
   h. Remove the transmission screws at the sunroof housing.
   i. Mask the roof panel around sunroof to prevent damaging paint.
   j. Always handle module by glass panel, and avoid squeezing module as this will bend components.
   k. Remove the sunroof module by lifting up and forward.

2. Cycle unit to rear until arm pin is clear.

3. Remove the cover plates. Usually the rear screw is a machine thread type; make sure to return screws to their correct locations.

4. Cycle forward to expose the opening in track which allows the lifter arms to disengage from trolley.

5. Remove the lift arms by sliding to the rear and lifting out at openings in track.

6. Cycle the trolley to its forward position, but DO NOT disengage the cable from the transmission.

7. Pull the trough and shield forward, then lift out.

8. Pull sunshade forward and lift rear guides out of openings in track.

To install:

9. Cycle trolley to forward position.

10. Rotate sunshade until rear guides fit through openings and into track slots. Inspect to insure that both rear guides have engaged correctly.

11. Slide sunshade to rear while keeping unit centered.

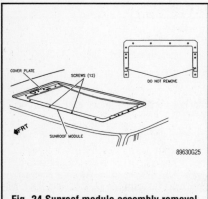

Fig. 24 Sunroof module assembly removal

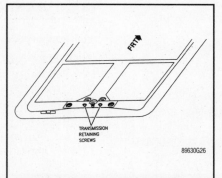

Fig. 25 Sunroof module assembly transmission retaining screws

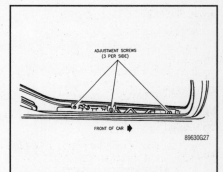

Fig. 26 Glass height and opening fit adjustment (1 of 2)

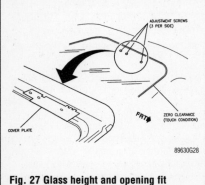

Fig. 27 Glass height and opening fit adjustment (2 of 2)

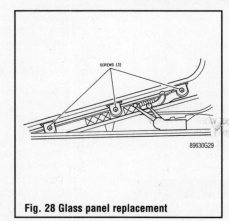

Fig. 28 Glass panel replacement

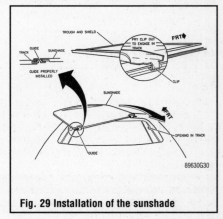

Fig. 29 Installation of the sunshade

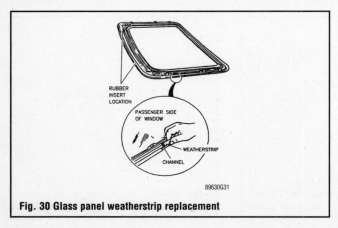

Fig. 30 Glass panel weatherstrip replacement

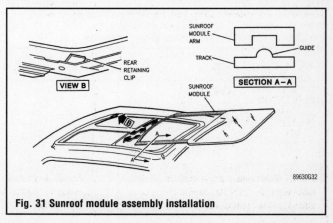

Fig. 31 Sunroof module assembly installation

12. Slide sunshade forward unit even with trolley.

13. Install the left guide shoe of trough and shield assembly into opening in track, and engage in slot in the track.

14. Position right guide shoe at opening in track. With a thin blade screwdriver pull out the spring clip on the right guide shoe so that right side of trough and shield assembly snaps into track slot.

15. Center and push trough and shield assembly into housing until seated.

16. Cycle trough and shield assembly to full rear travel.

17. Install the sunroof glass panel/module, as follows:

a. Insert the rear of module through roof opening taking care to index module on raised guides on track.

b. Slide module into sunroof opening taking care to avoid damage to finish. During the last 2 or 3 inches of travel, resistance will be felt as the module slides under its rear retaining clips.

c. Inspect to confirm that the module is under its clips, or noise will be created when the vehicle is driven.

d. Lower the glass panel.

e. Install the screws into the transmission.

f. Install the motor.

g. Cycle the glass panel fully to the rear, then forward ⅛ inch to take load off of the bumpers.

h. Install the module's rear screws to orient the unit.

i. Install the remaining screw.

18. Check for proper operation and alignment.

Air Deflector Assembly

▶ See Figure 32

1. Cycle glass panel to rear.

2. Push out the pin in the deflector lift arm with an angled tool (one pin per side).

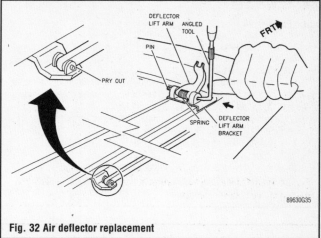

Fig. 32 Air deflector replacement

3. Remove the spring.

➡ Note the position of the spring before removal.

4. Raise the deflector lift arm to the vertical position, then snap the molded pin out of the bracket.

➡ To get a proper fit, you may need to squeeze the bracket arms together with pliers.

5. Installation is the reverse of the removal procedure. Be careful to install the spring in its original position.

INTERIOR

Instrument Panel and Pad

Due to the wide range of models and options, the instrument panel and pad removal procedure cannot cover every possible location for screw or clip locations. The car's instrument panel enables removal of control switches, instruments, gauges, and lights from the driver's side of the instrument panel. Trim panels that must be removed are held in place by bolts, screws and clips. These locations vary from model to model. After the removal of all the fasteners that you are aware of, if the cluster is still firmly attached, you probably missed a hidden fastener. If this happens, gently and carefully pry the area, looking for the location that doesn't flex. The location that does flex is where you'll find the fastener(s) you missed. Take great care with the plastic trim panels. Plastic trim panels are usually very hard plastic and extremely easy to crack. The following steps can be used to guide you through the removal and installation of the instrument cluster, but you will need to alter steps to your specific needs.

❊❊ WARNING

Servicing the instrument area requires disconnecting the negative battery cable. The electronics involved with an analog or digital dashboard are both sensitive and expensive. Use great care with these components. If equipped with an air bag, you MUST follow all DISARMING procedures, as described in Section 6.

REMOVAL & INSTALLATION

1986–91 Vehicles

▶ See Figures 33, 34, 35, 36 and 37

1. Disconnect the negative battery cable. If equipped with SIR, disable the SIR system as outlined in Section 6 of this manual.

❊❊ CAUTION

Some models covered by this manual may be equipped with a Supplemental Inflatable Restraint (SIR) system, which uses an air bag.

Whenever working near any of the SIR components, such as the impact sensors, the air bag module, steering column and instrument panel, disable the SIR, as described in Section 6.

2. Remove the steering column filler panel.

➡ For more information on instrument cluster removal, please refer to Section 6 of this manual.

3. Remove the instrument panel top cover-to-instrument panel screws.

4. If equipped with a twilight sentinel, pop up the photocell retainer and turn the photocell counterclockwise in the retainer and pull it down-and-out.

5. Slide the instrument panel top cover out far enough to disconnect the aspirator hose and the electrical connector, if equipped.

6. Remove the instrument panel top cover/pad from the instrument panel. If equipped with quartz electronic speedometer clusters, remove the steering column trim cover, so the shift indicator can be removed.

7. Remove all necessary sound insulators.

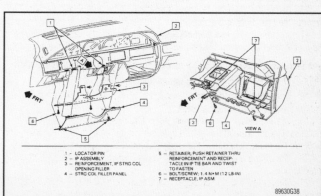

1 — LOCATOR PIN
2 — IP ASSEMBLY
3 — REINFORCEMENT, IP STRG COL OPENING FILLER
4 — STRG COL FILLER PANEL
5 — RETAINER; PUSH RETAINER THRU REINFORCEMENT AND RECEPTACLE IN IP TIE BAR AND TWIST TO FASTEN
6 — BOLT/SCREW; 1.4 N•M (12 LB-IN)
7 — RECEPTACLE, IP ASM

Fig. 33 Exploded view of typical steering column filler and reinforcement panels

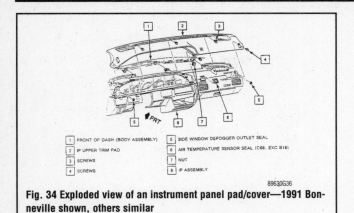

Fig. 34 Exploded view of an instrument panel pad/cover—1991 Bonneville shown, others similar

1. FRONT OF DASH (BODY ASSEMBLY)
2. IP UPPER TRIM PAD
3. SCREWS
4. SCREWS
5. SIDE WINDOW DEFOGGER OUTLET SEAL
6. AIR TEMPERATURE SENSOR SEAL (C68, EXC B18)
7. NUT
8. IP ASSEMBLY

89630G36

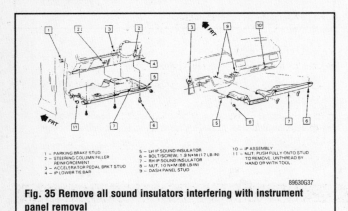

Fig. 35 Remove all sound insulators interfering with instrument panel removal

1. PARKING BRAKE STUD
2. STEERING COLUMN FILLER REINFORCEMENT
3. ACCELERATOR PEDAL BRKT STUD
4. IP LOWER TIE BAR
5. LH IP SOUND INSULATOR
6. BOLT/SCREW: 1.9 N•M (17 LB-IN)
7. RH IP SOUND INSULATOR
8. NUT: 10 N•M (88 LB-IN)
9. DASH PANEL STUD
10. IP ASSEMBLY
11. NUT: PUSH FULLY ONTO STUD TO REMOVE, UNTHREAD BY HAND OR WITH TOOL

89630G37

8. Remove the instrument cluster-to-instrument panel carrier screws. Pull the cluster housing assembly straight out; this will separate the electrical connectors from the cluster.

➡ **It may be helpful to tilt the wheel all the way down and pull the gear select lever to low, when removing the cluster.**

9. Disconnect the non-volatile memory chip, if equipped.
10. Remove the speedometer retaining screws and disconnect the speedometer cable or the electrical connection, if equipped.
11. Remove the speedometer assembly.
12. Remove the radio and heater and A/C control assembly, as outlined in Section 6 of this manual.
13. Remove the glove compartment door and/or glove compartment, as necessary.
14. Tag and unplug all necessary electrical connectors.
15. Unfasten the screws attaching the ALDL connector to the instrument panel (located near the dimmer module).
16. Detach the cigar lighter wires, then remove the ashtray. If necessary, remove the ashtray slide bracket.
17. If necessary, remove the fuse block from the instrument panel by pushing up on the lower tab to release, then push on the panel behind the instrument panel.

➡ **The retaining screws may be different sizes, so be sure to note their locations during removal.**

18. Unfasten the instrument panel support screws and mounting screws, noting their locations for installation.
19. Tag and detach the instrument panel electrical connectors. It may be necessary to use a small flat-bladed tool to push the locking tang(s) from the holes in the instrument panel, then slide the connector downward.
20. Unfasten any necessary steering column support or instrument panel bracket bolts.
21. Disconnect the side defogger hoses from the instrument panel outlet connections.
22. Remove any electrical harness retaining clips from the metal instrument panel bracket.

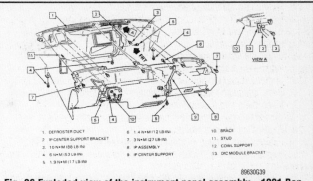

Fig. 36 Exploded view of the instrument panel assembly—1991 Bonneville shown

1. DEFROSTER DUCT
2. IP CENTER SUPPORT BRACKET
3. 10 N•M (88 LB-IN)
4. 6 N•M (53 LB-IN)
5. 1.9 N•M (17 LB-IN)
6. 1.4 N•M (12 LB-IN)
7. 3 N•M (27 LB-IN)
8. IP ASSEMBLY
9. IP CENTER SUPPORT
10. BRACE
11. STUD
12. COWL SUPPORT
13. DIC MODULE BRACKET

89630G39

23. After all retainers are removed, and connectors disengaged, remove the instrument panel from the vehicle. Be careful not to scratch the steering column, shift lever, or other components.

To install:

24. Carefully position the instrument panel in the vehicle.
25. Connect the side defogger hoses to the outlet connections. Attach all electrical connectors, as tagged during removal.
26. Install all bracket and steering column support bolts. Tighten the instrument panel bracket-to-steering column bolts to 20 ft. lbs. (27 Nm), the instrument panel stiffener rod screws to 14 inch lbs. (1.6 Nm) and the center support screw to 89 inch lbs. (10 Nm).
27. Install the instrument panel support screws in their proper locations.
28. Install the ashtray bracket and ashtray, then attach the electrical connector.
29. Install the screws attaching the ALDL connector and tighten to 17 inch lbs. (1.9 Nm).
30. Attach all electrical connectors, as they were tagged during removal.

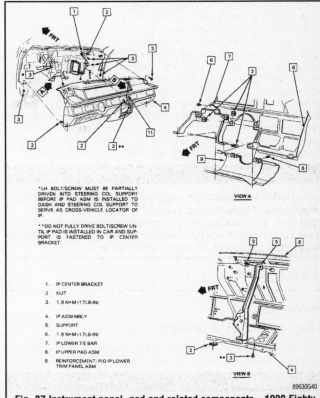

*LH BOLT/SCREW MUST BE PARTIALLY DRIVEN INTO STEERING COL SUPPORT BEFORE IP PAD ASM IS INSTALLED TO DASH AND STEERING COL SUPPORT TO SERVE AS CROSS-VEHICLE LOCATOR OF IP.

**DO NOT FULLY DRIVE BOLT/SCREW UNTIL IP PAD IS INSTALLED IN CAR AND SUPPORT IS FASTENED TO IP CENTER BRACKET.

1. IP CENTER BRACKET
2. NUT
3. 1.9 N•M (17 LB-IN)
4. IP ASSEMBLY
5. SUPPORT
6. 1.9 N•M (17 LB-IN)
7. IP LOWER TIE BAR
8. IP UPPER PAD ASM
9. REINFORCEMENT: P/O IP LOWER TRIM PANEL ASM

89630G40

Fig. 37 Instrument panel, pad and related components—1990 Eighty Eight shown

31. Install the glove compartment and/or glove compartment door, as necessary.

32. Install the radio and heater and A/C control assembly, as outlined in Section 6 of this manual.

33. Install the speedometer assembly. Connect the speedometer cable or the electrical connection, if equipped.

34. Reconnect the non-volatile memory chip, if equipped.

35. Install the instrument cluster and connect the electrical connections.

36. Install the instrument panel top cover and the shift indicator, if equipped.

37. Connect the aspirator hose and the electrical connections.

38. Replace the photo cell and retainer, if equipped with a twilight sentinel.

39. Replace the defroster grille and connect the negative battery cable.

40. If equipped with SIR, enable the system, as outlined in Section 6 of this manual.

1992–99 Vehicles

BUICK

▶ **See Figures 38 and 39**

1. Disconnect the negative battery cable. Properly disable the SIR system, as outlined in Section 6 of this manual.

❊❊ CAUTION

Some models covered by this manual may be equipped with a Supplemental Inflatable Restraint (SIR) system, which uses an air bag. Whenever working near any of the SIR components, such as the impact sensors, the air bag module, steering column and instrument panel, disable the SIR, as described in Section 6.

2. Remove the reveal cover and upper trim panels, as follows:

a. Remove the reveal covers by prying them up and carefully pulling forward.

b. Remove the fasteners, then carefully pull the upper trim plate up and remove the sunload and twilight sentinel by turning ¼ turn.

c. Remove the upper trim plate.

3. Remove the information center fasteners, then remove the center.

4. Remove the lower instrument panel trim plate by carefully prying it out.

5. Carefully pry out the air deflectors.

6. Unfasten the fasteners, then remove the instrument panel trim plate.

7. Remove the passenger inflator module.

8. Remove the knee bolster/deflector.

9. Place a protective cloth on the steering column to avoid scratching. Lower the steering column.

10. Unfasten the instrument panel fasteners. Pull the instrument panel slightly rearward.

11. Detach the electrical connector, including the antenna cable. Disconnect the vacuum line.

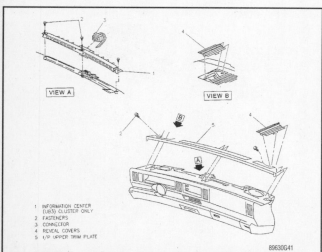

1 INFORMATION CENTER (UB3) CLUSTER ONLY
2 FASTENERS
3 CONNECTOR
4 REVEAL COVERS
5 I/P UPPER TRIM PLATE

89630G41

Fig. 38 Exploded view of the upper trim plate—1995 Buick shown, other years similar

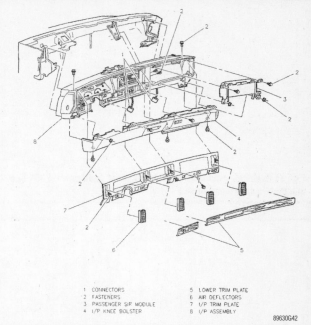

1 CONNECTORS
2 FASTENERS
3 PASSENGER SIR MODULE
4 I/P KNEE BOLSTER
5 LOWER TRIM PLATE
6 AIR DEFLECTORS
7 I/P TRIM PLATE
8 I/P ASSEMBLY

89630G42

Fig. 39 Exploded view of the instrument panel and related components—1995 Buick shown, other years similar

12. Carefully remove the instrument panel from the vehicle.

To install:

13. Carefully maneuver the instrument panel into the vehicle.

14. Attach the vacuum line connector and the electrical connectors.

15. Install the instrument panel fasteners, and tighten to 89 inch lbs. (10 Nm).

16. Raise the steering column.

17. Install the knee bolster/deflector.

18. Install the passenger inflator module.

19. Instal the instrument panel trim plates, using the reverse of the removal procedure.

20. Install the information center and secure with the retaining fasteners.

21. Properly enable the SIR system and connect the negative battery cable.

OLDSMOBILE

▶ **See Figures 40 and 41**

1. Disconnect the negative battery cable. Properly disable the SIR system, as outlined in Section 6 of this manual.

❊❊ CAUTION

Some models covered by this manual may be equipped with a Supplemental Inflatable Restraint (SIR) system, which uses an air bag. Whenever working near any of the SIR components, such as the impact sensors, the air bag module, steering column and instrument panel, disable the SIR, as described in Section 6.

2. Remove the console assembly, as outlined later in this section.

3. Remove the instrument cluster trim plate, as follows:

a. Remove the instrument panel molding fasteners (in the instrument panel compartment), then remove the molding by carefully pulling it rearward.

b. Unfasten the cluster trim plate-to-instrument panel fasteners.

c. Tilt the top of the trim plate rearward, then pull the bottom of the trim plate rearward.

d. Remove the HVAC control head and light switches from the connectors. Unplug the HVAC control head vacuum connector. Remove the control head and light switch by pushing one side outward.

e. Remove the trim plate.

4. Remove the upper trim pad, as follows:

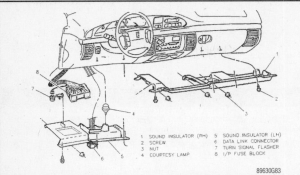

1 SOUND INSULATOR (RH)
2 SCREW
3 NUT
4 COURTESY LAMP
5 SOUND INSULATOR (LH)
6 DATA LINK CONNECTOR
7 TURN SIGNAL FLASHER
8 I/P FUSE BLOCK

89630G83

Fig. 40 Exploded view of the sound insulators' mounting—1995 Oldsmobile shown, other years similar

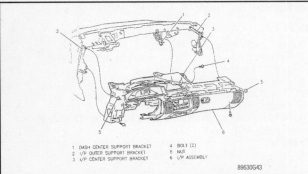

1 DASH CENTER SUPPORT BRACKET
2 I/P OUTER SUPPORT BRACKET
3 I/P CENTER SUPPORT BRACKET
4 BOLT (2)
5 NUT
6 I/P ASSEMBLY

89630G43

Fig. 41 Instrument panel mounting—1995 Oldsmobile shown, other years similar

   a. Carefully pull the molding rearward.
   b. Carefully pry the windshield defroster grille upward, with a suitable tool.
   c. Remove the sunload and twilight sentinel sensors by turning them ¼ turn to release.
   d. Remove the windshield defroster grille.
   e. Unfasten the upper trim pad fasteners, then remove the upper pad.
5. Remove the passenger inflator module.
6. Unfasten the retainers, then remove the sound insulators.
7. Remove the knee bolster and deflectors.
8. Remove the PRNDL cable.
9. Place a protective cloth on the steering column to prevent it from being scratched. Lower the steering column.
10. Unfasten the bolts attaching the instrument panel center bracket to the dash center support bracket. Remove the 10 nuts from the outer support brackets.
11. Remove the 12 fasteners from the instrument panel outer support brackets. Pull the instrument panel slightly rearward.
12. Detach the electrical connector, including the antenna cable. Disconnect the vacuum line.
13. Carefully remove the instrument panel from the vehicle.
To install:
14. Carefully maneuver the instrument panel into the vehicle.
15. Attach the vacuum line connector and the electrical connectors.
16. Install the instrument panel fasteners and bracket fasteners, and tighten to 84 inch lbs. (9.5 Nm).
17. Raise the steering column.
18. Connect the PRNDL cable.
19. Install the passenger inflator module.
20. Install the upper trim pad, as follows:
   a. Position the pad, then secure with the fasteners.
   b. Place the windshield defroster grille at the base of the windshield.
   c. Install the sunload and twilight sentinel sensors, if equipped.
   d. Press the defroster grille into place, carefully.
   e. Install the instrument panel molding by pushing forward to engage the clips.

21. Install the instrument cluster trim plate, as follows:
   a. Route the connectors through the holes in the trim plate.
   b. Position the trim plate to the instrument panel, and secure with the retaining fasteners. Tighten to 17 inch lbs. (1.9 Nm).
   c. Attach the wiring and vacuum connectors, then install the HVAC and light switch control heads.
   d. Install the instrument panel molding by carefully pushing forward to secure the clips.
   e. Install the instrument panel molding fasteners (in the instrument panel compartment).
22. Properly enable the SIR system and connect the negative battery cable.

PONTIAC

▶ **See Figures 42 and 43**

1. Disconnect the negative battery cable. Properly disable the SIR system, as outlined in Section 6 of this manual.

⁂ **CAUTION**

Some models covered by this manual may be equipped with a Supplemental Inflatable Restraint (SIR) system, which uses an air bag. Whenever working near any of the SIR components, such as the impact sensors, the air bag module, steering column and instrument panel, disable the SIR, as described in Section 6.

2. If equipped, remove the lower console assembly, as outlined later in this section.
3. If equipped with a console, remove the automatic transaxle control assembly.
4. Disconnect the release cables.
5. If equipped with a console, remove the automatic transaxle cable bracket.

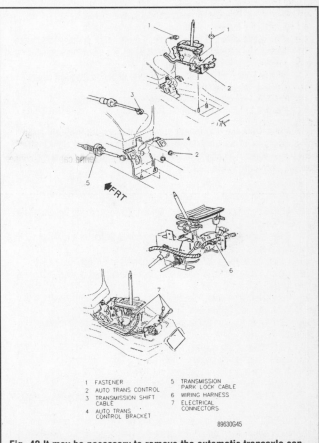

1 FASTENER
2 AUTO TRANS CONTROL
3 TRANSMISSION SHIFT CABLE
4 AUTO TRANS CONTROL BRACKET
5 TRANSMISSION PARK LOCK CABLE
6 WIRING HARNESS
7 ELECTRICAL CONNECTORS

89630G45

Fig. 42 It may be necessary to remove the automatic transaxle control and cable bracket

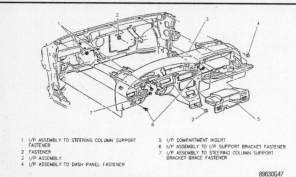

1 I/P ASSEMBLY TO STEERING COLUMN SUPPORT FASTENER
2 FASTENER
3 I/P ASSEMBLY
4 I/P ASSEMBLY TO DASH PANEL FASTENER
5 I/P COMPARTMENT INSERT
6 I/P ASSEMBLY TO I/P SUPPORT BRACKET FASTENER
7 I/P ASSEMBLY TO STEERING COLUMN SUPPORT BRACKET BRACE FASTENER

89630G47

Fig. 43 Exploded view of the instrument panel and related supporting components

6. Remove the instrument panel trim plate, as follows:

a. Remove the lower trim plate by prying up carefully. Pull the trim plate up, then rearward.

b. If equipped, detach the sub-woofer gain control switch connector.

c. Remove the upper cluster trim plate fasteners from the instrument panel.

➡**Be careful not to lose the interior lamps dimmer knob retainer!**

d. Remove the interior lamps dimmer and twilight sentinel control knob from the headlight/parking light switch.

e. Detach the cigar lighter connector.

f. Remove the instrument cluster trim plate.

7. Remove the steering column filler panel.
8. Lower the steering column.
9. Remove the glove compartment insert fasteners and insert by pulling rearward.
10. Remove the defroster grille by carefully prying upward.
11. Remove the fasteners from under the defroster grille.
12. Remove the fasteners from the steering column support bracket brace.
13. Remove the fasteners from the dash panel, the instrument panel support bracket and the steering column support.
14. Tag and detach all electrical connectors, including the antenna cable.
15. Disconnect the aspirator hose.
16. Carefully remove the instrument panel from the vehicle.

To install:

➡**When installing the instrument panel, if it does not properly align with the bottom of the windshield, loosen the center and right instrument panel support brackets to allow proper alignment and re-tighten after the assembly is aligned.**

17. Carefully maneuver the instrument panel into the vehicle.
18. Attach the aspirator hose and electrical connectors.
19. Install the fasteners to the steering column support and tighten to 106 inch lbs. (12 Nm).
20. Attach the instrument panel support bracket fasteners and tighten to 84 inch lbs. (9.5 Nm).
21. Install the dash panel fasteners and tighten to 27 inch lbs. (3 Nm).
22. Attach the fasteners to the steering column support bracket brace and tighten to 106 inch lbs. (12 Nm).
23. Install the glove compartment insert fasteners, after positioning and tighten to 17 inch lbs. (1.9 Nm).
24. Install the fasteners under the defroster grille, then position the grille and press it in place.
25. Raise the steering column.
26. Install the steering column filler.
27. Install the trim plate as follows:

a. Attach the cigar lighter connector.

b. Position the upper trim plate to the instrument panel, carefully inserting the tab.

c. Install the interior lamps dimmer and twilight sentinel control knob to the head/parking lamp switch. Properly align the retainer in the interior lamps dimmer knob before installing to insure proper retention.

d. Install the trim plate fasteners and tighten to 17 inch lbs. (1.9 Nm).

e. If equipped, attach the sub-woofer gain control switch connector.

f. Press the lower trim plate into place.

28. Install the automatic transaxle cable bracket and control assembly, if equipped.
29. If equipped, install the lower console.
30. Properly enable the SIR system and connect the negative battery cable.

Console

Take great care with the plastic trim panels. Plastic trim panels are usually very hard plastic and extremely easy to crack. The following steps can be used to guide you through the removal and installation of the console unit, but you may need to alter steps to your needs on your specific vehicle.

REMOVAL & INSTALLATION

Touring Design

◆ **See Figure 44**

TRIM PLATE

1. Disconnect the negative battery cable.
2. Remove the transaxle dial control, with the shifter in park. Lift up and move rearward to release the indicator from dial.
3. Remove the transaxle control indicator.
4. Remove the console compartment.
5. Remove the trim plate and sight shield screws.
6. Remove the fog lamp switch connector and the power seat switch connectors, if equipped.

To install:

7. Connect the fog light and seat switches.
8. Install the trim plate.
9. Install the console compartment.
10. Install the transaxle control indicator.
11. Install the transaxle control dial. The console trim plate, ashtray appliques and cup holder appliques are most likely serviced as a matched set.
12. Connect the negative battery cable.

CONSOLE ASSEMBLY

1. Disconnect the negative battery cable.
2. Remove the trim plate, as outlined in this section.
3. Unfasten all necessary console fasteners, screws, nuts.
4. Tag and detach the necessary electrical connectors.
5. Carefully remove the console assembly from the vehicle.
6. If the console is being replaced, transfer all brackets and other needed items to the new console.

To install:

7. Place the console in position.
8. Attach all electrical connectors, as tagged during removal. Install the console retaining nuts, screws and fasteners,
9. Install the trim plate, as outlined in this section.

Sport Design

◆ **See Figure 45**

BIN LID AND HINGE

1. Remove the armrest bin lid.
2. Remove console vent assembly
3. Remove the console center trim; detach the trim and rotate up.
4. Remove the duct assembly.
5. Remove the bezel/latch/cup holder assembly and unfasten the armrest bin lid hinge nuts.
6. Remove the hinge.

To install:

7. Install the hinge and retaining nuts, then install the cup holder assembly.
8. Install the duct assembly, by pulling it rearward into the proper position.
9. Install the console center trim plate; rotate it down into position and reattach.
10. Install the console vent assembly and bin lid.

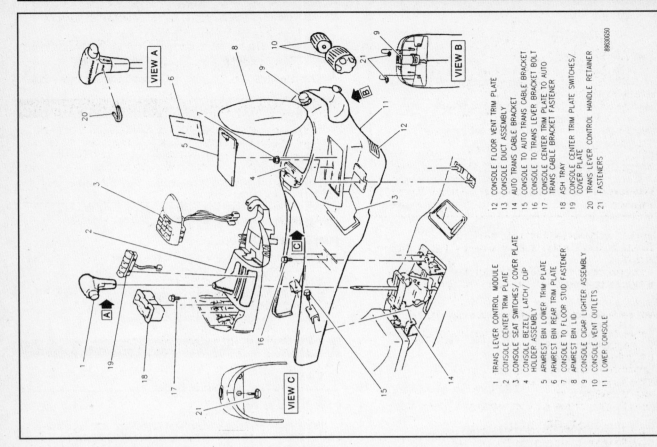

89630G50

1   TRANS LEVER CONTROL MODULE
2   CONSOLE CENTER TRIM PLATE
3   CONSOLE SEAT SWITCHES/ COVER PLATE
4   CONSOLE BEZEL/ LATCH/ CUP
    HOLDER ASSEMBLY
5   ARMREST BIN LOWER TRIM PLATE
6   ARMREST BIN REAR TRIM PLATE
7   CONSOLE TO FLOOR STUD FASTENER
8   ARMREST BIN LID
9   CONSOLE CIGAR LIGHTER ASSEMBLY
10 CONSOLE VENT OUTLETS
11 LOWER CONSOLE
12 CONSOLE FLOOR VENT TRIM PLATE
13 CONSOLE DUCT ASSEMBLY
14 AUTO TRANS CABLE BRACKET
15 CONSOLE TO AUTO TRANS CABLE BRACKET
16 CONSOLE TO AUTO TRANS LEVER BRACKET BOLT
17 CONSOLE CENTER TRIM PLATE TO AUTO
    TRANS CABLE BRACKET FASTENER
18 ASH TRAY
19 CONSOLE CENTER TRIM PLATE SWITCHES/
    COVER PLATE
20 TRANS LEVER CONTROL HANDLE RETAINER
21 FASTENERS

Fig. 45 Exploded view of the sport design center console—Pontiac shown

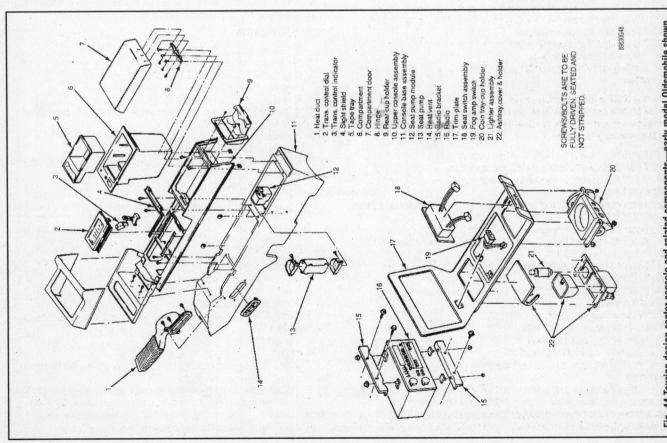

89630G48

1. Heat duct
2. Trans. control dial
3. Trans. control indicator
4. Sight shield
5. Tape tray
6. Compartment
7. Compartment door
8. Hinge
9. Rear cup holder
10. Upper console assembly
11. Console base assembly
12. Seat pump module
13. Radio bracket
14. Heat vent
15. Radio
16. Radio
17. Trim plate
18. Seat switch assembly
19. Fog amp switch
20. Coin tray-cup holder
21. Lighter assembly
22. Ashtray cover & holder

SCREWS/BOLTS ARE TO BE
FULLY DRIVEN, SEATED AND
NOT STRIPPED.

Fig. 44 Touring design center console and related components—early model Oldsmobile shown

CENTER TRIM PLATE

1. Unfasten the transaxle control lever handle retainer, then remove the handle from the shifter.
2. Open the lid and lift out the ash tray.
3. Remove the console trim plate by carefully prying it up.
4. Unfasten the console center trim plate-to-transaxle cable bracket bolts.
5. Rotate the console trim plate up.
6. Detach the connectors, then disengage the console center trim plate pivot arms by squeezing arms together.
7. Rotate the console center trim plate further, then pull forward.
8. Remove the center trim plate.

To install:

9. Install the console center trim plate, install and rotate into position. Engage console center trim plate pivot arms to pins, squeeze pivot arms together, align with pins, snap into place.
10. Attach the electrical connectors, then install the console center trim plate-to-transaxle cable bolts.
11. Install the console trim plate; press the plate firmly until seated.
12. Install the ash tray.
13. Install the handle to shifter, align the slot to keyway on shifter, then install the handle retainer.

CONSOLE DUCT ASSEMBLY

1. Remove the console vent assembly.
2. Remove the lower console.
3. Remove the armrest bin and cigar lighter.
4. Remove the center trim plate, as outlined in this Section.
5. Unfasten the duct assembly to lower console screws.
6. Remove the duct assembly.

To install:

7. Install the duct assembly and secure with the duct-to-lower console screws.
8. Install the console center trim plate.
9. Install the cigar lighter and armrest bin.
10. Install the lower console.
11. Install the console vent assembly.

CONSOLE VENT ASSEMBLY

1. Disconnect the outlets and pull rearward from the knob.
2. When installing; connect and align pin with hole in flow diverting knob.
3. Align the outlet with pivot arm, then press firmly until seated.

LOWER CONSOLE

1. Remove the console center trim, detach and rotate upwards.
2. Remove the armrest bin trim plate; lift the tab to remove.
3. Unfasten the lower console-to-transaxle cable bracket bolts.
4. Remove the lower console-to-transaxle control bolts.
5. Unfasten the lower console to floor stud nuts.
6. Carefully remove the lower console from the vehicle.

To install:

7. Maneuver the lower console into position, aligning the tabs on the transaxle control with lower console.
8. Install the bracket and cable bolts, and the floor stud nuts.
9. Install the armrest bin lower trim plate and console trim plate.

CONTROL LEVER HANDLE

1. Unfasten the transaxle control lever handle retainer.
2. Remove the transaxle control lever handle from shifter.

To install:

3. Install the transaxle control lever handle to shifter.
4. Align the slot in handle to keyway on shifter.
5. Install the transaxle control lever handle retainer.

Door Panels

REMOVAL & INSTALLATION

▶ **See Figures 46 thru 66**

The many different design interiors make it impossible to list each fastener location. The trim panels that must be removed are held in place by screws and clips. These locations vary from model to model. After removal of all the fasten-

Fig. 46 Pull the inside door handle out, unfasten the escutcheon retaining screw . . .

Fig. 47 . . . then remove the escutcheon from the door panel

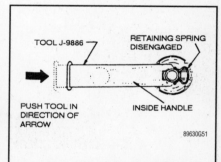

Fig. 48 Use the special tool to disengage the retaining clip behind the inside handle

Fig. 49 Carefully pry the switch plate from its mounting position

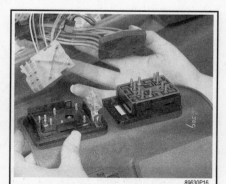

Fig. 50 Detach the power mirror switch and window switch electrical connectors

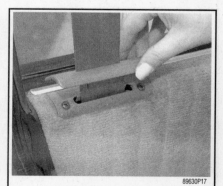

Fig. 51 Lift the seat belt escutcheon up and remove the 2 retaining screws

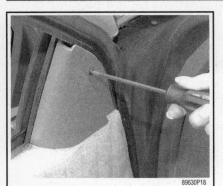

Fig. 52 Remove the mirror trim panel retaining screw . . .

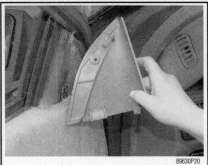

Fig. 53 . . . then lift the panel up to disengage the retainer and remove it from the door

Fig. 54 Pry the reflector from the side of the door panel

Fig. 55 Unfasten the 2 trim cover retaining screws, located at the bottom of the door panel . . .

Fig. 56 . . . then remove the lower trim cover

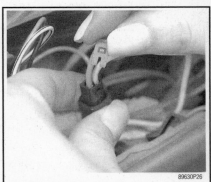

Fig. 57 As necessary, remove any electrical connector CPA clips . . .

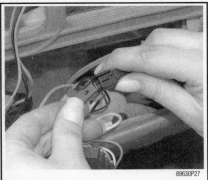

Fig. 58 . . . then unplug the electrical connector

Fig. 59 Unfasten the retaining screw, accessible after the mirror trim panel is removed

Fig. 60 Remove the door panel retaining screw located behind the reflector

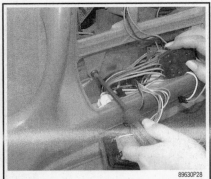

Fig. 61 Unfasten the mounting screw located under the switch plate

Fig. 62 Insert a trim panel removal tool behind the panel to disengage all of the trim panel retaining buttons

Fig. 63 Carefully pull the trim panel away from the door, making sure all the retainers and connectors are unfastened

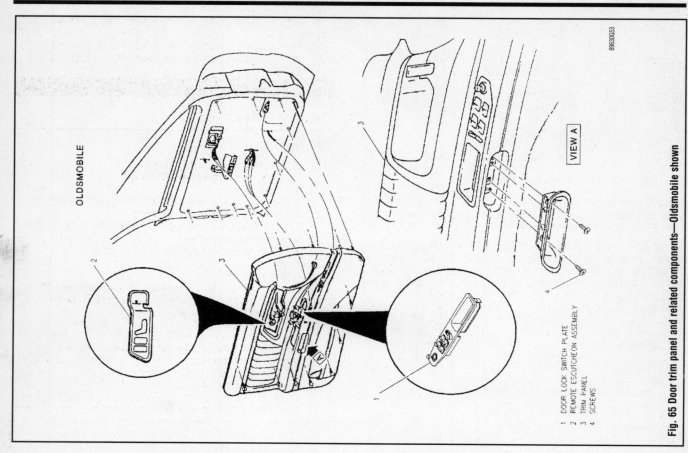

89630G53

1 DOOR LOCK SWITCH PLATE
2 REMOTE ESCUTCHEON ASSEMBLY
3 TRIM PANEL
4 SCREWS

Fig. 65 Door trim panel and related components—Oldsmobile shown

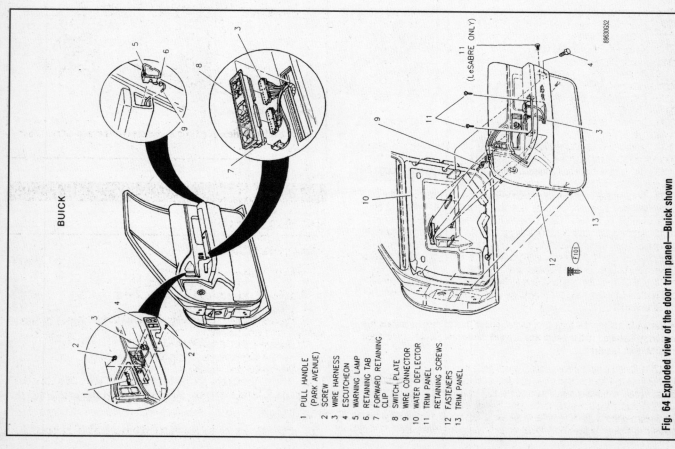

89630G52

1 PULL HANDLE (PARK AVENUE)
2 SCREW
3 WIRE HARNESS
4 ESCUTCHEON
5 WARNING LAMP
6 RETAINING TAB
7 FORWARD RETAINING CLIP
8 SWITCH PLATE
9 WIRE CONNECTOR
10 WATER DEFLECTOR
11 TRIM PANEL RETAINING SCREWS
12 FASTENERS
13 TRIM PANEL

Fig. 64 Exploded view of the door trim panel—Buick shown

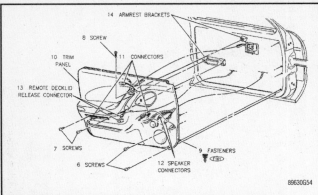

Fig. 66 Exploded view of the door trim panel—Pontiac shown

ers that you are aware of, if the trim panel is still firmly attached, you probably missed a hidden fastener. If this happens, gently and carefully pry the area looking for the location that doesn't flex. The location that does flex is where you'll find the fastener(s) you missed. Screws and retainers are usually hidden. Handle trim, reflectors, light lenses and other plastic pieces usually cover the main retaining screws. Take great care with the plastic trim panels. Plastic trim panels are usually very hard plastic and extremely easy to crack. The following steps can be used to guide you through the removal and installation of the trim panels, but you may need to alter these steps to your specific needs.

1. Disconnect the negative battery cable.
2. Pull the inside door handle to the open position, unfasten the screw and remove the handle escutcheon.
3. If equipped with manual locks, remove door inside locking rod knob.
4. If equipped with manual windows, insert a suitable window regulator handle removal tool behind the handle. Disengage the retainer, then remove the handle.
5. If equipped with power windows and locks, use a small flat-bladed pry-tool to carefully pry the switch plate up, then detach the power component electrical connectors.
6. If equipped, remove the screws inserted through door armrest and pull handle assembly into door inner panel or armrest hanger support bracket.
7. Lift the seat belt trim panel up and remove the hidden retaining screws.
8. Remove the outside side view mirror trim plate retaining screw. Lift the panel up to disengage the retaining clip, then remove the trim panel from the door.
9. On styles with courtesy lamps located in the lower area of the trim panel, disconnect the wiring harness at the lamp assembly.
10. If equipped, use a suitable tool to pry the reflector plate from the side of the door panel.
11. Remove bottom trim cover retaining screws, then remove the lower trim cover.
12. Remove any necessary electrical connector CPA clips, then unplug the electrical connectors.
13. On styles with integral armrests, remove the screws inserted through the pull cup into the armrest hanger support.
14. Unfasten the door trim panel retaining screws. The locations of the screws will vary depending upon the year of model of vehicle. The screws are usually hidden, so be sure to look carefully to make sure you don't miss any.
15. After all of the trim panel retaining screws are removed, slide a suitable trim panel removal tool between the door panel and door perimeter to carefully disengage all of the trim panel retaining buttons. Make sure to position the tool close to the fastener, or the trim panel may be damaged.
16. Carefully lift the trim panel away from the door, checking to be sure all of the retaining buttons and screws and electrical connectors are unfastened.

To install:

→**Before installing the door trim panel, check that all trim retainers are securely installed to the panel and are not damaged. Replace damaged retainers as required.**

17. Connect electrical components where present.
18. To install the door trim panel, pull door inside handle inward; then position the trim panel to the inner panel, inserting the door handle through the panel hole.
19. Position the trim panel to the door inner panel so that the trim retainers are aligned with the attaching holes in the panel, and tap the retainers into the holes with a clean rubber mallet. Install all previously removed items.

20. Install the remaining door panel components in the reverse order of removal.
21. After installation, connect the negative battery cable, then check for proper attachment and operation of electric components, if so equipped.

Door Locks

REMOVAL & INSTALLATION

▶ **See Figure 67**

1. Disconnect the negative battery cable.
2. Disconnect the trim panel and water deflector.
3. Disconnect the lock rods.
4. Cut out and remove the lock rod clips. They should be replaced with new ones, since they usually break during removal.
5. If equipped with power locks, detach the electric lock wiring connector.
6. Unfasten the retaining screws.
7. Remove the lock mechanism.

To install:

8. Install the lock mechanism.

A new service lock mechanism will have a block-out plug installed. Don't operate the lock or remove the plug until the lock mechanism is installed and the rod is connected to the lock.

9. Install the retaining screws.
10. Connect the electrical connectors.
11. Install the new lock clips to the rods and install the lock rods.
12. Remove the block-out plug.
13. Install the trim panel and water deflector.
14. Connect the negative battery cable.

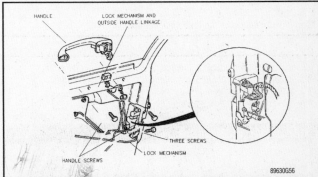

Fig. 67 Exploded view of a typical lock mechanism and outside door handle

Door Lock Cylinder

REMOVAL & INSTALLATION

▶ **See Figures 68 and 69**

1. Raise the glass to its full up position.
2. Disconnect the negative battery cable.
3. Disconnect the trim panel and water deflector.
4. Disconnect the lock rods.
5. Remove lock rod clips. They should be replaced with new ones. They usually break during removal.
6. Disconnect the electric lock wiring.
7. Remove the electric lock mechanism retaining screws.
8. Remove the lock mechanism.
9. Remove the lock cylinder retainer by prying out with a flat blade tool. Use care not to damage vehicle or cause personal injury when prying. Remove the lock cylinder.

To install:

10. Install the lock cylinder and electric lock mechanism, if equipped.

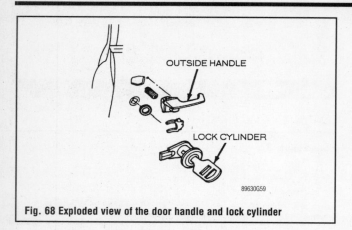

Fig. 68 Exploded view of the door handle and lock cylinder

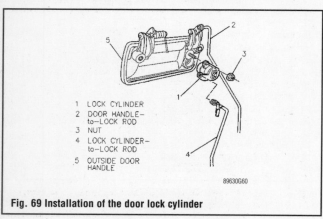

1 LOCK CYLINDER
2 DOOR HANDLE—
   to—LOCK ROD
3 NUT
4 LOCK CYLINDER—
   to—LOCK ROD
5 OUTSIDE DOOR
   HANDLE

Fig. 69 Installation of the door lock cylinder

11. Install the retaining screws.
12. Connect the electrical connectors.
13. Install the new lock clips to the rods and install the lock rods.
14. Install the trim panel and water deflector.
15. Connect the negative battery cable.

Door Glass and Regulator

REMOVAL & INSTALLATION

Power Window Assembly

CONVENTIONAL DESIGN

▶ See Figure 70

This procedure is for 1986–91 vehicles with the separate regulator design. If your vehicle has the modular design, follow those procedures regardless of year or model.
1. Remove door trim panel and water deflector.
2. Remove the speaker assembly, if necessary.
3. Tape or block window to door frame in fully up position.

➡ Many of the door components are fastened with rivets in place of screws. These rivets must be drilled out for removal and should be replaced with new rivets, NOT screws. Screws may be longer than rivets and will cause interference or, on thin panels, screws will pull loose under use.

4. Remove the regulator to door inner panel rivets using a ¼ inch drill.
5. If equipped with power locks, remove the lock-to-actuator inner panel rivets.
6. Remove the lock actuator.
7. Remove the regulator guide and block assembly from the lower sash by positioning the window halfway down, and pushing the regulator forward. After removal, tape the glass in the fully up position again.

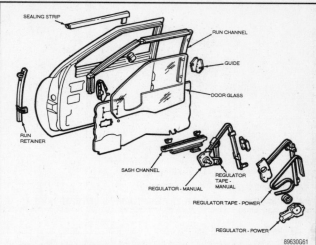

Fig. 70 Exploded view of the conventional window assembly and related components

8. Detach the electrical connector, then remove the regulator through the access hole.
To install:
9. Install the window.
10. Install the guide and block assembly to the regulator.
11. Position the regulator to the door, attaching the wiring connector. Install the regulator to the door using new rivets.
12. To adjust the window, move it upward into the door header.
13. Grasp the window and move it rearward and upward into the seal, to assure full engagement of the window to run channel.
14. Tighten the window-to-sash nuts.
15. Tighten front nut channel bolts.
16. Cycle the window up and down to check operation.
17. Install the speaker, water deflector and trim panel.

MODULAR DESIGN

▶ See Figures 71, 72, 73 and 74

This procedure is for the 1991 and newer modular design assembly. If your car has a separate regulator assembly, it may be removed using the conventional design system procedure, regardless of year or model.
1. Remove door trim panel and water deflector.
2. Remove speaker assembly, as needed.
3. Tape or block window to door frame in fully up position.

➡ Many of the door components are fastened with rivets in place of screws. These rivets must be drilled out for removal and should be replaced with new rivets NOT screws. Screws may be longer than rivets causing interference or on thin panels screws will pull loose under use.

4. Remove front channel assembly, remove the inner and outer belt strips.

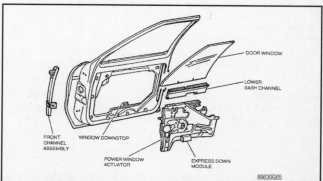

Fig. 71 Exploded view of the modular design door window assembly components

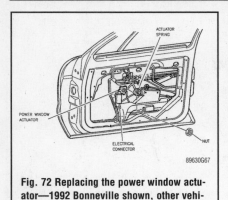

Fig. 72 Replacing the power window actuator—1992 Bonneville shown, other vehicles similar

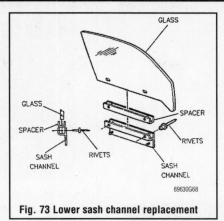

Fig. 73 Lower sash channel replacement

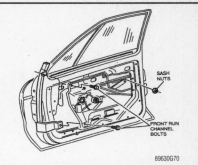

Fig. 74 Modular design front door glass adjustment—Bonneville shown, other models similar

5. Remove the sash nuts.
6. Carefully remove window through outboard side of door.

To install:

7. Install the window.
8. Install the inner and outer belt strips.
9. Install the sash nuts, but do not tighten.
10. Move window upward into door header.
11. Grasp window and move it rearward and upward into seal to assure full engagement of window to run channel.
12. Tighten the window to sash nuts.
13. Tighten the front nut channel bolts.
14. Cycle the window up and down to check operation.
15. Install the speaker, water deflector and trim panel.

Manual Window Regulator

▶ See Figures 75, 76 and 77

1. Remove door trim panel and water deflector.
2. Remove speaker assembly, as needed.
3. Tape or block window to door frame in fully up position.

➡**Many of the door components are fastened with rivets in place of screws. These rivets must be drilled out for removal and should be replaced with new rivets NOT screws. Screws may be longer than rivets causing interference or on thin panels screws will pull loose under use.**

4. Remove the regulator-to-door inner panel rivets using a ¼ in. drill.
5. Remove the lock-to-actuator inner panel rivets, if equipped with power locks.
6. Remove the lock actuator.
7. Remove the regulator guide and block assembly from lower sash by rotating regulator rearward 180 degrees.
8. Remove the regulator through the access hole.

To install:

9. Install the window.
10. Install the inner and outer belt strips.

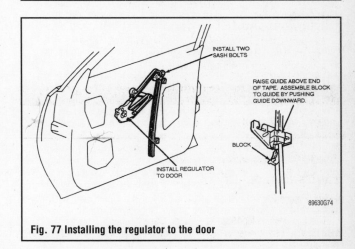

Fig. 76 Crank the handle to wind the tape into the regulator, then attach the end of the tape to the regulator's tabs

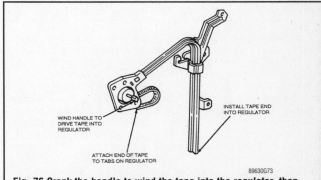

Fig. 77 Installing the regulator to the door

11. Install the sash nuts, but do not tighten.
12. Move window upward into door header.
13. Grasp window and move it rearward and upward into seal to assure full engagement of window to run channel.
14. Tighten the window to sash nuts.
15. Tighten front nut channel bolts.
16. Cycle the window up and down to check operation.
17. Install the speaker, water deflector and trim panel.

Window Actuator

The power window actuator motor assembly removal does not involve removing the regulator or window assembly on most models. If your model requires these components to be removed, follow the procedures for Glass and Regulator replacement.

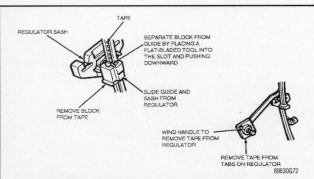

Fig. 75 Separate the block from the guide by placing a flat-bladed tool into the slot and pushing downward

REMOVAL & INSTALLATION

1. Remove door trim panel and water deflector.
2. Remove speaker assembly, as needed.
3. Detach the electrical connectors.
4. Unfasten the retaining screws or drill out the retaining rivets, as applicable.
5. Remove the actuator.

To install:

6. Install the actuator.
7. Make certain the teeth on the actuator align with teeth on the crossarm.
8. Install retaining screws.
9. Attach the electrical connector.
10. Check window for proper operation.
11. Install speaker assembly, water deflector and trim panel.

Windshield and Fixed Glass

REMOVAL & INSTALLATION

If your windshield, or other fixed window, is cracked or chipped, you may decide to replace it with a new one yourself. However, there are two main reasons why replacement windshields and other window glass should be installed only by a professional automotive glass technician: safety and cost.

The most important reason a professional should install automotive glass is for safety. The glass in the vehicle, especially the windshield, is designed with safety in mind in case of a collision. The windshield is specially manufactured from two panes of specially-tempered glass with a thin layer of transparent plastic between them. This construction allows the glass to "give" in the event that a part of your body hits the windshield during the collision, and prevents the glass from shattering, which could cause lacerations, blinding and other harm to passengers of the vehicle. The other fixed windows are designed to be tempered so that if they break during a collision, they shatter in such a way that there are no large pointed glass pieces. The professional automotive glass technician knows how to install the glass in a vehicle so that it will function optimally during a collision. Without the proper experience, knowledge and tools, installing a piece of automotive glass yourself could lead to additional harm if an accident should ever occur.

Cost is also a factor when deciding to install automotive glass yourself. Performing this could cost you much more than a professional may charge for the same job. Since the windshield is designed to break under stress, an often life saving characteristic, windshields tend to break VERY easily when an inexperienced person attempts to install one. Do-it-yourselfers buying two, three or even four windshields from a salvage yard because they have broken them during installation are common stories. Also, since the automotive glass is designed to prevent the outside elements from entering your vehicle, improper installation can lead to water and air leaks. Annoying whining noises at highway speeds from air leaks or inside body panel rusting from water leaks can add to your stress level and subtract from your wallet. After buying two or three windshields, installing them and ending up with a leak that produces a noise while driving and water damage during rainstorms, the cost of having a professional do it correctly the first time may be much more alluring. We here at Chilton, therefore, advise that you have a professional automotive glass technician service any broken glass on your vehicle.

WINDSHIELD CHIP REPAIR

▶ **See Figures 78 and 79**

➡**Check with your state and local authorities on the laws for state safety inspection. Some states or municipalities may not allow chip repair as a viable option for correcting stone damage to your windshield.**

Although severely cracked or damaged windshields must be replaced, there is something that you can do to prolong or even prevent the need for replacement of a chipped windshield. There are many companies which offer windshield chip repair products, such as Loctite's® Bullseye™ windshield repair kit. These kits usually consist of a syringe, pedestal and a sealing adhesive. The syringe is mounted on the pedestal and is used to create a vacuum which pulls the plastic layer against the glass. This helps make the chip transparent. The adhesive is then injected which seals the chip and helps to prevent further stress cracks from developing

➡**Always follow the specific manufacturer's instructions.**

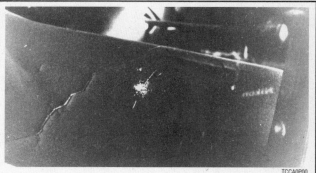

Fig. 78 Small chips on your windshield can be fixed with an aftermarket repair kit, such as the one from Loctite_

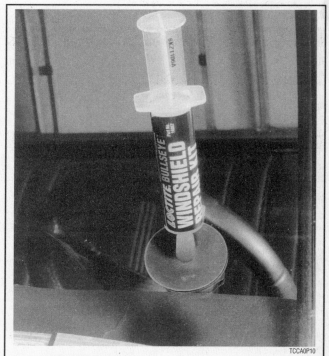

Fig. 79 Most kits use a self-stick applicator and syringe to inject the adhesive into the chip or crack

Inside Rear View Mirror

REMOVAL & INSTALLATION

▶ **See Figure 80**

The rear view mirror is attached to a support which is secured to the windshield glass. A service replacement windshield glass has the support bonded to the glass assembly. To install a detached mirror support or install a new part, use the following procedures to complete the service.

1. Locate the support position at the center of the glass 3 in. (76mm) from the top of the glass to the top of the support.
2. Circle the location on the outside of the glass with a wax pencil or crayon. Draw a large circle around the support circle.
3. Clean the area within the circle with household cleaner and dry with a clean towel. Repeat the procedures using rubbing alcohol.
4. Sand the bonding surface of the support with fine grit (320–360) emery cloth or sandpaper. If the original support is being used, remove the old adhesive with rubbing alcohol and a clean towel.

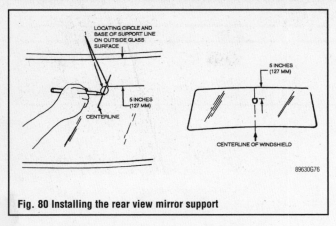

Fig. 80 Installing the rear view mirror support

5. Apply the adhesive as outlined in the kit instructions.
6. Position the support to the marked location with the rounded end UP.

✳✳ CAUTION

Do NOT apply excessive pressure to the windshield glass. The glass may break, causing personal injury.

7. Press the support to the glass for 30–60 seconds. Excessive adhesive can be removed after five minutes with rubbing alcohol.

Power Seat Motor

REMOVAL & INSTALLATION

▶ **See Figure 81**

The six-way power seat adjusters are actuated by three 12V, reversible permanent magnet motors with built in circuit breakers. The motors drive the front and rear vertical gearnuts and a horizontal actuator. When the adjusters are at their limit of travel, an overload relay provides stall torque, so the motors are not overloaded. Each motor can be serviced as a separate unit.

1. Disconnect the negative battery cable.
2. Remove the seat assembly from the vehicle as outlined in this section.
3. Remove the adjuster assembly from the seat.
4. Detach the feed wires from the motor.
5. Unfasten the nuts securing the front of the motor support bracket-to-inboard adjuster. Partially withdraw the assembly from the adjuster and gearnut drives.

6. Remove the drive cables from the motor. Completely disassemble the support bracket with the motors attached.
7. Grind off the peened-over ends of the grommet assembly securing the motor-to-support. Separate the motor from the support.
To install:
8. Drill out the top end of the grommet assembly using a ³⁄₁₆ inch (5mm) drill bit.
9. Install the grommet assembly-to-motor support bracket. Secure the motor with a ³⁄₁₆ inch (5mm) rivet.
10. Install the drive cables.
11. Install the motor-to-inboard adjuster.
12. Connect the motor feed wires and negative battery cable.
13. Install the adjuster assembly-to-seat bottom.
14. With an assistant, install the seat and check for proper operation.

ADJUSTMENT

Horizontal Actuator

▶ **See Figure 82**

1. Operate the seat to its full up position and about ¾ full forward.
2. Loosen the 2 actuator screws.
3. Pry out and, at the same time, energize the horizontal switch to move the seat fore and aft slightly.
4. After the gear teeth free-play has been eliminated, maintain the outward pressure and tighten the 2 actuator screws.

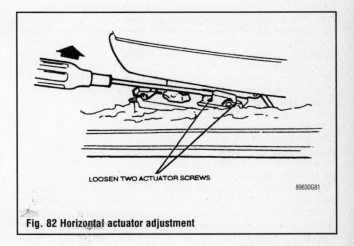

Fig. 82 Horizontal actuator adjustment

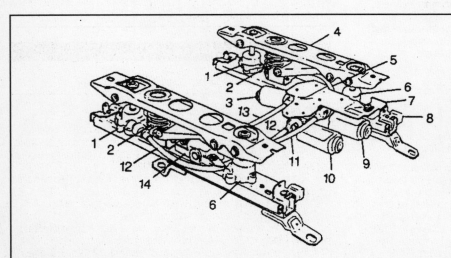

1. Rear gearnut drive
2. Assist springs
3. Horizontal adjuster motor
4. Adjuster assembly
5. Rear vertical gearnut assembly
6. Front gearnut drive
7. Motor support bracket
8. Lower channel stop
9. Front vertical gearnut motor
10. Rear vertical gearnut motor
11. Front vertical drive cable
12. Rear vertical drive cable
13. Horizontal drive cable
14. Horizontal adjustor drive

Fig. 81 Six-way power seat assembly

TORQUE SPECIFICATIONS

Component	ft. lbs.	inch lbs.	Nm
Exterior			
Door mounting bolts and nuts	35		47
Hood retaining bolts	21-24		29-33
Trunk hinge-to-lid attaching bolts	18-24		25-33
Interior			
Instrument panel and pad			
1986-91 vehicles			
Bracket-to-steering column bolts	20		27
Stiffener rod screws		14	1.6
Center support screw		89	10
1992-99 vehicles			
Buick instrument panel fasteners		89	10
Oldsmobile instrument panel fasteners		84	9.5
Pontiac			
Steering column support fasteners		106	12
Support bracket fasteners		84	9.5
Dash panel fasteners		27	3
Steering column support bracket brace		106	12
Glove compartment fasteners		17	1.9
Trim panel fasteners		17	1.9
Front and rear seat mounting bolts	31		42

89630C01

GLOSSARY

AIR/FUEL RATIO: The ratio of air-to-gasoline by weight in the fuel mixture drawn into the engine.

AIR INJECTION: One method of reducing harmful exhaust emissions by injecting air into each of the exhaust ports of an engine. The fresh air entering the hot exhaust manifold causes any remaining fuel to be burned before it can exit the tailpipe.

ALTERNATOR: A device used for converting mechanical energy into electrical energy.

AMMETER: An instrument, calibrated in amperes, used to measure the flow of an electrical current in a circuit. Ammeters are always connected in series with the circuit being tested.

AMPERE: The rate of flow of electrical current present when one volt of electrical pressure is applied against one ohm of electrical resistance.

ANALOG COMPUTER: Any microprocessor that uses similar (analogous) electrical signals to make its calculations.

ARMATURE: A laminated, soft iron core wrapped by a wire that converts electrical energy to mechanical energy as in a motor or relay. When rotated in a magnetic field, it changes mechanical energy into electrical energy as in a generator.

ATMOSPHERIC PRESSURE: The pressure on the Earth's surface caused by the weight of the air in the atmosphere. At sea level, this pressure is 14.7 psi at 32°F (101 kPa at 0°C).

ATOMIZATION: The breaking down of a liquid into a fine mist that can be suspended in air.

AXIAL PLAY: Movement parallel to a shaft or bearing bore.

BACKFIRE: The sudden combustion of gases in the intake or exhaust system that results in a loud explosion.

BACKLASH: The clearance or play between two parts, such as meshed gears.

BACKPRESSURE: Restrictions in the exhaust system that slow the exit of exhaust gases from the combustion chamber.

BAKELITE: A heat resistant, plastic insulator material commonly used in printed circuit boards and transistorized components.

BALL BEARING: A bearing made up of hardened inner and outer races between which hardened steel balls roll.

BALLAST RESISTOR: A resistor in the primary ignition circuit that lowers voltage after the engine is started to reduce wear on ignition components.

BEARING: A friction reducing, supportive device usually located between a stationary part and a moving part.

BIMETAL TEMPERATURE SENSOR: Any sensor or switch made of two dissimilar types of metal that bend when heated or cooled due to the different expansion rates of the alloys. These types of sensors usually function as an on/off switch.

BLOWBY: Combustion gases, composed of water vapor and unburned fuel, that leak past the piston rings into the crankcase during normal engine operation. These gases are removed by the PCV system to prevent the buildup of harmful acids in the crankcase.

BRAKE PAD: A brake shoe and lining assembly used with disc brakes.

BRAKE SHOE: The backing for the brake lining. The term is, however, usually applied to the assembly of the brake backing and lining.

BUSHING: A liner, usually removable, for a bearing; an anti-friction liner used in place of a bearing.

CALIPER: A hydraulically activated device in a disc brake system, which is mounted straddling the brake rotor (disc). The caliper contains at least one piston and two brake pads. Hydraulic pressure on the piston(s) forces the pads against the rotor.

CAMSHAFT: A shaft in the engine on which are the lobes (cams) which operate the valves. The camshaft is driven by the crankshaft, via a belt, chain or gears, at one half the crankshaft speed.

CAPACITOR: A device which stores an electrical charge.

CARBON MONOXIDE (CO): A colorless, odorless gas given off as a normal byproduct of combustion. It is poisonous and extremely dangerous in confined areas, building up slowly to toxic levels without warning if adequate ventilation is not available.

CARBURETOR: A device, usually mounted on the intake manifold of an engine, which mixes the air and fuel in the proper proportion to allow even combustion.

CATALYTIC CONVERTER: A device installed in the exhaust system, like a muffler, that converts harmful byproducts of combustion into carbon dioxide and water vapor by means of a heat-producing chemical reaction.

CENTRIFUGAL ADVANCE: A mechanical method of advancing the spark timing by using flyweights in the distributor that react to centrifugal force generated by the distributor shaft rotation.

CHECK VALVE: Any one-way valve installed to permit the flow of air, fuel or vacuum in one direction only.

CHOKE: A device, usually a moveable valve, placed in the intake path of a carburetor to restrict the flow of air.

CIRCUIT: Any unbroken path through which an electrical current can flow. Also used to describe fuel flow in some instances.

CIRCUIT BREAKER: A switch which protects an electrical circuit from overload by opening the circuit when the current flow exceeds a predetermined level. Some circuit breakers must be reset manually, while most reset automatically.

COIL (IGNITION): A transformer in the ignition circuit which steps up the voltage provided to the spark plugs.

COMBINATION MANIFOLD: An assembly which includes both the intake and exhaust manifolds in one casting.

COMBINATION VALVE: A device used in some fuel systems that routes fuel vapors to a charcoal storage canister instead of venting them into the atmosphere. The valve relieves fuel tank pressure and allows fresh air into the tank as the fuel level drops to prevent a vapor lock situation.

COMPRESSION RATIO: The comparison of the total volume of the cylinder and combustion chamber with the piston at BDC and the piston at TDC.

CONDENSER: 1. An electrical device which acts to store an electrical charge, preventing voltage surges. 2. A radiator-like device in the air conditioning system in which refrigerant gas condenses into a liquid, giving off heat.

CONDUCTOR: Any material through which an electrical current can be transmitted easily.

CONTINUITY: Continuous or complete circuit. Can be checked with an ohmmeter.

COUNTERSHAFT: An intermediate shaft which is rotated by a mainshaft and transmits, in turn, that rotation to a working part.

CRANKCASE: The lower part of an engine in which the crankshaft and related parts operate.

CRANKSHAFT: The main driving shaft of an engine which receives reciprocating motion from the pistons and converts it to rotary motion.

CYLINDER: In an engine, the round hole in the engine block in which the piston(s) ride.

CYLINDER BLOCK: The main structural member of an engine in which is found the cylinders, crankshaft and other principal parts.

CYLINDER HEAD: The detachable portion of the engine, usually fastened to the top of the cylinder block and containing all or most of the combustion chambers. On overhead valve engines, it contains the valves and their operating parts. On overhead cam engines, it contains the camshaft as well.

DEAD CENTER: The extreme top or bottom of the piston stroke.

DETONATION: An unwanted explosion of the air/fuel mixture in the combustion chamber caused by excess heat and compression, advanced timing, or an overly lean mixture. Also referred to as "ping".

DIAPHRAGM: A thin, flexible wall separating two cavities, such as in a vacuum advance unit.

DIESELING: A condition in which hot spots in the combustion chamber cause the engine to run on after the key is turned off.

DIFFERENTIAL: A geared assembly which allows the transmission of motion between drive axles, giving one axle the ability to turn faster than the other.

DIODE: An electrical device that will allow current to flow in one direction only.

DISC BRAKE: A hydraulic braking assembly consisting of a brake disc, or rotor, mounted on an axle, and a caliper assembly containing, usually two brake pads which are activated by hydraulic pressure. The pads are forced against the sides of the disc, creating friction which slows the vehicle.

DISTRIBUTOR: A mechanically driven device on an engine which is responsible for electrically firing the spark plug at a predetermined point of the piston stroke.

DOWEL PIN: A pin, inserted in mating holes in two different parts allowing those parts to maintain a fixed relationship.

DRUM BRAKE: A braking system which consists of two brake shoes and one or two wheel cylinders, mounted on a fixed backing plate, and a brake drum, mounted on an axle, which revolves around the assembly.

DWELL: The rate, measured in degrees of shaft rotation, at which an electrical circuit cycles on and off.

ELECTRONIC CONTROL UNIT (ECU): Ignition module, module, amplifier or igniter. See Module for definition.

ELECTRONIC IGNITION: A system in which the timing and firing of the spark plugs is controlled by an electronic control unit, usually called a module. These systems have no points or condenser.

END-PLAY: The measured amount of axial movement in a shaft.

ENGINE: A device that converts heat into mechanical energy.

EXHAUST MANIFOLD: A set of cast passages or pipes which conduct exhaust gases from the engine.

FEELER GAUGE: A blade, usually metal, or precisely predetermined thickness, used to measure the clearance between two parts.

FIRING ORDER: The order in which combustion occurs in the cylinders of an engine. Also the order in which spark is distributed to the plugs by the distributor.

FLOODING: The presence of too much fuel in the intake manifold and combustion chamber which prevents the air/fuel mixture from firing, thereby causing a no-start situation.

FLYWHEEL: A disc shaped part bolted to the rear end of the crankshaft. Around the outer perimeter is affixed the ring gear. The starter drive engages the ring gear, turning the flywheel, which rotates the crankshaft, imparting the initial starting motion to the engine.

FOOT POUND (ft. lbs. or sometimes, ft.lb.): The amount of energy or work needed to raise an item weighing one pound, a distance of one foot.

FUSE: A protective device in a circuit which prevents circuit overload by breaking the circuit when a specific amperage is present. The device is constructed around a strip or wire of a lower amperage rating than the circuit it is designed to protect. When an amperage higher than that stamped on the fuse is present in the circuit, the strip or wire melts, opening the circuit.

GEAR RATIO: The ratio between the number of teeth on meshing gears.

GENERATOR: A device which converts mechanical energy into electrical energy.

HEAT RANGE: The measure of a spark plug's ability to dissipate heat from its firing end. The higher the heat range, the hotter the plug fires.

HUB: The center part of a wheel or gear.

HYDROCARBON (HC): Any chemical compound made up of hydrogen and carbon. A major pollutant formed by the engine as a byproduct of combustion.

HYDROMETER: An instrument used to measure the specific gravity of a solution.

INCH POUND (inch lbs.; sometimes in.lb. or in. lbs.): One twelfth of a foot pound.

INDUCTION: A means of transferring electrical energy in the form of a magnetic field. Principle used in the ignition coil to increase voltage.

INJECTOR: A device which receives metered fuel under relatively low pressure and is activated to inject the fuel into the engine under relatively high pressure at a predetermined time.

INPUT SHAFT: The shaft to which torque is applied, usually carrying the driving gear or gears.

INTAKE MANIFOLD: A casting of passages or pipes used to conduct air or a fuel/air mixture to the cylinders.

JOURNAL: The bearing surface within which a shaft operates.

KEY: A small block usually fitted in a notch between a shaft and a hub to prevent slippage of the two parts.

MANIFOLD: A casting of passages or set of pipes which connect the cylinders to an inlet or outlet source.

MANIFOLD VACUUM: Low pressure in an engine intake manifold formed just below the throttle plates. Manifold vacuum is highest at idle and drops under acceleration.

MASTER CYLINDER: The primary fluid pressurizing device in a hydraulic system. In automotive use, it is found in brake and hydraulic clutch systems and is pedal activated, either directly or, in a power brake system, through the power booster.

MODULE: Electronic control unit, amplifier or igniter of solid state or integrated design which controls the current flow in the ignition primary circuit based on input from the pick-up coil. When the module opens the primary circuit, high secondary voltage is induced in the coil.

NEEDLE BEARING: A bearing which consists of a number (usually a large number) of long, thin rollers.

OHM: (Ω) The unit used to measure the resistance of conductor-to-electrical flow. One ohm is the amount of resistance that limits current flow to one ampere in a circuit with one volt of pressure.

OHMMETER: An instrument used for measuring the resistance, in ohms, in an electrical circuit.

OUTPUT SHAFT: The shaft which transmits torque from a device, such as a transmission.

OVERDRIVE: A gear assembly which produces more shaft revolutions than that transmitted to it.

OVERHEAD CAMSHAFT (OHC): An engine configuration in which the camshaft is mounted on top of the cylinder head and operates the valve either directly or by means of rocker arms.

OVERHEAD VALVE (OHV): An engine configuration in which all of the valves are located in the cylinder head and the camshaft is located in the cylinder block. The camshaft operates the valves via lifters and pushrods.

OXIDES OF NITROGEN (NOx): Chemical compounds of nitrogen produced as a byproduct of combustion. They combine with hydrocarbons to produce smog.

OXYGEN SENSOR: Use with the feedback system to sense the presence of oxygen in the exhaust gas and signal the computer which can reference the voltage signal to an air/fuel ratio.

PINION: The smaller of two meshing gears.

PISTON RING: An open-ended ring with fits into a groove on the outer diameter of the piston. Its chief function is to form a seal between the piston and cylinder wall. Most automotive pistons have three rings: two for compression sealing; one for oil sealing.

PRELOAD: A predetermined load placed on a bearing during assembly or by adjustment.

PRIMARY CIRCUIT: the low voltage side of the ignition system which consists of the ignition switch, ballast resistor or resistance wire, bypass, coil, electronic control unit and pick-up coil as well as the connecting wires and harnesses.

PRESS FIT: The mating of two parts under pressure, due to the inner diameter of one being smaller than the outer diameter of the other, or vice versa; an interference fit.

RACE: The surface on the inner or outer ring of a bearing on which the balls, needles or rollers move.

REGULATOR: A device which maintains the amperage and/or voltage levels of a circuit at predetermined values.

RELAY: A switch which automatically opens and/or closes a circuit.

RESISTANCE: The opposition to the flow of current through a circuit or electrical device, and is measured in ohms. Resistance is equal to the voltage divided by the amperage.

RESISTOR: A device, usually made of wire, which offers a preset amount of resistance in an electrical circuit.

RING GEAR: The name given to a ring-shaped gear attached to a differential case, or affixed to a flywheel or as part of a planetary gear set.

ROLLER BEARING: A bearing made up of hardened inner and outer races between which hardened steel rollers move.

ROTOR: 1. The disc-shaped part of a disc brake assembly, upon which the brake pads bear; also called, brake disc. 2. The device mounted atop the distributor shaft, which passes current to the distributor cap tower contacts.

SECONDARY CIRCUIT: The high voltage side of the ignition system, usually above 20,000 volts. The secondary includes the ignition coil, coil wire, distributor cap and rotor, spark plug wires and spark plugs.

SENDING UNIT: A mechanical, electrical, hydraulic or electro-magnetic device which transmits information to a gauge.

SENSOR: Any device designed to measure engine operating conditions or ambient pressures and temperatures. Usually electronic in nature and designed to send a voltage signal to an on-board computer, some sensors may operate as a simple on/off switch or they may provide a variable voltage signal (like a potentiometer) as conditions or measured parameters change.

SHIM: Spacers of precise, predetermined thickness used between parts to establish a proper working relationship.

SLAVE CYLINDER: In automotive use, a device in the hydraulic clutch system which is activated by hydraulic force, disengaging the clutch.

SOLENOID: A coil used to produce a magnetic field, the effect of which is to produce work.

SPARK PLUG: A device screwed into the combustion chamber of a spark ignition engine. The basic construction is a conductive core inside of a ceramic insulator, mounted in an outer conductive base. An electrical charge from the spark plug wire travels along the conductive core and jumps a preset air gap to a grounding point or points at the end of the conductive base. The resultant spark ignites the fuel/air mixture in the combustion chamber.

SPLINES: Ridges machined or cast onto the outer diameter of a shaft or inner diameter of a bore to enable parts to mate without rotation.

TACHOMETER: A device used to measure the rotary speed of an engine, shaft, gear, etc., usually in rotations per minute.

THERMOSTAT: A valve, located in the cooling system of an engine, which is closed when cold and opens gradually in response to engine heating, controlling the temperature of the coolant and rate of coolant flow.

TOP DEAD CENTER (TDC): The point at which the piston reaches the top of its travel on the compression stroke.

TORQUE: The twisting force applied to an object.

TORQUE CONVERTER: A turbine used to transmit power from a driving member to a driven member via hydraulic action, providing changes in drive ratio and torque. In automotive use, it links the driveplate at the rear of the engine to the automatic transmission.

TRANSDUCER: A device used to change a force into an electrical signal.

TRANSISTOR: A semi-conductor component which can be actuated by a small voltage to perform an electrical switching function.

TUNE-UP: A regular maintenance function, usually associated with the replacement and adjustment of parts and components in the electrical and fuel systems of a vehicle for the purpose of attaining optimum performance.

TURBOCHARGER: An exhaust driven pump which compresses intake air and forces it into the combustion chambers at higher than atmospheric pressures. The increased air pressure allows more fuel to be burned and results in increased horsepower being produced.

VACUUM ADVANCE: A device which advances the ignition timing in response to increased engine vacuum.

VACUUM GAUGE: An instrument used to measure the presence of vacuum in a chamber.

VALVE: A device which control the pressure, direction of flow or rate of flow of a liquid or gas.

VALVE CLEARANCE: The measured gap between the end of the valve stem and the rocker arm, cam lobe or follower that activates the valve.

VISCOSITY: The rating of a liquid's internal resistance to flow.

VOLTMETER: An instrument used for measuring electrical force in units called volts. Voltmeters are always connected parallel with the circuit being tested.

WHEEL CYLINDER: Found in the automotive drum brake assembly, it is a device, actuated by hydraulic pressure, which, through internal pistons, pushes the brake shoes outward against the drums.

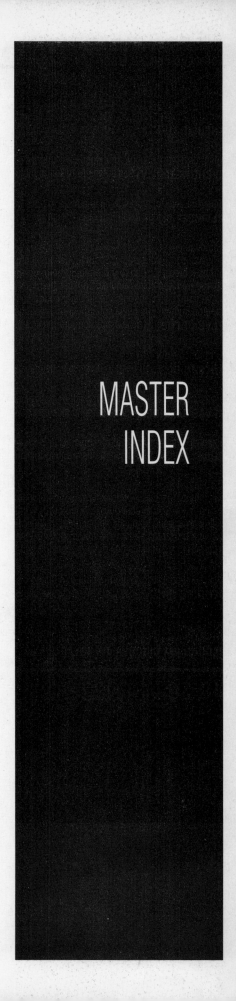

MASTER INDEX

ABS PUMP RELAY 9-39
   LOCATION 9-39
ABS SERVICE 9-38
   PRECAUTIONS 9-38
ADJUSTING LINK 8-15
   REMOVAL & INSTALLATION 8-15
AIR BAG—GENERATION 1 CORPORATE SYSTEM 6-8
AIR BAG—OLDSMOBILE INFLATABLE RESTRAINT (IR)
  SYSTEM 6-12
AIR CLEANER (ELEMENT) 1-14
   REMOVAL & INSTALLATION 1-14
AIR CONDITIONING COMPONENTS 6-16
   REMOVAL & INSTALLATION 6-16
AIR CONDITIONING SYSTEM (ROUTINE MAINTENANCE AND
  TUNE-UP) 1-30
   PREVENTIVE MAINTENANCE 1-31
   SYSTEM INSPECTION 1-31
   SYSTEM SERVICE & REPAIR 1-30
ALTERNATOR 2-11
   REMOVAL & INSTALLATION 2-12
   TESTING 2-11
ALTERNATOR FUNCTIONAL CHECK—1996–99 VEHICLES 2-12
ALTERNATOR PRECAUTIONS 2-11
   BELT TENSION ADJUSTMENT 2-11
ANTI-LOCK DIODE (DELCO VI AND DELCO BOSCH V ANTI-LOCK
  BRAKING SYSTEMS) 9-39
   LOCATION 9-39
ANTI-LOCK DIODE (TEVES MARK IV ANTI-LOCK BRAKE SYSTEM) 9-33
   LOCATION 9-33
AUTOMATIC TRANSAXLE 7-2
AUTOMATIC TRANSAXLE (FLUIDS AND LUBRICANTS) 1-39
   DRAIN, FILTER SERVICE & REFILL 1-39
   FLUID RECOMMENDATIONS 1-39
   LEVEL CHECK 1-39
AUTOMATIC TRANSAXLE ASSEMBLY 7-3
   ADJUSTMENTS 7-5
   REMOVAL & INSTALLATION 7-3
AVOIDING THE MOST COMMON MISTAKES 1-2
AVOIDING TROUBLE 1-2
BALANCE SHAFT 3-36
   REMOVAL & INSTALLATION 3-36
BASIC ELECTRICAL THEORY 6-2
   HOW DOES ELECTRICITY WORK: THE WATER ANALOGY 6-2
   OHM'S LAW 6-2
BASIC FUEL SYSTEM DIAGNOSIS 5-2
BASIC OPERATING PRINCIPLES 9-2
   DISC BRAKES 9-2
   DRUM BRAKES 9-2
BATTERY 1-17
   ADJUSTMENT 1-18
   BATTERY FLUID 1-18
   CABLES 1-19
   CHARGING 1-20
   GENERAL MAINTENANCE 1-18
   PRECAUTIONS 1-17
   REPLACEMENT 1-20
BATTERY CABLES 6-8
BELTS 1-20
   BELT ADJUSTMENT 1-20
   INSPECTION 1-20
   REMOVAL & INSTALLATION 1-21
BLEEDING THE ABS SYSTEM 9-35
BLEEDING THE BRAKE SYSTEM 9-7
   BENCH BLEEDING THE MASTER CYLINDER 9-9
   MANUAL BLEEDING 9-7
   PRESSURE BLEEDING 9-8
BLOWER MOTOR 6-14
   REMOVAL & INSTALLATION 6-14
BODY LUBRICATION 1-46
   ACCELERATOR LINKAGE 1-47
   BODY DRAIN HOLES 1-47

DOOR HINGES 1-46
HOOD 1-46
LOCK CYLINDERS 1-47
PARKING BRAKE LINKAGE 1-47
TRUNK LID 1-47
BOLTS, NUTS AND OTHER THREADED RETAINERS 1-5
BRAKE CALIPER 9-10
OVERHAUL 9-11
REMOVAL & INSTALLATION 9-10
BRAKE DISC (ROTOR) 9-13
INSPECTION 9-13
REMOVAL & INSTALLATION 9-13
BRAKE DRUMS 9-14
INSPECTION 9-15
REMOVAL & INSTALLATION 9-15
BRAKE FLUID RESERVOIR AND SEAL 9-28
REMOVAL & INSTALLATION 9-28
BRAKE LIGHT SWITCH 9-3
ADJUSTMENT 9-3
REMOVAL & INSTALLATION 9-3
BRAKE MASTER CYLINDER 1-44
FLUID RECOMMENDATIONS 1-44
LEVEL CHECK 1-44
BRAKE OPERATING SYSTEM 9-2
BRAKE PADS 9-9
INSPECTION 9-10
REMOVAL & INSTALLATION 9-9
BRAKE SHOES 9-15
ADJUSTMENTS 9-19
INSPECTION 9-15
REMOVAL & INSTALLATION 9-15
BRAKE SPECIFICATIONS 9-42
BUY OR REBUILD? 3-41
CABLES 9-22
ADJUSTMENT 9-23
REMOVAL & INSTALLATION 9-22
CAMSHAFT/BALANCE SHAFT BEARINGS 3-35
REMOVAL & INSTALLATION 3-35
CAMSHAFT, BEARINGS AND LIFTERS 3-35
INSPECTION 3-35
REMOVAL & INSTALLATION 3-35
CAMSHAFT POSITION SENSOR (ELECTRONIC ENGINE CONTROLS) 4-25
OPERATION 4-25
REMOVAL & INSTALLATION 4-25
TESTING 4-25
CAMSHAFT POSITION SENSOR (ELECTRONIC IGNITION
SYSTEMS) 2-10
CAPACITIES 1-50
CATALYTIC CONVERTER 4-11
INSPECTION 4-11
OPERATION 4-11
CHARGING SYSTEM 2-10
CHARGING SYSTEM PROBLEMS 2-18
CHASSIS GREASING 1-46
CIRCUIT BREAKERS 6-41
CIRCUIT PROTECTION 6-39
CLEARING CODES (DELCO VI AND DELCO BOSCH V ANTI-LOCK
BRAKING SYSTEMS) 9-38
CLEARING CODES (TROUBLE CODES) 4-39
COIL SPRINGS 8-12
REMOVAL & INSTALLATION 8-12
COMBINATION SWITCH 8-20
REMOVAL & INSTALLATION 8-20
COMPONENT LOCATIONS
EMISSION CONTROL AND ELECTRONIC ENGINE CONTROL
COMPONENT LOCATIONS—3.8L (VIN C) ENGINE 4-30
EMISSION CONTROL AND ELECTRONIC ENGINE CONTROL
COMPONENT LOCATIONS—3.8L (VIN K) ENGINE 4-31

FRONT SUSPENSION COMPONENT LOCATIONS 8-4
REAR SUSPENSION COMPONENT LOCATIONS 8-11
UNDERHOOD MAINTENANCE COMPONENT LOCATIONS—EARLY
MODEL 1-14
UNDERHOOD MAINTENANCE COMPONENT LOCATIONS—LATE
MODEL 1-12
CONSOLE 10-12
REMOVAL & INSTALLATION 10-12
CONTROL CABLES 6-16
ADJUSTMENT 6-16
REMOVAL & INSTALLATION 6-16
CONTROL PANEL 6-17
REMOVAL & INSTALLATION 6-17
COOLANT TEMPERATURE SENDER 2-16
OPERATION 2-16
REMOVAL & INSTALLATION 2-16
TESTING 2-16
COOLANT TEMPERATURE SENSOR 4-17
OPERATION 4-17
REMOVAL & INSTALLATION 4-18
TESTING 4-17
COOLING SYSTEM 1-41
COOLING SYSTEM INSPECTION 1-42
DRAIN & REFILL 1-43
FLUID RECOMMENDATIONS 1-41
FLUSHING & CLEANING 1-44
LEVEL CHECK 1-42
CRANKCASE VENTILATION SYSTEM 4-2
COMPONENT TESTING 4-2
OPERATION 4-2
REMOVAL & INSTALLATION 4-3
CRANKSHAFT DAMPER 3-30
REMOVAL & INSTALLATION 3-30
CRANKSHAFT POSITION SENSOR (ELECTRONIC ENGINE
CONTROLS) 4-26
OPERATION 4-26
REMOVAL & INSTALLATION 4-26
TESTING 4-26
CRANKSHAFT POSITION SENSOR (ELECTRONIC IGNITION
SYSTEMS) 2-10
CRUISE CONTROL SYSTEMS 6-18
CV-BOOTS 1-24
INSPECTION 1-24
CYLINDER HEAD (ENGINE MECHANICAL) 3-26
REMOVAL & INSTALLATION 3-26
CYLINDER HEAD (ENGINE RECONDITIONING) 3-44
ASSEMBLY 3-47
DISASSEMBLY 3-44
INSPECTION 3-45
REFINISHING & REPAIRING 3-46
**DELCO VI AND DELCO BOSCH V ANTI-LOCK BRAKING SYSTEMS
(ABS) 9-35**
DETERMINING ENGINE CONDITION 3-41
COMPRESSION TEST 3-41
OIL PRESSURE TEST 3-41
DIAGNOSIS AND TESTING (ELECTRONIC IGNITION SYSTEMS) 2-3
SERVICE PRECAUTIONS 2-3
DIAGNOSIS AND TESTING (TROUBLE CODES) 4-36
CIRCUIT/COMPONENT REPAIR 4-36
INTERMITTENTS 4-36
VISUAL/PHYSICAL INSPECTION 4-36
DIAGNOSTIC PROCEDURES 9-36
INTERMITTENT FAILURES 9-37
INTERMITTENTS AND POOR CONNECTIONS 9-37
DISC BRAKES 9-9
DISCONNECTING THE CABLES 6-8
DO'S 1-4
DON'TS 1-5

DOOR GLASS AND REGULATOR   10-18
  REMOVAL & INSTALLATION   10-18
DOOR LOCK CYLINDER   10-17
  REMOVAL & INSTALLATION   10-17
DOOR LOCKS   10-17
  REMOVAL & INSTALLATION   10-17
DOOR PANELS   10-14
  REMOVAL & INSTALLATION   10-14
DOORS   10-2
  ADJUSTMENT   10-2
DRIVE AXLE   1-11
DRUM BRAKES   9-13
ELECTRIC COOLING FAN(S)   3-22
  REMOVAL & INSTALLATION   3-22
  TESTING   3-22
ELECTRIC FAN SWITCH   2-17
  OPERATION   2-17
  REMOVAL & INSTALLATION   2-17
  TESTING   2-17
ELECTRIC FUEL PUMP   5-4
  REMOVAL & INSTALLATION   5-4
  TESTING   5-4
ELECTRICAL COMPONENTS   6-2
  CONNECTORS   6-4
  GROUND   6-3
  LOAD   6-4
  POWER SOURCE   6-2
  PROTECTIVE DEVICES   6-3
  SWITCHES & RELAYS   6-3
  WIRING & HARNESSES   6-4
ELECTRONIC BRAKE CONTROL MODULE (DELCO VI AND DELCO
  BOSCH V ANTI-LOCK BRAKING SYSTEMS)   9-38
  REMOVAL & INSTALLATION   9-38
ELECTRONIC BRAKE CONTROL MODULE (TEVES MARK IV ANTI-LOCK
  BRAKE SYSTEM)   9-32
  REMOVAL & INSTALLATION   9-32
ELECTRONIC BRAKE LAMP DRIVER MODULE (LDM)   9-39
  REMOVAL & INSTALLATION   9-39
ELECTRONIC CONTROL MODULE (ECM)   4-11
  OPERATION   4-11
  REMOVAL & INSTALLATION   4-12
ELECTRONIC ENGINE CONTROLS   4-11
ELECTRONIC IGNITION SYSTEMS   2-2
EMISSION CONTROL AND ELECTRONIC ENGINE CONTROL COMPONENT
  LOCATIONS—3.8L (VIN C) ENGINE   4-30
EMISSION CONTROL AND ELECTRONIC ENGINE CONTROL COMPONENT
  LOCATIONS—3.8L (VIN K) ENGINE   4-31
EMISSION CONTROLS   4-2
ENGINE (ENGINE MECHANICAL)   3-5
  REMOVAL & INSTALLATION   3-5
ENGINE (SERIAL NUMBER IDENTIFICATION)   1-7
ENGINE BLOCK   3-47
  ASSEMBLY   3-50
  DISASSEMBLY   3-48
  GENERAL INFORMATION   3-47
  INSPECTION   3-48
  REFINISHING   3-50
ENGINE IDENTIFICATION   1-10
ENGINE MECHANICAL   3-2
ENGINE OVERHAUL TIPS   3-42
  CLEANING   3-42
  OVERHAUL TIPS   3-42
  REPAIRING DAMAGED THREADS   3-42
  TOOLS   3-42
ENGINE PREPARATION   3-43
ENGINE RECONDITIONING   3-41
ENGINE SPECIFICATIONS   3-2
ENGINE START-UP AND BREAK-IN   3-52

BREAKING IT IN   3-52
  KEEP IT MAINTAINED   3-52
  STARTING THE ENGINE   3-52
ENTERTAINMENT SYSTEMS   6-19
EVAPORATIVE CANISTER   1-16
  SERVICING   1-17
EVAPORATIVE EMISSION CONTROLS   4-3
  OPERATION   4-3
  REMOVAL & INSTALLATION   4-4
  TESTING   4-4
EXHAUST GAS RECIRCULATION SYSTEM   4-7
  OPERATION   4-7
  REMOVAL & INSTALLATION   4-9
  TESTING   4-8
EXHAUST MANIFOLD   3-16
  REMOVAL & INSTALLATION   3-16
EXHAUST SYSTEM   3-39
EXTERIOR   10-2
FASTENERS, MEASUREMENTS AND CONVERSIONS   1-5
FILLING AND BLEEDING (DELCO VI AND DELCO BOSCH V ANTI-LOCK
  BRAKING SYSTEMS)   9-41
  SYSTEM BLEEDING   9-41
  SYSTEM FILLING   9-41
FILLING AND BLEEDING (TEVES II ANTI-LOCK BRAKE SYSTEM)   9-29
  SYSTEM BLEEDING   9-29
  SYSTEM FILLING   9-29
FIRING ORDERS   2-10
FLASHERS   6-41
  REPLACEMENT   6-41
FLUID DISPOSAL   1-36
FLUIDS AND LUBRICANTS   1-36
FLYWHEEL AND RING GEAR   3-39
  REMOVAL & INSTALLATION   3-39
FOG LIGHTS   6-38
  AIMING   6-38
  REMOVAL & INSTALLATION   6-38
FRONT COVER OIL SEAL   3-32
  REPLACEMENT   3-32
FRONT HUB, BEARING AND STEERING KNUCKLE   8-9
  REMOVAL & INSTALLATION   8-9
FRONT SUSPENSION   8-4
FRONT SUSPENSION COMPONENT LOCATIONS   8-4
FUEL AND ENGINE OIL RECOMMENDATIONS   1-36
  FUEL RECOMMENDATIONS   1-36
  OIL & FILTER CHANGE   1-37
  OIL LEVEL CHECK   1-37
  OIL RECOMMENDATIONS   1-36
FUEL FILTER   1-14
  REMOVAL & INSTALLATION   1-14
FUEL INJECTOR   5-7
  REMOVAL & INSTALLATION   5-7
  TESTING   5-7
FUEL LINES AND FITTINGS   5-2
FUEL PRESSURE REGULATOR   5-11
  REMOVAL & INSTALLATION   5-11
FUEL RAIL ASSEMBLY   5-8
  REMOVAL & INSTALLATION   5-8
FUEL TANK   5-13
FUSES   6-39
  REPLACEMENT   6-39
FUSIBLE LINKS   6-40
GASOLINE FUEL INJECTION SYSTEM   5-3
GAUGES   6-32
  REMOVAL & INSTALLATION   6-32
GENERAL DESCRIPTION (AIR BAG—GENERATION 1 CORPORATE
  SYSTEM)   6-8
  DISARMING THE SIR SYSTEM   6-11
  ENABLING THE SYSTEM   6-11

SERVICE PRECAUTIONS 6-11
SYSTEM COMPONENTS 6-9
SYSTEM OPERATION 6-9
GENERAL DESCRIPTION (AIR BAG—OLDSMOBILE INFLATABLE
RESTRAINT SYSTEM) 6-12
DISARMING THE IR SYSTEM 6-13
ENABLING THE SYSTEM 6-13
SERVICE PRECAUTIONS 6-12
SYSTEM COMPONENTS 6-12
GENERAL DESCRIPTION (CRUISE CONTROL SYSTEMS) 6-18
GENERAL DESCRIPTION (TEVES II ANTI-LOCK BRAKE
SYSTEM) 9-23
SYSTEM COMPONENTS 9-24
GENERAL DESCRIPTION (TEVES MARK IV ANTI-LOCK BRAKE
SYSTEM) 9-29
SYSTEM COMPONENTS 9-30
SYSTEM OPERATION 9-30
GENERAL ENGINE SPECIFICATIONS 1-11
GENERAL ENGINE TUNE-UP SPECIFICATIONS 1-30
GENERAL INFORMATION (CHARGING SYSTEM) 2-10
GENERAL INFORMATION (DELCO VI AND DELCO BOSCH V ANTI-LOCK
BRAKING SYSTEMS) 9-35
BASIC KNOWLEDGE REQUIRED 9-36
ENHANCED DIAGNOSTICS 9-36
ON-BOARD DIAGNOSTICS 9-36
GENERAL INFORMATION (ELECTRONIC IGNITION SYSTEMS) 2-2
SYSTEM COMPONENTS 2-2
SYSTEM OPERATION 2-2
GENERAL INFORMATION (STARTING SYSTEM) 2-14
GENERAL INFORMATION (TROUBLE CODES) 4-35
ELECTRICAL TOOLS 4-36
SCAN TOOLS 4-35
GRILLE 10-4
REMOVAL & INSTALLATION 10-4
HALFSHAFTS 7-6
OVERHAUL 7-9
REMOVAL & INSTALLATION 7-6
HEADLIGHT SWITCH 6-32
REMOVAL & INSTALLATION 6-32
HEADLIGHTS 6-33
AIMING THE HEADLIGHTS 6-34
REMOVAL & INSTALLATION 6-33
HEATER CORE 6-14
REMOVAL & INSTALLATION 6-14
HEATING AND AIR CONDITIONING 6-14
HOOD 10-2
ALIGNMENT 10-3
REMOVAL & INSTALLATION 10-2
HOSES 1-22
INSPECTION 1-22
REMOVAL & INSTALLATION 1-23
HOW TO USE THIS BOOK 1-2
HUB AND BEARINGS 8-16
REMOVAL & INSTALLATION 8-16
HYDRAULIC ACCUMULATOR 9-28
REMOVAL & INSTALLATION 9-28
HYDRAULIC UNIT 9-26
REMOVAL & INSTALLATION 9-26
IDLE AIR CONTROL VALVE 4-16
OPERATION 4-16
REMOVAL & INSTALLATION 4-17
TESTING 4-16
IDLE SPEED AND MIXTURE ADJUSTMENTS 1-29
IGNITION COIL 2-8
REMOVAL & INSTALLATION 2-8
TESTING 2-8
IGNITION LOCK CYLINDER 8-20
REMOVAL & INSTALLATION 8-20

IGNITION MODULE 2-9
REMOVAL & INSTALLATION 2-9
IGNITION SWITCH 8-20
REMOVAL & INSTALLATION 8-20
IGNITION TIMING 1-29
ADJUSTMENT 1-29
GENERAL INFORMATION 1-29
INSIDE REAR VIEW MIRROR 10-20
REMOVAL & INSTALLATION 10-20
INSPECTION 3-39
REPLACEMENT 3-40
INSTRUMENT CLUSTER 6-28
REMOVAL & INSTALLATION 6-28
INSTRUMENT PANEL AND PAD 10-8
REMOVAL & INSTALLATION 10-8
INSTRUMENTS AND SWITCHES 6-28
INTAKE AIR TEMPERATURE SENSOR 4-19
REMOVAL & INSTALLATION 4-20
TESTING 4-19
INTAKE MANIFOLD 3-11
REMOVAL & INSTALLATION 3-11
INTERIOR 10-8
JACKING 1-48
JACKING PRECAUTIONS 1-48
JUMP STARTING A DEAD BATTERY 1-47
JUMP STARTING PRECAUTIONS 1-47
JUMP STARTING PROCEDURE 1-47
KNOCK SENSOR 4-28
OPERATION 4-28
REMOVAL & INSTALLATION 4-28
TESTING 4-28
LIGHTING 6-33
LOWER BALL JOINTS 8-7
INSPECTION 8-7
REMOVAL & INSTALLATION 8-7
LOWER CONTROL ARMS 8-8
REMOVAL & INSTALLATION 8-8
MACPHERSON STRUT 8-5
OVERHAUL 8-6
REMOVAL & INSTALLATION 8-5
TESTING 8-5
MAINTENANCE INTERVALS 1-49
MAINTENANCE LIGHTS 1-34
RESETTING 1-34
MAINTENANCE OR REPAIR? 1-2
MANIFOLD ABSOLUTE PRESSURE SENSOR 4-22
OPERATION 4-22
REMOVAL & INSTALLATION 4-23
TESTING 4-23
MASS AIR FLOW SENSOR 4-20
OPERATION 4-20
REMOVAL & INSTALLATION 4-21
TESTING 4-21
MASTER CYLINDER 9-4
REMOVAL & INSTALLATION 9-4
NEUTRAL SAFETY SWITCH 7-2
REMOVAL & INSTALLATION 7-2
OIL PAN 3-28
REMOVAL & INSTALLATION 3-28
OIL PRESSURE SENDER 2-17
OPERATION 2-17
REMOVAL & INSTALLATION 2-17
TESTING 2-17
OIL PUMP 3-29
INSPECTION 3-29
INSTALLATION 3-30
REMOVAL 3-29
OUTSIDE MIRRORS 10-5

MIRROR FACE REPLACEMENT 10-5
   REMOVAL & INSTALLATION 10-5
OXYGEN SENSOR 4-14
   OPERATION 4-14
   REMOVAL & INSTALLATION4-15
   TESTING 4-14
PARKING BRAKE 9-22
PCV VALVE 1-14
   REMOVAL & INSTALLATION 1-14
PMV FLUID LEVEL SENSOR (DELCO VI AND DELCO BOSCH V ANTI-LOCK BRAKING SYSTEMS 9-41
PMV FLUID LEVEL SENSOR (TEVES MARK IV ANTI-LOCK BRAKE SYSTEM) 9-35
   REMOVAL & INSTALLATION 9-35
PMV RESERVOIR 9-35
   REMOVAL & INSTALLATION 9-35
POWER ANTENNA 6-22
   REMOVAL & INSTALLATION 6-23
POWER BRAKE BOOSTER 9-4
   REMOVAL & INSTALLATION 9-4
POWER SEAT MOTOR 10-21
   ADJUSTMENT 10-21
   REMOVAL & INSTALLATION 10-21
POWER STEERING GEAR 8-22
   REMOVAL & INSTALLATION 8-22
POWER STEERING PUMP (FLUIDS AND LUBRICANTS) 1-45
   FLUID RECOMMENDATIONS 1-45
   LEVEL CHECK 1-45
POWER STEERING PUMP (STEERING) 8-23
   REMOVAL & INSTALLATION 8-23
   SYSTEM BLEEDING 8-24
PRESSURE MODULATOR VALVE (PMV) ASSEMBLY (DELCO VI AND DELCO BOSCH V ANTI-LOCK BRAKING SYSTEMS) 9-40
   REMOVAL & INSTALLATION 9-40
PRESSURE MODULATOR VALVE (PMV) ASSEMBLY (TEVES MARK IV ANTI-LOCK BRAKE SYSTEM) 9-34
   REMOVAL & INSTALLATION 9-34
PRESSURE WARNING SWITCH 9-28
   REMOVAL & INSTALLATION 9-28
PROM/MEM-CAL/KS MODULE 4-13
   FUNCTIONAL CHECK 4-13
   REMOVAL & INSTALLATION 4-13
PROPORTIONING VALVES 9-5
PUMP AND MOTOR ASSEMBLY 9-28
   REMOVAL & INSTALLATION 9-28
QUICK-CONNECT FITTINGS 5-2
   REMOVAL & INSTALLATION 5-2
RADIATOR 3-20
   REMOVAL & INSTALLATION 3-20
RADIO 6-19
   REMOVAL & INSTALLATION 6-19
READING CODES (DELCO VI AND DELCO BOSCH V ANTI-LOCK BRAKING SYSTEMS) 9-37
READING CODES (TROUBLE CODES) 4-37
   1986-94 VEHICLES EXCEPT 1994 MODELS WITH 16-PIN DLC 4-37
   1994 VEHICLES WITH 16-PIN DLC AND ALL 1995-99 MODELS 4-39
REAR BALL JOINT 8-15
   INSPECTION 8-15
   REMOVAL & INSTALLATION 8-16
REAR CONTROL ARMS 8-14
   REMOVAL & INSTALLATION 8-14
REAR DEFOGGER SYSTEM 6-32
   OPERATION 6-32
   REPAIR 6-32
   TESTING 6-32
REAR MAIN OIL SEAL 3-37
   REMOVAL & INSTALLATION 3-37

REAR SUSPENSION 8-11
REAR SUSPENSION COMPONENT LOCATIONS 8-11
REGULATOR 2-14
   REMOVAL & INSTALLATION 2-14
RELIEVING FUEL SYSTEM PRESSURE 5-4
   PROCEDURE 5-4
ROCKER ARM (VALVE) COVER 3-7
   REMOVAL & INSTALLATION 3-7
ROCKER ARM/SHAFTS 3-9
   REMOVAL & INSTALLATION 3-9
ROUTINE MAINTENANCE AND TUNE-UP 1-12
SENDING UNITS 2-16
SERIAL NUMBER IDENTIFICATION 1-7
SERVICE PRECAUTIONS 5-3
SERVICING YOUR VEHICLE SAFELY 1-4
SIGNAL AND MARKER LIGHTS 6-35
   REMOVAL & INSTALLATION 6-35
SPARK PLUG WIRES 1-26
   REMOVAL & INSTALLATION 1-27
   TESTING 1-26
SPARK PLUGS 1-24
   INSPECTION & GAPPING 1-26
   REMOVAL & INSTALLATION 1-25
   SPARK PLUG HEAT RANGE 1-25
SPEAKERS 6-21
   REMOVAL & INSTALLATION 6-21
SPECIAL TOOLS 1-4
SPECIFICATION CHARTS
   ALTERNATOR FUNCTIONAL CHECK—1996-99 VEHICLES 2-12
   BRAKE SPECIFICATIONS 9-42
   CAPACITIES 1-50
   ENGINE IDENTIFICATION 1-10
   ENGINE SPECIFICATIONS 3-2
   GENERAL ENGINE SPECIFICATIONS 1-11
   GENERAL ENGINE TUNE-UP SPECIFICATIONS 1-30
   MAINTENANCE INTERVALS 1-49
   TORQUE SPECIFICATIONS (BODY AND TRIM) 10-22
   TORQUE SPECIFCATIONS (DRIVE TRAIN) 7-13
   TORQUE SPECIFICATIONS (ENGINE AND ENGINE OVERHAUL) 3-53
   TORQUE SPECIFICATIONS (SUSPENSION AND STEERING) 8-25
   VEHICLE IDIENTIFICATION CHART 1-8
STABILIZER SHAFT 8-8
   REMOVAL & INSTALLATION 8-8
STABILIZER SHAFT AND INSULATORS 8-15
   REMOVAL & INSTALLATION 8-15
STABILIZER SHAFT MOUNTING BRACKET 8-15
   REMOVAL & INSTALLATION 8-15
STANDARD AND METRIC MEASUREMENTS 1-7
STARTER 2-15
   REMOVAL & INSTALLATION 2-15
   SOLENOID REPLACEMENT 2-16
   TESTING 2-15
STARTING SYSTEM 2-14
STARTING SYSTEM PROBLEMS 2-18
STEERING 8-17
STEERING GEAR 1-46
   FLUID RECOMMENDATIONS & LEVEL CHECK 1-46
STEERING LINKAGE 8-21
   REMOVAL & INSTALLATION 8-21
STEERING WHEEL 8-17
   REMOVAL & INSTALLATION 8-17
STRUT 8-12
   REMOVAL & INSTALLATION 8-12
STRUT AND KNUCKLE SCRIBING 8-5
   PROCEDURE 8-5
SUNROOF 10-5
   MOTOR SYNCHRONIZATION 10-6

REMOVAL & INSTALLATION 10-5
TRACK ASSEMBLY SYNCHRONIZATION 10-6
SUPERCHARGER (ENGINE MECHANICAL) 3-19
REMOVAL & INSTALLATION 3-19
SUPERCHARGER (FLUIDS AND LUBRICANTS) 1-46
FLUID RECOMMENDATIONS 1-46
LEVEL CHECK 1-46
SYSTEM DESCRIPTION 5-3
SYSTEM TESTING (TEVES II ANTI-LOCK BRAKE SYSTEM) 9-25
CLEARING TROUBLE CODES 9-26
DEPRESSURIZING THE HYDRAULIC UNIT 9-25
DISPLAYING ABS TROUBLE CODES 9-25
FUNCTIONAL CHECK 9-25
INTERMITTENTS 9-26
SERVICE PRECAUTIONS 9-25
VISUAL INSPECTION 9-25
SYSTEM TESTING (TEVES MARK IV ANTI-LOCK BRAKE SYSTEM) 9-31
DIAGNOSTIC PROCEDURE 9-31
SERVICE PRECAUTIONS 9-31
TANK ASSEMBLY 5-13
DRAINING 5-13
REMOVAL & INSTALLATION 5-13
SENDING UNIT REPLACEMENT 5-14
TEST EQUIPMENT 6-5
JUMPER WIRES 6-5
MULTIMETERS 6-5
TEST LIGHTS 6-5
TESTING 6-6
OPEN CIRCUITS 6-6
RESISTANCE 6-7
SHORT CIRCUITS 6-6
VOLTAGE 6-6
VOLTAGE DROP 6-7
TEVES II ANTI-LOCK BRAKE SYSTEM 9-23
TEVES MARK IV ANTI-LOCK BRAKE SYSTEM 9-29
THERMOSTAT 3-10
REMOVAL & INSTALLATION 3-10
THROTTLE BODY 5-5
REMOVAL & INSTALLATION 5-5
THROTTLE POSITION SENSOR 4-24
ADJUSTMENT 4-25
OPERATION 4-24
REMOVAL & INSTALLATION 4-24
TESTING 4-24
TIMING CHAIN AND SPROCKETS 3-33
REMOVAL & INSTALLATION 3-33
TIMING CHAIN COVER 3-30
REMOVAL & INSTALLATION 3-30
TIRES AND WHEELS 1-32
INFLATION & INSPECTION 1-33
TIRE DESIGN 1-32
TIRE ROTATION 1-32
TIRE STORAGE 1-33
TOOLS AND EQUIPMENT 1-2
TORQUE 1-6
TORQUE ANGLE METERS 1-7
TORQUE WRENCHES 1-6
TORQUE SPECIFICATIONS (BODY AND TRIM) 10-22
TORQUE SPECIFCATIONS (DRIVE TRAIN) 7-13
TORQUE SPECIFICATIONS (ENGINE AND ENGINE OVERHAUL) 3-53
TORQUE SPECIFICATIONS (SUSPENSION AND STEERING) 8-25
TOWING THE VEHICLE 1-47
TRANSAXLE 1-11
TROUBLE CODES 4-35
TROUBLESHOOTING CHARTS
CHARGING SYSTEM PROBLEMS 2-18
STARTING SYSTEM PROBLEMS 2-18

TROUBLESHOOTING ELECTRICAL SYSTEMS 6-6
TRUNK LID 10-4
ALIGNMENT 10-4
REMOVAL & INSTALLATION 10-4
TURN SIGNAL SWITCH 8-19
REMOVAL & INSTALLATION 8-19
UNDERHOOD MAINTENANCE COMPONENT LOCATIONS—EARLY MODEL 1-14
UNDERHOOD MAINTENANCE COMPONENT LOCATIONS—LATE MODEL 1-12
UNDERSTANDING AND TROUBLESHOOTING ELECTRICAL SYSTEMS 6-2
UNDERSTANDING THE AUTOMATIC TRANSAXLE 7-2
VACUUM DIAGRAMS 4-41
VALVE BLOCK ASSEMBLY 9-27
REMOVAL & INSTALLATION 9-27
VALVE LASH 1-29
VEHICLE 1-7
VEHICLE IDIENTIFICATION CHART 1-8
WATER PUMP 3-23
REMOVAL & INSTALLATION 3-23
WHEEL ALIGNMENT (FRONT SUSPENSION) 8-10
CAMBER 8-10
CASTER 8-10
TOE 8-10
WHEEL ALIGNMENT (REAR SUSPENSION) 8-16
WHEEL BEARINGS 1-47
WHEEL CYLINDERS 9-20
OVERHAUL 9-20
REMOVAL & INSTALLATION 9-20
WHEEL LUG STUDS 8-3
REMOVAL & INSTALLATION 8-3
WHEEL SPEED SENSORS (DELCO VI AND DELCO BOSCH V ANTI-LOCK BRAKING SYSTEMS) 9-39
REMOVAL & INSTALLATION 9-39
WHEEL SPEED SENSORS RELUCTOR RING (DELCO VI AND DELCO BOSCH V ANTI-LOCK BRAKING SYSTEMS) 9-40
REMOVAL & INSTALLATION 9-40
WHEEL SPEED SENSORS (TEVES II ANTI-LOCK BRAKE SYSTEM) 9-27
REMOVAL & INSTALLATION 9-27
WHEEL SPEED SENSORS RELUCTOR RING (TEVES MARK IV ANTI-LOCK BRAKE SYSTEM) 9-34
REMOVAL & INSTALLATION 9-34
WHEEL SPEED SENSORS (TEVES MARK IV ANTI-LOCK BRAKE SYSTEM) 9-33
REMOVAL & INSTALLATION 9-33
WHEELS 8-2
WHEELS 8-2
INSPECTION 8-3
REMOVAL & INSTALLATION 8-2
WHERE TO BEGIN 1-2
WINDOW ACTUATOR 10-19
REMOVAL & INSTALLATION 10-20
WINDSHIELD AND FIXED GLASS 10-20
REMOVAL & INSTALLATION 10-20
WINDSHIELD CHIP REPAIR 10-20
WINDSHIELD WASHER MOTOR 6-27
REMOVAL & INSTALLATION 6-27
WINDSHIELD WIPER BLADE AND ARM 6-24
REMOVAL & INSTALLATION 6-24
WINDSHIELD WIPER MOTOR 6-26
REMOVAL & INSTALLATION 6-26
WINDSHIELD WIPER SWITCH 8-18
REMOVAL & INSTALLATION 8-18
WINDSHIELD WIPERS 1-31
ELEMENT (REFILL) CARE & REPLACEMENT 1-31
WINDSHIELD WIPERS AND WASHERS 6-23
WIRE AND CONNECTOR REPAIR 6-7
WIRING DIAGRAMS 6-42